Oxford Studies in British Church Music

THE SUCCESSION OF ORGANISTS

Lincoln Cathedral: Accounts of the Clerk of the Common Fund, 1563–4 (Bj.3.8, f.124v), reproduced by kind permission. See p. 155.

The Succession of Organists

OF THE CHAPEL ROYAL
AND THE
CATHEDRALS OF ENGLAND
AND WALES FROM *c.*1538

Also of the Organists of the
Collegiate Churches of Westminster
and Windsor, certain academic choral
foundations, and the Cathedrals
of Armagh and Dublin

WATKINS SHAW

CLARENDON PRESS · OXFORD
1991

Oxford University Press, Walton Street, Oxford OX2 6DP
Oxford New York Toronto
Delhi Bombay Calcutta Madras Karachi
Petaling Jaya Singapore Hong Kong Tokyo
Nairobi Dar es Salaam Cape Town
Melbourne Auckland
and associated companies in
Berlin Ibadan

Oxford is a trade mark of Oxford University Press

Published in the United States
by Oxford University Press, New York

British Library Cataloguing in Publication Data
data available

Library of Congress Cataloging in Publication Data
data available

ISBN 0–19–816175–1

Typeset by Hope Services (Abingdon) Ltd.
Printed in Great Britain by
Biddles Ltd, Guildford and King's Lynn

EDITOR'S FOREWORD

THE church music of Britain, like its church buildings and liturgical texts, is a national heritage that transcends religious controversy and the decline of faith. Unlike them—because of the ephemeral nature of music—it needs revival, interpretation, and advocacy if it is to be preserved and appreciated. Such processes must rest on a sound basis of fact and understanding. This series serves to encourage and present some of the best efforts of modern scholarship in the field.

The great Anglican cathedral tradition, with its roots in the Middle Ages, naturally takes the central place in this heritage. For centuries it has raised the music of worship to a high art, with its own style and history and its own series of composers, performers, and critics. It constitutes a school of musical art that is effortlessly distinctive, recognizably English, without being in the least nationalistic. Much though we may appreciate cathedral music as art, it also has a function in religious worship, and indeed in society. It shares this function with many other kinds of British church music—not all Anglican, not all English, not all achieving or even attempting high artistic value, but each playing a certain part in the life of a denomination and a community. The books in this series will all, in a variety of ways, link developments in church music with the life of the individuals and societies that produced them.

Watkins Shaw, in his research for this book, has examined the records of cathedrals and choral foundations more thoroughly, I suspect, than any musicologist has ever done before. In doing so, he has uncovered the working life of specialized communities, sheltered from society at large, for whom music was, or ought to have been, one of the chief justifications of their privileges. We might expect the organist to have been firmly seated at the centre of musical affairs. Dr Shaw's investigations reveal that this was rarely the case, and that the legal, institutional, and personal factors determining the organist's position varied widely among the different foundations, and from one period to another. His detailed accounts combine to build up, for the first time, a continuous and quite colourful picture of the musical life of these communities.

The picture that emerges, however, is only a background to Dr Shaw's main purpose, which has been to establish, as accurately as records permit, the names, biographies, and dates of office of all who have held the post of cathedral organist from the Reformation until the present time. Anyone who has had to make do with J. E. West's *Cathedral Organists Past and Present* will welcome a reference book that is comprehensive in its coverage, totally documented, and meticulously precise in its statements of fact. It is as useful for its outline of the musical history of each institution as for its information about hundreds of individual organists.

This book is the product of decades of painstaking research by one of today's leading authorities on English church music. What makes it doubly impressive is the fact that the author enjoyed no institutional help: he worked entirely in his spare time. It might seem rash to say that this book will never be superseded, but it is difficult to see where any future researcher could go to improve significantly on the amount and accuracy of Dr Shaw's information.

Urbana, Illinois
April 1990

NICHOLAS TEMPERLEY

PREFACE

In 1899 John Ebenezer West (1863–1929) published his *Cathedral Organists Past and Present* (London, Novello and Co. Ltd.), of which a 'new and enlarged edition' appeared in 1921. Not only did this contain a good deal of interest, but it came to be held in a certain affection.

It was therefore suggested that it might be possible to reissue it with an appendix containing additions and corrections and bringing the entries down to the present time. Where it rested on the careful work of J. C. Bridge for Chester Cathedral, and the even more admirable work of Sir Ivor Atkins for Worcester, that could certainly have been done. But after going no further than to compare West's entries at first hand with the archives of two other historic cathedrals, it became clear that, as he had not consulted original sources, there was much additional relevant information, and that this, together with the extensive modifications also required, could not well be dealt with in an appendix; that a good deal of explanation of much uncertain evidence would be needed; and that detailed, direct references to original authorities ought to be supplied. The time seemed ripe to start afresh, leaving his book a welcome pioneer work which remains our authority for certain information within West's own knowledge relating to men alive at the time of his two editions.

Consequently, the whole task of investigation has been undertaken *de novo*, the result being an independent book. But whatever one may feel to be the shortcomings of West's work after the passage of years, I myself am only too conscious of how the existence of his framework made my labours lighter, and no one can feel more indebted than I to his pioneering interest in the subject.

As my starting-point I determined on the period immediately succeeding the dissolution of the greater monasteries in 1538–9, during which no fewer than thirteen of the historic cathedrals were founded or refounded, a matter explained more fully in the Introduction below. The records of pre-existing institutions have been picked up from that point, and those of later ones from the date of foundation or elevation.

Institutions are included which, though not the sees of bishops, are otherwise akin to the historic cathedrals in constituting corporate, self-governing bodies with a perpetual succession, and enjoying, either by original charter or (as St John's College, Cambridge) by subsequent permanent endowment, a foundation for purposes of choral worship. Nine bodies are thus embraced, together with the collegiate churches of Manchester, Ripon, and Southwell prior to their becoming cathedrals. Such a feature distinguished Eton and Winchester Colleges from other public schools with chapels, choirs, and organs. But while Winchester

College still maintains this distinction, Eton College, by the closure of its choir school in 1968, has lost touch with this aspect. The Chapel Royal, though not resting on any corporate foundation, is included on account of its manifest historic pre-eminence.

Exploration of the careers of several figures necessarily led to first-hand work on the three prominent cathedrals of Ireland: Armagh, Christ Church, Dublin, and St Patrick's, Dublin. Provision for music in these cathedrals was on a generous scale throughout a long period of their history, analogous to that of the historic English cathedrals. However, the Church of Ireland as a whole lies outside my terms of reference, and so the material I have collected about these three cathedrals has been placed in an appendix.

Essentially my purpose has been to document each man's tenure from the cathedral (etc.) archives themselves. Where possible I have set this in an outline framework of his life and career, drawing on secondary sources. The amount of space allotted has no regular relation to a man's importance as a musician: much may be occupied because of difficulty in interpreting evidence which is baffling or elusive; or because the documents shed light not so much on an individual as on the varying conditions of cathedral work; or for no better reason than that I have found material (see, for instance, W. P. Propert, p. 254) fascinating in its own right. Nor have I sought to impose a consistent pattern on all entries. While it was far from my primary intention to provide data for a social history of a particular branch of the musical profession, I have not been unmindful, when selecting material, that the book might incidentally contribute to this by mentioning parentage and offspring; training and educational background; contributions outside cathedral work; types of qualifications acquired and at what age; relations with colleagues and superiors; temperament and character. But this could not be the place for details of compositions, which, except in rare instances shedding light on biography, are not mentioned. On the other hand, the publication of some important book or piece of scholarship is mentioned, not because one rates these things higher than composition, but because they are less usual in a cathedral organist.

The taking of a university degree in music in earlier times (by someone like Orlando Gibbons, for instance) is usually a matter for biographical notice, and from the later nineteenth century such degrees became one of the recognized avenues to a cathedral organ-stool. They are indeed more woven into the fabric of the organists' world than into that of any other musical performer, and constitute part of the picture incidentally unfolded here of a section of the musical profession. So I have chronicled them throughout.[1] With reference to the MA degree of the universities of Oxford

[1] It may not be inappropriate to interpolate a short explanation about early degrees in music, for it is evident that they are liable to be misinterpreted in the light of present conditions. At Cambridge, Dublin (Trinity College), and Oxford, until after the middle of the 19th century, the

and Cambridge, it will be understood that this is a matter of standing within the university, not the result of scholastic tests.

As to the multiplicity of professional diplomas in music which pervade the United Kingdom, I have, without disparagement, passed over them all except that of FRCO, the standard (though not obligatory) technical qualification of an organist, with the related choir-training diploma and the Archbishop of Canterbury's diploma in church music.

All persons living at the time of my enquiries were invited to complete a questionnaire for biographical purposes, and their replies now form part of Lcm, MS 6068. Some were only too modest about themselves, and this may have led to some apparent inequality of treatment, but for the decisions about what type of data to include, I am responsible. I am glad to say that all but two complied with my request. In one instance (Birmingham), my enquiries in several quarters failed to elicit an address; in another (St David's), to my regret, more than one application failed to secure a response.

The archives consulted contain certain information contributory to a history of the cathedral organs. I have alluded to this, however, only when it touches on a biographical point, or tells something of the conditions under which an organist worked.

Lists of documents consulted, together with abbreviations devised for adoption here, are given separately for each of the historic institutions covered. Instead of the customary conventional mark for the abbreviated ending of Latin words (a single concluding inverted comma), I have used a colon to avoid confusion with the end of a quotation. All quotations from original documents, if in English, are given with expanded contractions and with modern spelling and capitalization, while sums of money such as 'xl. xiijs. ivd.' are rendered as '£10. 13*s.* 4*d.*'. There are, however, two exceptions to this modernization: (1) in all verbatim quotations, proper names are transcribed exactly, lest it should be that I have been too free with any identification; and (2) any memorial inscription is exactly transcribed.

To avoid confusion between Old Style and New Style dates before the year 1753 (see p. xxx), the form 1648/9 has been adopted (as distinct from 1648–9, meaning period extending from 1648 to 1649). Because of possible conflict with occasional citations elsewhere of an Old Style date, I have preferred, *other than in main headings with dates of birth and death*, not to

requirements to be fulfilled were of the loosest: no residence was exacted (for no tuition was organized), association with the university was of the most nominal and fleeting character, and the degrees themselves possessed only an anomalous status within the university. Even after prescribed tests were framed (Cambridge, 1857; Dublin, 1861; Oxford, 1862), residence was still unnecessary until after 1893 at Cambridge, 1926 at Oxford, and 1982 at Dublin. When Durham University instituted music degrees at the end of the 19th century, these had no residential requirements, and continued thus until 1985. Degrees acquired under these conditions do not therefore necessarily imply a university education.

express my dates in the simple New Style form, especially in a work maintaining close contact with original documents.

In quoting from archives earlier than the Civil War, I have generally followed the practice of giving page or folio numbers, since these documents are not always easy to consult quickly. But for later events it is usually an easy matter to turn up the reference under the given date.

In the earlier period here covered, proper names took a variety of unstable forms, scribes often doing their best phonetically. For my headings I have usually conformed to modern accepted use for famous figures, and to any form now adopted for lesser figures in booklets published in association with any of the cathedrals, whether or not these seem to me well founded. I have used the Index of Names (below) as some guide to alternatives. But 'Smyth' and 'Smythe' have been converted to 'Smith': all three variants were commonly used as alternatives for one and the same person, and are unsafe means by which to differentiate between one man and another. No difference in pronunciation was involved (unlike today), and *DNB* acknowledges no Smyth(e) until the eighteenth century.

The problem of to what extent closely contemporary identity of name (allowing for variant spelling) implies an identity of person is not an easy one, especially at a time when sons often bore a father's Christian name. Are there, for instance, three men named William Inglott where, with mild reservation, I accept one? How many John Farrants were there? There is no single yardstick for consistency of treatment, and each instance must be considered on its own merits. Sometimes one may feel confident without disguising matters; sometimes one may be reasonably confident though bound to enter a caveat; sometimes one can simply draw attention to a mere possibility; yet again, the only approach is to set out uncertain evidence as fully as possible.

For biographical information beyond the cathedral (etc.) archives, if material happened to lie within my own sphere of knowledge, or original sources for it came readily to hand, I have made use of this, and there is in fact a fair amount of such information scattered over the book. The secondary sources on which I have otherwise drawn are cited fully in the Bibliography, and attention is directed to these at points of detail, but sometimes, to avoid repetition where reliance on them has been general and pervasive, I have indicated them in square brackets at the end of an entry.

My own primary work on the original documents was full of pleasure, gratefully recalled, particularly when undertaken in the very buildings to which they refer. I must place on record my warm thanks to the appropriate authorities, Chapter clerks, archivists, and librarians, both clerical and lay, many of them acting in honorary capacities, for kind facilities extended to me at the cathedrals of Armagh, Bristol, Canterbury, Carlisle, Chester,

Dublin (St Patrick's and Christ Church), Durham, Ely, Exeter, Gloucester, Hereford, London (St Paul's), Manchester, Norwich, Oxford (Christ Church), Peterborough, Ripon, Southwell, Wells, Winchester, Worcester, and York; similarly to those of Westminster Abbey, St George's Chapel, Windsor Castle, King's and Trinity Colleges, Cambridge, Eton College, and Magdalen and New Colleges, Oxford; and, further, to the officers of the County or Diocesan Record Offices preserving some or all of certain cathedral archives, namely at Maidstone (for Rochester), Chichester, Gloucester, Lichfield, Lincoln, and Salisbury; and to the National Library of Wales in which are deposited the archives of the cathedrals of Wales. All these, and their staffs, were invariably welcoming, and patiently answered any subsequent questions in correspondence. I also express my thanks to the archivists of Eton and Winchester Colleges for helpful correspondence. More than ordinary help was given by Mr C. B. L. Barr, MA (York Minster), Miss Barbara Dodwell, MA (Norwich Cathedral), Mrs A. M. Erskine, B.Litt., MA (Exeter Cathedral), the late Mr F. C. Morgan, MA, FSA, FLA, and Miss Penelope Morgan, MA, FLA (Hereford Cathedral), Mr Arthur Sabin, MA (Bristol Cathedral), and Mrs Joan Varley, MA, FSA (Lincoln Record Office).

For the necessary kind permission to base my work on the archives thus consulted, and, further, to make verbatim quotations from them when desired, I am grateful to the relevant authorities, whether entitled (as the case may be) the Lord Chamberlain's Office, the Dean and Chapter, the Dean and Canons, the Provost, the Master and Fellows, the Provost and Fellows, and the Church in Wales through the National Library of Wales. I also thank those persons who co-operated so helpfully by supplying the information on which I have based their brief biographies.

As I now conclude a task which has occupied me intermittently for many years, I am strongly reminded of Samuel Johnson's estimate of an historian: 'Great abilities (said he) are not requisite for an Historian . . . He has the facts ready to hand; so there is no exercise of invention. Imagination is not required in any high degree . . . Some penetration, accuracy, and colouring, will fit a man for the task, if he can give the application which is necessary.' (Boswell's *Life of Johnson*, AD 1763). Though not applicable to the higher branches of history as practised since his day, Johnson's unflattering assessment fits the kind of work I have attempted. But if, in spite of my endeavour to 'give the application which is necessary', inaccuracies have crept in, I beg the reader's indulgence, while trusting that my ample references will at least have kept my tracks open.

W.S.

30 April 1973

POSTSCRIPT

THE investigations on which the bulk of this book rests were carried out between 1961 and 1972, and its substance was written by 1973. In view of the passage of time, I have thought it well, in giving schedules of archives available to me, to indicate the respective years in which they stood thus.

For purposes of present publication I have taken note of resignations, deaths, and appointments since 1973. I have also fortunately been able to take advantage of the publication of Donovan Dawe's *Organists of the City of London, 1666–1850* (1983) and Andrew Ashbee's *Records of English Court Music*, i–iii (1986–9). One's indebtedness to Dr Ashbee and Mr Dawe is increased by the consideration that each had to shoulder personal responsibility for the publication of his work. In earlier years I ran into some difficulty in connection with the archives of St John's College, Cambridge, and I now feel much indebted to Mr Malcolm Underwood, the present archivist, for enabling me to overcome this. In addition I am grateful to Mr Brian Crosby, MA, for some further information about Durham Cathedral, and to Mr L. S. Colchester, BA, FSA, for help in connection with Wells Cathedral.

Finally I wish to thank Nicholas Temperley for some wise guidance, and also to recall the friendship of the late Walter Emery, at whose suggestion I began to undertake the work.

W.S.

30 September 1989

CONTENTS

List of Abbreviations and Symbols xvi

Introduction xviii

The Historic Constitutional Position of Cathedral Organist in England and Wales xviii

Archival Sources Discussed xxv

Dates of Tenure xxviii

Notes on Money and Dates xxix

1. THE CHAPEL ROYAL 1

2. CATHEDRALS OF ENGLAND AND WALES 21

Bangor 21

Birmingham 27

Blackburn 28

Bradford 30

Brecon (Diocese of Swansea and Brecon) 31

Bristol 32

Bury St Edmunds (Diocese of St Edmundsbury and Ipswich) 42

Canterbury 43

Carlisle 52

Chelmsford 59

Chester 60

Chichester 71

Coventry 83

Derby 85

Durham 87

Ely 96

Exeter 106

Gloucester 118

Guildford 129

Hereford 131

Leicester 144

Lichfield 146

Lincoln 154
Liverpool 164
Llandaff 165
London (St Paul's) 170
Manchester 183
Newcastle 192
Newport (Diocese of Monmouth) 194
Norwich 196
Oxford (Christ Church) 208
Peterborough 218
Portsmouth 225
Ripon 227
Rochester 232
St Albans 240
St Asaph 243
St David's 248
Salisbury 257
Sheffield 269
Southwark 271
Southwell 273
Truro 280
Wakefield 281
Wells (Diocese of Bath and Wells) 283
Winchester 292
Worcester 304
York 313

3. COLLEGIATE CHURCHES 325
Westminster Abbey 325
Windsor, St George's Chapel 341

4. ACADEMIC CHORAL FOUNDATIONS 355
Cambridge 355
King's College 355
St John's College 361
Trinity College 365

Eton College 372
Oxford 378
Magdalen College 378
New College 387
Winchester College 396

Appendices 403
I. Armagh Cathedral 403
II. Dublin 407
Christ Church Cathedral 407
St Patrick's Cathedral 416

Bibliography 427
Addenda 434
Index of Names 435

LIST OF ABBREVIATIONS AND SYMBOLS

*	Subject of an entry in another section herein.
§	Entry based on material supplied or approved by its subject.
←	First documented date, but likely to have been in office earlier (e.g. ← 1575).
→	Latest documented date, but likely to have continued in office thereafter (e.g. 1575 →).

b. born; bap. baptized; bur. buried; d. died.

Dates between 1 January and 24 March inclusive prior to 1753 are expressed as both Old Style and New Style, thus: 1641/2.

'Interregnum' as used here denotes the period, roughly from about 1645 (and certainly from 1649) until 1660–1, during which capitular records in general are intermitted on account of the Civil War, Commonwealth, and Protectorate.

'London' as used here in respect of births, baptisms, and deaths refers to the modern conurbation generally so understood, without reference to the counties to which its various parts historically belonged.

BMB	*British Musical Biography*, ed. J. D. Brown and S. S. Stratton (1897).
CA	Chapter Acts.
CB2	Second Cheque Book of the Chapel Royal (see p. 1).
Cfm	Cambridge, Fitzwilliam Museum.
Ckc	Cambridge, King's College Library.
CSPD	*Calendar of State Papers, Domestic.*
CTB	*Calendar of Treasury Books.*
Cu	Cambridge University Library.
D & C	Dean and Chapter.
DNB	*The Dictionary of National Biography* (including *The Twentieth Century Dictionary of National Biography* for relevant decades).
ECM	*English Church Music.*
GM	The *Gentleman's Magazine.*
Grove[1]	*A Dictionary of Music and Musicians*, ed. George Grove (1878–89). (Subsequent editions, 1900–54, indicated as *Grove*[2], etc.)
Gu	Glasgow University Library.
HAM (*HE*)	*Hymns Ancient and Modern, Historical Edition* (1909).
HMC	Historical Manuscripts Commission.
Lbl	London, British Library, Reference Division.
Lcm	London, Royal College of Music Library.
Lgh	London, Guildhall Library.
Llp	London, Lambeth Palace Library.
MB	*Musica Britannica.*
ML	*Music and Letters.*
MMR	The *Monthly Musical Record.*
Mpl	Manchester Public Library.

MR	*Music Review.*
MT	The *Musical Times.*
Mus. Op.	*Musical Opinion.*
NG	*The New Grove Dictionary of Music and Musicians*, ed. Stanley Sadie (1981).
Ob	Oxford, Bodleian Library.
Och	Oxford, Christ Church Library.
Pc	Paris, Bibliothèque nationale (fonds du Conservatoire national de musique).
PCC	(Public Record Office: will proved in the) Prerogative Court of Canterbury.
PMA	*Proceedings of the Musical Association.*
PR	Parish Register.
PRMA	*Proceedings of the Royal Musical Association.*
PRO	Public Record Office.
RSCM	Royal School of Church Music.
TCM	*Tudor Church Music.*
VCA	Vicars Choral Acts.
Venn	*Alumni Cantabrigienses*, ed. J. Venn and J. A. Venn, 2 parts (1922–53).
Wad	City of Westminster Archives Department, 160 Buckingham Palace Road, London SW1.
WW	*Who's Who.*
WWM	*Who's Who in Music*, 1st to 6th edns. (1935, 1937, 1950, 1962, 1969, 1972 (Burke's Peerage, Ltd.).
WWW	*Who Was Who.*
Y	York Minster Library.

INTRODUCTION

THE HISTORIC CONSTITUTIONAL POSITION OF CATHEDRAL ORGANIST IN ENGLAND AND WALES

On the accession of Henry VIII in 1509 there were 18 dioceses and 20 cathedrals in the province of Canterbury (the discrepancy arising because 2 bishops each had 2 cathedrals: Bath and Wells; Coventry and Lichfield), and 3 dioceses with a cathedral each in the province of York (the diocese of Sodor and Man having no cathedral). Of these 23 cathedrals, 13 had constitutions as bodies of secular clergy, but the other 10 were swept away by the dissolution of the monasteries because they had been cathedral priories. The loss of 2 such, at Bath and at Coventry, did not matter constitutionally, as the bishops still had a non-monastic cathedral (Wells and Lichfield respectively) whose continuity was undisturbed.

But it was necessary to refound the other 8, namely, Canterbury, Carlisle, Durham, Ely, Norwich, Rochester, Winchester, and Worcester, which all started a new life between 1538 and 1542 as foundations of Henry VIII, endowed merely with part of the assets of the monasteries he had suppressed. Out of the same proceeds he also founded 6 new dioceses with cathedrals in former monastic buildings, namely, Westminster (a foundation which lasted only ten years), Osney (shortly to be replaced by Christ Church, Oxford), Bristol, Chester, Gloucester, and Peterborough. All cathedrals founded or refounded by Henry are collectively known as cathedrals 'of the New Foundation', thus distinguished from those 'of the Old Foundation' whose constitutions he left undisturbed. We therefore have: cathedrals of the Old Foundation—Bangor, Chichester, Exeter, Hereford, Lichfield, Lincoln, Llandaff, London (St Paul's), St Asaph, St David's, Salisbury, Wells, York; cathedrals of the New Foundation—(*a*) former cathedral priories, now refounded: Canterbury, Carlisle, Durham, Ely, Norwich, Rochester, Winchester, Worcester; (*b*) former abbeys, now refounded as new cathedrals: Bristol, Chester, Gloucester, Peterborough (also Westminster, shortly to be dissolved, but later refounded as a collegiate church by Elizabeth I); (*c*) Christ Church, Oxford, a refoundation of Wolsey's Cardinal College on the site of St Frideswide's Abbey.

Cathedrals of the New Foundation

In the Middle Ages all adults engaged in singing the mass and the offices had from the first been in holy orders. But as time went on it became difficult to find sufficient singers thus qualified, and the foundations of Henry VIII therefore provided for choirs of whose adults some were in holy orders (minor, or 'petty', canons—*canonici minores*) and some were not (lay clerks—*clerici laici*). By this time, too, the organ had become a recognized element in musical worship, and the New Foundations provided for an organ-player. But Henry (or his advisers) arranged that one man was to do two jobs: an officer known as 'master of the choristers' (*magister choristarum*) was also to play the organ as required. He was to be additional to the minor canons and lay clerks, not one of their number. In succeeding years, before the Civil War, the role of the organ so increased that this officer began to be known unofficially as the organist, notwithstanding his statutory title of master of the choristers; there is still living (1990) one ex-cathedral organist, Dr Herbert Sumsion, who held his office by that title under the statutes of Henry VIII.[1] With minute literal variations, the formula used in those statutes for all his newly constituted cathedrals (and repeated with only slight differences in the later Marian statutes given to Durham Cathedral) was that the *magister choristarum* should be one of good character and upright life, skilled in singing and in organ-playing, who would diligently apply himself to teaching the boys, to playing the organ at proper times, and to singing the divine offices ('honestae famae, vitae probae, cantandi et organa pulsandi peritus, qui pueris docendis, organis pulsandis suo tempore, et divinis officiis cantandis studiose vacabit'). Appointment was to be 'per Decanum, aut eo absente per Vicedecanum et Capitulum'.

In early Stuart days it seems that conditions arose in certain New Foundation cathedrals which made it desirable to separate the work of master of the choristers from that of organist, and in 1620 a body of statutes for Norwich Cathedral was promulgated by James I which made this possible. As it happened, it had already been done (presumably *ultra vires*) at Norwich in 1591, when Richard Carlton, followed by Thomas Askew and George Sanders, became master of the choristers but not organist. The two posts were not reunited at Norwich until 1629. But at various times up to the nineteenth century there were again separate organists and masters of the choristers there. Then, in the reign of Charles I, new statutes both for Canterbury (January 1636/7) and Winchester (1638) allowed for separation of the two posts, so that Christopher Gibbons was organist of Winchester Cathedral, but not master of the choristers. In both instances the intention was that, if more suitable and skilful ('magis idoneus et peritior') than the organist, one of the minor canons or lay clerks might be master of the choristers. In 1666 statutes issued by Charles II made corresponding provision for Worcester Cathedral, while those for Ely Cathedral

[1] Strictly speaking, the statutes of Henry VIII are drafts only, lacking the Great Seal; nevertheless they were accepted as recognized authority: see A. Hamilton Thompson in the introduction to J. M. Falkner (ed.), *The Statutes of the Cathedral Church of Durham* (Surtees Society, 143; 1929).

recognized the existence of separate posts, albeit in a somewhat casual way (see p. 96).

Thus, with respect to cathedrals of the New Foundation, we find that, unless otherwise allowed by statute, the common form was a combination of the two posts under the title of master of the choristers. However, by the time of the Civil War there was a growing tendency, whatever the statutes might say, to use the term 'organist' in cathedral documents. Nevertheless, the position was that, if no one was separately named as organist in such cathedrals, then the officer designated master of the choristers also played the organ. Conversely, when the term 'organist' came into informal use, the holder of that post would also be master of the choristers if no one else was so named. From the seventeenth century some Chapter clerks and treasurers began to use the unambiguous expression 'master of the choristers and organist' (whatever the statutes might say), and where this is so, matters are self-evident. But at one time and another—the Norwich instance of 1591 being by far the earliest—many cathedrals of the New Foundation found it suitable to make separate appointments, whether allowed by statutes or not. Bristol, Carlisle, Gloucester, Christ Church, Oxford, and Rochester are the exceptions. It was not until Victorian days that the general practice of combined responsibility once more grew up, to prevail until today.

One must here allude to what happened at Westminster Abbey. Under the foundation of Queen Elizabeth I this was a collegiate church not a cathedral, but its constitution was akin to that of cathedrals of the New Foundation. So here, too, the duties of organist had at first been remitted to the master of the choristers. But Edmund Hooper, who had discharged both duties from 1585 under the title of *magister choristarum*, was made solely organist in 1606, with a new patent of appointment. His successor, John Parsons, discharged both duties, but with a patent expressly designating him not only as master of the choristers but specifically as organist. After him the separation continued, with the exception of the years 1621–3, until 1804, and so neither Orlando Gibbons nor Henry Purcell ever taught the Westminster Abbey choristers.

As we have seen, the masters of the choristers/organists of the New Foundations were specifically to be additional to the other adult members of the choral establishment, whether clerical or lay. Exceptions soon grew up. Both George Barcroft and John Amner, successive organists of Ely Cathedral, became also minor canons while still organist. After the Restoration the organist of Carlisle Cathedral was made a minor canon, though a layman, and this went on until 1833; but here it was simply a device to improve the organist's stipend, and amounted to the suppression of a minor canonry. At the Restoration, when no doubt recruitment was difficult, Peter Stringer, a former lay clerk, was appointed master of the choristers/organist at Chester and, taking holy orders, minor canon and precentor as well. Other early instances of the combination of a minor canonry with the post of organist occur at Canterbury (Marson), Chester (William Kay), and Peterborough (Roger Standish). An example in modern times is found at Durham, where A. D. Culley, minor canon from 1906, became also organist from 1907. This arrangement was regarded unfavourably by the Cathedrals Commission of 1921. None of these combinations seems to have given trouble, though obviously they must have depended on a deputy organist. But a dispute arose at Chester in 1737 in connection with Edmund Baker (see p. 67), and at Winchester two unhappy incidents grew up simply as a result of clerical confusion. There, from the start, in the twice-yearly roll-calls and in the accounts, the name of the master of the choristers/organist was entered at the head of the list of lay clerks. As it happened, most Winchester organists, from the end of the sixteenth century at least, down to 1849 were specifically appointed not only as organist but as lay clerk (if not already such), though this was contrary to the draft statutes. Even as late as 1849, 1865, and 1902, though S. S. Wesley, G. B. Arnold, and William Prendergast were not actually appointed as lay clerks, each was entered in official rolls at the head of the lay clerks' list, and it was not until 1907 that the Chapter corrected this anomaly deriving from the year 1541. This caused trouble in 1676, when it was conceived that Jewett ought to take his turn to sing in the choir, and a lay clerk named Webb had undertaken this for him (see p. 299). As late as the time of S. S. Wesley, the Winchester Chapter, somewhat ludicrously as one might now think, was attempting to make him sing in the choir when he was not playing the organ.

Cathedrals of the Old Foundation

Along with the English cathedrals of this group may be placed St David's Cathedral in Wales, which had an analogous constitution. The other cathedrals of Wales (Bangor, Llandaff, and St Asaph) were differently placed (see p. xxiv).

There is some misunderstanding about the historic position of the organists of the Old Foundation cathedrals, often expressed in such phrases as 'the organist was not a statutory officer', or 'the organist ranked in fact as one of the vicars choral'. The implication of these expressions is that the post of organist was unknown to the statutes of all these cathedrals; and, this being so, that it was necessary to make an appointment to a 'statutory' post of vicar choral. The facts are not so simple.

As to statutes, when these existed in codified form at all, namely, at Hereford (1637) and Lichfield (1693), the organist was specifically mentioned under that title. Elsewhere, the government of the cathedral being a matter of custom interpreted and regulated by visitations, injunctions, and precedents, it is wrong to think of any official as being either statutory or not. A true distinction is rather between endowed, freehold offices on the one hand, and appointments at the pleasure of the Dean and Chapter on the other. As to the organist's ranking as a vicar choral, this was at no time true of the great cathedral church of York, while at Hereford some organists were vicars choral, others were not.[2] At Lincoln two organists only, covering the years 1705–41, were 'junior vicars'. Hence John Bull (Hereford), William Byrd (Lincoln), and James Nares (York) were plain, straightforward organists, not vicars choral.

It is nevertheless true that, at the other six English cathedrals of the Old Foundation and at St David's, a regular association developed between the post of organist and the freehold of a vicar choral. But, except at St Paul's, this is far from saying that there was no official recognition of the organist as such. At Salisbury, for example, John Farrant was admitted vicar choral and organist in 1600; at Wells James Weare was admitted vicar choral and organist in 1608; at Exeter Arthur Cock became organist in 1589 with the reversion of a vicar's stall, and John Lugge had already been organist for some time before becoming a vicar in 1605; at the episcopal visitation of Chichester in 1613 Thomas Weelkes was formally cited as 'organist, instructor of the choristers, and Sherburne clerk' (these clerks were on a special foundation at Chichester, supplementary to the vicars); at St David's, where certain of his predecessors had been vicars, Henry Mordant was solely organist for some fifteen years before it was resolved in 1713 that he should succeed to the next vicar's place to fall vacant. At Lichfield, where the 1693 statutes made specific provision for an organist, those statutes went on to attach a vicar's stall to the post, so that here the link was indeed statutory; yet the organist did not lack statutory recognition as such. Only at St Paul's Cathedral, even down to the appointment of Goss, was no official cognizance taken of an organist, so that on occasions of formality such as an episcopal visitation no member of the Cathedral body was cited as organist. Here alone is it true to say that the organist ranked as a vicar choral.

Where, as in these six cathedrals, a firm association established itself by custom, or where, as at Lichfield, the association was established by statute, it grew out of convenience. A cathedral such as Lincoln had no need to economize, but less fortunate bodies like Chichester and Lichfield were glad to use this connection as a means of providing a substantial part of the organist's stipend and of getting a little extra work out of him. At Lichfield only £4 a year came to him as organist; the rest of his stipend came from his vicar's stall, and he was required to join in those parts of the service that were sung without organ. At Chichester in Thomas Weelkes's day it was enjoined that the organist should move from the choir-stalls to the organ

[2] It is relevant to note that, unlike elsewhere, membership of the Colleges of Vicars Choral at York and Hereford was restricted to men in holy orders.

and back again during the service as required. The Chapter minute of September 1616 (cited in full on p. 75) contains a strong hint of general practice elsewhere.

Vicars choral were members of endowed corporations. If Deans and Chapters chose to make use of a vicar's place to relieve themselves of a substantial part of the cost of an organist, it was hardly fair of them to expect him to do a vicar's work, and, as time went on and the duties of organist became more specialized and absorbing, there are no general signs that unreasonable demands were made. S. S. Wesley, for instance, was a vicar choral of Exeter Cathedral when organist there, and though there were indeed difficulties between him and the Chapter, they did not arise from this, and there was a considerable advantage in the arrangement. As vicar choral he held a freehold and enjoyed his share of the endowments, whereas simply as organist, unlike his brethren in the New Foundations, he was a servant at will. So it happened that when John Alcock gave up being organist at Lichfield, he sacrificed no more than £4 a year and continued as vicar choral for another forty years. This was inconvenient to the Chapter, which exacted a bond from Alcock's successor that he would not resign as organist without also resigning the vicar's place they had managed to find for him. Again, at St David's, after difficulties between Chapter and organist following the dismantling of the organ in 1864, W. P. Propert seems to have retained his freehold as vicar choral up to his death in 1906, and certainly continued to sing in the choir long after ceasing to be organist. It appears that Stainer, on appointment to St Paul's in 1872, attached some importance to the security which a vicar choralship would provide in the event of possible criticism. The converse position is illustrated by the plight of John Hutchinson, who was organist but not vicar choral of York Minster in the reign of Charles I. After cathedral bodies were abolished under Puritan rule, the Commonwealth committee handling cases of hardship considered it had no power to relieve him, as he was only a servant at pleasure.

Matters may now be summarized as follows: at York there was no connection between organist and vicar choral; at Hereford and Lincoln there was no regular connection; at Lichfield a statutory link existed from 1693 to 1959; at Chichester a Sherburne clerkship was annexed to the post of organist in 1685, but successive appointments were made under the title of organist only; at other cathedrals there grew up a customary connection, eventually broken in 1860 at Wells, 1876 at Exeter, 1888 at St Paul's, and at Salisbury some time after the death of A. T. Corfe in 1863. Appointments of organists were apparently in the hands not of the dean alone, but of the Dean and Chapter, saving only any rights possessed by a College of Vicars Choral in the event of its being desired to make the appointee a vicar.

Before leaving this question of the standing of the organist in cathedrals of the Old Foundation, one must draw attention to the unique instance of an organist who combined this post with that of canon and prebendary together with the dignity of precentor: T. H. Davis, organist of Wells cathedral, 1899–1933; canon, prebendary, and precentor, 1920–47.

There was no fundamental link between the post of master of the choristers and that of organist in cathedrals of the Old Foundation such as there was in those of the New Foundation, and practice varied a good deal. At Hereford the master of the choristers was never distinct from the organist after 1591. This was so also at Lichfield after the Restoration. On the other hand, at St Paul's, from the death of Sebastian Westcott in 1582 until the appointment of Martin in 1888, no organist except Jeremiah Clarke was master of the choristers. At Chichester, Lincoln, and Exeter matters fluctuated in varying degrees at various times, so that although Weelkes (Chichester), Byrd (Lincoln), and Langdon (Exeter) taught the choristers, not all their predecessors did so. After varied practice, the two offices came together at Wells in 1713 on the appointment of William Broderip; at Salisbury from the time of Giles Tomkins, who was master of the choristers before becoming organist; and at York from 1739 while Nares was organist. As in the New Foundations, the general practice of combined responsibility asserted itself in Victorian times.

It remains to speak of Bangor, Llandaff, and St Asaph Cathedrals. Having been staffed by secular rather than monastic clergy, rating thus as 'of the Old Foundation', these, like St David's Cathedral, were undisturbed at the Reformation. But during their early history they were less fortunately placed than St David's with regard to music. Before the Civil War they had no more than two, two, and four vicars choral respectively, and these did not constitute corporate bodies. Organists, singingmen, and boys were provided on a small scale in some informal way. However, Bangor and St Asaph received endowments under Acts of Parliament in 1685 and 1678 respectively for the maintenance of their choirs, including the organists (see pp. 21, 244) Llandaff, on the other hand, was forced to give up its choir in 1691 for want of income, and it was not until 1861 that an organist was once more appointed there.

Cathedrals of the Modern Foundation

Of the newly constituted cathedrals of dioceses created in the nineteenth and twentieth centuries, those of Manchester and Ripon already had an existing collegiate constitution providing for an organist (see pp. 183 and 227). At an early stage capitular bodies were envisaged for Liverpool and Truro. But the others, though now containing the bishop's cathedra, retained for many years the simple constitution of a parish church. The organists therefore stood in the customary position of a parish-church organist *vis-à-vis* the incumbent, though at Sheffield the involvement of the

Capital Burgesses (see p. 269) was an exception to this. Not until after the Cathedrals Measure (1934) were different constitutional arrangements made, with a provost at the head of each of these cathedrals, and the office of organist, however designated, regulated under bodies of statutes.

Present Titles of Office

At the present time, in statutes dated between 1963 and 1968, the cathedral officers charged with the duty of organist are officially mentioned by a variety of titles, of which 'master of the music' seems the most recently introduced. As a matter of information, not without interest, the exact terms of these various statutes are used below in respect of the present officer, notwithstanding that other designations may, of course, have come into customary use generally. In most instances the understanding is that this officer is responsible for the choir, even though the term used in the statutes may not specifically indicate that. However, the statutes for Liverpool Cathedral explicitly provide for separate posts of organist and 'choir director', while those for Gloucester and Manchester Cathedrals make permissive provision for separate appointments.

ARCHIVAL SOURCES DISCUSSED

As the core of this book is based on data derived from the archives of the ancient cathedrals, collegiate churches, and academic foundations, some information about the documents referred to may be not only useful but also interesting.

Capitular Foundations

1. *Chapter Act Books*. These are in effect the minute-books (occasionally but rarely so called) of the deans and canons of cathedral and collegiate churches, compiled (in Latin, for the most part, until the eighteenth century) by the Chapter clerk. (In a strict sense, 'acts' and 'minutes' are different things, and, indeed, from 1831 Wells Cathedral maintained a series of minutes distinct from the Act Books; but otherwise cathedrals did not maintain that distinction either in the titles or in the contents of their records, and in my own writing I have not hesitated to speak of an entry in an Act Book as a minute.) Most commonly, Chapter meetings were held monthly, though there were considerable variations; at Exeter they were weekly, while at Carlisle, in the early days, they were relatively infrequent. Unfortunately, few cathedrals still possess Act Books going back to the second half of the sixteenth century, and Chester, for example, has none earlier than 1648. Where they do survive, it is to these books that we should most readily turn for information about the appointment of organists or, in the cathedrals founded by Henry VIII, about the masters of the choristers/

organists. In some cathedrals early appointments were set out in a patent or an indenture recording a precise agreement. This, requiring a decision of Chapter, would be referred to in the Acts. Numerous instances are noted below, whether in cathedrals of the Old or of the New Foundation. But even where Act Books survive, by no means all cathedrals followed this practice, and it was in any event given up before the Civil War. Apart from patents, mention of organists' appointments is haphazard. Sometimes they have to be inferred when an organist is mentioned for the first time in some other connection, perhaps an admonition. On the whole (though there are interesting exceptions), early organists were rated fairly low by deans and canons, while the appointment of a simple bedesman in the Henrician cathedrals, being in the gift of the sovereign, would be punctiliously entered in the Acts. Again, in a cathedral of the Old Foundation, where perhaps an organist might also be a vicar choral, his admission as such might well be carefully minuted without any mention at that point of his post as organist.

Act Books, therefore, are not the certain source of information we could wish, although they tend to have a good deal to say where the organist gave trouble. A few cathedral Act Books, however, contain a good series of twice-annual roll-calls, in June and November, when the names and offices of all members of the cathedral body were listed, together with a note of whether they attended personally to answer their names. Much information concerning the personnel of Winchester Cathedral and St Patrick's Cathedral, Dublin is derived from these lists.

2. *Registers of patents and indentures.* It was sometimes the practice for copies of all documents issued under the capitular seal to be entered in a large register or ledger, in which, along with leases, presentations to livings, and so on, the documents issued to organists may be found. Such entries may correspond to, or enable us to infer, Chapter Acts, and are informative about conditions of appointment. They are, however, rare, the best survivals being at Ely and Norwich.

3. *Accounts.* As with Chapter Acts, early accounts were kept in Latin. Most usually they ran from Michaelmas to Michaelmas (29 September). A common practice was simply to enter the name of the man in office at the end of the accounting period. Only if, as happened from time to time, the yearly account shows 'To the organist: Mr Jones £7. 10*s*., Mr Smith £2. 10*s*.', can we infer that in a year ending at Michaelmas, Smith took over from Jones at Midsummer. More helpfully, some accounts show quarterly reckonings, so that if names are mentioned as well as the office, changes in appointments can be plotted more easily. Most useful of all, the treasurer of Durham Cathedral kept rough quarterly accounts in which, against the quarterly stipend, the recipient signed his name. Least helpful are those treasurers who entered simply 'To the organist'.

Under the heading 'Stipendia' or 'Solutiones', the organist (by whatever title he may be known) will probably be included with the other 'ministri inferiores'—the minor canons, vicars choral, and lay clerks. Some accounts give complete lists of the names of these, sometimes also of the choristers. If so, information about another part of some organist's career may be gleaned. But too often payments are summarized as 'to the six lay clerks' or 'to the eight chorister boys'. Other payments to the organist may be traced under some miscellaneous heading such as 'Extraordinary Payments' (*Extraordinary Solutiones*) or 'Fees and Tips' (*Feoda et Regarda*). These entries may cover payment for music-copying; or an augmentation of the statutory salary; expenses for a journey; and so on. Yet further information may be gathered under other headings: for example, 'Repairs' (*Reparationes*), which may mention builders' work on the organist's house, or mending and tuning the organ. At Lincoln Cathedral early accounts have a section headed 'Clerk of the Seals and Wax' under which payment was made to the organist (if also master of the choristers) for paper and ink used in teaching the boys.

Accounts of cathedrals of the New Foundation are fairly straightforward and uniform. Cathedrals of the Old Foundation had a more complicated financial structure, and may have had to keep more than one set of accounts for funds differently derived. One cannot feel quite sure, where the organist's stipend is concerned, that at York the surviving accounts give us the whole picture.

4. *Episcopal visitations*. Somewhat rarely, but occasionally usefully, there survive the questions asked by the bishop of the diocese at his periodic visitation of his cathedral church, together with the answers. These may mention the organist by name, or comment on his work. There may also be a list of all the members of the cathedral body.

5. *Records of minor corporations*. Where, in the cathedrals of the Old Foundation, the vicars choral constituted a college, they transacted business of their own. As they were deeply involved in the music of the cathedral and sometimes included the organist in their number, this may be germane to our purpose. There are useful Act Books for the Colleges of Vicars Choral at Hereford and Wells.

6. *Registers of baptisms, marriages, and burials*. Some cathedrals, though they were not parish churches, maintained registers of their own. In some others, part of the cathedral might have parochial status—the south aisle of Chester Cathedral (St Oswald's), for example, or the Lady Chapel of Ely Cathedral (Holy Trinity)—and so have its own registers. Elsewhere (Chichester, for instance), burials within the cathedral precincts were entered in the registers of the nearest parish church.

Academic Foundations

These have more limited archival material. For Trinity College, Cambridge the 'Conclusion Books' of the Seniority (roughly corresponding to cathedral Act Books) contain useful information; so also do some scattered entries in the Vice-President's Register of Magdalen College, Oxford. At Winchester College there are the yearly lists, or 'Long Rolls', of members of the College. But for the most part in these foundations we are dependent on the annual accounts, written up each year in a form very similar to those of the cathedrals, but tending to speak of four terms instead of quarters.

Cathedrals of the Nineteenth and Twentieth Centuries

Most of these were parish churches at the time of their elevation, and continued without constitutional change until after 1934. It seems that few records, if any, were kept, and in most instances it has proved impossible to reach primary documentation about appointments of the earlier organists. Correspondence with the cathedral authorities now forms part of Lcm, MS 6069.

DATES OF TENURE

It is by no means always easy to determine the exact dates on which an organist took up or relinquished the duties of his post. That problems arise at an early date, when records are imperfect, is not surprising. But they occur in quite recent instances also.

Some have arisen out of confusion between the date when an appointment was offered, accepted, and announced, and the date on which it became effective; and also because of a tendency to assume an unbroken chain of appointments, such as 'XYZ retired in 1906 and was succeeded by PQR', giving rise to the idea that PQR's duties began in 1906, which is by no means necessarily so. The dates variously given for S. H. Nicholson's tenure at Westminster Abbey are instructive:

Grove[5]	resigned 1927
Who Was Who, 1941–50	1918–1927
A House of Kings (London, 1966)	1918–1927
Gravestone in Abbey cloisters	1919–1928

The facts are that he was offered the appointment in 1918, took up duty in January 1919 following Bridge's retirement on 31 December 1918, proffered his resignation in 1927, and left in 1928. Another example concerns W. G. Alcock, who is usually stated to have given up at the Chapel Royal in 1916, started at Salisbury Cathedral also in 1916, and to have been succeeded at the Chapel Royal by C. H. Lloyd in that same year. What happened was that he tendered his resignation at the Chapel Royal by letter dated 1 November 1916 to take effect on 31 December that year, and that C. H. Lloyd's appointment to succeed him ran from 1 January 1917 (letter from Lord Chamberlain's Office to me, 6 October 1972). Yet in supplying information to *Who's Who*, Alcock himself said 'organist of Salisbury Cathedral 1916'. That there must be many such pitfalls is only too plain, however one may have tried to avoid them.

Concerning dates based on older archives, difficulties may be classified thus:

(*a*) Where surviving records are intermittent. Suppose a series of treasurer's rolls names XYZ for the quarter ending Midsummer 1596, and then breaks off until the quarter ending Christmas 1597, when PQR is named. In such cases I have shown the concluding date for XYZ as 1596→, and the opening date for PQR as ←1597.

(*b*) Where accounts show a change of organist at the quarter ending 25 December in, say, 1577. It may be pedantic, for the sake of the six remaining days of the calendar year, to give the new tenure as beginning in 1577, yet there is nothing else to be done.

(*c*) Where accounts are written up in yearly form, naming merely the organist in office at the end of the year. Thus at Westminster Abbey the accounts give Purcell's name for the stipend for the complete year ending Michaelmas 1695, and John Blow's for the complete year to Michaelmas 1696. But, apart from the absurdity of supposing that offices changed hands only on the same given day each year, we know in this instance that Blow did not begin duty until after Purcell's death on 21 November 1695. There are bound to be other instances which we have no means of checking.

(*d*) Where a cathedral followed the practice of passing formal resolutions about appointments once a year, as happened at Peterborough every June. But it would surely be wrong to assume that all organists there went in and out of office only in June.

(*e*) Where patents of appointments, as frequently happened, used the conventional formula 'on account of services already rendered and to be rendered', giving rise to a supposition that the document was issued to someone already in office from an earlier date. In some instances this may be so. But the phrase was a lawyer's way of covering all contingencies, and does not necessarily apply throughout. Particular instances are commented on below.

NOTES ON MONEY AND DATES

In pre-decimal coinage, 1*s*. (shilling) = 5p; 6*d*. (pence) = 2½p. The curious sums often mentioned below of 13*s*. 4*d*. and 6*s*. 8*d*. (and their multiples) derive from the obsolete medieval mark and noble respectively.

Until 1753 in England, unlike the Continent, the new year for legal, administrative, and financial purposes began on 25 March. Thus 28 February 1621 (Old Style, as to the Chapter clerks and treasurers of the cathedrals of the Church of England) is 28 February 1622 (New Style, reckoning the change of year from the preceding 1 January). Hence the convention: 28 February 1621/2. The opportunity was also taken in 1752 to adjust an accumulated difference of eleven days between the old (Julian) calendar and the new (Gregorian) calendar. But in historical writing, while the years prior to 1753 are commonly adjusted, the difference of eleven days is ignored. Thus, while 18 February 1652 OS should strictly become 1 March 1653 NS, in practice it is given simply as 18 February 1653, or, as we say here, 18 February 1652/3. This consideration relates to the date of Samuel Arnold's birth (see p. 335).

I

The Chapel Royal

The primary sources for appointments in the Chapel Royal until the late nineteenth century are (1) the so-called 'Old' Cheque Book, covering the years 1561 to 1744, and (slightly overlapping) (2) the 'Second' Cheque Book for the period 1721 to 1880. These were kept by an officer known as the clerk of the Cheque, usually one of the 'gentlemen' of the Chapel (see below). The originals are in the keeping of the Chapel Royal, St James's Palace, London SW1, and a microfilm of them is available for consultation in the Public Record Office, Kew (PRO 28/1). The first of them was published by the Camden Society (New Series 3) in 1872, edited by E. F. Rimbault.

Abbreviated references in this section:

OCB the Old Cheque Book (with page references to Rimbault's edition).

CB2 the second Cheque Book (with page numbers).

The Chapel Royal consists of a body of persons—the dean, the sub-dean, the chaplains, the priests in ordinary, the organist (who at present is also the choirmaster and composer), 'gentlemen', and 'children'—who form the ecclesiastical establishment of the Court (except in Scotland). In this sense in times past the Chapel Royal was required to accompany the monarch on state occasions, as when Henry VIII met Francis I at the Field of the Cloth of Gold, or when Charles I went ceremoniously to Canterbury to receive his bride on her way from France through Dover. In modern times the most public occasions on which members of the Chapel Royal appear are when the children and the organist go with the Queen for the distribution of the Royal Maundy money, or when, headed by the Bishop of London as dean, the whole choir attends her at the annual observance of Remembrance Sunday in Whitehall.

The adult male singers, now exclusively lay but formerly both ordained and lay, are designated 'gentlemen of the Chapel Royal', and the boys are termed the 'children'. For a long time the office of master of the children, which may be traced from pre-Reformation times, was a more important post than that of organist, and a summary list is given below (pp. 19–20). On the other hand, we have no names of any organists before the year 1575. The work of organ-playing seems to have been allotted to various gentlemen of the Chapel with some degree of informality until gradually a feeling of a definite post emerged. The earliest person actually designated organist in a document of official character is John Bull in May 1592. At exactly what point remuneration, independent of that of a gentleman, began to be attached specifically to the duty of organist does not transpire. The earliest reference to come to notice is in a document headed 'Establishment of our Chapels . . . at Whitehall', dated 1702 (Lbl, Add. MS 14407, f. 16^{v}). Doubtless drawn up for guidance at the accession of Queen Anne, this shows Blow and Croft ('1st' and '2nd' organist respectively) as having £11. 8*s*. 1½*d*. wages and £61. 11*s*. 10½*d*. board-wages each, with like sums also in their capacities as composers.

At various times there has been more than one organist, taking turns of duty. Indeed, the earliest identified organists of the Chapel, Tallis and Byrd, served jointly. This was particularly necessary when the posts were occupied by men who simultaneously held appointments elsewhere, like Thomas Tomkins. Such plurality is explained by the prestige and status of a Chapel Royal appointment, which was coveted as much for this as for purely professional reasons. From 1700 there has been a post of composer (later increased to two) in the Chapel Royal, first held by Blow (see list on p. 20).

An anecdote of Anthony Wood's (see under Ely Cathedral) suggests that ***Christopher Tye** may have been organist of the Chapel Royal. I prefer, however, to begin this record with the safely attested names of Tallis and Byrd.

Thomas Tallis 1575–85 (b. *c.*1505; d. London (Greenwich), 23 Nov. 1585). E. H. Fellowes (*Grove*[3]) gave reasoned grounds for believing Tallis was born about 1505. Baillie notes that already in 1531–2 he was 'joculator organorum' of Dover Priory, where he may have stayed until 1536–7 when he became a 'conduct' (lay singer) of St Mary-at-Hill, London. He left there during 1537–8, and is next heard of in 1540 when he received a gratuity on the dissolution of Waltham Abbey. Almost immediately he became a lay clerk of Canterbury Cathedral, where his name is found in a list *c.*1541 (Canterbury Cathedral, MS DE 164).

The exact date of his appointment as a gentleman of the Chapel Royal is unknown, but he took part in that capacity in the funeral of Henry VIII and the coronation of Edward VI in 1547 (Lafontaine 1909: 6, 7). In 1575, when they were granted a royal monopoly of printing music and music-paper, he and Byrd were named as 'two of the gentlemen of our Chapel'; but in the same year there appeared the *Cantiones Sacrae* composed by Tallis and Byrd, 'Serenissimae Regineae Maiestati a priuato Sacello generosis et Organistis'. This, then, is our evidence that Tallis and Byrd were both organists of the Chapel at least by 1575. Presumably Tallis remained until his death.

He was buried in the choir of Greenwich Parish Church. Presumably he died while serving the Queen at her palace of Greenwich. The record of his death (OCB, 4) reads: 'Tho. Tallis died the 23rd of November 1585 and Henry Eveseed sworn in his place the last of the same. Child there.' This refers, of course, to his place as gentleman. The last two words have been accepted too readily as testimony that Tallis himself had been one of the children of the Chapel; but they clearly point to Eveseed.

The inscription on his tomb is recorded thus by Strype (1720: ii, App. I: 92):

In the Chancel. A stone before the Rails, having a Brass Plate thus inscribed in old Gothic Letters.

Enterred here doth ly a worthy Wyght
Who for long Tyme in Musick bore the Bell:
His name to shew, was Thomas Gallys hyght,
In honest vertuous Lyff he dyd excell.

He serv'd long Tyme in Chapp . . with grete prayse,
Fower sovereygnes reignes (a thing not often seene),
I mean King Henry and Prynce Edward's Dayes,
Quene Mary, and Elizabeth our Quene.

He maryed was, though Children he had none,
And lyv'd in Love full thre and thirty Yeres,
With loyal Spowse, whos Name yclyipt was Jone
Who here entomb'd, him Company now bears,

As he did Lyve, so also did he dy,
In myld and quyet Sort (O! happy Man)
To God full oft for Mercy did he cry,
Wherefore he lyves, let Death do what he can.

'Gallys' is an obvious mistranscription of the 'old Gothic Letters'. The inscription was restored in 1935, but destroyed during World War II.

William Byrd 1575–*c*.1613. The Old Cheque Book records Byrd's admission as gentleman of the Chapel Royal as follows: '1569. Robt. Parsons was drowned at Newark upon Trent the 25th of January and Wm. Bird sworn gentleman in his place at the first [*sic*] the 22d of February following, A°. xiiij[to], Lincoln.' There is confusion here between the calendar year and the regnal year: 22 February 1569 (i.e., 1569/70) falls in the twelfth year of Elizabeth I, on the other hand, if the regnal year is correct, the calendar year should be 1571/2. (Not only does the Cheque Book seem to be muddled on this point between June 1568 and October 1573, but in some of its entries it does not maintain chronological sequence.) For Byrd's post as organist of the Chapel, see the evidence adduced above for Tallis. His two books of *Cantiones Sacrae* (1589, 1591) and of *Gradualia* (1605 (2nd edn., 1610), 1607) speak of these as composed by William Byrd, 'Organista Regio Anglo'. However, his publications of English part-music dated 1588, 1589, and 1611 speak only of his being a gentleman of the Chapel.

A document of 2 November 1615 (OCB, 74) refers to 'the now organists Edmund Hooper and Orlando Gibbons' in a context clearly implying that there were no others, and it is reasonable to suggest that by this time, when he would be more than 70 years of age, Byrd may have given up playing the organ in the Chapel, while retaining his status as one of the gentlemen.

See under Lincoln Cathedral.

John Blitheman ?–1591 (d. London, Whitsun 1591). The solitary reference to Blitheman in the Cheque Book (OCB, 5) records his death in 1591, but neither this nor his memorial inscription (see below) mention a Christian name. That of William was at one time attached to him, relying on a composition thus attributed in the Fitzwilliam Virginal Book. But there can be no doubt that we are concerned with a John Blith(e)man who appears to have joined the Chapel Royal as a gentleman in the reign of Mary I. He is not listed among the gentlemen at her coronation, but he is named on the occasion of her funeral in 1558 (PRO, E101/427/6; LC2/4(2)), and the name continues to occur in assessments of lay subsidies for members of the Chapel during Elizabeth's reign up to 1590 (e.g., PRO, E179/266/13). His inclusion in the roll of organists rests on his memorial inscription (see below), echoed in Wood (1815–20: i. 235, *sub* 'Bull'). There it is stated that John Bull 'was trained up under an excellent master named Blithman, organist of Queen Elizabeth's chapel who died much lamented in 1591'. A footnote by Bishop Tanner printed in Wood reads: 'John Blithman belonged to Christ Church quire, seems to have been master of the choristers 1564', and, indeed, someone of that name is found in Registrum A of Christ Church, Oxford for the years 1563–78, though not specially designated other than by standing at the head of the lay clerks. Perhaps his departure from Christ Church marks his assumption of the duty of an organist in addition to that of a gentleman of the Chapel Royal.

According to Williams (1893), Blitheman took the Cambridge degree of Mus.B. in 1586, but this is not mentioned in *Venn*.

Blitheman was buried in St Nicholas Olave Church, Queenhithe, London. The inscription to his memory is given thus in Stow's collections (Lbl, Harl. MS 538, f. 130^{v}):

> Blitheman an organist of the queen's chapel buried there in the year 1591 with this epitaph:
>
> Here Blitheman lies, a worthy wight, who feared God above,
> A friend to all, a foe to none whom rich and pore did love,
> Of Princes Chaple gentleman, unto his dienge daye
> Wher all toke greate delight to here him on the organs playe
> Whose passing skill in musykes arte, a scholar left behinde
> John Bull by name, his master's veyne expressing in eche kynde.
> But nothing here continuethe longe, nor resting place can have
> His sowle departed hence to heven, his body here in grave.

John Bull 1592–1613. Bull was sworn a gentleman of the Chapel Royal in January 1585/6 (OCB, 4). As with Tallis and Byrd, no specific date can be established when he became organist, but an OCB entry dated May 1592 speaks of 'Mr Bull, organist in her said Majesty's Chapel', and an account of the Easter Communion Service of 1593 mentions that 'Dr Bull was at the organ playing the offertory' (OCB, 150). By patent dated 13 April 1605, described as 'Doctor in Music and Organist of our Chapel', he was granted what was apparently a special annuity (PRO, E403/2454; information from Andrew Ashbee). He was still organist at the time of his leaving England in 1613.

It has sometimes been stated that Bull was organist of the Chapel Royal at first jointly with Blitheman and then in succession to him. While this is not impossible, there is no documentary evidence to support this.

See under Hereford Cathedral.

William Randall 1592–1604. Randall, who came from Exeter, was admitted as epistler of the Chapel Royal on 15 February 1584/5 (OCB, 4). At the funeral of Elizabeth I and the coronation of James I in 1603 he was listed as one of the gentlemen (Lafontaine 1909: 44; OCB, 128). He was specifically designated as organist when witnessing the admission of the sub-dean in July 1592 (OCB, 33). He died or resigned early in 1604, as implied by the entry dated 1 March 1603/4 of the swearing-in of Edmund Hooper 'in Mr Randall's room' (OCB, 6).

Early in 1601 Randall made an attempt, through royal representations, to secure readmission to his place in Exeter Cathedral (cf. the instance of William

Byrd at Lincoln q.v.) making out that he had been unjustly dispossessed on joining the Queen's service. But the Dean and Chapter of Exeter stood their ground, as appears from a copy letter in their archives (D&C Exeter, VC/22207) addressed to the Queen as follows:

It hath pleased your highness by your gracious letters to recommend unto us Mr Randall, a gentleman of your majesty's chapel, for the obtaining of that vicar's room . . . he enjoyed before his preferment to your highness' service, giving information that he was by us unjustly dispossessed of the same and that there hath been for the space of many years past certain vicars' rooms [appointments] kept void and the benefit thereunto appertaining enjoyed by others. May it therefore please your majesty of your gracious favour to take knowledge that his departure from the place was voluntary, void on his own resignation of the same to the use of one Roger Mudge, commended by Sir Walter Rayleghe, and took of the said Mudge £10 for the same, besides other money for certain implements in his chamber. And for the rooms which he reporteth to be now void, there are so many priests and lay vicars at this time in this church as were many years before his departure and as may be by their small revenues with any competencies of living maintained. And thus in all humility beseeching your highness to be pleased with this our due and dutiful answer we end with our daily and hearty prayers to almighty God for the continuance of your majesty's most happy reign over us and for your endless comfort in the kingdom of heaven. 28 Martii 1601.

Your majesty's most bounden and humble subjects
The Dean and Chapter of the Cath. Church of St Peter in Exon.

Attached to this is a paper with two paragraphs of memoranda, no doubt ammunition gathered before the letter was drafted. One of these is illuminating: 'William Randall, being possessed of a vicar's room in this church, was not sent for to serve in her Majesty's Chapel but made great suit that he might be of that place, and until he had obtained the same he served under Mr Byrde and had maintenance from him.' So far as one can tell, the Exeter authorities appear successfully to have withstood royal pressure in this matter.

Arthur Cock ***c.*****1601–5** (d. London, Jan. 1605). Cock was a chorister of Canterbury Cathedral, 1568–76. Then in 1578–9 he became a 'substitute' in the Cathedral choir, and not later than 1587 he became master of the choristers and organist (q.v.). Next he was appointed organist of Exeter Cathedral in April 1589 (q.v.). While at Exeter he obtained the Oxford degree of B.Mus. on 25 February 1593/4 (Wood 1815–20: i. 261), and he was still at Exeter when he joined the Chapel Royal.

On 3 March 1600/1 'Arte Cocke' was sworn 'gentleman in ordinary and organist (without pay) in her Majesty's said Chapel, until an organist place shall become void'. He was required to 'give his attendance, and to supply the wants of organists which maybe through sickness or other urgent causes . . . and at his own proper costs and charges'. The inequality of this bargain was somewhat rectified when, on 8 March 1601/2, 'Arthur Cock from Exon' was sworn into a vacancy as gentleman (OCB, 37, 6).

It would appear that at this time there were already three organists: Byrd, Randall, and Bull. It may be, therefore, that Cock was never anything but a deputy organist. However, his final entry in the Cheque Book reads: 'Arthur

Cock died the 26th of January 1604 [1604/5]; and Orlando Gibbons was sworn in his room the 21st of March following.' Admittedly, this says neither that Cock was organist nor that Gibbons succeeded him as such. Nevertheless, as Gibbons undoubtedly did become organist, it creates a certain presumption that Cock had filled such a post. If that is so, then for some time there must have been four organists available in the Chapel: Byrd, Randall, and Bull, together with Cock followed by Gibbons.

Edmund Hooper 1604–21. Hooper was sworn of the Chapel Royal on 1 March 1603/4 'in Mr Randall's room' (OCB, 6), and it may reasonably be presumed that he was not only a gentleman but also one of the organists from that time. On Bull's departure in 1613, Hooper, along with Orlando Gibbons, was allotted a substantial share of his unapportioned wages, a clear indication that the three of them had ranked together as organists. In 1615, in connection with a document setting forth how the duties of organist were to be shared, Hooper and Gibbons both signed as 'the now organists'. Again, in the list of gentlemen of the Chapel on the occasion of Queen Anne's funeral in 1618 both of them are marked 'organist' (Lafontaine 1909: 52); and in recording Hooper's death on 14 July 1621 OCB describes him as 'organist'. It is evident, therefore, that by now there was a much clearer consciousness of a definite position of organist in the Chapel.

See under Westminster Abbey.

Orlando Gibbons 1605–25 (bap. Oxford, 25 Dec. 1583; d. Canterbury, 5 June 1625). Orlando Gibbons, the youngest son of William Gibbons, a musician, was born in Oxford (baptized at St Martin's Church, Carfax) but brought up in Cambridge. Lists compiled by F. L. Clarke (see p. 355) show that from early 1596 to autumn 1598 he was a chorister of King's College, Cambridge under his elder brother Edward as master of the choristers. He matriculated as 'a sizar from King's' in 1598 (*Venn*). In Michaelmas and Nativity terms of the academic years 1601–2 and 1602–3 he received payments 'pro musica in festo Dominae Reginae' and 'pro musica in festo purificationis' (King's College, Bursar's Particular Books, under 'Feoda et Regarda').

As noted above under Cock, he was sworn of the Chapel Royal on 21 March 1604/5. One has little difficulty in regarding him as one of the organists from this date, particularly in view of his description as 'royal organist' when taking his Cambridge degree (see below). At the funeral of James I in May 1625 he was designated 'senior organist' (OCB, 156); but this record is not the same as a complete list of musicians at the funeral (Lafontaine 1909: 58) which places Thomas Tomkins (III) at the head of the list, with Gibbons among the gentlemen with the description 'privy organ'.

In 1619 Gibbons received a further royal appointment as musician for the virginals, and in the later part of 1623 he also became organist of Westminster Abbey (q.v.). He died suddenly in Canterbury, where he had gone with the Chapel Royal on the way to welcome the bride of Charles I in June 1625, and he is buried in the Cathedral there, which has an elaborate tablet to his memory together with a bust (of which a modern copy has been placed in Westminster

Abbey). There is a portrait of him (a copy of a lost original) in the Music School collection at Oxford (Poole 1912–25: i. 151).

In 1606 the Cambridge degree of Mus.B. was granted to him, 'regio organistae' (Wood 1815–20: 406). In 1607 he was apparently incorporated at Oxford as an MA of Cambridge, but this must surely be a mistake for Mus.B. (Foster 1887–92). When William Camden founded his history lectureship at Oxford in 1622, Gibbons, along with William Heather who then endowed a 'music master' and a music lecturer, received the Oxford degree of D.Mus. (Wood 1815–20: i. 406).

Of Gibbons's seven children, his second son Christopher became a musician and is noted separately below.

Fellowes 1951.

Thomas Tomkins (III) 1621–Interregnum. Thomas Tomkins, 'organist of Worcester', was sworn in the place of 'Edmund Hooper, organist' on 2 August 1621 (OCB, 10). It is not explicitly stated that he became a gentleman of the Chapel, but, along with Orlando Gibbons, he appears in the context of such when Thomas Peirs (Pearce) was sworn gentleman on 29 June 1620 (OCB, 47). One has no hesitation in identifying him as the 'Mr Tomkins' who, in 1625, received 40*s.* 'for composing of many songs against the coronation of King Charles I' (OCB, 58).

See under Worcester Cathedral.

Thomas Warwick 1625–Interregnum. On the death of Gibbons in June 1625, 'Thomas Warwick was sworn in his place as organist the first day of July following and to receive the pay of the pistoler [epistler]', and he was sworn a gentleman of the Chapel on 12 September (OCB, 11). On 29 March 1630 he came under the censure of Laud (in his capacity as dean of the Chapel) 'because he presumed to play verses on the organ at service time, being formerly inhibited by the Dean from doing the same, by reason of his insufficiency for that solemn service' (OCB, 78).

In a list of royal household musicians dated 1641 (Ashbee 1986–9: iii. 113) 'Mr Warwick' is named 'for the virginal'. In 1622 Thomas Tomkins dedicated to 'Mr Thomas Warwicke' his madrigal 'When I observe those beauty's wonderments'. He died before the Restoration, for in 1660 Christopher Gibbons succeeded Thomas Warwick 'deceased' as musician upon the virginals (ibid. i. 4). The statement that he was organist of Westminster Abbey (Wood MS Notes) is manifestly unreliable.

According to *DNB*, Thomas was the father of Sir Philip Warwick (1609–83), a royalist statesman of some importance. For a comment on his connection, if any, with Thomas Warrock (or Warwick), organist of Hereford Cathedral, see below (p. 134).

A memorandum of 1625 (OCB, 11) reads as follows: 'that Mr John Tomkins, Organist of St Paul, London, was sworn extraordinary gentleman of his majesty's Chapel for the next place of an organist there, or the place of Anthony Kirkby, which of them shall first fall void'. But no vacancy as organist occurred for him. However, he did not have to wait for Kirkby's place, being admitted epistler on 3 November 1626 and gentleman on 19 July 1627 (OCB, 12). As an organist he accompanied several members of the Chapel Royal to Scotland in 1633, along with his brother Giles, on the occasion of the King's visit (Ashbee 1986–9: iii. 71), but this was probably an *ad hoc* arrangement for the purpose. It must be regarded as very uncertain that **John Tomkins** was organist of the Chapel Royal, though no doubt his services may have been used.

See under St Paul's Cathedral, London.

On the re-establishment of the Chapel Royal after the Restoration there were three organists, and in an order dated 19 December 1663 it was provided that: 'Of the three organists two shall ever attend, one at the organ, the other in his surplice in the quire, to bear a part in the psalmody and service. At solemn times they shall all three attend . . . Other days they shall wait according to their months.' (OCB, 81.) Inasmuch as the first three organists after the Restoration all held regular appointments elsewhere, as did some of their successors, the requirement that two of them should always attend must have been difficult to satisfy; and a further requirement in the same order that 'No man shall be admitted gentleman of his Majesty's Chapel Royal but shall first quit all interest in other quires', must have been a dead letter.

There continued to be three organists until the death of Henry Purcell in 1695. Thereafter until the death of George Smart in 1867 there were two, and since that time there has been one only.

William Child (Post 1) **1660–97.** There is no formal record of Child's appointment as organist of the Chapel Royal, but in a list of 'The names of the Sub-dean, gentlemen, and others' who took part in the coronation of Charles II on 23 April 1661 (OCB, 128) he is designated such, and it is therefore likely that he was appointed before the end of 1660. At the coronation of James II in 1685 he was named by Sandford (1687) as 'Eldest Gentleman of the Chapel'. He retained office until his death (OCB, 21).

See under St George's Chapel, Windsor.

Christopher Gibbons (Post 2) **1660–76.** At some time in 1660 a note made in the royal household records reads: 'Mr Gybbons approved of by the King at Baynard's [?Barnard's] Castle, and an organ to be made for him' (Ashbee 1986–9: i. 3). This may imply Christopher Gibbons's appointment to the Chapel Royal. In any event, like Child, he is named as organist in the list of members of the Chapel at the coronation of 1661. His death on 20 October 1676 was entered in the Cheque Book, where he was described as 'organist of his Majesty's Chapel Royal' (OCB, 16).

See under Winchester Cathedral.

Edward Lowe (Post 3) **1660–82.** Lowe, like Child and Gibbons, was named as organist in the list of Chapel Royal musicians attending the coronation of 1661.

In recording his death at Oxford on 11 July 1682, the Cheque Book describes him as 'organist of his Majesty's Chapel Royal' (OCB, 17).

See under Christ Church Cathedral, Oxford.

John Blow (Post 2) **1676–1708** (bap. Newark-on-Trent, 23 Feb. 1649; d. London (Westminster), 1 Oct. 1708). Blow had been one of the children of the Chapel under Henry Cooke from about 1660 until his voice changed some time before Christmas 1664 (Ashbee 1986–9: i. 63). He was appointed a gentleman in March 1673/4, and succeeded Pelham Humfrey as master of the children in July 1674 (OCB, 15, 16; Ashbee 1986–9: i. 140). On the death of Christopher Gibbons in October 1676, Blow followed him as organist without delay. OCB (16) is not explicit about this, but it is put beyond doubt by a register kept by the serjeant of the Vestry (PRO, Reg. RG8/110, f. 20v). The tale of his Chapel Royal appointments, all of which he held until his death, is completed by his admission to a newly created post of composer in March 1699/1700 (OCB, 23; Obl, MS Mus. e.17).

He held various appointments in the secular part of the royal household. From Christmas 1668 he was a virginalist; in 1674 he succeeded Humfrey as composer in the private music for voices; and in 1695, jointly with Bernard Smith, he followed Henry Purcell as tuner of regals, organs, virginals, and wind instruments (Ashbee 1986–9: i. 134, 140; ii. 56).

Concurrently with these royal appointments, Blow was twice organist of Westminster Abbey (q.v.) first from 1668 to 1679, and again from 1695 until his death. In addition he became almoner and master of the choristers of St Paul's Cathedral in September 1687, holding this post until November 1703 (Lgh, MSS 25630/13, f. 231v; 25664/1, f. 202; 25738/3, p. 65).

Blow was the first holder of the Lambeth degree of Doctor of Music, which he received on 10 December 1677 (Llp, Faculty Office Muniment Book, 1669–79). He is buried in the north choir aisle of Westminster Abbey (Chester 1876). No inscription marks the grave, but a memorial on the north wall states that 'He was scholar to the excellent Musician Dr Christopher Gibbons and Master to the famous Mr H. Purcell and most of the Eminent Masters in Musick since.'

Henry Purcell (Post 3) **1682–95**. Purcell's appointment as organist of the Chapel Royal was dated 14 July 1682, and he was sworn on 16 September (OCB, 17).

See under Westminster Abbey.

Francis Pigott (Post 1) **1697–1704** (d. 15 May 1704). This is no doubt the Francis Pigott, one of the children of the Chapel, whose voice had changed by November 1683 (Ashbee 1986–9: i. 208). After having been organist of St John's College, Oxford, he became organist of Magdalen College in January 1686 (q.v.). He was appointed organist of the Temple Church, London in 1688. The agreement, dated 25 May 1688, between Pigott and the Societies of the Middle and Inner Temple is printed by Macrory (n.d.). For his salary of £50 (a generous sum at that time) he was to provide an organ-blower, and observe the improbable provision that he was to play 'in such manner and on such stops as shall be fitting, or as the said Treasurers (if they shall order anything therein) shall appoint'. He was not to be 'or undertake to be organist in any other church or chapel whatsoever'; but this did not prevent him from taking up duties in the Chapel Royal while retaining the Temple appointment until his death.

He was appointed organist extraordinary in the Chapel Royal in December 1695, and on 24 March 1696/7 he was sworn organist on the death of Child (OCB, 21). The following year he took the Cambridge degree of Mus.B. (*Venn*). His death is recorded in OCB (25).

William Croft and Jeremiah Clarke (Post 1 jointly) **1704–7.** On 7 July 1700 Croft and Clarke were both sworn gentlemen extraordinary with a promise of succession 'as organists according to merit', and in due course, on 25 May 1704, they were jointly admitted to the place made vacant by Pigott's death (OCB, 23, 25).

For Clarke, see under St Paul's Cathedral, London.

William Croft (Post 1 sole occupant) **1707–27** (bap. Nether Ettington, War., 30 Dec. 1678; d. Bath, Somerset, 14 Aug. 1727). Croft was brought up in the Chapel Royal choir under Blow. His voice had broken by April 1699 (Ashbee 1986–9: ii. 64). In 1699 William III, directing Blow to attend to the matter (ibid.) presented the organ in the former Queen Dowager's Chapel to the church of St Anne, Soho, Westminster, and Croft, when contributing complimentary verses about his old master to Blow's *Amphion Anglicus* in 1700, described himself as 'Organist of St Ann's'. The relevant page in the Vestry minutes of the church is now wanting, but an entry in the index to the volume reads '1700. Croft, Mr appointed organist [p.] 183' (Wad, MS A2202/2202a). (The two later references to him in these minutes, the second on his resignation in 1711, use the Christian name 'Philip'.) Croft's admission as gentleman and organist of the Chapel Royal jointly with Clarke has already been noted. The full place fell to him on Clarke's death, and in 1708 he succeeded Blow as both master of the children and composer of the Chapel (OCB, 25, 26). He also followed Blow as organist of Westminster Abbey (q.v.). In 1713 he took the Oxford degree of D.Mus., to qualify for which he wrote two odes, published under the title of *Musicus Apparatus Academicus*. His death 'at the Bath' was recorded in the *Daily Journal* for 18 August 1727.

Croft lies buried in the north choir aisle of Westminster Abbey, close to Purcell. A lengthy and elaborately worded memorial on a nearby wall proclaims: 'Harmoniam, A praeclarissimo modulandi Artifice, Cui alterum jam claudit latus, Feliciter derivavit.' This, which may be rendered as 'he happily derived his harmony from the pre-eminent master of composition who now lies at the other side of him', evidently refers to Blow. A portrait of Croft by Thomas Murray is in the Music School collection at Oxford (Poole 1912–25: i. 158).

John Weldon (Post 2) **1708–36** (b. Chichester, 19 Jan. 1676; d. London (Westminster), 7 May 1736). Weldon's place of birth is traced through Hawkins (1853: ii. 784). He was a chorister of Eton College when *John Walters was organist there, and the College accounts, 1689–1701, reveal the following payments relating to him:

1692–33. Allowed Mr Walter towards putting out Weldon the chorister for half a year at Michaelmas 1693, £5.

1693–4 . Allowed to Mr Pursell with Weldon the chorister for half a year ended at Lady Day 1694, £5.

He was organist of New College, Oxford, 1694–1701 (q.v.). In a competition advertised in the *London Gazette* in 1699 for setting Congreve's *The Judgment of Paris*, Weldon won the first prize of 100 guineas (Burney 1776–89: iv. 632).

On 6 June 1701 he was sworn gentleman extraordinary of the Chapel Royal; on Blow's death he became one of the organists; and when a second post of composer of the Chapel Royal was established, Weldon was admitted on 8 August 1715 (OCB, 23, 26, 28).

Along with these appointments he was organist of St Bride's in the City of London from June 1702 (Dawe 1983), and the Vestry minutes of St Martin-in-the-Fields, Westminster (to which George I presented an organ in 1726) speak of Weldon as being already organist there in January 1726/7 (Wad, MS F2006). In 1724 Weldon was among the subscribers to Croft's *Musica Sacra*. He retained all his posts until his death after a long illness, during which Jonathan Martin and William Boyce acted for him in the Chapel Royal (OCB, 51). He is buried at St Paul's, Covent Garden. His portrait is in the Music School collection at Oxford (Poole 1912–25: i. 159). It is curiously interesting to note that at the time of his death he lived in Downing Street (*General Evening Post*, 8–11 May 1736).

Maurice Greene (Post 1) **1727–55.** Greene was sworn both organist and composer of the Chapel Royal on 4 September 1727 (CB2).

See under St Paul's Cathedral, London.

Jonathan Martin (Post 2) **1736–7** (d. London (Westminster), 4 Apr. 1737, aged 22). The main authority for biographical information about Martin is Hawkins (1853: ii. 893), who says he 'had his education in the royal chapel under Dr Croft and soon after his decease was committed to the tuition of [Thomas] Roseingrave, then organist of St George's, Hanover Square; and having . . . qualified himself for choral duty, he became the deputy of Weldon as organist of the Chapel'. He was admitted organist of the Chapel Royal on 7 May 1736 (OCB, 51), and on 21 June it was agreed that he should occasionally compose for the Chapel, on consideration that William Boyce would sometimes take his duty as organist. According to Hawkins, Martin suffered 'under a pulmonic disposition'. He is buried in the west cloister of Westminster Abbey (Chester 1876).

John Travers (Post 2) **1737–58** (d. London (Westminster), June 1758). Hawkins (1853: ii. 910), informs us that Travers

received his education in music in the Chapel of St George at Windsor; and, being a favourite boy of Dr Henry Godolphin, dean of St Paul's, and provost of Eton college, was by him put apprentice to Maurice Greene; and about the year 1725 [actually in November 1726] became organist of St Paul's church, Covent Garden, and after that of Fulham.

The Vestry minutes of St Paul's, Covent Garden record that he was appointed on the recommendation of the Duke of Bedford 'and other persons of distinction' (Wad, MS H804). In 1727 the list of subscribers to the score of Handel's opera *Admetus* included the name of John Travers, 'sub-organist' of St Paul's Cathedral. He was admitted organist of the Chapel Royal on 10 May 1737 (OCB, 52), soon after which, as Hawkins remarks, 'upon some disgust, he quitted his place at Fulham'.

Hawkins further tells us that Travers 'commenced an early acquaintance with Dr Pepusch, and received some assistance from him in the course of his studies, but Burney (1776–89: iii. 61) says mordantly that he 'confined his studies to the correct, dry, and fanciless style of that master'. In the biographical notes to his *Cathedral Music* (1790: ii. 263), *Samuel Arnold says that towards the latter part of his life Travers was wont to pass one evening a week with Pepusch on musical researches. Travers eventually inherited part of Pepusch's library (Burney 1776–89: iv. 639). He is buried at St Paul's, Covent Garden.

The following entry, dated 1752, is found in CB2:

> Mr Traver's complaint
>
> I hereby certify that on a Sunday lately having with me two ladies, whose dress and appearance could be no objection to their admittance, I prayed the doorkeeper to admit these ladies into the Chapel, on which, without reply, he threw the door in my face. I tapped on the door again, but to my great surprise he said he knew me very well, but would not let in 'my mob', which occasioned the ladies to remark that they neither expected such behaviour at a place of devotion, nor at Court.
>
> John Travers

It may be remarked that Robert Wass and William Savage, both gentlemen of the Chapel who sang for Handel, also had encounters with this door-keeper, one Vaux by name.

James Nares (Post 1) **1756–83.** Nares was admitted organist and composer of the Chapel on 13 January 1756, and on 18 March 1757 he was further admitted to succeed Bernard Gates on his resignation as master of the children (CB2).

See under York Minster.

William Boyce (Post 2) **1758–79** (bap. London, 11 Sept. 1711; d. London (Kensington), 7 Feb. 1779). Boyce was baptized in the church of St James, Garlickhythe, London (Lgh, MS 9141). He became a chorister of St Paul's Cathedral under Charles King, and was subsequently an articled pupil of Maurice Greene, to whose *Forty Select Anthems* he was a subscriber in 1743.

He was appointed organist of Oxford Chapel, Cavendish Square, Westminster in 1734, and for some time before Weldon's death in 1736 he acted, along with Jonathan Martin, as organist of the Chapel Royal. In 1736 he became organist of St Michael's, Cornhill in the City of London, a post for which he had been an unsuccessful candidate in 1734 (Dawe 1983). On the death of Weldon in 1736 he was appointed one of the composers of the Chapel Royal, with an understanding that he would informally share duties with Martin (OCB, 51).

In 1749 he added to his existing appointments that of organist of All Hallows Great and Less, Thames Street (Dawe 1983). On 3 July 1749 he accumulated the Cambridge degrees of Mus. B. and Mus.D. (*Venn*). In 1755 he succeeded Greene as conductor of the Festivals of the Sons of the Clergy, having conducted the Three Choirs Music Meetings from 1737 (Pearce 1928; Lysons 1812). He was also Greene's successor as master of the king's music from 1755.

All these duties were clearly in conflict with each other, and early in 1758 trouble arose at All Hallows: 'Ordered at the said vestry the salary of Dr Boyce the organist be reduced to twenty pounds per annum from Lady Day next. Ordered that Dr Boyce have immediate notice of the above order and that he be at the same time requested to change Mr Bullbrick his deputy.' (Lgh, MS 824/1, 5 Jan. 1758.) However, he went on to become one of the organists of the Chapel Royal, admitted on 23 June 1758 (CB2). But on 21 March 1764 it was decided to dismiss him from All Hallows, and on 7 April 1768, after some dissatisfaction with his work, the Vestry of St Michael's, Cornhill agreed to treat a letter from him as his resignation (Lgh, MSS 819/2; 4072/2).

The three volumes of his influential anthology of English cathedral music appeared between 1760 and 1773. He was one of the subscribers to Burney's *History of Music* in 1776.

He is buried in the crypt of St Paul's Cathedral, where his memorial inscription reads: 'Happy in his compositions, much happier in a constant flow of harmony, through every Scene of Life, Relative or Domestic: the Husband, Father, Friend.'

His library and musical instruments were sold by auction in April 1779 (King 1963). A portrait of Boyce by Hudson is in the Bodleian Library, Oxford (Poole 1912–25: i. 162). Although this is sufficiently identified by the artist's inclusion of a copy of 'Solomon Serenata' in the sitter's hand, it is difficult to see in it the same person as is depicted in the engraving by Sherwin prefixed to the second edition of Boyce's *Cathedral Music.*

'Memoirs of Dr Boyce' by J. H. (i.e. John Hawkins), prefixed to 2nd edn. of Boyce's *Cathedral Music* (1788).

Thomas Sanders Dupuis (Post 2) **1779–96** (b. London, 5 Nov. 1733; d. London, 17 July 1796). According to DNB, Dupuis came of a family of Huguenot immigrants. An editorial note in volume 3 of his posthumous *Cathedral Music* (1797) records that as a boy he was in the Chapel Royal choir under Gates. When subscribing to volumes 1 and 2 of Boyce's *Cathedral Music* (1760, 1768) he was plain 'Mr Dupuis'; but in volume 3 (1773) he was 'Mr Dupuis, Organist of Charlotte-street Chapel, near the Queen's Palace'. He was admitted organist and composer of the Chapel Royal in succession to Boyce on 24 March 1779 (CB2, where his second name is spelt 'Saunders').

Along with Samuel Arnold, he was joint residuary legatee of Bernard Gates, who died in 1773 (Chester 1876). Thus these two men are linked to an earlier age of English music by the long life of Gates, who had been a pupil of John Blow. Dupuis displayed serious interests by subscribing to Burney's *History of Music*

(1776), the second edition of Boyce's *Cathedral Music* (1788), Arnold's *Cathedral Music* (1790), and that of William Hayes (1795). On 26 June 1790 he accumulated the Oxford degrees of B.Mus. and D.Mus., and in that same year he established a short-lived informal association of graduates in music called 'the Graduates Meeting' for periodic social intercourse (Lbl, Add. MS 27693).

His death followed a dose of opium, the obituary notice in *GM* remarking that 'although absolutely rendered unfit by severe illness, perhaps he took opium on this account, he would attend the Chapel-royal on Sunday the 10th instance, and it is supposed the exertion was fatal'. He was buried in the cloisters of Westminster Abbey. In the register his age at death is given as 60 (Chester 1876), and the mural tablet in the cloisters gives it as 66: both seem to be in error.

George Smart, who was an organ pupil of Dupuis, noted in his journal that he 'was rather a sharp master and would sometimes rap my fingers with his watch-chain, holding the watch in his hand'. Smart also records: 'During his first visit to this country, in 1790, Haydn came to the Chapel Royal. He was so pleased with Dr Dupuis' extempore fugues, that meeting the doctor as he came downstairs from the organ loft, after the service, he gave him two kisses in the Ambassadors' Court. This I saw him do.' (Cox and Cox 1907: 3–4, 59.) Against his list of London musicians in 1792 Haydn wrote: 'Dupuis a great organist', and put a ring round this entry (Landon 1959: 265).

GM, 1796, ii. 621–2.

Samuel Arnold (Post 1) **1783–1802.** Arnold was admitted organist and composer in succession to Nares on 1 March 1783 (CB2).

See under Westminster Abbey.

Charles Knyvett (Post 2) **1796–1822** (b. 22 Feb. 1752; d. London, 19 Jan. 1822). Knyvett, who was one of the principal alto singers at the Handel Commemoration in 1784, was admitted a gentleman of the Chapel Royal on 6 November 1786, becoming organist on 25 July 1796, and succeeding Arnold as composer on 27 December 1802 (CB2).

In 1808 he was succeeded as composer by his son William. The record of this in CB2 misleadingly describes Charles as 'deceased'. The explanation is that the entry was inserted out of sequence many years later. An error is found in the annual *Royal Kalendar* which shows him as organist and composer up to and including 1808; then names William Knyvett as organist and composer 1809–14 inclusive; and then gives Charles Knyvett as organist again from 1815, with William as composer. It seems evident that the compiler, when changing the Christian name of the composer in 1809, was misled into changing that of the organist also, a mistake which was corrected only in 1815. There are yet further biographical errors in *DNB*. Its statement that he resigned his post as gentleman in favour of his son Charles in 1808 is unsupported by CB2, and the remark that William Knyvett succeeded Arnold as composer is obviously wrong.

Knyvett died 'after a lingering illness' (*Annual Register*, 1822).

John Stafford Smith (Post 1) **1802–36** (bap. Gloucester, 30 Mar. 1750; d. London, 21 Sept. 1836). Smith was the son of *Martin Smith, organist of Gloucester Cathedral, where he was baptized. According to the *Harmonicon* (1833: 186), after some early instruction from his father he studied in London under Boyce. *Grove*[1], however, stated that he became a chorister of the Chapel Royal under Nares.

He was admitted a gentleman of the Chapel Royal on 16 December 1784, and a few months later he also became a lay vicar of Westminster Abbey. He was appointed organist of the Chapel on 1 November 1802, and on 14 May 1805 he was admitted master of the children (with the sinecure office of lutenist) on the death of *Edmund Ayrton. He resigned the latter post in 1817, but remained organist of the Chapel until his death. All references to his Chapel Royal appointments may be traced in CB2.

He revealed his historical interests as early as 1779, when he published *A Collection of English Songs . . . composed about the year 1500* which drew attention to the famous 'Agincourt Song'. His two-volume collection *Musica Antiqua* was published in 1812. He generously assisted Hawkins in writing his *History of Music*, some of the items in the appendix of which are taken from Smith's important library of early music (King 1963: 43).

The tune of the national anthem of the United States, 'The Star-Spangled Banner', is that of Smith's 'Anacreon in Heaven' or 'The Anacreontic Song', but it is uncertain whether the tune is Smith's own (see Sonneck 1914).

There is a memorial to Smith in Gloucester Cathedral.

Sir George (Thomas) Smart (Post 2) **1822–67** (b. London, 10 May 1776; d. London, 23 Feb. 1867). Smart, of whom Maclean (1908–9) provides an interesting pedigree, entered the Chapel Royal choir in 1783 and left at Christmas 1792. Apart from instruction from Edmund Ayrton, Dupuis, and Arnold (all Chapel Royal musicians), he had piano lessons from J. B. Cramer, and before leaving the choir he played a concerto by Dussek at the Italian Opera House. While still only a youth, he came into contact with Haydn on his second visit to London when, in an emergency, Smart volunteered to play the drums.

He became organist of St James's Church, Hampstead Road, London in 1791, and from 1794 he sang as a chorus bass in the Italian Opera and the Antient Concert. In 1797, among the subscribers to Dupuis's *Cathedral Music*, he was described as organist of Brunswick Chapel as well as of St James's, and when Arnold became organist of Westminster Abbey Smart deputized for him there. In 1810 he went to Dublin to conduct some concerts, and there received a knighthood at the hands of the Lord Lieutenant on 1 January 1811. An original member of the Royal Philharmonic Society, he conducted many of its concerts as well as the Lent oratorios in London theatres. He gave the first English performance of Beethoven's 'Battle' Symphony and *Christus am Oelberg*.

His appointment as organist of the Chapel Royal, to commence 1 April 1822, is entered in CB2 on 8 February, but according to his own account he was appointed on 25 January and began duties on 17 February. His diary lists charges amounting to £40. 12*s*. 10*d*. on taking up this office. In April 1838 he was further appointed composer to the Chapel on the death of Attwood.

When he became organist of the Chapel Royal he had a wider background of experience than any other holder of the post, and was indeed the most prominent English professional musician of the time. In 1823 he became one of the first members of the board of professors of the Royal Academy of Music, and in 1823–4 he conducted festivals at Liverpool, Bath, Newcastle, Norwich, and Edinburgh. He travelled a good deal on the Continent, becoming acquainted with many continental musicians, and it was at his house (91 Great Portland Street, London) that Weber died.

A cutting from the *Musical Examiner*, dated 16 December 1838 and preserved in William Ayrton's common-place book (Lcm, MS 1163), contains a bitter general attack on Smart, more specifically because, at the Chapel Royal on 2 December 1838, it noticed that he intruded into the Sanctus of Croft's Service in A a dominant seventh on G between 'Lord God of hosts' (E major) and 'heaven and earth' (C major), and another on F between 'the majesty of thy glory' (C major) and 'Glory be to thee' (A major).

On his death the second post of organist of the Chapel Royal lapsed.

Cox and Cox 1907; Maclean 1908–9; King 1950.

Thomas Attwood (Post 1) **1836–8**. Attwood, already one of the composers (from 1796), was appointed organist of the Chapel Royal on 19 September 1836 (CB2).

See under St Paul's Cathedral, London.

John Bernard Sale (Post 1) **1838–56** (b. Windsor, 24 June 1779; d. London (Westminster), 16 Sept. 1856). Sale was of the third generation of cathedral musicians. His grandfather was successively junior vicar of Lincoln Cathedral and lay clerk of St George's Chapel, Windsor, while his father John (1758–1827) 'was at one time a member of no fewer than five choirs, namely, Eton, Windsor, the Chapel Royal, St Paul's, and Westminster-abbey'. *GM* (the source of the previous quotation) appears to read as though he was simultaneously a member of all five choirs, whereas only joint membership of the first two or the last three, but not all five together, was possible. John Sale was also almoner and master of the choristers of St Paul's Cathedral, 1800–12 (q.v.).

J. B. Sale was a chorister of both St George's Chapel, Windsor and of Eton College from 1785. In 1800 he was appointed a lay vicar of Westminster Abbey, and was admitted a gentleman of the Chapel Royal on 10 January 1803. In 1809 he became organist of St Margaret's, Westminster. His appointment as organist of the Chapel Royal is dated 1 April 1838 (CB2). As a singer he is reputed to have been a powerful bass. A curiosity of his career is that in 1806 he was appointed to a second place as lay vicar of Westminster Abbey. As each place at that time involved half a year's duty, this arrangement meant that Sale served throughout the year.

In 1852, during the time that Smart and Sale were organists and Thomas Helmore was master of the children, Berlioz attended a service in the Chapel Royal, and observed that there were 'a few voiceless singers, eight choir-boys with too much voice, a primitive organ, and that is all there is to hear' (*Les Soirées de l'orchestre*, English trans. 1929).

GM 1856 (NS) 625; *Grove*[1].

George Cooper (Post 1) **1856–76** (b. London (Lambeth), 7 July 1820; d. 2 Oct. 1876). Cooper's father, also George, was assistant organist of St Paul's Cathedral. The boy's extemporization was on one occasion praised by Mendelssohn. He was appointed organist of St Benet's, Paul's Wharf, London when only 13½ years old. In 1836 he became organist of St Anne and St Agnes, and on Attwood's death in 1838 he became assistant organist of St Paul's Cathedral, his father resigning at that juncture. On his father's death in 1843, he succeeded to the posts of organist of the church of the Holy Sepulchre, Holborn and singing-master and organist of Christ's Hospital, London. On 29 September 1856, to take effect on 1 October (CB2), Cooper was appointed organist of the Chapel Royal as colleague to Smart, and after Smart's death he, like all his successors, became sole organist. Meantime, he retained his post at Christ's Hospital until his death.

He was an influential teacher of the organ, and author of *An Introduction to the Organ*. At the time of Stainer's appointment as organist of St Paul's Cathedral in 1872, Cooper undoubtedly was felt to have claims to succeed Goss, but he loyally continued as assistant to Stainer, a former pupil (Charlton 1984: 48–52). He is said to have had 'a strong taste for natural science, and divided his time between the organ, his ferns, and photography'. Information about Cooper's career is hard to document, and the article in *Grove*[1] which is drawn on here is anonymous and without references.

Charles Sherwood Jekyll 1877–91 (b. London (Westminster), 29 Nov. 1842; d. London, 7 Nov. 1914). Jekyll was a chorister of Westminster Abbey, where, from 1860 to 1875, he was later assistant organist. He was also organist of Acton Parish Church, 1860–1, and of St George's, Hanover Square, London from 1861.

CB2 records his appointment as 'organist and composer of H. M. Chapel Royal, St James' on 15 January 1877 in succession to George Cooper. But Cooper was not composer to the Chapel, and since the death of Smart there had been only one such, namely Goss. At this time services were also being held in the Banqueting House, Whitehall, the only surviving part of the former palace of Whitehall, and presently Jekyll assumed the duty of playing there. Concerning this, a note in CB2 reads: 'Mr Jekyll has since been appointed organist of the Chapel Royal, Whitehall, so that his present title is organist of H. M. Chapels Royal.' This plural form, referring to buildings rather than the establishment, and which had also been used without explanation in the entry of Cooper's appointment in 1856, has been in official use ever since.

In July 1880, following the death of Goss, the Chapel commissioners recommended that the two posts of organist, and those of composer, should all be combined in one joint office whose holder would 'be considered the leader of the choir . . . and generally responsible for the efficiency of the music' (CB2).

Jekyll retired on account of ill health in 1891, the same year in which the Chapel in Whitehall was closed.

BMB; MT, 56 (1915), 32.

William Creser 1891–1901 (b. York, 1844; d. 13 Mar. 1933). Creser was a chorister of York Minster. He took the Oxford degrees of B.Mus. and D.Mus. in 1869 and 1880, and held the FRCO diploma. At the age of 15 he became organist of Holy Trinity, Micklegate, York, and later of St Paul's, York. From 1863 to 1875 he was organist of St Andrew's, Grinton. More important positions then followed, at St Martin's, Scarborough (1875), where the service was 'chiefly of a Gregorian character' (Spark 1892: 65), and Leeds Parish Church (1881). Some account of his work there is given by Spark (168–9). He left Leeds on his appointment to the Chapel Royal in 1891, when, according to Sheppard (1894: ii. 348), he was chosen out of nearly 300 candidates.

Notwithstanding his selection from so wide a field, his regime was not a success. There were difficulties between him and the gentlemen throughout his time, and eventually the sub-dean reported a general impression in the musical profession that Creser was incompetent (*ML* 50 (1969), 346, quoting Lord Chamberlain's papers).

BMB; MT, 74 (1933), 370.

Sir Walter (Galpin) Alcock, MVO, 1902–16.

See under Salisbury Cathedral.

Charles Harford Lloyd 1917–19.

See under Christ Church Cathedral, Oxford.

(Edgar) Stanley Roper, CVO, 1919–53 (b. Croydon, Surrey, 23 Dec. 1878; d. London, 19 Nov. 1953). After serving as a chorister of Westminster Abbey, 1887–93, Roper attended the Royal Grammar School, High Wycombe, and then went up to Corpus Christi College, Cambridge as organ scholar, 1900–3. He held the John Stewart of Rannoch scholarship in sacred music, and took the degrees of BA (1902), Mus.B. (1903), and MA (1928). He also held the FRCO diploma.

He was successively organist of two London parish churches, St Paul's, Hammersmith (1903–12) and St Stephen's, Walbrook (1912–19); concurrently he was sub-organist of the Chapel Royal, 1905–16, organist of the Danish Service, Marlborough House, 1909–19, and assistant organist of Westminster Abbey from 1917.

On appointment as organist of the Chapel Royal in 1919, he continued as assistant at Westminster Abbey, latterly in an honorary capacity. From 1929 he was principal of Trinity College of Music, London, retiring in 1944. He was appointed MVO (4th class) in 1930, and promoted CVO in 1943, receiving the Lambeth degree of D.Mus in 1950.

Venn; MT, 95 (1954), 39; *ECM*, 24 (1954), 16; *WWW*, 1951–60.

§**(William) Harry Gabb, CVO, 1954–74** (b. Ilford, Essex, 5 Apr. 1909). Gabb studied at the Royal College of Music, 1927–8, and while there became organist of Christ Church, Gipsy Hill, London. He became sub-organist of Exeter Cathedral in 1929, and was appointed organist of Llandaff Cathedral in 1937. Almost immediately after the end of the war he returned to London as sub-organist of St Paul's Cathedral, a post which he continued to hold after becoming organist of the Chapel Royal. He took the FRCO diploma in 1931, and was appointed MVO (4th class) and CVO in 1961 and 1974 respectively. He received the Lambeth degree of Mus.D. in 1974.

§**Timothy (Robert Warwick) Farrell 1974–9** (b. Cape Town, 5 Oct. 1943). After leaving the Diocesan College, Cape Town, Farrell came to England to study at the Royal College of Music, and took the FRCO diploma in 1965. He was assistant organist of St Paul's, Knightsbridge, London, 1962–6, and of St Paul's Cathedral, 1966–7. From then until his appointment to the Chapel Royal he was sub-organist of Westminster Abbey. In 1975 he also became organist of the Liberal Jewish Synagogue, St John's Wood, London, and he continued in this post after leaving the Chapel.

§**Richard (John) Popplewell, organist, choirmaster, and composer from 1979** (b. Halifax, Yorks., 18 Oct. 1935). Popplewell was a chorister of King's College, Cambridge. He went to Clifton College with a music scholarship, and then to the Royal College of Music with an open scholarship in 1953. He returned to King's College in 1955 as organ student, but ill health prevented him from completing his university course. However, he was able to resume his musical career as assistant organist of St Paul's Cathedral, 1958–66. He was appointed organist of St Michael's, Cornhill, London in 1966, and moved from there to the Chapel Royal in 1979. He took the FRCO diploma in 1954, having already won the Sawyer prize at the early age of 14 when taking the ARCO diploma. Concurrently with his other appointments he has been on the staff of the Royal College of Music since 1962. (See Addenda, p. 434.)

MASTERS OF THE CHILDREN OF THE CHAPEL ROYAL SINCE THE REFORMATION

(* – also organist)

Richard Bower, 1545–63 (OCB, 1).
Richard Edwards, 1563–6 (OCB, 2).
William Hunnis, 1566–97 (OCB, 2).
Nathaniel Giles, 1597–1633 (OCB, 5).
Thomas Day, earlier than 1636 – Interregnum (OCB, 48).
Henry Cooke, 1660–72 (Ashbee 1986–9: i. 4).
Pelham Humfrey, 1672–4 (OCB, 15).
*John Blow, 1674–1708 (OCB, 16).
*William Croft, 1708–27 (OCB, 26).
Bernard Gates, 1727–57 (resigned) (CB2, 31).
*James Nares, 1757–80 (resigned) (CB2, 36).
Edmund Ayrton, 1780–1805 (resigned) (CB2, 45).
*John Stafford Smith, 1805–17 (resigned) (CB2, 52).
William Hawes, 1817–46 (CB2, 54).

Thomas Helmore, 1846–86 (CB2, 195).
No further appointments.

COMPOSERS OF THE CHAPEL ROYAL

(* – also organist)

Post 1, established 1700

*John Blow, 2 Mar. 1699/1700–8 (date to be understood from OCB, 22).
*William Croft, 1708–27 (OCB, 26).
*Maurice Greene, 1727–55 (CB2, 31).
*James Nares, 1756–83 (CB2, 36).
*Samuel Arnold, 1783–1802 (CB2, 46).
*Charles Knyvett, 1802–8, (CB2, 51).
William Knyvett, 1808–56 (CB2, 192, entered retrospectively).
John Goss, 1857–80 (CB2, 198).
No further appointments.

Extra Post

George Frideric Handel, 1723–59 (warrant of 25 Feb. 1722/3, PRO).

Post 2, established 1715

*John Weldon, 1715–36 (OCB, 28).
*William Boyce, 1736–79 (OCB, 51).
*Thomas Sanders Dupuis, 1779–96 (CB2, 45).
*Thomas Attwood, 1796–1838 (CB2, 49).
*George Smart, 1838–67 (CB2, 193).
Post vacant, 1867–77.
*Charles Sherwood Jekyll, 1877–91 (CB2, 204).
All Jekyll's successors as organist have also been composers.

2

Cathedrals of England and Wales

BANGOR

The Cathedral Church of St Deiniol

Main sources for this section (1964) (with National Library of Wales references):

Chapter Acts
1680–Aug 1747 (B/DC/V5).
Jan. 1746/7–1791 (B/DC/V3).
1791–1821 (B/DC/V4).
1821–1881 (B/DC/V2).
1882–1920 (B/DC/V1).

In view of the straightforward nature of these sources, and the ease with which each statement may be traced under the dates cited, it is unnecessary to give detailed references in the text below.

Though of ancient foundation, Bangor Cathedral had not acquired any endowed establishment for its music by the close of the Middle Ages. It remained without financial resources for music until 1685, when an Act of Parliament bestowed the tithes of the rectory of Llandinam on the Cathedral, in the first place for the upkeep of the fabric, and in the second for the maintenance of the choir. Before that date no records enable us to trace any organist (however remunerated) other than **Thomas Bolton ?–1645**. We owe our knowledge of him solely to the transcription (Willis 1721: 37) of a memorial inscription to him in the north transept of the Cathedral: 'Here lyeth the Body of Thomas Bolton, Organist of Bangor who dyed the 21st of Jan. 1644 [1644/5].'

The written records of the Cathedral begin with the Chapter Act Book opening in 1680, which contains the following minute dated 22 October 1689: 'That Hugh Johnson be one of the singingmen in the quire of the said Cathedral while a vicar-choral is organist there and no longer, and that he have a salary of eight pounds per annum paid him during the said time out of the tithe of Llandinam.' We are not told, however, who that vicar choral/organist was.

Thomas Roberts 1692–1705 (d. Bangor, 18 May 1705, aged 47). Roberts was appointed organist on 27 January 1691/2 at a salary of £14, and at the same time it was decided that the choir was to include four boys (appointed by the organist) and two men (presumably in addition to the two vicars choral). These resolutions are clearly an implementation of the opportunities offered by the Act of Parliament of 1685. On 30 May 1694 Roberts was granted an additional £4 a year 'in consideration of his care and diligence in his office and place'. A further means of improving his stipend was found on 20 October 1701, when it was ordered that: 'The organist shall instruct such boys in the art of singing as the

Bishop or Dean or the Chapter shall appoint out of the number of choristers. And if any boy so instructed by him be admitted a singingboy, the organist shall receive the second twenty shillings of such boy's salary for his pains.' This clearly implies the existence of a larger body of choirboys from whom stipendiary 'singingboys' were selected. By this time there were four, not two, singingmen.

Under the same date there are some interesting details about the music of the Cathedral. There was to be an anthem 'every Sunday when the sermon is in English and in the choir before noon and on the other Sundays in the afternoon'. The organist, men, and boys were required to attend on Sundays, Saturday afternoons, and holy days and eves, but they were allowed until the following Easter to prepare themselves for singing the services on these occasions; the men and boys must practise under the organist not less than twice a week. They must wear bands and not cravats in church.

These orders were reinforced on 14 July 1703, when the organist was told to have an anthem sung 'every Sunday, Holyday, and Vigil', and that he must teach 'three other services besides Tallis (whereof two at least be alternate or for sides)' for use on those days. Practices are to be 'always in the Cathedral and not in private houses'.

Willis (1721: 37) records this inscription: 'Here lyes, in Hopes of a joyful Resurrection, the Body of Tho. Roberts, the first endow'd Organist of this Cathedral since the Restoration, who dyed on the 18th Day of May, in the Year of our Lord 1705, and the 48th of his Age.' The expression 'endowed organist' was tendentious, or at least pitched rather high, for the Act of Parliament of 1685 did not specifically endow a post of organist as such.

——**Priest 1705–8.** Priest's appointment was minuted on 14 June 1705, when it was recorded that he had been recommended by 'Mr Hall, Organist of Hereford'. As an inducement he was promised an extra £5 at the end of a year, provided he had 'performed his duty to general satisfaction and done much in the way of improvement of the choir in point of singing with relation to services and anthems and chants'.

Note that a Nathaniel Priest became organist of Bristol Cathedral in 1710 (q.v.).

——**Smith 1708–10.** Smith was elected organist on 14 July 1708.

——**Ferrer 1710–12.** Ferrer was formally chosen organist on 19 September 1710, with a salary to run retrospectively from 1 May 1710.

John Rathbone 1712–21. The minute recording Rathbone's election on 6 May 1713 authorized his salary to run from All Saints' Day 1712. The provision made to Roberts in 1701 was extended further on 10 March 1715, when, to 'encourage the organist to take pains with the choristers and be very sedulous in teaching the boys to sing', he was allotted '10*s*. out of the second 20*s*. that every one of Dr Glynne's poor scholars [i.e., not singingboys] shall be paid hereafter'.

On 10 November 1718 the organist was instructed to teach the choir Rogers's Communion Service and also those by Tallis and Child 'as soon as they can be had'; further, 'Bird's Service' was to be added to 'the other four now performed'. Two new anthems were to be taught every year, 'as long as the present stock holds or new ones can be procured'.

Thomas Rathbone 1721–50 (d. Bangor, 1750). Thomas Rathbone was appointed organist on 22 November 1721, 'during pleasure of the Dean and Chapter'. He is doubtless the 'Thomas Rathbone, son of Mr Rathbone, organist' (his predecessor), who was admitted a singingboy on 21 October 1713. As organist he received £1 for every '£5 boy' (singingboy) and 10*s*. for every '40*s*. boy' (Dr Glynne's scholar) whom he taught. On the day his successor was elected, £5 was allotted to Rathbone's widow 'when the sub-treasurer shall think proper'.

Thomas Lloyd 1750–78. Lloyd's appointment (18 June 1750) was in the same terms as his predecessor's. He had been a singingboy (to 1731) and singingman (from 1732). Perhaps he may have been the son of John Lloyd, singingman, who, having received tempting offers from Bristol and Dublin, was allowed £5 a year extra to encourage him to stay at Bangor (Chapter minute, 21 Jan. 1719/20).

Richard Jarred 1778–82 (d. Bangor, 1782). On Jarred's election (13 October 1778) it was resolved that he should receive 'the yearly salary of forty guineas'. The name appears in the form 'Gerard' in the accounts for 1779.

William Shrubsole 1782–4 (b. Canterbury, Jan. 1760; d. London, 18 Jan. 1806). Shrubsole was baptized on 13 January 1760 at Canterbury, where his father was a farrier. He was a chorister of Canterbury Cathedral, 1770–7. His appointment at Bangor was enthusiastically minuted thus, under the date 26 September 1782:

> William Shrubsole was named organist with a salary of 40 guineas a year payable from the 22nd day of August last from which time he has attended the duties of the organist's place in a manner so satisfactory and promising that we think proper for his encouragement to direct the treasurer to pay him also the sum of eight guineas towards the expenses of his journey, the removal of his harpsichord and other effects from London to Bangor.

But within a year trouble developed. Shrubsole gave offence partly by frequenting dissenting meeting-houses and partly because of 'his close attention with one Abbot, late of this place'. Accordingly, the dean was empowered (16 October 1783) to dismiss Shrubsole either in the event of Abbot's returning to Bangor or if Shrubsole 'shall be found to frequent any conventicle or religious assembly where any thing is taught which is contrary to the doctrine or discipline of the Church of England'. One or other of these contingencies evidently arose, and the minutes of 24 December 1783 record Shrubsole's dismissal from the following Lady Day, with leave to go earlier if he so wished.

In 1784 he became organist of Spa Fields Chapel (Countess of Huntingdon's Connexion), Clerkenwell, London (*Grove*[2]), and his name as 'organist of Lady Huntingdon's Church' occurs in the list of subscribers to the second edition of Boyce's *Cathedral Music* in 1788. But his association with the Established Church was not at an end: in 1800 one 'Shrubsole' became organist of St Bartholomew the Less, London (Dawe 1983); and as this man died on 18 January 1806, he is undoubtedly our subject.

William Shrubsole was a friend of Edward Perronet (1726–92), author of the hymn 'All hail the power of Jesu's name', to which Shrubsole's tune 'Miles Lane' (first published in the *Gospel Magazine* for November 1779, where it is anonymous) is still widely sung.

He is buried in Bunhill Fields, Finsbury, London.

DNB.

Edmund Olive 1784–93 (d. Warrington, Lancs., 18 Nov. 1824). Olive's appointment, at first on probation, was minuted on 3 August 1784. In addition to the stipend of £42, he was allotted two further sums of £4 for teaching the boys and for tuning the organ. During his time at the Cathedral he was authorized to purchase Kent's and Nares's published anthems and Ebdon's *Cathedral Music.* He personally subscribed to the second edition of Boyce (1788) and to Arnold's *Cathedral Music* (1790). *BMB* states that, on his leaving Bangor in 1793, he became organist of Warrington Parish Church, Lancashire, where he died.

Joseph Pring 1793–1842 (b. London (Kensington), 15 Jan. 1776; d. Bangor, 13 Feb. 1842). Pring was one of three brothers who were choristers of St Paul's Cathedral while Robert Hudson was master of the choristers there (see also Isaac Pring, p. 392). He was an unsuccessful applicant for the post of organist of St Martin's, Ludgate, London in 1792 (Dawe 1983). He took up his duties at Bangor in 1793, but he was not formally admitted until 1810. He himself gives the following account of the circumstances:

> Mr Olive was elected Organist in 1784 and resigned in favour of his relative, Dr Pring, in 1793 . . . Dr Pring was appointed Organist of Bangor Cathedral by Bishop Warren on the 1st of April 1793, being at that time 17 years of age. He never, after that, made any application to the Chapter, *to secure* by their election, the *Permanency of his Situation*, until the necessity of such a measure was politely suggested to him by the present Bishop—and who, at a Chapter holden on the 26 [actually 28] Sept. 1810 made a proposition to that effect which was opposed by the Dean, on the principle of its not being a situation for life. This singular objection was, however, over-ruled by the Bishop and all the other members present [the Bishop of Bangor was a member of the Chapter in virtue of his office as Archdeacon of Anglesey]; the Dean, in consequence, withdrew his *dissent* and Dr Pring was on that day *unanimously elected*, Organist of the Cathedral.

This matter of formal election as organist became important two or three years later, when Pring went to law against the Dean and Chapter. He afterwards published an account of the suit (which much impoverished him) under the title *Papers . . . Respecting the Maintenance of the Choir of the Cathedral Church of Bangor. Collected and Arranged by Joseph Pring Mus. Doc. Oxon: Endowed Organist of Bangor Cathedral* (Bangor, 1819), from which the foregoing note has been quoted.

The facts were these: the Dean and Chapter proposed to promote an Act of Parliament empowering them to build a church to hold services in Welsh, to be paid for out of the tithes of Llandinam. Not without self-interest, yet rightly jealous of the music of the Cathedral, Pring stoutly opposed this and successfully obtained an order against it from the Court of Chancery. Furthermore, arising out of this, two-thirds of the tithes were redistributed for the benefit of the Cathedral's music under a new scheme. Pring bore the whole burden of this suit, without help from the singingmen and in the face of opposition from the vicars choral. As organist he did a good deal better out of the new scheme than formerly, but by no means as well as he had hoped; proportionately, though not absolutely, the singingmen benefited more. But what particularly annoyed him was that the three individuals who had actually opposed him in taking action—the precentor and the 'ecclesiastical vicars' (vicars choral), who were already well-remunerated members of the Cathedral—received no less than three-eighths of the new allocation, where before they had received nothing from this source. Nevertheless, it is too strong to say, as W. H. Husk does in *Grove*[1], that the Lord Chancellor 'set at nought' the express provisions of the Act of Parliament of 1685.

For some time Pring was also organist of Beaumaris Church, Anglesey, describing himself when subscribing to William Hayes's *Cathedral Music* in 1795 as 'organist of Bangor Cathedral and Beaumaris'. In January 1808 he proceeded B.Mus. and D.Mus. by accumulation at Oxford. He is buried in the Cathedral yard at Bangor.

Apart from J. S. Pring, who succeeded him as Cathedral organist, Joseph Pring had three other sons who all took holy orders, one of them, Charles, being for a time a chaplain of New College, Oxford, and another, Ellis Robert, similarly a clerk of Magdalen College.

James Sharpe Pring 1842–68 (d. Bangor, 1868, aged 57). Pring had been both chorister and assistant organist under his father. His appointment, in the first place on probation for a year, was minuted on 2 August 1842. West (1921) gives the date of death as 3 June 1868; *Grove*[2] as 3 January.

Robert Roberts 1868–71 (b. Llandegai, Bangor, 24 May 1840; d. Bangor, 9 Feb. 1871). Roberts was educated at the North Wales College for Schoolmasters, Caernarvon, on whose staff he afterwards served as 'Third Master' and music master (West 1921). Before his appointment to Bangor Cathedral, minuted on 4 August 1868, he had been assistant organist from November 1865.

Roland Rogers (1st tenure) **1871–91** (b. West Bromwich, 17 Nov. 1847; d. Bangor, 30 July 1927). Rogers received his early musical education from his father. His appointment at Bangor was minuted on 1 July 1871. Before then he was successively organist of St Peter's, West Bromwich (1858), St John's, Wolverhampton (1862), and Tettenhall Parish Church (1867). He took the Oxford degrees of B.Mus. (1870) and D.Mus. (1875). He left the Cathedral in 1891 because of difficulties placed in the way of his accepting outside work, and he became organist of St James's, Bangor. In 1906, however, he resumed his Cathedral post, holding this until his death.

WWW 1916–28; *BMB; MT* 47 (1906), 819; 68 (1927), 846.

Tom Westlake Morgan 1892–1906 (b. Congresbury, Somerset, 6 Aug 1869; d. ?1934). Morgan was a chorister of King's College, Cambridge, where he subsequently became pupil-assistant to A. H. Mann, while also organist of St Catharine's College. He later studied for a time at the Royal College of Music, and while there was organist of St John's, Wilton Road, London. In 1891 he became organist of St David's, Merthyr Tydfil, moving to Bangor Cathedral in the following year (minute of 1 July 1892). In the later part of 1907 he became organist of St Bride's, Fleet Street, London. After that his movements are unknown, though up to and including November 1934 his name is found in advertisements as chairman of the 'Victoria College of Music' (a proprietary body), wherein he is designated 'Mus. Doc.'. In his pamphlet on the Cathedral organs Leslie Paul, his eventual successor at Bangor, guardedly describes Morgan as 'a somewhat tragic figure'.

West 1921.

Roland Rogers (2nd tenure) **1906–27.**

See above.

§Leslie (Douglas) Paul 1927–70 (b. Bangor, 8 Mar. 1903; d. 12 Oct. 1970). After holding a music scholarship at Clifton College (1918–21), Paul went up to the Royal Academy of Music with an open organ scholarship, and then proceeded to Keble College, Oxford, 1922–5. He took the Oxford degrees of BA (1925), B.Mus. (1927), and MA (1929), and the Edinburgh degree of D.Mus. in 1951. He also held the FRCO diploma.

After teaching briefly at Winchester College (1924–6) and Warriston School, Moffat, Dumfries (1926–7), he returned to his native place as organist of Bangor Cathedral. He retired very shortly before his death.

Drennan 1970.

In 1970 Bangor Cathedral appointed John Hywel, M.Mus., lecturer in music at the University College of North Wales, to a newly created post of director of music in the Cathedral, and at the same time instituted, in co-operation with University College, an organ scholarship whose holder played for the Cathedral services. This was awarded to Andrew Goodwin (see below).

§Andrew (John) Goodwin, organist and master of the choristers from 1972 (b. Hillingdon, Middlesex, 11 Nov. 1947). On leaving Wolverhampton Grammar School, Goodwin proceeded to the University of Liverpool, 1967–70, where he read music (BA, 1970). He took the FRCO diploma in 1970. While still at school and university he was organist of St Paul's Church, Wolverhampton, 1964–6, and assistant organist of St John's Church, Wolverhampton, 1966–70. From 1970 to 1972 he was organ scholar (see above) at Bangor Cathedral, and in the latter year he took the degree of MA at the University of Wales.

John Hywel relinquished his post of director of music at the Cathedral in 1971, and from then until confirmed in the full appointment in September 1972, Goodwin was effectually in charge of the Cathedral music.

BIRMINGHAM

The Cathedral Church of St Philip

St Philip's Church was built in 1710–14 to serve the needs of the growing town of Birmingham, whose only church until then was St Martin's Parish Church. The first organist was ***Barnabas Gunn**, 1715–30. ***Jeremiah Clarke** (later of Worcester Cathedral) was organist of St Philip's, 1765–1803. When the diocese of Birmingham was created in 1905, the organist of St Philip's was Arthur Elmore (see below).

Arthur Elmore (1901) **1905–6** (d. 1932). Elmore was apparently a local amateur musician. He had been a pupil of C. W. Perkins, organist of Birmingham Town Hall. Before his appointment to St Philip's he was organist of St Thomas-in-the-Moors and St Edward's Churches, Birmingham. After leaving the Cathedral, he was organist of St Mary's Church, Acock's Green, Birmingham until his death.

West 1921; information from Mr Roy Massey.

Edwin Stephenson 1906–14 (b. Windermere, 1871; d. 20 Sept. 1922). Stephenson studied at the Royal College of Music. Before his appointment to Birmingham Cathedral he held organists' posts at Cartmel Priory Church (1888), Sunningdale Parish Church (1891), St Michael's, Brighton (1901), and Brighton Parish Church (1905). He left Birmingham to become organist of St Margaret's, Westminster.

West 1921; *MT,* 63, (1922), 807.

William Frederick Dunnill 1914–36 (b. Wakefield, 16 Mar. 1880; d. Birmingham, Oct. 1936). Dunnill was a pupil of *J. N. Hardy, and his assistant at Wakefield Cathedral. He afterwards held an organ scholarship at the Royal College of Music, and while there he was organist of Christ Church, Surbiton (1900) and St Luke's, Bromley (1901). In 1903 he became organist of Nottingham Parish Church, moving from there to Birmingham. He died suddenly in the vestry of Birmingham Cathedral.

West 1921; information from Mr Roy Massey.

§Willis Grant 1936–58 (b. Bolton, Lancs., 1 May 1907; d. 9 Nov. 1981). Grant was educated at Astley Bridge School and privately under *E. C. Bairstow. He took the Durham degrees of B.Mus. (1929) and D.Mus. (1934). He was assistant organist of Lincoln Cathedral, 1931–6. Concurrently with his two cathedral appointments he was successively lecturer in music at the University of Sheffield, 1934–47, and director of music at King Edward's School, Birmingham, 1948–58. In 1958 he was appointed professor of music in the University of Bristol, retiring in 1972.

§**Thomas (Newburgh) Tunnard 1958–67** (b. Lexham, near King's Lynn, Norfolk, 30 July 1918). Tunnard was a chorister of St George's Chapel, Windsor, 1928–32, and then went to Bedford School. After a year at the Royal College of Music he went up to New College, Oxford as Margaret Bridges music scholar, 1937–9 and 1945–6. He took the Oxford degrees of BA and B.Mus. in 1946. In that year he became organist of St Michael's-at-the-Northgate, Oxford, holding this post until he moved to Warwick in 1950 as organist of St Mary's Church and director of music at Warwick School. Concurrently with his appointment at Birmingham Cathedral he was director of music at King Edward's School. He was appointed one of Her Majesty's inspectors of schools in the Department of Education and Science in 1967.

Roy (Cyril) Massey 1968–74.
See under Hereford Cathedral.

§**David (Malcolm) Bruce-Payne 1974–7** (b. Banbury, Oxon., 8 Aug. 1945). After being a chorister of King's College, Cambridge, Bruce-Payne went to Bryanston School, and from there to the Royal College of Music as W. T. Best scholar (1964–8). He took the FRCO and CHM diplomas in 1968, and the London degree of B.Mus. in 1969. On leaving the Royal College of Music, he became second assistant organist of Westminster Abbey and taught at the Abbey Choir School until his appointment to Birmingham Cathedral. He was also director of music at King Edward's School, Birmingham from 1974 to 1976, and is now a senior lecturer at the Birmingham School of Music and director of music at St George's Church, Edgbaston, Birmingham.

Hubert Best 1978–85.
See p. ix.

§**Marcus (Richard) Huxley, organist from 1986** (b. Chelmsford, 11 Dec. 1949). From Brentwood School, Huxley went to Pembroke College, Oxford in 1968, winning a Heath Harrison scholarship in 1970, and taking the honour school of modern languages and the degree of BA in 1972 (MA, 1980). He then migrated to Worcester College, Oxford as organ scholar, and took the honour school of music in 1974. From 1974 to 1986 he was assistant organist of Ripon Cathedral, acquiring the FRCO diploma in 1976.

BLACKBURN

The Cathedral Church of St Mary the Virgin

The see of Blackburn was created in 1926, whereupon Blackburn Parish Church became the Cathedral. Former organists of the church named in this book are

J. J. Harris (1828), **Henry Coleman** (1912), and **C. Hylton Stewart** (1914). **Henry Smart** was organist from 1831 to 1836.

Hermann Brearley (1916) **1926–39** (b. Batley, Yorks.; d. Blackburn, 1940, aged 63). Brearley was a chorister of Lichfield Cathedral under *J. B. Lott. His early posts as organist were at Halstead, Essex and at Hastings, first at Holy Trinity Church, then at All Saints'. He was appointed to Blackburn Parish Church in succession to C. H. Stewart in 1916. There he soon acquired a reputation as a trainer of choral societies, among them for a number of years Dr Brearley's Contest Choir. He was municipal organist of Blackburn, 1922–30, and music master of Queen Elizabeth's Grammar School, 1918–38. In 1937 he became chorus-master of the Hallé Choir. For many years he taught singing at the Royal Manchester School of Music.

On his retirement from Blackburn Cathedral in 1939 he was given the title of organist emeritus and he took a less exacting post as organist of St Silas's Church, Blackburn, which he held at the time of his death.

Brearley took the Durham degree of B.Mus. (1900) and D.Mus. (1909), and he also held the FRCO diploma.

MT, 81 (1940), 320.

Thomas Lucas Duerden 1939–64 (b. Blackburn, 1898; d. Blackburn, 20 Mar. 1969). Duerden was educated at Church of England schools in Blackburn, and studied music under *C. H. Stewart and Dr F. H. Wood. Later he worked under *E. C. Bairstow, and took the Durham degree of B.Mus. in 1932. For some twenty years up to the time of his appointment to the Cathedral he was organist of St John's Church, Blackburn; he was also music master of Hutton Grammar School, Preston, 1932–47, and of Queen Elizabeth's Grammar School, Blackburn, 1938–63. On his retirement from the Cathedral he received the title of organist emeritus.

MT, 79 (1939), 129; information from Mrs T. L. Duerden.

§**John Bertalot 1964–83** (b. Maidstone, Kent, 15 Sept. 1931). Bertalot held an organ scholarship at the Royal College of Music before going up to Cambridge, where he was organ scholar of Corpus Christi College, 1955–8. He read music and proceeded to the degree of MA in 1961. He holds the FRCO and CHM diplomas (1955 and 1953). On leaving Cambridge he became organist of St Matthew's, Northampton in succession to *R. H. Joyce, moving from there to Blackburn Cathedral. He subsequently became organist of Trinity Church, Princeton, NJ, USA.

§**David (Anthony) Cooper, organist from 1983** (b. Derby, 14 Jan. 1949). Cooper was educated at Derby School, and then became organ scholar of Lincoln College, Oxford, 1967–70, where he read music (BA, 1970; MA, 1974). He also spent a year at the University of York. He obtained the FRCO diploma in 1970, followed by that of CHM in 1981. His early appointments were as music master of St Peter's School, York, 1971–3, and director of music at Queen

Elizabeth's Grammar School, Ashbourne, 1973–7. He entered cathedral work as assistant organist of Wells Cathedral, 1977–83. Concurrently with his post at Blackburn Cathedral he is music master of Queen Elizabeth's Grammar School there.

BRADFORD

The Cathedral Church of St Peter

Bradford Parish Church became the Cathedral when the diocese of Bradford was founded in 1919. An earlier organist of some slight note is **Joseph Bottomley**, 1807–20 (see also Sheffield Cathedral).

Henry Coates (1893) **1919–38** (b. Bradford, Yorks., Nov. 1855; d. Bradford, 9 Feb. 1940). Coates came from a well-known West Riding musical family; the distinguished tenor John Coates (1865–1941) was his cousin. Henry was a chorister in Bradford Parish Church, and a pupil of A. R. Swaine, a local musician. He also studied for a time under E. J. Hopkins in London. After some years as assistant organist at the parish church, he was appointed organist of St John's, Horton Lane, Bradford in 1886. In October 1893 he moved to the parish church, and thus became the first organist of the Cathedral, where he remained until his retirement at the end of 1938. He is commemorated in the new Song School of the Cathedral.

Bradford Telegraph and Argus, 19 Dec. 1938, 13 Jan. and 9 Feb. 1939, 10 Feb. 1940; *Yorkshire Observer*, 14 Jan. 1939, 10 Feb. 1940.

§**Charles Hooper 1938–63** (b. Plymouth, Devon, 28 Dec. 1896; d. Baildon, Shipley, Yorks., 1963). Hooper was educated at Plymouth Grammar School, and owed his early music training to Harry Moreton, organist of Plymouth Parish Church. After some years in schoolteaching, Hooper became music adviser to Bradford Education Committee in 1936, and music adviser and inspector of schools to Leeds Education Committee in 1947, from which post he retired in 1961. He took the degrees of Mus.B. (Dublin, 1935), Mus.D. (Manchester, 1940), and MA in Education (Leeds, 1942).

§**Keith (Vernon) Rhodes 1963–81** (b. Bradford, Yorks., 4 Mar. 1930). Rhodes was educated at Grange Grammar School, Bradford and the University of Leeds (B.Mus., 1952). He was an organ pupil of *Melville Cook, and holds the FRCO, CHM, and ADCM diplomas. Before appointment to Bradford Cathedral he was organist of Menston Parish Church, West Yorkshire, 1958–60, and Heaton Parish Church, Bradford, 1960–3. From 1955 to 1973 he was music master of Grange Grammar School, and he was on the staff of the Royal Manchester/Northern College of Music from 1975 to 1984. Since then he has been director of music at Ashville College, Harrogate. His resignation from Bradford

Cathedral was occasioned by a change of policy for music in worship which he felt unable to accept.

§**Geoffrey John Weaver 1982–6** (b. Bath, Somerset, 31 Dec. 1943). From the City of Bath Boys School, Weaver went to Gonville and Caius College, Cambridge, 1962–5, where he read music and took the degree of MA, followed by a year at the University of Bristol. After leaving Bradford he became a lecturer in the Selly Oak Colleges, Birmingham.

§**Alan Graham Horsey, organist and choirmaster from 1986** (b. Fordingbridge, Hants, 2 July 1955). After leaving Bishop Wordsworth's School, Salisbury, Horsey went to the Royal College of Music, where he won the Walford Davies prize for organ performance. When taking the FRCO diploma in 1975 he won three prizes and the Coventry Cathedral recital award. He added the CHM diploma in 1977. In 1977–8 he was organ fellow of Leeds Polytechnic and Parish Church, and he then became organist of St James's Church, Muswell Hill, London, 1979–85.

BRECON

The Cathedral Church of St John the Evangelist

(Diocese of Swansea and Brecon)

The bishopric of Swansea and Brecon was set up in 1923, after the disestablishment of the Church of Wales. The ancient church of Brecon, which in pre-Reformation days had been a Benedictine priory church, became the Cathedral.

John Humphrey Carden 1923–56 (b. Row, Dunbartonshire, 21 June 1886; d. Brecon, 21 Sept. 1957). Carden was a chorister of Hereford Cathedral, and subsequently served his articles there to *G. R. Sinclair. Before his appointment to Brecon Cathedral he was organist of St Peter's Church, Hereford. He retired in 1956.

Information from Mrs J. H. Carden.

§**David Gwerfyl Davies 1956–63** (b. Merthyr Tydfil, 1 Feb. 1913). After attending Merthyr Tydfil County Grammar School, Davies studied at University College, Cardiff (1932–7), where he read music and took the degree of BA in 1937. Subsequently, in 1954, he took the degree of Mus.B. at Trinity College, Dublin, and he also holds the FRCO diploma. He was organist of various parish churches in Leicester and Birmingham before his appointment to Brecon, where he was also music master at Brecon Grammar School. In 1963 he became music adviser to the City of Leicester Education Authority.

§**(Michael) Bryan Hesford 1963–6** (b. Eccles, Lancs., 19 July 1930). Hesford received his general education at William Hulme's Grammar School, Manchester, and studied music privately under (among others) Caleb Jarvis of Liverpool and Marcel Dupré. Before appointment to Brecon he was sub-organist of Newcastle Cathedral, 1959–60, and organist of Wymondham Abbey, 1960–3. He left Brecon on appointment as organist of St Margaret's Priory and Parish Church, King's Lynn. Subsequently he was organist of several other important parish churches, including that at Skaanevik, Norway. He was editor of *Musical Opinion*, 1976–85, and of the *Organ*, 1976–80. He holds the degrees of MA, Ph.D., and D.Mus. of the Geneva Theological College, USA.

§**David (Patrick) Gedge, organist and master of the choristers from 1966** (b. London, 12 Mar. 1939). On his mother's side, Gedge is a great-nephew of *H. S. Middleton. He was educated (as a chorister of Southwark Cathedral) at St Olave's Grammar School, London, and subsequently at the Royal Academy of Music and the University of London Institute of Education. He was awarded the Turpin prize with the FRCO diploma in 1962. From 1957 to 1962 he was organist of St Mary the Virgin, Primrose Hill, London, and from 1962 until his appointment to Brecon he was organist of Selby Abbey. As a boy he sang the treble solo the first London performance of Britten's *St Nicolas* in Southwark Cathedral.

BRISTOL

The Cathedral Church of the Holy and Undivided Trinity

Main sources in this section (1962) (with Bristol Record Office references):

Chapter Acts

CAx Extracts from minutes of Chapter relating to appointments of minor officers, 1542–1752; an eighteenth-century transcript by Dean Beeke of summary extracts from Chapter minutes no longer surviving (DC/A/12/1).

CA1 Chapter minutes, 1663, 1666–83 (in full from Nov. 1672 only, with index 1666–72, 1714–51 (DC/A/8/1).

CA2 Chapter minutes, 1751–1800 (DC/A/8/2).

CA3 Chapter minutes, 1801–8 (DC/A/8/3).

CA4 Chapter minutes, 1818–31 (DC/A/8/4).

CA5 Chapter minutes, 1831–41 (DC/A/8/5).

CA6 Chapter minutes, 1841–57 (DC/A/8/6).

CA7 Chapter minutes, 1858–79 (DC/A/8/7).

CA8 Chapter minutes, 1879–1900 (DC/A/8/8).

Treasurer's Accounts

Ac1 1550–6 (DC/A/9/1/1).

Ac2 1556–70 (DC/A/9/1/2).

Ac3 1557, 1590–2, 1595 (DC/A/9/1/3).

Ac4 1572–93 (DC/A/9/1/4).

Ac5 1602–19, 1621—32 (DC/A/9/1/5).

Ac6 1603–4, 1608, 1611, 1613–15, 1617–19, 1620–41 (DC/A/9/1/6).

Ac7 1660–80, 1679–83 (DC/A/9/1/7).

Ac8 1682–1715 (DC/A/9/1/8).

Ac9 1740–54 (DC/A/9/1/9).

Registers of Baptisms, Marriages, Burials

PR Printed as *The Bristol Cathedral Register 1669–1837*, transcribed by C. R. Hudleston (Bristol, 1933).

Bristol Cathedral was founded by Henry VIII in June 1542 for his newly established bishopric of Bristol. He granted it the buildings of the surrendered Victorine abbey of St Augustine. Its fairly modest musical establishment included six choristers, and the draft statutes provided that the duties of the master of the choristers should include those of an organist (see above, p. xix). Bristol is one of the few Henrician cathedrals in which, throughout its history, there has been no break in the duality of this office. From 1836 to 1897 the diocese of Bristol was merged with that of Gloucester, but the Cathedral retained its status.

John Senny ?1542–5. Willis (1727: 759–60) names Senny as 'chartulary' master of the choristers. No such statement can be traced in the charter of foundation. However, Willis goes on to give the names not only of Senny but of the minor canons, gospeller, epistler, and the six lay clerks. He cannot have invented all this. So I assume he may be quoting some document now lost, something like the 'Book of Portions' for Winchester Cathedral. Senny may thus be accepted as master of the choristers (and therefore organist) from the date of foundation until shortly before the appointment of his successor. Possibly relevant to him is a bequest of Canon Roger Hughes who, by his will made on 24 December 1545, left to a certain Mr Laurence the sum of 5*s*. 'for the debts of Senyes' (information from Mr Arthur Sabin).

Humphrey Walley 1545–50. CAx quotes the issue of letters patent of the office of master of the choristers to Walley on 5 October 1545. Ac1, the earliest extant volume of treasurer's computa, shows him under the title of 'teacher of the choristers' at a stipend of £10 for the year ending Michaelmas 1550.

Walter Gleson 1551–?69. Gleson's letters patent as master of the choristers were granted on 31 July 1551 (CAx), and he may be presumed to have taken up duty a little before then. He seems to have been a valued member of the Cathedral body. On 10 October 1547 'Walter Gleson, formerly a lay clerk' was granted 'the office of one of the six clerks' by letters patent. This is unexplained. It has been suggested that it may refer to a pre-dissolution office in the abbey connected with the chapel of the Blessed Virgin Mary; but that would be exceptionally anomalous. On the other hand, one might think at first sight that it cannot be synonymous with lay clerk, for he is expressly described as 'formerly a lay clerk'. But what else can it mean? It could be that, for some special reason, his post of lay clerk was now dignified by conveyance under patent (a quite unusual proceeding for such an appointment). Be this as it may, he certainly continued to be paid as a lay clerk (see Ac1, year ending Michaelmas 1550) until becoming master of the choristers. The accounts disclose that from 1549 he had also been Chapter clerk, and he evidently continued in that capacity while master of the choristers and even later (the accounts sometimes carelessly having 'clericus capelle' instead of 'clericus capituli').

In the year ending Michaelmas 1558 (Ac2) we find payments to Gleson as master of the choristers for one quarter only (correctly pro rata, £2. 10*s*.), with £3 for special services, and a sum of £1. 10*s*. shared between John Palmer and Thomas Gunter 'pro informatione choristarum' in Gleson's place for three quarters. The archives are not full enough to explain the state of affairs from this point until after Michaelmas 1569. But it may be deduced that, while remaining in possession of his post, some recognized arrangement was made whereby others helped him and had a share of the stipend. At the same time, varying sums were allotted to him for unspecified services 'in choro festis diebus' or 'pro dilgentia sua'. These latter payments continue irregularly up to 1607, along with his pay as Chapter clerk well into the time of Elway Bevin (Ac2, 3, 5). The names of those assisting him in addition to Palmer (who did most of the work) and Gunter are Peter Bassett and James Purvage. The total sums allotted to Gleson and to them in any one year never amounted to the full £10 stipend of the post. Possibly this state of affairs is an early example, of which there are several even down to the first part of the twentieth century, of attempts to meet the problem created by freehold tenure when the occupant becomes too old for work (unless he is willing to relinquish his rights). In Gleson's case the hypothesis must seem to be that, by the time of Farrant's appointment in 1570, he had surrendered his patent.

Richard Linsey 1569–70. After a lapse of twelve years, the accounts for the twelve months ending Michaelmas 1570 (Ac2) record payment of the full stipend (£10) to a single man. Though no record survives of a patent of appointment to him, this is perhaps sufficient indication to justify Linsey's inclusion here.

John Farrant (I) 1570–1. Letters patent were granted to Farrant as master of the choristers on 4 December 1570 (CAx). He could not have been at Bristol for more than a few weeks before this, since Linsey had been paid up to Michaelmas. Beyond a mention of the appointment of his successor, there is no further reference to him at Bristol.

In the absence of conclusive proof, it is not unreasonable, on the basis of the sequence of dates, to suggest as a hypothesis that the career of this man (perhaps born *c.*1545 and aged about 90 when he died) was as follows: organist of Ely Cathedral (q.v.), Michaelmas 1566 to Michaelmas 1568, then organist of Bristol Cathedral for a few months, 1570–1; lay vicar choral of Salisbury Cathedral from October 1571, and later master of the choristers and organist there until dismissal in February 1591/2 (q.v.); and next, vicar choral in holy orders and organist of Hereford Cathedral, March 1591/2 to December 1593 (q.v.).

We pick him up again at Wells, where in January 1593/4 he was admitted an ordained vicar choral of the Cathedral, and collated to the rectory of Allerton in July 1594. But when the time came for him to be 'perpetuated' as vicar choral, six of his fellows declared their disapproval of his character, and he was confirmed by a majority of two only. His last mention as a vicar choral at Wells is dated 1 April 1599, when he was granted twenty days' leave of absence; but we know that he was rector of Allerton until into the year 1607, a successor to 'Dom John Farrant, the last incumbent' being collated in October. (Wells Cathedral, CA1, ff. 93^{v}, 98, 101, 121; CA2, f. 210.)

Finally, that date, coupled with his being in holy orders, makes it possible that he was the John Farrant, 'clerk of Great St Bartholomew's', who was appointed music master of Christ's Hospital, Newgate Street, London on 10 June 1607. Taking the identity for granted, it must be assumed that he was by now a widower, as the endowment of this post required its holder to be unmarried. At first he met with some success, and his salary was twice increased. But in 1613 old traits reappeared, and he was censured for neglect of duty, 'ill carriage and behaviour', and abuse of the governors. Then he was arrested for debt in 1616 and asked to be allowed to resign, saying he was 'very hard of hearing and his sight doth decay and his whole body so weak and feeble'. When he did resign in January 1617/18 he was generously given a pension, an allowance for coal and wood, and a room near the kitchen with a way into the garden. While in retirement, he married a second wife, Dorothy, on 29 October 1621, his marriage allegation describing him as a bachelor, aged 54 'or thereabouts', a little odd for a man who in 1616 had been weak and feeble (Lgh, MSS 5160/1; 10091/3).

Following dissatisfaction with his eventual successor, Farrant proposed his own reappointment in January 1624/5, and this was accepted because, in the words of the minutes, 'the children were better taught and instructed when the said John Farrant exercised in the said place than by any other that hath sithence succeeded him'. However, despite the requirement that the singing-master should be unmarried, the Hospital Court evidently valued him enough to turn a blind eye, being content to secure a bond that his wife would quit the Hospital within three months of his death. The name Dorothy in the bond is sufficient evidence to link him to the marriage of 1621.

Except in connection with the ill behaviour of some inebriated young fellows who, foolishly encouraged by the maidservant, insulted the Farrants in the cloisters at Michaelmas 1630 (for which they had to beg pardon, and on account of which the girl was dismissed), we hear no more of him until March 1634, when his deputy, referring to him as an 'aged master', petitioned for some recompense, and again in December 1634, when, on the appointment of a successor, he was reported as 'deceased' (Lgh, MS 12806/3, 10 June 1607, 9 Nov. 1608, 15 Jan. 1612/13, 20 Jan. 1615/16, 9 Jan. 1617/18, 21 Jan. 1624/5, 9 Oct. 1630; MS 12806/4, 12 Mar. 1633/4, 23 Dec. 1634). This reconstruction involves acceptance that he was some 90 years old when he died. Though unusual, this was not unknown in such early days; compare, for instance, *William Child, who died in his 91st year. It also has to be recognized that the Salisbury John Farrant was a layman, while the Farrant of Hereford had to be in holy orders to be a vicar choral there. There was hardly time for a man to qualify in this way between 9 February and 24 March. One tentatively suggests that he was admitted at Hereford on the understanding that he would become ordained. Probably this would not be very difficult to achieve: there were no particular qualifications then needed for ordination, and the distinction between lay and ordained men in cathedral choirs generally was probably very little marked. There is no extant Hereford Bishop's Register for the years in question which might settle the point, but on resignation from Hereford Cathedral he was recognized as 'clericus'. The age given at his marriage in 1621 is certainly a problem. No man then aged 54 could have been a lay vicar of Salisbury Cathedral in 1571, let alone organist of Ely Cathedral in 1566. But at that time people had very imperfect reckonings of dates of birth, and it is conceivable that it was loosely given. (The bride, by the way, was aged 33.) Lastly, it must be acknowledged that the signature of the 1621 bridegroom is unlike that to the Salisbury Cathedral indenture of 1592 as illustrated in Robertson (1938: 156); but the latter is more in the way of stylized calligraphy than a signature, and nearly thirty years and illness had intervened.

These are undeniable difficulties, and one must also bear in mind that identity of name and conjunction of dates are not necessarily conclusive, as witness a former mistaken belief that Charles Quarles of Trinity College, Cambridge, and Charles Quarles of York were one and the same person (see pp. 319 and 366). Yet, even in the face of these problems, it still seems not impossible, though unproven, that we have here the unusual career of a single figure spanning the years 1566 to 1634. If that is so, we note how remarkably quickly he was able to move from one appointment to another, and observe that the authorities took no care to enquire about earlier records.

Anthony Prinn 1571–7. CAx refers to the grant to Prinn on 5 October 1571 of a patent of the office of master of the choristers 'of the same tenor as that granted to Farrant'. He received the annual stipend up to Michaelmas 1577 (Ac4). With regard to payments as master/instructor of the choristers thereafter, the accounts reveal the following inconclusive state of affairs for years ending at Michaelmas:

		Payments for
1578	Humphrey Bussell	9 months
	Giles Painter	3 months
1579	Laurence Clarke	3 months
1580–1	No accounts extant	
1582	Anthony Prinn 'for the charge laid out by him in his journey in providing some meet choristers for our choir'.	5*s*.
1583	Anthony Prinn	3 months
1584	No accounts extant	
1585	Dominus Moore and Richard Miro	6 months
	Elway Bevin	6 months

Elway Bevin 1585–1638 (bur. Bristol, 19 Oct. 1638). There is no formal record of Bevin's appointment, but he began to receive his stipend from Lady Day 1585 (see above). He came from Wells Cathedral where he had been appointed a lay vicar choral on 10 May 1579 (Wells VCA, f. 54). On 2 January 1580/1 (Wells CA1, f. 15^{v}) he was accused of not having communicated for four years (a period which, oddly, goes back beyond his appointment in 1579) and was suspended from his emoluments until he mended his ways ('quousque se ipsum reformaberit in hac parte'). On 27 October 1582 he was again deprived of his emoluments for three months for refusing to install another vicar, and he was compelled to acknowledge his fault before the Chapter. But the punishment was later reduced to a fine of 3*s*. 4*d*. (Wells CA1, ff. 20, 21). He is last noted at Wells on 30 July 1583 in connection with a grant to the College of Vicars Choral (Wells Charter, 799).

On 3 June 1605 (Rimbault 1872: 42) Bevin was admitted a gentleman extraordinary of the Chapel Royal, and he combined this status with his duty at

Bristol. There is no evidence in support of a statement sometimes repeated that he was expelled from the Chapel Royal as a papist.

He was in office at Bristol at the time of Archbishop Laud's visitation of 1634. In reply to the articles of enquiry about the organist (note the use of the term), the Dean and Chapter said: 'And for the organist, he is a very old man who, having done good service in the church, is not now able to discharge the place, but that he is holpen by some other of the quire.' (HMC, App. to 4th Report, 1874.) Again, referring to the choristers, they replied: 'But the weakness, through age of their master causeth that they be not so well ordered or instructed as they otherwise should, but for help hereof are committed to the care of some other of the quire.' (Ibid.)

On 14 February 1637/8 the Chapter, long forbearing, 'ordered and decreed that Elway Bevin be removed, expelled, and dismissed from his office of organist and master of the choristers' (CAx). The registers of St Augustine the Less, Bristol note the burial there on 19 October 1638 of 'Mr Ellaway Bevin'. Six children of his had been baptized in that church between May 1590 and July 1603.

The statement given in several reference books that he was of Welsh extraction derives from Wood (MS Notes). His theoretical work, *A Briefe and Short Introduction to the Art of Musicke*, in which he speaks of his 'tired brain', was published in 1631.

Edward Gibbons is sometimes mentioned (e.g. by Boyce, *Cathedral Music*, i, p. viii) as having been organist of Bristol Cathedral at about this time. This goes back to Wood (1815–20: i. 258): 'Edward Gibbon . . . He was now or about this time, the most admired organist of the cath. ch. at Bristol.' But up to 1598 Edward Gibbons was at King's College, Cambridge as a lay clerk (College Mundum Books), and then at Exeter Cathedral as a vicar choral. More significantly, the succession of organists for this period at Bristol leaves no dates unaccounted for.

Arthur Phillips 1638–9. Phillips's formal admission is dated 1 December 1638 (CAx). It is possible that he may have served for a few months before this. His identification with the Arthur Phillips (allowing for common alternative spellings) who was organist of Magdalen College, Oxford, from 1639 is assumed in *DNB*, and there is obvious likelihood of this.

Thomas Deane 1640–68. Deane was admitted on 11 December 1640 (CAx). Allowance must be made for the possibility that he had started duty somewhat earlier. After the abolition of cathedral bodies by the Long Parliament, he received a grant of £5 from the Trustees for the Maintenance of Ministers in February 1658/9 (Matthews 1948). As shown in Ac7, he survived to resume his post after the Restoration of 1660.

Paul Heath 1669–82. Heath's admission was minuted on 13 May 1669 (CAx). It proved an unsatisfactory appointment. After admonitions, matters came to a head as revealed by the following minute of 13 December 1682 recorded in CAx:

It appearing to the Dean and Chapter that Paul Heath, organist and master of the choristers, hath had several admonitions for keeping a disorderly alehouse, debauching the choirmen and other disorders there, and neglecting the service of the church; and being now credibly informed that the said Paule Heath doth still keep ill-order in his house, and hath suffered one Bouch, a barber, to trim in his house on the Lord's Day, commonly called Sunday (and according to report hath allowed several town-dwellers to sit tippling in his house till they were drunk, or very much gone with liquor, one of them being found there dead, and hath often suffered illegal games there), the said Dean and Chapter . . . did . . . order and decree to remove, expel, and dismiss the said Paul Heath from his said office and place of organist and master of the choristers.

In the accounts for the year ending Michaelmas 1684 (Ac8) there is the memorandum: 'de stipendio Pauli Heath organistae et magistri choristarum ab antiqua debit £19 cum augmentatione ei concessa £22' ('£19 owing of old in relation to the stipend of Paul Heath, organist and master of the choristers, with £22 augmentation granted to him'). No successor was immediately appointed: in 1683 a new organ was being built; for the year 1683–4 a certain David Edwards was paid £2 simply as assistant organist; and no one is named in the accounts ending in 1685 and 1686.

Joseph Gibson 1686–1700. Gibson received his first stipend for the full accounting year 1686–7, and his tenure up to Michaelmas 1700 is attested in Ac8.

Stephen Jefferies (II) 1700–10. There was a lay clerk of Gloucester Cathedral, Stephen Jefferies junior, who in 1697 was admonished 'for the neglect of his service in the quire, and his often repair to the organ loft' (Gloucester CA2), and who was no doubt the son of *Stephen Jefferies (I) the organist there. It seems likely that this may be our present subject, who was formally admitted at Bristol Cathedral on 23 June 1701 (CAx) and whose stipend runs to Michaelmas 1710 (Ac8). One notes that a Stephen Jefferies became organist of Frome Parish Church, Somerset in July 1710 (the *Organ*, 52, p. 2).

Nathaniel Priest 1710–34. No record of Priest's admission survives, but his stipend ran from Michaelmas 1710 to Michaelmas 1734 (Ac8, 9). In 1719, having 'somehow gotten into the favour of some of the Chapter', he put himself forward to succeed Golding as organist of St George's Chapel, Windsor, but the post went to John Pigott, nephew of one of the other canons (Windsor Records, IV.B.18, f. 110). In 1734 he subscribed to Croft's *Music Sacra*. It has been stated (*MT*, 48 (1907), 705) that he was also organist of both All Saints' and Christ Church, Bristol as well as of the Cathedral. It will be observed that someone with the same surname (Christian name unknown) was organist of Bangor Cathedral, 1705–8 (q.v.).

James Morley 1734–55 (d. Bristol, Sept. 1755). Morley was admitted on 30 December 1734 (CA1). He was buried on 22 September 1755 (PR). In 1753–4 (Ac9), besides his fee as master of the choristers and organist, he was paid

£14. 6*s*. 8*d*. for two 'secondarii' (assistants), an arrangement which continued at least until Langdon's time.

George Combes (1st tenure) **1756–9** (d. Bristol, Feb. 1769). Combes, who until then had been organist of Wimborne Minster, was admitted on 24 June 1756. In the course of his first Bristol period he was associated with the performances of Handel's music in the Cathedral during August 1758 (Deutsch 1955: 803); and on 16 August 'L'allegro ed il penseroso' was given in the Assembly Room 'for the benefit of Mr Combe, organist of the Cathedral'. After resigning his post at Bristol in 1759, he returned (see below) to hold office again from 1765, being readmitted on 24 June with the additional post of lay clerk—presumably to increase his remuneration (CA2). The burial on 22 February 1769 of George Combes, 'the worthy organist of this church', is noted in PR.

Edward Higgins 1759–64 (d. Bristol, 8 Aug. 1769). Higgins was admitted on 29 January 1759 (CA2). On 1 December 1764 the following Chapter minute was adopted: 'As it is imagined [*blank*] Higgons, organist of this Cathedral Church is about to quit the same it is ordered that [*blank*] Combes be immediately sent for and appointed organist in the stead of the said Mr Higgons.' He can be identified as the Edward Higgins who thereupon entered the choirs of Christ Church and St Patrick's Cathedrals, Dublin in 1765. The burial on 12 August 1769 of Edward Higgins 'vicar-choral of St Patrick's, Dublin, and formerly organist of this church', is found in the Bristol PR. His gravestone gives the date of death.

George Combes (2nd tenure) **1765–9**.

See above.

Edward Rooke 1769–73 (d. Bristol, 24 Apr. 1773). Rooke's admission is dated 8 March 1769 (CA2). One of the same name had been a lay clerk, 1759–62.

According to *BMB*, Charles Wesley, son of the hymn-writer, was taught by Rooke. Samuel Wesley, the future composer, wrote to Charles (his brother) on 20 April 1773: 'I saw Mr Rooke last Tuesday, he looks very bad' (Lbl, Add. MS 35013, f. 2). *Farley's Bristol Journal*, 1 May 1773, notes Rooke's death. He was buried in the Cathedral precincts (PR).

Samuel Mineard 1773–7. Nothing is known of Mineard save the dates of his tenure. His formal admission was on 23 June 1773, and he gave up his post by resignation minuted on 3 December 1777 (CA2).

Richard Langdon 1777–81. The minutes of Langdon's appointment and resignation are respectively dated 3 December 1777 and 25 June 1781 (CA2).

See under Exeter Cathedral.

Rice Wasborough 1781–1802 (d. Bristol, 11 Apr. 1802, aged 54). Wasborough's appointment is noted in a minute dated 25 June 1781 (CA2). He is buried in the south aisle of the Cathedral, and there is a mural monument near his grave.

Joseph Kemp 1802–7 (b. Exeter, 1778; d. London, 22 May 1824). Kemp was a pupil of William Jackson of Exeter Cathedral. He was elected organist of Bristol Cathedral on 23 June 1802 (CA3). His tenure, though not long, was evidently successful. West (1921) records that he was presented with a gold medal by the Dean and Chapter in 1803 'for his unremitting attention to the improvement of the choir of this church'. (This is obviously a quotation from some unspecified document. It is not found in CA3.) On his resignation he moved to London, where he produced two musical entertainments for the theatre. In 1808 and 1809 he took the Cambridge degree of Mus.B. and Mus.D. He devised a curious 'New System of Musical Education' (published *c.*1810–19) involving the use of simple apparatus and intended for group instruction. In 1814 he settled in Exeter, but spent the years 1818–21 in France.

DNB: Venn.

John Wasborough 1807–25 (d. Bristol, 17 Dec. 1825, aged 54). Wasborough's election 'in the room of Mr Joseph Kemp resigned' is dated 30 November 1807 (CA3). He was the eldest son of Rice Wasborough (see above). He resigned shortly before his death, and was buried in the south choir aisle of the Cathedral. His name was added to his father's memorial.

John Davis Corfe 1825–76 (b. Salisbury, 1804; d. Bristol, 23 Jan. 1876). Corfe was the eldest son of *A. T. Corfe and brother of *C. W. Corfe. He was admitted on 23 June 1825 (CA4), and resigned a few weeks before his death. On the foundation of the Bristol Madrigal Society in 1837 he became its first conductor, continuing as such until 1865. There is a memorial window to him in the south choir aisle of the Cathedral.

DNB.

George Riseley 1876–98 (b. Bristol, 28 Aug. 1845; d. Bristol, 12 Apr. 1932). Riseley had been a chorister in Bristol Cathedral under his predecessor, to whom he was articled from 1862. His early organ posts included All Saints', Clifton, Bristol, and in 1870 he was appointed organist of Colston Hall. The minute of his appointment at the Cathedral is dated 11 January 1876 (CA7). After some years he became irregular in fulfilling the duties of the post. The matter was taken to law with a view to his dismissal, but he was eventually allowed to retire with a small annuity. The story is sensitively recounted in Fellowes (1946: 74–7).

Like most cathedral organists of his day, Riseley conducted local choral and orchestral societies. These deserve mention in his case because of their multiplicity: Bristol Orpheus Society (1878), which attained the appellation 'Royal' under him; Bristol Society of Instrumentalists (1887); Bristol Choral Society, which he founded in 1889; and the Bristol Triennial Musical Festivals, 1898–1911. A conspicuous piece of work was his inauguration in 1877 of a series of Monday Popular Orchestral Concerts, for which he personally shouldered financial responsibility. Outside Bristol, Riseley taught the organ for a time at the Royal Academy of Music from 1893, and he also conducted the Alexandra Palace

Choir and the Queen's Hall Choral Society in London. He was sheriff of the City of Bristol for two years, 1909–11.

BMB; MT, 40 (1899), 81; 73 (1932), 464.

Sir Percy (Carter) Buck 1899–1901. When, on account of Riseley's unsatisfactory discharge of duty, the Dean and Chapter wished to terminate his appointment, it was found that the statutes imposed certain procedures upon them, and, up to a point, offered some protection to the master of the choristers and organist as a member of the foundation. They therefore determined, perhaps questionably, that the next organist should not be appointed to the foundation. But this did not deter a good field of candidates, yielding a short list (besides Buck) of *A. W. Wilson, Hubert Hunt (see below), *Basil Johnson, and *F.J.W. Crowe. The dean was anxious not to have too austere a musician. After expressing this point of view in a letter to E. H. Fellowes, then precentor, he voiced misgivings about Buck by saying: 'Now I hear your friend Buck is a contrapuntist' (Fellowes papers, Oriel College, Oxford). Nevertheless, Buck was appointed by minute of 26 March 1899 (CA8).

See under Wells Cathedral.

Hubert Walter Hunt 1901–45 (b. Windsor, 12 July 1865; d. Bristol, 7 Oct. 1945). Hunt was the son of Thomas Hunt, who became lay clerk of St George's Chapel, Windsor (1864) after serving in a similar capacity at Carlisle and Worcester Cathedrals. While at Carlisle he married the sister of *John Naylor. Hubert was a chorister of St George's, Windsor, 1874–80, under *G. J. Elvey. He served his apprenticeship first to Elvey and then to *Walter Parratt, and studied the violin under J. S. Liddle and J. T. Carrodus.

Before appointment to Bristol, Hunt was organist of Clewer Parish Church (1883), Christ Church, Clapham, London (1886), and St Jude's, South Kensington, London (1887). While in London he was a member of the Blagrove String Quartet, and he continued his chamber-music playing in Bristol as a founder member of the Bristol Gentleman's Musical Club (now the Bristol Music Club).

Hunt was probably the latest survivor of the type of cathedral organist who took no formal musical examinations and relied entirely on his apprenticeship as a qualification. He received the Lambeth degree of D.Mus. in 1929, and was made an honorary FRCO in 1939. His son Edgar played a notable part in the revival of the recorder in England.

MT, 48 (1907), 714; 86 (1945), 349; *WWW* 1941–50.

(Reginald) Alwyn Surplice 1946–9.

See under Winchester Cathedral.

§(Arthur) Clifford Harker 1949–83 (b. Newcastle upon Tyne). Harker attended Dame Allan's School, Newcastle upon Tyne, and then studied at the Royal College of Music. In 1935 he became assistant organist of Newcastle Cathedral, and was appointed organist of St Andrew's Church, Newcastle in 1938. From

1946 to 1949 he was organist of Rugby Parish Church. He holds the FRCO diploma (1933), and took the Durham degree of B.Mus. in 1947. In 1975 he received the honorary degree of M.Mus. from the University of Bristol. Following retirement from the Cathedral, he became organist of the Lord Mayor's Chapel, Bristol in 1984.

§Malcolm (David) Archer, master of the choristers and organist from 1983 (b. Lytham, Lancs., 29 Apr. 1952). From King Edward VII School, Lytham, Archer went to the Royal College of Music (with the R. J. Pitcher scholarship awarded by the RCO), and from there to Jesus College, Cambridge as organ scholar, 1972–5. There he read music and took the degrees of BA (1975) and MA (1977). He took the FRCO diploma in 1974, and the postgraduate certificate in education in 1976. While assistant director of music at Magdalen College School, Oxford, 1976–8, he was also assistant organist of Hampstead Parish Church and St Clement Danes Church, Strand, London. From 1978 until his appointment to Bristol Cathedral he was assistant organist of Norwich Cathedral. (See Addenda, p. 434.)

BURY ST EDMUNDS

The Cathedral Church of St James

(Diocese of St Edmundsbury and Ipswich)

When the diocese of St Edmundsbury and Ipswich was founded in 1914, St James's Parish Church, Bury St Edmunds, became the Cathedral.

Charles John Harold Shann (1896) **1914–37** (b. Leeds, 24 Mar. 1868; d. Bury St Edmunds, 3 Mar. 1938). Shann studied at the Royal College of Music. His first post was at Driffield, Yorkshire 1892–6, and he was appointed to St James's, Bury St Edmunds in 1896, holding office there when the church was raised to cathedral status.

Information from Mr Wilfred Mothersole, Bury St Edmunds; Thornsby 1912.

Edward Percy Hallam 1937–57 (b. Nottingham, 4 Sept. 1887; d. Bury St Edmunds, 12 Oct. 1957). Hallam was articled to J. K. Pyne at Manchester Cathedral, and his first organ post was at St Chad's, Ladybarn, Manchester. He went to Bury St Edmunds in 1909 as organist of St Mary's Church, moving to the Cathedral on Shann's retirement. He took the Durham degree of B.Mus. in 1907, and held the FRCO diploma.

Information from Mr Wilfred Mothersole; *MT*, 98 (1957), 633.

§(Thomas Frederick) Harrison Oxley 1958–85 (b. Sheffield, 3 Apr. 1933). After attending King Edward's School, Birmingham, and studying concurrently at the Birmingham School of Music, Oxley went up to Christ Church, Oxford with an open scholarship in music, 1951–5. He proceeded to the Oxford degrees of BA (1954), B.Mus. (1955), and MA (1959), having taken the FRCO diploma (Turpin prize) in July 1951 before going up to Oxford. While at school he was organist of St Mary and St Ambrose Church, Edgbaston, Birmingham, 1949–50, and assistant at Birmingham Cathedral, 1950–1. From 1953 to 1955 he was assistant organist and then acting organist of Christ Church Cathedral, Oxford. Along with his post at Bury St Edmunds, he was on the staff of Silver Jubilee Boys Secondary Modern School, Bury St Edmunds (1958–60) and of Thetford Boys Grammar School (1960–1).

Being convinced of the suitability of a treble line of the choir shared by boys and girls, in demonstration of this he maintained for fourteen years a Cathedral choir so constituted, and when, upon a change of clergy, it was decided that girls should be dispensed with, he resigned, pursuing thereafter an independent free-lance career.

§**Paul Trepte, organist and master of the choristers from 1985** (b. Morley, Yorks., 24 Apr. 1954). Trepte went to New College, Oxford as organ scholar from Batley Grammar School, reading music and taking the degree of MA. He also holds the FRCO diploma. He was assistant organist of Worcester Cathedral, 1976–81, and then, until taking up his appointment at Bury St Edmunds, organist and director of music at St Mary's Church, Warwick. In the summer of 1989 it was announced that he was to become organist of Ely Cathedral in 1990. (See Addenda, p. 434.)

CANTERBURY

The Cathedral and Metropolitical Church of Christ

Main sources in this section (1963):

Registers of Patents, etc.

Reg. 1	1541–51.
Reg. 2	1567–9.
Reg. 3	1589–96.
Reg. 4	1596–1601.
Reg. 5	1601–7.

Chapter Acts

CA1	1561–8.
CA2	1568–81.
CA3	1581–1607.
CA4	1608–28.
CA5	1670–1710.
CA6	1711–26.
CA7	1727–46.
CA8	1746–60.
CA9	1761–75.
CA10	1794–1824.
CA11	1824–54.
CA12	1854–84.
CA13	1885–94.
CA14	1895–1910.

Treasurer's Accounts

Ac1a	Bound papers, 1541–67 (so labelled, but actually to 1575), with gaps.
Ac1b	Bound papers, 1576–1642, with gaps.
Ac2a	Fair-copy accounts 1–25, 1547–8 to 1616–17, with gaps.
Ac2b	Fair-copy accounts 26–47, 1617–18 to 1641–2, with gaps.
Ac2c	Fair copy accounts 48–50, 1660–1, 1661–2, 1662–3.
Ac3	Account books, annually from 1670–1.

Registers of Baptisms, Marriages, Burials

PR	Printed as *The Register Booke of the . . . Cathedrall . . . Church of Christe of Canterbury, 1584–1878* (Harleian Society, 1878).

After the dissolution of the Benedictine cathedral priory of Canterbury in 1538, Henry VIII refounded it in March 1540/1 to continue as the cathedral church of the archbishop. As befitted the cathedral of a primatial see, the musical establishment was generous, and included as many as ten choristers under a master. As in all other of his foundations, the draft statutes provided that the function of organist was to be discharged by the master of the choristers (see p. xix). In January 1636/7 new statutes were promulgated which recognized that, if required, the organist might be a separate person from that of the master of the choristers. As we shall see, from the death of Marson in 1632 until the death of William Pysing in 1684, the two posts were indeed separate, and they were also regarded as distinct at later dates.

William Selbye *c.*1541–84 (the last few months jointly with Matthew Godwin) (d. Canterbury, 1584). 'Mr Selbye' is found in Ac1a (f. 1[v]), for the accounting year ending Michaelmas 1543, as master of the choristers. He is also named in a list of members of the foundation *c.*1541 (Cathedral Archives, DE 164) in which *Thomas Tallis is named as lay clerk. It is therefore reasonable to assume that he held office from the date of Henry's foundation. On 25 November 1547 William Selbye was granted a patent of the post of master of the choristers and organist (Reg. 1 f. 181). This must not be taken to indicate a new appointment, but simply that, for some reason (perhaps the accession of a new king), it was thought fit to confirm his tenure. It is therefore curious to find in the fair-copy accounts (Ac2a) that Thomas Bull was paid as master of the choristers (and therefore organist) from the accounting year 1554–5. Meanwhile, for example in 1557–8 (Ac1a), Selbye headed the list of lay clerks with an extra payment. This state of affairs continues until the end of the accounting year 1563–4. Then, following a gap in the accounts, Selbye is once more found as master of the choristers from Michaelmas 1564 (Ac2a) to Michaelmas 1579 (Ac2a), when there is an intermission in the accounts until after his death (see below, under Cock).

There are no Chapter Acts earlier than 1561 to throw light on this apparent break in his tenure, and those for 1561–8 are silent about it. But on the occasion of Archbishop Parker's visitation of his cathedral in September 1560, Thomas Bull is named as one of the lay clerks, and Selbye as *magister choristarum* (Parker 1928: 632). This leaves no doubt that, even though Bull may have been doing the work and was paid for it, Selbye remained legally in the office under the terms of his patent for life. Woodruff and Danks (1912: 449, 461) suggested that Selbye may have given up temporarily for religious reasons under Mary I (1553–8); but against this it must be pointed out that he served meanwhile in the choir without apparent scruple. Moreover, these authors make the extraordinary assertion that Selbye 'was not a statutable officer'.

In his last year, as will be noted under Godwin, he shared his post with a younger man. An amusing titbit is provided by a census of householders of *c.*1565 (Cathedral Muniment Z.Z.1) which recorded that William Selbye had not only a son Robert, aged 13 and a king's scholar, and a maid, aged 14, but also '1 dog'.

Matthew Godwin 1584–5→ (First few months jointly with William Selbye). CA3 (f. 28) records an agreement dated 15 February 1583/4 'that Matthew Godwin shall be joined in patent with Mr William Selbye in the office of organist and master of the children'. This no doubt dealt with Selbye's infirmity or old age. Four months later, on 20 June 1584, a new patent was authorized for Godwin alone on Selbye's death (CA3, f. 30). At some date unknown, but certainly before the end of 1586, Godwin migrated to Exeter Cathedral.

See under Exeter Cathedral.

Arthur Cock ←1587–8. Cock(e) is named as master of the choristers in Ac1b for 1587–8 (there are no earlier accounts than this after 1578–9, nor any later ones until 1589–90). On 6 February 1587/8 he was granted an increase in salary from £12 to £15 (CA3, f. 80). Earlier he had been named as chorister in the accounts for 1568–9 (Ac1a), 1572–3 (Ac2a), 1574–5 (Ac1a), 1575–6 (Ac1b), and as a 'substitute' (deputy for a minor canon) in those for 1578–9 (Ac2a).

See under the Chapel Royal.

George Juxon 1589–90→. With the exception of the year 1589–90 (Ac2a), there are no surviving accounts between Cock's time and the year 1598–9 (Ac1b), when Marson's name (see below) is entered. For that solitary year 1589–90 George Juxon is named as master of the choristers. He was already a lay clerk in 1578–9 (Ac2a). I have not traced any references to him in CA3 or Reg. 3 and 4, but he was officially summoned as master of the choristers and as a lay clerk to the archbishop's visitation in June 1589 (Llp, Whitgift's Register, f. 255). The statement made by Woodruff and Danks (1912: 462), that in 1590 Thomas Stores was paid as organist, is a mistake for a payment to an organ-blower, 1589–90.

George Marson ←1598–1632 (b. Worcester, 1571 or 1572; d. Canterbury, 3 Feb. 1631–2). As mentioned under Juxon, Marson first appears as master of the choristers in the accounts for the quarter ending Christmas 1598 (Ac1b). On 26 February 1603/4 he was granted a patent of the office of 'master of the singing boys and organist' in consideration of his good and faithful service both in teaching the boys and in playing the organ (Reg. 5, pp. 182–3). This accords with a Chapter resolution dated November 1603 (CA3, f. 237).

From 1604 Marson combined his work with the post of minor canon, and from 1607 till shortly before his death he was rector of St Mary Magdalene, Canterbury (*NG*), an almost unique instance of a cathedral organist who was simultaneously parson of a parish.

In evidence given in connection with certain legal proceedings, Marson stated his age in August 1621 as 49, and his birthplace as Worcester (Cathedral Archives, X.11.14, f. 45^{v}); and in March 1621/2 (X.11.19, f. 36^{v}) he said he was 50. In the first statement he said he had been in Canterbury for twelve years, but in the second, fourteen years. His burial on 5 February 1631/2 is entered thus in PR: 'George Marson, once one of the Petticanons of this Church, Master of the Choristers, and Organist also of this Church'.

Venn notes a George Mersham of Trinity College, Cambridge who took the Mus.B. degree in 1598, and it may be that this is our subject. West (1921), however, gave the date of the degree as 1601.

It was during Marson's time that the Chapter House was fitted up for the preaching of sermons, whereupon it began to be known as the 'sermon house', and an organ was installed there for the congregational metrical psalms (Woodruff and Danks 1912: 452). It is not clear at what point it was recognized that playing this organ formed no part of the duty of the statutory master of the choristers and organist. But from 1625–6 until 1631–2 (Ac2b) an 'extraordinary payment' was made jointly to Marson and Francis Plomer, a lay clerk, for playing the psalms in the sermon house ('pro eorum diligentia in domo concionali et pro modulatione psalmorum et organorum').

Latterly, from 1627–8, although Marson remained officially responsible for them, the teaching of the choristers was given over to William Pysing (AC2b).

Valentine Röther 1632–7→. On Marson's death, the posts of master of the choristers and organist were separated. The former position went officially to William Pysing, whose remuneration is duly noted in the accounts in its regular place between the minor canons and the lay clerks. The organist's stipend, however, is entered among miscellaneous items under some such heading as 'Feoda et Regarda'.

There are no accounts for 1632–3 and no Chapter Acts from 1628 until 1670, but Röther may be presumed to have been appointed on Marson's death. He is described in the accounts (Ac2b) in 1633–4 and later as 'organista in choro' ('organist in the choir'). This is to distinguish the organist at the statutory choral services from the organist of the sermon house ('organista in domo concionali'), now Francis Plomer.

Röther's name appears in the accounts for the last time in 1636–7 (Ac2b); those for 1637–8 and 1638–9 are missing.

Thomas Tunstall ←1639–Interregnum. When the accounts resume in 1639–40 (Ac2b), Tunstall is named as 'organist in the choir' while Pysing and Plomer continue in their respective posts. Tunstall was formerly a lay clerk (see Ac1b, 1633–4). The latest extant accounts before the Civil War are for 1641–2, showing Tunstall, Pysing, and Plomer as before.

Thomas Gibbs 1661–3→. Immediately following the Restoration, there was a vacancy in the main post of organist, though, as the accounts for 1660–1 reveal (Ac2c), both Pysing and Plomer lived to resume their offices. However, in 1661–2 (Ac2c) Thomas Gibbs received the stipend of organist under 'Extraordinary Offices', while Plomer, under 'Feoda et Regarda', was designated 'quondam organista in domo capitulari' ('formerly organist in the Chapter House [i.e., sermon house]'). After Michaelmas 1663 there are no further accounts until 1670–1. Someone with the same name was organist of Norwich Cathedral, 1664–6 (q.v.).

Richard Chomley *c*.1669–75. West (1921) states that Chomley was appointed in 1669, but the first mention I have discovered of him is in the resumed accounts for 1670–1 (Ac3), when he is named as organist with Pysing still as master of the choristers. His last payment was at Christmas 1675. On 9 December of that year the Dean and Chapter received his request that 'by reason of age and other infirmities' he might resign his post and move to London or elsewhere. He was allowed a further quarter's stipend *ex gratia*, given £10 towards the cost of his removal, and a small pension of 25*s*. (CA5).

Robert Wren 1675–91 (d. Canterbury, Sept. 1691). Wren was elected organist at the same Chapter meeting as his predecessor's resignation was accepted. He was one of the lay clerks, and had been a chorister under Pysing. He may well have been connected with the family of Wren associated with the music of Rochester Cathedral in the late seventeenth century. In the accounting year 1684–5 (Ac3) Wren assumed the duty of master of the choristers, Pysing having died and been buried in the cloisters on 6 March 1683/4 (PR). (The William Pysing who continued thereafter as a lay clerk must have been his son.)

Wren was in office when, in 1684, 'Father' Smith rebuilt and enlarged the Cathedral organ built by Lancelot Pease in 1662. There was some trouble about the resulting instrument, and Smith was apparently asked to attend to it. In a characteristic letter to the dean (Tillotson), Smith wrote from Durham on 9 July 1686 to say that an immediate visit was impossible. He goes on:

> I hope you will excuse me, as for your organ I have done my endeavour to have served you with a good sound organ, but when I left Canterbury Mr Wren being not well and had a distemper in his eye that I could not show him so well of the variety of stops than otherwise I would have done, as for the trumpet stop being a thing that it will not always stand in tune than other stops, but I will show him when it please God [for me] to come to Canterbury that he shall tune it so well as myself.

The complete letter, in original spelling, will be found in Freeman (1977: 71).

I take it that a payment of £10 for two years' salary to 'Mr Smith the organist' in Ac3 (1690, 1691) perhaps refers to 'Father' Smith's fee for organ maintenance.

Nicholas Wooton 1692–8 (d. Canterbury, Apr. 1700). Wooton was appointed organist and master of the choristers, and also a lay clerk, on 1 December 1692 (CA5). On 27 June 1698 (CA5) it was resolved that: 'forasmuch as Nicholas Wooton, organist of this church, hath left and deserted that place . . . he be amoved and the place be void'. Nevertheless, when he died some two years later, he was buried within the Cathedral on 19 April 1700 (PR).

A glimpse of the Cathedral's musical practice during Wooton's time is provided by a Chapter order of 28 May 1696 'that every Sunday morning Tallis his Te Deum and Creed be used, and the Jubilate chanted, and that in the evening Batten's Service be sung' (CA5).

From March to September 1698 **William Porter** acted as organist and received the stipend (Ac3).

Daniel Henstridge 1698–1736 (1718–36 nominally only). With three dissentient voices, Henstridge was 'chosen probationer organist for a trial period of half a year to Midsummer Chapter next' in November 1698 (CA5). He was obliged to 'assist [William] Porter so far as he is capable in instructing him upon the organ' (this might have been more happily phrased), and 'to teach the King's scholars to sing Tallis his Service'.

Twenty years later, age was beginning to tell on Henstridge, as the following extract from CA6, dated 5 December 1718, shows:

Mr Dean acquainting the Chapter that the organist Mr Henstridge was desirous to resign his place of master of the choristers, Mr William Raylton, one of the substitutes of this church, is now chosen into the office of master of the choristers; he undertaking both to teach the boys and to play on the organ constantly in the choir from both which this Chapter is willing to excuse the said Mr Henstridge on account of his age and infirmities.

By this arrangement, though being relieved of the duty of both offices, Henstridge technically relinquished that of master of the choristers alone. He continued to receive the stipend of organist, presumably as a form of pension.

See under Rochester Cathedral.

William Raylton 1736–57 (d. 1757). Raylton was probably a chorister in the Cathedral, for on 5 December 1713 the Chapter resolved (CA6) that 'ten guineas be paid to Mr [William] Crofts for teaching Railton'. Traces of his connection with *Croft survive in a manuscript, now in Manchester Public Library (BRm 340 Rb 15), endorsed 'The organ book of William Raylton when under Dr Croft's tuition', and another, now in the Nanki Music Library, Tokyo (N–3, 35), headed 'William Raylton His [Book] 170[0]', apparently given to him by Croft.

On 5 December 1718 he became master of the choristers and acting organist in succession to Henstridge, in circumstances set forth above. In July 1720 (CA6) he was promoted from 'substitute' to lay clerk. But he had been troubled by debts, and on 4 July 1719 the Chapter minutes read as follows (CA6):

Upon petition of Wm. Railton, substitute and master of the choristers, representing his debts to be £21 and his creditors to be uneasy and pressing; The Dean and prebendaries are once more disposed to assist him with £16, viz: the quarter's stipend arising from the vacant place of Thomas Barham, lay clerk deceased, at Midsummer 1719 being £4. 10*s*. and out of the money in the church chest £11. 10*s*. But Mr Treasurer is to be satisfied that this our last intention of relief to this man be answered by payment of his debts to Mr Plot and Mr Poley and by purchasing the harpsichord mentioned in his note.

When Henstridge at long last died, Raylton was given the actual office of organist; but the minute of his appointment (CA7, 25 June 1736) reflects obvious dissatisfaction with the way in which the duties of organist had lately been discharged: 'Whenever he has leave to be absent from his duty of organist, we expect him to provide and pay a more sufficient person to do that office than has of late been allowed to do it.'

Samuel Porter 1757–1803 (b. Norwich, 1733; d. Canterbury, 11 Dec. 1810). Porter was a chorister in St Paul's Cathedral, and a pupil there of Maurice Greene, for whose final quarterly stipend Porter signed at Christmas 1755 (see p. 177). There is no reference to his appointment to Canterbury in CA8, but in June 1757 (CA8) it was resolved that 'Until such time as we can make a proper addition to our organist's income, Dr Tanner be desired to accept of him for a tenant in his house lately occupied by Mr Coke, and that the rent of it be paid by our Treasurer out of the Common Stock.' He retired in 1803, and was buried in the cloisters on 18 December 1810, aged 77 (PR). A mural tablet has the following inscription: 'Sacred to the memory of Samuel Porter organist of this cathedral for the space of 47 years. (and was scholar to Dr Maurice Greene.) He died Decr. 11. 1810, aged 77 years.'

He was a subscriber both to the first and second editions of Boyce's *Cathedral Music* in 1760 and 1788. His son W. J. Porter, who became chaplain to Viscount Fitzwilliam and headmaster of King's School, Worcester, published some of his father's music together with a portrait of him. W. J. Porter owned two sets of manuscript part-books in the hand of John Gostling (Obl, Tenbury MSS 797–803 and 1176–82), and these may have come to him through his father, who worked at Canterbury while Gostling's son William was minor canon there.

Highmore Skeats (I) 1803–31 (d. Canterbury, 1831). According to West (1921), Skeats was a chorister in Exeter Cathedral and then vicar choral of Salisbury. His father, certainly, was a lay vicar choral of Salisbury, for among the subscribers to Arnold's *Cathedral Music* in 1799 there are named 'Mr Skeats, Senr., Lay Vicar of the Cath. of Salisbury', and 'Mr Skeats, Junr., Organist of the Cathedral, Ely'. He succeeded Langdon as organist of Ely Cathedral in 1778 (q.v.). While there he subscribed not only to Arnold's *Cathedral Music* but to the second edition of Boyce's *Cathedral Music*, 1788. He moved to Canterbury as organist in 1803, his appointment (CA10) being joined with that of lay clerk, doubtless as a means of improving the stipend. (For his son, see under St George's Chapel, Windsor.)

It was during Skeats's time, in about 1827, that pedals were first added to the Cathedral organ. W. H. Longhurst, whose father installed them, recalled that Skeats would not use them, and would say to his pupil T. E. Jones: 'Here, Jones, come and show these things off, I never learned to dance.' (Compare a similar anecdote relating to John Amott of Gloucester, q.v.).

Thomas Evance Jones 1831–72 (b. 1805; d. Canterbury, 1872). Jones became a chorister in Canterbury Cathedral in 1813, and was appointed a lay clerk in 1822. In 1830, a little before Skeats's death, he took over the post of master of the choristers, then held by Stephen Elvey. His appointment as organist was formally minuted on 25 November 1831 (CA11). Jones was buried at St Martin's Church, Canterbury.

William Henry Longhurst 1873–98 (b. Lambeth, 6 Oct. 1819; d. Canterbury, 17 June 1904). Longhurst was a chorister of Canterbury Cathedral under Skeats, and was then a pupil of *Stephen Elvey and of T. E. Jones, whose assistant he became in 1836, holding a lay clerkship at the same time. In 1842 he refused an offer of the post of organist of Carlisle Cathedral. On the death of T. E. Jones, the Chapter decided not to advertise the vacancy publicly but to make private enquiries about a successor, and Longhurst was formally admitted on 31 January 1874 (CA12). When he retired in 1898 he had been in the service of the Cathedral for seventy years. He was buried at Harbledown, Canterbury.

In 1866, while still assistant organist, Longhurst was one of the first successful candidates for the fellowship of the (Royal) College of Organists. He was about to take steps to obtain an Oxford degree in music when this came to the notice of Ouseley, and he was recommended for the Lambeth degree of D.Mus., which he received in 1875, much to the disgust of *MT* which objected to the degree and thought that Longhurst should not have accepted it. He also had a further doctorate (1886) from the University of Trinity College, Toronto (*not* the University of Toronto, to which, however, the University of Trinity College became federated in 1904).[1]

In November 1897 the Dean and Chapter of Canterbury resolved to relieve Longhurst of his duties by appointing a deputy or acting organist, but when the matter was put to him he agreed to resign from 25 March 1898. A somewhat fulsome account of Longhurst, from which certain details above have been taken, is contained in the *Precentor*, May and June 1902.

Harry Crane Perrin 1898–1908 (b. Wellingborough, Northants., 1865; d. in England, *c.*1953, aged 88). Perrin was successively organist of St Columba's College, Rathfarnham, Dublin (1886), St John's Church, Lowestoft (1888), and St Michael's Church, Coventry (now Coventry Cathedral), where he succeeded *A. H. Brewer in 1892. From there he moved to Canterbury (CA14, pp. 106, 137) and then, on his resignation in 1908, to Montreal, to become professor of music at McGill University and director of the McGill Conservatorium of Music. He retired in 1929.

Perrin held the FRCO diploma, and took the Dublin degrees of Mus.B. and Mus.D. in 1890 and 1901.

West 1921; archivist of McGill University, Montreal.

Clement Charlton Palmer 1908–36 (b. Barton-under-Needwood, Staffs., 1871; d. Canterbury, 13 Aug. 1944). On Perrin's resignation, the Dean and Chapter appointed ***S. H. Nicholson** from a short list of candidates which included not only Palmer but also *C. H. Moody, *T. W. Morgan, and *F. W. Wadely. Almost immediately, however, Nicholson sought leave to withdraw in order to become organist of Manchester Cathedral, whereupon Palmer was appointed (CA12).

Palmer received his early training at the Derby School of Music, and went to Repton School. He was briefly organist of St Leonard's Church, Wichmore (1887) and of St Andrew's, Pau (France) (1888). He then became assistant organist of Lichfield Cathedral (1890–7), holding also the post of organist of Holy Trinity Church, Burton-on-Trent from 1891. In 1897 he moved to Ludlow Parish Church in succession to *Ivor Atkins, remaining there until his

[1] In 1885 the University of Trinity College, Toronto took steps to hold examinations in England for its degrees in music, and it was no doubt in this connection that Longhurst was given his degree, for he became one of the examiners and was thus involved in the controversy surrounding these *in absentia* degrees, which were regarded as 'bogus' by the graduates in music of Oxford, Cambridge, and Durham, and outside the powers of the University. They were withdrawn for English candidates in 1891. (Information from the Office of Statistics and Records, University of Toronto.)

appointment to Canterbury. He held the FRCO diploma, and took the Oxford degrees of B.Mus. (1891) and D.Mus. (1896).

West 1921; *WWW*, 1941–50.

§**Gerald (Hocken) Knight, CBE 1937–52** (b. Par, Cornwall, 27 July 1908; d. London (Paddington), 16 Sept. 1979). Knight was educated at Truro Cathedral School, and in 1922 he was articled to *H. S. Middleton at Truro Cathedral. In 1926 he went up to Peterhouse, Cambridge as a choral exhibitioner, and afterwards to the Royal College of Music and the College of St Nicolas of the School of English Church Music (now the Royal School of Church Music), then at Chislehurst, of which he was one of the earliest students.

From 1931 to 1937 he was organist of St Augustine's Church, Queen's Gate, London, and in 1932 he also became tutor in plainsong at the College of St Nicolas. In 1937 he was appointed to Canterbury Cathedral.

Meanwhile he remained closely in touch with the School of English Church Music, and when that organization moved to Canterbury after World War II, he became warden of the College of St Nicolas, combining this post with his Cathedral work from 1945 to 1952. After the death of *S. H. Nicholson in 1947, Knight was one of the three honorary associate directors of the Royal School of Church Music, and in 1952 he resigned his post at Canterbury Cathedral to become its director immediately before its move from Canterbury to Addington Palace, Croydon.

Knight took the English tripos and the Cambridge degrees of BA (1930), Mus.B. (1932), and MA (1933), and won the John Stewart of Rannoch scholarship in sacred music in 1927. He took the Archbishop of Canterbury's diploma in church music (ADCM) in 1937, being already FRCO (1935, Lafontaine prize) and CHM. In 1961 the Archbishop of Canterbury (Fisher) conferred on him the Lambeth degree of D.Mus. as one of his very latest archiepiscopal acts; it is understood that Knight had earlier excused himself from this honour on professional grounds. In the New Year Honours of 1971 he was appointed CBE, and he retired from the directorship of the Royal School of Church Music at the end of 1972.

§**Douglas (Edward) Hopkins 1953–5** (b. London (Dulwich), 23 Dec. 1902). Hopkins was educated first in the choir of St Paul's Cathedral and then at Dulwich College, the Royal Academy of Music, and the Guildhall School of Music. He was sub-organist of St Paul's Cathedral under *Stanley Marchant, 1927–46, and he was appointed to the staff of the Royal Academy of Music in 1935.

In May 1946 he took up the post of organist of Peterborough Cathedral, and in January 1953 he moved to Canterbury Cathedral, where he remained until 1955. From 1956 to 1965 he was director of music at St Felix School, Southwold, and in December 1965 he became organist of St Marylebone Parish Church, London.

Hopkins took the FRCO diploma in 1926, followed by the London degrees of B.Mus. (1932) and D.Mus. (1936).

Sidney (Scholfield) Campbell, MVO, 1956–61.
See under St George's Chapel, Windsor.

§**(Edward) Allan Wicks, CBE, 1961–88** (b. Harden, near Bingley, W. Yorks., 6 June 1923). Wicks, the son of a clergyman, was educated at St John's School, Leatherhead and at Christ Church, Oxford, of which he was a scholar. He took the Oxford degrees of BA (1947) and MA (1950), and the FRCO diploma (1948). On coming down from Oxford he was sub-organist of York Minster, 1947–54, and organist of Manchester Cathedral, 1954–61. He received the Lambeth degree of Mus.D. in 1974, the honorary degree of D.Mus. from the University of Kent in 1985, and was appointed CBE in the Birthday Honours of 1988, shortly before his retirement at the conclusion of the Lambeth Conference of that year.

§**David (Andrew) Flood, organist from 1988** (b. Guildford, Surrey, 10 Nov. 1955). From the Royal Grammar School, Guildford, and after a year at the Royal School of Church Music, Flood went up to Oxford as organ exhibitioner of St John's College, 1974–7, where he read music, and then spent a year at Clare College, Cambridge. He took the Oxford degrees of BA (1977) and MA (1981), and holds the diplomas of FRCO (1976) and CHM (1975). He was assistant organist of Canterbury Cathedral from 1978 to 1986, before being appointed organist of Lincoln Cathedral, from which post he moved back to Canterbury in September 1988.

CARLISLE

The Cathedral Church of the Holy and Undivided Trinity

Main sources in this section (1961):

Chapter Acts

CA2	Register II, Thomas Tallentyre, 1570–8.
CA3	Register III, John Smythe, 1579–96.
CA4	Register IV, 1609–18.
CA5	Register V, 1618–21 (including matter to 1627).
—	Register VI not located.
CA7	Register VII, 1636–44.
CA8	Register VIII, 1661–8.
CA9	Register IX, 1668–1703.
CA10	Register X, 1703–51.
CA11	Register XI, 1752–92.
CA12	Register XII, 1792–1833.
CA13	Order Book, 1834–55.
CA14	Order Book, 1855–74.
CA15	Order Book, 1874–1901.
CA16	Order Book, 1901–8.
CA17	Minute Book, 1906–14.

Account Books

Ac1a	Audit Books, 1667–92.
Ac1	Discharge Book I, 1677–90.
Ac2	Discharge Book II, 1691–1710.
Ac3	Discharge Book III, 1711–30.
—	Discharge Book IV not located.
Ac5	Discharge Book V, 1751–70.

Before the Reformation, Carlisle Cathedral was the Augustinian cathedral priory of St Mary. Following its dissolution, Henry VIII refounded it as the cathedral church of the bishopric in May 1541. It was the smallest of his creations, and its musical establishment included no more than six choristers under their master. The draft statutes of 1545 enjoined that the duty of organist was to be discharged by the master of the choristers (see above, p. xix). At no time in the history of Carlisle Cathedral have the duties of master of the choristers and organist been separated.

Thomas Southwicke ?–1587 (d. Carlisle, 1587). No name of any master of the choristers has been established for the earliest years of the Cathedral's existence. The first mention of any such is in a roll-call of members of the foundation *c.*1580–1 (CA3, f. 174[v]): 'Singingmen | 1. Thomas Southwicke et Mr of the Choristers'. Though he was thus listed among the lay clerks, by statute the master of the choristers should have been additional to them. As will be noted under his successor, Southwicke had assistance in his last years, which suggests that he may by then have been an old man who had perhaps been long in office. He died in 1587: an entry in CA3 (f. 166) dated 11 December speaks of 'the office of master of the choristers being void by the death of Thomas Southwicke'.

Robert James 1587–?95. James had been a lay clerk of the Cathedral. An order in CA2 (f. 144) dated 21 December 1578 reads as follows:

> That Robert James now one of the singingmen . . . to that end he shall do his best endeavours towards furnishing and adorning the choir with musical song and playing of the organs we do give and grant unto him the sum of five marks [£3. 6*s*. 8*d*.] by year during the life natural of the said Robert James. And further after the natural death of Thomas Southwick now master of the choristers we do give and grant unto him the said office together with the fee of £9. 15*s*.

The order goes on to say that James was to have the appointing of new choristers instead of Southwicke. He was eventually admitted to the full post of master of the choristers on 11 December 1587, and he was still in office in 1594 according to the roll-call for that year (CA3, ff. 166, 174).

Robert Dalton (I) ?1595–?; James Pearson ←1610–1627→; Robert Dalton (II) ←1641–1644→. The Chapter Register covering the period 1594–1609 (slightly overlapping CA3) has been missing at least since the eighteenth century. There is, however, an index to it preserved at the end of CA3, giving skeleton details together with page references to the missing Register. The following are the relevant extracts relating to these three men:

CA3	*Reference to Missing Register, 1594–1609*	
f. 194[v]	Doctor Parkins instituted Dean.	pp. 24, 25
	(*b*) Mr Dalton, Mr of the Choristers [and others] all admitted	ibid.
f. 195[v]	(*c*) An act for Mr Rob Dalton and allowance for James Pearson	p. 261
f. 196	The admission of Robert Dalton chorister.	p. 277
f. 198	(*d*) James Pearson admitted Mr of the Choristers.	p. 241
Ibid.	James Pearson suspended for being absent from the church 14 days without leave.	p. 247
f. 199	(*e*) Conferring upon James Pearson singingman toward the bettering of his wages, 26*s*. 8*d*.	p. 252

f. 200	(*a*) Robte Dalton Mr of the Choristers to have £3. 6*s*. 8*d*. augmented in his wages which Robert James lately has.	p. 261
Ibid.	(*c*) James Pearson 40*s*. allowance for pricking of books and songs.	ibid.
f. 200ᵛ	Robt Dalton Mr of the Choristers motion for augmentation of wage which was in part granted upon the supers[eding].	p. 268
f. 202	James Pearson elected sub-deacon.	p. 281
f. 202ᵛ	(*e*) Robert Dalton of the age of five years and a half admitted chorister.	p. 283

Examination of both CA3 and CA4 shows that items are by no means always in chronological order. It seems possible to make sense of this index to the missing register only by assuming likewise. However, the first item, entered on the same page as the institution of Dean Parkins (Perkins), can hardly refer to anything other than the year of that institution, 1595. For the rest, the following provisional reading is suggested:

(*a*) Robert Dalton receives an increase of stipend. Though he is referred to as master of the choristers, the sum of 5 marks is the same amount allotted to James in 1578 as Southwicke's deputy. I take it that Dalton now stood in a similar relation to James. (*b*) In 1595 Dalton succeeds James. (*c*) James Pearson, who has some association with Dalton, shows promise and is paid extra and undertakes music-copying. (*d*) Pearson then becomes master of the choristers (as we shall see from CA4, at some date not later than 1610). (*e*) Meanwhile, a special point is made of electing an unusually young chorister (hence the careful citation of his age) named Robert Dalton, who may perhaps prove to be Robert Dalton (II). (Could this possibly have been a device whereby the Chapter provided for an orphan on his father's death?) How the admission on f. 196 fits in is obscure; it is just conceivable that it might record the formal admission of this boy but entered out of sequence when he was rather older and had effectively become a chorister. All this is speculative but not unreasonable; the actual sequence of James–Dalton–Pearson does not seem to be in doubt.

Moving to the firmer ground of the lists of members of the foundation, we find James Pearson entered regularly as master of the choristers from the earliest such list, dated June 1610 (CA4, p. 490), in which Robert Dalton is a chorister, to the latest, dated 1627 (CA5).

During this period the Dean and Chapter became dissatisfied with the men of the choir, and on 23 June 1624 (CA5, p. 841) they ordered that the minor canons and lay clerks must 'endeavour themselves to perfect in singing' or else they would have no wages (was this not *ultra vires*?) after St Clement's Day (23 November).

Meantime, Robert Dalton (II) had been elected sub-deacon and singingman in June 1615 (CA4, p. 543), but on 8 October 1621 (CA5, p. 817) he did 'freely and voluntarily resign' the place of singingman. However, when CA7 first gives a list of members (June 1641, p. 123), Robert Dalton (II) is entered as master of the choristers, and remains so up to June 1644. This was the year of the parliamentary decree suspending the Prayer Book services. By the side of his name (and others) in this last list, a later hand, no doubt after the Restoration, has written the word 'mort'.

It was in the time covered by Pearson and Dalton (II) that three army officers reported their sly opinion that at Carlisle Cathedral, 'the organs and voice did well agree, the one being like a shrill bagpipe, the other like the Scottish tone' (Lbl, Lansdowne MS 213).

John Howe ←1665–92. Howe appears in the first surviving roll-call after the Restoration, dated 1665 (CA8), as minor canon and master of the choristers, and Ac1a, 1, and 2 show him thus continuously from Michaelmas 1675 to 1692. Though a minor canon, he was not necessarily in holy orders. This link between a minor canonry and the post of master of the choristers/organist continued at Carlisle until the end of Thomas Hill's time, and certainly neither he nor Greatorex were clergymen. It amounted to the diversion of a minor canon's stipend (£8 per annum) to augment that of the master of the choristers, now at the rate of £10.

In 1676–7 Howe was deputy treasurer of the Cathedral, and in the same year he was paid £1 as a personal book allowance ('procurand: libris musicis'), which was continued from year to year (Ac1, 2) and which went on being paid as late as Hill's day. It was quite separate from the purchase of music-books for the choir. On 12 April 1679 there is a payment of £1 'to Mr John How for his son's teaching at Durham Singing School'.

Unfortunately, John Howe finished his career in ill favour. On 26 September 1692 he was admonished because he had 'for several years' neglected 'to attend the duty of his ofice in his own proper person'. The next day he submitted his resignation, both as minor canon and organist, on account of 'age and other infirmities' (CA9). But, as we shall see, the minute recording his successor's admission tells a different story.

Timothy Howe 1692–*c.*1732. No doubt this was the boy, son of John Howe, who was sent to Durham to learn singing in 1679. He first received pay, both as minor canon and master of the choristers like his father, at Christmas 1692 (Ac2). It was not until 25 November 1693 that he was formally admitted to office. CA9 contains the following entry of that date:

> Whereas Mr John How senior, late organist of the Cathedral Church of Carlisle, did deservedly incur the displeasure of the Dean and Chapter . . . by his disrespectful carriage to Christopher Musgrave, Esq., Member of Parliament for the said City, I, Timothy How (son of the said John), being now to be admitted into the said office of organist do acknowledge the displacing of my said father (upon the aforementioned account) to have been most just and reasonable and do hereby promise never to be guilty of the like disrespect to so worthy patrons and friends to the established church as the said Mr Musgrave and his family have always proved themselves.
>
> Timothy How

Howe was then sworn and admitted minor canon and organist. But he had to be admonished three times, in 1719, 1720, and 1721/2, for negligence in teaching the boys (CA10).

Abraham Dobinson 1733–48. Howe was last present at a roll-call in November 1732. In June 1733 no one is named as organist. Dobinson is entered as master of the choristers beginning with the roll-call for November 1733, and from June 1734 as minor canon also. In the roll-call for November 1748 he is marked 'dead' (CA10).

Charles Pick 1749–81. By a minute of 12 January 1748/9 the Chapter resolved to appoint Pick with an additional allowance of £7. He was sworn and admitted organist, master of the choristers, and minor canon on 23 June 1749 (CA10). At the June roll-call of 1781 his name is marked 'dead' (CA11).

Thomas Greatorex 1781–*c*.1784 (b. North Wingfield, Derbys., 5 Oct. 1758; d. Hampton, Middx., 17 or 18 July 1831). In Greatorex, Carlisle Cathedral for the first time appointed a musician of more than local repute. He came from a comfortable family background, his father being the Anthony Greatorex of Riber Hall, Matlock who, as 'Organist of Northwingfield', subscribed to the first edition of Boyce's *Cathedral Music* and who himself was the boy's first teacher. In 1772 he became a pupil of *Benjamin Cooke. From 1774–6 he was at Hinchinbrook House, Huntingdonshire as the protégé of the Earl of Sandwich, one of the founders of the Antient Concert in London.

He was admitted organist, master of the choristers, and minor canon of Carlisle Cathedral in November 1781, at the same time as a Mr Anthony Greatorex was admitted precentor, minor canon, and sub-sacrist (CA11). He was listed for the last time in the roll-call for November 1784. It is said that he sought appointment to Carlisle because his health required northern air. During his time there he spent many evenings in philosophical discussions with the dean, Archdeacon Paley, and others.

After leaving Carlisle, Greatorex travelled abroad, making the acquaintance of Charles Edward, the 'Young Pretender', on whose death he inherited some manuscript music (one surviving item, an opera by Galuppi, is now in the Bodleian Library, Tenbury MS 1060–2). In 1793 Greatorex became conductor of the Antient Concert, and later conducted the Birmingham Triennial Festivals. In 1819 he became organist of Westminster Abbey, holding the post until his death.

He held conservative views on music, considering Haydn's *The Creation* 'too theatrical for England'. His organ-playing has been described thus: 'His style was massive; he was like a Briareus with a hundred hands, grasping so many keys at once that surges of sound rolled from his instrument in awful grandeur'. (Gardiner 1838–53: i.)

As a keen botanist he became a fellow of the Linnean Society (1801); he was also interested in astronomy, and was elected a fellow of the Royal Society in 1819 on his discovery of a method of measuring the altitude of mountains. Among the effects sold after his death was a bookcase with manuscripts of Handel's works transcribed by J. C. Smith and the copyists associated with him. This bookcase and collection is now in the Fitzwilliam Museum, Cambridge.

GM gives the date of death as 18 July, but the inscription on his tomb in the west cloister of Westminster Abbey reads 17 July.

GM, 101 (1831), 280; Phillips 1864: i. 143.

Thomas Hill 1785–1833. Hill was admitted minor canon, master of the choristers, and organist on 23 June 1785 (CA11). In recording his remuneration, Ac5 uses the term 'lay canon', thus supporting what has been said above under John Howe.

A minute in CA12 dated June 1817 records how

> Mr Thos Hill the organist was reprimanded for tippling and frequenting the cockpit and as he had very often been admonished on the same account he was distinctly informed that if in future he should be found to offend again in any one instance either as to being present tippling in an alehouse or at the cockpit he should be dismissed without further enquiry, at the same time he was fined in the sum of five guineas to be applied to charitable purposes.

Richard Ingham 1833–41 (b. 1804; d. 1841). Ingham's appointment was minuted at the November Chapter, 1833 (CA12). At this point the combination of a minor canonry with the post of organist was discontinued. West (1921) gives the date of Ingham's birth and death, and states that before his Cathedral appointment he was organist of St Mary's Church, Gateshead.

James Stimpson 1841 (b. Lincoln, 29 Feb. 1820; d. Birmingham, 4 Oct. 1886). Stimpson was the son of a lay vicar of Lincoln Cathedral who had moved to Durham, where the boy became a chorister in the Cathedral (1822). After being articled to Ingham at Carlisle Cathedral in 1834, he was appointed organist of St Andrew's Church, Newcastle upon Tyne in 1836. He played both violin and double-bass.

At the Cathedral roll-call on 23 June 1841 (CA13) Ingham was marked 'sick'; yet on the same day (perhaps the minutes were written up some time later) Stimpson was appointed 'in the room of Richard Ingham deceased'. This is the only roll-call in which Stimpson's name appears; no organist is mentioned in November 1841.

Following this very brief spell as organist of Carlisle Cathedral, he became organist of Birmingham Town Hall in 1842. While in Birmingham he was also organist of various churches, among them St Martin's (1852–6). He was both founder of the Birmingham Festival Choral Society and its first conductor, 1843–55; thus it was that he trained the chorus and played the organ for the original performance of Mendelssohn's *Elijah* in 1846.

MT, 27 (1886), 668; *BMB*.

Henry Edmund Ford 1842–1909 (b. Warlingham, Surrey, 6 Aug. 1821; d. Carlisle, 3 Nov. 1909). Ford was a chorister and assistant organist under *Ralph Banks at Rochester Cathedral. His earliest appointment was as organist of Gillingham Parish Church. For a few weeks after Banks's death he acted as organist of Rochester Cathedral, and on 29 November 1841 the Rochester Chapter 'ordered that Mr H. E. Ford be paid £20 for his services as organist in this Cathedral since the decease of Mr Banks; and that in consideration of Mr Ford's good conduct and to mark the Chapter's sense of his commendable industry and exertions he be presented with an additional sum of £20' (Rochester CA12).

He was provisionally appointed organist and master of the choristers of Carlisle Cathedral in January 1842 (CA13), and was confirmed as such at the

June Chapter, 1842. In 1891 he was granted the Lambeth degree of D.Mus. He retired from active duty in 1902, though he retained the actual post of organist until his death. Thus, on a technical point, he holds the record—sixty-seven years—for length of tenure in a single cathedral post.

MT 50 (1909), 243, 786.

After Ford's retirement in 1902, **E. G. Mercer** was appointed to act as organist. He had been organist of St Michael's, Chester Square, London. When Mercer left Carlisle to join the music staff of Harrow in 1904, **S. H. Nicholson** was appointed to follow him. When Nicholson left for Manchester Cathedral in 1908, **Theodore Hunter Hastings Walrond** took over. Walrond (b. Glasgow, 1872; d. 1935), who was educated at Rugby and Balliol College, Oxford, had for a short time assisted Nicholson at Carlisle. When, following Ford's death, Wadely was offered the permanent post in 1910, the Chapter thought it suitable to congratulate Walrond on coming second in the competition conducted by *T. Tertius Noble. On leaving Carlisle, Walrond entered the service of the Board of Education, rising to be one of His Majesty's principal inspectors of schools, and retiring in 1933.

Frederick William Wadeley, OBE, 1910–60 (b. Kidderminster, Worcs., 30 July 1882; d. Carlisle, 28 May 1970). Wadely was the son of W. E. Wadely, a friend and contemporary of Elgar, who had been an articled pupil of *William Done and was organist of St John the Baptist's Church, Kidderminster for over fifty years. F. W. Wadely attended King Charles I Grammar School, Kidderminster, and received his earliest musical education from his father. After an early appointment as organist of Wolverley Parish Church, Worcestershire (1895), he went up to Cambridge as organ scholar of Selwyn Hall (now College) in 1900, and held the John Stewart of Rannoch scholarship in sacred music, 1901–3. He studied for a short time at the Royal College of Music, and was appointed organist of St Andrew's Church, Uxbridge, Middlesex in 1903. A year later he returned to his native county as organist of Malvern Priory Church, 1904–10.

In February 1910 (CA17) he was chosen organist of Carlisle Cathedral out of a field of 113 candidates. He held office for fifty years, so that he and Ford between them spanned 118 years.

Wadely took the Cambridge degree of BA and Mus.B. in 1903, proceeding MA in 1907 and Mus.D. in 1915. He also held the FRCO diploma. In 1955 he was appointed OBE, and in 1966 was made an honorary freeman of the City of Carlisle.

West 1921; *Venn; MT*, 111 (1970), 738.

§(Robert) Andrew Seivewright, master of the music from 1960 (b. Plungar, Leics., 22 Apr. 1926). Seivewright, whose father was vicar of Plungar, was educated at Denstone College, Staffordshire and at King's College, Cambridge, where he read music. He then studied for a year at Bretton Hall College of Music, Art, and Drama near Wakefield, and obtained the diploma in education of the University of Leeds (1952). He took the Cambridge degrees of BA and MA in 1950 and 1952 respectively.

In 1952 he became music master of Ermysted's Grammar School, Skipton, and in 1956 he went to Pontefract as organist of the parish church and music master of Pontefract Grammar School. He remained there until he took up his appointment at Carlisle Cathedral in 1960.

CHELMSFORD

The Cathedral Church of St Mary the Virgin, St Peter, and St Cedd

St Mary's Parish Church became a cathedral when the diocese of Chelmsford was founded in 1914. The earlier dates of tenure cited below have been either confirmed or corrected from issues of the *Cathedral Parish Magazine* or the *Cathedral News* by the kindness of Mr Eric Reed.

Frederick Robert Frye (1876) **1914–42** (b. Brook, near Ashford, Kent, 1851; d. Aug. 1942). Frye was a pupil of *F. E. Gladstone, among others. He became organist of New Romney Parish Church in 1870, and in 1876 he began his long connection with Chelmsford. His continuous record as organist of the parish church (later the Cathedral) there extends over sixty-five years, the longest active tenure recorded in this book. He retired in June 1942.

Frye took the FRCO diploma in 1879, and the Cambridge degree of Mus.B. in 1887. Towards the end of his career he was elected vice-president of the Royal College of Organists.

Venn; MT, 83 (1942), 352; *WWW*, 1941–50.

Following Frye's resignation in 1942, interim arrangements were made at Chelmsford Cathedral. **Mrs A. L. Harrison**, formerly assistant organist there, filled the vacancy until a new organist was appointed at the end of 1944.

(James) Roland Middleton 1945–9.

See under St Asaph Cathedral.

§(William) Stanley Vann 1949–53 (b. Leicester, 15 Feb. 1910). Vann received his early education at Alderman Newton's Grammar School, Leicester and Leicester College (the present Polytechnic). He took the London degree of B.Mus. (1947), and holds the FRCO diploma. He was assistant organist to *G. C. Gray at Leicester Cathedral from 1931 to 1933, before his appointment to Gainsborough Parish Church in 1933. From there he moved to Holy Trinity, Leamington Spa (1939–49). He left Chelmsford to become master of the music of Peterborough Cathedral in 1953, and retired in 1977. In 1971 he received the Lambeth degree of Mus.D.

Derrick (Edward) Cantrell 1953–62.
See under Manchester Cathedral.

Philip (Stevens) Ledger, CBE, 1962–5.
See under King's College, Cambridge.

§**John (William) Jordan 1965–81** (b. Birmingham, 24 Nov. 1941). Jordan attended King Edward's School, Birmingham from 1952 to 1959, and was a chorister of Birmingham Parish Church (1951–4) and of Birmingham Cathedral (1954–6). He went up to Emmanuel College, Cambridge where he held the organ scholarship from 1959 to 1962. He read music and took the Cambridge degrees of BA (1962), Mus.B. (1963), and MA (1966). He took the FRCO diploma with Limpus and Read prizes in 1961. He was appointed assistant at Chelmsford Cathedral in 1963, and succeeded to the full post in 1965. After leaving Chelmsford Cathedral he took up free-lance work, largely dividing his time between the Yamaha School of Music, Kuching, Malaysia and the UK.

Additional information from Associated Board of the Royal Schools of Music.

§**Graham (John) Elliott, master of the music from 1981** (b. Abergavenny, 10 Nov. 1945). Elliott was educated at King Henry VIII School, Abergavenny (1959–64) and the Royal Academy of Music (1964–5). He then became resident organ student at St George's Chapel, Windsor (1965–7). While still at school he had been organist of the priory church, Abergavenny (1960–4), and after leaving Windsor he was sub-organist of Llandaff Cathedral from 1967 to 1970. During this period he took the degree of B.Mus. (University of Wales, 1970). He was organist of St Asaph Cathedral, 1970–81, and took the further degrees of MA and Ph.D. (Wales) in 1982 and 1985 respectively.

CHESTER

The Cathedral Church of Christ and the Blessed Virgin Mary

Main sources in this section (1961) (with Chester Record Office references):

Chapter Acts
CA1 1648–73 (EDD/3913/3/2).
CA2 1674–95 (EDD/3913/3/3).
CA3 1694–1747 (EDD/3913/3/4).
CA4 1747–1816 (EDD/3913/3/5).
CA5 1816–94 (EDD/3913/3/6).
CA6 1841–85.

Accounts
1542–59 (beginning Oct. 1541) (EDD/3913/1/1).
1561–84 (EDD/3913/1/2).
1584–1610 (EDD/3913/1/3).
1611–43 (EDD/3913/1/4).
1664–94 (EDD/3913/1/5).
1694–1706 (EDD/3913/1/6).
1706–25 (EDD/3913/1/7).
1725–47 (EDD/3913/1/8).

Registers of Baptisms, Marriages, and Burials
PR 1687–1812; printed by the Parish Register Society, 1904.

On establishing the new see of Chester, Henry VIII founded Chester Cathedral in July 1541, granting it the buildings of the surrendered Benedictine abbey of St Werburgh. The choir included eight choristers under a master. By the draft statutes of 1544 the duties of organist were to be discharged by the master of the choristers (see p. xix). By local usage for nearly four centuries the lay clerks of Chester Cathedral were known as 'conducti' (anglicized as 'conducts').

For the first hundred years or more of its history, our only knowledge of the masters of the choristers/organists is derived from the quarterly treasurer's accounts, and these have many gaps. Until after 1660, therefore, it is impossible to say with precision when several of these officers were appointed, or for how long they served.

John Byrchley 1541–50. Byrchley had been schoolmaster of the former monastery, and on its dissolution he received a pension from the Court of Augmentations (J. C. Bridge 1913, quoting PRO, Augmentation Office, Misc. Books, 250–6). In connection with the new Cathedral his name is found on the first page of the earliest extant treasurer's account: 'Item the 3rd day of November [1541] to John Byrchelaye for the tabling of 8 children of our choir the space of 3 weeks.' In the very earliest accounts he is termed 'organ-player' against his stipend, but beginning with the accounting year 1544–5, when the accounts take a more regular shape (perhaps as a result of the promulgation of the draft statutes), his name, not designated by any office, comes between the sub-deacon and the lay clerks, the place at which one would expect to find the *magister choristarum*. His stipend at this juncture, however, was £8 a year, the same as the deacon and sub-deacon, less than the statutory fee of £10, but this may reflect his enjoyment of a pension from Augmentations. His last recorded payment is at Christmas 1550.

Thomas Barnes 1551–6→. Barnes, previously a lay clerk, received his first pay as master of the choristers at Lady Day 1551. He is properly designated *magister choristarum*, and has the regular £10 a year. In the accounting year 1555–6 he is grouped as one of the six lay clerks, though receiving £10 as against the £6. 13*s*. 4*d*. of the other five. Michaelmas 1556 is the last account in which he is named; the accounts are then intermitted until 1558. In the year to Michaelmas 1556 there was a minor canon of the same name.

Richard Saywell ←1558–64→. When the accounts resume for the quarter ending Christmas 1558, Saywell, like Barnes before him, is shown as one of the six lay clerks but with the larger stipend of master of the choristers. J. C. Bridge (1913) states that he was previously a lay clerk. It may be noted that a John Sewell or Saywell appears as a chorister in 1564. The last quarter for which Richard Saywell receives the stipend of master of the choristers is that ending Michaelmas 1564, after which there is no further account until the quarter ending Lady Day 1567, when 'Myster Saywell' is merely a lay clerk, remaining so until accounts break off after Michaelmas 1585 and he disappears. I cannot find evidence for Bridge's statement that he shared his successor's stipend.

Robert White 1567–8→. In the accounts at Lady Day 1567 there is no explicit entry for a master of the choristers, but a 'Mr Whyt' is entered after the Cathedral schoolmaster with a quarter's stipend of £4. 3*s.* 4*d.* At Midsummer and Michaelmas we find 'Mr/Magister Whit' designated as master of the choristers with the same stipend—much larger than his predecessors'. After Michaelmas 1567 the accounts are intermitted, and White's name is not found again. J. C. Bridge (1913) notes, however, that in both 1567 and 1568 he was paid for taking part in the music of the Chester miracle plays.

There is not much room to doubt that, though no Christian name is given, this is the Robert White who was formerly at Ely Cathedral and afterwards at Westminster Abbey. The dates fit, and his stipend at Chester suggests a man of some repute. Bridge observes that the title 'Mr' or 'Magister' denotes a university graduate, which the Westminster White certainly was; but this is not conclusive when it is noted that Saywell was termed 'Mayster' in 1567. The really strong testimony is that of *Thomas Tomkins (III), who wrote against Robert White's name in his copy of Morley's *Plaine and Easie Introduction* the description: 'First of Westchester & Westminster'—'Westchester' being the old name for Chester (see Stevens 1957: plate facing p. 29).

See under Ely Cathedral.

Robert Stevenson ←1571–97→. When the accounts resume for the quarter ending Christmas 1571, Stevenson is found as master of the choristers, the stipend having now reverted to the standard £10 per annum. He is named in the accounts until Michaelmas 1597, after which they are intermitted once more.

For the quarter ending Christmas 1596 the accounts accord the master of the choristers the style of 'magister doctor'. This, then, is the Robert Stevenson who took his degree of B.Mus. at Oxford in 1587, having been a student for thirty-three years, and who proceeded D.Mus. in 1596. Giving these details, Wood (1815–20: i. 239, 272) states that Stevenson was also admitted BA in 1587 but did not complete the formality of 'determination'. I am not persuaded that the graduate in music was the same man as this putative BA.

It was during Stevenson's time at Chester that the obligation was laid on the master of the choristers and organist to write out 'from time to time all necessary song books' in return for an increase of £2. 6*s.* 8*d.* in stipend (Burne 1958: 84). The accounts reveal several payments for paper to 'prick songs upon for the choir', and even for 'a pint of ink to prick songs for the choir, 6*d.*'.

Thomas Bateson ←1601–8. The next extant account is for the quarter ending Christmas 1601, and here Bateson is named as master of the choristers. When he published his 'First set' of madrigals in 1604, he described himself as 'Organist of the Cathedral Church of Christ in the City of Chester'. At this time one of his colleagues on the musical staff of the Cathedral was another madrigal-composer, Francis Pilkington, a minor canon.

The latest payment recorded to Bateson at Chester is at Michaelmas 1608, after which the accounts break off for nine months. But he is then found as vicar choral and organist of Christ Church Cathedral, Dublin in the first quarter of

1609 (q.v.). On publishing his 'Second set' of madrigals in London in 1618, he described himself as 'Bachelor of Music, Organist and Master of the Children of the Cathedral Church of the Blessed Trinity [Christ Church], Dublin'. Hawkins (1853: ii. 505) is surely right in suggesting that this degree may have come from Trinity College, Dublin, but there are no College registers for this period; the dates cited by various authorities have no foundation whatever, nor is it likely that he is the 'Bateson' who proceeded BA and MA in 1619 and 1622 (Burtchaell and Sadleir 1935).

Bateson remained in Dublin until his death in 1630, having made his will (from which J. C. Bridge 1913 printed an extract) on 2 March 1629/30.

John Allen 1609–13. Following a gap in the accounts after Michaelmas 1608, Allen was paid as master of the choristers for the quarter ending Michaelmas 1609. If he was the John Allen who had been a chorister under Bateson (accounts for 1601–2), he was no great age on appointment. He last received his stipend for the quarter ending Midsummer 1613. One presumes he is the John Allen who was granted the Oxford B.Mus. degree in 1612 (Clark 1887: 148). (This has escaped the notice of Wood 1815–20.) If that is so, it is worth remarking that Chester Cathedral had a good share of musicians who sought the vague status at this early date of a graduate in music: Allen, Stevenson, and Pilkington (a minor canon), from Oxford; White, from Cambridge; Bateson (after leaving Chester), supposedly from Dublin.

Michael Done 1613→. Done's name occurs as a chorister in the accounts at Michaelmas 1597, during Stevenson's time. Two others with this surname, William (afterwards lay clerk) and John, were also choristers, while the names of Richard Done (1578) and John Done (1583 and 1588) are found in the accounts as rendering various services to the Cathedral. Michael Done received his first payment as master of the choristers for the quarter ending Michaelmas 1613. There are no surviving accounts for the financial year 1613–14, but at best his tenure was so short as to suggest a purely temporary arrangement, unless he died fairly young.

Thomas Jones 1614–31→. Following the gaps in the accounts after Michaelmas 1613, Jones's name occurs as master of the choristers for the quarter ending Christmas 1614. He had been a chorister—the third in succession, apparently, to become master—between 1604 and 1610, and so was very young to have charge of the choristers. As it turned out, he was admonished at the episcopal visitation of 1623 because 'the defect of the organist or his neglect in tutoring the choristers' had 'insufferably impeached and impaired the service of God and almost utterly spoiled the children'. (Burne 1958: 100).

An interesting item among the miscellaneous payments in the accounts for 1618 is 6*s*. 'given to the organist to drink with the music that played the 5 of Nov in the choir'—a reference to the Thanksgiving Service on the anniversary of the Gunpowder Plot, and the instrumental players employed on that occasion.

It is probably he who, in an indenture of February 1625/6, is mentioned as 'Thomas Johnes, of the city of Chester, Bachelor of Music' (*Cheshire Sheaf*, 11 February 1891).

During Jones's time the accounts begin to use the term 'organist' instead of 'master of the choristers', an interesting indication of the way in which the office was coming to be regarded, notwithstanding the terminology of the draft statutes.

Richard Newbold ←1637–43. After Midsummer 1631, the latest quarter in which Jones is named, the next extant account is at Christmas 1637, when Newbold appears. A further evolution of the office now transpires, for not only, like Jones before him, is he designated as organist in the regular order of precedence among the statutory officers observed in the accounts, but, under 'Miscellaneous Payments', he receives extra, non-statutory remuneration for teaching the choristers. His last payments are at Lady Day 1643.

Randolph Jewett 1643–? Jewett received a quarter's stipend at Midsummer 1643, the latest extant account before the suppression of Prayer Book services by parliamentary edict. But there is an earlier special payment of £1 'To Mr Jewet for his services in the quire by Mr Sub-dean's appointment, Sept. 29' (1642; to be found under payments 'A fest: Na: Johis: Bapt:'). Together with payments 'to his majesty's footmen' (26 September) and 'to the ringers at his majesty's being here' (27 September), this points to some special music performed on the occasion of the visit of Charles I that year. Jewett, who came of a Chester family, was at that time in the service of the cathedrals of Dublin.

See under St Patrick's Cathedral, Dublin.

Peter Stringer 1660–73 (b. Chester, Oct. 1617; d. Chester, June 1673). When the Cathedral resumed its functions after the Restoration, it appointed as its master of the choristers and organist one of the most faithful of all its servants. Christened at St John's Church, Chester on 30 October 1617, Peter Stringer had been a chorister (accounts for Midsummer 1627) and then a lay clerk (accounts for Michaelmas 1637). In December 1657 he shared with six other 'poor officers' the sum of £10 allotted by the Trustees for the Maintenance of Ministers (Matthews 1948). Speaking of the Civil War, J. C. Bridge (1913) says that during the siege of Chester Stringer figured in the returns as having '6 in family and one measure of corn'.

The inscription on his wife's memorial in November 1660 (see below) indicates that he was by then both precentor and organist of the Cathedral. But it is not until 3 October 1662 that the Chapter Acts record his appointment as a minor canon (saying nothing about the post of organist). The earliest available post-Restoration account runs from Christmas 1664, and this duly shows his stipend (£39) as precentor, master of the choristers, and organist, due at Michaelmas 1664. From 1666 onwards he was also deputy treasurer of the Cathedral. (For a bid to tempt him to Manchester in that year, see p. 184.)

In 1673, when the dean wished to ascertain certain former customs of the Cathedral, it was to 'Mr Chanter Stringer' along with the sub-dean that he applied for information, they being 'the most ancient stagers now resident in this church', whose memories went back to the early 1630s (CA1, June 1673). The correspondence will be found in Burne (1958).

The dean's letter is dated 9 June. When the Chapter assembled for its Midsummer meeting, it recorded the death of Stringer and a tribute to him in the following terms (CA1, 25 June 1673):

> it hath pleased God to take out of this life our faithful and beloved Chanter Mr Peter Stringer, Petty Canon of this Church, Organist and Master of the Choristers which offices he hath discharged with great fidelity on his part and approbation on ours and who for several years last past has been thought worthy to be our [deputy] Receiver and Treasurer of the revenue thereof, which administration he hath very laudably executed and performed.

Ormerod (1882) is in error in stating that there is a memorial to Stringer in the north transept of the Cathedral. The memorial there was to Stringer's wife, who died in November 1660. Bridge (1913) quotes the complete inscription, which describes her as 'Conjux fidissima Petri Stringer clerici hujus ecclesiae precentoris et organistae.'

John Stringer 1673–86 (d. Chester, 1686). The son of Peter Stringer, this is perhaps the John Stringer noted in the accounts for 1664 and 1666 as a king's scholar. He was appointed organist and master of the choristers as well as (deputy) treasurer by the same Chapter minute that recorded his father's death. Peter Stringer's post of precentor went to William Otty (CA1, 30 July 1673). CA2 (28 November 1679) records that:

> whereas it appears to us that there hath been a great neglect in the teaching of the choristers for want of a convenient place to meet in, we do hereby appoint that room over the great porch on the south side of the great Church be made use of by Mr John Stringer the organist and master of the choristers to teach the said choristers and that the said Mr Stringer every day in the week except Sundays do there meet the said choristers to instruct them for half an hour after ten of the clock prayers and for an hour after four of the clock prayers according to the present Bishop's injunctions.

However, in 1683 John Stringer resigned as master of the choristers but remained organist, so bringing about a *de facto* separation of duties which was to endure for some time. William Otty was then made master of the choristers (CA2, 29 November 1683).

William Kay 1686–99 (d. Chester, Nov. 1699). On 28 June 1686 it was ordered that 'Mr William Kay be admitted one of the petty canons of this Church in the room of Mr Garencieur and that he be organist also in the room of Mr John Stringer deceased' (CA2). Otty remained master of the choristers and proved troublesome. The boys set on a pupil of Kay's, and, far from stopping them, Otty 'encouraged and bid those under his charge beat the other'. When reproved by the dean, he added rudeness to his offences and went on to threaten the organist's boy. As a result he was suspended for a week (during which Kay took over his duties) until he apologized (CA2, April–May 1694).

Kay's burial is recorded in PR on 12 November 1699. As he was in holy orders, and considering the instability of surname, it is possible that he was the William Key(s)/Kay formerly of St Asaph and Manchester (q.v.).

John Monnterratt 1699–1705. Monnterratt had been admitted a lay clerk on 28 June 1686 (CA2), and in that capacity had been admonished on 28 November 1687 after accusation 'of several vicious and debauched acts' (CA2). But this did not stand in the way of his appointment as organist, though the Chapter minute of 20 November 1699 is significantly worded: 'And Mr J. Monnterratt be organist during pleasure in the room of Mr Key [*sic*] lately deceased' (CA3). He received his last payment as organist at Lady Day 1705. In view of the varied forms of this unusual name (even 'Demonterat' and 'Montrot' are found), it may be pertinent to record that the library of Stoneleigh Abbey contains a manuscript endorsed 'The Song Book of Mr Montriot', *c.*1711.

Edmund White 1705–15. At this juncture there is a trace of what seems to be some slight choice or competition as to the appointment of organist. The accounts contain an entry dated 26 May 1706: 'To Mr Lamb [perhaps of Lichfield, q.v.] for his journey to Chester, when designed to be organist, £1.' As it was, however, White not only succeeded Monnterratt as organist but William Otty also as master of the choristers. At Midsummer and Michaelmas 1705 he was paid for the reunited duties, but from the second half of the next accounting year, 1705–6, circumstances evidently arose in which the teaching of the boys was once more committed to Otty, a state of affairs which, as the accounts show, continued till November 1708.

Meanwhile, for a whole year from Michaelmas 1707 White's duties as organist had been performed by Rathbone, one of the lay clerks, (who himself was later dismissed on 31 May 1712 on account of 'many very great misdemeanours and enormities'). This was because White was dismissed on 16 September: 'for that, being entrusted to instruct a young gentlewoman (of an ancient and right worshipful family) in music, [he] endeavoured to engage her affections by kissing, courting, and the like dalliances unknown to her parents, and mentioned a match with her, which particulars when convened he doth deny, only frivolously pretended the mention of marriage was in jest' (CA3). Though White was restored to his post the following May, Rathbone, according to the accounts, continued at the organ till Michaelmas, 1708.

At last White came to a disgraceful end, having been 'heretofor several times admonished concerning many very great misdemeanours and enormities by him committed', and was finally dismissed on 9 April 1715 because 'a bastard child hath been lately filiated upon him and he hath fled and absconded from the same' (CA3).

Samuel Davies 1715–21→. Nothing is known of Davies save that his name is given in an episcopal visitation of 1716, and begins to be shown in the accounts from Summer 1715 as both organist and master of the choristers, posts which were never again separated at Chester.

After Michaelmas 1721 the name of the organist is not entered against the office in the accounts until Lady Day 1727. Then, and again at Midsummer 1727, **Benjamin Worrall** signed for the quarterly stipend. He was already in the choir as a lay clerk, and he returned to that capacity for the quarter ending the following Michaelmas. This seems to have all the appearance of a temporary arrangement to cover a short vacancy. J. C. Bridge (1913) notes that Worrall died in 1730.

Edmund Baker 1727–65 (d. Chester, Feb. 1765). West (1921) says Baker was a pupil of *John Blow. If so, presumably he was the 'Edmond Baker, late a child of Her Majesty's Chapel Royal', whose voice had changed by the end of 1710 (Ashbee 1986–9: ii. 148). Owen and Blakeway (1825: ii. 226) state that he was a friend of T. A. Arne, and had been the first organist appointed upon the erection of a new organ in St Chad's Church, Shrewsbury in 1716. The minute of his appointment to be 'organist and teacher of the singing boys' of Chester Cathedral, dated 5 April 1727, notes that besides the normal stipend, he was to have the salary and house of a conduct 'during pleasure' (CA3). He first received his stipend for the quarter ending Michaelmas 1727. The link with a place of conduct (i.e. lay clerk) was to lead to trouble. The situation is not clear, but as Baker was evidently a young man already established in his profession, it may be that this was done to tempt him by a better stipend (organist, £12; master of the choristers, £10; lay clerk, £10 together with a house)—yet, as organist and master of the choristers, he should have had a house independently of this. It is difficult to suppose that there was a real intention for him to sing in the choir, for the style of eighteenth-century cathedral music would often preclude an organist from so doing. None the less, an attempt was made in 1737 to exact such an obligation from him, when 'in time of divine evening service . . . [he] was sent to by the senior prebendary to sing an anthem (which he had some times before done) and absolutely refused to do so', whereupon he was admonished. The record of this (CA3, 21 May 1737) carefully recites the aforementioned condition of appointment, including the phrase 'during pleasure and not otherwise'.

It is a little surprising to find that in the early part of the eighteenth century anthems at Chester Cathedral were sung from the organ-loft until a Chapter minute of 9 March 1735/6 ordered that they were to be sung in the choir 'and not in the organ loft unless it be upon a trial of a new one'—a somewhat curious proviso.

Burney (1785) tells us that Baker was his music master at Chester where Burney was a king's scholar. It was in 1741 that Handel, waiting to cross to Ireland, asked Baker to arrange for some singers and players to run through parts of *Messiah* for him (ibid.).

In 1747 (CA4, 6 October) the dean complained about Baker's work, referring to 'the unskilfulness of the boys in singing' and 'a general complaint that they knew but little and could not well be taught'. But by the time of his death in February 1765 he was not without favour, for the Dean and Chapter resolved to pay his burial fees, and his daughters were allowed £2. 10*s*. as a half-year's payment in lieu of a house. He was buried in the south choir aisle of the Cathedral, where his tombstone is now slightly mutilated.

Edward Orme 1765–76 (b. Chester; d. Chester, 25 Mar. 1777, aged 61). Orme was the son of Charles Orme, a Chester painter, as appears by the record of his admission as freeman of the city on 13 July 1747. In recording the interment of Baker, PR notes: 'Mr Orme elected organist in the room of Mr Baker deceased, June 15 1765.' CA4 minuted the appointment on 28 November, the accounts showing that he had been paid from 25 March. Like Baker, he was allowed a house and given a place as conduct.

In 1733 Norroy King of Arms appointed him to be deputy herald for Cheshire and North Wales jointly with Francis Bassano, to whom he was apprenticed. At that time he would be no more than about 17 years of age. Bassano, who was Orme's godfather, died in 1747, and presumably Orme then became sole deputy herald. He was painting armorial bearings as late as 1773, the year in which he was sheriff of the City of Chester. There is an oil-painting of him by Delacour in the Freemasons' Hall, Chester (Bridge 1913; Wagner 1967: 372).

In 1772 Orme organized the earliest Chester Musical Festival. It would seem that he resigned as organist shortly before his death from gout in 1777. He was buried in the Cathedral. For his monument, see under Edward Bailey below.

John Bailey 1776–1803 (b. Chester, 1749; d. Chester, 26 Nov. 1823, aged 73). On admission as freeman of the city on 8 April 1779, John Bailey was described as 'organist', son of John Bailey of Chester, felt maker'. Although it appears from the accounts that he had taken up duty in 1776, it is not until 17 July 1777 that his formal appointment is recorded as 'organist on probation, conduct, and assistant teacher of the boys' (CA4). The expression 'assistant teacher' is mysterious.

Salisbury (1880: 9) gives the following account of him:

> John Bailey, elder brother of Edward Bailey, was born at Chester in the year 1749. He loved music from childhood, and possessing an excellent soprano voice, he was received into the choir of Chester Cathedral at the early age of seven, as a probationer; in 1760 [*recte* 1761] he was duly installed as a chorister, and had a foundation scholarship given to him at the King's School. Under proper tuition he soon became proficient in the art of music, delighting the lovers of anthem singing in the admirable manner in which he fulfilled his part of that noble service of praise. He was articled to Mr Edward Orme, the then organist, and continued to be his assistant till 1776, when the Dean and Chapter promoted him to the chief post, just then vacated by his old master. The dignified office he held with credit and distinction till his death in 1803.

This last date is wrong. A memorial inscription (see under Edward Bailey below) records his death in 1823, and implies that he resigned as organist in 1803.

Edward Bailey 1803–23 (b. Chester, 1758; d. Chester, 4 Nov. 1830). Edward was the younger brother of his predecessor. He was admitted freeman of the city on 8 April 1784, and it is not impossible that he is the Edward Bailey who was organist of St Asaph Cathedral, 1785–91 (q.v.). It seems that he simply slipped into his brother's place at Chester without formality, there being no minute of his appointment in CA4. The accounts, however, show payment to him from Michaelmas 1803. Salisbury (1880: 9) says that 'Edward Bailey, born at Chester in the year 1758 . . . gained a high reputation as a chorister at Chester Cathedral. He rivalled his brother John . . . in the richness of his voice, and possibly in musical taste also, but being his brother's pupil and assistant, we must not put him above his master.'

He retired as organist in 1823, and the Cathedral granted him a pension (CA5, 4 July), the first instance of such a thing at Chester. A large memorial in the north transept of the Cathedral records the following family items among others: (1) 'Edward Orme late Organist of this Cathedral died 25th March 1777 Aged 61.' (2) 'Mary the Wife of John Bailey Organist of this Cathedral and Niece to the above Edward Orme died 30th April 1792 Aged 42.' (3) 'Edward Bailey late Organist of this Cathedral for 22 years [*recte* 20] died 4th Novr 1830 aged 72.' (4) 'John Bailey Husband of Mary Bailey and Organist of this Cathedral for 27 years died 26th Novr 1823 aged 73.'

George Black 1823–4 (on probation only). Black was appointed on 4 July 1823 (CA5), but did not continue in the post after the expiry of his probationary year.

Thomas Haylett 1824–40 (b. Chester, 6 Oct. 1843). There is no minute of Haylett's appointment, but he can be traced in the accounts from 1824 to Michaelmas 1840. On his retirement the Cathedral did not follow the precedent of Edward Bailey's case, and he was not offered a pension.

J. C. Bridge (1913) quotes a reminiscence contributed to the *Chester Courant* on 20 March 1899 by a certain Charles Stanyer: 'Haylett was a very good performer, a thorough master of the theory of music. His voluntaries, very frequently, were *extempore*, particularly those before the morning service, and it was a great musical treat to listen to his playing. The concluding voluntaries were the fugues of Bach, Handel and others.' One must realize that, at the time in question, 'the fugues of Bach' probably refers to 'the 48' rather than to the organ works requiring full pedal compass.

Frederick Gunton 1840–77. Though Gunton began to receive pay from the quarter ending Christmas 1840, by some lapse he was not formally admitted until 13 July 1853 (CA6).

During his time the stipend of the organist was put on what may be regarded as a more professional footing. Haylett had been paid an official stipend of £12 as organist and £10 as master of the choristers, plus an 'extra allowance' of £38 and (like the lay clerks) a variable gratuity of about £40. By Chapter minute of 25 November 1843 all this was consolidated into a recognized annual salary of £100.

See under Southwell Cathedral.

Joseph Cox Bridge 1877–1925 (b. Rochester, 16 Aug. 1853; d. St Albans, 29 Mar. 1929). Bridge was the younger brother of *J. F. Bridge, and son of John Bridge, lay clerk of Rochester Cathedral. He was a chorister there under *John Hopkins, and later he was assistant to his brother at Manchester Cathedral. He then went up to Oxford as undergraduate organist of Exeter College, 1871–6, and took the degrees of BA (1875) and B.Mus. (1876). After a year as assistant to Gunton at Chester Cathedral, he was elected master of the choristers and organist there in 1877 (CA6), and took the FRCO diploma in 1879. Also that year he revived the Chester Musical Festival (of which he wrote a short history), and he directed these triennial events until 1900. Meanwhile, having taken the Oxford degrees of MA (1878) and D.Mus. (1885), he was appointed in 1908 to follow *Philip Armes as professor of music (non-resident) in the University of Durham. On retirement from Chester he became director of studies at Trinity College of Music, London, retaining this post and his Durham appointment until his death.

Bridge was elected FSA in 1905. In addition to his work on the organists of Chester Cathedral (1913), he contributed a useful paper on 'Ludlow and the Masque of Comus' to the *Journal of the Chester Architectural . . . Society*. His paper on 'The Chester Recorders' (PMA, 27 (1901)) was a pioneer essay, written before such instruments became of common interest.

There is a memorial window to Bridge in Trinity College of Music, and a plaque under the organ-loft of Chester Cathedral.

MT, 70 (1929), 463; *WWW*, 1929–40.

John Thomas Hughes 1925–30 (b. Chester; d. Chester, 27 Feb. 1934, aged 68). Hughes was a chorister in the Cathedral choir under Gunton, and later served his articles to J. C. Bridge. During the latter period he was also organist of Holy Trinity Church, Chester for a time. He then became Bridge's assistant, and while holding that post he succeeded the celebrated W. T. Best as organist of West Derby Parish Church, Liverpool, a post he occupied for twenty-four years up to 1909. From then on, Hughes combined his work as assistant to Bridge with that of 'nave organist' of the Cathedral, officiating at the evening services of congregational character held in the nave. He became organist of the Cathedral in March 1925, and retired in September 1930.

Cheshire Observer, 3 Mar. 1934.

(Arthur) Charles (Lestoc) Hylton Stewart 1930–2.
See under Rochester Cathedral.

§Malcolm (Courtenay) Boyle 1932–49 (b. Windsor Castle, Berks., 30 Jan. 1902; d. 3 Apr. 1976). Boyle was the son of a lay clerk of St George's Chapel, Windsor Castle, and was educated first as a chorister of Eton College and then in the College itself. In 1918 he won the Goss scholarship to the Royal Academy of Music. He became assistant organist of St George's Chapel in 1924, and rendered valuable service there in the years between the death of *Walter Parratt and the appointment of *H. W. Davies. He left Windsor to become organist of Chester Cathedral when Hylton Stewart succeeded Davies at Windsor. Subsequently he became director of music at King's School, Canterbury (1951–4) and at Nottingham High School (1954–7). He was organist of West Bridgford Parish Church, Nottinghamshire, 1957–61, and of Sandiway Parish Church, Cheshire from 1965.

Boyle took the FRCO diploma in 1921 and the Oxford degree of B.Mus. in 1932.

J(ames) Roland Middleton 1949–63.

See under St Asaph Cathedral.

John (Derek) Sanders 1963–7.

See under Gloucester Cathedral.

§**Roger (Anthony) Fisher,** master of the choristers and **organist from 1967** (b. Woodford Green, Essex, 18 Sept. 1936). Fisher attended Bancroft's School, Woodford Green and then proceeded to the Royal College of Music, 1955–9, winning the Tankard prize for organ-playing. He went up to Christ Church, Oxford as organ scholar, 1959–62, reading music and taking the Oxford degrees of BA (1962) and MA (1966). He obtained the FRCO diploma in 1959, and also holds that of CHM. Before his appointment to Chester he was organist of St Mark's, Regent's Park, London, 1957–62, and assistant organist of Hereford Cathedral, 1962–7.

CHICHESTER

The Cathedral Church of the Holy Trinity

Main sources in this section (1965) (with West Sussex County Record Office references):

Chapter Acts

CA1 1545–1618 (Cap. I/3/1); calendered by W. D. Peckham, Sussex Record Society, 58 (1959).
CA1b 1618–42; recovered from miscellaneous documents, and calendered by W. D. Peckham, ibid.
CA2 1660–1710 (Cap. I/3/2).
CA3 1710–39 (Cap. I/3/3).
CA4 1739–74 (Cap. I/3/4).
CA5 1775–1801 (Cap. I/3/5).
CA6 1802–48 (Cap. I/3/6).
CA7 1849–76 (Cap. I/3/7).
CA8 1874–1901 (Cap. I/3a/1–2); a rough notebook.

Communar's Accounts

Ac2 Extracts from old registers, Act Books, computa, etc. (Cap. I/23/2).
Ac3 1556–85 (Cap. I/23/3).
Ac4 1585–1641, 1660–1701 (Cap. I/23/4).

Episcopal Visitations

EV1 Harsnett, 1613, Episc. I/18/31.
EV2 Harsnett, 1616, Episc. I/18/33.
EV3 Carleton, 1619, Episc. I/20/9.
EV4 Carleton, 1622, Episc. I/20/10.

Wills in the Dean's Peculiar Court

STD I/3 (Weelkes).
STD I/6 (Pearson).
STD I/8 (Capell).

Registers of Baptisms, Marriages, and Burials

PR Registers of St Peter's (the 'subdeanery parish').

The see of Chichester dates from very early Norman times. The Cathedral, one of the Old Foundation, acquired a body of vicars choral whose common life can be traced to the fourteenth century. They achieved incorporation in 1465, and received statutes from Bishop Sherburne in 1534. A few years earlier (1526) Sherburne had founded four 'Sherburne clerkships' to supplement the number of vicars; these were held by laymen, whose appointed stipend was better than that of the lay vicars who began to be employed in the absence of an adequate supply of suitably ordained vicars choral.

The first known posts of master of the choristers and organist at Chichester appear to have been held by vicars or by Sherburne clerks. From the time of Jacob Hillarye (1599), the organist was regularly appointed to a Sherburne clerkship, so affecting an economy in stipend; in 1685 such a post was definitely annexed to the post of organist. Eventually, in 1767, the three other Sherburne clerkships (already amalgamated to two) were merged with the surviving posts of lay vicar choral.

Although at Chichester the lay vicars were not members of the College of Vicars Choral, they and the Sherburne clerks appear to have lived along with the priest-vicars in Vicars' Court, half of which pleasingly survives, just inside the Canon Gate. For information about the vicars, see Peckham(1937).

William Campion *temp.* late Henry VIII. On St Thomas's Day (21 December) 1543 Campion was paid 6*s*. 8*d*. 'for organs in the choir', and 3*s*. 4*d*. 'for organs in the Lady Chapel'. At the same time he received his stipend as vicar choral (Ac2, f. 57). There are similar payments at Midsummer and Michaelmas 1544 (Ac2, ff. 59v–60).

Thomas Brodehorne (alias Goring) ←1550–7→. At Midsummer 1550 Thomas Brodehorne, a vicar choral, received 6*s*. 8*d*. 'for the organs' (Ac2, f. 69v). When a regular series of accounts becomes available from the year Michaelmas to Michaelmas 1555–6, Brodehorne, a lay vicar, receives a total of £4. 13*s*. 4*d*., of which 23*s*. 4*d*. was for 'beating the organs'. He is named also for the year 1556–7; but the account for 1557–8 does not give the name of the organ-player, though Brodehorne is still a lay vicar. In 1558–9 he is no longer found at all (Ac3). For his alternative name of Goring, see the grant to him of a lease dated 25 April 1557 (CA1). The teacher (or master) of the choristers in 1555–6 and 1556–7 was Richard Base, a lay vicar; he was succeeded in 1558–9 by William Payne, who was admitted a Sherburne clerk on 28 December 1558 (CA1).

Michael Woodes ←1565–9. After 1556–7, the accounts (Ac3), though continuous, furnish no organist's name for a number of years. In 1560–1 there is the curious entry (f. 47v), 'et pro solut Edwardo Piper pro usu organorum a xiijs. iiijd.' (Piper was a lay vicar who in 1562–3 was paid as master of the choristers).

In 1565–6 Michael Woodes is named as organist (Ac3), and he is included in a return (CA1) dated 7 October 1568 made by the Dean and Chapter to the Exchequer. At that date William Payne was master of the choristers. On 13 September 1569 Woodes was admitted a lay vicar as from Michaelmas. He continued to draw his stipend to the end of the accounting year 1568–9; the accounts for the next year do not include a fee to the organist.

Clement Woodcock 1570–89. In the accounts for 1571–2 Clement Woodcock, 'organist', received £2. 3*s*. 4*d*. for 'fee and benevolence during pleasure'. It so happens that he received exactly the same amount in 1570–1 without any description or details, so it would seem that he was doing the work from that time.

Meanwhile, William Payne was dismissed as teacher of the choristers on 5 May 1571 (CA1), and on 21 November Woodcock is mentioned in that capacity (CA1). On 1 April 1574, described as 'clerk', Woodcock was admitted vicar choral; and a year later, on 2 May 1575, he was admitted fully and also allowed 13*s*. 4*d*. a year 'quamdiu deservierit in loco organiste' ('for as long as he deserves it in the position of organist'), which seems to represent a saving to the Cathedral. He appears to have given up the post of teacher of the choristers, since this was granted to Christopher Paine on 2 May 1580.

In January 1587/8 there is the interesting entry in CA1 that 'Mr Clement Woodcocke shall be pardoned his perditions [fines for absence] every Sunday and holy day for nine of clock services only'. It is possible that this is a reference to his conflicting duty as vicar choral and organist (cf. Hugh Davis of Hereford). On 2 May 1589 he once more assumed the work of master of the choristers, following the death of Christopher Paine. Almost immediately after this (1 August 1589), Woodcock was presented by the Chapter to the rectory of Rumbaldswyck; but he held this for only a few months, as the records state that he was buried on 9 February 1589/90 (PR).

It is worth noting that a Clement Woodcock was a clerk of King's College, Cambridge in 1562–3 (College Mundum Books).

After Woodcock, we have no knowledge of any organist at Chichester until the end of 1599. In January 1594/5 we hear of a master of the choristers, John Cowper (or Cooper), who was then already in office. Cowper had been a lay vicar since 2 May 1587. His successor as master of the choristers from 25 May 1597 was Thomas Lambert, a lay vicar since 10 October 1598 (CA1). It is possible, of course, that Cowper and Lambert may also each have held the post of organist.

Jacob Hillarye ←1599–?1601. Hillarye, already a lay vicar from 2 May 1590 and a Sherburne clerk from 21 January 1591/2, was admitted to the joint post of master of the choristers and organist on 21 January 1599/1600, the appointment dating from 21 December 1599. He remained in the choir after giving up as organist and master of the choristers, and was still a lay vicar in 1610 (all these references are from CA1). He was buried on 18 August 1632 (PR). His appointment marks the earliest association between a Sherburne clerkship and the post of organist.

Thomas Weelkes 1602–23 (d. London, 30 Nov. 1623). Nothing certain is known of Weelkes's origins. He may or may not have been the Thomas Wikes who was a chorister of Winchester Cathedral in 1583 and 1584 (Winchester CA1). The first ascertainable fact about him is that he was organist of Winchester College from Christmas 1598 (q.v.).

There is no minute of his appointment at Chichester; but in the accounts for the year ending Michaelmas 1602 there is an item of 13*s*. 4*d*. under 'solut: Tho [*a word struck through*] organist:', and in the following year there are items of 13*s*. 4*d*. to Thomas Weelkes 'pro feod: organist:', and £4. 4*s*. 'eidem Thome informator choristarum', this latter sum being made up of a fee of 42*s*., 'benevolence of 20*s*., and 22*s*. 'for the choristers garden' (Ac4). It may well be that he took up his work at Chichester in October 1601. To support this, it may be noted that this is the point at which, in the Winchester College accounts, the College organist's stipend drops from 13*s.* 4*d.* quarterly to 10*s.*; and that a vacancy in a Sherburne clerkship—and we know that Weelkes held one—occurred at Chichester in September 1601 as a result of the death of John Base, alias Martyn.

On 13 July 1602 Weelkes took the Oxford degree of B.Mus. (Wood 1815–20: i. 295). It was no doubt a mark of his Wykehamist connection that the 'grace' for this (12 February 1601/2) described him as 'e Collegio Novo' and it declared him to have been 'sedecim annos in studio et praxi Musices'. His first child, Thomas, was baptized at Chichester on 9 June 1603 (PR), following the father's no doubt hasty marriage to Elizabeth Sandham at All Saints' Church, Chichester on 20 February 1602/3. On the publication of his *Ayeres or Phantasticke Spirites* in 1608, he described himself as 'Gentleman of his Majesty's Chapel, Bachelor of Music, and Organist of the Cathedral Church of Chichester', but there is no documentary record of his appointment to the Chapel Royal.

The second half of his career at Chichester was troublesome. At the episcopal visitation of 1613 'Thomas Weelkes, organist, instructor of the choristers, and Sherburne clerk', was charged with 'a public fame', which he denied (EV1). Worse was to come at the visitation of 1616, when it was asserted that 'he hath been and is noted and famed for a common drunkard and a notorious swearer and blasphemer. His usual oaths are that which is most fearful to name, by the wounds, heart, and blood of the Lord.' (EV2.) The eventual upshot of this was that the bishop deprived him of his posts as Sherburne clerk and instructor of the choristers on 16 January 1616/17 (EV2). Nothing was said about his post as organist. On 3 May 1617 one John Fidge was admitted as master of the choristers; but no action seems to have been taken about Weelkes's Sherburne clerkship, for Fidge was merely promised the next lay vicarship to fall vacant (CA1). Weelkes evidently continued as organist, for the accounts, which do not often mention such officers by name, do actually give his name for the year ending Michaelmas 1622; further, the register of his wife's burial on 7 September 1622 describes him as 'Mr Tho: Welkes organist of the Cathedriall Church'.

Further trouble came at the visitation of 1619, when it was again alleged that he was a drunkard, and very often came 'so disguised either from the tavern or ale house into the quire as is much to be lamented, for in these humours he will both curse and swear most dreadfully and so profane the service of God (and especially on the Sabbath days) as is most fearful to hear' (EV3). Note how it does not seem to have been recognized at this visitation that, following his deprivation, he had no legal standing as Sherburne clerk; but at the visitation in October 1622 the three other such clerks named him as 'Mr Thomas Weelkes who was one of our foundation of Bishop Sherburne's clerks but being expelled by your Lordship's predecessor Bishop Harsnett in his last visitation since which time we never knew him admitted' (EV4). This is an interesting instance of the illegal retention of a troublesome, though gifted, musician in the face of an explicit sentence of deprivation.

Weelkes died in London, and was buried on 1 December 1623 at St Bride's Church, Fleet Street. His will, dated 30 November 1623, was proved at Chichester on 5 December 1623.

Some details of the conditions of Weelkes's post at Chichester are not without interest. Harsnett's injunctions of 1611 ordered that the master of the choristers was to devote at least three hours a day to teaching the choristers (CA1). In May 1616 the Chapter resolved that the four senior choristers should have an hour's singing instruction from Weelkes at 9 a.m. and at 3 p.m. each day, in each case before service; and that the juniors should have two hours' from 8 a.m. and 2 p.m. (CA1). In September 1616 it was enjoined (CA1)

That the organist remain in the choir until the last psalm be sung, then he go up to the organs, and there having done his duty, to return into the choir again to bear his part all along [on pain of 3*d.* fine]. This is thought a meet manner in all double choirs, much more is it necessary in all half choirs such as ours is.

William Eames 1624–35. Eames, having been elected organist on 20 January 1623/4, was formally admitted as such and also as Sherburne clerk on 1 March in that year. It is extremely likely that, after the resignation of John Fidge as lay vicar on 14 October 1624, Eames was also master of the choristers; the terms of a complaint addressed by him to the Chapter on 8 March 1630/1, in which, *inter alia*, he claimed 12*s.* for 'Richard's first quarter's wages after his admission as a chorister', seem to support this. His conduct was not altogether satisfactory: on 20 January of that year he had to be warned, along with others, to attend to his duty, and on 3 May 1631 he and the succentor were told to reconcile their differences. On 20 January 1634/5 John Fidge (perhaps a second of that name?) took over the post of instructor of the choristers; he had been a Sherburne clerk since 1632. Finally, on 19 December 1635, Eames was expelled from the office of organist (all references from CA1b). A William Emes was organist of Winchester College from about 1606 (q.v.) and one cannot rule out the possibility that this was the same person.

Thomas Lewes 1636–?. Lewes (for so he signed, though the Chapter clerk wrote his name as 'Leues') was admitted organist and Sherburne clerk on 2 May 1636. One can almost certainly detect an echo of trouble with Eames, his predecessor, in his being required to give a written undertaking that if he resigned the organist's place, he would also resign that of Sherburne clerk (CA1b).

The Sherburne foundation accounts for 1641 contain the following exceptional and interesting entry about the repertory:

Organistae pro Antiphonis transcribend: 10*s*.

O give thanks	Dr Giles
O give thanks	Dr Munday
Holy, Lord God Almighty	[No composer named]
Behold, it is Christ	[No composer named]
Sing joyfully unto God.	[No composer named]

Lewes was one of eight Chichester minor officials among whom the Trustees for the Maintenance of Ministers ordered £8 to be divided in 1658 (Matthews 1948), and this makes it reasonable to suppose that he was alive to resume his post after the Restoration. No further appointment is mentioned in CA3 until 1668; meanwhile the accounts (Ac4) record the organist's stipend without giving a name.

On 14 September 1661 John Floud, one of the Sherburne clerks, became master of the choristers in place of John Fidge, but by 16 January 1662/3 Floud was dead, and George Hush took his place as Sherburne clerk (CA2). It is not clear who then became master of the choristers until 1668.

Bartholomew Webb 1668–73. Webb was admitted organist on 1 September 1668 (CA2). A further minute (10 October 1668) notes his admission as both organist and master of the choristers. That he was also a Sherburne clerk is revealed in the list of those present at the installation of the bishop on 24 March 1669/70 (CA2).

Thomas Lewis 1673–4 (d. Chichester, July 1674). Lewis was appointed for one year on 10 October 1673 (CA2), and at the same time John Turner, a Sherburne clerk, was made master of the choristers. Lewis was buried on 22nd July 1674 (PR). The provisional nature of his appointment suggests that he was a young man, not Thomas Lewes (above) reappointed under a slightly varied name.

John Reading 1675–?1676. Reading's appointment was recorded by Chapter minute on 4 January 1674/5 (a meeting dated and continued from 28 December: CA2). He was made both organist and master of the choristers, and was allotted a Sherburne clerkship. Some have identified him with the John Reading who was appointed organist of Winchester Cathedral in 1675 (q.v.). On the face of things, this seems a reasonable supposition, especially as there is no mention of him at Chichester after that time; yet I feel considerable reservation about the identification. For one thing, the next organist of Chichester Cathedral was not appointed until 1677; if Reading left late in 1675, it would be necessary to presume that some person unknown officiated there meanwhile, and of this there is no sign. Names of officers are not given in Ac4, but the details of payments to the organist at this time are as follows:

Year (Michaelmas–Michaelmas)	Official payment 'Stipendia'	Additional payment 'Regarda et Benevolentia'
1673–4	13*s*. 4*d*.	£8. 10*s*.
1674–5	13*s*. 4*d*.	£8. 10*s*.
1675–6	13*s*. 4*d*.	£8. 10*s*.
1676–7	nil	£6. 13*s*.
1677–8	13*s*. 4*d*.	£28. 10*s*.

Although the remuneration attached to the post of master of the choristers (£2. 2*s*. + £5) remains uniform throughout all these years, payments to the organist seem to point to continuity of office up to Michaelmas 1676, interim arrangements 1676–7, and a new appointment from Michaelmas 1677. As far as it goes, this seems to separate the Chichester Reading from his Winchester namesake.

Another small point: one John Reading was master of the choristers at Lincoln Cathedral from 1670 (q.v.); the accounts there show him in office for the year 1674–5, but not thereafter. This suggests that it was maybe the Lincoln Reading, not the Chichester one, who moved to Winchester late in 1675. But the matter is incapable of proof either way; certainly it is a strong coincidence if two men of the same name held office simultaneously at neighbouring cathedrals. I merely suggest reserve on the subject.

Note that neither the Chichester nor the Winchester musician should be confused with yet another John Reading who was master of the Lincoln choristers from 1702 to 1707 (q.v.), and identified by Hawkins (1853: ii. 771) as the 'Organist of St John's, Hackney; educated in the Chapel Royal under the late Famous Dr John Blow', who published *A Book of New Anthems* (*c*.1715). Note that *DNB* is in error in stating that this last John Reading was *organist* of Lincoln Cathedral. Before going to Lincoln, he was organist of Dulwich College, 1700–2, and at the time of his death he held simultaneous posts at St Mary Woolnoth, St Mary Woolchurchhaw, and St Dunstan's-in-the-West.

Samuel Pearson (or Peirson) 1677–1720 (b. Newark-on-Trent, Notts., *c*.1645; d. Chichester, July 1720). Pearson was admitted as organist on 10 October 1677 (CA2). The minute does not mention the post of master of the choristers or a Sherburne clerkship. It was in his time (1685), however, that the Chapter definitely annexed such a clerkship to the organist's post. In 1683 Gilbert Coningsby was admitted master of the choristers; when he resigned, after some trouble, Thomas Blyfer was appointed (January 1686–7), but on 10 October 1688 Coningsby returned (CA2).

Two interesting directions about anthems are found in the Chapter minutes during Pearson's time. On 2 August 1708 it was ordered that 'anathemata [*sic*] carmine composita' were to be sung in the choir on Sunday, Tuesday, and Thursday mornings; and on 5 October 1709 that 'the verse anthems shall be sung in the course appointed . . . but if [a vicar] is absent or disabled by a cold, he may provide a substitute'. It was also ordered that the 'new chanting' of the Psalms should be performed daily (CA2).

Pearson seems to have been something of a non-juror at heart. On 28 January 1710/11 he was suspended for three months for having said that 'the late King William [III] was a pickpocket; that he had seen the king at his Chapel and he had no more religion than a dog'.

On 1 January 1715/16 he presented the Cathedral library with a theological book by Henry More, inscribing it as the gift of 'Samuel Pearson, gentleman, born at Newark, Notts., organist forty years and more, aged near seventy'. In his will, dated 20 October 1718 and proved 22 March 1720/1, he desired 'that the four choral vicars of the Cathedral Church of Chichester do bear the pall', and also that 'the rest of the members of the quire do attend and use the ceremony as usual at such funerals when sung to church'. He was buried on 28 July 1720 (PR).

Thomas Kelway 1720–44 (b. Chichester, Aug. 1695; d. Chichester, 21 May 1744). One of the five sons of Thomas Kelway, priest-vicar choral of Chichester, 1694–1736, another of whom, Joseph (d. 1782), became a well-known musician, Thomas Kelway junior was admitted chorister on 13 October 1704, and was appointed organist 'during pleasure' on 1 August 1720. Many years later, as if to rectify an oversight, he was admitted 'absolutely' (CA3, 1 August 1733). Some years afterwards, he made a nuisance of himself to the porter of the Close, Thomas Burgess, and on 3 January 1736/7 (CA3) it was

> objected to the said Thomas Kelway, That he . . . was frequently guilty of disturbing the said Thomas Burghess and making him arise out of his bed at unreasonable hours in the night time to let him . . . out and in at the said Cannon-gate. And the said Dean admonished the said Thomas Kelway to live more regular and keep better hours for the future.

Kelway died on 21 May 1744, and was buried on 23 May (PR). His memorial is in St Clement's Chapel in the Cathedral; unfortunately, when the lettering was recut in 1846, the year of death was wrongly changed to 1749, and this error was carried forward to *The Poetical Works of Charles Crocker* (1860). Crocker (1797–1861) was a virger of the Cathedral, an amateur of letters, who wrote the following verses on Kelway:

> Kelway! thy memory, fresh as vernal day,
> In many a heart's most secret holiest call
> Where love of sacred song delights to dwell,
> Lives—and shall live while music holds her sway
> Within these hallowed walls, where day by day,
> Year after year, he plied the wondrous art
> Which bids the spirit from its prison start,
> And soar awhile to happier realms away.
> His strains full oft—still fall upon the ear
> Of those who tread yon aisle, while, at their feet,
> His name and record of his hope appear.
> Peace to his ashes—be his slumbers sweet,
> Till that glad morn when he shall wake to hear
> The angel choir in nightless Heaven's bright sphere.

Thomas Capell 1744–76 (d. Chichester, May/June 1776). Capell, who had already been master of the choristers for some years, was admitted as organist also on probation on 1 August 1744, and was rapidly confirmed in the appointment on 10 October (CA4).

In December 1751 he took an apprentice, Thomas Tremaine (see below); the articles were for seven years, and the consideration was £59 (*Sussex Record Society*, 28 (1922), 191).

After nearly twenty years in office, his health failed, and on 20 January 1767 the following minute (CA4) was passed:

> Whereas Thomas Capell, organist and master of the choristers of this Cathedral, hath been visited by sickness by which he hath been for upwards of two years last past rendered utterly incapable of attending his duty in the said several offices which have ever since been supplied by Richard Hall the younger on very moderate terms . . . And to the end that the said several offices may be henceforth supplied with as little loss as may be to the said Thomas Capell during such his sickness and confinement, and the better to encourage the said Richard Hall's continuance and regular performance . . . [therefore the Dean and Chapter] have spontaneously agreed to augment the salaries and payments for the said several offices to seventy pounds a year from St Thomas's Day [21 December] last.

Accordingly, Capell was allotted the sum of £40, and Hall that of £30. Hall was dismissed in 1771, and Thomas Tremaine, Capell's former apprentice, was admitted as deputy on 16 May. He too was dismissed on 25 March 1775 (CA5), and William Walond took his place from that date by a minute of 2 May.

Capell made his will on 31 May 1776, and was buried on 3 June (PR).

William Walond 1776–1801 (d. Chichester, 9 Feb. 1836). Walond quietly slipped into Capell's shoes without any formal minute of appointment. In 1794 he gave up his post as teacher of the choristers, and this office was assumed by Thomas Barber, a lay vicar, £15 a year being deducted from Walond's stipend (CA5). As 'organist of Chichester' Walond subscribed to William Hayes's *Cathedral Music* in 1795. *Grove*[1] notes the date of his death, saying that after his retirement he lived in Chichester in extreme poverty.

James Targett 1801–3 (b. near Kidderminster, Oct. 1778; d. Chichester, 15 May 1803). Targett was admitted as organist on probation on 6 May 1801 in place of Walond 'resigned', and as master of the choristers in place of Barber 'removed' (CA5). He was buried on 18 May 1803 (PR). Giving details of Targett's birth and death, West (1921) states that he was a chorister of the Cathedral.

Thomas Bennett 1803–48 (b. Fonthill, Sussex, *c.*1779; d. Chichester, 21 Mar. 1848, aged 69). Bennett was admitted organist and master of the choristers on probation on 1 August 1803, and was confirmed in these appointments on 2 May 1817 and 20 January 1819 respectively (CA6). As a boy he had been a chorister of Salisbury Cathedral under Joseph Corfe. On 3 May, 1813 he was allowed a daily quartern-loaf from the 'Bread Account' in augmentation of salary, and in 1830 his stipend was increased by £10 a year 'on account of additional duty'. He died on 21 March 1848, and was buried in the Cathedral graveyard; his memorial inscription should read '45' years as organist, but it has been wrongly cut as '15'.

Grove[1].

Henry Roberts Bennett 1848–61. Bennett was admitted on probation 'in the room of his late father' on 6 July 1848, and was confirmed in his appointment on 1 August 1849 (CA6). He was the brother of *Alfred Bennett of New College. West (1921) states that he had been a chorister in Magdalen College Chapel, Oxford. He submitted his resignation on 10 October 1860, to take effect from the following January (CA7). He moved to St Andrew's, Wells Street, London to replace his successor at Chichester.

Philip Armes 1861–3. Armes was admitted organist and master of the choristers on probation on 21 January 1861, and was confirmed in his appointment on 1 August. His resignation was minuted on 20 January 1863 (CA7).

See under Durham Cathedral.

Edward Henry Thorne 1863–70 (b. Cranborne, Dorset, 9 May 1834; d. London, 26 Dec. 1916). Thorne was an articled pupil of *G. J. Elvey at Windsor. He was elected organist and master of the choristers after ten years as organist of Henley Parish Church. After leaving Chichester he was organist of St Patrick's, Hove (1870), and then of three London churches in succession: St Peter's, Cranley Gardens (1873), St Michael's, Cornhill (1875), and St Anne's, Soho (1891). It was at the last that he established the reputation which that church long enjoyed for its performances of Bach's choral and organ music. Thorne held the FRCO diploma, and in 1913 the Lambeth degree of D.Mus. was conferred on him.

BMB; MT, 58 (1917), 68; *Grove*[3].

Francis Edward Gladstone 1870–3. Gladstone's election as organist and master of the choristers was minuted on 20 January 1870 (CA7).

See under Llandaff Cathedral.

James Kendrick Pyne 1873. Pyne was elected organist and master of the choristers on 2 May 1873, the day on which Gladstone's resignation was minuted (CA7). He took his oath on 10 October 1873. He had already ceased to be organist as early as 20 January 1874 (see below under Stewart).

See under Manchester Cathedral.

Charles Henry Hylton (or Hilton) Stewart 1874–5 (b. Bath, 20 May 1849; d. Chester, 7 Apr. 1922). Stewart went up to Christ's College, Cambridge in 1870, but migrated to St Catharine's as choral scholar and organist in 1871. He took the Cambridge degrees of BA (1874) and MA (1877) (*Venn*).

During the last part of Pyne's brief term of office Stewart in fact filled his place; and in accepting Pyne's resignation the Dean and Chapter resolved that they thank Stewart 'for the efficient manner in which he has conducted the services and maintained the choir, and they beg him to continue to them the benefit of his invaluable aid until Lady Day' (CA7, 20 January 1874). In due course, on 2 May 1874, Stewart was himself appointed Cathedral organist. He resigned in the later part of 1875 to take holy orders, and eventually became minor canon and precentor of Chester Cathedral (1877–89). He was subsequently vicar of New Brighton, Birkenhead (1889), and rector of Bathwick, Bath (1904). Upon his retirement he was made an honorary canon of Chester (1916). (For his son, Charles Hylton Stewart, see p. 239.) The surname, as given officially in *Crockford's Clerical Directory*, is simply 'Stewart', *not* 'Hylton Stewart'.

Daniel Joseph Wood 1875–6. The minute of Wood's appointment (CA7), dated 17 September 1875, reads as follows: 'Mr Daniel Joseph Wood of Church Precincts, Boston, Bachelor of Music, be appointed organist of the Cathedral in the room of Mr C. H. Stewart who has resigned.' Wood took his oath as organist and master of the choristers on 20 January 1876.

See under Exeter Cathedral.

Theodore Edward Aylward 1876–86. Aylward was appointed, on the recommendation of *Walter Parratt, by a minute dated 31 August 1876 (CA8).

*Langdon Colborne and *C. Lee Williams were the runners-up. Aylward took his oath on 20 January 1877.

See under Llandaff Cathedral.

Frederick John Read (1st tenure) **1887–1902** (b. Faversham, Kent, Dec. 1857; d. Chichester, 28 Jan. 1925). Among Read's teachers were *C. W. Corfe and *J. F. Bridge. In 1876 he was appointed organist of Christ Church, Reading, where he remained until his appointment to Chichester Cathedral. In 1886 he joined the staff of the Royal College of Music. After giving up his Cathedral post in 1902, Read settled in London. He was reappointed to Chichester Cathedral in 1921, and continued in the post until his death. He took the Oxford degrees of B.Mus. and D.Mus. in 1876 and 1891, and held the FRCO diploma.

BMB; MT, 66 (1925), 268.

Frederick Joseph William Crowe 1902–21 (b. Weston-super-Mare, Somerset, 1 Jan. 1864; d. ?Chichester, 9 Apr. 1931). After serving as a chorister of Wells Cathedral, Crowe was assistant organist there to *C. W. Lavington. Later he studied singing under Carpi in Milan. In 1882 he became organist of Ashburton Parish Church, Devon, moving in 1890 to St Mary Magdalene, Torquay, and from there to Chichester Cathedral. He retired on account of ill health in 1921. At some time he was a captain in the local Volunteer National Reserve. His varied interests are represented by his fellowships of the Royal Astronomical Society (1906) and the Royal Historical Society (1906). He is buried in the north transept of the Cathedral, and a memorial tablet to him there was presented by the students of Bishop Otter College.

MT, 46 (1905), 88; 72 (1931), 463; *WWW* 1929–40.

Frederick John Read (2nd tenure) **1921–5.**

See above.

Marmaduke Percival Conway 1925–31.

See under Ely Cathedral.

Harvey Grace 1931–8 (b. Romsey, Hants, 25 Jan. 1874; d. Bromley, Kent, 15 Feb. 1944). On his appointment to a cathedral post in his late 50s Grace brought to it a range of experience of an unusual kind. As a boy he had sung in the choir of Romsey Abbey, and he went on to study under *A. M. Richardson, taking the FRCO diploma in 1905. He held several church organists' posts in succession, of which the more important were, first, St Agnes's, Kennington, and second, St Mary Magdalene's, Munster Square, London. But an activity of a very different kind, by which he set great store, was his successful training for many years of a Working Girls' Choir, culminating in a series of festivals in the Albert Hall, 1925–33; he based this and much kindred work on the Tonic Sol-fa method. In 1910 he began a twelve-year series of contributions to *Musical Opinion* under the psueudonym 'Autolycus', and his long connection with the *Musical Times* began in

1913 with a famous series called 'The Compleat Organist'. In 1918, by which time he was already assistant editor of the *Musical Times*, he succeeded W. G. McNaught as editor. He retained this post until the day of his death, contributing a great deal to the journal under the name of 'Feste'. These activities caused him to relinquish his post at St Mary Magdalene's in 1925, but after six years he accepted the appointment at Chichester Cathedral. In 1932 he received the Lambeth degree of D.Mus. After leaving Chichester he joined the governing body and teaching staff of Trinity College of Music (1939), and later—to some extent as a piece of wartime service—he was organist of East Grinstead Parish Church.

His books included not only *The Compleat Organist* (1920) and *The Training and Conducting of Choral Societies* (1938), but *French Organ Music* (1919), *The Organ Works of Bach* (1922), and *A Musician at Large* (1928). He collaborated with Walford Davies in *Music and Worship* (1934), and among his contributions to *Grove*[3], the article on César Franck is worthy of particular mention. He also edited Rheinberger's organ sonatas.

Grace's likeness in stone may be seen (through field-glasses) on the parapet of the south transept of Chichester Cathedral, as he happened to be in office when this was being restored.

MT, 85 (1944), 73; *Grove*[5].

Horace Arthur Hawkins 1938–58 (b. Southborough, Kent, 1880; d. Hurstpierpoint, Sussex, 23 Jan. 1966, aged 85). As a boy Hawkins was trained at St Saviour's Choir School, Eastbourne. Later he had piano lessons from Miss Hamilton Stirling, a pupil of Clara Schumann. He took the FRCO diploma in 1909.

His earliest post was as organist of St Paul's, Southampton, after which he became assistant to *W. Prendergast at Winchester Cathedral and then spent eight years at St Andrew's, Worthing. Next he became organist of the English church, St George's, in Paris. During this time he took the French *baccalauréat* and studied under Widor and the Solesmes Fathers. On his return to England Hawkins was appointed director of music at Hurstpierpoint College, holding this post for twenty-two years before moving to Chichester. A feature of his period at the Cathedral was the ceremonial use on festal days of music for organ and brass.

MT, 99 (1958), 626; 107 (1966), 241.

§John (Anthony) Birch 1958–80 (b. Leek, Staffs., 9 July 1929). Birch was at Trent College, Derbyshire, 1942–7, before going to the Royal College of Music (1947–8 and 1950–3), where he held a scholarship and won prizes for organ-playing. He took the FRCO diploma in 1955, having already acquired that of CHM in 1952. He was organist of St Thomas's Church, Regent Street, London, 1950–3, and of All Saints', Margaret Street, 1953–8. He was also sub-organist of the Chapel Royal, 1957–8. In 1959 he joined the staff of the Royal College of Music, and from 1966 he has been organist to the Royal Choral Society. In 1967 he was appointed organist of the University of Sussex, Brighton, and in 1971 visiting lecturer in music, the year in which he received the honorary degree of MA from the University.

When the Cathedral bell tower was restored, a likeness of Birch was among those carved on the parapet (see under Grace above).

He left Chichester to settle in London. In 1982 he succeeded Sir George Thalben Ball as organist of the Temple Church, and in 1984 he was also appointed curator-organist of the Royal Albert Hall. The Lambeth degree of D.Mus. was conferred on him in 1989.

§**Alan (John) Thurlow, choirmaster and organist from 1980** (b. Woodford Green, Essex, 18 May 1947). From Bancroft's School, Woodford, Thurlow went to Sheffield University, where he read music (BA, 1968) and then went for further study to Emmanuel College, Cambridge, 1968–71. He was University organ scholar of Sheffield Cathedral, 1967–8. He took the FRCO diploma in 1972, holding already the CHM diploma. From 1963 he was organist of St Barnabas's Church, Woodford. He became sub-organist of Durham Cathedral in 1973, moving from there to Chichester in September 1980.

COVENTRY

The Cathedral Church of St Michael

The diocese of Coventry was established in 1918, the bishop taking St Michael's Church as his cathedral. This fine medieval building was destroyed by an act of war in November 1940. A new building, linked to its ruins by a paved way, was consecrated in 1962. Technically speaking, this is not a new cathedral church but an extension to the one so parlously damaged in World War II.

Some notable organists of St Michael's before it became a cathedral were: **Thomas Deane, 1733–49; Capel Bond, 1750–90; *Sir Herbert Brewer, 1886–92; *H. C. Perrin, 1892–8.**

Walter Hoyle (1898) **1918–27** (b. Exeter, 1873; d. 1934). Hoyle was an articled pupil and then assistant to *D. J. Wood at Exeter Cathedral. He held the FRCO diploma. I am indebted to Mr David Lepine for information about the year of Hoyle's death.

Harold (William) Rhodes 1928–33 (b. Hanley, Staffs., 15 Sept. 1889; d. Sanderstead, Surrey, 27 Feb. 1956). Rhodes received his musical education at the Royal College of Music, which he entered in 1904 and where he held open scholarships in organ-playing and in composition. From 1908 to 1910 he was assistant to *Walter Parratt at St George's Chapel, Windsor. He was then successively music master at Lancing College (1910–12) and organist of St John's Church, Torquay (1912–28). His appointment to Coventry Cathedral was announced in the June issue of *MT*, 1928. *H. W. Sumsion, who had originally accepted the post, asked to be released so that he could take up the appointment at Gloucester Cathedral created by the sudden death of Brewer.

Rhodes became organist of Winchester Cathedral in 1933 (q.v.), remaining there until his retirement in 1949. He held the FRCO diploma, and took the London degrees of B.Mus (1911) and D.Mus. (1923).

Grove[5]; *MT*, 97 (1956), 213; *ECM*, 26 (1956), 41; *WWW*, 1951–60.

Alan Stephenson 1933–40 (b. 5 July 1891; d. Heysham, Lancs., 1 May 1950). Stephenson was trained as an organist at Burnley Parish Church, and became organist of St Andrew's, Shifnal in 1912. In 1913 he was appointed organist of Gainsborough Parish Church, Lincolnshire, where he remained until his appointment to Coventry. After the bombing of Coventry Cathedral put an end to his work there, he became organist of Lancaster Priory. He took the Oxford degree of B.Mus. in 1911, and held the FRCO diploma.

Drennan 1970.

§David (Foster) Lepine 1961–72 (b. Sidcup, Kent, 27 Dec. 1928; d. Buckland, Glos., 24 Mar. 1972). After leaving King's School, Canterbury in 1947, Lepine studied at the College of St Nicolas (Royal School of Church Music) and then went up to St Chad's College, Durham as a music scholar (1949–52), where he read music and took the degree of BA in 1952. In 1953 he was appointed director of music at Dean Close School, Cheltenham. In 1961 he took up the joint appointment of organist of Coventry Cathedral and music adviser to the City of Coventry Education Committee. The conjunction of these two posts ended in 1963, when he became solely organist of the Cathedral. Meanwhile, having already taken the CHM diploma in 1953 (Brook prize), Lepine took the FRCO diploma (Limpus prize) and the Durham degree of MA in 1961. He died suddenly while visiting Buckland Church.

§Robert (George) Weddle 1972–7 (b. Amersham, Bucks., 19 Dec. 1941). After attending the Leys School, Cambridge, Weddle spent some time at the Hill School, Pottstown, Pa., USA with an English Speaking Union scholarship, and then went up to Magdalene College, Cambridge as music exhibitioner and organist. He read music, and took the Cambridge degrees of BA (1963) and MA (1968). He holds the certificate in education of the University of Cambridge (1964), and won the Brook prize with the choirmaster's diploma of the RCO in 1969.

From 1964 to 1972 he was sub-organist of Coventry Cathedral and assistant music master at King Henry VIII School, Coventry. He took up duties as organist of Coventry Cathedral immediately on Lepine's sudden death. After leaving Coventry he was director of music at Edinburgh Academy, 1977–80, and since 1980 he has been *professeur de la maîtrise et des chorales* at the Conservatoire national de région in Caen, Normandy, and organist of St Pierre de Caen.

§Ian (Donald) Little 1977–83 (b. St Austell, Cornwall, 26 Feb. 1953). As a boy Little was a chorister of Chester Cathedral, and then held organ scholarships at

Truro School, the Royal College of Music, and Pembroke College, Cambridge. At Cambridge he read music and took the degrees of BA (1975), Mus.B. (1976), and MA (1979). With the FRCO diploma he was awarded the Turpin prize (1972). Immediately on leaving Cambridge in 1976 he became sub-organist of Coventry Cathedral, succeeding to the full post in 1977. In 1984 he became director of music at Dean Close School, Cheltenham.

§**(Anthony) Paul Wright, organist and choirmaster from 1984** (b. Taplow, Bucks., 28 Aug. 1951). After leaving Desborough School, Maidenhead, Wright was organ scholar of St Catharine's College, Cambridge, where he read music and took the degrees of BA (1973) and MA. While at Cambridge he took the FRCO and CHM diplomas. He then became organist of St James's Church, Gerrards Cross, Buckinghamshire, and carried out free-lance work. From 1982 until his appointment to Coventry Cathedral he was director of music to the Methodist Association of Youth Clubs.

DERBY

The Cathedral Church of All Saints

The bishopric of Derby, founded in 1927, is one of the most recently created English bishoprics. All Saints' Parish Church (in pre-Reformation times a royal free chapel with a collegiate constitution under a dean) became the Cathedral of the new diocese.

Arthur Griffin Claypole (1921) **1927–9** (b. Peterborough, 1882; d. Derby, 30 June 1929). Claypole was educated at Peterborough Cathedral under *Haydn Keeton, and later at the Royal Conservatory, Leipzig. In 1902–3 he was assistant organist of Peterborough Cathedral, and from 1904–11 he was music master of Kent College, Canterbury. In 1912 he became organist of St Luke's Church, Derby. During World War I he was interned, like *P. C. Hull, under conditions of great hardship at Ruhleben in Germany. He became organist of All Saints', Derby in 1921, and resigned early in 1929, shortly before his death. Claypole took the Durham degrees of B.Mus. (1902) and D.Mus. (1910), and held the FRCO diploma (1903).

Thornsby 1912; *MT*, 70 (1929), 751; *Derbyshire Advertiser*, 5 July 1929; unidentified newspaper cutting communicated by Derby borough librarian; information from Mr Wallace Ross.

Alfred William Wilcock 1930–3 (b. Colne, Lancs., 21 Oct. 1887; d. 26 Oct. 1953). Wilcock was a pupil of *J. K. Pyne at Manchester Cathedral. In 1913 he took the Durham degree of B.Mus., following this with the Mus.D. of Manchester University in 1917. He took the FRCO diploma in 1908. He was on the staff of the Royal Manchester College of Music, 1918–33, and was also at various times from 1922 dean of the faculty of music in the University of

Manchester. He retained his Manchester posts while he was organist of Derby Cathedral, but relinquished these on his removal to Exeter Cathedral, where he was organist from 1933 until his retirement in 1952. There is a memorial to him, near to that of S. S. Wesley, in Exeter Cathedral.

WWM[1]; *MT*, 94 (1953), 582.

George Handel Heath-Gracie 1933–58 (b. Gosport, Hants; d. Devonshire, 20 Apr. 1987, aged 94). Heath-Gracie was educated at Bristol Grammar School and received his musical training under *Hubert Hunt at Bristol Cathedral. After early appointments in Bristol and Frome, he became organist of St Peter's, Brockley, Kent in 1918, a post he combined with that of music master at the Mercers' School, Holborn, London, and in which he remained until his appointment to Derby Cathedral. He took the FRCO diploma in 1915 and the Durham degree of B.Mus. in 1932.

MT, 74 (1933), 733; 128 (1987), 346.

§Wallace (Michael) Ross 1958–83 (b. Yeovil, Somerset, 19 Sept. 1920). Ross was at Rugby School until 1938, when he went to the Royal College of Music before going up to Balliol College, Oxford in 1939 as organ scholar. At Oxford he read Greats as well as music, taking the degrees of BA and MA together after the war, and that of B.Mus. in 1950. He took the FRCO diploma in 1950, and won both the Limpus and Read prizes; he also holds the CHM diploma.

From 1947–8 he was articled to *H. A. Hawkins of Chichester, and then became director of music at Pocklington School, Yorkshire and assistant organist of Beverley Minster, 1948–50. Next he became music master of Alderman Newton's School, Leicester and one of the assistant organists of Leicester Cathedral, 1951–4. He moved to Gloucester in 1954 as assistant organist of the Cathedral and director of music at the King's School, retaining these appointments until taking up his post at Derby Cathedral. While at Derby he was also music master of Sturgess Boys School. Outside his school and church work, Ross maintained an active interest in brass bands and ensembles.

§Peter (David) Gould, master of the music from 1983 (b. Portsmouth, 9 Feb. 1952). From Portsmouth Technical High School Gould went to the Royal Academy of Music, 1970–3, where he won various prizes, and then spent a year at Bretton Hall College, Wakefield. He took the FRCO diploma in 1974. Before his appointment to Derby Cathedral he was assistant organist of Wakefield Cathedral. Along with his Cathedral appointment he works as a teacher of singing for Derbyshire Local Education Authority.

DURHAM

The Cathedral Church of Christ and the Blessed Virgin Mary

Main sources in this section (1961):

Chapter Acts

CA1	1578–83.
CA2	1619–38.
CA3	1639–61.
CA4	1660–88.
CA5	1690–1729.
	1725–41, 1741–74, overlapping and duplicating CA5, 6.
CA6	1729–77.
CA7	1778–96.
CA8	1774–99, overlapping and duplicating parts of CA6, 7.
CA9	1800–18.
CA10	1819–29.
CA11	1829–38.
CA12	1838–47.
CA13	1847–56.
CA14	1856–67.

Account Books

A broken annual series giving details quarter by quarter for years ending Michaelmas 1558, 1563–5, 1567, 1569, 1570–2, 1577, 1578, 1580, 1581, 1588, 1589, 1595, 1597, 1598, 1600, 1604, 1610, 1613, 1615, 1617, 1633, 1634, 1636, 1661, 1662, 1664–9, 1672, 1674–80, 1683–9, through to 1704.

Account Rolls

A broken series of annual summaries (as distinct from the more detailed Account Books) covering the period from 1547–8 to 1606–7. More than 20 of these rolls are for years not covered by the Account Books.

Miscellaneous

PR Registers of baptisms, marriages, and burials, printed as *The . . . Registers of the Cathedral Church . . . at Durham 1609–1896* (Harleian Society, 1897).

Mickleton Durham University Library, Mickleton MS 32, f. 55^v. A late 17th-century memorandum in Latin by James Mickleton (d. 1693), cited here in English where appropriate. Some extracts in English are in Fowler (1902).

The Account Rolls came to light subsequent to my own investigations, and I am indebted to Mr Brian Crosby for information about them.

After the dissolution of the Benedictine cathedral priory of Durham, Henry VIII refounded it in 1541 to continue as the cathedral of the bishop. The provision for a choir was on a generous scale, only slightly less than that of the two largest of his cathedral foundations, Canterbury and Winchester. It included ten choristers under a master. There is no trace of any Henrician draft statutes, but one may confidently assume that, as with all other cathedrals of the New Foundation, it was intended that the master of the choristers should play the organ (see p. xix). Under statutes eventually promulgated in 1555 under Philip and Mary,[1] it was in fact provided that the work of organ-playing was to be included in the duties of the master of the choristers, the wording of the statutes at this point (Cap. xxvii) being, to all intents and purposes, identical with that of Henry's draft statutes for the other New

[1] As a technical point of legal interest whereas Henry's draft statutes had lacked full force of law, these statutes for Durham Cathedral were issued under seal and by parliamentary authority.

Foundation cathedrals. But they continue with a provision unique to Durham, namely:

And that he may give his labour the more diligently to the discipline and instruction of the boys, we permit him to be absent from choir upon ordinary weekdays, so that he be bound to serve in choir and at the organs every Sunday and feast-day and on double feasts as above. And on the days when he is permitted to be absent we will that some other person with knowledge of organ-playing be appointed from among the minor canons or [lay] clerks by the precentor to play . . . (Translation by J. M. Falkner.)

John Brimley 1541–76 (d. Durham, 13 Oct. 1576). *Mickleton* says that Brimley was organist and master of the choristers 'tempore Henry 8'. The earliest relevant extant document of the refounded Cathedral is the summary account-roll for 1547–8, which names him as master of the choristers (and so also organist) at £10 per annum. In view of his known association (see below) with the cathedral priory, there is no doubt that he was such from the time of the refoundation. His gravestone in the Galilee Chapel is engraved thus:

John Brimleis body here doth ly
Who praysed God with hand and voice
By musickes heavenlie harmonie
Dull myndes he maid in God rejoice
His soul into the heavens is lyft
To prayse him still that gave the Gyft.
Obiit Ao. Dni. 1576 Octo. 13.

The registers of St Nicholas's Church record the burial of 'John Brymley, singing man of the Cathedral Church of Durham', on 14 October 1576.

We know that he had been cantor of the priory before its surrender. At Whitsun 1537 there is a note of his stipend: 'Et sol: Joh'i Brymley, cantori £4' (Fowler 1900: 703). A reference to him as 'the master of the Song School (called Mr John Brimley) . . . playing upon a pair of fair organs the time of our Lady's mass', found in *The Rites of Durham* (1593), refers to this pre-dissolution period of office (Fowler 1902: 43).

Brimley was involved in questioning following the Northern Rebellion of 1569, and his signed deposition still exists (Consistory Court Deposition Book, V2, f. 184^{v}). He is described as 'master of the choristers in the Cathedral Church of Durham' and as 'gentleman of the City of Durham, aged 67':

(*Item 5*). He remembereth well that he was twice at mass when Robert Peirson with Homes sang the same within the said Cathedral Church but he sang not himself at them but played organs and did divers times help to sing salvaes at mattins and evensong and played on the organs and went in processions as others did . . . (*Item 9*). He instructed the choristers in such things as they did in the choir pertaining to service at that time but not since nor before.

The deposition concludes: 'he trusteth that he is pardoned by the Queen's majesty's free pardon', and is followed by his signature in the form 'John Brymley'. His continuance in office implies that pardon was granted.

William Browne (1st tenure) **1576–88**. After a break, the accounts resume for the year ending Michaelmas 1577, when William Browne received pay as master of the choristers from 20 November 1576. When, after a further gap, the accounts resume for the year ending Michaelmas 1581, he is again named, and the account-roll for 1577–8 shows him as still in office to the end of that year.

But thereafter we enter on a period of uncertainty. In such accounts as survive, Browne's name is not found again until the year 1598–9. Fowler (1902) assumes that the men who received payment as master of the choristers in the meantime merely acted for Browne, who, on this reading, continued in office throughout. There is silent support for this in *Mickleton*, who mentions no one but Browne between Brimley and Edward Smith.

In 1588–9 Robert Maysterman, who was also a lay clerk, signs for payment as master of the choristers (but at a reduced rate) at Christmas, Lady Day, and Midsummer. Against the third payment is noted 'solut: eidem in pleno'. He died in that same year; but the reduced stipend suggests that he was simply acting temporarily. For the quarter ending Midsummer 1589 William Smith, a minor canon, also signs for a similar reduced payment (£1. 5*s*.) as joint master of the choristers, and in the last quarter to Michaelmas 1589 he alone signs for the same sum. Thereafter, while allowing for gaps, his name can be traced continuously in the account-books or -rolls as receiving the full stipend of £10 as master of the choristers until at least Michaelmas 1598, rather too long a span for a man who was merely acting for Browne while the latter retained his rights. With this necessarily intricate explanation, I have provisionally allotted two separate terms to Browne, regarding Maysterman as merely temporary and including Smith in the record. For Browne, see more fully below.

William Smith 1589–98 (bur. Billingham, Co. Durham, 21 Jan. 1604). As already noted, Smith took over from Maysterman after a slight overlap in 1589. Signatures in the accounts make it fairly clear that he is the William Smith/ Smyth(e) found therein as a minor canon from 1576–7 up to 1599–1600. On 6 November 1599 he was presented by the Dean and Chapter to the living of Billingham (Reg. 6, f. 91[v]). Whether or not he was merely acting for Browne, his skill was clearly an advantage to the Cathedral. In a document endorsed 'Paid 28 September 1589' (Miscellaneous Charter 3198, quoted in Fowler 1900: 733), he wrote to the Dean and Chapter thus:

> May it please you to understand right worshipful that whereas you have one pair of organs which standeth above the choir door, and hath not been played upon this many years for lack of mending, I have bestowed a week's labour in mending the sound board, the wind stop, the spring wires, and in tuning the pipes, so that I have made them in that good order as now they will much delight both the auditory and the player because they yield the principalest and imperial sound of all the rest. And if it seem strange unto your worships that I have taken in hand to do it, you shall understand I have had some practice in mending of an instrument, and also I have given diligence in marking men of greater skill that hath been here in time past when they have been recompensed five marks or forty shillings for less pains than I have taken (which I refer to the choir) so that now I leave my pains to your considerations, for because I did not so much seek after the recompense of reward as I did

the excellency of the instrument regard, and as also that you should see my readiness and good will to endeavour myself in what soever I may profit our Church.

Yours in whatsoever he is able
Will[i]am Smythe petticanon.

The accounts for the year 1588–9 include a payment of 30*s*. for this work.

This William Smith must not be confused, as he has been in the past, with another of similar name (1603–45), also a minor canon (but not organist), who was the composer of the celebrated Preces and Responses by 'William Smith of Durham'.

William Browne (2nd tenure) **1598–1607→**. The account-roll for 1598–9 discloses William Browne once more as master of the choristers. He also held a lay clerk's place. Subsequent signatures for receipt of payment show that this post-1598 Browne is the same as the pre-1588 man. William Smith meanwhile stands at the head of the minor canons. *Mickleton* describes Browne as 'musice artis magister, sed homo et magister severus' ('master of music, but a severe man and teacher') and goes on to say that, among others, he taught his successor, Edward Smith. A break in the accounts after the roll for 1606–7 means that the end of his tenure cannot be determined exactly. (For the possibility of his subsequent connection with York Minster, see p. 316.)

In the absence of a Chapter minute or patent of appointment, we cannot know what his position—if any—may have been at Durham during the years for which Maysterman and Smith were paid, or whether, as is more likely, he went elsewhere. If so, and if in 1576 he had been given an appointment for life (a common form of words at the time), it is legally conceivable, though not very probable, that, while sacrificing payment, he relied on this life tenure to keep his place warm while he spent some years elsewhere.

Edward Smith ←1608–12. When, after a gap of two years, the accounts resume in the form of the book for 1609–10, Smith, like his predecessor, is found as both lay clerk and master of the choristers. But he was already organist when he married in October 1608 (St Nicholas's Church Register; information from Brian Crosby). One infers from *Mickleton* that he remained in office until his death, and PR records: 'Edward Smythe organist of this church buried the 4 day of February Anno D Jacobi 9° [1611–12]'.

Mickleton suggests that something of an interregnum then ensued. He observes that 'next to the aforesaid Edward Smith there succeeded a certain Dodshon who officiated as organist about a year and a half'. *Mickleton*'s use of the word 'officiated' in connection with 'a certain Dodshon' does not suggest a permanent appointment. One Francis Dodgson was organist of Southwell Collegiate Church from about 1617 to 1622 (see p. 275).

Richard Hutcheson 1613–Interregnum (d. Durham, 7 June 1646). Though the Cathedral documents more often than not use the form 'Hutchinson', the holograph signatures are in the form 'Hutcheson'. In citing Chapter Acts below, I have reproduced the form given therein. *Mickleton* gives both forms of the name.

The appointment of Hutchinson/Hutcheson may be traced from Miscellaneous Charter 5916 (reference from Brian Crosby), and the account-book for 1614–15 shows that he also held a lay clerk's place. His tenure was full of incident during the period 1626–8, and the Chapter Acts, though not troubling to record the appointment of an organist at this time, have much to tell us about this. He went to gaol, ran into debt, haunted alehouses, broke the head of an estimable lay clerk with a candlestick, 'wounding him very dangerously', was suspended from teaching the choristers; and yet the Dean and Chapter continued to bear with him, and he held office for some thirty years, a period during which the music of the Cathedral reached a peak. Indeed, when matters came to such a pass that charge of the choristers was taken away from him and given to a reliable lay clerk, one Henry Palmer, his services were still called upon

> 'three times in every week . . . from twelve of the clock unto the beginning of Evening prayer . . . to teach the choristers to play upon the virginals or organs and to be also ready . . . when the said Henry Palmer shall request him thereto to hear the said choristers sing unto the said organs or to hear them play them, for their skill and fitness in singing of any anthem of church service (CA2, 7 May 1628).

Notwithstanding that a debt of £10 was cancelled on this consideration, not many weeks later, on 8 July, it was thought necessary to suspend him for an unspecified reason 'from any further service or dealing in the church'. Nevertheless, on 23 November a Chapter minute reads: 'Richard Hutchinson restored this day to the organist place in this church . . . to be continued upon certain conditions agreed on.'

An interesting little detail of his time is contained in a Chapter order to pay 'John Moore for turning over the organ book, when Mr Hutchinson playeth upon the organs 26*s*. 8*d*. paid by 6*s*. 8*d* a quarter' (CA2, 3 April 1627).

Mickleton describes him as 'prae-excellens organista' (which perhaps explains the forbearance shown), and records the date of his death. He also remarks that 'from time to time the other William Smith [i.e., William Smith junior who was the son of Christopher Smith] officiated for him'. This William Smith junior is the composer of the well-known Preces and Responses. On the very same day that the Chapter agreed to pay someone to turn over the pages for Hutcheson, it granted to this William Smith the sum of £2 'for his painstaking in the time Mr Hutchinson, organist, was in the gaol'.

For this period in general at Durham, see Shaw (1963–4).

John Foster 1660–77 (d. Durham, 20 Apr. 1677). The earliest post-Restoration accounts, 1660–1, have a blank under 'master of the choristers', and Foster's name does not appear until 1661–2. But *Mickleton* clearly states that he entered upon his duties at Christmas 1660. He may safely be presumed to be the same 'John Foster, chorister of the Church of Durham', to whom, with the date 1638, a Communion Service is ascribed in Durham Cathedral, Music MS A5. His death, and burial on the next day, is noted in PR.

Alexander Shaw 1677–81. Shaw appears to have been both a king's scholar (CA4) and chorister (Accounts, 1660–1 to 1663–4), and then to have had one of the two places (perhaps at this time sinecures) of sackbut-player ('tubicini') from 1664–5. It is possible that he was the 'Mr Shaw' who was organist of Ripon Collegiate Church from about 1674 (see p. 228). *Mickleton* says that he was 'made or elected' organist of Durham Cathedral after the death of John Foster. He describes him as 'junior'; thus he may have been the son of Alexander Shaw who became Cathedral bell-ringer in 1660, and continued in the service of the Cathedral after the younger man ceased to be organist there.

With Shaw's appointment, the duties of organist and master of the choristers were divided for a time. The accounts for the quarter ending Michaelmas 1677, which is when he first appears, show that he was organist only, with a stipend of three-quarters of the whole, while the work of master of the choristers was given to John Nicholls, the senior lay clerk, with a stipend of one-quarter. This arrangement continued throughout Shaw's time, and Nicholls was followed in June 1681 by Robert Tanner (*Mickleton*). Nicholls was already master of the school 'pro plano cantu et arte scribendi' in Palace Green, the ancient foundation of Cardinal Langley.

Shaw lost no time in marrying his predecessor's widow, Eleanor, on 29 November 1677 (PR). Some of his music-copying (1678 and 1679) still survives in Durham Cathedral, Music MS A4. *Mickleton* notes that he was expelled for 'contumeliousness before Christmas Eve 1681'.

William Greggs 1681–1710 (b. ?York; d. Durham, 15 Oct. 1710, aged 47). Greggs became organist and master of the choristers at Christmas 1681 (*Mickleton*). CA4 records that it was agreed on 1 December 1686 'that Mr Greggs the organist have leave for three months to go to London to improve himself in the skill of music'. *Mickleton* says that Gregg(s) was made master of the school on Palace Green by the Bishop of Durham in 1690. This explains the entry in CA5, dated 24 September 1711, which reads: 'Ordered William Greggs patent from the Bishop of the Song School—pro plano cantu—to be confirmed gratis.' This is a mysterious posthumous registration of a post which by that time was on the point of expiry.

Greggs's epitaph on the south exterior wall of the church of St Mary the Less, Durham records his death on 15 October 1710, 'in the 48 year of his age'. The inscription, now only partly legible, formerly read: 'Son of Jo. Greggs, gent. of York, a sufferer for K.C.I [King Charles I].' This York connection, confirmed by *Mickleton*, who describes Greggs as 'Eboracensis', appears to identify him with the William Greggs who was admitted singingman of York Minster on 5 September 1670 (York CA) and master of the choristers there from Candlemas 1676 to Whitsun 1681 (York Ac2). But, if this is so, the age recorded on his memorial must be inaccurate.

James Heseltine 1711–63 (d. Durham, 20 June 1763). Heseltine was one of the children of the Chapel Royal; the sub-dean certified the changing of his voice on 19 December 1707 (Ashbee 1986–9: ii. 91). He was therefore one of the latest boys to come under *John Blow. His appointment at Durham is entered thus in CA5 under 20 January 1710/11: 'Mr Heseltine of London admitted organist of this church and master of the boys in the place of Mr Greggs deceased at £70 per annum salary to commence Lady Day next.' Not much earlier he had been appointed organist of St Katherine-by-the-Tower, London from 1709 (Dawe 1983), 'the duty of which he executed by deputy' (Hawkins 1853: ii. 800). The Dean and Chapter of Durham agreed on 22 April 1723 (CA5) 'That the organist have leave to go to London for six weeks'.

At first Heseltine's work seems to have earned approval. On 26 May 1711 he was given a gratuity of 5 guineas which was afterwards renewed and then (3 July 1721) put on a permanent footing 'so as the same be no precedent to the succeeding organists' (CA5). But there was trouble in August 1727, when Heseltine was summoned before the Chapter for 'notoriously abusing' Dr Mangey, one of the prebendaries; upon his refusing to make submission, he was suspended unless he asked Mangey's pardon within a week, which he seems to have done, as no more is heard of the affair. Hawkins suggests there were other troubles, for 'Having, as he conceived, been slighted, or otherwise ill treated by the Dean and Chapter, he in revenge tore out of the church-books all his compositions that were there to be found.' Be this as it may, he married the daughter of Sir George Wheler, one of the prebendaries, in 1730. He subscribed to Croft's *Musica Sacra* in 1724, Greene's *Forty Select Anthems* in 1743, and to the first edition of Boyce's *Cathedral Music* in 1760. There is an autograph letter from Heseltine to one Mickleton, dated 2 March 1715/16, promising to furnish manuscript copies of church music from Durham, presumably for Tudway's collection (Lbl, Harl. MS 3779).

Heseltine is buried in the Galilee Chapel of the Cathedral (PR). There is a portrait of him in the Music School collection at Oxford (Poole 1912–25: i. 160), presented by Philip Hayes.

Thomas Ebdon 1763–1811 (d. Durham, 23 Sept. 1811, aged 73). West (1921) states that Ebdon was the son of Thomas Ebdon, 'cordwainer'. He was a chorister in the Cathedral under his predecessor, and his name is stated to be carved on the screen separating the north aisle from the choir. On 1 October 1763 the Chapter resolved to allow him £20 for acting as organist from Midsummer to Michaelmas following Heseltine's death, and on the same day he was elected and appointed organist by the dean (CA6). He was at that time a lay clerk, but he resigned his place as such on 28 September 1764 (CA6). Together with various other musicians, he was involved in conducting the Newcastle Subscription Concerts from 1783. He is buried in St Oswald's churchyard, Durham. The Thomas Ebdon who was minor canon and sacrist of the Cathedral from 1812 to 1849 was his son.

Ebdon subscribed to the second edition of Boyce's *Cathedral Music* (two copies), and also to Burney's *History of Music* (1776). His own published church music (2 vols., 1790–1811) is described as 'composed for the use of the choir of Durham'.

Charles Erlin Jackson Clarke 1811–13. On 20 November 1811 (CA9) 'Mr Charles Clarke' was appointed organist and sworn in. He resigned late in 1813. *See under Worcester Cathedral.*

William Henshaw 1814–62 (b. Marylebone, London, 1792). Henshaw was sworn in as organist of Durham Cathedral on 1 January 1814 (CA9). On 27 September 1862 (CA14) the Chapter agreed that 'Dr Henshaw having resigned his office as organist in the Cathedral . . . a retiring pension for life of £260 be granted to him in testimony of the conduct, zeal and ability with which he has discharged his duties for nearly fifty years.' This was remarkably generous treatment for the time, and tends to support the statement in *BMB* that 'he brought the choir to a high state of efficiency which made it celebrated throughout Britain'. Nothing is known of his early years nor, in spite of his long period of office, about his time in Durham (though doubtless something could be gleaned from local newspapers), save that he was made D.Mus. of the University of Durham by diploma in 1860.

According to *Grove*[2] (*sub* 'Armes'), he died on 14 November 1862; but the minute of 22 November 1862 appointing his successor speaks of him not as 'deceased' but as 'resigned'. It was his wife not he (as stated by *BMB* and West 1921) who was buried at Clapham on 30 September 1877 (footnote to Harleian Society edition of PR).

Philip Armes 1863–1907 (b. Norwich, 29 Mar. (*Grove*[2])/15 Aug. (*DNB*) 1836; d. Durham, 10 Feb. 1908). Armes was a chorister first of Norwich Cathedral (1846–8) under *Z. Buck, and then of Rochester Cathedral (1848–50) under *J. L. Hopkins. He was afterwards articled to Hopkins. He became organist of Holy Trinity Church, Milton, Gravesend in 1854 or 1855, and then of St Andrew's, Wells Street (a very fashionable London church) in 1857. In 1861 he became organist of Chichester Cathedral (q.v.). As a factor which perhaps weighed in this appointment, it is related in *MT* (41 (1900), 81) how the dean observed: 'Mr Armes, I think you hold an Oxford degree.' His appointment at Durham was minuted in November 1862 (CA14), and he seems to have taken up duties in 1863.

When the University of Durham instituted its external degrees in music, Armes conducted the earliest examinations in 1890 and was appointed resident examiner. Seven years later his position was dignified by the title of professor of music, a post which he held till his death. *Grove*[2] noted that in 1903 he was playing first viola in the Durham Orchestral Society.

Armes held the Oxford degrees of B.Mus. (1858) and D.Mus. (1864), and was created MA of Durham in 1891. He was also an honorary FRCO. There is a memorial to him in the west cloister of the Cathedral.

Grove[3]

Arnold Duncan Culley 1907–32 (b. 9 Mar. 1867; d. Seipton, Ludlow, 3 Dec. 1947). After attending Great Yarmouth Grammar School, Culley studied at the Royal College of Music, where he was the first holder of the Norfolk and Norwich scholarship. After early appointments at St Peter's, Hammersmith (1884) and Christ Church, Surbiton (1889), he went up to Cambridge as organ scholar of Emmanuel College in 1891. Following his ordination in 1894 he became curate of the Chapel Royal, Brighton, and was then appointed deputy priest-vicar choral of Exeter Cathedral (1897). He went to Durham as minor canon and precentor in 1906, and succeeded Armes as organist the following year, retaining his minor canonry and precentorship. On retirement from Durham he became rector of Burwarton with Cleobury North, Shropshire, 1932–41.

He took the Cambridge degrees of BA and Mus.B. in 1895, followed by that of MA in 1898, having taken the FRCO diploma in 1887.

MT; 89 (1948), 62; *WWW*, 1941–50; *Crockford's Clerical Directory*.

Sir John Dykes Bower, CVO, 1933–6.

See under St Paul's Cathedral, London.

§Conrad (William) Eden, TD, 1936–74 (b. Hants, 1905). Eden was a chorister of Wells Cathedral, and a pupil there of *T. H. Davis. He then went to Rugby School and the Royal College of Music, followed by three years in Oxford as organ exhibitioner of St John's College, 1924–7. He was appointed organist of Wells Cathedral in 1933, the year in which he took up his Oxford degree of B. Mus., and moved from there to Durham three years later. He received the honorary FRCO diploma in 1971, and the Lambeth degree of Mus. D. on his retirement in 1974.

Richard (Hey) Lloyd 1974–85.

See under Hereford Cathedral.

§James (Bennett) Lancelot, master of the choristers and organist from 1985 (b. Kent, 2 Dec. 1952). Lancelot was a chorister of St Paul's Cathedral, London, 1961–6, before going to Ardingly College with a music scholarship. After a year's scholarship at the Royal College of Music, 1970–1, he went up to Cambridge as organ student of King's College, 1971–4. There he read for part I of the classical tripos and part II of the music tripos, taking the degree of BA in 1974 (subsequently MA) and that of Mus.B. in 1975. In 1969 he had taken the FRCO diploma (Turpin prize), followed by that of CHM in 1971. He was assistant organist of St Clement Danes, Strand, London and of Hampstead Parish Church, 1974–5, and then, from 1975 until his appointment to Durham, sub-organist of Winchester Cathedral.

ELY

The Cathedral Church of the Holy and Undivided Trinity

Main sources in this section (1963) (with Cathedral Muniment reference where appropriate):

Register of Patents

LB Ledger Book I, 1543–1614 (2/4/1).

Chapter Acts

CA1 'A Registre for the Church of Ely', 1550–1643 (2/1/1).

CA2 1660–1729 (2/1/2).

CA3 1729–69.

CA4 1770–1804.

CA5 1805–41.

CA6 1863–88.

CA7 1888–1915.

CA8 1915–32.

Accounts

Ac1 Computi Receptorum; a series of annual accounts to Michaelmas, running intermittently from 1542–3 to 1607–8, housed in two boxes (3/3/1–12, 3/3/13–20).

Ac2 Computi Receptorum; an intermittent series of 13 annual accounts, 1589–90 to 1623–4 (3/4/1–20).

Ac3 Accounts, 1597–1635, with gaps (3/1/5).

Ac4 'Great Book of Ely'; accounts, 1603–4 to 1676–7 (3/1/2).

Miscellaneous

PS Parliamentary Survey (6/2/15).

PR Holy Trinity Parish Register of baptisms, marriages, and burials for residents of Cathedral precincts.

Watkins MS compilation by Thomas Watkins (precentor, 1736–76), 'Members or Officers of the Cathedral Church of Ely, 1544 to the present time' (i.e., *c.*1764).

Ely Cathedral was refounded by Henry VIII in August 1541 to take the place of the surrendered Benedictine cathedral priory. The foundation included eight choristers under a master, on whom the draft statutes laid the duty of organist (see p. xix). Listing officers of the foundation, statutes issued in 1666 enumerated an organist and a master of the choristers separately. But there was no statute dealing with the duties of the former, while that for the master of the choristers simply remarked that he was to be skilled in organ-playing.

William Smith 1541–2. We learn of Smith from a document entitled 'The Book of the erection of the King's new College at Ely' (Cambridge, Corpus Christi College, MS Misc. XX, p. 293, printed in Bentham 1812: Appendix, p. 40). It includes the entry: 'A Scole Master for the Queristers, William Smith the elder. £10.' The designation, 'the elder', distinguishes him from William Smith the younger, whose name is found in the list of singingmen. Arkwright (1893) thought that, after being succeeded by Christopher Tye as master of the choristers, Smith became simply a singingman. It was thus that he interpreted the name William Smith in Ac1 to Michaelmas 1543. But this name is not distinguished as elder or younger, and it seems reasonable to presume that the elder had died, and that the younger remained in the choir. (See Addenda, p. 434.)

Christopher Tye 1542–61 (d. ?1572). The earliest surviving receiver's account at Ely (Ac 1) runs from Michaelmas to Michaelmas 1542–3: this records a complete year's salary to 'Christopher Tye, gent, magistro choristarum'. He is also found in the next extant account, 1546–7; then, following another gap, the account for

1560–1 contains an entry for half a year's salary only. In July and November 1560 (Register of Richard Cox, Bishop of Ely) he had been ordained deacon and priest; and in the same year he was presented to the rectory of Doddington-cum-Marche.

About a year before, that is on 23 May 1559, Tye received a grant of the office of organist and master of the choristers at Ely for life, with power to distrain on the manor of Sutton for his stipend (LB, f. 15). When printing this document in full, Arkwright (1893) considered that it indicated that Tye occupied an exceptional position. But this is not an uncommon form of grant at this period, and the power to distrain was only a means of guaranteeing security (see, for example, Thomas Grew of Norwich and Edmund Hooper of Westminster Abbey). The date of the grant (as with the letters patent given to Richard Fisher of Worcester, 3 April 1559) suggests that the early months of the reign of Queen Elizabeth I were the occasion for putting the appointment on a documented footing.

F. L. Clarke's Year Lists of King's College, Cambridge (see p. 355) disclose the name 'Tye' among the choristers for 1509–12, and then among the clerks, 1528–35. In 1536 the name Richard Tye occurs; in 1537 both Richard and Christopher Tye; in 1538 and 1539 Christopher Tye; and from 1540 to 1546, Richard Tye. When Christopher took the Cambridge degree of Mus.B. in 1536, the 'grace' mentioned his having taught boys. In 1545 he proceeded Mus.D. at Cambridge, when he was allowed the academic dress of a doctor of medicine (Cambridge University, Grace Book Delta). According to Wood (1815–20: i. 127), he was incorporated as D.Mus. at Oxford in 1548.

There is indirect evidence that he was a member of the Chapel Royal throughout the reign of Edward VI; and indeed in 1553, on the title-page of his famous 'Acts of the Apostles', he described himself as 'one of the Gentlemen of his graces most honourable Chapel'. This, of course, was while he held office at Ely. Fuller (1662) says that he was 'probably the organist' of the Chapel Royal, while Wood (MS Notes) asserts that 'he was chief organist of Edward 6, and first organist of Elizabeth'. No definite appointments of Chapel Royal organists as such are known from this period, but it does not seem unreasonable to suppose that, though neither he nor anyone else was 'organist of the Chapel Royal' at that time, he was one of those who, as suitably qualified gentlemen, played for the services from time to time during his tour of duty there.

After taking holy orders, he held, in addition to Doddington, the livings of Newton-cum-Capella, close by, and Wilbraham Parva, near Cambridge, but he gave up both of these before his death. This must have taken place before 15 March 1572/3, on which date the Bishop of Ely collated one Hugo Bellett to the rectory of Doddington explicitly stated to be vacant by the death of Christopher Tye, doctor of music (Cu, Diocesan Archives, G1/8, f. 165).

Fuller's (1662) inclusion of Tye among the worthies born at Westminster has no significance, for it was his method to classify in this way those whose birthplaces were unknown to him.

Robert White *c.***1561–6** (d. London (Westminster), Nov. 1574). Following the accounts for 1560–1 (already quoted under Tye), there is a gap until the year ending Michaelmas 1563 (Ac1), when payment is recorded to 'magistro Roberto Whyte, musice bachalario, magistro choristarum'. It is reasonable to assume that he followed Tye sometime during the accounting year 1561–2. There is no trace of the issue of a patent to him. The accounts for the year ending 1564 and 1566 are now wanting, while those for 1565 give no details of the master of the choristers. However, White's continuing presence at Ely in December 1565 is reliably inferred from the entry of his daughter's (Margery's) baptism in PR. Accepting that he became organist of Chester Cathedral about Christmas 1566 (q.v.) his departure from Ely may be placed at the end of 1566.

It can hardly be doubted that Robert White, organist of Ely Cathedral, was the same as Robert White, organist of Westminster Abbey, 1570–4 (q.v.). As already noted, Robert White had a daughter called Margery while he was at Ely; and the will of Robert White of Westminster, bachelor of music, dated 7 November 1574 (proved in the court of the Dean and Chapter of Westminster), refers to a daughter Margery. Furthermore, in her will dated 21 November 1574 the widow of the Westminster White speaks not only of her mother 'Katherin' Tye (a significant Ely connection in itself), but of her sister Mary Rowley; and we know that Christopher Tye's daughter Mary married a certain 'Roberte Rowlye' at Ely on 12 August 1560. These facts are sufficient to identify Robert White of Westminster as a former organist of Ely Cathedral, and show that he was Tye's son-in-law. Nor is there any real room for doubt that the Westminster organist was the 'Mr Whit' who was formerly organist of Chester Cathedral (q.v.). *Thomas Tomkins (III), writing in the margin of his copy of Morley's *Plaine and Easie Introduction*, entered against the name of White the legend: 'first of Westchester & Westminster' (see facsimile in Stevens 1957, facing p. 29); 'Westchester' is the old name for Chester. Such dates as we have are consonant with successive moves from Ely to Chester and from Chester to Westminster, and the outline of White's career may therefore be taken to be thus: Ely, *c.*1561–6; Chester, 1567–8 or later; Westminster Abbey, 1570–4. He took the Mus.B. degree at Cambridge on 13 December 1560, the 'grace' describing him as the 'son of Robert'. He was buried in St Margaret's, Westminster on 11 November 1574. For a valuable basis of biographical fact, see Arkwright (1898).

An early tribute to White is contained in Och, Music MSS 984–8 (*c.*1581): 'Maxima musarum nostrarum gloria White / Tu peris, aeternum sed tua musa manet.' ('Thou, O White, greatest glory of our muses, / dost perish, but thy muse is everlasting.')

John Farrant (I) 1566–?70. The account for the year ending Michaelmas 1567 (Ac1) contains the entry 'Mro Johni Farond mro choristarum £10'. On 9 December 1567 (CA1, p. 32) the Chapter resolved to issue letters patent of the office of organist and master of the choristers to Farrant, and the patent itself bears the date 10 December 1567 (LB, f.84). It does not mention life tenure; Farrant was to teach the boys not only singing but instrumental music; Ac1 discloses his payment for the year ending Michaelmas 1568, but a gap in the series at that point leaves the date of his departure conjectural.

For discussion of the presumed identity of John Farrant (I), see under Bristol Cathedral.

William Fox 1571–9 (d. Ely, Sept. 1579). Willis (1742) refers to an account for the year (?ending) 1572 which gave Fox's stipend as £13. 6*s*. 8*d*. There are at present no extant accounts between those for 1567–8 and 1572–3. In the latter, 'Mr Fox' is named, with the stipend as given by Willis. Fox's patent, in terms similar to Farrant's, is dated 30 October 1572 (CA1, p.35; LB, f.102ᵛ). *Watkins* notes his burial on 10 September 1579.

George Barcroft 1580–1610. Barcroft's patent of appointment is dated 10 January, 25 Elizabeth (1583 NS) (Lb, f.138ᵛ), when he is decribed as 'in artibus baccalaureus', but his stipend goes back to the later half of the accounting year ending Michaelmas 1580 (Ac1). He continued to be paid up to Midsummer 1610 (Ac4). From the accounting year 1592–3 (Ac1) he was also a minor canon (or 'vicar', as the inaccurate usage then was at Ely).

Venn records a George Barcroft who was a sizar of Trinity College, Cambridge in 1574 and who took the degree of BA in 1577–8, identifying him not only with the Ely organist and minor canon but as having been ordained priest on 30 August 1590 by the Bishop of Peterborough and as being vicar of Dullingham, Cambridgeshire in 1589. One would like to feel sure that two separate individuals are not confused here. There was also a George Barcroft, lay clerk of Durham Cathedral, who died in February 1638/9 (Durham University Library, Michaelmas MS).

The statement sometimes found that one Thomas Barcroft was organist of Ely Cathedral in 1535 rests on a misunderstanding on the part of Thomas Tudway (Lbl, Harl. MS 7340, f. 31). Thomas Barcroft was a lay clerk of Ely during the time of George Barcroft and John Amner.

John Amner 1610–41 (bap. Ely, 24 Aug. 1579; d. Ely, July 1641). There is no record of a patent for Amner, but he received his stipend as *informator choristarum* (and therefore as organist) from Michaelmas 1610 (Ac4). On 1 March 1617 he was ordained deacon by the Bishop of Ely in Ely Chapel, Holborn, London, and thereafter combined the two posts of 'vicar' (i.e., minor canon) and master of the choristers/organist. He took the Oxford degree of B.Mus. in May 1613 (Wood 1815–20: i. 351), and the Cambridge degree of Mus.B. in 1640 (*Venn*). Amner was buried on 28 July 1641 (PR).

Robert Claxton 1641–62 (d. Ely, *c.*Feb. 1668). Claxton had been a lay clerk from the accounting year 1624–5 (Ac4). From 1636 he taught the choristers to play the viol, for which he received an additional 10*s*. a year. On his becoming master of the choristers and organist from Michaelmas 1641 (Ac4), he retained his post of lay clerk and continued to be paid as 'master of the viols'. His patent as master of the choristers and organist was granted on 20 October 1641 (CA1, p. 145). He continued to receive his various stipends to Michaelmas 1643, when the accounts are intermitted following the suspension of cathedral bodies; but his name reappears in the accounts ending at Michaelmas 1660.

He appears to have remained at Ely during the Interregnum. The parliamentary survey of the Close (PS) speaks of 'the singing school, and anciently a school to teach children to read, is now in the tenure of Robert Claxton'. It describes

Claxton's house as 'a pretty house', consisting of two rooms as well as 'another room with a parlour taken out of it for a place to play upon the violin'—no doubt a music room. In January 1645, in a petition to the Committee for Sequestrations, he claimed arrears of stipend since Michaelmas 1644 at £28. 16*s*. per annum; and in 1659 the Trustees for the Maintenance of Ministers granted him £9. 6*s*. 8*d*. (Matthews 1948).

The last payment to him as master of the choristers and organist is at Christmas 1662. Between then and his death in 1668 he retained his post as lay clerk and also received an allowance of £10 under various covers: for example, 'allowed to Mr Claxton his stipend for the choristers' (Ac4, 1663); 'being infirm and under an apoplexy' (1664); 'by consent' (1665); and 'eleemosynae' (1666 and 1667). *Watkins* records his burial on 2 March 1668.

John Ferrabosco 1663–82 (presumed b. Greenwich, Oct. 1626; d. Ely, Oct. 1682). John Ferrabosco was the last notable English representative of a family of musicians that can be traced back to Bologna at the end of the fifteenth century; he was the grandson of Alfonso Ferrabosco (d. 1588) who was represented in *Musica Transalpina* (1588). The English members of the clan, employed by the royal household, settled in Greenwich, where a certain John Ferrabosco, very likely our present subject, was baptized on 9 October 1626. Perhaps this court connection accounts for the royal intervention in securing a university degree for him (see below).

Ferrabosco received his first payment at Ely for the quarter ending March 1663 (Ac4); and the accounts up to the following Michaelmas record a special grant to him of £5 'at his coming down to Ely'. CA2, under the date 23 June 1663, ordered 'that Mr Ferrabosco shall have (in consideration of his pains in pricking out of books) ten pounds, to provide his chamber of necessaries'. Ac4, in the year 1664–5, contains the intriguing entry: 'To Mr Ferrabosco for his expenses at several music meetings in the last two years, 17*s*.' Though the term 'music meeting' was common in the eighteenth century, its occurrence at this early date is striking.

With Ferrabosco's arrival at Ely, the accounts break the total stipend into two parts: £7. 10*s*. for work as organist, and £2. 10*s*. as master of the choristers. A new arrangement was made in the quarter ending Michaelmas 1669, when one 'Mr Jackson' (sometimes identified as *John Jackson of Wells Cathedral) became master of the choristers, and John Ferrabosco, as organist, was recompensed by the sinecure office of cook at £1. 10*s*. In the quarter ending Christmas 1670 Jackson was replaced by John Blundeville, a new lay clerk, and Blundeville in his turn was succeeded by Robert Robinson in the quarter ending Michaelmas 1674. (For Blundeville, see also p. 159.)

In 1671 Ferrabosco received the Cambridge degree of Mus. B. on the direction of Charles II (*Venn*), and the Cathedral accounts for 1670–1 contain the entry: 'To Mr Ferrabosco for his degree of Bachelor of Music £3.' He married Anne Burton at Ely on 28 June 1679, and they had a son John (August 1679, May 1682: PR).

Ac4 comes to an end at Michaelmas 1677. *Watkins* says that Ferrabosco was buried at the charge of the Chapter (Audit Book 1682, not now extant), and that letters of administration of his estate were granted on 27 November 1682. He was buried on 15 October 1682 (PR).

Upon Ferrabosco's death, there was a brief interregnum before the arrival of his successor. During this time a young lay clerk named Thomas Bullis acted as organist; on 14 June 1683 (CA2) the Chapter resolved 'that besides the £5 given to young Bullis for his services during the vacancy of the organist's place, there be £5 given to his father as a testimony of the kindness of the Dean and Chapter'. Several years earlier, while Robinson was still master of the choristers, there was an extra payment for two quarters in the accounting year 1676–7 to 'Mr Bullis' (i.e, the father, Thomas Bullis) for teaching the choristers. This was continued, so far as can be ascertained, until Hawkins arrived (*Watkins*).

James Hawkins (I) 1682–1729 (d. Ely, 18 Oct. 1729). Atkins (1918: 34) identifies Hawkins with a chorister of Worcester Cathedral, 1671–4. On the other hand, assertions that he was a chorister of St John's College, Cambridge, though unsupported, may well be more likely. For reasons discussed below (p. 362), he can hardly be other than the Hawkins (no Christian name given) who was organist of that College in 1681.

CA2 contains no record of his appointment at Ely, and accounts fail us for the period. We must therefore rely on *Watkins* for the date. He says that Hawkins's stipend first ran from Michaelmas 1682, and it is clear that the duties of organist and master of the choristers were now reunited.

Within a relatively short time Hawkins sought to develop a music-teaching connection outside Ely, and on 14 June 1684 (CA2) the Chapter passed the following resolution:

> Agreed at the request of the organist that he have liberty to be absent at Bury [Bury St Edmund's] for the teaching of children there in music three days in a fortnight and no more. Provided that he take care for the supply of his two places of organist and informator in his absence, and that this liberty and allowance be continued to him at Michaelmas and no longer, except renewed again by the Dean and Chapter.

This activity seems to have led to trouble, and fourteen years later the Chapter resolved as follows (CA2, 14 June 1698):

> Ordered that Mr Hawkins our organist shall not be allowed to absent himself from the services of the church one day, or to teach any person to sing, or play, in the country, unless he carefully teach the choir at home three afternoons, at least, in every week; and unless the proficiency of the choir be very evident, and a sensible progress be made, as well by those of the lay clerks, who are willing to learn, as by the children, within the space of three months next ensuing.

Hawkins was also active as a music-copyist, wishing to enrich the repertory of the Ely choir; but the Chapter applied a brake on 23 October 1693, when it was ordered 'that the organist shall not be allowed any bill for pricking books, setting any chorus or composing any anthems or doing anything else for the church unless his design shall be first allowed before he performs it'. On his own account, Hawkins was a diligent collector of church music, and copied out a great deal in scores now deposited by the Cathedral in Cu. Some of this he rescued from fragments of old part-books. This side of his activities was particularly useful to Thomas Tudway, who mentioned him as 'honest James Hawkins' in his correspondence with Humfrey Wanley (Lbl. Harl. Ms 3782). Tudway attempted to persuade Wanley to acquire Hawkins's manuscript score of Tallis's forty-part motet.

During Hawkins's time the official choir school appears to have fallen into disuse, if not decay, and on 14 June 1696 he was allowed 20*s*. a year 'in consideration of his finding a schoolroom in which he teaches the choir to sing'. Towards the end of his life the Chapter granted him (25 November 1727, CA2) the sum of £21 'in consideration of his present difficult circumstances, and of his long services to the church'. The following was the inscription on his tomb in the south transept of the Cathedral, as recorded by Bentham: 'Under this marble (Among many of his relations) Lieth the body of James Hawkins, B.M., 46 Years Organist of this Church; Eminent in his Profession, Regular in the discharge of his Duty, Chearful and friendly in his Deportment. He died the 18th of October 1729, In the 67th year of his Age.'

For his son James Hawkins (II), see under Peterborough Cathedral.

Thomas Kempton 1729–62 (bap. Ely, 3 May 1702; d. Ely, 16 June 1762). Kempton's appointment as Hawkins's successor was formally minuted on 25 November 1729 (CA3), when his emoluments were set out as follows: £20 as organist, plus £10 'bounty'; £10 as *informator choristarum* (the ancient statutory salary); £2 'for playing the [metrical] psalm before the sermon'; £1 'for finding a singing-school'; 5*s*. quarterly for every chorister during his first year as such; 1*s*. 'at the entrance of every one into his singing school'. On 25 November 1737 Kempton was further allotted a bedesman's place, no doubt simply as a way of augmenting his stipend. He is buried in St Mary's Church, Ely, where the tombstone gives his age wrongly as 68. West (1921) noted in 1899 that some of Kempton's descendants had sung in the Cathedral choir 'until recently'.

John Elbonn 1762–8 (d. Ely, 7 June 1768). Elbonn was admitted organist and master of the choristers on 25 November 1762 as from Michaelmas of that year (CA3). His emoluments were the same as Kempton's had been. There is a memorial plaque to Elbonn on the exterior wall of the Lady Chapel of the Cathedral.

David Wood 1768–74. Wood was formally admitted on 14 June 1768 (CA3) as from 29 June, on the same terms as Elbonn's. Page's *Harmonia Sacra*, ii (1800), prints an anthem by David Wood, 'Gentleman of the Chapel Royal and Vicar Choral of St Paul's Cathedral'; this is perhaps a clue to Wood's later career. A David Wood was admitted a gentleman of the Chapel Royal on 8 April 1774, and died in 1786 (CB2).

James Rodgers 1774–7. On 14 June 1774 (CA4) the Chapter took the interesting step of ordering 'that the following advertisement be inserted on Saturday next in the Cambridge Journal, and on Tuesday next and the two next succeeding Tuesdays in the St James's Chronicle':

Organist

Wanted immediately an organist in the Cathedral Church of Ely. No person will be elected, unless he is well skilled in, and used to Church Music, and can produce a sufficient testimonial of his good life and conversation. Any person by applying to Mr John Knowles of Ely may be informed of all further particulars relating to this matter.

The formal appointment of Rodgers was minuted on 7 September 1774, dating his emoluments from Midsummer. He left for Peterborough Cathedral (q.v.). He also had a bedesman's place (CA4).

(Richard) Langdon 1777–8. 'Mr Langdon' was appointed 'in place of James Rodgers' on 25 November 1777 (CA4), and was sworn in on the following day.

See under Exeter Cathedral.

Highmore Skeats (I) 1778–1803. Highmore Skeats was appointed organist, master of the choristers, and bedesman 'in the room of Mr Langdon' on 14 June 1778 (CA4).

See under Canterbury Cathedral.

Highmore Skeats (II) 1803–30. Although the elder Skeats was appointed organist of Canterbury Cathedral by minute dated November 1803 (q.v.), the Ely Chapter Acts make no mention of any change until 25 November 1804 (CA4), when his resignation was recorded and Highmore Skeats 'junior' was appointed 'probationary organist'. This is obviously a formal minute, passed at the annual audit, regularizing an existing situation.

See under St George's Chapel, Windsor.

Robert Janes 1830–66 (b. 3 Feb. 1806; d. Ely, 10 June 1866). Janes was a sol-fa scholar (i.e., chorister) of Dulwich College, and was articled to *Zechariah Buck at Norwich in 1824. He was appointed organist of Ely Cathedral by minute dated 25 November 1830 (CA5). Like so many of his predecessors, he held a bedesman's place, and it is interesting to note that he also held the position—no doubt a sinecure—of bridge-keeper.

At the time of his appointment to Ely, the organ was still that which had been built by Gerard Smith in James Hawkins's time at the end of the seventeenth century and was afterwards repaired by Green and by Byfield. Dickson (1894), who mentions its unusual compass ('AA to *d* in alt'), describes how 'some of the front pipes had settled down so much at the feet that the precaution of tying them in their places with cords had been thought necessary'.

Dickson also states that Janes had a very large teaching-practice in Norfolk and Suffolk, and in later years was wont to relate how he rode long distances on horseback to fulfil his engagements, attaching a pair of lamps to his saddle like pistol-holsters to light his lonely road at night through the Fen country. It was said that his income at this time could not have been expressed in less than four figures.

BMB.

Edmund Thomas Chipp 1866–86 (b. London, 25 Dec. 1823; d. Nice, 17 Dec. 1886). Chipp was the eldest son of T. P. Chipp (1793–1870), the most noted English orchestral drummer of his day. Edmund was a chorister in the Chapel Royal under William Hawes, and he also studied the violin under eminent masters. From 1843 to 1845 (*BMB*, 1843–55) he was a violinist in the Queen's private band. Meanwhile he held a succession of organ appointments in London, including Albany Chapel, Regent's Park (1843), St Olave's, Southwark (1847), St Mary-at-Hill (1852), and Holy Trinity, Paddington (1856). Concurrently with these last two posts he also succeeded W. T. Best as organist of the Royal Panopticon from 1855. In addition he played the violin in the orchestras of the Royal Italian Opera, the Philharmonic Society, and the Sacred Harmonic Society.

In 1862 he moved to Ireland as organist of the Ulster Hall and St George's Church, Belfast (1862–6); after brief appointments in Dundee and Edinburgh (1866), he was sworn in as organist of Ely Cathedral on 14 June 1867 (CA6). Stephens (1882) states that he actually succeeded Janes in November 1866, which may well have been the case. In December 1878 and again in November 1879 the Chapter allowed £20 for a deputy during Chipp's 'enforced absence and vacation'.

Chipp held the Cambridge degrees of Mus.B. (1859) and Mus.D. (1860) (*Venn*). Towards the end of his life he was made an honorary FRCO. He is buried in Highgate Cemetery, London.

Grove[1]; West 1921; *DNB*; *BMB*; *MT*, 28 (1887), 43.

Basil Harwood 1887–92. Harwood's appointment was minuted on 21 February 1887, and he was sworn in on 15 November of that year (CA6).

See under Christ Church Cathedral, Oxford.

Thomas Tertius Noble 1892–8 (b. Bath, 5 May 1867; d. Rockport, Mass., 4 May 1953). When he was only 14 years old, Noble became organist of All Saints' Church, Colchester. He then went to the Royal College of Music in 1885, where he was successively exhibitioner and scholar. He was briefly organist of St John's Church, Wilton Road, London in 1889, before becoming assistant to C. V. Stanford at Trinity College, Cambridge, 1890–2. He was appointed organist of Ely Cathedral by Chapter minute dated 22 August 1892, and was sworn in on 25 November 1893 (CA7). He was subsequently organist of York Minster, where he established his reputation, and in 1913 he was invited to take charge of the music at the rebuilt St Thomas's Episcopal Church, New York. He retired in 1943.

Noble was made an honorary FRCO in 1905, and held the honorary degrees of MA (Columbia University of New York, 1918) and D.Mus. (Trinity College, Hartford, 1926). He received the Lambeth degree of D.Mus. in 1932.

BMB; *Grove*[3]; *ECM*, 23 (1953), 126; *MT*, 94 (1953), 281.

Sir Hugh Percy Allen, GCVO 1898–1900. Allen was elected organist on 4 January 1898, but was not sworn in until 26 November 1900, only three weeks before the election of his successor (CA7).

See under New College, Oxford.

Archibald Wayett Wilson 1901–18. Wilson's election as organist took place on 17 December 1900, and he was sworn in on 14 June 1902 (CA7).

See under Manchester Cathedral.

Noel Edward Ponsonby 1919–26 (b. Cambridge, 14 Jan. 1891; d. Oxford, 10 Dec. 1928). Ponsonby, whose father was rector of St Mary-le-Bow, London, was a chorister of St George's Chapel, Windsor Castle under *Walter Parratt, and then went to Repton School. He became organ scholar of Trinity College, Oxford in 1909, and took the degrees of BA and B.Mus. (1914), and MA (1916). For two periods, first at the Royal Naval College, Dartmouth (1912–14) and then at Marlborough College (1914–18), he worked as a director of music, embarking upon cathedral work as organist of Ely Cathedral in 1919. He was elected on 8 November 1918 and sworn in on 25 November 1919 (CA8). In 1926 he moved to Christ Church Cathedral, Oxford, but died at the early age of 37. It will be noted that at three points his career was identical with that of *Basil Harwood: Trinity College, Oxford; Ely; and Christ Church, Oxford. His son Robert, who eventually followed in parental footsteps as organ scholar of Trinity College, Oxford, was controller of music for the BBC, 1977–85.

West 1921; *WWW*, 1916–28; *MT*, 70 (1929), 79; *ECM*, 17 (1947), 12, 30.

Hubert Stanley Middleton 1926–31. Middleton was elected organist of Ely Cathedral on 9 March 1926 and was sworn in on 25 November 1927 (CA8). He submitted his resignation on 7 November 1930, and this was accepted on 11 January 1931 (CA8).

See under Trinity College, Cambridge.

Marmaduke Percival Conway 1931–49 (b. London, 1885; d. Douglas, Isle of Man, 22 Mar. 1961). Conway studied at the Royal College of Music. He was successively organist of Upperton Congregational Church, Eastbourne, 1900–2, assistant organist of St Saviour's, Eastbourne, 1902–9, and organist of All Saints', Eastbourne from 1908. He was assistant organist of Wells Cathedral, 1920–5. He was then organist of Chichester Cathedral until moving to Ely in 1931, having been elected organist of the Cathedral on 12 December 1930 (CA8). He remained at Ely until his retirement.

Conway took the FRCO diploma in 1904, followed by the Oxford degree of B.Mus. in 1907 and the Dublin degree of Mus.D. in 1914.

Thornsby 1912; *MT*, 102 (1961), 309.

Sidney Scholfield Campbell, MVO, 1949–53.

See under St George's Chapel, Windsor.

Michael (Stockwin) Howard 1953–8 (b. London, 14 Sept. 1922). Howard was educated at Ellesmere College and the Royal Academy of Music (scholar), where he studied under G. D. Cunningham and William Alwyn. He later worked privately with Ralph Downes and Marcel Dupré. From September 1943 to March 1944 he was organist of Tewkesbury Abbey, but he returned to London and was appointed organist of Christ Church, Woburn Square, 1945–50. After leaving Ely he once more settled in London, working mainly as a conductor and lecturer.

MT, 87 (1946), 361.

§**Arthur (William) Wills, organist and choirmaster from 1958** (b. Coventry, 19 Sept. 1926). Wills received his education at St John's School, Coventry and at the College of St Nicolas (Royal School of Church Music), Canterbury. He was sub-organist of Ely Cathedral before succeeding to the full post. From 1953 to 1965 he was director of music at the King's School, Ely, and in 1964 he joined the staff of the Royal Academy of Music.

Wills took the Durham degrees of B.Mus (1953) and D.Mus. (1957). In addition to the FRCO and CHM diplomas (1948 and 1949), he also holds that of ADCM (1951). He is the author of a volume in the Yehudi Menuhin Music Guides series entitled *Organ* (1984).

In the summer of 1989 it was announced that Wills intended to retire in 1990, and that he would be succeeded by Paul Trepte (see under Bury St Edmund's (Cathedral). (See Addenda, p. 434.)

EXETER

The Cathedral Church of St Peter

Main sources in this section (1963):

Chapter Acts

CA1	1537–66.
CA2	1607–28.
—	1630–5.
—	1635–43.
CA5	1643–60.
CA6	1661–7.
CA7	1667–77.
CA8	1677–85.
CA9	1685–95.
CA10	1695–1708.
CA11	1708–16.
CA12	1716–27.
CA13	1727–39.
CA14	1739–44.

19 further volumes: 1744–53; 1753–62; 1763–70; 1770–7; 1777–84; 1784–91; 1791–8; 1798–1805; 1805–10; 1810–16; 1817–22; 1822–7; 1828–32; 1832–8; 1838–42; 1842–51; 1851–9; 1859–69; 1869–76.

Accounts of the Dean and Chapter

Ac1	Christmas 1602–Michaelmas 1625.
Ac2	Michaelmas 1625–67.

Accounts of the Vicars Choral

VC/Ac1	1586–7 to 1606–7.
VC/Ac2	1606–7, 1621–45.

Miscellaneous

SWP	Records connected with the suit *in re* Withers and Parsons, culled from documents now no longer extant (Cathedral Muniment 7155/1).
Mon.	*Monumentarium*; a 20th-century survey of all the monumental inscriptions in the Cathedral compiled by V. Hope.
PR	Registers of baptisms, marriages, and burials in the Cathedral, printed as *Registers of Baptisms, Marriages and Burials of the City of Exeter*, i (Devon and Cornwall Record Society, 1910).

Exeter has been the seat of a bishop since 1050, when Edward the Confessor removed the see from Crediton. The first Bishop of Exeter, Leofric, displaced a Benedictine monastery and established a secular cathedral in that year. Like other cathedrals of the Old Foundation, it developed a body of vicars choral, and at least by the year 1388 they were living a common life in a hall or houses. They received their charter of incorporation in 1401, and a body of statutes in 1405. Laymen were admitted as vicars at Exeter after the Reformation, when there were insufficient men singers in holy orders; but by royal mandate of 1613 they ceased to be members of the College, though they continued to participate in the election of the *custos* and to share in certain tithes. It will be found that many of the Exeter organists—indeed, all of them from Colby to Angel—were lay vicars choral. There was also a period when the office of succentor (or sub-chanter, as it used to be called) was held by the Exeter organists, although it is usually regarded as a clerical office, the deputy of the precentor (or chanter) and his counterpart among the vicars. The Exeter choir also included some supplementary singers called 'secondaries', below the rank of vicar choral (cf. 'poor clerks' at Lincoln Cathedral).

At Exeter the post of master or instructor of the chorister boys was distinct from that of organist, though in practice the two were often combined in one person.

There is unfortunately no trace of any organist of Exeter Cathedral until we reach the name of Thomas Heath (see below). I have omitted detailed documentary references after the appointment of Richard Henman (see below), as all citations may be traced under the appropriate dates in the Chapter Acts.

Thomas Heath 1558–? Heath's appointment for life (subject to good behaviour) as clerk of the chapel of the Blessed Virgin Mary, organist and *informator puerorum* at an annual salary of £10 is recorded in CA1 (f.131[v]) under the date 23 July 1558. As security for payment he was granted the right of distraint on the manor of Clyst Honiton. There is an interesting postscript to a letter dated 29 May 1557 (CA1 f. 117) dealing with the negotiations leading to his appointment:

> Touching Mr Heath of whom ye have written to our trusty brethren Mr Subdean and Mr Holwell, he being such a man as you report, we shall be glad to have him here, and so to conclude with him accordingly, praying you to send him with as much speed as you can, trusting that we shall so continually find him to be such one as you in your letters have gentilly praised him.
>
> To the right worshipful brother Mr John Rixman, Chanter of the Cathedral Church of Exeter now being in London deliver these.

This gives a strong hint that he may have been the same Thomas Heath who had been lay vicar and master of the choristers of Westminster Abbey (q.v.).

There are no surviving details of his tenure at Exeter, though we know from *SWP* that he was alive in 1582.

Matthew Godwin ?–1586 (d. Exeter, 12 Jan. 1586 or 1587). The sole details known to us about Godwin's connection with Exeter Cathedral are derived from the charming memorial to him on the north nave wall. This attests to his having been organist there for some time before his death in January 1586 (OS?), and to his identification with the Matthew Godwin, organist of Canterbury Cathedral from 1584 (q.v.). The memorial, which is in colour, depicts him in academic dress kneeling in prayer before an organ. The inscription is as follows: 'Matthei Godwin adolescentis pii mitis ingeniosii musicae bacchalaurii dignissimi scientissimi Ecclesiarum Cathed.: Cantuar: et Exon.; Archimusici. Æternae memoriae posuit G: M: ER: vixit annos XVII: menses V: Hinc ad coelos migravit XII Januarii, 1586.' ('Erected by G: M: ER: to the everlasting memory of Matthew Godwin, a good, gentle, clever youth, bachelor of music, most worthy and expert chief musician of the Cathedral Churches of Canterbury and Exeter. He lived 17 years and 5 months, and departed hence to heaven on 12 January 1586.')

There is something very puzzling about this record of his age: even allowing that the date of death might have been January 1586 NS (though OS is more probable), he would have been born in August 1568, and therefore only in his sixteenth year when he succeeded to the sole charge at Canterbury on Selbye's death. Were it not for the word 'adolescens', one might suppose that the roman figures XVII represent an error made during some restoration of the memorial. With regard to the degree mentioned in the inscription, it may be noted that a Matthew Godwyn took the Oxford B.Mus. on 24 July 1585 (Wood 1815–20: i. 230), having been twelve years a student. Identity of surname brings to mind the fact that the Dean of Canterbury from 1567 to 1584 was Thomas Godwin, later Bishop of Bath and Wells, and that his son Francis, later Bishop of Hereford, was sub-dean of Exeter from 1587 to 1601. As Matthew Godwin's memorial is somewhat exceptional, one wonders whether some relationship with these cathedral dignitaries may account for it.

Arthur Cock 1589–1602 (d. London, 26 Jan. 1605). It seems reasonable to suppose that this is the Arthur Cock(e) who had been a chorister of Canterbury Cathedral and then organist there in 1587–8 (q.v.).

SWP (f.146^{v}) records Cock's appointment as organist of Exeter Cathedral at £5 a year on 19 April 1589, with reversion to the vacant lay vicar's stall, and also (f.236^{v}) his subscription to the statutes on 21 June 1589. VC/Ac 1 (f.29) notes the receipt of a fee of 13*s.* 4*d.* for his admission as lay vicar, 1588–9. On 25 February 1593 (OS?) he took the Oxford degree of B.Mus. (Wood 1815–20: i. 261), and on 13 June 1597 Elizabeth, daughter of 'Art Cocke', was baptized in Exeter Cathedral (PR). When the Exeter treasurer's accounts begin at Christmas 1602, Cock has vanished (Ac1).

See under the Chapel Royal.

John Lugge 1602–Interregnum. There are no Chapter Acts available to record Lugge's appointment, but he is entered as organist in the earliest surviving treasurer's account, namely, for the quarter ending Christmas 1602, which he signed. He continued to receive the stipend up to 1645, when the accounts break off. Meanwhile, however, a number of deputy organists received payment as follows: Peter Chambers, 1608; Greenwood Randall, 1610 and 1630; Thomas Gale, 1628 (lay vicar) and 1634 (priest-vicar); George Moore, 1635 (lay vicar); William Wake, 1635–42 (lay vicar); John Mayne, 1642 (priest-vicar). Lugge himself became a lay vicar on 24 June 1605 (VC/Ac 1, f. 62^{v}).

The surname was already known at Exeter in connection with one Thomas

Lugge, a lay vicar from 1570 (Chanter 1933), who may have been our subject's father. Among the seven children born at Exeter to John Lugge and his wife Rebecca, one Robert (born 1620) can perhaps be identified with the Robert Lugge who became organist of St John's College, Oxford in 1638.

In 1618 John Lugge ran into trouble on account of his religious tendencies. His brother Peter, a Spanish sympathizer, wrote a letter to him (dated 10 December 1617) which was intercepted, and the Bishop of Exeter, Cotton, was asked to report. He was able to affirm (24 January 1617/18) that Lugge retained none of his Popish sympathies, though his religion (in Cotton's words) was 'as the market goes'. Lugge himself averred that he had had nothing to do with his brother for seven years and had never promised him to become a Romanist. At the same time the vicars of Exeter Cathedral certified that Lugge had received Holy Communion and that he attended church daily with them (*CSPD*, James I, 1611–18: 517).

As we have seen, Thomas Heath was both master of the choristers and organist. What arrangements were made at Exeter for teaching the choristers after his death is obscure; provisionally one may assume that the organist discharged this duty. But in 1608, during Lugge's tenure, Edward Gibbons (who, though a layman, held a priest-vicar's place by dispensation) was appointed 'teacher of the choristers' on 25 June (CA2), and remained so until the Interregnum.

A note in VC/Ac2 (f. 119) testifies that Lugge was at Exeter as late as 1647. However, he is not named by Matthews (1948) as one of the Exeter choir musicians who were awarded grants by the Trustees for the Maintenance of Ministers on 23 October 1655.

William Hopwood 1661–4 (bap. Exeter, 4 Nov. 1641; d. Westminster, 13 July 1683). This is presumably a son of the William Hopwood, priest-vicar of Exeter, to whom the Trustees for the Maintenance of Ministers allotted £5 on 23 October 1655 (Matthews 1948; see also *Devon & Cornwall Notes and Queries*, 16: 187). There is no formal record of his appointment, but Ac2 shows that he received his salary from Midsummer 1661 up to Christmas 1664. He had already been appointed lay vicar on 6 October 1660 (Chanter 1933), 'on the death of John Lugge' (which merely means that Lugge had died at some time during the Interregnum, not in 1660). On 25 October 1664, described as a 'a bass from Exeter', he was admitted a gentleman of the Chapel Royal, and his death is recorded in the Cheque Book (Rimbault 1872). He is buried in the east cloister of Westminster Abbey, where he was a minor canon (Chester 1876).

Hopwood was organist only. Thomas More (lay vicar, 1635; priest-vicar, 1660–71, according to Chanter 1933) was appointed master of the choristers by Chapter minute of 1661, holding the post until 1664 (CA6). He died (*Mon.*) on 1 November 1671, aged 60. He was succeeded by William Wake, already mentioned as deputy organist for Lugge, appointed on 9 July 1664. He had been a lay vicar from 1640, and became a priest-vicar in 1660 (Chanter 1933). Wake resigned as master of the choristers on 4 August 1683; at the time of his death on 6 May 1687, aged 88, he was succentor, having been a member of the Cathedral body for seventy-two years (*Mon.*).

Thomas Mudd 1665. Although he was appointed organist of Exeter Cathedral in March 1664, Mudd drew the official salary as organist for no more than the single quarter from Christmas 1664 to Lady Day 1665; Hopwood, his Exeter predecessor, received his stipend up to Christmas 1664 (Ac2). The Chapter minutes (CA6, 5 March 1663/4) record Mudd's appointment as follows: 'Item, they ordered Mr Mudd to be one of the organists, and to sing in the choir, and to have £20 per annum for his salary [*interlined*: 'quam diu se bene gesserit'] and £4 for his clothes and charges.' This reads as though he had come from a long distance and, being destitute, had to be fitted up with clothing. The expression 'one of the organists' strikes the eye: apparently Mudd worked along with Hopwood until Christmas 1664, for though he was not allotted the official stipend, he began to draw 'extraordinary payments' on 14 March 1663/4. The solitary signature in the Exeter accounts (Lady Day 1665, Ac2) not only discloses the Christian name of the Exeter 'Mr Mudd' as Thomas but, when compared with signatures in the Peterborough accounts, conclusively identifies him with a petty canon of Peterborough Cathedral, 1662–4; and, further, it seems to have been this Peterborough Thomas Mudd who, as we shall see, had a brief and unsatisfactory career as organist of Lincoln Cathedral in 1663.

Before referring to the Peterborough and Lincoln episodes, it should be noted that this minute of March 1663/4 is not the first mention of 'Mr Mudd' at Exeter, for on 6 April 1661 the Dean and Chapter of Exeter 'ordered £3 to be given to Mr Mudd together with the remainder of the money formerly given him to bear his charges in his journey from London' (CA6, f. 141). Although no Christian name is mentioned here, one naturally assumes that this refers to the Thomas Mudd who became organist of Exeter Cathedral three years later.

Meanwhile, he may be traced to Peterborough and Lincoln Cathedrals. At Peterborough (q.v.) he was appointed a petty canon by Chapter minute of 15 August 1662. The quarterly accounts at Peterborough (Ac2) are signed by his own hand from Michaelmas 1662 to Christmas 1663; but for the two quarters ending Lady Day and Midsummer 1664 his name was written on his behalf by someone else, showing that he was not present to receive his pay in person. This fits in with the Exeter minutes and accounts for March 1663/4.

We are assuming that this is the Thomas Mudd, son of John Mudd, who had been organist of Peterborough Cathedral, 1631–2 (q.v.), and who was now seeking renewed employment there after some sojourn in an unexplained capacity at Exeter which he quitted in 1661. Whether or not he procured the necessary holy orders for the post of minor canon, in 1663 he was playing fast and loose with the Peterborough authorities by seeking appointments at Lincoln and Exeter.

He was paid as organist of Lincoln Cathedral only for the half-year ending 1 May 1663, and conducted himself disgracefully there (q.v.). His subsequent tenure at Exeter was even shorter, and a successor was appointed in March 1665. Nevertheless, that is not the end of him there, for on 26 August 1665 the Chapter voted him £20 for some unspecified purpose (CA6, p. 566), after which he at last vanished from the Exeter records.

This means that he could have been the Thomas Mudd who was appointed master of the choristers at York in 1666 and who died at Durham in 1667 (see

p. 317). If these identifications are accepted, then his unsatisfactory career may be summarized thus: son of John Mudd, organist of Peterborough Cathedral; successively chorister (1619) and organist (1631–2) there; next heard of in Exeter in 1661; returned to Peterborough in 1662 with a minor canon's appointment, nominally held until 1664 but meanwhile organist of Lincoln Cathedral during the first part of 1663, and then found at Exeter Cathedral, 1664–5; finally made a brief appearance for one month at York in 1666, and died at Durham in 1667, apparently without a regular appointment.

Theodore Colby 1665–74. Colby had earlier been organist of Magdalen College, Oxford, 1660–4 (q.v.).

His appointment as organist of Exeter Cathedral at a salary of £50 is dated 25 March 1665 (CA6). A few days later (1 April) he was voted £5 'towards his charges in coming from London and riding up'. His early work clearly met with approval: on 23 December 1665 it was resolved that his rent should in future be paid by the Chapter; on 26 January 1666/7 he was granted an annuity of £4; and on 2 March 1666/7 he was confirmed in his appointment for life. It was part of the agreement that he was to teach the organ to 'such persons of the choir' as the Chapter should direct and that he should accept a place as vicar choral. His total emoluments amounted to the considerable sum of £58, and on 6 April 1667 this was increased by a further £2. On 20 September 1667 he was duly admitted a lay vicar choral.

However, Colby's career came to an unsatisfactory end. First, in 1668 the Chapter advanced him two substantial sums (£47. 16*s*. 6*d*. and £30) 'toward the supplying of his present necessities'. Then, on 8 August 1674, 'upon Mr Colbie's absenting himself, they pronounced the organist's place of this church to be void', but they considerately agreed to vote £30 for the benefit of his children (CA7).

Henry Hall (I) 1674–9. Hall was appointed organist of Exeter Cathedral by Chapter minute dated 8 August 1674 (CA7); he was also a lay vicar choral. He left shortly before 14 June 1679, having apparently been absent for some time, leaving behind him a debt to one Charles Ford, which the Chapter discharged (CA8).

See under Hereford Cathedral.

Peter Pasmore 1679–94 (d. Exeter, Apr. 1713). Some details of Pasmore's career are of exceptional interest. As a chorister in Exeter Cathedral he formed the ambition to go to London to study under *John Blow. Perhaps he was influenced in this by Hall, who was himself an admiring pupil of Blow. However this may be, a long Chapter minute dated 20 December 1676 recounts that

> Whereas Peter Pasmore one of the choristers of this Cathedral Church desires to improve his skill on the organ for the service of the quire. In order whereunto he hath agreed with Mr [*blank*] Blowe the king's organist to teach and fully instruct him in that art and is to pay him for it twenty pounds, to wit, ten pounds in hand and th'other ten pounds when he is fully taught. We do order and decree that the said Peter Passmore shall have leave and liberty to travel to London to that purpose and to be absent here for one year and that he

shall have given him from the Dean and Chapter the sum of forty shillings, to defray the expenses of his journey to London, and the sum of ten pounds to pay the said Mr Blow for the first payment aforementioned. And that he shall enjoy the profits of his place in this quire notwithstanding his absence during that time to learn as aforesaid, and that no advantage to be taken of his absence to that purpose for that time. But that for his support and maintenance during that time his place in this quire shall be made worth twelve pounds to be paid him for that one year. He the said Peter Passmore, giving bond to the Chapter to imploy the money aforesaid to the uses aforesaid and to return again at the end of the said time or within some further time to be hereafter (if it be forethought fit) allowed him, to and for the service of this quire.

On 28 December 1678 Pasmore was given £2 to pay for his journey home, and on 1 February 1678/9 £5 was lent for the same purpose. On 15 February he was admitted vicar choral in Hall's place; on 29 March 1679 he was allowed the £10 needed to pay Blow; and, finally, on 14 June he was admitted organist 'upon Mr Henry Hall's departing his place of organist'. At the same time, John White was allowed £3 'for his attendance and playing the organ for some time in Mr Hall's first absence'.

Regular provision was later made for a deputy organist to play 'in the organist's absence and upon special occasions requiring the organist's presence in his stall [as vicar choral]', and John White was appointed at a salary of £20 on 23 October 1680. Pasmore seems to have kept in touch with London, for it was resolved on 14 February 1684/5 that 'upon information of Mr Pasmore the organist's being sick in London they [the Chapter] dispensed with his longer stay here till he recover his health to return'.

Two Chapter minutes of 26 July and 2 August 1690 touch on the danger of French invasion in those days: 'Mr Pasmore, organist, being desired by the Deputy Lieutenant to take a commission and go towards the enemy and for a party of the posse, Ordered leave be given him so to do and to have [?] supply; and: 'They allowed Mr Pasmore, organist, five guineas towards his expenses in his commission . . . he having taken on him a commission of Cornet.'

In 1693 he took over the tuning of the organ; but not long after, on 4 August 1694, he was appointed priest-vicar choral and therefore had to seek holy orders and relinguish the post of organist. The following year he added to his duties those of clerk and overseer of the works. (These details about Pasmore may all be traced in CA6, 7, 8.) He was buried on 30 April 1713 (PR).

Richard Henman 1694–1741. Henman was admitted organist and lay vicar choral on 22 September 1694 (CA9). He may have been either the Richard Henman who was a chorister in the Chapel Royal until 1692 (Ashbee 1986–9: ii. 45), or the Richard Hinman who was admitted chorister of Rochester Cathedral under Henstridge in December 1680 (Rochester CA2). In either case, he was no credit to his teacher, and one wonders why he should have been appointed. Numerous other men mentioned in this book have shown instability of character, but none of them, so far as we know, have been incompetent musicians—indeed, sometimes quite the reverse. But on 19 July 1695 the Exeter Chapter admonished Henman 'To make himself capable and to qualify himself for his continuance in that place (complaint being made by the choir of his unfitness)'; and again on 10 August

1695: 'upon complaint of Mr Henman the organist's inabilities they admonished him to qualify himself for the performance of that office by Easter next'. His entire career at Exeter was disastrous, absence, incompetence, and bad language towards Hicks (the master of the choristers) being alleged against him (CA10–11, *passim*, Feb. 1697/8–Oct. 1714).

In 1716, as shown by a separate document (D&C Exeter, 5370/22), Henman, with an eye to his own profit, initiated a petition pointing out that there were only eight lay vicars (including himself) to occupy ten places, and going on to claim for himself a share in the emoluments of the two vacancies. His petition was refused, the seven other vicars saying that they had to do the work of nine, while Henman enjoyed his vicarship in addition to his stipend as organist. The interest of this incident lies in its implication that though the organist counted as one of the lay vicars, he did not by then share in their turns of duty as such.

On 8 February 1734/5 the Chapter ordered Henman's pay as organist to be stopped till further order; when it was restored on 24 May, £2. 2*s*. was deducted and given to John Sanders who had been playing in his place. On 11 October a permanent quarterly deduction of £2. 2*s*. was authorized so that Sanders should play when he was needed (this was later raised to £3. 3*s*. in April 1736 and £4 in May 1739). On 10 June 1738 Henman's pay was stopped entirely until he attended in person.

The arrangement with Sanders came to an end on 4 January 1740/1, when the Chapter resolved that anyone approved to supply the organist's place should have the profits of a lay vicar's stall and 'also the allowance now paid to Sanders out of Henman's pay'. John Silvester now became deputy organist. Finally, patience with Henman was at last exhausted. On 27 June 1741 it was

> decreed that Mr Richard Henman (for his long absence and disorderly life) be removed from the place of organist . . . but they [the Dean and Chapter] ordered that he shall still have the same sum out of the organist's salary that he now receives [this proved to be the lay vicar's stipend] provided he continue to pay annually such debts as he hath charged his said place with the payment of.

(For all these details, see CA11–14, *passim*.)

John Silvester 1741–53 (d. 1753). Silvester was appointed organist on 27 June 1741, the date of Henman's dismissal; he was allotted the balance of the fee and became a vicar choral. From June 1741 he also received £6 a year for helping Hicks, the master of the choristers, but this was withdrawn on 23 February 1742/3 (when he began to have the full salary as organist) because Hicks had received 'little or no assistance from him'. Before long he was forced to abscond for debt, and on 8 December 1744 the Chapter 'allowed him to be absent from the service of the church till Lady Day next to give him an opportunity in the meantime to make his peace with his creditors'. Arrangements were made for him to have a deputy, whose stipend was to be deducted from his own.

In 1745–6 Silvester was summoned no fewer than five times to attend the Chapter under pain of suspension, and on 3 September 1748 he was made to wait on the bishop to beg pardon for neglect of duty. The same minute discloses that Silvester had recently been in prison (for debt, as it would seem).

Richard Langdon 1753–77 (b. Exeter; d. Exeter, 8 Sept. 1803, aged 74). Langdon was a relative (almost certainly a grandson) of Tobias Langdon, vicar choral of Exeter Cathedral, 1683–1712; he was evidently the Richard Langdon 'of the Close' who married Susanna Evans on 28 August 1770 (PR). (For a point of identification dependent on his wife's Christian name, see under Armagh Cathedral.)

He was a chorister of the Cathedral, and in 1744 the Chapter arranged for him to have organ lessons from Hicks, the master of the choristers. On 16 and 23 June 1753 he was admitted as lay vicar and organist of the Cathedral, posts specifically stated to be vacant on the death of Silvester. He was given leave on 21 October 1758 'to take Eastcott the chorister an apprentice for seven years'. He was rebuked on 3 March 1759 'for his frequent absence from the church and for not obeying the sub-chanter's orders'. However, not long afterwards (7 April 1759) he was granted leave of absence for five weeks; and on 8 May 1762 he was appointed *informator puerorum* and (though a layman) sub-chanter (succentor) in place of John Hicks, who resigned because of age. Langdon had by then taken the Oxford degree of B.Mus. (1761). On 8 January 1774 it was ordered 'That the organist shall, in future, in virtue of his office and at his own expense, prick the organ parts of such anthems, services, and other church music as he shall introduce'. This may have been intended not simply as an economy measure but also as a curb on the amount of new music used, for the occasion was also taken to revive an older provision, namely, that 'no church music shall henceforth be pricked by the organist at the expense of the Chapter without a particular order from them for that purpose'. However, when Langdon's *Divine Harmony . . . with several other Pieces of Sacred Music composed by the most eminent Masters* was published in 1774, the Chapter agreed (29 October) to take six copies of it. Langdon himself was a subscriber to Boyce's *Cathedral Music* in 1760, and to Burney's *History of Music* in 1776.

After twenty-four years, he resigned all his Exeter offices, for undisclosed reasons, in October 1777. It is usually assumed that he is the Langdon who, on 25 November 1777, was formally admitted organist of Ely Cathedral (q.v.) and who was similarly admitted organist of Bristol Cathedral on 3 December 1777 (q.v.). He may safely be taken to be the Richard Langdon who was organist of Armagh Cathedral, 1782–94 (q.v.), and it appears that he left Armagh for reasons of health. There was evidently some question of his becoming organist of Peterborough Cathedral in 1784 (q.v.), but it seems that nothing came of this.

Langdon died in 1803, and the memorial to him in St Martin's Church, Exeter reads as follows: 'Richard Langdon Batchellor of Music died the 8th of Septr. 1803. aged 74.'

William Jackson 1777–1803 (b. Exeter, 29 May 1730; d. Exeter, 5 July 1803). Jackson's father was a grocer. The boy was initially taught music by Silvester, and then he went to London at the age of 18 to study under *John Travers. He settled in Exeter as a private teacher, and in October 1777 he became organist and master of the choristers of the Cathedral, holding a lay vicar's stall and also the office of sub-chanter. According to his own diary, he found the choir in a low state of proficiency.

Both before and after his Cathedral appointment, he enjoyed considerable success as a composer of music for a number of London stage productions. At one time doubt was cast on the authenticity of the famous Service in F which bears his name—a doubt arising, seemingly, because Paddon (see below), who published a volume of Jackson's church music, did not include it. But Jackson's diary leaves no room for doubt on the subject (see extracts in the magazine entitled the *Leisure Hour*, 1882).

Jackson had considerable interests outside music. In 1792 he founded a literary society in Exeter, and he was an amateur landscape-painter. He was friendly with Sheridan, Gainsborough, and Reynolds. His literary publications include *Thirty Letters of Various Subjects* (1782; 3rd edn., 1795), *Observations on the Present State of Music in London* (1791), and *Four Ages, together with letters on various subjects* (1798). He was a subscriber to Burney's *History of Music* in 1776, and he reviewed this in two articles for the *Critical Review* (Lonsdale, 1965: 344–6). There is a glimpse of him in Fanny Burney's diary, under the date 28 December 1782:

> Our dinner party consisted merely of Mr West . . . Mr Jackson of Exeter, and Miss Reynolds . . . Mr Jackson . . . is very handsome, and seems possessed of much of that ardent genius which distinguished Mr [Arthur] Young; for his expressions, at times, are extremely violent, while at other times he droops, and is so absent that he seems to forget not only all about him, but himself. (*The Diary and Letters of Madame d'Arblay*, ed. Charlotte Barrett (1842–6).)

Burney himself, in *Rees's Encyclopaedia*, said of Jackson that his qualities of 'genius, judgment, taste' were 'strongly alloyed by a mixture of selfishness, arrogance and an insatiable rage for superiority'. Burney also contributes the gem that Jackson 'latterly dined on milk-porridge and drank water. The experiment proved fatal.'

He is buried in St Stephen's Church, Exeter, where there is this memorial inscription to him in the vestry:

> William Iackson born in this city XXIX May MDCCXXX died V July MDCCCIII. In the science of music an eminent professor, whose genius united elegant expression, pure and original melody, with peculiar delicacy of harmonic combination. In painting, in literature, in every liberal study that enlightens the intellect, or expands the heart, his attainments were rare and distinguished: a writer, novel and acute in observation, a correct and discriminating critic, endeared to his select associates by a conversation and demeanour of impressive and fascinating simplicity.

Mackerness 1956–8.

James Paddon 1803–35 (d. Exeter, 14 June 1835, aged 67). According to *BMB*, Paddon was educated in the Cathedral choir, and became a lay vicar choral in 1793. His formal appointment as organist and *informator choristarum* is recorded on 30 July 1803, and that as sub-chanter on 12 April 1804. On 26 November 1808 he was granted permission 'To use the organ in the church for the instruction of his apprentices on Tuesdays and Saturdays from nine to ten and from the end of morning service to one in the afternoon.' Recording his death in June 1835, a minute of August 1835 discloses that Paddon received 100 guineas premium for an apprentice, and that his emoluments as organist, sub-chanter, and *informator* amounted to 100 guineas a year, and as lay vicar to 'about' £70. He is buried in the nave of the Cathedral.

Samuel Sebastian Wesley 1835–41. Wesley was formally elected at a Chapter meeting on 15 August 1835. He was organist, sub-chanter, *informator*, and lay vicar.

On 16 May 1840 the Chapter passed what, on the face of it, seems an unreasonable resolution, namely, that 'Dr Wesley be informed that he is not to give lessons on the organ either to his apprentices or to any other person, the order not being meant to extend to a prohibition to the apprentices to practise any service for use in the church.' In June 1840 he was reminded that his private engagements should not interfere with his attendance at the weekly Saturday Chapter meetings. A year later (June 1841) it was reported that Wesley had been absent for more than a week without notice, leaving a young, inexperienced pupil to play in his stead. Finally, following a dispute about the rebuilding of the organ, he was asked to resign, which he did on 20 November 1841.

See under Gloucester Cathedral.

Alfred Angel 1842–76 (b. *c.*1816; d. Exeter, 24 May 1876). When seeking a successor to Wesley, the Chapter called in *Stephen Elvey of New College, Oxford to adjudicate; his choice fell on Alfred Angel, 'assistant organist at Wells'. Like his four predecessors at Exeter, Angel was master of the choristers, but, unlike them, he was not appointed succentor. At the time of Angel's appointment (April 1842), the Chapter recorded its wish to break the long association between the posts of organist and lay vicar; nevertheless, he was immediately made a 'secondary' and, in 1864, a lay vicar.

Angel's terms of appointment stressed his share in the training of the chorister boys in morals, manners, and religious devotion. It was implied that access to the organ for purposes of teaching apprentices was to be subject to the same limitation as had been imposed on Wesley. The full choir was to be practised even in music already known, and the introduction of new music required Chapter approval. It was ordered that the music for the week and allotment of solos should be decided at Saturday Chapter meetings.

Daniel Joseph Wood 1876–1919 (b. Brompton, Kent, 25 Aug. 1849; d. Exeter, 27 Aug. 1919). Wood was a chorister of Rochester Cathedral, where he later became assistant organist. He then held a series of parish-church appointments (New Brompton, 1864; Cranbrook, 1866; Lee, 1868), leading to that at Boston, Lincolnshire in 1869. While there he took the Oxford degree of B.Mus. in 1874, and also the FRCO diploma (1873). In September 1875 he was appointed organist of Chichester Cathedral (q.v.), but less than a year later he moved to Exeter as organist and master of the choristers (but not lay vicar), his appointment being minuted on 22 July 1876. In 1896 he received the Lambeth degree of Mus.D.

West 1921; *MT*, 60 (1919), 555.

Sir Ernest Bullock, CVO, 1919–27

See under Westminster Abbey.

Sir Thomas (Henry Wait) Armstrong 1928–33.

See under Christ Church Cathedral, Oxford.

Alfred William Wilcock 1933–52.

See under Derby Cathedral.

§Reginald Moore 1953–7 (b. Bramley, near Leeds, 19 May 1910; d. Exeter, 25 May 1968). Moore was a chorister in Leeds Parish Church, and subsequently a pupil of *E. C. Bairstow at York. He took the FRCO diploma in 1933, and the Durham degree of B.Mus. in 1952.

His first appointment was as assistant organist of Salisbury Cathedral, 1933–47. From 1947 to 1952 he was on the music staff of Winchester College. While at Exeter Cathedral he was also part-time director of music at the University College of the South West of England (afterwards the University of Exeter). From 1965 he was lecturer in music at the University of Exeter and from 1967 until his death he was acting head of the department of music.

§Lionel (Frederick) Dakers, CBE, 1957–72 (b. Rochester, Kent, 24 Feb. 1924). Dakers was educated at Rochester Cathedral School, and later studied under *E. C. Bairstow at York Minster before proceeding to the Royal Academy of Music. He took the Durham degree of B.Mus. in 1951, and holds the diplomas of FRCO (1945) and ADCM (1952).

His first organ post was at All Saints' Church, Frindsbury, Rochester, 1939–42. After the war he was successively organist of Cairo Cathedral (1945–7), Finchley Parish Church (1948–50), and assistant organist of St George's Chapel, Windsor (1950–4), combining the last post with a position on the music staff of Eton College (1952–4).

He was organist of Ripon Cathedral from 1954 to 1957, when he moved to Exeter Cathedral. While at Exeter he was also lecturer in music at St Luke's College of Education, 1958–70. He left Exeter in January 1973 to succeed *G. H. Knight as director of the Royal School of Church Music. He received the Lambeth degree of Mus.D. in 1979, was appointed CBE in 1983, and retired in 1989.

§Lucian Nethsingha, organist from 1973 (b. Colombo, Ceylon, 3 May 1936). Nethsingha received his early education at St Thomas's College, Colombo before studying at the Royal College of Music, London under Ralph Downes. From 1956 to 1959 he was at King's College, Cambridge, where he read music and took the degree of BA (later MA). He acquired the FRCO diploma in 1958. Immediately on leaving Cambridge he became organist of St Michael's College, Tenbury, which he left at the end of 1972 on his appointment to Exeter.

GLOUCESTER

The Cathedral Church of St Peter and the Holy and Indivisible Trinity

Main sources in this section (1962) (with Gloucester County Record Office references where appropriate):

Chapter Acts

CA1 1616–87.
CA2 1688–1739.
CA3 1740–74.
CA4 1775–1807.
CA5 1807–38.
CA6 1839–62.
CA7 1863–92.
CA8 1893–1915.

Treasurer's Accounts

1609–34 (D936 A1/1).
*c.*1612–14 (D936 A/22).
1634–64 (D936 A1/2).
1664–84 (D936 A1/3).

Miscellaneous

PR Registers of baptisms, marriages, and burials in the Cathedral.
Episcopal and metropolitical visitations of the Cathedral (transcripts made by F. S. Hockaday and others).
Parliamentary Survey, 1649 (D936 E/1).

On his establishment of the new diocese of Gloucester, Henry VIII founded Gloucester Cathedral in August 1541, granting it the buildings of the surrendered Benedictine abbey of St Peter. Its musical establishment included a master of the choristers and eight choristers. Following the usual form of the draft statutes of Henry's cathedrals, the master of the choristers performed the duty of organist (see p. xix).

We have no knowledge of the masters of the choristers during the first twenty years of the Cathedral's history. At the episcopal visitation of 1542 no reference was made to this office; but as a master of the choristers was not mentioned in answer to the enquiry about vacant posts, it may be assumed that one had been appointed.

Robert Lichfield *c.*1562–83 (d. Gloucester, 6 Jan. 1583). Robert Lichfield, master of the choristers, was mentioned in the metropolitical visitations of 1576 and 1580. He is buried in the south transept of the Cathedral, where the inscription on his tomb (not recorded by Bigland 1792), now greatly mutilated, reads: 'Here lyeth under this marbel stone, Robart Liechfi[eld,] Organist and Maister of the Choresters of this Cathedral Church 20 years. He dyed the 6 of January 1582.'

Lichfield's will, which he signed 'Rob. Lychfyllde', is now in Gloucester City Library. It records his wish 'to be buried in the Cathedral Church of Gloucester amongst my old acquaintances and friends of the choir', to whom he left 6*s*. 8*d*. He bequeathed his musical instruments and books to his widow and children, and also land in the parish of Sparkbrook. The document is damaged where the day of the month is written, but it can only be iij January, 25 Elizabeth, i.e., 1582/3, which confirms the date on the tombstone as OS.

Elias Smith ←1605–20 (d. Gloucester, 1620). One Elias Smith is mentioned as a lay clerk in the episcopal visitation of 1594; in the visitation of 1605 he is named as master of the choristers. The record of his successor's appointment indicates that he died in office.

Philip Hosier 1620–38 (d. Gloucester, 1638). The earliest extant Chapter Act Book (CA1), which begins with Laud's reign as dean on 25 January 1616, records, over Laud's signature, that Hosier was admitted 'in locum organistae et choristarum instructoris . . . in loco Elias Smith mortui' on 19 October 1620 (f. 15v). He was ordained deacon on 23 September 1621 (Diocesan Records, General Act Book, vol. 142a). On 11 August 1628 (CA1, f. 35v) he was ordered 'one day in every week to catechise and teach the children in the principles of the Christian religion'.

Berkeley Wrench 1638–9. The treasurer's accounts for the year 1638–9 give a hint, at this early date, of competition for the vacancy on Hosier's death in the shape of payments to someone from Coventry and a man named Wall. Wrench, who was admitted on 29 November 1638 (CA1, f. 56), Hosier now being 'defunct', is presumably the same Berkeley Wrench, chorister, who on 23 June 1629 'freely and voluntarily surrendered his place of a chorister'. Numerous members of the Wrench family held Cathedral offices, both high and low. Thus, when Elias Wrench was prebendary and treasurer in 1629, one of his sons, Simeon, surrendered the post of porter, and another, Berkeley, gave up that of sexton—both on the same day that chorister Berkeley Wrench left the choir. It is not impossible that these positions were being treated as sinecures.

John Okeover (or Oker) 1640–?1661. On 14 November 1639 (CA1, f. 57v) the Dean and Chapter resolved 'that upon the admitting of an able and sufficient organist, the place being now void', the stipend should be increased by £6. 13*s*. 4*d*. per annum. This suggests that they were looking for, or perhaps already had their eye on, a candidate of proved experience, and 'Johannes Okeover' was admitted on 25 April 1640 (CA1, f. 59). (For discussion of the alternative form of the surname, see under Wells Cathedral.)

The Gloucester Cathedral Chapter Acts break off after 1641 until the Restoration. However, in 1642 a marriage licence was issued to John Okeover and Mary Mills, both of Gloucester (Diocesan Record Office). It is also apparent that Okeover served in the Civil War on the parliamentary side (unusual, one thinks, for a cathedral officer), and then returned to Gloucester. The parliamentary survey of the Close noted in November 1649 that the 'grand old and ruinous building . . . commonly called the Firmery and the chambers over the same' were 'now in the possession of John Oker, late organist of the said Cathedral Church'. On 28 March 1651 the Trustees for the Maintenance of Ministers (Llp. MS 978, f. 221) noted that 'John Oker, organist and master of the choristers of the late Cathedral Church of Gloucester', had drawn their attention to certain uncollected arrears of tithe from an impropriate rectory, and that as 'the said Mr Oker is very well affected to the Parliament, having been in arms for them, and that he is in a necessitous condition, it is therefore ordered that he shall have one year's rent'. Perhaps he is the 'John Oker of the City of Gloucester' who on 21 August 1654 was admitted a freeman of the city without fee (Gloucester Roll of Freemen). In 1655 he applied to become a bedesman of the suspended Cathedral, and was granted such a place in November 1656 (Llp, MSS 967, p. 163; 1021, f. 69), the month in which John, son of John Oker and his wife Mary, was baptized in the church of St Mary-de-Lode, Gloucester. Further, in March 1657/8 he received 25*s*. from the Trustees for the Maintenance of Ministers as one of the 'poor officers' of the Cathedral (Matthews 1948).

It may well be that, as with Randolph Jewett at St Patrick's Cathedral, Dublin (q.v.), the Cathedral authorities expected Okeover to resume his post after the Restoration. But for some years thereafter there was an unsettled period in relation to the master of the choristers/organist. In the accounts for 1660–1 the name has been heavily scored through, though the Christian name 'Johi' can be made out. In 1661–2 that of Robert Webb is written, but this was obviously inserted at some later time. Yet Okeover was still about, for those same accounts contain details of payments made to him through one of the canons; for example, 'to Dr Washbourne in part for Oker's pricking some anthems to the organ, £1'. In 1662–3 once more no name occurs against 'magister choristarum', and '£0' is significantly entered in the money column.

However, for each of those three years Richard Elliott, one of the lay clerks, was paid for teaching the boys, but without formal status. The visitation of 1661 contains no reference to an organist or master of the choristers; but that of 1663 says that there is 'at present no organist', though 'there was lately an organist . . . who is lately gone away', and 'one of the singingmen [Richard Elliott] teacheth the choristers for which he receiveth pay', having done this 'ever since His Majesty's most happy restoration . . . being two whole years'.

On the strength of the obliterated Christian name in the 1660–1 accounts, the observations in the visitation of 1663, the payment to Okeover for writing out organ-parts, and the oddly emphatic £0 for the accounting year 1662–3, I tentatively suggest that Okeover may still have been thought of as master of the choristers/organist up to Michaelmas 1662, though it was necessary to pay Elliott for doing some of the work.

The puzzling question of whether he is the John Okeover of Wells Cathedral, is discussed on p. 286.

1662–3 was evidently a year of makeshift, the accounts disclosing the following payments:

To the organist from Mr Dean, 10*s*. and 10*s*. more from the Church.
To the organist, 5*s*. [and three similar payments].
To the organist, 10*s*.
Given to the Worcester organists and choirmen, £1.

But at length there seemed prospect of a stable appointment. In the accounts for 1663–4 we read of the payment of £4. 10*s*. to **Robert Webb**, 'pbat: organist:' (probationer organist). But in that very same year there are also the following disbursements:

Sent to the organist being sick, 2*s*. 6*d*.
More to the organist, 5*s*.
More to the organist, 5*s*.
Paid towards the burial of the organist, 10*s*.
For a shroud for the organist, 4*s*.
Paid more towards his funeral for ringing, beer and cakes, 11*s*. 6*d*.
Paid for transporting the organist child to her mother per the Crow [stage coach] and a man with her to take care of her, 15*s*.
Given to Cowles his wife for keeping the organist's child four weeks, 5*s*.

As late as 15 May 1672 the Cathedral was still honourably discharging Webb's liabilities: 'Paid Mr Marston per order of Chapter for Robert Webb, late organist to the Church £3. 10*s*.' So Webb died before he could be confirmed in office.

Thomas Lowe 1665–6. Lowe was paid as organist for the latter part of the accounting year 1664–5, also taking over the teaching of the choristers from Elliott; he was formally admitted on 8 August 1665 (CA1). The accounts show that in June 1665 he had been paid £10 'for and towards his charge in removing from Salisbury', which suggests a connection with *Edward Lowe, who was brought up at Salisbury.

Lowe's tenure began full of expectation. The episcopal visitation of December 1665 refers to him thus: 'We have an organist competently skilful to perform his duty (required by statute) and we hope our future experience of him may inable us to give him our commendation of his diligence in teaching the choristers.' He busied himself copying music, for which he was paid £5 in December 1665. His name appears again when the December 1665 visitation was continued in February 1665/6, but on 9 April there is the entry in the accounts: 'Paid Mistress Lowe for her transport to London, £2. 10*s*', from which we conclude that Lowe had died. It seems that he had asked for an advance of salary, for when the treasurer came to write up his accounts, he entered under January 1665/6: 'Paid Mr Lowe the organist to have been deducted out of his salary £10.' It is pleasing to note that the Cathedral bore this charge.

Daniel Henstridge 1666–73. Henstridge's appointment was minuted on 6 December 1666 (CA1), but the accounts for 1664–84 show a payment to him in the year 1665–6 which seems to cover three quarters of the accounting year.

See under Rochester Cathedral.

Charles Wren 1674–8. Wren's appointment was minuted on 19 January 1673/4 (CA1).

See under Rochester Cathedral.

Daniel Roseingrave 1679–81. There is no formal record of Roseingrave's appointment, and, indeed, when Stephen Jefferies was appointed in May 1682, the Chapter clerk took no cognizance of him (see below). Nevertheless, not only is Roseingrave named in the accounts as master of the choristers for the three complete accounting years 1678–9, 1679–80, and 1680–1, but he is included as organist in the list of members of the Cathedral body cited at the visitation of 1679. As early as 10 April 1679 (CA1) he was admonished for beating and wounding one of the choir.

See under St Patrick's Cathedral, Dublin.

Stephen Jefferies (I) 1681–1712 (d. Gloucester, 25 Jan. 1713, aged 54). It is possible that this may be the 'Jeferies' who was organist of Winchester College, 1678–80 (q.v.). In a posthumous note, Hawkins (1853: ii. 769) says that Jeffries (*sic*) was a pupil of Michael Wise and only 20 years of age on his appointment to Gloucester, which Hawkins puts at 1680. The accounts, however, clearly show Roseingrave's payments for the accounting year 1680–1, and Jefferies received his first stipend in 1681–2. His appointment was formally minuted on 17 May 1682 (CA1) as organist and master of the choristers 'in loco Caroli Wren mortui', presumably because Roseingrave's appointment had never been formally recorded. The baptisms of Jefferies' son and several daughters are entered in PR. The son, John, died in 1693 when only 1 year old. (For a reference to an apparently older son, Stephen Jefferies (II), see under Bristol Cathedral.)

Jefferies himself was an unruly character. In January 1683/4 (CA1) he was admonished for neglect and unreasonable absence. Then, in February 1688 (CA1, 8 February 1687/8), an astonishing incident occurred:

> Mr Subdean pronounced against Mr Stephen Jefferies, organist of this Church . . . for that he . . . did upon Thursday last in the morning (being the Thanksgiving day) immediately after the sermon ended and the Blessing given, play over upon the organ a common ballad in the hearing of 1500 or 2000 people . . . And further . . . the said Stephen Jefferies . . . did after Evening Prayer, as soon as the last Amen was ended, in the presence and hearing of all the congregation, fall upon the same strain, and on the organ played over the same common ballad again; insomuch that the young gentlewomen invited one another to dance, and the strangers cried it were better that the organs were pulled down than that they should be so used, and all sorts declared that the Dean and Chapter could never remove the scandal if they did not immediately turn away so insolent and profane a person out of the Church.

Nevertheless, forbearance was exercised, and he continued in his place. He was further admonished for neglect in teaching the choristers on 5 December 1699 (CA2). Hawkins (1853: ii. 770) recounts a ridiculous anecdote about him:

> The choirmen of Gloucester relate that, to cure him of a habit of staying late at the tavern, his wife drest up a fellow in a winding-sheet, with directions to meet him with a lanthorn and candle in the cloisters through which he was to pass on his way home; but that, on attempting to terrify him, Jeffries [*sic*] expressed his wonder only by saying, I thought all you spirits had been abed by this time.

He was buried in the cloisters on 28 January 1712/13 (PR); the memorial inscription, giving the date of death (25 January), is noted in Bigland (1792). For some considerable time before his death he had been unable to discharge his duties (see below under Hine), but the Dean and Chapter generously allowed him to keep his house and half his salary.

William Hine 1713–30 (acting organist from 1707) (b. Brightwell Oxon.; d. Gloucester, 28 Aug. 1730, aged 43). *Philip Hayes, whose father was a pupil of Hine, states in a note (Lbl, Add. MS 33235, f. 2) that Hine was born at Brightwell, Oxfordshire, and that he was a pupil of both 'Mr Hite [*Thomas Hecht] organist of Magdalen College, Oxford, and of *Jeremiah Clarke'. He appears to have been the William Hine who was appointed clerk of Magdalen College, Oxford in 1705, and whom Bloxam (1853–7) identified with the 'Hyne' or 'Hind' who became a chorister there in 1694. In 1705, according to Bloxam, this Hine was removed from his clerkship 'propter fornicationem, manifestam et scandalosam'. If this is our Hine, then he later lived this down satisfactorily.

The Gloucester Cathedral accounts disclose payments to him from October 1707 for playing the organ; indeed, the first of these entries speaks of 'Mr Hynde the new organist', though in fact Jefferies was still in office. Then, on 2 June 1710 (as recorded in CA2), the Dean and Chapter, 'being sensible of the good service and constant attendance of Mr Hines in the place of organist', promised him the succession to the post when it should become vacant. Meanwhile 'Stephen Jeffries now disabled to perform that office' was allowed to keep his house and have £25 a year. The same sum was to be paid to Hine so that 'he who performs the whole duty' should not have less 'than he who executes no part of the office'.

Hine was among the subscribers to Croft's *Musica Sacra* in 1724. Arnold (*Cathedral Music*, iii. 226) tells us that Hine was an accomplished singer who performed 'elegantly in a feigned Voice, and was esteemed an excellent Teacher of singing, &c.'. Philip Hayes (Lbl, Add. MS 33235) says that Hine was

> an excellent organ player, as I have frequently heard my father and others who knew him say, but being fixed in a place not very prone to encourage musical abilities, found himself neglected, which made him the less solicitous about improving those talents that nature had given him, and thereby became a lost man to the musical world, who otherwise would have done the greatest honour to it.

Arnold transmits the same sentiment in Gibbonian phrase: 'Mr Hine's talents shone conspicuously even in a place not prone at that time to encourage music.'

On 21 September 1710, not long after he had settled in Gloucester. Hine married Alice Rudhall, daughter of the bell-founder Abraham Rudhall, in the Cathedral. Hine's memorial, on the east wall of the cloister, is inscribed thus:

> M.S. Gulielmi Hine hujusce Ecclesiae Cathedralis Organistae et Choristarum Magistri Qui morum candore et eximia in arte coelesti peritia omnium amorem et admirationem venerandi autem Decani et Capituli gratium (voluntario Stipendii incremento testatum) meritissimo affectus est. Morte praematura ereptus Obiit Aug. 28vo Anno: Christi 1730, Aetatis 43.

An unidentified portrait, presented to the Music School collection at Oxford by Philip Hayes, has been supposed to be a likeness of Hine (Poole 1912–25: i. 159; Mrs Poole misnames him 'John Hine').

Barnabas Gunn 1730–9 (d. Birmingham, 6 Feb. 1753). When St Philip's Church, Birmingham (now Birmingham Cathedral) was completed in 1714, Gunn was appointed its first organist in 1715 (I am grateful to Mr Roy Massey for this information). He was formally admitted as organist of Gloucester Cathedral on 14 December 1730 (CA2).

After leaving Gloucester in 1739, Gunn returned to Birmingham. At his death, *Aris's Birmingham Gazette* for 12 February 1753 described him as 'Post Master of this Town, and Organist to both Churches' (i.e., St Philip's and St Martin's); and on the title-page of his *Six Solos for the Violin and Violoncello* (1745) he is designated as 'Organist of St Philip's and St Martin's, Birmingham'. He is buried at St Philip's.

In 1751 a satirical pamphlet appeared entitled *The Art of Composing Music by a Method entirely New*, written in such a way as to suggest that Gunn was the author, and describing him as 'Organist, P—t M—r, and Box-maker at B—m'. The pamphlet advocated the composition of music by squirting ink-marks on ruled paper by means of a supposititious machine, the 'Spruzzarino'—a sarcastic reference to what *William Hayes, the true author, thought of Gunn's music. Gunn rose to the occasion with good humour in 1752 by publishing (likewise anonymously) his *Twelve English Songs . . . Set to Musick by the New-invented Method of Composing with the Spruzzarino*. Hayes's pamphlet makes clear that the Barnabas Gunn who was organist of Chelsea Hospital from 1730 to 1753 was our present subject, his duties there being performed by a deputy.

Beginning in 1748, Gunn organized a series of summer concerts (after the style of those given in Vauxhall, London) at Duddeston Gardens, near Birmingham (later known as Vauxhall Gardens). He continued these until his death, stated to be from consumption, in 1753 (W. Bennett 1933).

Martin Smith 1739–81 (d. Churchdown, Gloucester, 13 Apr. 1786). Smith, who was formally admitted on 16 June 1740 (CA2), received his full salary for the accounting year 1739–40, and was paid £2. 2*s*. 'for his travelling charges from London'. He was a subscriber to Greene's *Forty Select Anthems* (1743). In spite of his long tenure, little is known of him save that he was the father of an estimable son, *John Stafford Smith. According to reminiscences derived from his successor (see *Gloucester Journal*, 7 January 1832), Smith had been a pupil of *Maurice Greene. He resigned on 29 November 1781 (CA4).

William Mutlow 1781–1832 (b. Gloucester, 22 Apr. 1760; d. Gloucester, 1 Jan. 1832). There are early traces of the Mutlow family in the Gloucester Cathedral PR from at least 1668, when Miles Mutlow married Maria Banknett on 29 February 1667/8. William Mutlow was baptized at St Nicholas's Church. He was an apprentice of Martin Smith, and in the accounting year 1780–1 he assisted him by teaching the choristers. The minute of his appointment as organist is dated 18 December 1781 (CA4).

In 1790 he conducted the Gloucester Music Meeting (the Three Choirs Festival) for the first time, something that no previous Gloucester organist had done (Shaw 1954: 23). A portrait of Mutlow now in the practice-room of the Cathedral shows him as very fat. The following account by Phillips (1864: ii. 59), obviously highly coloured but no doubt embodying some element of truth, fairly evidently relates to Mutlow:

Mr Braham [the celebrated singer] was a man generally of most reserved manners . . . yet no one entered more into a jest than he did . . . One of a laughable character occurred at a celebrated triennial festival, in connection with the conductor, who was organist of the cathedral. He chanced to be a gentleman of eccentric habits and appearance, very short and fat, an epicure of no ordinary stamp, the length of whose arm was as near as possible the measure of his baton. Though an especial favourite with Madam Malibran, she delighted to play him all sorts of tricks, at which he never took offence. On the occasion of a morning performance, of selected sacred music, Madame Malibran and Braham had to sing a duett [*sic*], John Loder being leader of the orchestra; the three consulted together as to what trick they could play the conductor, and one having been agreed upon, the morning performance arrived, all went very well, the band and singers going on smoothly in one time while the conductor beat another—that was of little consequence in those days. At length came the duett by Malibran and Braham, which had a long symphony preceding it; the conductor, with more than ordinary energy in honour of so grand an occasion, waved his baton in the air, till down it came as a signal for the first chord, but not a semblance of sound issued from the orchestra. 'Hallo!' shouted the conductor, with a raised head in amazement, 'can't you all see? Now, then, we'll try again'. He did, and the result was the same. 'Why, what the devil's the matter?—are you all mad?' cried the little fat man, the huge drops falling from his forehead, which, as he drew his handkerchief to remove, the symphony began, to his great astonishment, and almost defied his beating a bar correctly till it had nearly finished, the singers almost fainting with suppressed laughter at the success of the trick they had so ingeniously planned.

. . . He was, however, a kind, good-tempered soul, that took all that happened in the best part, and when the festival had terminated said, 'some very droll things have occurred this week; but never mind, come and dine with me, and we'll enjoy the haunch of venison, and drink success to the next festival in some of the finest port wine in England'.

Mutlow's name is among the subscribers to the second edition of Boyce's *Cathedral Music* (1788) and to Arnold's *Cathedral Music* (1790). It will be observed that Martin Smith and Mutlow between them cover very nearly a hundred years in office.

Gloucester Journal, 7 Jan. 1832.

John Amott 1832–65 (b. Monmouth; d. Gloucester, 3 Feb. 1865, aged 66). Amott was organist of the abbey church (St Chad's) in Shrewsbury from 1820 to 1832, having previously been a pupil of Mutlow (Stephens 1882). He was appointed to Gloucester by minute dated 13 April 1832 (CA5). Brewer (1931) relates how Amott used to keep the organ pedals at Gloucester covered by a board, allowing his choristers to see them occasionally as a treat. His musical direction of the Three Choirs Festival was undistinguished (Shaw 1954: 45, 75), but he was its faithful historian, reissuing Lysons's *Annals* with notes by Rimbault and bringing them down to the year 1864. Stephens (1882) is the authority for his place of birth.

Samuel Sebastian Wesley 1865–76 (b. London, 14 Aug. 1810; d. Gloucester, 19 Apr. 1876). Wesley was the illegitimate son of Samuel Wesley, the composer, and grandson of Charles Wesley, the great hymn-writer. His half-brother Charles became sub-dean of the Chapel Royal, and his sister Eliza was organist of St Margaret Pattens Church in the City of London.

It is usually stated that S. S. Wesley became one of the children of the Chapel Royal under William Hawes in 1819, but the following letter (now in the Royal College of Organists) from his father to Hawes discussing his admission to the Chapel Royal choir is dated 28 November 1817:

Dear Sir,

Pray accept my best thanks for your extremely kind offer relative to my little Boy. He is a very apprehensive child and very fond of music; how far he may have Talent and Voice sufficient to do Credit to your valuable Instruction, experiment will best shew: his Temper and Disposition I believe to be good, wanting only due Direction, and I know him to be susceptible of kindness, which with you I am confident he will meet . . .

Your greatly obliged
S. Wesley.

Wesley began his career as an organist at St James's Chapel, Hampstead Road, London in March 1826. There then followed appointments at St Giles's, Camberwell (1829), St John's, Waterloo Road London (also 1829), and Hampton-on-Thames Parish Church (1830). For some time he held the last post—as evening organist only—together with the one at Camberwell. He then moved to Hereford Cathedral as organist in 1832 (q.v.), and to Exeter Cathedral in 1835 as organist and succentor (q.v.). He took the Oxford degrees of B.Mus. and D.Mus. by accumulation in 1839. In 1841 he was invited to open the new organ in the recently consecrated parish church of Leeds, and he accepted the offer of the post of organist there at a stipend of £200 per annum, guaranteed for two years. There, from 1842, under the celebrated Walter Hook, Vicar of Leeds and afterwards Dean of Chichester, he laid the foundation of a strong musical tradition which endures to this day.

After seven years at Leeds, 'and not until there had been some friction between the vicar and himself' (Spark 1892: 167), Wesley became organist of Winchester Cathedral (1849), combining this from 1850 with the work of organist of Winchester College (q.v.). During his Winchester period he had several pupils and assistants whose names will be found elsewhere in this book: G. B. Arnold, T. E. Aylward, G. M. Garrett, F. E. Gladstone, and J. K. Pyne. On Amott's death in 1865, he was asked by the Dean and Chapter of Gloucester to advise on a successor; having indicated that he himself would like the post, he was then appointed by minute dated 18 February 1865 at a stipend of £150 together with a house, and £25 for an assistant if required (CA7)

Wesley was the foremost English organist of his day. Of his extemporization, Bumpus (1972: ii. 494) quotes a pupil (unnamed) as saying: 'His spontaneous introductions to anthems he liked cannot easily be forgotten. They were always in harmony with the leading subjects of the composition, ever adding new beauties to the thoughts and works of the original writers.' A knowledgeable account of his playing was contributed to *MT* (17: 490) by William Spark (1823–87), a former pupil and assistant:

As an organist, Wesley, in his prime, stood first and foremost. He was unquestionably one of the earliest and most successful performers of John Sebastian Bach's grand organ pedal fugues; and he was the first to introduce a greatly varied style and expression, and to infuse orchestral combinations and colouring into organ playing; he was a splendid choir accompanist; and, lastly, he was certainly one of the finest and most dignified extempore players of his day and generation.

It was at Exeter that he first began to feel and rebel against the frustrations of the work and the lack of recognized status of a cathedral organist which he was to experience throughout his life, and to which he gave vigorous literary expression in three manifestos: the preface to his Service in E (published while he was at Leeds, and reprinted in *MT*, 48 (1907), 662, 797); *A few words on Cathedral Music and the Musical System of the Church with a plan of reform* (1849); and *Reply to the Inquiries of the Cathedral Commissioners* (1854). The conditions imposed on the use of the organ at Exeter Cathedral (q.v.) certainly seem irksome and unnecessary. Yet it must be recognized that Wesley himself was not easy to get on with, and that, in spite of his high ideals with regard to cathedral services, he seems to have become careless and indifferent about his routine cathedral work. At Winchester Cathedral he was more than once admonished for quite inexcusable attitudes (q.v.), and Brewer (1931: 3) states that Wesley left the singing of Gloucester Cathedral choir at a very low ebb. Nor did he rise to the responsibilities of a conductor of the Three Choirs Festival, for in 1874 it was reported in *MT* that 'assuredly more slovenly singing we have rarely heard within the walls of a cathedral'.

Several times he came forward for a university position—the Edinburgh chair of music in 1841, 1844, and 1845; the Oxford chair in 1848; and the Cambridge chair in 1856. In 1873 he received a Civil List pension, choosing this, so it is said, in preference to a knighthood.

Wesley was buried in the Old Cemetery, Exeter. There are memorials to him in Hereford, Exeter, Winchester (giving the wrong date of his resignation there), and Gloucester Cathedrals and in Leeds Parish Church. The commemorative plaque on No. 8 Kingsgate Street, Winchester gives the wrong date of his appointment to Winchester College. A portrait of Wesley, painted in 1849 by W. R. Briggs, RA, is now in the Royal College of Music.

Horton, forthcoming.

Charles Harford Lloyd 1876–82. Lloyd was appointed under Chapter minute dated 2 May 1876 (CA7), with a stipend of £150 as organist and £50 as master of the choristers.

See under Christ Church Cathedral, Oxford.

Charles Lee Williams 1882–96 (b. Winchester, 1 May 1853; d. Gloucester, 29 Aug. 1935). Williams (or Lee Williams has he came to be known) was the son of the Revd David Williams, formerly fellow of New College; he became a chorister of New College (1862–5) under *G. B. Arnold, whom he followed to Winchester as a pupil (while at Winchester College) and later as assistant at the Cathedral. His earliest appointments were as organist of Upton Church, Torquay (1870); of St Columba's College, Rathfarnham, Dublin (1872); and of Llandaff Cathedral (1876). He took the Oxford degree of B.Mus. in 1876, and he held the FRCO diploma.

The minute of his Gloucester appointment is dated 30 June 1882 (CA7). He retired on account of ill health in 1896. In 1929 he received the Lambeth degree of D.Mus.

MT, 76 (1935), 944.

Sir (Alfred) Herbert Brewer 1897–1928 (b. Gloucester, 21 June 1865; d. Gloucester, 1 Mar. 1928). Brewer, the son of a Gloucester hotel-keeper, was a chorister of the Cathedral, 1877–80, and then studied under C. H. Lloyd, holding organists' posts briefly at St Catherine's and St Mary-de-Crypt Churches, Gloucester. From 1882 to 1885 he was organist of St Giles's Church, Oxford; during this same period he held an organ scholarship at the Royal College of Music for one year and then was organist of Exeter College, Oxford for two years.

His first important post was as organist of St Michael's Church, Coventry (afterwards Coventry Cathedral) in 1886, followed by that of music master of Tonbridge School (1892). The Dean and Chapter of Bristol, mistaken in their belief that they could dismiss their organist except after prescribed admonitions, invited Brewer to replace him in 1895, but this could not take effect. However, following Lee Williams's resignation at Gloucester in December 1896, Brewer was appointed to succeed him in June 1897 (CA8, 15 December 1896).

Brewer had many successful pupils, including *A. P. Porter, *R. Tustin Baker, *Sir John Dykes Bower, and his own successor, H. W. Sumsion. Another was Herbert Howells who, in *DNB*, pays particular tribute to his master's skill as a performer. Herbert Byard, alluding to the scarcity of opportunities for hearing orchestral music sixty years ago, wrote of Brewer's choice of voluntaries thus: 'Brewer played a lot of transcriptions after Sunday evensongs; I must have learned the themes of quite a number of Haydn and Beethoven symphonies, not to mention some of his *tours de force*, like Elgar's Coronation March and the Hungarian March from Berlioz's "Faust", from listening to him; and very grateful I was.' (The *Organ*, 51 (1972), 144.) In choosing orchestral transcriptions, Brewer was typical of his period; but his manner of playing them, perhaps from the full score, is still admiringly recollected as outstanding.

Brewer held the Dublin degree of Mus.B and the Lambeth degree of D.Mus. (1905), and received a knighthood in 1926. He was sheriff of the City of Gloucester, 1922–3.

Grove[3]; *MT*, 69 (1928), 367; *DNB*, 1923–30; *WWW*, 1916–38; Brewer 1931.

§Herbert (Whitton) Sumsion, CBE, 1928–67 (b. Gloucester, 19 Jan. 1899). Sumsion was a chorister of Gloucester Cathedral under Brewer, and was subsequently an articled pupil and assistant. He later studied at the Royal College of Music (composition and pianoforte), and held posts as organist of Christ Church, Lancaster Gate, London and as director of music at Bishops Stortford College.

In 1926 he was appointed to teach composition at the Curtis Institute, Philadelphia. Shortly before Sumsion's return to England in 1928, having accepted the post of organist of Coventry Cathedral, Brewer suddenly died, whereupon the Dean and Chapter of Gloucester appointed Sumsion as his successor, and he was released from his intended post at Coventry. In 1935 he also became director of music at Cheltenham Ladies College, retaining this post until 1968.

He took the Durham degree of B.Mus. in 1920, and the FRCO diploma in 1916; in 1947 he received the Lambeth degree of D.Mus., and in the Birthday Honours of 1961 he was appointed CBE.

Grove[3]; *WW.*

§**John (Derek) Sanders, organist and master of the choristers from 1967** (b. Woodford, Essex, 26 Nov. 1933). After attending Felsted School, Essex, Sanders went to the Royal College of Music with a scholarship (1950–2) and then to Gonville and Caius College, Cambridge as organ scholar (1952–6). At Cambridge he read music, proceeding to the degrees of BA (1955), Mus.B. (1956), and MA (1959). He took the FRCO diploma in 1955. From 1958 to 1963 he was assistant organist of Gloucester Cathedral and director of music at King's School. In 1963 he became organist of Chester Cathedral, where he remained until his return to Gloucester. (See Addenda, p. 434.)

GUILDFORD

(I) The Pro-Cathedral Church of the Holy Trinity, 1927–1961

The diocese of Guildford was founded in 1927. As in similar instances, a leading parish church was raised to cathedral status, but since at Guildford the prospect was envisaged of a newly built cathedral, this was strictly a pro-cathedral, though it was hardly ever spoken of thus.

§**John Albert Sowerbutts, MC,** (1924) **1927–46** (b. London, 1 Feb. 1892; d. 15 Sept. 1970). Sowerbutts was educated at St Olave's Grammar School, London, and from 1911 to 1914 studied at the Royal Academy of Music. From 1914 to 1924 he was on the music staff of Winchester College, but his time there was interrupted by the Great War, during which he won the Military Cross. He took the London degree of B.Mus. in 1919, and held the FRCO diploma. In 1924 he left Winchester and returned to the Royal Academy of Music as a member of the professorial staff, also becoming organist of Holy Trinity Church, Guildford, shortly to be designated the Pro-Cathedral. He retired from the Royal Academy of Music in 1967.

§**Peter Goodman 1946–51** (b. Welling, Kent, 23 Oct. 1921). After having been a chorister of New College, Oxford, Goodman went to Magdalen College School, Oxford before winning an organ scholarship to the Royal College of Music in 1939. He held this until 1942, together with (1940–2) the organ scholarship of Gonville and Caius College, Cambridge. He took the Cambridge degree of

Mus.B. and the FRCO diploma in 1943, having received the Brook prize with the CHM diploma in 1941.

For a short time from 1945 he was organist of Abbassia Garrison Church, Cairo. After leaving Guildford, where he also taught at the Royal Grammar School, he was organist of Holy Trinity Church, Kingston-upon-Hull, 1951–61. From 1955 to 1974 he was head of music at Kingston High School, Hull, and he has been city organist of Hull since 1957.

Ronald Walter Dussek 1951–60 (d. 30 Dec. 1961, aged 70). Dussek, who was of the same family as the Czech composer J. L. Dussek, was a pupil of *G. F. Huntley at St Peter's Church, Eaton Square, London, first as a chorister and then as assistant organist. He was successively organist of Epsom Parish Church (1923) and St Mary's, Southampton, where he followed *H. D. Statham in 1928, before becoming precentor of Radley College in 1933. On retirement from Guildford he was given the title of organist emeritus.

ECM, 32 (1962), 11; *MT*, 103 (1962), 116.

Barry (Michael) Rose 1960–1. On the retirement of R. W. Dussek, the provost of the Pro-Cathedral, looking ahead to the forthcoming consecration of the new Cathedral and the establishment there of a musical tradition, made an apparently unorthodox choice of a relatively untried man (compare Dean Strong and H. G. Ley at Christ Church, Oxford) as organist, with a view to his forming a choir and transferring to the new Cathedral in a few months' time, which transfer duly took place in May 1961, though the provost who planned this was not himself appointed dean.

See immediately below.

(II) The Cathedral Church of the Holy Spirit

Barry (Michael) Rose 1961–74

See under St Albans Cathedral.

Philip (John) Moore 1974–82.

See under York Minster.

§Andrew (Thomas Seager) Millington, organist from 1983 (b. Willenhall, Staffs., 2 May 1952). From Hanley Castle Grammar School and King's School, Worcester, Millington went up to Downing College, Cambridge as organ scholar, 1971–4, reading music and proceeding to the degrees of BA (1974) and MA (1978). He took the FRCO diploma in 1972.

After a short spell as assistant music master at Malvern College, he became assistant organist of Gloucester Cathedral, also teaching at King's School, 1975–82.

HEREFORD

The Cathedral Church of St Mary the Virgin and St Ethelbert the King

Main sources in this section (1965):

Chapter Acts
CA1 1512–66.
CA2 1566–1600.
CA3 1572–1603 ('Quarto Act Book').
CA4 1600–22; 1660–1712.
CA5 1712–68.
CA6 1768–1801.
CA7 1801–17.
CA8 1814–34.
CA9 1834–44.
Quarto Act Books 1785–96 and 1796–1814 have not been examined.

Vicars Choral Acts
VCA 1573–1661.
VCA2 1660–1717.
VCA3 1717–87.

Miscellaneous
Other documents cited according to reference numbers in the Cathedral Archives, as A-2601, etc.

The history of Hereford Cathedral, one of the Old Foundation, goes back at least to the twelfth century, and its College of Vicars Choral was incorporated in 1396. Throughout its history, membership of the College at Hereford (as at York) was restricted to persons in holy orders, a matter not without significance when considering the biography of John Farrant (see p. 34). They were sustained by endowments termed 'vicarages'. After the Reformation the ancient customs of the Cathedral were codified into statutes delivered by Elizabeth I in 1583. 'Statuta circa pietatis exercitis' ordained that the musical establishment was to consist of twelve vicars choral, four sub-canons (lay singers representing the pre-Reformation deacons and sub-deacons), seven choristers, and 'unum qui pueros in musicis instruat et organa pulset' ('one who should teach the boys and play the organ'). New statutes were given in 1637 by Charles I, and details about the stipend of the master of the choristers were inserted into the provisions relating to the vicars choral. He was not necessarily of their number; but, in addition to 4 marks (£2. 13*s*. 4*d*.) annually from the Chapter, he was to receive £8 from the College of Vicars Choral and, if he wished, he might dine with them at their common table. This explains the reference below, under Thomas Warrock, to 'their organist', and, under Hugh Davis, to their relief from a yearly charge.

Thus the position of organist and master of the choristers of Hereford Cathedral was formally recognized by statute. At various times its holder was also a vicar choral, but this was by no means necessarily so, as, for example, in the case of John Bull. Although the statutes of 1583 united the duties of organist and master of the choristers in one person, there were brief periods in the late sixteenth century when the work was for some reason divided.

John Hodges 1538–*c.*1583 (from 1582 jointly with John Bull). Hodges' admission as organist is dated 3 October 1538 (CA1, f. 82), with a fee of £8 a year. On 23 September 1549 (CA1, f. 101) he was granted leave of absence until Christmas. For a time he must also have had charge of the choristers, for on 4 October 1540 'John Hoge', as instructor of the choristers, accepted two boys (CA1, f. 85ᵛ). However, on 27 July 1543 Richard Ledbury (alias Ludby) replaced Hodges as instructor of the choristers (CA1, f. 90). Hodges was appointed verger on 21 March 1551, and is referred to as both organist and verger on 5 July 1562 (CA1, ff. 106ᵛ, 167ᵛ). On 11 December 1581 (CA2, f. 96) Thomas Mason (see below) was appointed master or instructor of the choristers with a fee of 40*s*. 'during pleasure' of the Chapter. It is not known how long Ledbury had held the post. By 1582, as it would seem, Hodges was perhaps getting past his work, and in that year John Bull was appointed to share the duties of organist.

John Bull 1582–6 (at first jointly with John Hodges) (b. *c.* 1562; bur. Antwerp, 15 Mar. 1628). The name John Bull is first found at Hereford Cathedral on 31 August 1573 when the Chapter admitted 'quendam Johannem Bulle' as a chorister (CA3, f. 12); and one assumes this is the future organist. Later, when he was sworn as a gentleman of the Chapel Royal, it was noted that he had been a 'child there', that is to say a chorister of the Chapel. If so, and if our identification is correct, then this must have been after he was a chorister at Hereford. At some time he seems to have been a pupil of *John Blitheman, whose memorial inscription (recorded by Stow, (Lbl, Harl. MS 538, f. 130ᵛ) stated that he 'a scholar left behind John Bull by name'.

On 24 December 1582 a minute (CA2, f. 104ᵛ) in Latin (of which this is a rendering) recorded:

> The aforesaid day and place the venerable Dean and Chapter (having received letters from the honourable Henry Sydney, knight of the honourable Order of the Garter, Lord President of the Marches of Wales, in favour of John Bull, skilled in music) granted to the same John Bull letters patent of the office of organist in the said Cathedral Church either jointly with John Hodges the present organist or immediately after the death of the said Hodges, during the natural life of the same Bull, to occupy for himself with all fees pertaining to the same office.

Shortly afterwards, by minute of 21 January 1582/3 (CA2, f. 104ᵛ), the Chapter deliberated about the negligence of Mason, the master of the choristers, and gave the post to Bull, allowing Mason to draw the stipend for another six months. But Bull himself was not perfect, and on 1 February 1584/5 the Chapter decided that since he had been absent for longer than the month which the dean had allowed him specially, the posts of both organist and master of the choristers were vacant (CA2, f. 117). This evidently blew over and no fresh appointment was made, but still more trouble arose in 1585. A rather incoherent minute of 5 June (CA3, f. 104) recounts that, having disobeyed and insulted the precentor, Bull went off without excuse, and records that, for these reasons as well as 'pro diversis aliis suis offensis', he was suspended until such time as the precentor interceded for him. We are not told when that was.

Not long after this, Bull was sworn a gentleman of the Chapel Royal in January

1585/6 (Rimbault 1872: 4). His tenure as master of the choristers and organist at Hereford seems to have ended in the summer of 1586 (see below under Warrock). Nevertheless, he retained some connection with Hereford. VCA1 (p. 59) records the grant to Mr John Bull on 16 September 1587 of 'the 4th chamber on the north side of the quadrangle' of the College of Vicars Choral; and as late as 18 January 1590/1 the vicars 'granted unto Mr John Bull one of the gentlemen of Her Majesty's chapel the great upper chamber behind the College hall (appointed heretofore for the reader of the divinity lecture) at the request of my Lord's grace [the Archbishop] of Canterbury'.
He took the Oxford degree of B.Mus. on 9 July 1586, and incorporated as D.Mus. on 7 July 1592 (Wood 1815–20: i. 235, 258), having taken the Cambridge degree of Mus.D. *c.*1590–2 (*Venn*).

By May 1592 he had already become one of the organists of the Chapel Royal (q.v.), and in 1596, on the Queen's recommendation, he was also appointed first professor of music at Gresham College, London, with permission to lecture in English not Latin. He resigned that post on his marriage in 1607.

In 1613, by which time he had already travelled in France, Germany, and Spain, he suddenly quitted England 'without licence' (Rimbault 1872: 7), serving in Brussels from September of that year to August 1614 as one of the organists of the Archduke's Chapel, and then from 1617 until his death as organist of Antwerp Cathedral. James I was understandably vexed at this defection, and on the King's behalf the Archduke was informed that, so far from Bull's having left 'for any wrong done to him, or for matter of religion, under which feigned pretext he now sought to wrong the reputation' of James, his departure had been to escape punishment 'for his incontinence, fornication, adultery, and other grievous crimes' (Lbl, Add. MS 6194). He was further characterized to the Archduke by the British envoy as 'vile and abject' (PRO, State Papers (Flanders), quoted fully by Hoppe 1954).

The date of his birth is calculated from the inscription on his portrait in the Music School collection at Oxford: 'Ano aetatis suae 27, 1589.' The fringed hood in which he is depicted has been stated (Poole 1912–25: i. 152) to be that of the livery of the Merchant Taylors Company, to which he was admitted in 1606. However, Thurston Dart has suggested that it may have been that of Bull's Cambridge doctorate. If so, this degree must have been earlier than the date suggested in *Venn*. He died in poverty in Antwerp, where he is buried in the Cathedral precincts.

His skill as a keyboard-player was legendary. The story goes that someone, hearing an unseen but astonishing player, declared it was 'either Dr Bull or the devil'. Wood (1815–20) puts this more suavely by remarking that he 'was so much admired for his dexterous hand on the organ, that many thought there was more than man in him'.

Thomas Warrock 1586–?1589. On 8 April 1586, before Warrock had been officially appointed organist, the Dean and Chapter resolved to grant him ('at the instance of John Scudamore, Esq.') the organist's customary fee of £2. 13*s*. 4*d*. for one year from March 1586 'in subsidia sustentationis sue' (CA2, f. 122). Apparently, Thomas Mason (mentioned above in connection with Bull) was acting organist at this time, described in a minute of 25 June 1586 as 'tunc organistam' when allotting him not only a second vicarage on account of his teaching the choristers, but also, for no explicit reason, 40*s.* in augmentation of his stipend for a single year. At the same time Warrock's £2. 13*s.* 4*d.* is mentioned in a way that suggests that he was diligently improving his organ-playing (CA2, ff. 122–3). There is no record of any formal admission of Mason as organist—evidently this arrangement with him was a temporary one until Warrock was ready to take over—and eventually, on 30 September 1586, Warrock was admitted to the combined offices of organist and master of the choristers (CA2, f. 124ᵛ).

By minute dated 27 September 1588 the vicars choral resolved that 'if Thomas Warrock their organist doth depart herehence to remain in any other place and so be absent from this church, not regarding his duty to do the service of the organist that he shall have no wages or allowance out of their vicarages during the time of his absence as he have had this year' (VCA1, p. 70). There is a similar reference with regard to John Fido in December 1596. The words 'their organist', while on the face of things suggesting that the vicars had an organist independent of the Dean and Chapter, must rather be understood in relation to their contribution to the stipend of the Cathedral organist, later formally embodied in the statutes of 1637 (see p. 131 above).

On 10 November 1589 (CA2, f. 140) Thomas Madokes, a vicar choral, was appointed master of the choristers, and so one assumes that Warrock had ceased to be organist by then, especially given the further mention of Thomas Mason at the time of John Fido's appointment (see below). It is significant that the vicars choral on 13 November 1589 appointed 'Sir Thomas Mason the subchanter' to be their organist 'for this said one whole year', giving him a fee of 40*s.* and remitting a debt of 32*s.* (VCA1).

West (1921) thought Thomas Warrock of Hereford was the same as the Thomas Warwick who was organist of the Chapel Royal in the reign of Charles I (q.v.). *Grove*³, on the other hand (*sub* 'Warwick'), states that the Hereford musician was the father of the Chapel Royal organist. The first statement is unlikely, while the second, though not impossible, lacks documentation. The name Warrock is not uncommon in the Hereford Chapter Acts before the Civil War.

John Fido (1st tenure) **1591–2**. The minute of Fido's appointment as organist is dated 22 March 1590/1 (CA2, f. 143ᵛ). It was made as a result of a recommendation from Whitgift, Archbishop of Canterbury. Mason appears to have been acting organist at the time, as he had been before Warrock's admission: the minute contains a provision that nothing in this grant shall subtract from the stipends already granted to Thomas Mason and Thomas Madokes, vicars choral, for playing the organ and teaching the choristers—perhaps a reference to some unexpired portion of their temporary terms. Though it is not explicitly stated, one assumes that Fido took over both offices.

John Farrant (I) 1592–3. Farrant's admission, both as organist and vicar choral, is dated 22 March 1591/2 (CA2, f. 145). As a vicar choral of Hereford he must have taken, or have been about to take, holy orders, a point discussed above. In VCA1, under the date 13 May 1592, there is a note of the grant to him of 'the lower chamber behind the hall next unto the saffron garden for his use to teach and instruct the choristers'. Evidently he was master of the choristers also. On 6 November 1592 (CA2, f. 147) he was granted a deacon's (sub-canon's) stall, presumably to augment his stipend. His bad language—in keeping with his presumed identity with the elder John Farrant of Salisbury—got him into trouble on 14 February 1592/3, when the vicars fined him for abusing William Vicary 'with filthy, unhonest and contumelious words which are not to be named', and also admonished him, under pain of deprivation, for similar behaviour to the *custos* of the College at supper. His resignation as vicar choral and organist was minuted on 24 December 1593, when he was described as 'clericus' (CA2, f. 151). (For a discussion of the presumed identity of John Farrant (I), see under Bristol Cathedral.)

John Fido (2nd tenure) **1593–5**. On the day of Farrant's resignation, John Fido, 'laicus', was appointed organist. Presently, on 22 February 1594/5 (VCA1), the vicars choral resolved 'not to allow John Fido not [*sic*] to be our organist neither to pay him any wages therefore neither to admit him to come to our house or commons. This act was made against him for that he gave out most slanderous words against the said custos and company.' They further decided, on 1 March, to fine him 10*s*. should he ever enter the College.

Fido can then be traced as master of the choristers and organist of Worcester Cathedral from March 1595 until Michaelmas 1596 (q.v.).

John Gibbs 1595–?1596. On 24 March 1594/5 Gibbs was admitted as organist on a year's probation, and granted a deacon's stall in augmentation of stipend (CA2, f. 156). The vicars choral (VCA1, 19 August 1595) agreed to pay '40*s*. every year towards Mr Gybbes the organist's commons so long as we shall have our common table for £6 a year and also so long as he shall be a commensal at our table'. It may be noted that a certain John Gibbs became almoner and master of the choristers of St Paul's Cathedral in 1613.

John Fido (3rd tenure) **1596–7**. For a third time Fido became organist of Hereford Cathedral. The vicars choral resolved to reappoint him on 22 December 1596, and he was admitted on a year's probation by the Chapter on 7 January 1596/7 (CA3, f. 172), on condition that he behaved himself meanwhile. At the same time he was admitted to a deacon's stall. But in less than a year, on 14 May 1597, he was described as organist and admitted as master of the choristers (CA2, f. 163^{v}; CA3, f. 172^{v}). He finally quitted Hereford in 1597, and he might well be the John Fido in deacon's orders who was chosen vicar choral of Wells Cathedral in November 1605 (Wells CA2, f. 193). Eventually he found his way back to Worcester, where he became a minor canon of the Cathedral and rector of St Nicholas's Church (1615–36). He was still alive in 1639 (Atkins 1918: 36–7).

William Inglott 1597–1609→. Inglott was admitted organist on 1 October 1597 (CA2, f. 165^{v}), and he remained in office until at least Michaelmas 1609, when the accounts (A-R595) record payment to him for teaching the choristers. One is much inclined to presume that this is the William Inglott who was twice organist of Norwich Cathedral, though there is no signature to prove it, and the Hereford Chapter Acts shed no light on the date or circumstances of his departure.

See under Norwich Cathedral.

Hugh Davis ←1630–44 (d. Hereford, 1644). The Chapter Acts make no further mention of an organist from the time of Inglott's appointment until after the Restoration of Charles II. Hugh Davis became a vicar choral on 25 June 1605 (CA4, f. 31), and, according to Wood (1815–20: i. 410), he took the Oxford degree of B.Mus. on 12 July 1623 as a member of New College. Wood's description of him as 'organist of the Cathedral Church of Hereford' may well refer to this date, but we do not know precisely when he was appointed. It may have been about 1611, the year in which William Inglott became organist of Norwich Cathedral for the second time. The only specific trace of Davis as organist in the Hereford archives is contained in VCA1. The following entry, dated 7 July 1630, shows that at Hereford the combination of a vicar's post with that of organist was no mere convenience for salary purposes, but involved the performance of conflicting duties. How this was resolved in other instances—for example, that of Farrant—we do not know:

> Enacted . . . that Mr Hugh Davis for that he is a senior . . . and doth ease the house in the yearly charge and payment for the organist which the College must undergo if he were a stranger. Therefore the Custos and Vicars now at his request . . . do agree that Mr Hugh Davis shall be spared out of the choir and not be pricked [marked absent] but accounted as present at the psalmody and Gloria Patri so that he be ready in the organ loft to play before the reading of the first lesson every morning and evening prayer and attend his duty there.

On 5 May 1637 'Mr Hugh Davis, bachelor in music and senior of the said College', was elected by the vicars choral as perpetual *custos*; VCA1 further records the election on 6 April 1644 of a *custos* in place of 'Mr Hugh Davis, deceased'. He is wrongly described by Havergal (1869) as having been at one time organist of New College, Oxford.

John Badham 1660–88 (d. Hereford, 1688). Badham was admitted vicar choral on probation on 27 September 1660 (CA4), and the accounts for the year ending Michaelmas 1661 (A-R609) record payment of £6 'To Mr Badham the organist by consent of the Chapter by reason of his poverty and necessity'—a reference perhaps to his circumstances under the Commonwealth and Protectorate—thus enabling us to assume his appointment as organist at about the same time. On 19 June 1662 a Chapter minute (CA4) fixed the organist's stipend at £12 a year. A long entry in VCA2, dated 12 July 1665, reads thus:

> An agreement was made by the Custos and Vicars with Mr Badham one of their fellows concerning his demands whatsoever in regard of former and future service at the organ as followeth:
>
> First that in consideration Mr Badham hath for some years past supplied the duty of organist whereby the College hath been eased of the pension which an organist not being vicar may pretend unto [*see above under Davis*]. The College doth remit unto him £10

resting in his hands being due to them for the installation of . . . the now Lord Bishop of Hereford.

And in consideration of future service the steward of the College rents is appointed to pay him quarterly . . . so long as the Dean and Chapter shall continue him upon the duty [of organist]. . . .

In consideration whereof Mr Badham . . . doth hereby promise . . . at such times as he may be spared from the organ to be present in the choir and assistant in all the service there incumbent upon him as vicar. . . .

He appears to have aspired to be a composer, for the accounts to Michaelmas 1666 note a payment to him of 10*s*. 'for encouragement for making an anthem' (A-R611).

In 1674 a calamitous occurrence nearly burnt down the Vicars' College. On 6 November 1674 VCA2 records that Badham was admonished for permitting his 'maidservant and [her] children to lodge in his chamber in the College, who by their great neglect and carelessness had brought the said College into great danger by fire'.

At the episcopal visitation of 1677–8 it was ordered, as entered in VCA2 in April 1678, that the organist 'shall duly and diligently teach the choristers to play upon the organs and other instruments of music'; and further:

That Mr John Badham, organist, taking to his assistance Mr Robert Griffiths, one of the vicars-choral, shall set the song books belonging to the choir into a good and perfect order and shall represent weekly unto the Lord Bishop or the Hebdomadary how far the said work is advanced and when it shall be completely finished the Dean and Chapter are to give them a reasonable satisfaction for the same.

Badham's death in 1688 is noted by Havergal (1869).

Henry Hall (I) 1688–1707 (d. Hereford, 30 Mar. 1707). Hall is described in Wood (MS Notes) as 'born at New Windsor in Berks . . . now living aged 40 or thereabouts'. He was a Chapel Royal chorister, and his voice had broken by Christmas 1672 (Ashbee 1986–9: i. 121). It may be that he was the 'Mr Hall' who was briefly organist of Wells Cathedral in 1674 (q.v.). He was organist of Exeter Cathedral, 1674–9 (q.v.).

At Hereford he is first mentioned on 27 June 1679, when he was granted £20 a year (a larger salary than Badham's), 'he assisting the organist, instructing the choristers thrice a week and assisting in the choir' (CA4). At the same time the vicars choral allowed him chambers and commons in their College (VCA2, 27 June 1679). He must quickly have acquired holy orders, for on 27 December 1679 (CA4) Henry Hall, 'clericus', was elected vicar choral; VCA2 records his perpetuation as such on 21 January 1680/1. On 15 September 1688 he was appointed organist (CA4).

Some verses by him, wherein he laments his isolation at Hereford, are prefixed to Blow's *Amphion Anglicus* (1700);

This while you spread your Fame, at Home I sit
Amov'd by Fate from Melody and Wit
No Chanting at St Paul's regales my Senses,
I'm only vers'd in Usum Herefordensis.

From these verses, and others contributed to Purcell's *Orpheus Britannicus* (1696), it is evident that he and Purcell were fellow-pupils under Blow:

> We learnt together, but not learnt alike:
> Though equal care our Master might bestow
> Yet only Purcell e'er shall equal Blow.

Hall was buried in the cloisters of the Vicars' College at Hereford (Havergal 1881).

Henry Hall (II) 1707–14 (d. Hereford, 21 Jan. 1714). It appears that this was the son of his predecessor. In minuting his appointment on 5 June 1707, CA4 describes him as 'nunc vel nuper oppidi de Ludlow'. Like his father, he was something of a versifier. No doubt *DNB* is right in attributing the greater part of this verse to the younger man, though it is clearly wrong in assigning to him the lines prefixed to *Orpheus Britannicus* and *Amphion Anglicus*. Most of his verse, including a ballad 'All in the land of Cyder', is found in an anthology entitled *The Grove*, published in 1721. *DNB* urbanely remarks that Hall's verses were 'admired for their ease and brilliancy in an age that was not repelled by their coarseness'. He was buried near his father (Havergal 1881).

Edward Thompson 1714–18. Thompson was elected organist on 24 March 1713/14 (CA5), and moved to Salisbury Cathedral during 1718.
See under Salisbury Cathedral.

Henry Swarbrick 1720–54 (d. Hereford, June 1754). Swarbrick's election as organist is dated 10 November 1720 (CA5). Nothing is known of what earlier arrangements were made after Thompson's departure. In September 1729 Thomas Swarbrick (Schwarbrook), the Midlands organ-builder, received a contract to tune and repair the Cathedral organ (A-4930); and in November 1752 Henry Swarbrick, declaring himself to be the nephew of the organ-builder, petitioned to take over this work, having done it for many years without pay (A-4930). Consequently the Chapter agreed to make terms with him about the care and tuning of the organ. He was buried on 23 June 1754 (Havergal (1881), and his executrix was allowed the stipend up to Michaelmas (CA5). Swarbrick was one of the subscribers to Croft's *Musica Sacra* in 1724.

Richard Clack 1754–79 (d. Hereford, 1779). When Clack was appointed on 6 July 1754, he was given the duty of cleaning and tuning the organ, his salary to run from Michaelmas (CA5). He seems to have served at a time when the vicars choral were very slack. In 1758 the dean complained thus: 'I am fully persuaded, upon enquiry, that there is no cathedral choir in England so much neglected in this respect as that of Hereford, and when the number of vicars provided for that service in our church is considered such neglect must appear so much the more inexcusable, as well as more indecent.' The dean ends by a reference to 'the indecency of seeing the Psalms and Hymns [canticles?] so often left to be chanted by the boys only' (VCA3). Clack himself was admonished for negligence in teaching the choristers on 9 November 1764 (A-5661), and he received a further admonition (CA5) on 24 March 1766 'to attend personally divine service every day in the week except Wednesdays and Fridays as his predecessors have done and teach the choristers of the said church three times a week at least'. He became a vicar choral in July 1769, and was perpetuated a year later (VCA3).

In 1776 Clack subscribed to Burney's *History of Music*. He resigned in person on 11 November 1779 (CA6), and his burial in the Cathedral that same year is noted in Havergal (1881).

William Perry 1779–89 (d. 1789). Perry was appointed at the same Chapter meeting that received Clack's resignation. On 23 December 1785 (CA6) he had to be ordered to teach the choristers regularly. Later, on 9 December 1788, he was excused attendance on Wednesdays and Fridays during the winter quarter 'on account of his bad state of health'.

Miles Coyle 1789–1805. Coyle was appointed on 7 March 1789 (CA6) 'in place of the late Mr William Perry'. There can be little doubt that he was the 'Mr Coyle, Organist, Ludlow, Salop', who subscribed to the second edition of Boyce's *Cathedral Music* in 1788. On 14 November 1794 a Chapter order required the organist 'to play on Sundays when the Bishop, Dean, or Residentiary enters the choir and on the other days except when his attendance is dispensed with'. On 26 October 1795 he had to be told that he was expected to play a voluntary on the next 'Holiday', and on 28 November he was fined for not performing his office on two Sundays in accordance with the order of 1794. Coyle followed this up by a petition dated 12 December 1795 (CA6): 'The organist in consideration of his time being much occupied with pupils, requests the Dean and Chapter to dispense with his playing a voluntary before the Communion Service on Holidays, except on Christmas Day, the State Holidays, and when the Bishop visits or confirms.' His request was granted.

Charles James Dare 1805–18 (d. 1820). On the day of Dare's election 'in the room of Mr Coyle' (CA7, 26 November 1805), it was ordered that the organist should play between the Third Collect and the Litany. At the time of his appointment, Dare was assistant organist of Westminster Abbey and organist of Margaret Street Chapel, Cavendish Square, London. His application was supported by a testimonial signed by, among others, Sir William Parsons (master of the king's music), *Robert Cooke, and *Thomas Attwood (A-4905). In spite of this, however, he proved unsatisfactory, and on 10 December 1816 £40 augmentation of salary was withdrawn 'until he shall perform his duty or provide an assistant to be approved by the Chapter'. Worse was to follow, and misconduct led to his being given notice on 13 November 1817 (CA8). The following reminiscence comes from Gretton (1889: 8):

> Another not infrequent offender against 'Church Discipline' was Dare the organist; his command of the instrument often stood him in good stead. His bibulous tendencies earned him the rheumatic gout; his gout made him indolent and unlocomotive, consequently it now and then happened that he was behind his time. I think I hear him now crawling upstairs into the organ loft, which was perched between the nave and the choir, while the Psalms were being chanted; gradually and stealthily he manipulated the keys, till at once he

broke into the note of the chant. It was something wonderful, and doubtless often saved him from a wigging from the residentiary.

According to West (1921), Dare died in 1820.

Aaron Upjohn Hayter 1818–20 (b. Gillingham, 16 Dec. 1799; d. Boston, USA, 28 July 1873). Hayter, 'late of Salisbury Cathedral', was unanimously appointed organist of Hereford Cathedral on 24 March 1818 (CA8). He had been a chorister and pupil under *A. T. Corfe at Salisbury, and his father Samuel had been organist at Mere, Wiltshire. Sad to say, he, like his predecessor, disgraced himself, and he was given notice on 26 June 1820. His letter, humbly begging, not without dignity, for forgiveness and mercy, dated 24 May, still survives (A-5979). He was able to surmount this setback in his career, and after a period as organist of the collegiate church of Brecon, 1820–35, he emigrated to the United States, where he was organist of Grace Church, New York, 1835–7, and Holy Trinity, Boston from 1837. He was also organist and conductor of the Handel and Haydn Society of Boston, 1839–48. Two of his sons became musicians.

Perkins and Dwight 1893; West 1921.

John Clarke-Whitfeld (formerly Clarke) 1820–32 (b. Gloucester, 13 Dec. 1770; d. Holmer, near Hereford, 22 Feb. 1836). On his matriculation at Magdalen College, Oxford on 30 May 1793, Clarke-(Whitfeld) was described as 'son of John, of St Mary's, Gloucester' (Foster 1887–92). When appointed organist and master of the choristers of Hereford Cathedral in June 1820 (CA8), he had a varied career behind him.

The *Annual Biography* for 1837 says 'Dr Whitfeld's early fondness for music induced him to resign a legacy from his grandmother to educate him for *any other* profession.' It goes on to say that he 'was placed under Dr William Hayes at Oxford', but this seems unlikely, as he was only 7 years old when *William Hayes died. Both *DNB* and *GM* state that he was educated musically under *Philip Hayes at Oxford. At the time of his matriculation he was already organist of Ludlow Parish Church, to which he was appointed in 1789 (Macray 1894–1915). Early authorities such as *GM* and the *Annual Biography* state that he took his B.Mus. degree at Oxford, but Foster (1887–92) does not record this. However, there would be little point in his matriculating from Ludlow as a non-resident unless he proposed to take a music degree, and his autobiographical notes (Gu, MS R.d.85) state that he took the degree in that year, 1793.

He then moved to Ireland, first as organist of Armagh Cathedral, 1794–7, and then as master of the choristers of Christ Church and St Patrick's Cathedrals, Dublin, 1797–8 (q.v.). He was granted the Mus.D. degree of Trinity College, Dublin by diploma by private grace on 10 October 1795. In the autobiographical material in volume 2 of his *Cathedral Music* he said that he left Dublin 'owing to the Irish rebellion'.

From 1799 to 1820 he was organist of St John's and Trinity Colleges, Cambridge (q.v.) under the joint arrangements then prevailing. On settling in Cambridge he secured recognition of his academic status by becoming Mus.D. by incorporation: by grace of Senate on 14 December 1799 (*Venn*) he was received 'ut iisdem anno ordine at gradu apud nos Cantabrigienses, quibus est apud suos Dublinienses'. He stated in his autobiographical notes that he took the Oxford degree of D.Mus. (by incorporation?) in 1810, but no official record is preserved. On the death of his maternal uncle in 1814, he assumed the additional surname of Whitfeld; but his expectation of financial inheritance was disappointed, and he found himself in debt 'owing to a Chancery suit and the unfeeling conduct of a relative'. During his Cambridge period he set some of Walter Scott's poems to music, and his numerous letters to Scott are now in the National Library of Scotland (*Annual Biography*, 1837; Spink 1970). Soon after moving to Hereford he was elected (non-resident) professor of music in the University of Cambridge 'by a majority in the Senate 'of more than 100'.

He tendered his resignation at Hereford in April 1823, but withdrew it in June. On 16 June 1832 the Chapter passed the following minute:

In consequence of the long and increasing deterioration in the choral services of the Cathedral proceeding as they are aware from Dr Whitfeld's infirm state of health which has for a long period experienced the forebearance of the Chapter; the Dean and Chapter now feel it to be their indispensable duty to communicate to him their decision that the office of organist will be vacant at Midsummer next. Should it be a matter of convenience to Dr Whitfeld to be relieved from his responsibility at any earlier period the Dean and Chapter will be ready to concur in any suitable arrangement.

On 25 June he was granted an annual allowance of £40 'in proof of [the Chapter's] kindly feelings towards him'. (For which £40, however, see below, under S. S. Wesley.)

Clarke-Whitfeld retained his Cambridge professorship until his death in 1836. On the east wall of the Bishop's Cloister of Hereford Cathedral there is the following inscription:

Sacred to the memory of John Clarke Whitfeld Esqr. Mus Doc in the three universities and professor in that of Cambridge Born Dec 13. 1770 Died Feb 22. 1836 aged 65. He left to his family the inheritance of a fair and honourable name and to the many who knew and loved him a memory without stain as the father the gentleman and the friend.

Samuel Sebastian Wesley 1832–5. The appointment of 'Mr Wesley the organist of Hampton Church near London' as organist of Hereford Cathedral was minuted on 10 July 1832 (CA8). His emoluments were fixed at £52, together with £8 from the vicars choral and a further £40 to be paid by the Chapter after the death of Clarke-Whitfeld. Soon after his arrival in Hereford in October 1832, he wrote to his mother thus: 'I find that much teaching may be had within fifteen miles of Hereford. I should of course have been better pleased to have lived quietly, without this tiresome and degrading occupation. The salary at the Cathedral is, however, insufficient. (Lbl, Add. MS 35019.)

The Cathedral organ was then in the hands of the builders, and Wesley occupied himself with composing his famous anthem 'The Wilderness' in readiness for the reopening: 'Yesterday the organ at our Cathedral . . . was opened under the conduct of Mr S. Sebastian Wesley . . . never were the full powers of the beautiful instrument more successfully and skilfully developed.' (*Hereford Journal*, 7 November 1832.)

On 4 May 1835 he married Marianne Merewether, sister of the Dean of Hereford. The ceremony took place not in the Cathedral but in the church of Ewyas Harold, and apparently without the attendance of the bride's brother, all of which suggests some secrecy about the event.

Wesley's resignation as organist of Hereford Cathedral is recorded on 2 September 1835 (CA9). There was an unpleasant aftermath to his tenure when, on 11 January 1836, the Chapter considered a letter from him claiming that he ought to have received £100 a year besides 'a place of abode', whereas he had had only £52, paying £30 thereof for lodgings. The Chapter quite properly declined to discuss the matter.

See also under Gloucester Cathedral.

John Hunt 1835–42 (b. Marnhull, Dorset, 30 Dec. 1806; d. Hereford, 17 Nov. 1842). After receiving Wesley's resignation on 2 September 1835, the Hereford Chapter resolved (22 September) that a new organist would be 'responsible for the instruction of the vicars-choral, deacons [sub-canons], and choristers and for the due preparation of each for the performance of the choral services'. On 1 October 1835 John Hunt, 'a [lay] vicar-choral of Lichfield', was appointed on a year's probation; but he was confirmed in office as early as 12 November 1835 (CA9). He had been brought up as a chorister and articled pupil of *A. T. Corfe at Salisbury, and moved to Lichfield in 1827.

He died on 17 November 1842, after falling over a dinner-wagon laden with plates and glasses which had been left in a dark part of the cloisters after an audit dinner. His adopted nephew, a chorister, died three days later from the shock of his uncle's death, and was buried in the same grave. There is a memorial to Hunt and the boy in the western window of the north choir aisle of the Cathedral. After his death a volume of his songs, with a eulogistic memoir, was published by subscription in 1843.

George Townshend Smith 1843–77 (b. Windsor, 14 Nov. 1813; d. Hereford, 3 Aug. 1877). The son of E. W. Smith, lay clerk of St George's Chapel, Windsor, Smith was a chorister there, and later a pupil of Samuel Wesley. Before his appointment to Hereford he was organist of Eastbourne Old Parish Church and of St Margaret's, Lynn. He was chosen organist of Hereford Cathedral on 5 January 1843 (CA9) out of 42 candidates, at a salary of £100 less £25 per annum to Hunt's widow.

He was a man of some antiquarian tastes, perhaps derived from his father, who was the transcriber of Purcell's *Dido and Aeneas* and *Circe* (now Lbl, Add. MSS 31450, 15979, and 33237). G. T. Smith was the owner of the manuscript of Roger North's *Memoirs of Music*, now in the library of Hereford Cathedral.

He is commemorated by a stained-glass window in the north transept clerestory, and also by a plaque recording that 'he honourably and conscientiously discharged the office of organist of this Cathedral for upwards of 34 years'.

Grove[1].

Langdon Colborne 1877–89 (b. London (Hackney), 15 Sept. 1835; d. Hereford, 16 Sept. 1889). Colborne was a pupil of *George Cooper. He became organist of

St Michael's College, Tenbury in 1860, moving from there to Beverley Minster (1874), Wigan Parish Church (1875), and Dorking Parish Church (1877) before his appointment to Hereford. He took the Cambridge degree of Mus.B. in 1864, and received the Lambeth degree of Mus.D. in 1883. There is a memorial window to him in the north transept clerestory of the Cathedral.

BMB.

George Robertson Sinclair 1889–1917 (b. Croydon, 28 Oct. 1863; d. Birmingham, 7 Feb. 1917). Sinclair's father was director of public instruction in India. He himself was a chorister of St Michael's College, Tenbury, and then studied for a time at the Royal Irish Academy of Music under *Robert Stewart. In 1879 he became assistant to *C. H. Lloyd at Gloucester Cathedral. From 1880 to 1889 he was organist of Truro Cathedral, at first before the consecration of the present building. He brought fresh vitality to bear on the Three Choirs Festivals at Hereford, introducing, for example, the music of Wagner. From 1899 until his death he conducted the Birmingham Festival Choral Society. He was an honorary member of the Royal Academy of Music, and an honorary FRCO. In 1899 he received the Lambeth degree of D.Mus.

Sinclair was an intimate friend of Elgar, who dedicated 'Pomp and Circumstance' March No. 4 to him. His initials, 'GRS', are found on Variation XI of Elgar's 'Enigma Variations, Op. 36, which (it is generally, though not universally, accepted) immortalizes Sinclair's bulldog, Dan. There is a memorial to him in the south choir aisle of the Cathedral, declaring that 'his lofty character, devotion to duty, and passionate love of his profession won for him universal affection and esteem'.

Grove[2].

§Sir Percy (Clarke) Hull 1918–49 (b. Hereford, 27 Oct. 1878; d. Farnham, Surrey, 31 Aug. 1968). Hull became a chorister of Hereford Cathedral in 1889 under Sinclair (who, as he said, 'chopped us up very fine'), and was assistant organist there from 1896. He was interned at Ruhleben during the 1914–18 war, but was released in time to be appointed Sinclair's successor in 1918. He became an honorary FRCO in 1920, and in 1921 received the Lambeth degree of D.Mus. In 1947, following the revival of the Three Choirs Festivals after World War II, he received a knighthood.

After retirement as organist of the Cathedral (with the title of organist emeritus), he retained his life appointment as sub-canon, though without active duties. He was the last holder of this ancient office, mentioned on p. 131 above. There is a memorial to him in the Bishop's Cloister, close to that to Clarke-Whitfeld.

(Albert) Meredith Davies, CBE, 1950–6.
See under New College, Oxford.

§(Alfred) Melville Cook 1956–66 (b. Gloucester, 18 June 1912). Cook was a chorister of Gloucester Cathedral, 1923–8, and was subsequently (1929–32) an articled pupil there under *H. W. Sumsion, and assistant organist from 1932 to 1937. He was also organist of All Saints' Church, Cheltenham, 1935–7. In 1937 he became organist of Leeds Parish Church. He left Hereford to become organist of All Saints' Church, Winnipeg, moving a year later to the Metropolitan United Church, Toronto. On retirement in 1986 he returned to England. He took the FRCO diploma with the Harding prize in 1931, and the Durham degrees of B.Mus. and D.Mus. in 1934 and 1941 respectively.

§**Richard (Hey) Lloyd 1966–74** (b. Stockport, 25 June 1933). Lloyd was a chorister of Lichfield Cathedral, 1942–7, and was educated subsequently at Rugby (1947–51) and at Jesus College, Cambridge, where he was organ scholar, 1952–5. He read music and holds the Cambridge degree of MA as well as the FRCO diploma. From 1957 to 1966 he was assistant organist of Salisbury Cathedral. In 1974 he moved to Durham on his appointment as organist of Durham Cathedral, and in 1985 he became deputy headmaster of Salisbury Cathedral School. Ill health brought about his early retirement in 1988.

§**Roy (Cyril) Massey, organist from 1974** (b. Birmingham, 9 May 1934). Massey was educated at Moseley Grammar School, Birmingham and the University of Birmingham (1953–7). He was an organ pupil of *David Willcocks. He took the Birmingham degree of B.Mus. (1956), and holds the diplomas of FRCO (1956), CHM (1957), and ADCM (1963). He was organist of St Alban the Martyr, Bordesley, Birmingham, 1953–60, and of St Augustine's, Edgbaston, Birmingham, 1960–5. He then became warden of the Royal School of Church Music and organist of Croydon Parish Church, 1965–8. He was organist of Birmingham Cathedral, 1968–74, and also director of music at King Edward's School. (See Addenda, p. 434.)

LEICESTER

The Cathedral Church of St Martin

(formerly Collegiate Church, 1922–6)

While still yet in the diocese of Peterborough, St Martin's Parish Church, Leicester became a collegiate church in 1922 under the Bishop of Peterborough as dean. Following the establishment of the diocese of Leicester in 1926, it was hallowed as the Cathedral in February 1927.

Charles Hancock (1875) **1922–7** (b. London (Islington), 4 Jan. 1852; d. Leicester, 6 Feb. 1927). After leaving the choir of St George's Chapel, Windsor, Hancock served articles to *G. J. Elvey there, and went on to become his assistant. He took the FRCO diploma in 1872 and the Oxford degree of B.Mus.

in 1874. Appointed to St Martin's, Leicester in 1875, he was in office when the church became collegiate in 1922. His death occurred a few days before the formal act raising it to cathedral status.

BMB.

§**Gordon (Archbold) Slater, OBE, 1927–31** (b. Harrogate, 1 Mar. 1896; d. Lincoln, 26 Jan. 1979). Slater studied under *E. C. Bairstow at York. His first appointment was to be organist of Boston Parish Church, Lincolnshire, 1919–27. He was organist of Leicester Cathedral from 1927 until January 1931, having been chosen out of a field of 149 candidates (information from the honorary archivist). In 1931 he took up the post of organist of Lincoln Cathedral, which he retained until his retirement in June 1966.

In addition to the FRCO diploma, Slater took the Durham degrees of B.Mus. (1915) and D.Mus. (1923). He was Ferens fine art lecturer at University College, Hull in 1946, and in that year he was also made a Justice of the Peace for Lincoln. In 1974 he was appointed OBE.

WWW, 1971–80.

§**George (Charles) Gray 1931–69** (b. Nutfield, Surrey, 7 Oct. 1897; d. Leicester, 24 Mar. 1981). Gray was educated at Rotherham Grammar School, Yorkshire, and was articled to *E. C. Bairstow at York Minster from 1919 to 1922. While there he was organist of St Michael-le-Belfry, York, 1920–2, and then moved to Leeds as organist of St Martin's Church, 1922–3. From 1923 to 1926 he was organist of Alnwick Parish Church, and from 1926 to 1930 of St Mary-le-Tower, Ipswich. He took up duty at Leicester Cathedral early in 1931 and retired at Easter 1969.

Gray obtained the Lafontaine prize with the FRCO diploma in 1920, and won the silver medal of the Worshipful Company of Musicians in 1922. He took the Durham degree of B.Mus. in 1927. In 1942 he was made a lay canon of Leicester Cathedral, and in 1965 the University of Leicester conferred on him the honorary degree of M.Mus. He received the Lambeth degree of Mus.D. in 1968.

§**Peter (Gilbert) White, master of the music from 1969** (b. Plymouth, 21 Jan. 1937). After leaving Plymouth College, White studied at both the Royal Academy of Music, where he held an organ scholarship, and the Royal School of Church Music, 1954–6; he then went up to St John's College, Cambridge as organ student, 1956–60. At Cambridge he read music and won the Stewart of Rannoch scholarship in sacred music, taking the degrees of BA (1959), Mus.B. (1960), and MA (1964). He also holds the diplomas of FRCO (1956) and CHM (1959).

He was assistant organist of Chester Cathedral, 1960–2, and then became headquarters choirmaster at the Royal School of Church Music. He left that post in 1966 to become director of music at the Merchant Taylors' School, London. On his appointment to Leicester Cathedral he also became head of music at Alderman Newton's School, subsequently moving to the staff of the City of Leicester School.

LICHFIELD

The Cathedral Church of The Blessed Virgin Mary and St Chad

Main sources in this section (1966):

Chapter Acts		*Miscellaneous*	
CA4	IV, 1521–60 ('The Red Book').	P2	Affidavit of Thomas Cotterell, 14 Aug. 1728.
CA5	V, 1537–1621 (intermittent).	P3	Letter of George Lamb, 4 Oct. 1728.
CA6	VI, 1628–37.	P6	Petition of sub-chanter and vicars choral relating to John Alcock, endorsed 'Michaelmas 1758'.
CA7	VII, 1660–1734.	SB	Subscription Book, 1660–1753.
CA8	VIII, 1740–95.	PR	Registers of baptisms, marriages, and burials in the Cathedral.
CA9	IX, 1795–1820.		
CA10	Hebdomadary Chapter Acts, (i) 1709–26, (ii) 1726–58, (iii) 1758–72.		

Lichfield first became a see in AD 670 under Chad, Bishop of the West Saxon diocese of Mercia. Later, the bishopric came to have two sees, one in the cathedral church of Lichfield, the other in the Benedictine cathedral priory of Coventry, and the bishop was known as 'of Coventry and Lichfield'. The dual title was retained after the dissolution of Coventry Cathedral Priory by Henry VIII (cf. Bath and Wells), though from 1660 it became 'of Lichfield and Coventry'. In the nineteenth century Coventry was made part of the diocese of Worcester, and from that time the simple title of Bishop of Lichfield was used.

Lichfield Cathedral, one of the Old Foundation, remained undisturbed in its constitution at the Reformation. Its body of vicars choral was already in existence in 1315, when the vicars had their common buildings hard by the Cathedral. After the Reformation the vicars, like those at Exeter, could be either in holy orders or laymen, but the Lichfield vicars were distinctive in that, up to the 1930s, each was constitutionally regarded as the vicar of an individual prebendary, as in the very early Middle Ages, and was admitted to 'the stall of the vicar choral of the prebend of Longdon', or what ever it might be (see below, under A. P. Porter).

The Cathedral Muniments are by no means deficient in documents pre-dating the Civil War, but, unfortunately, these disclose no information about organists or masters of the choristers. Two Act Books covering 1521–60 and 1628–37 record installations of vicars choral, but have nothing to tell us about organists or masters of the choristers; another, covering 1537–1621, is almost entirely a transcript of lease-indentures. There is little doubt that the organist/masters of the choristers of this period were vicars choral. We only know of two such officers before the Civil War, and they are not named in the Cathedral Muniments. Michael East described himself as master of the choristers of Lichfield Cathedral on the title-pages of his fourth and subsequent madrigal books. Presumably he was appointed after 1610, when the title-page of his third madrigal book carried no such description. In 1606 he inscribed his second madrigal book from Ely House, Holborn, London.

Watkins's notes at Ely Cathedral (q.v.) record a Michael East who was lay clerk there from the quarter ending March 1609 to Midsummer 1610, and again for the single quarter ending Michaelmas 1614. The Lichfield East no doubt remained in office until 1644, when the choral services were stopped. His will was proved on 9 May 1648 (PCC, Essex, f. 77). He had a son, Michael, who was 4 in 1650 (*CSPD*, Interregnum G220, nos. 125, 127, 131), and in December 1656 the Trustees for the Maintenance of Ministers granted £3 to a Michael East of Lichfield (Matthews 1948). There was a Michael East among the lay vicars choral of Lichfield immediately after the Restoration, presumably (since he was not newly installed) the same man reinstated. Among the choristers trained by the elder Michael East as master of the choristers *c.*1630 was Elias Ashmole.

Henry Hinde ←1630–?1641. Elias Ashmole, who was born in Lichfield in 1617, observed in his autobiography that 'being competently grounded therein [i.e., in music], I became a chorister in the Cathedral Church [of Lichfield] . . . Mr Michael East, Bachelor of Music, was my tutor for song and Mr Henry Hinde, organist of the Cathedral (he died the 6th of August 1641?) taught me on the virginals and organ.' Hinde, then, is the first organist of Lichfield Cathedral who can be named; we do not know his immediate successor.

Ashmole records how, immediately after the Restoration, services again began to be said in the Cathedral on 16 June 1660; but the building was in a very poor condition, and there probably was no organ music for some time, perhaps not until 1669, when Bishop Hackett, who had a new organ built, reconsecrated the Cathedral. Hackett also set on foot a move to furnish a regular body of statutes for the Cathedral, though these were not issued until 1693, after his death. The provisions concerning the vicars choral contain the following (rendered from the Latin):

> We appoint one organist and the same to be a lay vicar in our Cathedral Church, that in those parts of the Services which are only to be sung he may join with the rest and in those where the organ is to be used he may play upon that . . . For salary [in addition to his stipend as vicar] he shall yearly receive . . . four pounds.

William Lamb (I) ?–1688 (d. Lichfield, 2 Mar. 1688). In a list of vicars dated 24 August 1683, written on the reverse of the title-page of the *primus contratenor* part of Barnard's *Cathedral Music*, now in the Cathedral library, the name 'Mr Lamb sen[ior]' is designated 'organist'. Later, the legend 'Dyed Mar. 2 1687/8' was added to it. The last name on this list is 'Mr Lamb jun[ior]'. I take these to be, respectively, William Lamb (I), admitted vicar choral of the prebend of Pipa Minor on 7 September 1660, and William Lamb (II) (see below), admitted vicar choral of the prebend of Eccleshall on 7 September 1682.

William Lamb (II) 1688–? (d. Lichfield, ?1713). The reverse of the title-page to Barnard's *Cathedral Music* (see above) supplies us with three further lists of vicars. One, dated 19 March 1687/8, contains 'Mr Lamb'; another, 12 February 1698/9, 'Mr Lamb organist'; and a third, undated, also 'Mr Lamb organist'.

These must refer to William Lamb (II), admitted vicar choral in 1682. His stall of vicar choral (Eccleshall) was filled by Thomas Hill on 30 September 1713 (CA7), by which time one assumes that Lamb was dead. His post as organist, however, had been filled by 1712 at the latest.

George Lamb ←1711–49 (d. Lichfield, Dec. 1749). George Lamb was admitted lay vicar of the stall of Tachbrook on 25 March 1709 (SB). CA10 (i) records on 21 March 1711/12, that 'George Lamb the organist' was required to live permanently in his house as vicar, though he himself said it was too small for his family. In 1714, on the occasion of a visitation, it was alleged (CA7) that he 'Led a wicked unchaste life, being charged by common fame with lying with several women one of which as we have heard has lately fathered a bastard child upon him.' On 5 January 1721/2 (CA7) he moved from the stall of Tachbrook to that of Longdon.

Two remarkable documents crop up in 1728. A certain Thomas Cottrell of Halesowen, Staffordshire had been employed to repair the organ. On 24 August he made affidavit (P2) against George Lamb, asserting that the latter had more or less compelled him to hand over half of the £40 he had received for his work. 'Damn you', Lamb allegedly said to the organ-builder, 'if you will not pay me half you are allowed for mending the organ it shall never be approved of [meaning, no doubt, that Lamb would not certify the work as satisfactory] and then according to your agreement you will have nothing for your pains.' Further, Cottrell said, Lamb had deliberately damaged the pipes and then incited Cottrell to steal some out of the little organ in the Lady Chapel to build him a house organ. When Cottrell said he would be hanged for this, Lamb allegedly replied: 'Damn you, never fear it, for they will never miss them.'

To this, Lamb replied with vigour and at great length on 4 October (P3) to the effect that Cottrell had misrepresented himself as an organ-builder, and that he had in fact asked for Lamb's help to cover up for him. Lamb then proceeded to enlarge the field of conflict by rounding on his enemies among the vicars, four of whom—he says—had tried to father a bastard child on him. One of them, Perkins by name, he attacked for drunkenness and filthiness (he 'bepissed his bed'), and another, Hains, for buggery and slander. How it was all resolved does not transpire.

Lamb was buried in the Cathedral on 23 December 1749.

John Alcock 1750–65 (b. London, 11 Apr. 1715; d. Lichfield, Feb. 1806). Alcock was born near St Paul's Cathedral. His date of birth is contained in a letter now in the Bodleian Library (Montague MS d.6, f. 30). He was a chorister of St Paul's under Charles King ('my most kind and ingenious master'), as he mentions in a letter of 25 January 1791 printed by T. F. Bumpus (1903: iii. 47). In 1729 he was apprenticed to John Stanley, of whom, in the preface to his collection of anthems published in 1771, he speaks as 'my worthy friend and master, the inimitable Mr Stanley', and then, in 1736, applied unsuccessfully for the organist's post at the London churches of St Antholin, Budge Row, and St Giles, Cripplegate (Dawe 1983). His first appointment was as organist of St Andrew's Church, Plymouth, where a newly installed organ was opened on 30 November 1737. In 1741 he moved to Reading, and 'Mr John Alcock, Organist of St Laurence in Reading', subscribed to Greene's *Forty Select Anthems* in 1743.

On 19 January 1749/50 (CA10, ii) he was appointed lay vicar of the stall of Longdon in Lichfield Cathedral, 'the same being vacant by the death of George Lamb the late vicar thereof'; he was installed on 22 January (CA7), and appointed Cathedral organist the next day (CA10, ii). At the September audit of 1754 he was given leave of absence 'to teach his scholars either at home or in the country' without being mulcted, provided that his son, 'or other skilful person', supplied his place (CA7).

In 1752, having noticed, as he says, the 'numberless mistakes' in the manuscript part-books of many cathedrals (but not Lichfield!), he conceived a scheme of publishing one Service per quarter, engraved in score and figured to the organ, beginning with 'Mr *Tallis's*; Mr *Bird's* (in all the Six Parts); *Dr Gibbons's; these will be transposed one note higher*', and working through Rogers, Blow, Purcell, and others to Charles King's Service in F (see the prospectus bound with Alcock's *Divine Harmony* (1752) in Lbl, and printed by J. S. Bumpus 1972: 257–9). As a specimen of style, he had his own Service in E minor engraved. But nothing came of this plan; and when Alcock heard that *Maurice Greene intended to publish an anthology of cathedral music, he handed over to him his transcripts of Services by Tallis, Byrd, and Gibbons (see his remarks in Lbl, Add. MS 23624, f. 2). As is well known, the eventual outcome of Greene's design was Boyce's *Cathedral Music*, to which Alcock subscribed in 1760–73.

In June 1755 he took his B.Mus. degree at Oxford (Foster 1887–92). By 1758 trouble had developed in his work at Lichfield: at Michaelmas ten vicars choral sent a long petition to the Chapter protesting about Alcock's conduct. They complained that if they asked him to play more slowly, he played 'so slow that their breath will not serve to hold out the long, loitering, dragging notes'; but if they asked him to play faster, he would play so quickly that 'the choir cannot sometimes articulate half the words'. It was also requested that 'he may not hereafter mock and mimic with his voice any of the vicars, as he frequently has done, in the Responses, and even in the Confession. That he may not show his splenetic tricks upon the organ to expose or confound the performers, or burlesque their manner of singing.' Finally, it was demanded 'that he may have some regard to the sacredness of the place and the solemnity of the worship; so that we may . . . attend on the service of God without distraction' (P6). No doubt it was as a result of this that at the September audit of 1760 (CA8) the Chapter, 'upon complaint made by the Sub-chanter and body of the vicars-choral against Mr John Alcock', admonished him for having 'frequently interrupted the decency of public worship . . . by playing improperly, indecently and perversely on the organ with design to confound and prevent the vicars from the due performance of their duty'. He was warned to behave himself in future.

After he had ceased to be organist of the Cathedral, Alcock recorded his own complaints about his working conditions in his argumentative and self-justificatory preface to his *Six and Twenty Select Anthems in Score* (1771; dated from Lichfield Close):

when I was Organist and Master of the Boys . . . I was forced to teach the lads every day . . . and also to attend the Church, as often, being not permitted to go out of town, to my scholars in the country, more than two days, in a fortnight or three weeks [*but see the Chapter minute of September 1754 already quoted*]; although I had only one scholar in the town for the first seven years . . .

'Tis incredible what a number of base artifices have been practised by some people belonging to this Cathedral, in order to prejudice me, in my profession, and distress my family, for no cause whatever: Nay even my son, as soon as ever he began to play for me, was turned out from being a chorister, though he had been in the choir but two years, and his voice (which was a very useful one) not the least fallen . . . Also, though he always officiated for me, yet I forfeited the same money, when I went out of town, as if the duty had been totally neglected; albeit the salary then was only four pounds per annum, besides the vicar's place; and there was much more duty when I was organist, than now, being obliged always to play a voluntary after Morning and Evening Prayers, even in the severest cold weather, when, very often, there was only one vicar, who read the Service, and an old woman at church, besides the choristers; which not only brought, but fixed the rheumatism so strongly upon me, that I am seldom free from pain, and sometimes confined to my bed, for eight or ten days together, though I never had the least complaint of that kind, till then; and no body can live more regular than I have always done, as every one of my acquaintance, can testify; I likewise played the organ all Passion Week, (except Good Friday), both which customs had ever since been discontinued . . .

DNB states that he resigned as Cathedral organist in 1760; but of this there is no trace in the surviving archives. It appears that he became organist of Sutton Coldfield Church in 1761, but there is no reason why he should not have combined this with his Cathedral post, provided he supplied the required deputies. The next organist of Lichfield Cathedral was not appointed until 1765, and I see no reason to suppose that Alcock did not remain in office until shortly before then. His son, by this time organist of Newark Parish Church, Nottinghamshire, was paid £4 on 25 May 1764 for tuning the Lichfield organ (CA10, iii). There was (see below under William Brown) a short vacancy before his successor was appointed, and this was filled by **Thomas Edmonds**, a vicar choral. It also appears that Alcock latterly had not been master of the choristers.

It may well have been about the time he ceased to be Cathedral organist that he took the D.Mus. degree at Oxford. Foster (1887–92) is only able to cite '176–'. In his publication of 1771 Alcock speaks of the degree as being taken during his time as Cathedral organist, and in the letter cited above which supplied his date of birth, written on 4 April 1803, he spoke of 'having been created a Doctor of Music almost 40 years at Oxford'. This accords reasonably well with the year 1765 as given in *GM* (1806); but the Chapter Act appointing his successor in September 1765 (see below) speaks of him as 'Mr' Alcock.

In September 1770 the inexplicable Chapter order is recorded (CA8) 'that the seat which Dr Alcock quits be set to William Jackson'. But he continued to hold a place as vicar choral, and for a time (as he recorded in 1771) he combined this with the duties of organist both at Sutton Coldfield and Tamworth. Stephens (1882) gives his dates at Sutton Coldfield as 1761–86, and at Tamworth as 1766–90. In 1776, described simply as 'Dr Alcock, Litchfield', he subscribed to Burney's *History of Music*, while in 1790 and 1795, described as a vicar choral of Lichfield, he subscribed to Arnold's and William Hayes's *Cathedral Music* respectively. The Chapter treated him well in his later years, passing a minute in September 1790 (CA8) so that he was not mulcted for his absences, 'as he constantly attends when able'.

Under the pseudonym of John Piper, Alcock was the author of a novel, *The Life of Miss Fanny Brown*, containing much patently autobiographical matter, shedding light on cathedral conditions. The National Portrait Gallery possesses a photograph of an unattributed portrait of Alcock, *c.*1766, the present whereabouts of which is unknown.

He died at Lichfield, where the Cathedral register has this entry: 'John Alcock, Doctor of Music, Senior Lay Vicar of this Cathedral Church and formerly organist of Plymouth and Reading. Buried February 23 1806 Aged 91.'

William Brown 1765–1807 (b. Worcester, *c.*1737; d. Lichfield, Mar. 1807, aged 70). The terms of Brown's election as organist no doubt reflected the Chapter's dislike of a constitutional arrangement whereby, having made Alcock a vicar in order to appoint him organist, they were compelled to allow him to continue as vicar when his duties as organist had come to an end. It was also thought fit to lay down precise conditions about absence:

The Dean and Chapter unanimously elected William Brown of the City of Worcester to succeed Henry Wood as a lay vicar [of the prebend of Wolvey] upon his giving security that he will resign the vicar's place in case he shall at any time hereafter resign the organist's place if the Dean and Chapter shall elect him into the said office or place of organist.

The Dean and Chapter immediately afterwards elected the said William Brown their organist in the room of Mr Alcock at the usual salary of four pounds a year, provided he give a bond not to resign the organist's place without resigning the vicar's place at the same time.

That when the said Mr Brown is absent from church on the teaching of scholars that he shall be entitled to his commons and not be marked absent, but he is not to be entitled to this privilege except when he is attending scholars.

That a present of ten guineas be made to Mr Edmonds for his care of the organist's place during the vacancy. (CA8, 27 Sept. 1765.)

Brown also assumed the post of master of the choristers, which had, apparently, been divorced from the office of organist for some time:

Ordered that Mr Fletcher [Chapter clerk] do for the future pay Mr Bird [Francis Bird, lay vicar] six pounds a year out of the choristers' rent in consideration of his having been Master of the Boys and his voluntarily resigning the office in favour of Mr Brown, and that Mr Fletcher do pay the said Mr Brown four pounds, the remaining part of the said salary, and no more, during the lifetime of the said Mr Bird . . . it being intended and ordered that Mr Bird is to have six pounds a year out of the salary for his life.

In 1779 Brown was relieved of a duty about which Alcock had so bitterly complained: it was ordered on 24 September 'that for the future the service be read in Passion Week in a parochial way, and that the organ is not to be used in Passion Week' (CA8).

In 1771 he subscribed to Alcock's *Six and Twenty Anthems*, and in 1788 to the second edition of Boyce's *Cathedral Music.*

The Cathedral register records his burial thus: 'William Brown, native of

Worcester, for 42 years organist and vicar-choral of this Cathedral. Aged 70. Buried March 11, 1807.' A tablet, high on the wall in the south-east corner of St Stephen's Chapel, speaks of him as 'highly esteemed as a musician and as a man'.

Samuel Spofforth 1807–64 (b. Southwell; d. Lichfield, 6 June 1864, aged 84). Spofforth was the younger brother of Reginald Spofforth the glee-writer, and they were both choristers of Southwell Minster under their uncle, Thomas Spofforth. From 1798 to 1807 Samuel was organist of Peterborough Cathedral (q.v.). In connection with his appointment there, the Chapter of Southwell Minster granted him the sum of £4. 3*s*. 7*d*. 'for his journey to Peterborough on account of his diligent services to the church'. (Southwell CA13, 18 October 1798). He had been admitted a chorister of Southwell on 18 April 1793, and left the choir there on 19 April 1798 (James 1927).

At Lichfield 'Samuel Spofforth of Peterborough' was elected organist and lay vicar of the prebend of Wolvey, 'vacant by the death of William Brown', on 6 June 1807 (CA9).

The Cathedral register notes his burial on 13 June 1864, aged 84. He had been organist of Lichfield Cathedral for fifty-seven years, and a cathedral organist for sixty-five years.

Thomas Bedsmore 1864–81 (b. Lichfield, 26 Dec. 1833; d. Lichfield, 9 June 1881). Bedsmore was a chorister of Lichfield Cathedral and then an articled pupil of Samuel Spofforth. He was appointed assistant organist of the Cathedral in 1849, and organist of St Chad's, Stow, Lichfield in 1854. After his appointment as Cathedral organist he also became organist of St Mary's, Lichfield and of Barton-under-Needwood Parish Church. He took the FRCO diploma in 1865.

A memorial brass on the wall of the north choir aisle describes him as 'Thomas Bedsmore who for seventeen years was Organist of this Cathedral. He was also Captain of the E or Lichfield Company, 5th Battalion Staffordshire Rifle Volunteers.'

Stephens 1882.

John Browning Lott 1881–1924 (b. Faversham, Kent, 1849; d. Buxted, Sussex, 29 Sept. 1924). Lott was a chorister of Canterbury Cathedral under *T. E. Jones and *W. H. Longhurst. T. F. Bumpus (1903: ii. 16) relates how it was Lott who gave the alarm at choir practice when a fire broke out at the east end of Canterbury Cathedral on 3 September 1872. After early appointments as organist of St Dunstan's and St Paul's Churches, Canterbury, he became Longhurst's assistant in 1873. In 1875 he became organist of Margate Parish Church, moving to Lichfield in 1881.

Sir William Harris (*MT*, 89 (1948), 55) recorded how Lott, on being asked whether it was true he had worked under a precentor named Abraham, replied (evidently relishing the reference to his own name): 'Yes, but he had *all* the cattle' (alluding to Genesis 13).

Lott took the Oxford degree of B.Mus. in 1876, and also held the FRCO diploma.

BMB; *MT*, 65 (1924), 1037.

Ambrose Probert Porter 1925–59 (b. Coleford, Glos., 1885; d. 1970). Porter was educated at Bell's Grammar School, Coleford, and was subsequently a pupil of *A. H. Brewer at Gloucester Cathedral. At an early age he was organist of Newland Parish Church, Gloucestershire. He then became assistant to Brewer, 1907–13, moving from there to St Matthias's, Richmond, Surrey, where he remained until his appointment to Lichfield. He took the Oxford degree of B.Mus. in 1913, and held the FRCO diploma.

Like all his predecessors from 1693, he was lay vicar choral as well as organist, holding the stall of Wolvey which, from the time of William Brown, had been regularly allotted to that officer. The statutes of 1905, under which he was appointed, virtually repeated the provisions of 1693: 'The Organist by virtue of his appointment is a lay vicar, and shall have a stall assigned to him accordingly, so that he may take part in singing with the choir when the organ is not used.' When Porter retired in 1959, by which time new statutes had come into force, this long-standing arrangement came to an end.

WWM.

§Richard (George) Greening 1959–77 (b. Sunningwell, Berks., 17 Nov 1927; d. Oct. 1979). Greening was a chorister of New College, Oxford, and afterwards a private pupil of *H. K. Andrews. He went up to New College in 1948, taking the Oxford degrees of BA (1951), B.Mus. (1952), and MA (1955). In 1952, on taking the FRCO diploma, he was awarded the Harding prize.

After a period as organist of St Giles's Church, Oxford, 1950–5, he became assistant to *W. H. Harris at St George's Chapel, Windsor, 1955–9. During this time he was also organist of the private chapel in Windsor Great Park. In 1961 he joined the staff of the Birmingham School of Music, continuing there after resigning from the Cathedral in 1977.

Greening was the first organist of Lichfield Cathedral not to hold a vicar's stall. His stipend, however, still included, as an indentifiable element, the old sum of £4 allocated to the organist under Bishop Hackett's statutes.

§Jonathan Rees-Williams, organist and master of the choristers from 1978 (b. St Helier, Jersey, 10 Feb. 1949). Rees-Williams was educated at Kilburn Grammar School, London, the Royal Academy of Music (various prizes), and New College, Oxford (organ scholar, 1969–72). He read music, taking the degrees of BA (1972) and MA (1976), having already acquired the FRCO diploma in 1968. In Michaelmas term 1972 he was acting organist of New College; he then became assistant organist of Hampstead Parish Church and St Clement Danes, Strand, London until 1974, when he was appointed assistant organist of Salisbury Cathedral, where he remained until moving to Lichfield.

LINCOLN

The Cathedral Church of the Blessed Virgin Mary (Lincoln Minster)

Main sources in this section (1965) (with Lincolnshire Archives Office references):

Ledger Books of Patents, &c.
LB1 1560–76 (Bij/2/4).
LB2 1568–87 (Bij/3/17).
LB3 1587–1607 (Bij/2/5).

Chapter Acts
CA1 1520–45 (A/3/5).
CA2 1546–59 (A/3/6); CA1 and 2 are calendared by R. E. G. Cole (Lincoln Record Society, 12, 13, 15).
CA3 1559–98 (A/3/7).
CA4 1562–84 (A/3/8).
CA5 1598–1640, 1660–9 (A/3/9).
CA6 1670–1702 (A/3/11).
CA7 1702–5 (A/3/12).
CA8 1706–52 (A/3/13).
CA9 1731–61 (A/3/14).
CA10 1762–89 (A/3/15).
CA11 1790–1811 (A/3/16).
CA12 1811–53 (A/3/17).

Accounts
Ac1 1525–95 (Bj/3/8).
Ac2 1531–96, drafts (Bj/5/12).
Ac3 1548–77 (Bj/3/6).
Ac4 1601–27 (Bj/3/9).
Ac5 1603–41 (Bj/3/10).
Ac6 1661–70 (Bj/3/11).
Ac7 1670–82 (Bj/3/13/12).
Ac8 1682–94 (Bj/4/1).

Registers of Baptisms, Marriages, and Burials
Parish Register of St Margaret-in-the-Close, Lincoln (Lincoln Record Society, 2).

The history of Lincoln Cathedral begins in early Norman times, when Remigius, Bishop of Dorchester, was ordered by William the Conqueror to move his see to Lincoln. The building of the Cathedral was started in 1073. It is a cathedral of the Old Foundation, ranking, together with York and Salisbury, as pre-eminent among them.

Some of the terms used at various times at Lincoln call for explanation. As at Salisbury, final responsibility for the choristers rested on one of the canons, who, in this capacity, was known as 'master of the choristers'; we shall not, however, be concerned with this use of the title. The musician who actually taught the choristers was known as the 'master', 'teacher', 'instructor', or 'schoolmaster' of the choristers. There was also a third officer, called the 'seneschal' or 'steward' of the choristers, whose duties were those of an administrator of their endowed income. The men of the choir were divided into two groups: 'senior vicars choral' and 'junior vicars choral'. The vicars choral had a common hall from the early fourteenth century, and were incorporated as a college in 1441. From the time of the Reformation, only the former were in holy orders. Latterly the expression 'lay vicar choral' came to be applied to the junior vicars. Below both of these groups there was at one time a category of 'poor clerks' (*pauperes clerici*, or *clerici secundi formi*). The singingboys were of two foundations, the choristers proper, who can be traced back to 1258, and the 'chanters' (derived from a pre-Reformation chantry) on the foundation of Sir Bartholomew, Lord of Burgersh (1345).

Thomas Appleby (1st tenure) **1537–9**. Appleby was first appointed on a year's probation in April 1537, following the death of **Robert Dove**, who had been master of the choristers (CA1, 24 October 1528) and also, according to *Valor Ecclesiasticus* (1535), organist. Appleby's full admission on 23 April 1538 as both organist and master of the choristers is recorded in CA1 (f. 159). In 1539 (July, according to Flood 1925) he left his post at Lincoln, and it has generally been presumed that he was the 'Applebie' (no Christian name given) who in that year became instructor of the choristers at Magdalen College, Oxford (Bloxam 1853–7: ii. 187), where he was succeeded in 1541 by John Sheppard. However that may be, it is certainly reasonable to identify him with the Thomas Appleby who held office again at Lincoln from 1541 (see below).

James Crawe 1539–?1541. Crawe's letters patent of appointment as organist and master of the choristers, dated 4 October 1539, divide his annual remuneration for organ-playing into two parts—40*s*. for playing at the daily Mary Mass, and 13*s*. 4*d*. for playing at double feasts, Sundays, and feasts of nine lessons. By a minute of the same date (CA1, f. 169^{v}) he was granted a further 13*s*. 4*d*. which was not to be included in his patent; presumably this was personal to him and not pertaining to the office. He was required not only to teach the boys both singing and organ-playing, but also, 'especially two or three of them . . . to play on the instruments called clavicords', the boys to find 'the instruments called clavicords at their own proper cost and expense'.

Thomas Appleby (2nd tenure) **1541–60→**. The minute of Appleby's reappointment is dated 26 November 1541 (CA1, f. 193) and provides for a patent in the same terms as Crawe's. He was allowed the chamber over the outer gate of the choristers' house. His services were evidently well approved, for on 12 February 1558/9 it was resolved to grant him the next vacancy in the office of seneschal (or steward) of the house of choristers, to which he was in fact admitted on 18 August 1559. Flood (1925) thought that Appleby gave up his duties as master of the choristers in 1559, but this is not so; he has misunderstood the appointment of the precentor to the post of master of the choristers, which must be read in the sense of the note on p. 154 above. The last to be heard of Appleby is when, on 3 March 1560, he complained that in consequence of a reduction in the choristers' revenues, the number of boys had fallen from nine to six.

William Byrd 1563–72 (d. 4 July 1623, aged 80). Byrd was appointed organist and master of the choristers by letters patent under a minute of 24 April 1563 (CA3, f. 27^{v}; CA4, f. 4^{v}), his salary dating from 25 March 1563. The remuneration, £6. 13*s*. 4*d*. in each capacity, was quite sizeable for someone only a little over 20 years of age. Earlier, on 6 February 1562/3, the Chapter had granted him the rectory of Hainton, Lincolnshire, for a term of forty-one years (CA3, f. 27; CA 4, f. 4^{v}). Throughout his time at Lincoln, successive annual payments to him in the accounts of the Common Fund for paper and ink indicate that he was not only the music teacher, but also the general schoolmaster of the choristers.

His stipend was derived from more than one of the Cathedral accounts (see Shaw 1967). The frontispiece to the present volume reproduces the entry in the accounts of the Common Fund for the year ending Michaelmas 1564. A transcript (expanding abbreviations without distinction, but leaving the conventional contractions 'solut:' and 'allocat:') is as follows: 'Et solut: Willelmo Birde magistro choristarum pro feodo suo tam pro lusu organorum quam pro erudicione eorundem choristarum ad lxvjs. viijd. per annum ei per capitulum allocat: viz. in all—[?] inde per tempus compoti ultimi xxvjs. viijd. ei solut: ex revene ducatus Lancastre—xls.' ('and paid to William Birde master of the choristers for his fee for playing the organs and for teaching those choristers at 66*s*. 8*d*. a year allowed him by the Chapter, namely the allowance since the time of the last account, 26*s*. 8*d*. having been paid to him from the revenue of the Duchy of Lancaster—40*s*.').

On 19 November 1569 he was summoned before the Chapter and, for reasons not precisely specified ('ob quasdam causas eidem objectas', is the phrase used), his salary was suspended. However, at his humble entreaty ('ad humilem instantiam dicti Willelmi Byrde') he was released from this at the end of July (CA3, f. 66[v]; CA4, f. 44). Directions about his duties at the organ during Morning and Evening Prayer were issued at Michaelmas 1570: he was to play before the chanting ('ante inchancionem') of the canticles and during the singing of the anthem ('necnon tempore psallendi le anthem una cum choro psallente idem') (CA3, f. 68; CA4, f. 45[v]).

Byrd married while he was at Lincoln, and two of his children, Christopher and Elizabeth, were baptized there. And during this period he was sworn a gentleman of the Chapel Royal on 22 February 1569/70 (for a problem about this date, see p. 3).

He left Lincoln for London at the end of 1572, and recommended Thomas Butler, a poor clerk (see below), as his successor (CA3, f. 72[v]; CA4, f. 50). Perhaps, however (whether disingenuously or not), he really meant Butler to be only his deputy; though the Cathedral did not seem to think so. Evidently Byrd's view became known, for as late as *c*.1700 Thomas Ford, chaplain of Christ Church, Oxford, noted that Byrd was organist of Lincoln Cathedral, 'which he kept by Butley his suppletio [?] when organist of Queen Elizabeth's Chapel' (Ob, MS Mus. e.17). Be this as it may, the Cathedral certainly saved £3. 6*s*. 8*d*., the difference between Butler's initial stipend and Byrd's.

A year later, on 2 November 1573, the Chapter met to consider letters received on Byrd's behalf from certain noblemen and members of the Queen's Council, and somewhat grudgingly granted him an annual payment of £3. 6*s*. 8*d*. (perhaps significantly, the sum by which Butler's remuneration had been reduced), to start on 25 March 1574 (CA3, f. 75; CA4, f. 52[v]); this was later embodied in a patent dated 15 January 1576/7 (LB1, f. 61[v]; LB2, f. 46[v]). The accounts (Ac2) show that this payment ceased after the accounting year 1581–2. (For details of the Lincoln documents, with facsimile, see Shaw 1967.)

In 1577, in a joint petition to the Queen with Tallis, Byrd spoke of how, with his family commitments, he was the poorer for 'being called to Her Majesty's service from Lincoln Cathedral, where he was well settled' (Hatfield House MSS, CP 160, 134). They were rewarded by a lease.

From 1572 Byrd's whole life was bound up with the Chapel Royal under Elizabeth I and James I, and he retained his position despite his unconcealed sympathy for the old religion. He was organist of the Chapel in both reigns (q.v.). In his will he expressed a wish to be buried at Stondon Massey, where he had property. His pedigree and coat of arms were recorded at the herald's visitation of Essex in 1634 (printed by the Harleian Society, 13, p. 366).

Thomas Butler 1572–97. As already noted, Butler's appointment was made on Byrd's suggestion, and was dated 7 December 1572 (CA3, f. 72v; CA4, f. 50). On 20 September 1580 he was admonished by the Chapter for negligence in his teaching, as disclosed at the bishop's visitation (CA3, f. 89; CA4, f. 64v). It is significant that his patent of appointment as both organist and master of the choristers, dated 4 February 1582/3 (LB2, f. 89v), was not granted until the annuity to Byrd had been discontinued; at the same time his stipend was increased to what Byrd's had been up to 1572. On 9 November 1584 his pay both as organist and poor clerk was suspended until such time as he did his duty not only on Sundays and feast-days but on vigils and weekdays; it was restored on 4 December (CA3, f. 97v). Ten years later he was in trouble again (11 January 1594/5, CA3, f. 121), and was admonished for not teaching 'some of those most apt' to play the organ to take his place when he was absent. On 30 June 1597 (CA3, f. 125v) he voluntarily relinquished the posts of organist and master of the choristers. It should be noted that some of the Lincoln documents render the surname as 'Boulter'.

It was during Butler's time, in the year 1594–5, that the master of the choristers began to have the duty of teaching the boys to play the viol; he was reimbursed for the cost of strings (Ac1, under 'Custos et Expensae').

A Chapter minute of 26 January 1593/4 (CA3, f. 118v) speaks of John Hilton (see under Trinity College, Cambridge) as having been recently organist of the Cathedral. This cannot be taken literally, as Butler was continuously in office (not always satisfactorily) until his resignation in 1597. But his patent did permit him to execute his office by deputy with the consent of the Dean and Chapter; and, as Hilton was clearly a musician of competence, he may have acted as organist, which would explain the loose designation referred to. It is worth noting that in the accounting year 1590–1 (Ac1) the small sum allowed to the master of the choristers for paper and ink used in teaching was paid to Hilton instead of Butler (accounts for the next three years are wanting).

William Boys 1597. Boys was appointed on probation for one year (CA3, f. 125v) on 30 June 1597, but he served only a few months.

John Allen 1597–9. Allen was appointed on 16 December 1597 (CA3, f. 126v). No details about him are known. He was not appointed on probation, and, like his predecessors, he was both organist and master of the choristers.

Thomas Kingston 1599–1616. A certain Thomas Kingstone served his apprenticeship to *Edward Manestie, then master of the Magnus Song School, Newark-on-Trent, from 1593; on Manestie's departure for Southwell Minster in 1595, he abated two years of his apprentice's service, leaving him with only three more to serve (Jackson 1964: 72). It is very likely that this 'Kingstone' is our present subject.

His admission as organist and master of the choristers of Lincoln Cathedral on 24 September 1599 (CA5, f. 9v) was in the first instance on a year's probation. His patent was eventually issued on 1 October 1601 (LB3, f. 58). On 30 March 1611 a long complaint about him was entered in the Chapter Acts (CA5, f. 82):

> that he hath for many a long time and often been negligent in the execution of the duties of his office as well in teaching the choristers and in unreasonable beating of them as in playing upon the organs and also that he contemptuously some few days past did behave himself before the said Dean and Chapter in using contemptuous words and behaviour towards them and in calling Mr Dye [John Dye, since 2 March 1610/11 seneschal of the choristers] ass and otherwise divers times abuse the singingmen and others in words and deeds.

Kingston acknowledged his offence and was admonished. But the trouble was not at an end, for on 26 September 1612 (CA5, f. 89) he was called upon to surrender his patent as organist and teacher of the choristers in exchange for a new one as organist only. It was ordered 'that he shall not at any time hereafter meddle with the teaching of the choristers'. His new patent is dated 5 October 1612 (LB3, f. 31v). Thomas Stanley was made teacher of the choristers in his place. Kingston misbehaved himself again, and on 27 September 1615 (CA5, f. 112v) a complaint was lodged that he was 'very often drunk and that by means thereof he hath by disorderly playing on the organs put the quire out of tune and disordered them'. He was ordered to behave for one year or be dismissed. Meanwhile Stanley was not doing well with the choristers, and he too had to be admonished on 24 March 1615/16 (CA5, f. 115v).

Whether dismissed or not, Kingston had departed by October 1616, when his successor was admitted. It looks very likely, therefore, that he was the Thomas Kingston who appears at York in August of that year (q.v.) especially in view of the similar behaviour at both cathedrals. If this reconstruction of his career is correct, then he seems to have rounded it off by a return to Newark, where in 1633 one Thomas Kingstone was admitted master of the Magnus Song School, and where he was eventually buried on 17 November 1641 (Jackson, 1964: 73–5).

John Wanless 1616–63. Wanless was admitted as organist (Stanley still being master of the choristers) on 28 October 1616 (CA5, f. 122v); presumably Kingston was finally dismissed. A year later, on 30 September 1617 (CA5, f. 129v), Wanless's salary was fixed at £20, and on 25 September 1620 he was granted an extra £3. 6*s*. 8*d*. He was allotted the Gatehouse Chambers (i.e., the gatehouse to Vicars' Court) at a rent of 10*s*. on 5 February 1624/5, and on 1 October 1636 he was appointed to take charge of the Scripture library for the choristers at £2 a year (CA5, f. 195).

Meanwhile Stanley, who had been accused of negligence and allowing rudeness among the choristers (CA5, f. 139v, 2 Oct. 1619), had been replaced by Ralph Standish in the accounting year 1624–5 (Ac4; perhaps Standish was related to the Peterborough family of that name), and he, in turn, by Henry Mace, who was appointed teacher of the choristers on 2 October 1632 (CA5, f. 177). In the accounting year 1634–5 (Ac5) John Heardson took this post, presumably retaining it until the Interregnum.

In 1658 Wanless received a grant of £2 from the Trustees for the Maintenance of Ministers (Matthews 1948). After the Restoration he reappears in the accounts for 1660–1 as organist, and in 1661–2 as poor clerk also. In 1661–2 John Blundeville is named in the accounts as teacher of the choristers (see also pp. 100 and 318). Wanless's death is inferred from the payment, made in the accounting year 1662–3, of half a year's salary to Henry Wanless for 'John Wanless *defunct*, lately organist and poor clerk'.

Six of John Wanless's children were baptized at St Margaret-in-the-Close, Lincoln between 1628 and 1641: Thomas, John, Mary, Henry William, and Edward. His wife Mary died on 19 December 1641. On 19 October 1626 (CA5, f. 161^{v}) a Christopher Wanless was elected chorister, and a Thomas Wanless likewise on 30 September 1633 (CA5, f. 181). This could be the Thomas Wanless who is mentioned in the minutes (Lbl, Harl. MS 1911) of the London Corporation for Regulating the Art and Science of Music on 3 February 1662/3. A John Wanless became Burgersh chanter on 1 October 1636, as did an Ezekiel Wanless on 14 July 1639 (CA5, ff. 194^{v}, 202). The son Henry, to whom the half-year's salary was paid in 1662–3, became an innkeeper, and was appointed by patent to be constable of the Close of Lincoln on 19 September 1670. Another Thomas Wanless (conceivably Henry's son) was admitted Burgersh chanter on 2 April 1677 (CA6), and one of that name was playing the organ on 12 November 1689 when John Cutts struck John Jameson (see below); was this perhaps the Thomas Wanless who became organist of York Minster (q.v.)?

It may be that the whole Wanless group of cathedral musicians (Lincoln, Ripon, York) was of Durham origin. The register of leases granted by the Dean and Chapter of Durham records a grant of property in Claypath (Durham City) on 18 December 1593 to one Edward Wandlesse. In 1632–3 a certain Thomas Wanless (or 'Wandles'), MA, was precentor of Durham; and in 1609–10 and 1633–4 two boys called Henry Wanles (or 'Wandles') were choristers of Durham. Thomas Wanless, precentor of Durham; John Wanless, organist of Lincoln; and Henry Wanless, organist of Ripon, could all have been brothers, possibly the sons of Edward of Claypath, who might have been the great-grandfather of Thomas Wanless of York. Matthews (1948) records how Thomas Wanless, precentor of Durham, was called 'Chevalier Wandles' for his being sequestered and imprisoned at Hull for loyalty to the King during the Civil War. The various phonetic transcriptions of the name are well illustrated in the Ripon Cathedral PR, which records the burial, on 25 May 1690, of 'Mrs Ellen Goodman from Wath, daughter of Mr Wansley once organist of Ripon'.

Thomas Mudd 1662–3. There are only two references to Mudd in the official archives of Lincoln Cathedral, both in Ac6. The first records the payment to Mr Mudd, formerly organist ('Mro Mudd nup: organist'), of his half-year's stipend to St Philip's and St James's Day 1663; the other establishes his connection with Peterborough, and records the payment of 30*s*. the same year to Mr Mudd, formerly organist, for his expenses in riding from Peterborough to Lincoln ('pro expensis suis in equitando a civitate Petriburgens: ad civit: Lincoln:').

His behaviour during his short tenure at Lincoln is described in two letters from Featley (alias Fairclough), the precentor, to Dean Honywood. These letters, no longer extant, are printed thus by Maddison (1889):

14 March 1662/3. Mr Mudd hath been so debauched these assizes, and hath so abused Mr Derby the organ builder that he will hardly be persuaded to stay and finish his work unless Mudd be removed. And I have stuck in the same *Mudd* too; for he hath abused me above hope of pardon. I wish you would be pleased to send us down an able and more civil organist.

16 March 1662/3. Yesterday Mr Mudd showed the effects of his last week's tipling, for when Mr Joynes was in the midst of his sermon Mudd fell a-singing aloud, insomuch as Mr Joynes was compelled to stop; all the auditory gazed and wondered what was the matter, and at length some near him, stopping his mouth, silenced him, and then Mr Joynes proceeded: but this continued for a space of near half a quarter of an hour. So that now we dare trust him no more with our organ, but request you (if you can) to help us to another; and with what speed may be.

See under Exeter Cathedral.

Andreas Hecht 1663–93 (d. Lincoln, Mar. 1693). Hecht (or Height) received £10 as his stipend for the last three months (i.e., from June 1663) of the accounting year 1662–3 (Ac6). There is no formal record of his appointment. In the correspondence with Dean Honywood cited above (under Mudd) it is disclosed that Hecht, a Dutchman, was the dean's choice in preference to Featley's suggestion of John Hinton of Newark (letter of 21 March 1662/3, quoted by Maddison 1889). Hecht was buried in the Minster on 31 March 1693 (ibid.)

John Blundeville continued as master of the choristers until 1667, when William Turner (afterwards Dr William Turner, a gentleman of the Chapel Royal and vicar choral of St Paul's Cathedral) took over, to be succeeded in his turn, on 7 June 1670, by John Reading (see under Chichester and Winchester Cathedrals). Reading's duties were defined as teaching the choristers and Burgersh chanters 'to write, cast accounts, and to sing pricksong'. Reading was followed by William Holder (poor clerk, 1675) in 1675–6, and John Cutts was appointed on 4 January 1683/4. (These successive appointments, when not recorded in CA6, may be traced through the accounts.)

A certain John Jameson, a former chorister and now clerk of the Revestry, was at this time a centre of trouble. On 22 March 1669/70 (CA5) it was recorded that he took out a writ at Westminster 'to sue Mr Heicht for striking him in the church'. When told that he should have sued in the court of the Dean and Chapter, he impudently replied that he did not think he would have justice done him there. Nothing more was heard of this affair. But in 1689 he himself was struck in the Cathedral by John Cutts, the master of the choristers, when Thomas Wanless, 'being playing on the organ', and Henry Wanless were witnesses. Accordingly, Cutts was suspended on 12 November 1689. In 1690 the vicars proposed that the mastership of the choristers should be divided into two posts, one for vocal teaching, the other for instrumental, and that they should both be annually elective. Under this arrangement, Thomas Norris was the first master or teacher of vocal music (CA6, 1690, *passim*).

Thomas Allinson 1693–1705 (d. Lincoln, 1705). On 3 April 1693 Thomas Hecht, 'filius Andreas Hecht nuper organist defuncti', was appointed to succeed his father 'cum approbatione totius chori'; but on 5 May it was recorded that Hecht junior 'declinavit the office', whereupon Allinson was appointed with similar approbation (CA6). A condition of his appointment was that he should teach a chorister to play the organ. In November 1702 another John Reading was appointed master of the choristers in song in succession to William Norris, retaining the post until 1707. This John Reading had been a pupil of Blow, and was later organist of St John's, Hackney, London.

Maddison (1889) states that Allinson was buried in the Minster in February 1704/5.

George Holmes 1705–20 (d. Lincoln, 1720, aged 40). There is no formal record of Holmes's appointment, but he received salary for the full accounting year 1705–6. On 7 November 1707 he was appointed a junior vicar, presumably in augmentation of his stipend (CA8). He was also a master of the Company of Ringers, as recorded on the wall of the Ringers' Chapel. A manuscript in the British Library (Add. MS 31446) at one time contained the legend 'George Holmes his Book, 1698 at my Lord Bishop of Durham's', and it has been suggested that this is the Lincoln George Holmes and that he was at one time organist to the Bishop of Durham.

Holmes's grave may still be seen in the north walk of the cloisters, beneath the Wren Library. It is inscribed: 'Hear lyeth the Body of George Holms late Organist of this Church who died Ao. Dni. 1720 Aetat 40.' John Reading was followed as master of the choristers (vocal music) by Thomas Weeley, during whose period of office (1709–31) the practice of having a separate instrumental teacher, dating from 1690, was given up.

Charles Murgatroyd 1721–41 (d. 4 Sept. 1741, aged 52). Murgatroyd, who was admitted organist 'cum approbatione chori' on 31 July 1721 and junior vicar on the same day (CA8), was doubtless the Charles Murgatroyd who was succeeded at York Minster that year by William Davis (q.v.).

On 26 July 1731 a Chapter minute ordered that 'the organist do constantly play a short voluntary before the Second Lesson'. On 24 March 1732/3 (CA8) Murgatroyd was suspended from duty, and it was ambiguously decreed that 'the profits arising from his places . . . shall from this time be paid unto Mr Wise one of the junior vicars of the said Cathedral Church, and to be applied towards the payment of his debts and the necessary support of his family'. Samuel Wise was appointed to act for him. However, Murgatroyd was still in office in 1741, the year of his death as recorded by Maddison (1889).

In 1731 Stephen Harrison followed Weeley as master of the choristers.

William Middlebrook 1741–56. Middlebrook was admitted on 26 October 1741 'on the death of Charles Murgatroyd', but he was not made a junior vicar (CA8).

He had been a Burgersh chanter (1717) and chorister (1720) under Holmes (CA8). In 1743 he was one of the subscribers to Greene's *Forty Select Anthems*.

Lloyd Raynor 1756–84. Raynor was admitted organist on 11 September 1756 (CA9). He was a chorister in 1746, when, on his admission on 3 May, he was described as 'about ten years old'. Since then he had been master of the Magnus Song School, Newark-on-Trent (Jackson 1964: 199). Soon after Raynor took office at Lincoln, John Cowper became master of the choristers (1757–99) in succession to Harrison. On his death (6 February 1799, aged 67), Cowper was described in *GM* as having served the Cathedral for sixty years.

In 1771 Raynor disgraced himself. On 10 September (CA10) the precentor

> made a complaint against Lloyd Raynor the organist for negligence and not attending his duty whereby the hymns [i.e., the canticles] are obliged to be chanted and that because that in the course of his playing the organ he either by design or negligence interrupts the junior vicars in their singing anthems and more particularly on Tuesday the third instant when Mr Binns was singing the anthem he played the organ in the tune of a different anthem whereby the singer was interrupted and the choir put to confusion.

This, by the way, seems to imply that already by this date the senior vicars of Lincoln, that is, those in holy orders, no longer sang as members of the choir; compare, however, the minor canons of Norwich as late as 1795.

Raynor was eventually dismissed on 17 September 1784 for having 'in the grossest manner abused and insulted the Dean and made use of several menacing and threatening expressions to him' (CA10). However, he was generously treated: a resolution dated 29 October 1784 allowed him £10 of his yearly stipend in return for good behaviour. But, sad to say, this was discontinued on 5 March 1785.

John Hasted 1784–94. Hasted was admitted on 29 October 1784 (CA10). Meanwhile, John Cowper was still master of the choristers. On 15 September 1794 the chancellor reported to the Chapter that 'John Hasted the organist had absented himself from his duty and never attended the Cathedral since the fifth day of July last and had withdrawn himself from the place' (CA11).

George Skelton 1794–1850. On the same day as the report of Hasted's misdemeanours, George Skelton, 'of the city of Lincoln', was admitted organist. He had been Burgersh chanter and chorister (CA10, 29 April 1782, 10 September 1785). On his resignation in 1850, after fifty-six years of service, he was permitted to retain his salary of £80 (CA12). His son, G. J. Skelton, became organist of Holy Trinity Church, Hull (West 1921).

In 1799 Benjamin Whall succeeded Cowper as master of the choristers. He, like Skelton, retired in 1850 (CA12).

John Matthew Wilson Young 1850–95 (b. Durham, 17 Dec. 1822; d. West Norwood, Surrey, 4 Mar. 1897). On Young's appointment, the offices of organist and 'instructor of the boys' were united at a total salary of £100 (CA12). He had been a 'professor of music' at St Peter's College, York (Stephens 1882). West

(1921) notes that it was in Young's time that organ pedals were first used at Lincoln. The memorial to him in the Minster speaks of 'a musician devoted to the reverent and impressive rendering of Divine Service'. T. F. Bumpus (1903: i. 132) records the following interesting remarks about Young's playing from the old open scores with figured organ bass: 'Like those of his old friend, Dr E. J. Hopkins, Mr Young's accompaniments were almost always independent of the voices, and some of the feeblest passages in the services and anthems of Kent, Clarke-Whitfeld, and others of the late Georgian school, were rendered palatable by his musician-like organ parts.' Young exerted himself in the direction of speech-rhythm chanting of the Psalms, boldly reducing the number of notes in the standard Anglican chant. He was a British Israelite—a somewhat curious adherence for a cathedral organist.

West 1921; information from Dr G. A. Slater.

George John Bennett 1895–1930 (b. Andover, Hants, 5 May 1863; d. Lincoln, 20 Aug. 1930). Bennett was a chorister of Winchester College, and after leaving the Quiristers' School there, he studied at the Royal Academy of Music. He then worked abroad in Berlin and Munich, where he studied composition under Rheinberger. (These foreign studies were made possible by Messrs Novello and Co. Ltd.) In 1887 he joined the staff of the Royal Academy of Music, and from 1890 he held posts as organist of various London churches, among them St John's, Pimlico. Following his appointment to Lincoln he conducted the musical festivals there in 1896, 1899, 1902, 1906, and 1910. In 1925 he was sheriff of the City of Lincoln, and in 1927 he was master of the Worshipful Company of Musicians.

Bennett took the Cambridge degrees of Mus.B. (1888) and Mus.D. (1893), and also held the FRCO diploma. His memorial in Lincoln Cathedral has the following tribute: 'His fine qualities both personal and artistic were dedicated with inflexible integrity to the services of this Cathedral and to the music of his time.'

Grove[3]; *MT*, 71 (1930), 896; *WWW*, 1929–40; *Venn*.

Gordon (Archbold) Slater, OBE, 1931–66.

See under Leicester Cathedral.

(Joseph) Philip Marshall 1966–86.

See under Ripon Cathedral.

David (Andrew) Flood 1986–8.

See under Canterbury Cathedral.

§Colin (Stephen) Walsh, organist from 1988 (b. Portsmouth, Hants, 26 Jan. 1955). After leaving Portsmouth Grammar School, Walsh became organ scholar at St George's Chapel, Windsor and then went up to Christ Church, Oxford as organ scholar, 1974–8, reading music and taking the degree of BA (later MA). In

1976 he took the FRCO diploma with the Turpin prize. On leaving Oxford he became assistant organist of Salisbury Cathedral, moving to St Albans Cathedral as organist in 1985, and to Lincoln Cathedral in 1988.

LIVERPOOL

(I) The Pro-Cathedral Church of St Peter

When the diocese of Liverpool was founded in 1880, St Peter's Parish Church became the bishop's see. It remained the Pro-Cathedral for thirty years (1880–1910) until the Lady Chapel of the present Cathedral was ready for use. St Peter's Church was subsequently pulled down. Its earlier organists included ***Robert Wainwright**, 1775–82, and ***Richard Wainwright**, 1782–1804.

Frederick Hampton Burstall 1880–1910 (b. Liverpool, 29 Jan. 1851; d. Liverpool, 1916). Burstall was a pupil of a certain Dr Rohner at Liverpool, and his first two posts as organist were at Childwall Parish Church (1870) and Wallasey Parish Church (1876). He became organist of St Peter's, Liverpool on the formation of the diocese in 1880, and transferred to the new Cathedral when the Lady Chapel was ready. One of the processional crosses of the Cathedral is a memorial to him.

BMB; West 1921; Chapter clerk of Liverpool Cathedral.

(II) The Cathedral Church of Christ

The 1968 statutes for Liverpool Cathedral provide for two principal musical offices, one of organist, the other of choir director. Except for the years 1955 to 1982, these have been held conjointly.

Frederick Hampton Burstall 1910–16.

See above.

Walter Henry Goss-Custard 1917–55 (b. St Leonards-on-Sea, 7 Feb. 1871; d. St Leonards-on-Sea, 6 July 1964). Goss-Custard, whose father Walter was also an organist, was the great-nephew of *John Goss, and his brother Reginald was a well-known London organist. W. H. Goss-Custard was a pupil of E.H. Lemare. At the age of 15 he became organist of Christ Church, Hastings (1887), and then of Holy Trinity, Hastings (1891). His successive London appointments were as organist of St John's, Lewisham, 1902, of St Saviour's, Ealing, 1904–17, and also to the Royal Philharmonic Society, 1914–17.

At the time of Goss-Custard's appointment to Liverpool Cathedral, the notable Willis organ there was only in the course of construction and was not completed until 1920. He had a considerable share in its design.

Goss-Custard took the Oxford degree of B.Mus. in 1895. He was made an honorary FRCO in 1926, and received the Lambeth degree of D.Mus. in 1953. He retired to his birthplace.

West; *Grove*³; *MT*, 96 (1955), 652.

§**(Christopher) Noel Rawsthorne 1955–80** (b. Birkenhead, Lancs., 24 Dec. 1929). Rawsthorne was a chorister in Liverpool Cathedral, and, after attending Liverpool Institute High School, he proceeded with an exhibition to the Royal Manchester College of Music. He was appointed assistant organist of Liverpool Cathedral in 1949, and took the FRCO diploma in 1953. A Gulbenkian scholarship enabled him to study under Germani in Italy and Dupré in France.

§**Ian (Graham) Tracey, organist from 1980; choir director from 1982** (b. Liverpool, 27 May 1955). Tracey was educated at The Highfield School, and first studied the organ under Noel Rawsthorne. From 1973 to 1975 he attended Trinity College of Music, London and in the later months of his time there he won a scholarship to study under Isoir and Langlais in Paris. He qualified as a teacher at St Katharine's College, Liverpool in 1976, and in the same year he became assistant organist of Liverpool Cathedral, succeeding to the full post in 1980. Among various appointments concurrent with this, he is consultant organist of St George's Hall, Liverpool.

LLANDAFF (CARDIFF)

The Cathedral Church of St Peter and St Paul

Main sources in this section (1964) (with National Library of Wales references):

Chapter Acts
1573–1664 (LL/Ch/1).
1573–1722, embodying transcript of earlier volume (LL/Ch/4).
1722–1817 (LL/Ch/5).

Proctor-General's Accounts
1682–3 and 1683–4 (LL/Ch/3621–2).

Though it is of ancient foundation, there are no Chapter Acts of Llandaff Cathedral before 1573, and for the ensuing twenty years they are but fragmentary. There are no financial records to supplement our knowledge until the years 1682–3 and 1683–4. On 30 June 1608 a minute was passed granting '**Rese** the organist' a stipend of £7 per annum as organist. The meeting does not seem to have been regularly constituted, for a marginal note records that 'the Chapter did disagree and not consent to this act'.

It may be noted that in two lists of members of the Cathedral, dated 1604 and 1610 respectively, two vicars choral and six 'cantors' (singingmen) are named for each year, but no cognizance is taken of boys or organist. Rese is not one of the 'cantors'.

George Carr 1629→. At a meeting on 3 September 1629 the Bishop and Chapter admitted George Carr 'to be their organist in the said Cathedral Church as probationer for one year and afterwards for so long a time as the said Bishop and Chapter shall think fit. And he is to have eight pounds per annum and to begin at Michaelmas next to come.' There are no further references to an organist before the Chapter Acts break off in 1645.

After the Restoration an attempt was made to organize a choir, for on 7 July 1670 the Chapter ordered

> That Mr Proctor General shall pay unto six men intended for the quire of this church for their better encouragement to fit themselves for the same the sum of forty shillings apiece and to the preparing boys for the quire as aforesaid the sum of twenty shillings apiece. And further enjoined both the said men and boys being then present in the Chapter House to use all diligence to fit and perfect themselves for the service aforesaid. And Gabriell Thomas upon diligently preparing himself for the quire is also to have 40*s*.

——Wrench 1672. The first mention of any organist since George Carr occurs in 1672, when on 9 July it was ordered 'that Mr Wrench the organist shall have four pounds quarterly, Mr Lewis the singingman the same and the six other singingmen the twentyfive shillings quarterly and four singing boys twelve shillings and sixpence for the ensuing year'. The following year (2 July 1673) Wrench and Lewis were allotted only £3 each quarterly. The minutes for this date and for 5 July 1673 reveal that the organist and choir rehearsed twice a week under Lewis. In 1674 Lewis was succeeded by one Paine as instructor of the choir.

Two stray accounts for 1682–3 and 1683–4 show that an organist was being paid £12 per annum, but no name is given.

Llandaff Cathedral was now passing through difficult times. Unlike St David's Cathedral, it had no ancient choral endowments; unlike the cathedrals of Bangor and St Asaph, it was not granted anything by Act of Parliament. On 3 July 1691 the following momentous minute was passed:

> the said Archdeacon and Chapter being fully met in Chapter and considering the small revenues of this church and the irregular management of the quire thereof by the singingmen and singing boys belonging to the same voted the quire singing to be put down and discontinued and their respective salaries to be for the future withdrawn but considering the indigency of some of the singingmen, 'tis referred to the discretion of the Proctor General to give and bestow to such of them as he shall judge meet provided he gives no sum to either of them exceeding one year's salary.

The same day the said Archdeacon and Chapter appointed 'Mr William Deane, deacon, to give the singing psalms in the quire of the church and that he should be allowed four pounds yearly for such his service over and above the eight pounds formerly allowed him by the Chapter for keeping school.'

By the middle of the nineteenth century the Cathedral was to a large extent ruinous. At the enthronement of Bishop Ollivant on 13 March 1850 'the National Schoolmaster . . . gave out a Psalm, which was sung by about a dozen of his scholars, a bass viol being the only instrument then in the possession of the Cathedral', as the bishop himself recalled in his visitation charge of 1869. Under his leadership the Cathedral was restored, and in 1861 a newly built organ was opened.

John Bernard (or Bernhardt) Wilkes 1861–5 (b. Leominster, 2 May 1823). Wilkes's elusive biography has been intensively investigated in the *Bulletin of the Hymn Society of Great Britain and Ireland*, 171 (April 1987) and 174 (January 1988). It appears that he was born into a Moravian family. He studied at the Royal Academy of Music, and then seems to have become organist at Monkland, Herefordshire, where he came to the notice of Sir Henry W. Baker, the moving spirit behind *Hymns Ancient and Modern*. Prior to his appointment at Llandaff Cathedral on its restoration, he was organist of St David's, Merthyr Tydfil from 1854, when for the first time an organ was installed there. Chapter records show that he submitted his resignation from the Cathedral in December 1865, after which he lapses into obscurity, perhaps settling in London.

Francis Edward Gladstone 1866–70 (b. Oxford, 2 Mar. 1845; d. Hereford, 5 Sept. 1928). Gladstone's father, the Revd J. E. Gladstone, was a cousin of W. E. Gladstone, the famous Victorian prime minister. The boy was a pupil of *S. S. Wesley at Winchester Cathedral, 1859–64. In the next twenty years he held a number of organ posts in fairly rapid succession: Holy Trinity, Weston-super-Mare, 1864; Llandaff Cathedral, 1866; Chichester Cathedral, 1870 (q.v.); St Patrick's, Hove, 1873 (following *E. H. Thorne); St Peter's, Brighton, 1875; St Mark's, Lewisham, 1876; Norwich Cathedral, 1877; and Christ Church, Lancaster Gate, London, 1881–6.

Gladstone subsequently joined the Roman Catholic Church, and was director of music at St Mary-of-the-Angels, Bayswater, London, 1887–94. He retired to live at Hereford. He took the Cambridge degrees of Mus.B. (1876) and Mus.D. (1879).

Grove[2]; West 1921; *WWW*, 1916–28; *Venn*; *MT*, 69 (1928), 943.

Theodore Edward Aylward 1870–6 (b. Salisbury, 28 Feb. 1844; d. ?Cardiff, 3 or 6 Feb. 1933). Aylward was the great-great-nephew of *Theodore Aylward. His father, William Price Aylward, was organist of St Martin's and then St Edmund's Church, Salisbury, and mayor of the city in 1868–9. According to *BMB* (which gives his Christian names as Theodore Price), T. E. Aylward was one of seven children who became professional musicians. He was an articled pupil of *S. S. Wesley at Winchester and Gloucester, his first post being at St Matthew's,

Cheltenham. For some months during 1866 he was organist of St Columba's College, Rathfarnham, Dublin before returning to Salisbury. He was appointed to Llandaff Cathedral in 1870, moving from there, like his predecessor, to Chichester Cathedral in 1876 (q.v.). In 1886 he went back to Wales as organist of St Andrew's, Cardiff and the public hall there. He retired in 1925.

Aylward was the owner of the copy of the 1558 edition of the Genevan Psalter now in the Henry E. Huntingdon Library, California.

BMB; *Grove*[2]; *MT*, 48 (1907), 728; 74 (1933), 273.

Charles Lee Williams 1876–82.

See under Gloucester Cathedral.

Hugh Brooksbank 1882–94 (b. Peterborough, 13 Sept. 1854; d. Cardiff, 28 Apr. 1894). Brooksbank was a chorister in St George's Chapel, Windsor, and then served his articles to *Haydn Keeton at Peterborough. Following early appointments at St John's Church, Peterborough and Trinity College, Glenalmond, he went to Oxford as undergraduate organist of Exeter College, taking the degree of B.Mus. and the FRCO diploma in 1874. He was organist of St Alban's Church, Birmingham for one year before his appointment to Llandaff Cathedral. There is a memorial plaque to him in the Cathedral.

MT, 35 (1894), 415; *BMB*; information from Dr W. R. Pasfield.

George Galloway Beale 1894–1936 (b. London, 1868; d. Llandaff, 7 Sept. 1936). Beale was educated at Marlborough College and studied music under *J. F. Bridge at Westminster Abbey. He became organist and assistant master at St John's School, Leatherhead and then organist of St John's Church, Paddington, London before moving to Llandaff, where he remained until his death.

MT, 77 (1936), 945; *WWW*, 1929–40.

(William) Harry Gabb, CVO, 1937–46.

See under the Chapel Royal.

§(Albert) Vernon Butcher 1946–9 (b. East Rudham, Norfolk, 11 Apr. 1909). From the Strand School, Brixton, London, Butcher went up to Brasenose College, Oxford as organ scholar, 1927–30, and afterwards studied at the Royal College of Music, 1930–2. He took the FRCO diploma (Lafontaine prize) in 1929, and proceeded to the Oxford degrees of BA (1930), B.Mus. (1932), MA (1934), and D.Mus. (1940). He was director of music at Chigwell School, Essex from 1930, organist of Llandaff Cathedral, 1946–9, director of music at Wrekin College, Shropshire, 1949–53, and subsequently at Worcester College for the Blind, retiring in 1974.

Thomas Hallford 1949–50 (d. Llandaff, 15 Jan. 1950, aged 35). Hallford was a pupil of *E. C. Bairstow, and took the Durham degrees of B.Mus. (1936) and

D.Mus. (1949). He held the FRCO diploma (Lafontaine prize, 1931) with that of CHM. Before taking up his post at Llandaff in January 1949, he had been successively organist of the parish churches of Malton (1932), Alnwick, and Brighton.

MT, 91 (1950), 74; *ECM*, 20 (1950), 38.

Eric Arthur Coningsby 1950–2 (b. Whadden, Cambs., 2 Jan. 1909; d. 1955). Coningsby became a choral clerk of Trinity College, Cambridge in 1927, and took the natural sciences tripos (part I) in 1929, proceeding to the degrees of BA (1930), MA (1936), and Mus.B. (1937). He took the FRCO diploma in 1945. He was at one time organist of St Barnabas's Church, Cambridge. In 1944 he became a songman of York Minster and, in 1945, assistant music master at Uppingham. Before his appointment to Llandaff he was organist of Folkestone Parish Church. Ill health compelled him to leave Llandaff in 1952, but in 1954 he resumed work as organist of Grimsby Parish Church.

ECM, 26 (1956), 12; records of Trinity College, Cambridge.

Charles Kenneth Turner 1952–7 (b. Liverpool, 1903; d. Mansfield, Notts., 2 Jan. 1959). Turner was educated at the Merchant Taylors' School, Great Crosby, Liverpool and subsequently at the Guildhall School of Music and Drama London (Carnegie scholar), where he obtained prizes both in organ-playing and singing. He took the FRCO diploma in 1923, followed by that of CHM in 1949, and he obtained the London degree of B.Mus. in 1942.

His early organ posts were: Brasted Parish Church, Sevenoaks, Kent (1918–24); Walton-on-Thomas Parish Church (1924–9); St John's, Redhill, Surrey (1929–34); St Peter's, Croydon (1934–7). In 1937 he returned to St John's, Redhill, where he remained until his appointment to Maidstone Parish Church, Kent, 1945–52.

He combined his post at Llandaff Cathedral with that of organist of Llandaff Parish Church. He left Llandaff to become organist of Mansfield Parish Church, Nottinghamshire, retaining this post until his death.

Information from Mrs C. K. Turner.

§(Eric) Howard Fletcher 1957–8 (b. Westcliff-on-Sea, Essex, 19 Dec. 1933). Fletcher was educated at Haileybury and Imperial Service College (1947–52) and at Pembroke College, Cambridge (1952–4). He took the FRCO diploma in 1954, and the Cambridge degrees of BA (1957), Mus.B. (1957), and MA (1961).

§Robert (Henry) Joyce 1958–73 (b. Tynemouth, Tyne and Wear, 20 Oct. 1927). Joyce was educated at Tynemouth High School, 1939–44, the Royal College of Music, 1944–6 and 1949–50, and at Corpus Christi College, Cambridge, where he was organ scholar, 1946–9. He holds the FRCO and CHM diplomas, as well as the ADCM (1953). He took the Cambridge degrees of BA (1949), Mus.B. (1951), and MA (1954). His first organ post was at All Souls', St Margarets, Twickenham in 1945–6. Immediately before his appointment to Llandaff he was organist of St Matthew's, Northampton from 1950. He is now a senior lecturer at the Welsh College of Music and Drama, Cardiff.

§**Michael (John) Smith, organist and master of the choristers from 1974** (b. Wanstead, Essex, 7 June 1937). From Wanstead County High School, Smith went up to Christ Church, Oxford with a state scholarship in 1955, becoming organ scholar while he was there. He read music (BA, 1958; MA, 1965), and took the further degree of B.Mus. in 1959. He also holds the diplomas of FRCO (1957, with the Limpus prize), CHM (1959), and ADCM (1963). In 1973 he took the Edinburgh degree of D.Mus.

After a year at the University of London Institute of Education, his first appointments were as organist and choirmaster of Pontefract Parish Church and head of music, King's School, Pontefract, 1960–4. From 1965 to 1966 he held similar posts at Louth Parish Church and King Edward VI Grammar School, Louth, and then, from 1967 until taking up his post at Llandaff, he was assistant organist of Salisbury Cathedral.

LONDON

The Cathedral Church of St Paul

Main sources in this section (1966) (with Guildhall Library references):

Dean's Registers
DR1 Sampson (25,630/1).
DR3 Nowell II (25,630/3).
DR4 Nowell III (25,630/4).
DR5 Overall (25,630/5).
DR7 Donne (25,630/7).
DR13 Stillingfleet (25,630/13).
DR15 Sherlock II (25,630/15).
DR16 Godolphin I (25,630/16).
DR22 Butler II (25,630/22).
DR29 Newton II (25,630/29).
DR32 Pretyman/Tomline II (25,630/32).

Muniment Books
MB1 1660–95 (25,664/1).
MB2 1695–1733 (25,664/2).
MB3 1733–60 (25,664/3).
MB6 1796–1826 (25,664/6).
MB7 1826–54 (25,664/7).
MB8 1854–1912 (25,664/8).

Minute Books
M1 1660–4 (25,738/1).
M2 1664–85 (25,738/2).
M3 1686–1728 (25,738/3).

Acquittances for Stipends and Augmentations
Ac1 1669–71 (25,650/1).
Ac2 1670–87 (25,650/2).
Ac3 1686–97 (25,650/3).
Ac4 1699–1707 (25,650/4).
Ac5 1707–17 (25,650/5).
Ac6 1717–34 (25,650/6).
Ac7 1735–65 (25,650/7).

Declarations of Assent
(25,801).

In the Middle Ages, long before a distinct position of organist developed, St Paul's Cathedral, one of the Old Foundation, appointed an almoner to look after and educate eight boys fit for the service of the church—mainly in lighting and extinguishing tapers. There was also a separate office of master of the song school, held by the precentor. But, by a gradual process of assimilation, the almoner came to have immediate charge of the choristers, and in the course of time (at least by about 1530) came to be known as almoner and master of the choristers. His duties as almoner disappeared at the Reformation, but the double title persisted until the post was abolished in 1872. The almoner and master of the choristers, who may or may not have been also a vicar choral, enjoyed a tenure conferred by patent. We can therefore trace an unbroken succession of almoners from the middle of the sixteenth century; and, as the office was of some significance and held by several notable musicians, a complete list of holders from that time is given in summary form below (p. 182).

By contrast with this well-defined early status, a definite post as organist of St Paul's was slow to emerge and, even then, was for long on an informal footing. When the musical developments of the later Middle Ages began to require an organ-player, someone was found from the existing musical establishment; and even from the late sixteenth century, when the work of an organist became increasingly significant, he continued at St Paul's to be drawn from the ranks of the vicars choral, deriving thus his security of tenure and status in the Cathedral body. Unlike the almoner and master of the choristers, the organist had no appointment dignified by patent. The tiny—nay, derisory—additional stipend of 2*s*. per annum (which continued until the early eighteenth century) is sufficient indication that the work was rated little above that of a vicar choral. It is striking to find such an arrangement, in the great Cathedral of the metropolis, contrasting with Lincoln (also a cathedral of the Old Foundation), where the organist was separately remunerated and, from early days, appointed by patent.

Long after a fairly substantial 'augmentation' of salary granted to the organist of St Paul's became a regular feature in the eighteenth century, the old practice of giving him a vicar's place for his basic stipend and status was kept up. Goss retained his freehold as vicar choral until his death in 1880, although he resigned as organist in 1872. In his report on the choir, made just before Goss retired, W. C. F. Webber, succentor, referred to the six vicars choral, 'one of whom, as there is no other provision, must be the organist' (Simpson 1873: p. xli). Sir George Martin was the first organist of St Paul's who was not a vicar choral.

For these reasons it would be a misconception to think of anyone as the appointed organist of St Paul's until at least the later seventeenth century; one must only think of persons who played the organ. And those records of the Cathedral which pre-date the Civil War do not contain any such names. In 1562 Bishop Grindal issued injunctions dealing with the use of the organ, but his visitation of 1561 did not distinguish a player by name among the thirteen minor canons and six vicars choral (Frere 1910: i. 152, 191). Such stray references as we possess have to be gleaned, with greater or lesser reliability, from sources external to the Cathedral. These mention the following: **John Redford** (d. 1547), almoner and vicar choral, who is spoken of as organist of St Paul's by, for example, Hawkins (1853: i. 367; ii. 537 n.). While it may be imprudent to attach that title to him, his output as an organ composer makes him a likely candidate among the vicars to have been allotted duty at the organ. **Sebastian Westcott(e)** (d. 1582), a vicar choral by 1547, who may have succeeded Redford as almoner in that year; his patent, though not issued until 1 February 1553/4, clearly implies that 'John Redfurthe' was his predecessor. Not long afterwards he refused to subscribe as required by the Elizabethan Act of

Uniformity, and it must surely be he who, in that connection, was referred to as 'Sebastian qui organa pulsabat apud D. Paulum Londini' in a report dated 1561, now in the Vatican (Catholic Record Society, 1 (1905), 21). By the Queen's favour he seems to have been allowed to remain in his post of almoner until his death. (For both Redford and Westcott, see A. Brown 1948 and 1949, and also Flood 1925.) But though the report in the Vatican alludes to his playing the organ, the looseness of the prevailing arrangements is shown by the statement in *NG* (*sub* 'Redford') that **Philip Ap Rhys** played the Cathedral organ after Redford's death. Furthermore, **Henry Mudd**, who, at the episcopal visitation of July 1674 (Lgh, MS 9537/3, f. 4), was listed among the vicars choral, is stated in *NG* to have been described in 1573 as 'organ player' of St Paul's, and in 1574 as a vicar choral there. *NG* identifies him with Henry Mudd, parish clerk (but organist, 1580–6, according to Smith 1964) of St Dunstan-in-the-West, London. **Thomas Morley**, in a reference relating to 1591, is mentioned by Nichols (1788–1821: iii. 108) in his 'Description of Q. Elizabeth's entertainment at Elvetham' (Hampshire) thus: 'A notable consort of six musicians so highly pleased her that she gave her name to one of those pavans made long since by master Thomas Morley, then organist of Paul's Church.' A letter written from the Low Countries by one Paget, dated 3 October 1591 (*CSPD*, Elizabeth, 1591–4: 106), refers to 'one Morley that playeth upon the organs in poules [St Paul's] Cathedral', and an associated document (ibid. 117) mentions 'Morley the singing man', which suggests—as is very likely—that he was a vicar choral, even though he cannot otherwise be traced as such. Indeed, his name is not among the six vicars choral listed at the episcopal visitation of 1598 (Lgh, MS 9537/19). (For other information about Morley, see under Norwich Cathedral.)

Some indication of the state of affairs with which the organ-players had to contend in late Elizabethan times is provided by the submission of Thomas Harrold, vicar choral, at the visitation of 1598 (Lgh, MS 25,175, mem. 31) when he said:

> The organs are so misused in the blowing, and other ways with jogging the bellows, that the bellows be broken and the wind is not sufficient to give sound to the instrument . . . The organ loft is greatly abused by the bell ringers letting up of many people for money, to the decay of the instrument, the pipes being many of them under feet, and the hazarding of the people underneath.

John Tomkins (d. 1638) is referred to in the Old Cheque Book of the Chapel Royal (Rimbault 1872: 11) under the date 1625 thus: 'Memorandum, that Mr John Tomkins, Organist of St Paul London, was sworn extraordinary gentleman of his Majesty's Chapel'; and then under 1626: 'Frauncis Wiborowe died . . . 28 October, and John Tomkins, Organist of St Paule, was sworn in his place the third of November following, pisteler.' We know he was a vicar choral of St Paul's, as he was mentioned in this capacity in an indenture of 20 December 1628, with Adrian Batten as his colleague (DR7). His tombstone in St Paul's Cathedral described him as 'organista sui temporis celeberrimus' ('most celebrated organist of his time'), and recorded that he had served the Cathedral (though not specifically as organist) for nineteen years (Dugdale 1658: 101). Otherwise, all that we know is that in 1636, in reply to Archbishop Laud's articles of enquiry, the College of Minor Canons of

St Paul's said that there was 'a very sufficient organist', but did not give a name (HMC, App. to 4th Report, 1874). (For earlier information about John Tomkins, see under King's College, Cambridge.) **Adrian Batten** (1591–1637), according to the late testimony of Boyce (*Cathedral Music*, ii), was 'Organist, and Vicar Choral of the Cathedral Church of St Paul, London, in the reigns of King Charles the First and Second.' After having been a lay vicar of Westminster Abbey from 1614, Batten certainly did become a vicar choral of St Paul's; but as he died in 1637, he could not have held office under Charles II. **Martin Peerson** (d. 1651), almoner and master of the choristers 1625–50, is described in the burial register of St Faith's Church (Lgh, MS 8882) under the date 15 January 1650/1 as 'sometime organist of the quire of the Cathedral Church of St Paul's'. But by the time of Laud's enquiry of 1636, the reply of the minor canons (see above, under John Tomkins) clearly distinguishes between Peerson, 'mr of the children', and the 'very sufficient' but anonymous organist.

Albertus Bryne ←1660–8 (duties broken off by the Fire of London). So far as records are concerned Bryne is only named as organist of St Paul's from the year 1668–9 (Ac1, the earliest extant relevant account), when, besides his stipend as vicar choral, he was credited with 2*s*. for the year as organist 'for pittance and [con]cession'. But a document conjecturally dated May 1661 (summarized in *CSPD*, Charles II, 1660–1: 25) reads as follows:

To the King's Most Excellent Majesty. The humble petition of Albertus Bryne.

Sheweth that your late Majesty's Royal father . . . was pleased in his lifetime to make choice of your petitioner to be organist of the cathedral church of St Paul's, London, in which said place he was by your said late Royal father confirmed when your petitioner was about the age of seventeen years.

And since then he hath so industriously practised that science that he hath very much augmented his skill and knowledge therein. And therefore most humbly presents himself to serve your Majesty as organist in your Majesty's Chapel at Whitehall.

Bryne was not successful in this bid for royal favour, but the petition seems to fix the date of his appointment to St Paul's before the abolition of the services of the Book of Common Prayer by the Long Parliament in 1644. That he was connected with St Paul's in some freehold capacity at this time, no doubt as vicar choral, is implied by the fact that he was granted £4 by the Trustees for the Maintenance of Ministers on 26 April 1655, and a further £2 on 6 November 1657 (Matthews 1948). On the strength of this, it may safely be assumed that he was restored as vicar choral in 1660 and began work as organist again. From the surviving records, he is the first person who is known to have received any pay, however small, explicitly as organist of St Paul's.

During the Interregnum he had subsisted as a teacher of music. Playford's *Musical Banquet* (1651) lists him as available to teach the organ or virginals in London. Among his pupils at this time was the sister of Susanna Perwick, in whose biography (*The Virgin's Pattern* (1661) by Daniel Batchiler), he is described as 'that velvet-fingered organist'.

The Great Fire of London interrupted the functioning of the Cathedral from

September 1666, whereupon (though retaining his position and stipend) Bryne took up work as organist of Westminster Abbey (q.v. for the documentation of this part of his career).

The last trace of him at St Paul's is the record of his stipend having been paid in January 1670/1 (Ac1), when his duties were still in abeyance. This raises a curious question, because at Westminster Abbey (q.v.) some money was 'allowed to Mr Bryan's executor' at Christmas 1668, by which time, then, one must accept that he was dead. One possible explanation of the St Paul's payments is somewhat discreditable, and is therefore put forward only speculatively. After the Great Fire, while the Cathedral officers were dispersed, payments were sometimes signed for by representatives. As we shall see, Bryne appears to have had a son of the same Christian name. Can it be that the signatures now in the accounts for 1668–9 onwards are those of the son, who suppressed the news of his father's death and collected his salary? In any event, there is no known record of the death. Hawkins (1853: ii. 713) says Bryne was buried in Westminster Abbey, but this is not supported by the burial register.

As to Bryne's origins, Thurston Dart (*ML*, 50 (1969), 514) put forward the ingenious hypothesis that he may have been born in the Spanish Netherlands of an English father. This is based on 'the uncertain spellings of his surname (attempts to reproduce the Dutch "Bruyn"?), together with his most unusual Christian name (virtually confined to the area ruled by the Spanish viceroy in Brussels during Sweelinck's lifetime, the Archduke Albert)'.

In a letter dated 10 January 1671/2 'a young man one Albertus Bryan', presumably the son of the St Paul's organist, was recommended by the Archbishop of Canterbury to become fellow and organist of Dulwich College; he was duly elected. He resigned on 17 September 1674 (Dulwich College Register and archives). Perhaps he was the Bryne/Bryan who was organist of All Hallows, Barking-by-the-Tower from about 1676 to his death in 1713 (Dawe 1983).

Isaac Blackwell 1687–99 (d. 1699). Early in 1687 steps were taken to reassemble the choir of St Paul's after the destruction of the Cathedral in 1666. In January 1686/7 *Michael Wise was appointed almoner and master of the choristers, and on 7 February Blackwell was admitted vicar choral on probation (MB1). On 22 November 1687 he signed for the 2*s*. pay of the organist, over and above his stipend as vicar choral (Ac3). His name is among the vicars listed as having been summoned to Bishop Compton's visitation in September 1695 (Lgh, MS 9531/18), and payments to him as vicar choral, with organist's 'pittance', can be traced up to 13 October 1697, after which the record is interrupted until a new series of acquittances begins in September 1699 (Ac4). It is reasonable to assume that he remained in office until 1699, to be succeeded by Clarke (see below). Blackwell was thus the first organist of Wren's noble building, and presumably played 'Father' Smith's newly built organ when the choir was opened on 2 December 1697.

Before his appointment to St Paul's he was organist of St Dunstan-in-the West (1674) and St Michael's, Cornhill (1684), and he retained these posts, together with his work at the Cathedral, until his death (Dawe 1983).

Jeremiah Clarke 1699–1707 (d. London, 1 Dec. 1707). Clarke was one of the children of the Chapel Royal, and sang at the coronation of James II in 1685 (Sandford 1687). His voice was already broken by 26 April 1691, when he was referred to as 'late child of the Chapel' (Ashbee 1986–9: ii. 45). He may thus be presumed to have been born about 1673–4. His first appointment was as organist of Winchester College, 1692–5 (q.v.).

Confusing statements have been made about the dates of Clarke's appointments as almoner and master of the choristers, as organist, and as vicar choral of St Paul's. For the first Hawkins (1853: ii. 784) gives 1693; for the second, *Grove*[1–5] gives 1695, while for the third *Grove*[1–4] gives 1705. The first of these is impossible, for Clarke was at Winchester until 1695, and *John Blow was almoner from 1687–1703. Hawkins does add, however, that Blow resigned in Clarke's favour, out of regard for his friendship. As pure conjecture, it is possible that Hawkins had heard some garbled story which might originally have told how Blow got his old pupil to assist him in his unusually multifarious duties by carrying out those at St Paul's some years before Clarke formally succeeded him. The facts are that the Dean and Chapter resolved on 28 November 1703 'that a patent be made to Mr Jeremiah Clarke of the office of almoner in the same form as the patent was made to Dr Blow who is to surrender his patent', and that Clarke's indenture is dated 11 January 1703/4 (M3; DR15).

As for the date of appointment as organist, Isaac Blackwell, as we have seen, can be traced at least until October 1697, after which the extant accounts fail for a time. However, in view of the link with a vicar choralship, one can only assume that 6 June 1699, the date of Clarke's appointment as vicar choral on probation, explicitly 'on the natural death of Isaac Blackwell' (MB2), also marks the date of his formal assumption of the duties of organist; and in fact on 22 December 1699 he signed the acquittance book as 'organist' (Ac4). As not uncommonly happened, however, he had actually been doing duty for some months before that formality. In March 1698/9 'Mr Clarke the organist' is mentioned in the Wren accounts for St Paul's Cathedral (*Wren Society Proceedings*, 15), when the keys for the organ-loft were made for him. His appointment as almoner and master of the choristers in November 1703 has already been mentioned. On 3 October 1705 (MB2) approval was given to the belated formality of confirming him in his vicar's place. Up to his final payment at Michaelmas 1707 (Ac4), Clarke merely received, as organist, the pitiful sum of 2*s*. in augmentation of his stipend as vicar choral.

Meanwhile, together with *William Croft, he had been sworn gentleman extraordinary of the Chapel Royal on 7 July 1700, with a joint reversion of an organist's place, to which they succeeded in May 1704 (q.v.). On the title-page of *A Choice Collection of Ayres for the Harpsichord* (1700) by Blow, Pigott, Clarke, and Croft he is described as 'Composer of the Music used in the Theatre Royal'—that is, Drury Lane.

Clarke died by his own hand at his house in St Paul's churchyard on the site of the present Chapter House. Hawkins (1853: ii. 784 n.) relates how John Reading, organist of St John's, Hackney, happened to be passing when he heard a shot, went in, and found his friend dying. There are conflicting accounts of the date, but W. B. Squire in *DNB* argues conclusively for 1 December 1707. Clarke was buried in St Gregory's vault in the crypt of St Paul's on 7 December (Lgh, MS 18,932). Letters of administration were granted to Clarke's sister, Ann, who was married to Charles King, his successor as almoner.

Richard Brind 1708–18 (d. London, Mar. 1718). Hawkins (1853: ii. 767) informs us that Brind was 'educated in St Paul's choir, and afterwards organist of that cathedral and Dr Greene's master'. Elsewhere (ibid. 859) he described him as 'no very celebrated performer'.

Brind was admitted vicar choral on probation on 4 March 1707/8, though the actual record (MB2, f. 69[v]) has clearly been entered out of order under the year 1710. The date is clear enough on his declaration of assent (Lgh, MS 25,801)—the same day on which Charles King was appointed Clarke's successor as almoner. His first payment as vicar choral, with 'augmentation' as organist (now increased to £25 per annum), was received on Lady Day 1718 (Ac5); the latest payment to him, 25 March 1718, was receipted by his executor (Ac6).

Brind was buried in St Gregory's vault in the Cathedral on 18 March 1717/18.

Maurice Greene 1718–55 (b. London, 12 Aug, 1696; d. 1 Dec. 1755). The son of Thomas Greene, DD, rector of St Olave Jewry, London, and grandson of John Greene, recorder of the City of London, Maurice Greene was unlike most earlier cathedral organists in coming from a professional family of recognized standing. Hawkins (1853: ii. 800) states that he entered the choir of St Paul's as a chorister under Jeremiah Clarke, and was later apprenticed to Brind. In 1714 he was appointed organist of St Dunstan-in-the-West (Dawe 1983). The *Post Boy* for 5 December 1717 carries his advertisement soliciting parishioners' votes for his candidature as organist of St Andrew's, Holborn. The Vestry minutes (Lgh, MS 4251) record his election on 17 February 1717/18, but no more than a few weeks later, on 3 April 1718, the same minutes declare the post to be vacant following Greene's 'election' to St Paul's; he was permitted to draw his salary up to 4 May 1718.

His admission as vicar choral of St Paul's on probation is recorded on 20 March 1717/18 (MB2), and he drew his first salary at Midsummer 1718 (Ac6), at which point the augmentation as organist rose to £50 a year. Hawkins (1853) appears to think that the joining of a vicar's place to the post of organist was a novelty specially created in Greene's favour, but, as we have seen, this is not so. When subscribing to Croft's *Musica Sacra* in 1724 he described himself as 'Organist of St Paul's'. Nevertheless, in accordance with the constitutional arrangements of the Cathedral, he was named simply as one of the six vicars choral at the episcopal visitation that year (Lgh, MS 9537/30).

In 1727 Greene became one of the composers and organists of the Chapel Royal (q.v.), and in 1730, the year in which he took his Mus.D. degree, he was made professor of music at Cambridge (*Venn*). To all these posts he added that of master of the king's music in 1735, the first cathedral organist to hold that office. He was a founder-member of the Royal Society of Musicians in 1738.

In 1750, on the death of his uncle, John Greene, serjeant-at-law, he inherited Bois Hall in Essex. Though retaining all his appointments, he was now able to enjoy greater leisure, and he formed a plan of publishing in score an anthology of standard cathedral music, and of presenting a copy to every cathedral. The scheme had not been carried out by his death, and he bequeathed the materials to *William Boyce, enjoining him not to publish any of his (Greene's) works, though without laying any specific obligation to carry out the plan.

Greene last signed for his salary in person at St Paul's at Christmas 1754. The acquittance for the following four quarters was signed by his executor, and the last of these (Christmas 1755) was also signed 'S. Porter'—no doubt the *Samuel Porter who was later organist of Canterbury Cathedral. He was buried at St Olave Jewry, where the Parish Register records him as being in his sixtieth year (Lgh, MS 4415). The actual date of death was found inscribed on his coffin when, on the demolition of St Olave's, Greene's remains were reinterred in St Paul's Cathedral in 1888.

There is a fine portrait of Greene in his doctor's robes, attributed to Joseph Highmore, which now belongs to his descendants in the Festing family (Greene's daughter having married the son of Michael Christian Festing); it gives no indication of the deformity from which he is said to have suffered. Another portrait, by Hayman, now in the National Portrait Gallery, shows him in the company of his friend John Hoadly, the bishop's son.

DNB.

John Jones 1755–96 (d. London, 17 Feb. 1796, aged 67). Jones, who had been a chorister of the Cathedral under Greene, was admitted vicar choral on probation on 23 January 1756 (MB3), and was paid his first quarter's salary as organist and vicar at Lady Day 1756 (Ac7). He was already organist of the Temple Church (Middle Temple) and of the Charterhouse from 1749 and 1753 respectively (Dawe 1983). On subscribing to the first edition of Boyce's *Cathedral Music* in 1760, he was described simply as 'organist of the cathedral church of St Paul, London, &c.', but in 1795, as a subscriber to Hayes's *Cathedral Music*, he was cited fully as 'organist of St Paul's Cathedral, the Charter House, and the Temple'. He was buried in the Charterhouse cloister (*Register of Charterhouse Chapel*, Harleian Society, 1892).

The *English Musical Gazette* for 1 January 1819 contains a misleading statement about Jones: 'as he could not play from score, he employed himself in arranging the anthems in two lines. The same book is now in use in the cathedral.' This misinterprets the well-known fact that, from the seventeenth century, all English organists used skeleton scores on two staves; and indeed, as the quotation innocently reveals, this particular short score remained in use at St Paul's during Attwood's time.

Thomas Attwood 1796–1838 (b. London, 23 Nov. 1765; d. London (Chelsea), 24 Mar. 1838). Attwood's father was a coal-merchant who played the trumpet and the viola. The boy became a chorister in the Chapel Royal, and in 1783 the Prince of Wales (later George IV) arranged for him to go to Naples to study. From there he went to Vienna in 1787, where he had some instruction from Mozart, who declared that 'Attwood is a young man for whom I have a sincere affection and esteem, he conducts himself with great propriety, and I feel much pleasure in telling you, that he partakes more of my style than any scholar I ever had, and I predict, that he will prove a sound musician.' (Kelly 1829: i. 228.)

Back in England, as 'Mr Attwood jun.' of Pimlico, he subscribed to the second edition of Boyce's *Cathedral Music* in 1788, and for the next few years he was music master to the Duchess of York and the Princess of Wales. Concerning this, *GM* remarked that 'when differences at Carlton House began to assume a serious form, he was continually placed in situations of a very trying kind'.

In 1792 Attwood began to write music for the London stage. Then, in 1796, he succeeded Jones as organist of St Paul's, admitted as vicar choral on probation on 21 March (MB6). In June of that year he became one of the composers to the Chapel Royal (CB2), and in 1821 George IV made him organist of the chapel in Brighton Pavilion. He was one of the original teachers at the Royal Academy of Music on its foundation in 1823. To all these posts he added that of one of the organists of the Chapel Royal in 1836 (q.v.).

Attwood enjoyed the friendship of Mendelssohn, who stayed with him at Norwood and dedicated his 'Three Preludes and Fugues' to him. He is buried in St Paul's Cathedral.

GM, 1838, i. 549; *DNB*.

Sir John Goss 1838–72 (b. Fareham, Hants, 27 Dec. 1800; d. London (Brixton), 10 May 1880). The son of an organist, Goss was also a nephew of John Jeremiah Goss, an alto in the three choirs of the Chapel Royal, St Paul's Cathedral, and Westminster Abbey. He himself became a chorister in the Chapel Royal in 1811, and when his voice broke he studied under Attwood. In 1821 (Stephens 1882) he became organist of Stockwell Chapel, London, and in January 1825 he was appointed the first organist of the new church of St Luke, Chelsea, London. He joined the staff of the Royal Academy of Music as a teacher of harmony in 1827.

He was appointed a vicar choral of St Paul's on 1 May 1838 (MB7) on succeeding Attwood as organist, and in 1856 he was also appointed one of the composers of the Chapel Royal (CB2). He became FRCO in 1866. In 1872, following the Thanksgiving Service at St Paul's for the recovery of the Prince of Wales (Edward VII) from a serious illness, Goss was knighted. He then retired from the post of organist (having submitted his resignation the preceding December), but retained his life freehold as vicar choral (though without active duties). In 1876 he received the honorary degree of Mus.D. from the University of Cambridge—the first instance of the conferment of an honorary degree (in the modern sense) on one who was, or had been, a cathedral organist. The memorial to him in the crypt of the Cathedral reads: 'His virtues and kindness of heart endeared him to his pupils and friends, who have erected this monument in token of their admiration and esteem.'

Conditions at St Paul's in his time were not easy. When he was appointed, the succentor (E. G. A. Beckwith) and William Hawes (almoner and master of the choristers) were at loggerheads, with legal proceedings threatened between them. Matters were at such a pitch that the Chapter directed Goss 'to play only such music as was enjoined by two other of the minor canons whose judgment was apparently trusted, and to observe "the strictest secrecy" about the whole matter' (Prestige 1955: 21). It must be remembered, of course, that Goss had nothing to do with training the choir or with the choice of music.

Of Goss as an organist, Stainer, his successor, said that it was very difficult to pass an opinion:

The organs of his youth were very different instruments from those of our own time, and if he were not a brilliant performer from a modern point of view, it is equally certain that many of our young organists would be utterly unable to produce the fine effects which Goss produced on an organ having two octaves of very clumsy pedals, a gamut-G swell, a 16 ft. (CCC) great organ manual, and two or three unruly composition pedals. He always accompanied the voices (especially when soli) with thoroughly good taste, and his extempore voluntaries were sometimes models of grace and sweetness. (Quoted by J. S. Bumpus 1972: ii, 527.)

DNB.

Sir John Stainer 1872–88 (b. London (Southwark), 6 June 1840; d. Verona, 31 Mar. 1901). Stainer was the younger son of the parish schoolmaster of St Thomas's, Southwark. On his mother's side he inherited some Huguenot blood. His father was musical and possessed a chamber-organ.

The boy joined the choir of St Paul's Cathedral, completing his probation in June 1849 (Charlton 1984: 13), and he sang at the funeral of the Duke of Wellington. Before leaving the choir school he became organist of St Benet's and St Peter's, Paul's Wharf, and during this period, thanks to the generosity of Maria Hackett, he had organ lessons from *George Cooper at the church of the Holy Sepulchre. His skill in improvising was soon noticed, and he was chosen by Sir Frederick Ouseley to become the second organist of St Michael's Church and College, Tenbury in 1857. Ouseley encouraged Stainer's career, and he took the Oxford degree of B.Mus. in 1859.

In 1860 he became organist of Magdalen College, Oxford (q.v.), and while holding this post, he took the opportunity, as a member of St Edmund Hall, to take the degrees of BA (1864), D.Mus. (1865), and MA (1866). In 1870 he obtained the FRCO diploma.

He began work at St Paul's Cathedral on Lady Day 1872, and, unlike his immediate predecessors as organist, he was given charge of the choir (Chapter minutes, 2 and 22 December 1871). It has been widely said, and is no doubt true, that, realizing the difficulties he faced in remedying a deplorable situation, he asked, for the sake of the security of tenure it conferred, to be given the next vicar's stall to fall vacant. Despite the wish of the Dean and Chapter at this juncture to sever the link between the post of organist and that of a vicar choral (Frost 1925: 24), he was so admitted on 30 December 1872 (MB8). He also wisely asked that he should be spared all criticism for two years, undertaking that at the end of this time his results would give complete satisfaction. In the event, the standard of the choir more than fulfilled his promise (Prestige 1955: 151–2).

In 1883 he assumed the additional post of H. M. inspector of mùsic in training college and elementary schools, through which he exerted a crucial, far-reaching influence in rejecting the so-called 'fixed doh' method propagated by his predecessor, J. P. Hullah, in favour of the 'moveable doh' as expounded by John

Curwen. He retained this post until his death, but, having lost the sight of one eye as a child, strain on the other caused him to retire from St Paul's in June 1888, by which time he had succeeded in setting a new standard for cathedral worship throughout the country. He received the honour of knighthood in July 1888. He then settled in Oxford, and from 1889 to 1899 was professor of music in the University.

Stainer received numerous honours, including the honorary degrees of D.Mus. and DCL from the University of Durham (1885 and 1895 respectively), the honorary fellowsip of Magdalen College, Oxford in 1892 (the first college ex-organist, either in Oxford or Cambridge, to be similarly honoured), and he was also a member of the Legion of Honour. There are memorials to him in Holywell Church, Oxford (in whose churchyard he is buried), St Paul's Cathedral (east wall of north transept), and St Michael's Church, Tenbury. There is a portrait of him at Magdalen College, and copies of a family portrait by Von Herkomer are now in the Music School collection at Oxford and in the possession of the Worshipful Company of Musicians.

DNB; *MT*, 42 (1901), 297.

Sir George (Clement) Martin, MVO, 1888–1916 (b. Lambourne, Berks., 11 Sept. 1844; d. London, 23 Feb. 1916). As a young man, Martin was organist of Lambourne Parish Church and a private pupil of Stainer. In 1871 he became private organist to the Duke of Buccleuch at Dalkeith. In 1874 he was appointed master of song at the choir school of St Paul's Cathedral, and two years later he became sub-organist there. In 1868 he took the Oxford degree of B.Mus., and in 1875 he became FRCO. In 1883, while still sub-organist, he received the Lambeth degree of D.Mus.

He was appointed organist of St Paul's on Stainer's retirement, and in that capacity, he was responsible for the music for the Thanksgiving Service on the steps of the Cathedral to mark Queen Victoria's Diamond Jubilee in 1887; he was knighted in that year. In November 1902 he was appointed MVO (4th class), and in 1912 received the honorary degree of D.Mus. from the University of Oxford.

MT, 57 (1916), 185; *WWW*, 1916–28.

Charles Macpherson 1916–27 (b. Edinburgh, 10 May 1870; d. London, 28 May 1927). Macpherson's father was the Edinburgh burgh architect. Charles was educated in the choir of St Paul's Cathedral, and when he was 17 he became organist of St Clement's, Eastcheap, London. In 1890 he went to the Royal Academy of Music. From 1887 he was private organist to Sir Robert Menzies at Weem, Perthshire, and then to Mme de Falbe at Luton Hoo, Bedfordshire from 1889. He was appointed sub-organist of St Paul's Cathedral in 1895, and succeeded to the full post on Martin's death. In 1919 he received the honorary degree of D.Mus. from the University of Durham.

West 1921; *MT*, 68 (1927), 655, *WWW*, 1916–28.

Sir Stanley (Robert) Marchant, CVO, 1927–36 (b. London, 15 May 1883; d. London, 28 Feb. 1949). As a boy, Marchant was a chorister of Christ Church,

Lancaster Gate, London. He then won the Goss scholarship to study at the Royal Academy of Music. In 1899 he became organist of Kemsing Parish Church, but he returned to London in 1903 as organist of Christ Church, Newgate Street, moving to St Peter's, Eaton Square in 1913. In 1903 he also became one of the assistant organists of St Paul's Cathedral, and when Macpherson succeeded Martin as organist in 1916, Marchant became sub-organist. When he himself was appointed organist of the Cathedral in 1927 on Macpherson's death, he was the third sub-organist in succession to be so appointed.

Meanwhile he had joined the staff of the Royal Academy of Music, where he became warden in 1934. In 1936 he resigned from St Paul's on his appointment as principal of the Academy. In 1937 he was elected King Edward professor of music in the University of London, retiring from that post in 1948. He remained principal of the Royal Academy of Music until his death; during World War II, in spite of severe arthritis, he returned to play the organ at St Paul's while his successor was in the RAF.

He took the FRCO diploma in 1902, and the Oxford degrees of B.Mus. and D.Mus. in 1909 and 1914. In 1942 he was created MA of Oxford by decree. He was elected a fellow of the Society of Antiquaries in 1933. He was knighted in 1943, having already been appointed CVO on the Jubilee of George V in 1935. In 1946 he was elected an honorary fellow of Pembroke College, Oxford.

Marchant's exceptionally attractive personality made a great impression on all who knew him. J. A. Westrup observed that 'the stale gibe that organists live only in their organ-lofts was quite untrue of Marchant. He was a man of wide interests—particularly in painting, in which he himself had no small skill.'

MT, 90 (1949), 105; *ML*, 30 (1949), 201; *WWW*, 1941–50.

§**Sir John Dykes Bower, CVO, 1936–67** (b. Gloucester, 13 Aug. 1905; d. Orpington, Kent, 29 May 1981). Dykes Bower, the son of a Gloucester medical practitioner, was educated at Cheltenham College and learnt to play the organ under *A. H. Brewer. He went up to Cambridge in 1922 as organ scholar of Corpus Christi College, holding also the John Stewart of Rannoch scholarship in sacred music. Having read classics as well as music, he took the degrees of BA (1925), Mus.B (1928), and MA (1929).

In 1926 he followed another Cambridge man, Hubert Middleton, as organist of Truro Cathedral (succentor also in 1928), from where he moved to New College, Oxford in 1929. He then became organist of Durham Cathedral in 1933, and followed Marchant at St Paul's in 1936. He retired on 31 December 1967, and was knighted in the New Year Honours of 1968.

On settling in London he joined the staff of the Royal College of Music. He was a fellow of Corpus Christi College, Cambridge, 1934–7, became an honorary FRCO in 1939, and received the Oxford honorary degree of D.Mus. in 1944. He was appointed CVO in the Coronation Honours of 1953, and in the last year of his life he was made an honorary fellow of his old college in Cambridge.

The name 'Dykes', originally a second Christian name in the family but later part of the surname, indicates a relationship to J. B. Dykes, the Victorian hymn-tune composer.

§**Christopher (Hugh) Dearnley, organist from 1968** (b. Wolverhampton, 11 Feb. 1930). Dearnley was educated at Cranleigh School and at Worcester College, Oxford, where he was organ scholar, 1948–52. He took the Oxford degrees of BA, B.Mus. (1952), and MA (1955), and holds the FRCO diploma. In 1987 he received the Lambeth degree of D.Mus. He was assistant organist of Salisbury Cathedral, 1954–7, and then succeeded to the full post, which he held until moving to St Paul's. He is the author of *English Church Music 1650–1750* (1970).

In the summer of 1989 he announced his intention to retire in February 1990, 'to pursue his professional career in lecturing and teaching in the service of the Church in Australia', and **John Scott**, sub-organist of the Cathedral, was appointed to be his successor. (See Addenda, p. 434.)

ALMONERS AND MASTERS OF THE CHORISTERS OF ST PAUL'S CATHEDRAL SINCE THE REFORMATION

John Redford, appointment implied in Westcott's indenture; d. 1547.

Sebastian Westcott, indenture dated 1 February 1553/4 (DR1, f. 276), but presumably succeeded on Redford's death; further indenture, 1 December 1559 (DR 1, f. 377ᵛ); d. 1582.

Thomas Giles, indenture dated 22 May 1584 (DR3, f. 188) to 'Thomas Gyles . . . who doth now teach the quiristers'; presumably succeeded on Westcott's death; date of death unknown.

Edmund Pearce, indenture dated 11 May 1599 (DR4, f. 154) granting the office 'as soon as the said Almonership . . . shall become void'; date of death unknown.

John Gibbs, indenture dated 24 December 1613 (DR5, f. 308), 'late master of the choristers of the collegiate church of St Peter in the city of Westminster'; known to have been alive in June 1624.

Martin Peerson, indenture dated 3 April 1626 (DR7, f. 62ᵛ) describing him as 'bachelor of music'; already styled almoner in a deed of 23 June 1625 (*MMR*, 85 (1955), 176); d. 1651.

Interregnum.

Randolph Jewett, 1660, nominally to 1675, but Cathedral destroyed by fire in 1666 (see p.418).

Michael Wise, 1686–7 (see p.264).

John Blow, 1687–1703 (see p.9).

Jeremiah Clarke, 1703–7 (see above).

Charles King, 1707–48, indenture dated 4 March 1707/8 (DR16); d. 1748.

William Savage, 1748–73, indenture dated 5 April 1748 (DR22); d. 1789.

Robert Hudson, 1773–93, indenture dated 5 January 1774 (DR29); d. 1815.

Richard Bellamy, 1793–1800, indenture dated 12 February 1794 (DR32); d. 1813.

John Sale, 1800–12 (Dawe 1983); d. 1827.

William Hawes, 1812–46 (Prestige 1955); d. 1846.

Hawes was really the last of the line. On his death the post was assumed by Archdeacon Hale, canon of St Paul's, who held it until 1853. He was succeeded by J. H. Coward, one of the minor canons, who held it until the office was abolished in 1872 (Prestige 1955: 48–9). Meanwhile, on Hawes's death, William Bayley instructed the choristers in singing until 1858, followed by Frederick Walker (J. S. Bumpus 1891: ii). After the abolition of the almonership, a choir school was instituted, and in 1874 George Martin was appointed its music master (Prestige 1955: 151, 156).

MANCHESTER
The Cathedral and Collegiate Church of St Mary, St Denys, and St George
(formerly a Collegiate Church, Manchester College)

Main sources in this section (1967) (with Cathedral Archive reference where appropriate):

Chapter Registers and Minutes
'A Register Booke for the Colledge of Christ in Manchester founded by Kinge Charles the 2d of Octobr Ao. dni. 1635'.
CA1 1635–41, 1662–1714 (MS 21/1).
CA2 1714–1870 (MS 21/2).
CA3 1871–1907 (MS 21/3).
CA4 1907–32 (MS 21/4).
CA5 1932–47 (MS 21/5).
Miscellaneous
PR The Parish Registers of the Collegiate Church, partly transcribed in Lancashire Parish Register Society, 59 (1919).
The foundation charter of Charles I (modern transcript) (MS75).

Manchester Parish Church, orginally dedicated to St Mary, was granted a collegiate constitution, with a warden and fellows, in 1421. The warden held the cure of souls as rector of the parish; the fact that the church retained its parochial function was not without importance to the organist (see under Sudlow and Harris, below). The College was dissolved in 1547 under Edward VI; refounded by Philip and Mary; continued under Elizabeth I, though its possessions were vested in the Crown from her accession until the grant of a new charter (under the title of Christ's College) in 1578; and fell into evil days under Warden Murray (1608–34), when it was reported in 1633 that Manchester Collegiate Church 'was found to be altogether out of order, where there is neither singingmen, nor quiristers, nor organ fit to be used' (*CSPD*, Charles I, 1633–4: 444). Matters were eventually settled by a new charter of foundation under Charles I, dated 30 September 1635. There are only scanty records of the College from 1557 to 1635, and, such as they are, they tell us nothing of any organist. (For these historical facts, see Hibbert 1834.)

The foundation of Charles I, entitled Christ's College, provided for a warden, four fellows, two chaplains in holy orders, four singingmen (either clerical or lay), and four boys 'skilled in music'. Among the officers of the College, there was to be an instructor of the choristers, an organist, and a bailiff, each to be elected annually in December from among the four singingmen.

Early in the reign of Victoria the title of warden and fellows was changed to that of dean and canons. Then, in 1847, the church, still on the foundation of Charles I, became the Cathedral of the new diocese of Manchester. From the time of J. J. Harris in the nineteenth century, the organist finally ceased to be one of the four singingmen, and thus became an additional officer of the establishment, not on the Caroline foundation (see particulars of the post circulated at the time of the 1908 vacancy).

The 1968 statutes for Manchester Cathedral provide that the organist may also be 'master of the choir', and until Robert Vincent left (1980, see below), the posts were held by one and the same person; separate appointments have obtained since then.

John Leigh 1635–8. At the first December meeting of the new College, 7 December 1635, John Leigh was elected organist, having been admitted a singingman on 21 October (CA1). On 24 September 1636 he was 'convened solemnly in the Chapter House for drunkenness', and admonished 'to relinquish that his accustomed sin'. There is no note of an election in 1636 and 1637, and one presumes that the same officers continued. He was elected bailiff in 1638, and on 14 July 1641 was again in trouble for his drunkenness.

The Leighs had a family connection with the College. The Elizabethan foundation had both a Robert and a Charles Leigh as singingmen in 1578 (Hibbert 1834). The Parish Registers of March 1620/1 record the burial of 'Charles Leigh of Manchester the elder, Receiver of the College', and in December 1623 that of a child of 'Charles Leigh one of the singingmen of the College'. Four Leighs are named in the charter of 1635: Charles Leigh the elder, John Leigh, Charles Leigh the younger (singingmen), and Charles Leigh (singingboy). The elder Charles Leigh was elected master or instructor of the choristers in December 1635, and the younger Charles Leigh was appointed bailiff. An Edmund Leigh was chosen chorister on 9 July 1641 in place of his brother Charles (CA1).

William Carter 1638–66 (d. Manchester, Apr. 1666). In December 1638 Carter was elected as both organist and master of the choristers. These posts are not mentioned again in the annual elections until after the Restoration. When minutes were then resumed, Carter was re-elected to both offices in December 1662, 1663, 1664, and 1665 (CA1). 'William Carter, organist of Christ College in Manchester', was buried on 30 April 1666 (PR).

——Turner 1666–9 (d. early 1669). On 26 June 1666 (CA1) 'Peter Stringer, Organist of Chester, was then elected Organist for the Collegiate Church of Manchester, the place being vacant by the death of Will Carter, provided that he come and continue resident here within two months notice given him of this election.' This minute reads like a bid, unsought by Stringer, to tempt him away from Chester, where his service was, by all accounts, devoted (q.v.). Nothing came of this. At their December meeting of 1666 the Manchester authorities appointed 'Mr Turner singing man and organist in the room of Mr Stringer'. Turner took the oath as singingman on 2 May 1667. He was dead by 22 February 1668/9, when his successor as singingman was appointed.

William Key(s) 1669–79. On 28 April 1668 Keys was elected singingman and made instructor of the boys, receiving 'from every boy out of his stipend twenty shillings per annum' (CA1). Further, on 1 October it was resolved that he should be 'desired to take pains with the other singingmen and to instruct them further in quire service and that the Chapter will determine what shall be allowed by each of them to Mr Key for his encouragement in that work'. Evidently a definite attempt was being made to improve the choir. Keys seems to have succeeded Turner as organist without any formality, as one infers from this minute of 19 June 1679:

> Mr William Keys and Nehemiah Grimshaw's places being void, the former by removal to the organist's place in the cathedral of St Asaph . . . Richard Booth was chosen singingman into the said Wm Keys' place and William Smith into the said Nicholas Grimshaw's place . . . also the said Richard Booth was then chosen Organist and Bailiff . . . and the said Wm Smith was chosen Instructor of the Choristers.

The remainder of Keys's career, under the name of 'Key' or 'Kay', is more conveniently dealt with under St Asaph Cathedral (q.v.).

Richard Booth 1679–96 (d. Manchester, Sept. 1696). At first (see above under Keys), Booth was organist only. After a time, William Smith, the master of the choristers, ran into trouble for 'immodest carriage towards women, excessive drinking and neglect of his duty in instructing the choir' (CA1, 26 September 1682). On 22 April 1685 his place as singingman was declared void, and it was ordered 'that Mr Booth, being now organist and teacher of the boys, shall constantly teach and instruct them two days a week'.

Booth himself was in trouble for drunkenness on 28 June 1688. He was buried on 14 September 1696 (PR), and at the time of his death he held the office of bailiff.

Edward Tetlow 1696–1702 (d. 1702). On 3 October 1696 (CA1) it was 'Agreed that Edward Tetlow be nominated and elected singingman and organist into the place of Richard Booth deceased for the space of six months, to be organist and so to continue if we find him fit and qualified, allowing him the same stipend of £15 per annum as Mr Booth had.'

James Holland 1702–4. Holland was appointed organist on 24 October 1702 in the place of Edward Tetlow, 'deceased'. Note that it was not explicitly stated that he was given a singingman's post. But the appointment was not a success. On 1 June 1704 the following minute was recorded (CA1):

> James Holland being accused of the detestable crime of adultery and absconding for the same to the total neglect of his office and duty to the church which he has highly scandalised thereby, and having either neglected or been unable to qualify himself for the

office of an organist as he promised at his coming into that place, the said place or office is hereby declared void.

Edward Edge 1704–14 (d. 1714). When Edge was appointed organist on 10 June 1704 (at £15 per annum, like Holland), again nothing was said about a singingman's place (CA1). On 25 January 1705/6 we learn about the master of the choristers for the first time for some years, when William Strugnall was appointed singingman and 'to instruct and teach the choir'. On Strugnall's death, Edward Betts (see below) was made singingman and teacher of the boys on 10 October 1706.

Edward Betts 1714–67 (d. Manchester, 18 Apr. 1767). Betts, already master of the choristers (see above), succeeded Edge as organist on 18 September 1714, when the minute recognizes the practice of making the organist additional to the singingmen: 'Mr Edward Betts resigned his place of singingman and was chosen organist in the room of Mr Edward Edge, deceased' (CA1). This was followed by a minute passed at the December Chapter of 1727 (CA2): 'It was agreed that there shall be an organist distinct from a singingman who shall constantly attend upon the duty of the choir and have a salary appointed for him.' However, this minute was at some time deleted; and on 8 June 1728 what might seem to be a redundant minute at such a time of year was passed, electing Betts as organist (could this possibly be a second man of the same name, or was it merely to set the record straight?). Subsequently, at every December Chapter from 1728 to 1766 inclusive Betts was elected.

It was during Betts's time that the parish began to make an addition to the organist's salary, presumably for parochial services, at the rate of £5 per annum. Hudson (1917), who notes this, also states that Betts died on 18 April 1767 and was buried in the nave of the church. He must have been an old man by then, bearing in mind that he was first elected master of the choristers in 1706.

John Wainwright 1767–8 (probably bap. Stockport, Cheshire 14 Apr. 1723; bur. Stockport, 28 Jan. 1768). 'Mr John Wainright' [*sic*] was elected singingman and appointed organist and instructor of the choristers on 12 May 1767, 'in the room of Edward Betts, deceased' (CA2). *NG* speaks of him as having been 'settled in Manchester about the middle of the 18th century', a statement which may arise from the note, dated Christmas Day 1750, in the pocket-book of John Byrom (1692–1763), and quoted in *HAM(HE)* (84) thus: 'the singing men and boys with Mr Wainwright came here [to Byrom's house in Hanging Ditch, Manchester] and sang "Christians, awake" [presumably to Wainwright's famous tune].' This seems to imply some kind of association, even if unofficial, between Wainwright and the Manchester choir before his appointment in 1767, perhaps assisting Betts in his old age. It is also consonant with the baptism of his son Richard in Manchester in 1757. As to 'Christians, awake', it should be noted that *HAM(HE)* says *categorically* that this hymn was sung not only in Manchester on Christmas Day 1750, as Byrom relates, but also in Stockport. It would be very desirable if that statement could be traced to some authority.

The registers of St Mary's, Stockport (now in the County Record Office,

Chester) attest to Wainwright's burial there on 28 January 1768, describing him as 'of Manchester, organist'; the fact that he was brought from Manchester to Stockport for interment supports the supposition that he was 'John, son of John Wainwright, joiner, and Mary his wife, of Stockport', who was baptized there on 14 April 1723.

In 1903 a tablet to Wainwright's memory was erected in St Mary's, Stockport, stating that he was 'sometime organist of this church'. There is no evidence to support this, only a supposition that such a man was likely to have been organist there. Mr Ronald Heys of Stockport, who has carefully examined the church-wardens' accounts from 1683 onwards, confirms that they contain no reference to Wainwright nor to any organ earlier than 1772, when 5 guineas was spent on its repair.

Robert Wainwright 1768–1775 or 1777 (b. 1748; d. Liverpool, 15 July 1782). According to the usual works of reference, Robert Wainwright, presumably the son of his predecessor, was born in 1748. His place of birth is sometimes stated as being Stockport, but the registers of St Mary's Church there contain no record of his baptism in the years 1747–9. He was elected singingman and appointed organist and instructor of the choristers at Manchester on 18 February 1768 (CA2). In April 1774 he took the degrees of B.Mus. and D.Mus. by accumulation at Oxford, giving his age as 23 (Foster 1887–92: ii).

On 1 March 1775 'Robert Wainwright Doctor in Music' was elected organist of St Peter's Church by the Common Council of Liverpool (Liverpool Town Books, xi. 696, now in the Liverpool Record Office). Nevertheless, as late as the annual audit on 23 December 1776, the Manchester CA record 'Dr Wainwright' as still in office: either he still held his posts there, with his brother Richard (see below) as deputy; or, and this is perhaps more likely, this was an understandable error on the part of the Chapter clerk when dealing with men of the same surname.

According to Miller (1804), in 1776 Robert Wainwright was a candidate for the new post of organist of Halifax Parish Church, and at the trials his execution was so rapid that Snetzler, the organ-builder, ran about exclaiming: 'Te tevil, te tevil, he run over te keys like von cat; he vill not give my piphes room for to shpeak.' (The Halifax post was awarded to F. W. [Sir William] Herschel, later the distinguished astronomer. Note that *DNB* gives the date of this Halifax appointment as 1775, not 1776 as implied by Miller.)

Robert Wainwright's burial is recorded in the registers of St Peter's, Liverpool (Liverpool Record Office).

Richard Wainwright 1775 or 1777–82 (bap. Manchester, 8 July 1757; d. Liverpool, 20 Aug. 1825). There can be little doubt that this is the Richard Wainwright who was elected chorister of Manchester Collegiate Church on 6 January 1768 (CA2), and the 'Richard, son of John and Ann Wainwright', who was baptized at St Ann's Church, Manchester on 8 July 1757. The statement that he was at one time organist of St Ann's appears incapable of verification. There is no specific record of his actual appointment as organist of the Collegiate Church, but he is listed as organist and instructor of the choristers at the December audit of 1777.

He may have been his brother's deputy for some time, or, as already observed, the corresponding entry for 1776 may have been careless.

Having succeeded his brother at Manchester, he was to do likewise at Liverpool. On 4 September 1782 a meeting of Liverpool Common Council ordered 'that Mr Richard Wainwright be and he is hereby appointed the organist at the Parish Church of St Peter in this town in the place of his late brother Dr Robert Wainwright deceased at the yearly salary of forty pounds' (Liverpool Town Books, xii. 310). He resigned this post in October 1804, and went to live at Preston (ibid. xiv. 28). However, he eventually returned to his former appointment, and at its meeting on 4 March 1812 the Common Council resolved 'that Mr James Salmon be dismissed from his situation of organist of Saint Peter's Church . . . and Mr Richard Wainwright appointed in his room' (ibid. 367).

Grove[1] gives the date of his death, presumably in Liverpool. The registers of St Peter's, Liverpool do not record his burial.

Griffith James Cheese 1783–1804 (d. Manchester, 2 Nov. 1804). On Wainwright's resignation, the parish (not the Collegiate) officials were anxious to publicize the vacancy, and Hudson (1917) quotes the following from the parish accounts: '1782. Oct. 19. Paid advertising for an organist in 2 London papers, each thrice . . . £1. 7*s*. 6*d*.'.

The election of 'Mr Cheese' as organist and instructor of the choristers was minuted by the Chapter on 2 January 1783 (CA2), and the parish paid 'G. J. Cheese, organist', at a new increased rate of £15 a year from the same date. By 1795 the parochial salary had gone up to £45 (Hudson 1917). His annual election is recorded for the last time in December 1803.

As an exception, one succumbs to temptation by mentioning the undated publication of an *Anthem for the use of Sunday Schools as performed by the Children of that Charity in the Collegiate Church of Manchester* 'by J. Cheese, Organist', a cantata with accompaniment for strings, flutes, trumpets, and drums.

His Christian names are never given in the Chapter minutes, but they are recorded in full in the entry of his death and burial in PR. Hudson (1917) says that he was buried in the nave of the Collegiate Church, but the grave does not now seem to be marked.

He was the author of a posthumous publication entitled *Practical rules for playing and teaching the pianoforte and organ . . . likewise useful information to teachers and pupils born blind* (London, *c*.1804–8) by 'the late G. J. Cheese, organist of the Collegiate Church of Manchester'. This work, with its insistence not only on the capacity of the blind to learn music but also to be successful teachers of it, gives ground for the supposition that Cheese himself was, or became, blind. It is curious that *BMB* identifies the author of this book with a certain Griffith James Cheese (b. 2 May 1751; d. 10 Nov. 1804) who was organist at Leominster, and does not mention the Manchester connection.

William Sudlow 1804–48 (b. Manchester, 1772; d. Manchester, 1848). According to Hudson (1917), William Sudlow was the 'Son of William Sudlow, a music dealer in Hanging Ditch [a few steps from the north porch of the Cathedral] who was at one time in partnership with William Wainwright, another son of John Wainwright, and a well known double-bass player.' He was born, according to *BMB*, in 1772. He was elected singingman and organist of the Collegiate Church in December 1804, and received his parish salary (£45) from the beginning of 1805. But from January 1834 the parish authorities asserted their independence: three years earlier, the churchwardens decided 'to allow out of the parish rates the sum of £40 per annum towards the support of a singing master', and from April 1831 J. J. Harris (see below) was appointed for this work. In January 1834 the stipend of parish organist was taken away from Sudlow, increased to £50, and given to Harris, who received a further increase (to £75) in 1843 (Hudson 1917). Meanwhile, Sudlow remained Collegiate organist, and was in office when the church became the Cathedral.

For many years there had been two organs on the choir-screen at Manchester—the small 'Father' Smith instrument and the 'parish organ' of two manuals. For the Manchester Musical Festival of 1828 the latter instrument was removed to the west end and enlarged. After the Festival it was decided to leave it in its new position, and it remained there until disposed of in 1861. This decision may well have been a factor behind Harris's appointment as 'parish organist'. But it is only by a loose use of terms that he could be regarded, as some works of reference have it, as deputy organist to, or joint organist with, Sudlow.

Joseph John Harris 1848–69 (b. London, 1799; d. Manchester, 10 Feb. 1869). *Grove*[1] says that Harris was a chorister of the Chapel Royal under John Stafford Smith and then became organist of St Olave's Church, Southwark (1823), moving from there to Blackburn Parish Church (now Blackburn Cathedral) in 1828. As we have already seen (above under Sudlow), he had been parish choirmaster and organist at Manchester from 1831 and 1834 respectively. He was also a singingman of the Collegiate Church, a post which he relinquished on succeeding Sudlow as organist of the Cathedral on 31 May 1848 (CA2).

Sir (John) Frederick Bridge, CVO, 1869–75. Bridge took the oath of office on 20 December 1869 (CA2).

See under Westminster Abbey.

James Kendrick Pyne 1876–1908 (b. Bath, 5 Feb. 1852; d. Ilford, Essex, 3 Sept. 1938). Pyne came from a family of musicians; his father and grandfather, both named James Kendrick Pyne, were professionals, the latter a pupil of Samuel Wesley and later organist of Bath Abbey for fifty-three years. The famous singer Louisa Pyne was our subject's cousin.

Pyne was articled to *S. S. Wesley at Winchester while he was still very young, and he moved with his master to Gloucester, where he became assistant organist of the Cathedral. In May 1873 he was elected organist of Chichester Cathedral, but he remained there for less than a year (q.v.). He then went to Philadelphia, USA as organist of St Mark's Church, with a salary, according to S. S. Wesley, of the huge sum of £800 a year (letter of 28 December 1873 to Mrs Rance Phipps, Gloucester City Library, Gloucestershire Collection, S23.17). But he returned to England in 1875, having been appointed organist of Manchester Cathedral by resolution dated 21 September 1875 (CA3). He also became city organist (1877) and University organist (1903), retaining both these posts after his retirement from the Cathedral in 1908. In 1900 he received the Lambeth degree of D.Mus. (not from the University of London as variously stated), and for some periods between 1909 and 1926 he held office as dean of the faculty of music at the University of Manchester. He was created an official MA in 1924. He retired from his University posts in 1927, but he remained city organist until his death. He formed a collection of old musical instruments, and was elected FSA in 1920.

As a player, Pyne was noted not only for the cathedral style he inherited from S. S. Wesley, and his skill in improvising, but also as a recitalist. *Grove*[5] has this to say:

> His very exceptional gifts led many great foreign musicians, when visiting Manchester, to ask him to play to them. Busoni got him to play a number of Bach organ works, of which he was making pianoforte transcriptions, in order to come to a decision in the matter of texture. Pyne's registration was as striking for its appropriateness, whether in simple or complex music, as his style was brilliant, and in the feathery lightness of his staccato touch he was quite the equal of Bonnet and other great French players.

He had, indeed, a marked interest and skill in playing French organ-music, and became both *officier d'Académie* and *officier de l'instruction publique*.

MT, 79 (1938), 787; *WWW*, 1929–40; *Grove*[5].

Sir Sydney (Hugo) Nicholson, MVO, 1909–18. The minute offering Nicholson the post of organist of Manchester Cathedral is dated 1 June 1908 (CA4). He is referred to as 'organist-elect of Canterbury Cathedral'.

See under Westminster Abbey.

Archibald Wayett Wilson 1919–43 (b. Pinchbeck, Lincs., 8 Dec. 1869; d. 17 Aug. 1950). A son of the vicar of Horbling, Lincolnshire, Wilson studied at the Royal College of Music, and then became organist of St Paul's Church, East Molesey in 1887. He went up to Oxford as organ scholar of Keble College in 1890, and read modern history, taking the Oxford degrees of B.Mus. (1891), BA (1893), D.Mus. (1897), and MA (1913). He also held the FRCO diploma (1889).

After teaching for two years at Temple Grove Preparatory School, Eastbourne, he moved to St Leonard's, Sussex as organist of St John's Church in 1896. He then followed *H. P. Allen in two successive appointments, at St Asaph Cathedral in 1898 and Ely Cathedral in 1901. In 1919 he left Ely for Manchester Cathedral (resolution dated 2 October 1918, CA4). He retired at Easter 1943 with the title of organist emeritus.

Manchester Guardian, 18 Aug. 1950; Drennan 1970.

Norman Cocker 1943–53 (b. Sowerby Bridge, Yorks., 30 Nov. 1889; d. Manchester, 15 Nov. 1953). Cocker, the son of a dental surgeon, was a chorister of Magdalen College, Oxford, and then went up to Merton College as organ scholar (1907–9). Between then and joining the army in 1916, he taught at Magdalen College School and was organist of St Philip and St James's Church and Manchester College, all in Oxford.

In 1920 he was appointed sub-organist of Manchester Cathedral (CA4). The Revd Victor Dams, succentor (afterwards precentor) from 1920, gives the following account of the interview:

CANON SCOTT: I notice that you did not take your degree at Oxford. Why was that, Mr Cocker?
COCKER: I was sent down.
CANON SCOTT: Sent down, Mr Cocker?
COCKER: Yes, I didn't do any work.
They appointed him on the spot.

But within a short time he moved to London as organist of St Peter's, Eaton Square (1921). This fashionable milieu was far from his taste, and two years later he returned to his former post in Manchester, serving as sub-organist there throughout the rest of Wilson's tenure. There appears to be no actual minute of his appointment as Cathedral organist, merely an expression of intention to appoint him, made in 1942 when Wilson's retirement was being discussed (CA5). He had already played a leading part in the design of a new organ for the Cathedral.

During the inter-war years Cocker was also organist of Holy Innocents' Church, Fallowfield, Manchester for some time, as well as organist of various cinemas (Kingsway, Manchester; Regal, Altrincham; Art, Bury)—a combination unique in the annals covered here. The *Manchester Guardian* stated that 'he was a brilliant amateur conjuror and a very fine cook, and spent much time on a model theatre which he used for designing stage-sets'.

In March 1951 the University of Manchester conferred on him the honorary degree of MA, a distinction regarded with some amused detachment by one who cared not at all for conventional forms or status.

Manchester Guardian, 16 Nov. 1953; *ECM*, 24 (1954), 15; personal letter from the Revd Victor Dams; information from Mr Simon Lindley.

(Edward) Allan Wicks, CBE, 1954–61.

See under Canterbury Cathedral.

§Derrick (Edward) Cantrell 1962–77 (b. Sheffield, 2 June 1926). Cantrell went up to Keble College, Oxford as organ scholar from King Edward VII School, Sheffield. He holds the FRCO diploma (1949), and took the Oxford degrees of BA (1950), B.Mus. (1951), and MA (1956). His first appointment was as organist of the church of the Holy Rude, Stirling (1950–3), from where he moved to Chelmsford Cathedral. While at Manchester Cathedral he was also on the staff of the Royal Manchester (later the Royal Northern) College of Music from 1963, and he remained there as a senior lecturer after leaving the Cathedral.

§Robert William Vincent 1977–80 (b. Medan, Sumatra, 14 Aug. 1941). Vincent was a music scholar at Ardingly College, Sussex, and then, after a year at the

Guildhall School of Music and Drama, London, went up to Magdalen College, Oxford as organ scholar in 1961, reading music and taking the degree of MA. He also holds the FRCO diploma. He was director of music at Malet Lambert Grammar School, Hull from 1964 to 1967, and afterwards, until his appointment to Manchester, organist and master of the music of St Martin-in-the-Fields, London. While there he taught at the Guildhall School of Music and Drama, 1968–77, and was head of the junior department. On leaving Manchester he became director of music at Whitgift School, Croydon.

§**Stephen (Drew) Pinnock 1980–1** (b. Redhill, Surrey, 9 June 1946). After leaving Dover Grammar School, Pinnock was an articled pupil of *Allan Wicks at Canterbury Cathedral, 1965–8, before proceeding to read music at the University of Leeds, 1968–71. He took the FRCO diploma in 1970, and the Leeds degree of BA (with Frank Toothill Memorial prize) in 1971. After a year at Cambridge, where he took the certificate in education, he became assistant director of music at Whitgift School, Croydon in 1972, and was then assistant organist of Manchester Cathedral from 1975 to 1980. The Cathedral statutes permit the separation of the offices of organist and master of the choristers, and this situation has obtained since Pinnock's appointment as organist in 1980. After leaving Manchester he has been successively director of music at Ardingly College, 1981–9, and thereafter at King's School, Canterbury.

§**Gordon (Brodie) Stewart, organist from 1981** (b. Dundee, 12 Nov. 1952). From Morgan Academy, Dundee, Stewart went to the Royal Manchester/Royal Northern College of Music, 1970–5. Having won a Sir James Caird scholarship in 1973, he was enabled to study for a further two years at the Geneva Conservatoire, where he won the Prix Otto Barblan and the Premier Prix de virtuosité in 1977. While in Geneva he was organist of the American Church. From 1977 until taking up his appointment at Manchester he was organist of Bowdon Parish Church, Cheshire. He is organ tutor at both the University of Manchester (from 1980) and the Royal Northern College of Music (from 1985).

NEWCASTLE

The Cathedral Church of St Nicholas

St Nicholas's Parish Church became a cathedral when the diocese of Newcastle was founded in 1882. The most eminent of its early organists was **Charles Avison**, who held office from 1736 till his death in 1770.

William Jamson Ions (1857) **1882–94** (b. Newcastle-upon-Tyne, 3 Nov. 1833; d. Newcastle-upon-Tyne, 30 Mar. 1906). Ions was a chorister in St Nicholas's Church under his elder brother, Thomas Ions, D.Mus. (Oxon.), who was then organist of the church, and was later articled to him. He became assistant organist in 1850 and then went to Germany to study (1852–4). He succeeded his brother as organist in 1857. His retirement in 1894 was brought about by deafness.

BMB; West 1921.

George Frederick Huntley 1894–5 (b. Datchet, Bucks., 31 May 1859; d. Hemel Hempstead, Herts., 4 Aug. 1913). Huntley studied under *Haydn Keeton and *G. J. Elvey, and took the Cambridge degrees of Mus.B. (1887) and Mus.D. (1894) as well as the FRCO diploma. He was organist of St George's, Campden Hill, London in 1880, and then of St Andrew's, Astley Place, Westminster in 1890. After his brief tenure at Newcastle Cathedral he returned to London as organist of St Peter's, Eaton Square. *MT* (96 (1955), 30) reproduces an amusing 'musical letter' of *W. G. Alcock which contains a reference to Huntley.

BMB; *MT*, 54 (1913), 606 (where it is stated that he went to Newcastle in 1893); West 1921.

John Edward Jeffries 1895–1918 (b. Walsall, Staffs., 18 Oct. 1863; d. Walsall, 11 May 1918). Jeffries was a choirboy under his father, an amateur musician, at St Paul's Church, Walsall. He studied at the Royal College of Music, and held the FRCO diploma. He succeeded his father as organist in 1881, remaining at Walsall until his appointment to Newcastle.

BMB; West 1921.

William Ellis 1918–38 (b. Tow Law, Co. Durham, 13 Oct. 1868; d. Hexham, 1947). Ellis was a pupil of *Philip Armes at Durham Cathedral. He became organist of Elvet Wesleyan Church, Durham when he was only 13 years old. In 1887 he was appointed organist of St Nicholas's Church, Durham, and he moved to Richmond, Yorkshire as organist of the parish church there in 1894. In 1903 he returned to Durham as sub-organist to his old master at the Cathedral, and he remained there until his appointment to Newcastle.

Ellis took the FRCO diploma in 1891 and the Durham degree of B.Mus. in 1893. In 1929 he was granted the Lambeth degree of D.Mus.

West 1921; *MT*, 79 (1938), 849; information from Mr Colin Ross.

Kenneth Forbes Malcolmson 1938–55.

See under Eton College.

§Colin (Archibald Campbell) Ross 1956–66 (b. Brecon, 7 Dec. 1911). Ross was educated at Christ College, Brecon and was an articled pupil of *J. H. Carden at Brecon Cathedral, 1927–30. He was then articled to *P. C. Hull at Hereford Cathedral, 1930–5, and became assistant organist there, 1935–40. After studying at the Royal College of Music, 1941–2, he became a *répétiteur* at Sadler's Wells Opera House. He was organist of St Barnabas's Church, Tunbridge Wells, 1945–8, and then went to Australia to be organist of St Paul's Cathedral, Melbourne, 1948–51. He resigned his post at Newcastle in December 1966, moving to Worthing as music master of the Boys High School there, and retiring in 1969. He holds the diplomas of FRCO (1934), CHM (1955), and ADCM (1956).

§**Russell (Arthur) Missin 1967–87** (b. Wisbech, Cambs., 15 July 1922). Missin was assistant organist of Ely Cathedral in 1945, and became organist of Oakham Parish Church, 1950–6. From there he moved to St Mary's Church, Nottingham, holding this post (1957–67) along with that of organist to the University of Nottingham. He holds the diplomas of FRCO (1947), CHM (1947), and ADCM (1951). In 1987, shortly after his retirement from the Cathedral with the title of master of the music emeritus, he took the degree of doctor in theology (church music) of the Geneva Theological College, USA.

§**Timothy (Graham) Hone, master of the music from 1987** (b. Hinckley, Leics. 27 Aug. 1957). From the John Cleveland College, Hinckley, Hone proceeded to Peterhouse, Cambridge as organ scholar, 1976–80. There he read music, winning the Barclay Squire prize and taking the degrees of BA (1979), Mus.B. (1980), and MA (1982). He took the FRCO and CHM diplomas in 1981. He was sub-organist of Leeds Parish Church, 1980–1, and of Coventry Cathedral, 1982–7.

NEWPORT

The Cathedral Church of St Woolos

(Diocese of Monmouth)

When the diocese of Monmouth was created in 1921, St Woolos's Parish Church, Newport became the Pro-Cathedral. Plans to build a new cathedral were set on foot, but in 1949 these were abandoned, and St Woolos's became the cathedral.

John Augustus Gaccon (1894) **1921–34** (b. Cardiff, 5 Nov. 1869; d. Newport, Mon., 28 Apr. 1934). Gaccon appears to have received his musical training locally, and took the FRCO diploma in 1908. He was for a short time organist of St John the Baptist's Church, Newport before his appointment to St Woolos's in 1894. From about 1895–6 he was also music master at Newport High Schools, holding these posts until his death. On the presentation of an organ to the town, he was appointed borough organist of Newport in 1925.

Information from Mr J. G. Gaccon.

Cyril James Ball 1934–41 (b. Wellington, Shropshire, 6 Apr. 1905; d. 6 Nov. 1975). After education at Queen Mary's Grammar School, Walsall, Lady Lumley's Grammar School, Pickering, and Archbishop Holgate's School, York, Ball served his articles to *E. C. Bairstow at York Minster, 1924–8. He took the

FRCO diploma in 1927 (Lafontaine prize and silver medal of the Worshipful Company of Musicians), the Durham degree of B.Mus. in 1928, and the CHM diploma in 1929. He spent some time in private practice as a teacher of music before his appointment to St Woolos's Cathedral. While there he was also music master of Newport Grammar School and borough organist of Newport.

After leaving Newport he entered Edinburgh University and took the degrees of BD and D.Mus. in 1947. He was then ordained in the Church of Scotland and served for a year (1947–8) as assistant minister at Dunfermline Abbey. From 1948 to 1952 he was county music organiser for Caithness, and from 1952 to 1959 he served as minister of Hutton and Corrie, Dumfriesshire. In 1957 he took the Edinburgh degree of Ph.D. From 1959 to 1967 he was head of the music department at Winneba Training College, Ghana. Thereafter he returned to Scotland.

Dates of birth and death from records of the Church of Scotland; other information from Mrs C. J. Ball.

Charles St Ervan Johns 1941–63 (b. Manchester, 22 Oct. 1896; d. Newport, Mon., 6 July 1963). Johns was educated at Swansea Grammar School and was a chorister in St James's Church there. He held early organ appointments at St Barnabas's and St James's Churches, Swansea and at St Mary's, Chepstow. In 1921 he was appointed to St John's, Maindee, Newport, where he remained until his appointment to St Woolos's in 1941. In that same year he also became borough organist of Newport, and in 1945 he was appointed music adviser to the borough. Johns held the FRCO diploma (1917).

Information from Mrs C. St Ervan Johns.

§Donald William Bate 1964–78 (b. Cardiff, 14 Sept. 1912). Bate attended Cardiff High School and received his musical training privately. Prior to his Cathedral appointment he was organist of the church of the Resurrection, Ely, Cardiff (1937–47), St Catherine's, Cardiff (1948–9), and Llanishen Parish Church, Cardiff (1949–63). He won the organ prize at the Welsh National Eisteddfod in 1938, and holds the FRCO diploma (1958). For many years prior to 1967 he held a post with the Electricity Board.

§Christopher Michael John Barton, organist and master of the choristers from 1979 (b. London, 8 Feb. 1956). Barton won an organ scholarship to Trent College, Nottingham from the Royal Grammar School, High Wycombe, and then proceeded to Worcester College, Oxford as organ scholar, 1975–8. There he read music, and took the degrees of BA (1978) and MA (1982). He holds the diplomas of FRCO (1980), CHM (1976), and ADCM (1982).

NORWICH

The Cathedral Church of the Holy and Undivided Trinity

Main sources in this section (1963) (with Norfolk Record Office references):

Registers of Patents	
LB1	First Ledger Book, 1538–*c.*1566 (DCN 47/1).
LB2	Second Ledger Book, 1558–66 (DCN 47/2).
LB3	Third Ledger Book, 1565–1621 (DCN 47/3).
LB4	Fourth Ledger Book, 1621–65 (DCN 47/4).
LB5	Fifth Ledger Book, 1668–87 (DCN 47/5).
LB6	Sixth Ledger Book, 1687–98 (DCN 47/6).
LB7	Seventh Ledger Book, 1698–1715 (DCN 47/7).
LB8	Eighth Ledger Book, 1715–27 (DCN 47/8).
Chapter Acts	
CA1	Chapter Book I, 1566–1614 (DCN 24/1).
CA2	Chapter Book II, 1614–49 (DCN 24/2); CA1 and 2 are partly transcribed in Norfolk Record Society, 24, 1953.
CA3	Chapter Book III, 1660–91 (DCN 24/3).
CA4	Chapter Book IV, 1691–1732 (DCN 24/4).
CA5	Chapter Book V, 1733–94 (DCN 24/5).
CA6	Chapter Book VI, 1795–1833 (DCN 24/6).
Account Rolls	
AR	Rolls 11–75, 75a, 76–82, for accounting years ending at Michaelmas 1550–1668, with gaps (DCN 10/1, *but each renumbered since 1963*).
Account Books	
Ac1	Bound volume of accounts, 1580–1 to 1646, with intermissions (DCN 10/2/1). (More careful inspection may close some gaps in Account Rolls above.)
Ac2	Audit Book, 1638 and 1660–9 (DCN 11/1).
Miscellaneous	
Misc. Lib. I/II	Bound volumes of miscellaneous documents (DCN 29/1–2).
CB	Choristers' Book no. 18 (DCN 39/4).
PR	Registers of baptisms, marriages, and burials in the parish of St Luke's, Norwich (the Cathedral parish), in the care of the Cathedral sacrist.

Almost immediately following the dissolution of the Benedictine cathedral priory of Norwich in 1538, Henry VIII reconstituted it in May of that year as the cathedral church of the bishopric. The musical establishment included a master of the choristers and eight choristers. The draft statutes (Misc. Lib. II) prescribed that the duties of the master of the choristers should include that of an organist (see above p. xix). For some reason the Cathedral was once more refounded by Edward VI in 1548, but without the issue of any statutes. Some statutes were drafted under Elizabeth I (Lbl, Stowe MS 128, *c.*1569–74; English transcription by Francis Blomefield (1705–52)) which, though never formally promulgated, show what was in mind:

Item, we will that there shall be a schoolmaster of the choristers, who shall be a man of honest life and godly religion, skilful in prick-song, descant, and playing of the organs. His office shall be to teach the choristers to read, write, sing, and play, until they be perfect in the same, and he shall be bound to serve in the choir as other singingmen do, and to play on the organs when and as often as it shall be thought convenient by the precentor or his substitute, and he shall provide such songs as shall be fit and convenient to furnish the choir.

The reference to an obligation to compose is particularly interesting and unusual. A further provision in this draft gives some idea of how the services were envisaged at the time when Thomas Morley was in office (see below). Dealing with Morning and Evening Prayer, it decreed that 'it shall suffice to have the service in plain note, without any parts [i.e., harmonized settings] on the working days, with a psalm in metre at the beginning and ending of prayer and also before and after sermons and lectures'. Eventually, statutes of legal force were promulgated in 1620 under James I, and the separate posts of organist and master of the choristers became permissible, though not obligatory. Statute 14 enjoined that the organist 'do wear a surplice and be present in the choir at the time of the celebration of the prayers until it is time for him to go to the organ'.

Thomas Grew 1542–50→. Grew is the first master of the choristers (and therefore organist) on the foundation of Henry VIII of whom we have any record. His patent (LB1, f. 31) is dated 18 March 1541/2, and is in English. Since it represents the earliest extant patent for such a post in any cathedral of the New Foundation, it is worth quoting from. Grew is described as 'of Windsor in the County of Berkshire', and his appointment was to take effect from Michaelmas 1542. Subject to good behaviour, he was granted for life 'the office and service of master, instructor, and teacher of eight singing children within the said Cathedral Church, with the finding and teaching of the same children together with the house or mansion called the Wardroper's house within the site of the said Cathedral Church'. For his duties, it was laid down that he should

daily minister and serve in the Cathedral Church in the time of divine service there to be celebrated with singing, plainsong and descant, and playing on the organs according to his knowledge and cunning . . . find eight children apt to singing and meet and convenient to service, minister, and sing plainsong and descant . . . well and sufficiently find with meat and drink and clothes and all other things to them necessary as well for their service and ministration in the said church as otherwise . . . well and sufficiently instruct and teach them in singing, plainsong, and descant.

When a boy died, Grew was allowed six weeks in which to replace him. His annual stipend of £34 was secured as a charge on the manor of Martheham in Norfolk; this sum included the costs of maintaining the eight boys.

Grew was still in office at Michaelmas 1550 (AR11), but it appears that he died or vacated his post not later than Michaelmas 1554 (see below).

Edmund Inglott 1555–83 (or possibly Edmund Inglott (I), 1555–8; Edmund Inglott (II), 1559–83). In AR12 and 13, for the year ending Michaelmas 1555, Edmund Inglott received pay for himself and the boys for what appears to be only three quarters of the year, which suggests a vacancy in the post up to Christmas 1554. With one exception, the same name is found regularly (allowing for occasional breaks in the series of AR) as far as March 1583 (AR32). The exception is the year 1558–9, when the stipend was inexplicably divided between two of the canons, John Barrett and Henry Mannell (who also received the pay of some singingmen). This raises a very slight possibility (no more) that there may perhaps have been a break in service between two men of the same name. (See reference below, under William Inglott, to an 'Edmund Inglott junior'.)

On 31 December 1560 (LB2, f. 42^v) a patent of appointment to the post of master of choristers was granted to 'Edmund Englott of Norwich'. He was assigned a house and garden 'now in the occupation of the said Edmund Englott'. Of his annual stipend of £36. 13*s*. 4*d*., all but £10 was for the boys' keep. While this patent may, of course, confirm a fairly recent appointment, that is not necessarily so. It might have resulted from the accession of Elizabeth I, an occasion which appeared to result in the need for some form of confirmation. (Compare Sebastian Westcott as almoner of St Paul's Cathedral (q.v.) or Christopher Tye and Richard Fisher at Ely and Worcester Cathedrals respectively (q.v.).)

In 1561 Edmund Inglott ran a dagger into Henry Smith (a lay clerk) and drew blood ('et super eum extravit sanguinem'). He himself was set upon by inhabitants of the Close. On another occasion he got into trouble with Dr Gascoigne for placing his dung-heap against Gascoigne's wall (Court Roll of Amners, quoted by Saunders 1932). He does not seem to have been a very estimable character, for in his answer to the metropolitical visitation of 1567 (Strype 1821: iii. 159–61), George Gardiner, one of the canons, complained that 'there is a master of the choristers but that the choristers are very evil ordered', and later added that 'Edmund England [*sic*], master of the choristers, is suspected for bearing and carrying tales betwixt gentlemen; and by that means causeth unquietness'.

The Dean and Chapter were surprisingly free in granting reversions to Inglott's post (something the draft Elizabethan statutes sought to prohibit). In 1564 a reversion was granted to Thomas Tusser (LB1, f. 388^v), and a year later another reversion, effective after the death of both Inglott and Tusser, was given to Thomas Dalyce (LB2, f. 128^v). The transcript of this is endorsed 'vacat quia Dalyce mortuus est'. Next (see below) comes a reversion to Thomas Morley in 1574, followed in turn, on 6 May 1579, by yet another, this time to William, 'son of Edmund Inglott' (LB3, f. 115^v). Still further, an entry in CA1 (f. 61^v, 23 May 1580) purports to record an actual patent, not a mere reversion, of the same post to Lionell and Hamont Claxton; it is difficult to make any sense of this. However, by the time Edmund Inglott's tenure came to its end, only two of these reversionaries were still alive, namely, Thomas Morley and William Inglott.

Thomas Morley 1583–7 (b. *c.*1557; d. ?London, *c.*1602). Morley was granted the reversion of the post of master of the choristers by patent dated 16 September 1574 (LB3, f. 82). AR32 shows that he took up the appointment from March 1583, the date to which Edmund Inglott had received pay. In the patent of 1574 Morley is described as the son of Francis Morley of Norwich, 'beer-brewer'. It may be noted that from Michaelmas 1562 to Michaelmas 1566 one Francis Morley is named in AR as Cathedral virger. A special payment ('reddit resolut:') made by the Cathedral in 1575–6 (AR27) to 'domino Morley' might possibly concern Thomas, who by then was in possession of the right of reversion. Early in his time as master of the choristers he had some kind of suit with John Amery, a lay clerk, towards the costs of which the Dean Chapter saw fit to allow him 10*s*. (AR33). His employment with the Cathedral ceased with his stipend at Michaelmas 1587 (AR35), and the last occasion on which his name is mentioned in the Norwich Muniments is when his 'house, chambers, and dorter' in the Close were leased in May 1587 to one Thomas Brown (CA1, f. 87). (Fuller discussion of his association with Norwich will be found in Shaw 1965.)

Making due allowance for the absence of direct proof, it seems reasonable to conclude that he is the Thomas Morley who had become connected with St Paul's Cathedral by 1591 (q.v.) and who was sworn a gentleman of the Chapel Royal on 24 July 1592 (Rimbault 1872: 5); presumably he was also the Oxford B.Mus. of 8 July 1588 (Wood 1815–20: i. 241), author of *A Plaine and Easie Introduction to Practicall Musicke* (1597), editor of *The Triumphes of Oriana*, and distinguished composer. The date of birth of that famous figure is reckoned as 1557 from the note endorsed on 'Domine non est exaltatum' (Ob, MS Mus. e.1–5): 'Thomas Morley aetatis suae 19 anno domini 1576'. Without allowing for well-known vagueness about personal age at that time, this would make him between 16 and 17 years old at the time of the Norwich reversionary grant. We may well suppose that, as a Norwich boy, he had been in the Cathedral choir and that this reversion might have been intended as a way of securing his future services in his home town.

It should not be overlooked that at the episcopal visitation of St Paul's Cathedral in July 1574, a certain Thomas Morley was third on a list which is clearly that of the ten choristers (Lgh, MS 9537/3, f. 4). This may be nothing but a coincidence of names. On the other hand, if it does refer to our subject, perhaps he had been 'pressed' into the choir of St Paul's from Norwich. Certainly, by 1574 his voice must have been well on the way towards breaking; but that development used to take place later than at present.

If we accept these matters of identity, then in 1591 he played a mysterious, perhaps duplicitous, part as a sympathizer to obtain information against English Catholics (see David Brown 1959). In 1597, in his *Plaine and Easie Introduction*, he referred to indifferent health. Five years later, on 7 October 1602, his place in the Chapel Royal was filled (Rimbault 1872: 6), and there is good ground for presumption that he was the Thomas Morley whose widow was granted letters of administration in the Prerogative Court of Canterbury on 25 October 1603.

It has been suggested that he was at some time organist of St Giles, Cripplegate, London. This is on the evidence of the burial there, on 14 February 1588/9, of 'Thomas, the son of Thomas Morley organist' (Lgh, MS 6419/1). But it is likely that 'organist' is used here simply as a personal description of his occupation, not as an indication that he was organist of the church. A musician of St Paul's Cathedral might well have been resident in the parish.

William Inglott (1st tenure) **1587–91** (d. Norwich, 1621). William was the son of Edmund Inglott (see above). He is known to have been a chorister under his father in 1567–8 (certificate to Queen Elizabeth, LB2, f. 1), and was later at various times a lay clerk. There was also a brother (or an uncle), Edmund Inglott junior, a lay clerk in 1578–9 who obtained a lease of 'the great garden within the close' on 25 September 1573 (CA1, f. 37).

In 1582–3 a gratuity of 60*s*. was paid to 'William Inglott son of Edmund Inglott' for his faithful service in the choir, and a similar payment (80*s*.) was made in 1584–5 (AR32, 34); these may indicate some special treatment in the light of his patent of reversion (already mentioned above, under his father), dated 1579. However, it seems that he was not immediately available on Morley's departure, because a special payment was made to Leonard Walker, a lay clerk, for teaching the choristers from Midsummer to Michaelmas 1587 (AR35). An entry in CA1 (f. 92[v]) of the formal grant to Inglott of the office of organist (*sic*), dated 8 May 1588, testifies that he took up duties during that accounting year. His latest payment for this period of office was for the quarter ending Midsummer 1591. A curious feature in this accounting year, 1590–1 (AR37), is that the choristers were boarded out with various people at £4 per annum (see below, after William Cobbold).

Henry Baker 1591–(not later than) 1594. At this point new arrangements were made whereby, from Michaelmas 1591 (AR38), the work of master of the choristers, informally divorced from that of organist, was assumed by Richard Carlton, madrigal-composer and one of the minor canons, who retained his duties until February 1604/5 (CA1, f. 153), when he was succeeded as master of the choristers by Thomas Askew, a lay clerk. Meanwhile the work of organist was allotted to Baker, whose appointment seems to have been at will, if we are to judge by the note, 'ex consideratione decani', against the record of his payment for 1591–2 (AR38). Unfortunately, the account-roll for 1592–3 is missing, and that for 1593–4 (AR39) is too badly worn to be read, so we do not know for how long this arrangement lasted.

William Cobbold 1595–1609→ (b. Norwich, Jan. 1560; d. Beccles, Norfolk, 7 Nov. 1639). No accounts exist after Michaelmas 1594 until Michaelmas 1597, but LB3 (f. 175[v]) records the grant of a patent as organist (*sic*) to Cobbold on 13 December 1594, with a stipend of £4 a year to run from Lady Day 1595. Corresponding payments are duly noted in AR40–50. The account-rolls break off again after 1608–9 (AR50), and resume only in 1612–13 (AR51), when Cobbold, having in the meantime given way to William Inglott, appears only as a singingman. But there is a puzzle about his status. In 1620, following the grant of statutes by James I, all members of the foundation were required to take a fresh oath, and the list in CA2 reads thus:

Mr { Wm Cobbold
Wm Inglot } Organists

Can it be that Cobbold only made way on the understanding that he retained his legal status? Did William Inglott, when he left in 1581, retain some right to claim his place back again? Whatever the circumstances, so far as the accounts are concerned, Cobbold remained a lay clerk until 1638, when they break off until 1660.

Cobbold was baptized at St Andrew's Church, Norwich on 5 January 1560. The inscription on his tomb in the parish church of Beccles reads: 'Here lyeth the body of William Cobbold, sometime Organist of Christ Church, in Norwich, who died the 7th November 1639. The body rests below But the soule above Sing heavenly anthem, Made of peace and love.' By his will dated 4 August 1637 (Fellowes 1921: 246) he left 20*s*. to the '[minor] canons, singingmen and choristers of the Cathedral of Christ Church within the choir', and 1*s*. to each of the two organ-blowers. 'Christ Church' was at that time an informal appellation of Norwich Cathedral.

William Inglott (2nd tenure) ←**1611–21**. It is hard to think that this is not the same William Inglott who held office from 1587 to 1591. His career during the intervening years is obscure, and we do not know why he left Norwich. The appearance of a William Inglott as organist of Hereford Cathedral in 1597 (q.v.) tempts one to think that he may have made his way there.

On resuming (if that is the right assumption) work at Norwich, he was organist only, not master of the choristers as well, as formerly. His patent is dated 1 June 1611 (LB3, f. 287), but this is not necessarily the date he took up his duties. On his death a fine memorial to him was erected on the south pillar of the organ-screen, where it may still be seen. It reads:

Here Willyam Inglott Organist doth rest
whose ARTE in musique this Cathedrall blest
ffor Descant most, for Voluntary all
He past on Organ, songe, and Virginall,
He left this life at AGE of sixtie seaven
and now 'mongst angells all sings [*illegible*[1]] in heaven
His fame flies farr, his name shall never die
See ART and AGE here crowne his memory.

Non digitis Inglotte tuis terrestia[2] tangis
Tangis nunc digitis Organa cessa[3] poli

Buried the last day of December 1621. This erected the 15 day of June 1622.

Versions of this are to be found in *The Posthumous Works of Sir Thomas Browne*, 1712 (engraving, p. 62), and in Hawkins (1853: ii. 770).

The engraving in Browne shows a further inscription: 'Ne forma hujusce Monumenti injuria Temporum pene deleti dispereat exculpi curavit W Croft, Reg: Capellae in arte Musica Discipul: praefectus.' ('Lest the inscription of this monument (almost destroyed by the ravages of the times) should be lost, William Croft, master of the children of the Chapel Royal, caused it to be recut.') Hawkins records this also, but reads 'Gul. Croft' for 'W Croft', 'ornavit' for 'curavit', and adds some punctuation. Oddly, however, it is not now to be seen. Any such restoration by Croft must have been between 1708 and 1712.

[1] This word appears to be 'faint', but the engraving renders it 'St', and Hawkins 'first'.

[2] The ending of this word seems doubtful.

[3] So the word appears to read; but 'celsa' as in the engraving and Hawkins yields good sense. The Latin may be translated as follows: 'Inglott! thou dost not play the organs on earth; now dost thou play them in heaven.'

Richard Gibbs 1622–Interregnum. Gibbs was sworn in as organist on 16 June 1622 (CA2, f. 43). At about the same time, George Sanders succeeded Thomas Askew as master of the choristers. However, from Michaelmas 1629 (AR68) the two posts were once more united in the person of Gibbs. Apparently to cover a situation which already existed, a minute was passed in June 1642 (CA2, f. 162) to the effect that 'the house within the precincts where Richard Gibbs, organist, now liveth, was assigned unto him for the house of the master of the children'.

It appears that Gibbs was not well served by his deputy, Peter Sandley, a lay clerk. Even before Gibbs's appointment, Sandley had been ordered 'for and in regard of his malpertness and sauciness in his carriage by words towards Mr Dean that he shall henceforth demean himself as is fitting for him in his place' (CA2, f. 25ᵛ). Now, however, on 29 May 1639, Gibbs was admonished 'for that in his absence an unfit man being by him appointed to be at the organ, there was a great confusion on the choirs, he should henceforth in his absence appoint a sufficient man to do his office there: and that he should look better to the education of his boys'. At the same time, Sandley was admonished 'upon his fault of distemper in drink when he undertook to play on the organ in the absence of the organist, from henceforth to carry himself with more sobriety' (CA2, f. 140ᵛ).

Payments to Gibbs can be traced as far as Michaelmas 1646 (Ac1) after Prayer Book services were suspended in 1644 under parliamentary edict. In 1649 the parliamentary survey listed the 'house of the organist and master of the choristers, Richard Gibbs'.

Richard Ayleward (1st tenure) **1661–4** (b. Winchester, 1626; d. Norwich, 15 Oct. 1669). Ayleward had been a chorister of Winchester Cathedral before the Civil War, and his father continued as a minor canon there after the Restoration. Twice during the Interregnum the father, also named Richard, had received payments from the Committee for Sequestrations (Matthews 1948). The younger Ayleward was admitted as organist and master of the choristers at Norwich on 12 March 1660/1, and shortly afterwards he was assigned a house (CA3). For a brief period before Ayleward's appointment Peter Sandley had been teaching the boys, and in November 1661 he was granted £4 for this work (CA3).

Ayleward gave up his post during the accounting year 1663–4 (Ac2). In June 1664 the Dean Chapter voted to 'Mr Ayleward, late organist', the sum of £5 'for some service formerly done and to be forthwith done by him in this church' (CA3), and the accounts for that year include an even more mysterious payment to Mr Kent (one of the canons) 'for what he laid out for sending for Mr Ayleward at the Assizes'. (See below, after Thomas Gibbs.)

Thomas Gibbs 1664–6. Gibbs, who may or may not have been connected with Richard Gibbs (see above), was formally admitted as organist and master of the choristers on 12 September 1664, when he was allotted Ayleward's house (CA3). He was buried, having died of plague, on 16 July 1666 (PR). A gratuity of £2 was made to his widow. Someone of the same name was organist of Canterbury Cathedral from 1661 (q.v.).

Richard Ayleward (2nd tenure) **1666–9.** Whatever his business at the Assizes may have been (see above), Ayleward was reappointed to follow Gibbs and was formally admitted on 5 December 1666, when he also took over his old house (CA3). On his death in 1669 he was buried in the north aisle of the Cathedral, where the inscription on his tombstone, as recorded by Blomefield (1805–62), formerly read:

Here lyeth interred the body of Richard Yleward, Organist of this place, who was born at Winchester, and died here the 15th of October, An. Dom. 1669.

Here lyes a perfect Harmonie
Of faith, & Truth, & Loyaltie;
And whatsoever Virtues can
Be reckon'd up, was in this Man.
His sacred Ashes here abide,
Who in God's Service liv'd and Dy'd;
But now by Death advanced higher,
To serve in the Celestial Quire.
God Save the King.

Thomas Pleasants 1669–89 (d. Norwich, 6 Aug. 1689, aged 40). The accounts for the year ending Michaelmas 1669 (Ac2) note the payment of 5*s*. to Pleasants 'for his attendance at the Audit'. This may be a reference to some kind of interview at one of the periodic roll-calls of the Cathedral body. On 5 December 1669 it was resolved that he should have £20 per annum 'so long as he shall execute the place of organist of this church though he be not admitted organist' (CA3). This must have covered some kind of probation before his permanent admission, which took place in February 1670/1 (CA3). He was not master of the choristers initially, but he followed John Jackson in that post in October 1672 (CA3). He was buried in the north transept of the Cathedral (PR).

The name 'Tho: Pleasants of Norwich and Norfolk' is found in the list of subscribers to Mace's *Musick's Monument*, 1676. His son William became the first organist of St Peter Mancroft, Norwich, where he was buried in October 1717 (Newman 1932).

James Cooper 1689–1720 (d. Norwich, 26 Jan. 1721). Cooper was admitted organist and master of the choristers on 18 September 1689 (CA3). A curious resolution of 3 December 1720 (CA4) suggests that he had managed to acquire extended official accommodation: 'It shall not be in the power of any succeeding Dean to grant any more houses or rooms in the organist's house to any succeeding organist than was formerly granted to the organists (Mr Cooper's predecessors) in 1661.'

Cooper is buried at the foot of William Inglott's memorial. He paid for an additional stop on the organ, and in his will he bequeathed £5 to the Cathedral choir (Mann MS Notes).

Humphrey Cotton 1720–49 (bap. Norwich, 14 Jan. 1693; d. Norwich, 19 Sept. 1749). Cotton, the son of a Norwich freeman, was baptized at St Peter Mancroft, where he was also organist, in succession to William Pleasants, from 1717 to 1720 (Newman 1932). He was admitted organist of the Cathedral on 29 December 1720 (CA4), and his patent was issued on 16 February 1721 (LB8).

On 25 August 1722 he was elected freeman of the city as the son of his father. Like Garland, his successor at the Cathedral, he gave many concerts in the city (Mann MS Notes).

Thomas Garland 1749–1808 (bap. Norwich, 5 July 1731; d. Norwich, 23 Feb. 1808). Garland was baptized in the Cathedral (PR); his father was a tailor who lived in the Lower Close. He was only 18 when he was appointed organist, a post which he held for fifty-nine years. I sought a record of his appointment in CA5, but failed to observe it. According to the quotation below, he was a pupil of *Maurice Greene. He was a subscriber to the first edition of Boyce's *Cathedral Music* (1760–3) and to William Hayes's *Cathedral Music* in 1795; he also subscribed to Burney's *History of Music* (1776).

An anonymous account of the choir and its music during Garland's time is found in *The English Choral Service, its Glory, its Decline* (London, 1845; quoted without source in J. S. Bumpus 1972: ii. 355). The mention of Vaughan as 'first boy' fixes the date of the circumstances described at about 1795:

> Well do I remember, says an ear-witness, the delight with which I used to listen to the Service in Norwich Cathedral, when the Minor Canons, eight in number, filed off into their stalls, Precentor Millard at their head, whose admirable style and correct taste as a singer I have never heard surpassed; Browne's majestic tenor; Whittingham's sweet alto; and Hansell's sonorous bass; while Walker's silver tone, and admirable recitation, found their way into every corner of the huge building. Vaughan was then first boy, who acquired his musical knowledge and pure style under his master, Beckwith. Frequently it would happen that the entire music of the day was written by members of the choir, for Garland, the organist (a pupil of Greene) was a composer of no mean talent. Beckwith, then master of the boys, was a most accomplished extempore player on the organ, and his well known anthem. 'The Lord is very great', sufficiently attests his talent as a writer for the Church, and of the minor canons and lay clerks four had produced services.

John ('Christmas') Beckwith 1808–9 (b. Norwich, *c.*1750 or *c.* 1759; d. Norwich 3 June 1809). Beckwith's father and grandfather had both been lay clerks of the Cathedral. The father, Edward, was also organist of St Peter Mancroft from 1780 to his death in 1793 (having acted as such from 1769), and master of the Cathedral choristers from 1759. Our present subject had been apprenticed to *William Hayes at Magdalen College, Oxford in 1775 (Macray 1894–1915: v. 22); the College registers call him 'John William Beckwith'. In 1782–3 he also did some music-copying, under *Philip Hayes, for New College, Oxford. In *William Crotch's manuscript memoirs (Norfolk Record Office, MS 11244) there is the following interesting recollection (p. 34): 'August 1783. Met John Beckwith, afterwards organist at Norwich and Dr of Music, he was now asst. to Dr Hayes. He presented me with D. Scarlatti's Lessons, and I well remember him playing the Cat's Fugue in a most masterly style.'

He succeeded his father as organist of St Peter Mancroft in 1794, and accumulated the Oxford degrees of B.Mus. and D.Mus. in 1803. His formal admission as Cathedral organist is dated 12 August 1808 (CA6), by which time he had already succeeded his father as master of the choristers. He retained his post at St Peter Mancroft until his death. It is thought that the informal second forename may indicate that he was born on 25 December.

Eaton (1872: 23) provides some account of Beckwith, drawing on the recollections of James Taylor (1781–1855), a blind Norwich musician. Referring to Beckwith's playing at St Peter Mancroft before his appointment to the Cathedral, Eaton gives a fulsome description of how, when extemporizing a fugue and after having 'given out the subject and replied to it in the regular way', Beckwith would treat it, 'if possible, by inversion, reversion, augmentation and diminution, carrying it through a course of modulation till he came to the *knot*, when he would bring the replies in close and closer, till Taylor was in a rapture of delight'. On his death, *GM* (1809, p. 589) declared: 'For the bold and striking genius with which he conceived, the correct and brilliant manner in which he executed, and the uncommonly rich, classical, original, and truly scientific style in which he performed his inimitable voluntaries, he may be pronounced to be almost without a rival.' The preface to his book *The First Verse of every Psalm of David, with an Ancient or Modern Chant, in Score* (1808) draws on what he learnt under William Hayes.

The registers of St Peter Mancroft, where he is buried, give his age at death as 58, while the *Norfolk Chronicle*, 10 June 1809, says 'aged 49'.

John Charles Beckwith 1809–19 (b. Norwich, July 1788; d. Norwich, 5 Oct. 1819). The elder son of his predecessor, J. C. Beckwith was admitted organist and master of the choristers on 4 September 1809 (CA6). From June of that year he was also organist of St Peter Mancroft. For two years before his death he was incapacitated by illness (Kitton 1899: 2). He was buried at St Peter Mancroft by the side of his father.

Zechariah Buck 1819–77 (b. Norwich, 9 Sept. 1798; d. Newport, Essex, 5 Aug. 1879). Born of humble parents, Buck was taken into the choir of Norwich Cathedral in October 1808 by Thomas Garland, who heard him singing in the street. After leaving the choir in Midsummer 1815 (CB), he served articles to J. C. Beckwith, becoming assistant organist and finally succeeding his master in 1819. Thereupon he made a tour of most of the English cathedrals to learn by hearing other choirs. In 1853 he was granted the Lambeth degree of Mus.D. He retired in 1877, having completed almost seventy years of unbroken connection with the Cathedral. He died at the home of his eldest son, Dr H. J. Buck. His second son was Sir Edward Buck, KCSI, honorary fellow of Clare College, Cambridge, and the third son became a clergyman.

He has passed into legend as a celebrated trainer of choirboys. He exacted long hours of singing-drill and rehearsal, at the same time appealing to the boys' imagination in order to bring out the meaning of what they sang. Concerning the style of performance of those days (not entirely confined to Norwich, it may be said, but cultivated there to a high degree), one of Buck's choristers and lay clerks, James Valentine Cox, described how (about 1840–50)

> everything was done in the most florid style, viz., grace notes, cadenzas, 'shakes' (single, double, and triple), while time was not much considered. Indeed, some of the treble solos were nearly sung *ad libitum* . . . In the anthems I have heard three boys making 'shakes' simultaneously, and not only the boys but the lay clerks used to 'shake' most extensively. There was one lay clerk—Mr William Smith—who had a good 'shake', so he was

requested not to forget it at the service, as the ladies admired it. I have known him begin a solo with an elaborate 'shake' and end with one—besides introducing two or three in the middle of the anthem. (Kitton 1899: 24.)

As an organist, his most celebrated performance was of the 'Dead March' in *Saul*. George Grove (ibid. 25) recorded that

it was always a grief to him [Buck] when it was played too strictly according to Handel's intentions. He liked that *rolling confused sound* which is got by *good big handfuls* of chords in the bass (old [*]Pratt, of Cambridge University, used to lay the whole of his left arm down the keys, I believe). He complained bitterly that all the grand effect was gone when he played without that.

In the later part of his time as organist, however, Buck rarely played. It is on record that one of his pupils, Bunnett, on the expiry of his articles of apprenticeship in 1855, 'entered into partnership with Dr Buck . . . for twenty-two years, during which time he ably discharged practically the chief duties of cathedral organist' (*MT*, 48 (1907), 382).

Buck had large numbers of articled pupils, including *Robert Janes, *F. C. Atkinson, and *George Gaffe, as well as A. R. Gaul, Edward Bunnett (just mentioned), and W. R. Bexfield (once admired composers of religious music) and also, of greater lustre, *A. H. Mann. He was extremely generous to his pupils, often giving a boy's parents the apprentice fee allowed by the Dean and Chapter. He would also lend them money to start their careers; and during the season before the expiry of their articles, he would take them to London 'in order that they might attend concerts and hear all the best music in vogue, he defraying all expenses involved by their two or three weeks' visit to the Metropolis' (Kitton 1899: 57).

Francis Edward Gladstone 1877–81.

See under Llandaff Cathedral.

Frederick Cook Atkinson 1881–5 (b. Norwich, 21 Aug. 1841; d. East Dereham, Norfolk, 30 Nov. 1896). Atkinson was an articled pupil of Zechariah Buck, and took the Cambridge degree of Mus.B. in 1867. He was appointed to Norwich Cathedral after serving as organist of Manningham (St Luke's?) Church, Bradford, Yorkshire. After leaving Norwich he was in Cheltenham for a few months before taking up the post of organist of St Mary's Church, Lewisham, near London.

BMB; Kitton 1899; West 1921.

Francis ('Frank') Bates 1886–1928 (b. March, Isle of Ely, 13 Jan. 1856; d. 11 May 1936). Bates received his early education at March Grammar School, but he seems to have obtained his musical education mainly by his own endeavours. He became organist of St Baldred's Episcopal Church, North Berwick when he was 17, and while he was there he obtained the Dublin degree of Mus.B. (1880), moving to St John's Episcopal Church, Princes Street, Edinburgh in 1882, and taking the further degree of Mus.D. in 1884. He was chosen organist of Norwich

Cathedral in December 1885 out of a short list of three candidates selected from 168 applicants. On retirement he was granted the title of organist emeritus.

BMB; West 1921; Bates 1930; *MT*, 77 (1936), 561.

§**Heathcote (Dicken) Statham, CBE, 1928–66** (b. London, 7 Dec. 1889; d. Norwich, 29 Oct. 1973). Statham was the son of H. Heathcote Statham, FRIBA, architect and author of *The Organ and its Position in Musical Art*. He received his early education as a chorister of St Michael's College, Tenbury (1900–5), and then went to Gresham's School, Holt. He proceeded to Gonville and Caius College, Cambridge with an open scholarship in music (1908), and took the degree of Mus.B. in 1911. He studied for a year under *Walter Parratt at the Royal College of Music in 1912.

In 1913 he became organist of Calcutta Cathedral, returning to England to be organist of St Michael's College, Tenbury, 1920–5. While there he took the Cambridge degree of Mus.D. (1923) as well as the FRCO diploma (1921). In 1926 he became organist of St Mary's, Southampton, where he remained until his appointment to Norwich Cathedral; he was the last to hold office at Norwich as master of the choristers and organist under the Jacobean statutes of 1620. He conducted at all the Norwich Musical Festivals held during his time there. During World War II he conducted three seasons of concerts with the London Symphony Orchestra in London. He retired from Norwich Cathedral at the end of 1966 with the title of organist emeritus, and was appointed CBE in the New Year Honours of 1967.

§**(Henry) Brian Runnett 1967–70** (b. Tyldesley, Lancs., 20 Jan. 1935; d. Lichfield, 20 Aug. 1970). After attending Waterloo Grammar School, Liverpool, Runnett was a Lancashire County scholar in music at the Matthay School of Music, Liverpool, 1950–5. He was then assistant organist of Chester Cathedral, 1955–60, proceeding to St John's College, Cambridge as organ student, 1960–3. He took the Durham degree of B.Mus. in 1958, followed by the Cambridge degrees of BA (1963) and MA (1967); he also held the FRCO and CHM diplomas.

He was lecturer in music and organist at the University of Manchester from 1963 to 1966. Concurrently with his Cathedral appointment he held a part-time lecturership in music at the University of East Anglia. He was killed in a road accident.

§**Michael (Bernard) Nicholas, organist from 1971** (b. Isleworth, Middlesex, 31 Aug 1938). Nicholas was a Middlesex County scholar at the City of London School, 1950–7, as well as a junior exhibitioner of Trinity College of Music, 1950–6. He then went up to Jesus College, Oxford as organ scholar, 1957–60. At Oxford he read music, taking the degrees of BA (1960) and MA (1964). He also holds the FRCO diploma (1958) and that of CHM (1963).

Before going up to Oxford he was organist of Hanworth Parish Church, Middlesex, 1956–7. Subsequently he was organist of Louth Parish Church, 1960–4. From 1965 to 1971 he was organist of St Matthew's, Northampton and director of music at Northampton Grammar School.

OXFORD

The Cathedral Church of Christ (Christ Church)

Two primary archival sources have been drawn upon for this section: Chapter Registrum A, 1547–1619; and the treasurer's Disbursement Books. The first contains certain yearly lists of members of the foundation to 1580 (some lists in Ob, Wood MS c.8 appear to be based on these rather than to constitute independent evidence). The second provides a series of accounts divided annually into four 'terms' or quarters. For the most part these run from Michaelmas to Michaelmas, but for a time from 1659 they adopt the calendar year. Apart from an isolated account, *c.*1548, and some gaps, these books provide material from the accounting year 1577–8 onwards, and have been relied on down to the time of William Crotch (resigned 1807; see below). From then to 1909 the dates given authoritatively by T. B. Strong, Dean of Christ Church, G. E. P. Arkwright's *Catalogue of Music in the Library of Christ Church Oxford* (1915) i, p. viii, have been used.

Christ Church was the latest of Henry VIII's cathedral foundations. When he established the bishopric of Oxford in 1542, the former Benedictine abbey church of Osney, near Oxford became the Cathedral. However, the see was moved to Oxford in 1546, and the buildings at Osney were allowed to fall into ruin.

Meanwhile Thomas Wolsey had sought to transform St Frideswide's Monastery in Oxford into a grandiose college, to be called Cardinal College. His statutes, among lavish provision for musical personnel, envisaged sixteen choristers together with a well-qualified person ('unus aliquis musices peritissimus') to teach them. One of the twenty clerks ('omnes musices periti') was to be organist. Under this foundation, John Taverner was appointed master of the choristers in November 1526, to be followed in May 1530 by John Benbow of Manchester (*TCM*, i). Taverner was in fact organist as well as master of the choristers.

Wolsey's disgrace and death (1530) put an end to this college, but in 1532 the King used the partly completed buildings for 'King Henry the VIII his College', of which one of the priests was charged to teach grammar and singing to the choristers. The projected statutes of this foundation do not mention organ-playing.

Finally, on transference of the see, Christ Church, part cathedral, part college, was created in November 1546 to succeed the King's College under the style 'Ecclesia Christi Cathedralis Oxon: ex fundatione Regis Henrici Octavi'. A memorandum of 1 October 1546 speaks, *inter alia*, of a master of the choristers at a stipend of £13. 6*s*. 8*d*., an organ-player (stipend, £10), and eight choristers. But the King died before any statutes were formulated, so that until 1867 the house was governed by custom only. (For these constitutional details, see *Statutes of the Colleges of Oxford* 1853; H. L. Thompson 1900; and Wood 1786–90: 433. The date 1867 was kindly supplied by the Revd Dr Henry Chadwick.)

West (1921) thought that John Benbow remained as master of the choristers (and organist) from 1530 to 1564, in other words, through all these changes. But as I read such records as remain, which are scanty enough, it seems that from the date of Henry's foundation of the Cathedral, the two posts were separated for some fifty years. In the earliest surviving Disbursement Book, *c.*1548, the list of 'inferior ministers' of the house does not particularize their several posts, but Benbow, though at the head of the list of ten clerks, is singled out to receive £3. 6*s*. 8*d*. per quarter. This sum accords with the yearly stipend proposed for the master of the choristers by the memorandum of 1 October 1546 (see above). Otherwise, the earliest Disbursement Book is for the year ending Michaelmas 1578, by which time Benbow has disappeared. However, there are four early lists of the foundation, 12 March 1549/50, 1 October 1550, 1551, and 1552, in Registrum A. These also do not distinguish particular offices. Nevertheless, the first has 'Mr Benbow' at the head of the clerks, the second and third 'Robertus Benbow', and the fourth 'Benbow'. I take it that Robert (perhaps alias John?) Benbow was the earliest master of the choristers of the Cathedral, but for reasons about to be advanced below, I take the earliest organist to be Bartholomew Lant.

Bartholomew Lant ←1550–89. Just as 'Benbow' at the head of the list of ten clerks in the 1548 account seems to occupy a special position, so 'Bartelme Lant', who signed the account in person, also seems to have some extra status among the clerks, for he receives an additional payment of 6*s*. 8*d*. His name is found among the clerks in the lists in Registrum A already referred to (see above), running (with gaps) from October 1551 to 1578 (latterly with a junior of the same surname). And when the continuous series of Disbursement Books begins in 1577–8, he stands after the four priests and before the clerks at an individual salary of 50*s*., corresponding to the yearly stipend of £10 envisaged in the memorandum of 1546. His name occurs regularly up to and including the quarter ending March 1589, though on some occasions the stipend was in fact signed for by 'J. Lant'. Not only does this salary make it fairly obvious that he was organist, but, significantly, in the quarter ending Christmas 1586 the clerk adds 'org:' after the name.

Bartholomew Lant had no immediate successor, so far as one can tell, for though the accounts are virtually complete from 1589 to 1605, no one is either named as organist or credited with any distinguishing stipend during the whole of that period. Meanwhile, it may well be that *John Blitheman was master of the choristers (as in Wood 1815–20: i. 235 n.). Registrum A shows 'Blytheman' or 'Blitheman' from December 1563 to December 1578, at first among the priests but marked 'loco minist:', and then, from 1569, at the head of the clerks. Only a surname is given.

Disbursement Books are wanting for a good deal of this period, but eventually these show the following as masters of the choristers: John Barber, (quarters ending) Christmas 1577; Thomas Maycock, March 1578 to Christmas 1580; Henry Hayes, March 1582 to Michaelmas 1585; William Maycock, Christmas 1585 to Christmas 1593; Henry Hayes, March 1594 to Christmas 1596; John Matthew, March 1597 to Michaelmas 1603; Henry Hayes, Christmas 1603 to March 1604; John Marson, Midsummer 1604 to March 1605.

Leonard Major 1605–8. In the quarter ending March 1605, when Major's name appears for the first time, the designation 'organista' is plainly found in the

Disbursement Book. Unlike Lant, however, Major is not listed among the clerks; evidently the post was now considered additional to them. Like Lant, however, he received a quarterly stipend of 50*s*. His latest signature is at Midsummer 1608.

Thomas Blagrove succeeded Marson as master of the choristers in March 1605; he was followed by Oliver Braye at Michaelmas 1607.

William Stonard 1608–31→. Stonard signed the accounts for the first time at Michaelmas 1608, when Braye was still master of the choristers. From the quarter ending Christmas 1608, however, Stonard combined both posts, as all of his successors have done. He took the Oxford degree of B.Mus. in December 1608 (Wood 1815–20: i. 324). West (1921) stated that he died in 1630, but he was paid his stipend until at least Michaelmas 1631. No Disbursement Books survive for the years beginning Michaelmas 1631 to 1640. A person named William Stonnard had been a lay clerk of Ely Cathedral from 1583.

Edward Lowe ←1641–82 (b. Salisbury, *c.*1610; d. Oxford, 11 July 1682). Wood, who was personally acquainted with Lowe, says that he was 'of Salisbury' (Wood 1815–20: i, *sub* 'Stonard') and had been 'bred a chorister there' by John Holmes (Wood MS Notes, f. 87v). That Lowe had been a chorister of some cathedral is clear from his own remark in his *Short Direction* (see below) that he had 'seen, understood, and bore a part in the same [the cathedral service] from his childhood'. Lowe mentions his cousin Humphrey Hyde in Lbl, Add. MS 29396 (ff. 63v–65). Following these clues, *DNB* identifies him with Edward Lowe, born in the parish of St Thomas, Salisbury, probably the son of John Lowe 'of New Sarum and the Inner Temple' by his second wife, Elizabeth, daughter of Thomas Hyde, DD.

The gap in the series of annual accounts at Christ Church, beginning at Michaelmas 1631, makes it impossible to determine when Lowe became organist; but his signature is found when the accounts resume for the year beginning Michaelmas 1641. It occurs for the last time in June 1682. He remained in Oxford during the Interregnum, and played a leading part in the weekly concerts described by Wood (1891–1900: i).

The annual accounts of the vice-chancellor of the University of Oxford name Lowe as University organist in 1657–8, when he received £4. 13*s*. 4*d*. for his current salary and some arrears. He kept this post until his death.

Immediately upon the Restoration, Lowe was active in reviving the cathedral service, and to this end he published (under the initials 'E.L.') *A Short Direction for the Performance of Cathedral Service* (Oxford, 1661) with the object of assisting those who had no knowledge of earlier practice. When a revised *Book of Common Prayer* was promulgated in 1662, he modified his work accordingly, under the title of *A Review of Some Short Directions* (1664). Meanwhile, on John Wilson's resignation as professor of music, Lowe succeeded to the office in 1661 (Wood 1796: ii/2. 894); but in Lbl, Add. MS 29396 he speaks of not having been 'installed' (whatever that may mean) until 1671.

To his three Oxford posts, Lowe added a Court appointment as one of the three organists of the Chapel Royal (q.v.) early enough after the Restoration to be listed as such at the Coronation of Charles II on 23 April 1661.

Wood (1815–20) says that he was 'judicious in his profession but not graduated therein', and (1786–90: 513) that he is buried in the Divinity Chapel of Christ Church Cathedral.

William Husbands 1684–92. There is some obscurity about the exact date of Husbands's appointment. After Lowe's death, one Robert Thynne signed for the organist's stipend for the rest of 1682 and the whole of 1683. Husbands then signed for the January–March quarter of 1684, but Thynne again signed for the remainder of that year. After that, Husbands's name is there regularly until March 1692, although for the January–March quarter of 1691 a certain Charles Husbands (no doubt a son) signed for William's music-copying. In 1691 William Husbands became one of the clerks of Christ Church.

Richard Goodson (I) 1692–1718 (d. Oxford, 13 Jan. 1718, aged 62). Goodson first signed for his stipend for the quarter ending Midsummer 1692. Before that he had been organist of New College from 1682 (q.v.). West (1921) stated that he had been a chorister in St Paul's Cathedral. He was professor of music at Oxford, to which post he was elected on 19 July 1682 (Wood 1796: ii/2. 894). Hawkins (1853: ii. 768) calls him a bachelor of music. Foster (1887–92) has no knowledge of this, but notes that he was admitted to the privileges of the University on 15 July 1682. He succeeded Lowe as University organist.

Goodson is buried in the Cathedral, and his epitaph in the south choir aisle, as recorded by Hawkins (1853), reads as follows: 'H.S.E. Richardson Goodson, Hujus Ecclesiae organista, Hujus Academ. Mus. Praelector Utriq: Deliciae et Decus. Ob. Jan. 13 1717–8.' Foster (1887–92) notes his age at the time of death as 62.

Richard Goodson (II) 1718–41 (d. Oxford, 9 Jan. 1741). If one did not know the date of the elder Goodson's death (see above), it would be difficult to say from the Disbursement Books exactly when the younger man took over from his father, so alike are the signatures. Note, however, that Stephens (1882) (who does not give any authority) dates the younger Goodson's appointment from 1716, 'on recession of his father'.

Hawkins (1853) states that Richard Goodson (II) had earlier been organist of Newbury Church, Berkshire, the first to be appointed there. He succeeded his father as professor of music on 27 January 1717/18 (Wood 1796: ii/2. 894).

Goodson (II) took the Oxford degree of B.Mus. in March 1716/17 (Foster 1887–92), and subscribed to Croft's *Musica Sacra* in 1724. Hawkins (1853) notes the date of death as 9 January 1740/1; Foster (1887–92), following Wood (1786–90: 515), gives it as 7 January.

Richard Church 1741–76 (d. Oxford, 20 July 1776, aged 77). *Philip Hayes, in the course of the memoir prefixed to his father's *Cathedral Music* (1795), stated that Church was an apprentice of *William Hine at Gloucester Cathedral, and that 'he was esteemed a good musician but not a very brilliant player'. He was organist of New College from Christmas 1731 (q.v.), and also a clerk of Magdalen College from 1732 to 1766 (Bloxam 1853–7: ii. 91).

He first signed the Christ Church Disbursement Books for the quarter ending Michaelmas 1741, but he retained his post at New College. When he subscribed to Alcock's *Six and Twenty Select Anthems* in 1771, he described himself as 'Organist of Christ Church and New College, Oxford'. Mary Church (his wife or daughter) signed for his stipend at Christ Church at Christmas 1775 and Lady Day 1776. He was buried at St Peter's-in-the-East (where he was also organist) on 23 July 1776.

Thomas Norris 1776–90 (b. Mere, Wilts., Aug. 1741; d. Himley, Staffs., 3 Sept. 1790, aged 50). Norris was brought up as a chorister of Salisbury Cathedral, and enjoyed an early reputation as a treble soloist. He seems to have settled in Oxford about 1765, and on 19 October that year he was admitted to the privileges of the University (Foster 1887–92) proceeding shortly afterwards to the B.Mus. degree. There is no official record of this, but his exercise, publicly performed (as regulations required) on 16 December 1765, is now Ob, MS Mus. Sch. d. 94. He became organist of St John's College in 1766. Bloxam (1853–7: ii. 109) identifies him with the Thomas Norris who was a clerk of Magdalen College, 1771–90, stating that he only attended the College to draw his pay, going there accompanied by his servant carrying his surplice and hood.

The Christ Church Disbursement Books show that Norris succeeded Church from Lady Day 1776, and a Chapter order of 17 April 1776 notes that 'Mr Norris the organist' had agreed that '£30 a year should be paid out of his salary to Mr Church the late organist' (Chapter Minute Book, 1735–86, communicated by Dr Henry Chadwick). Mee (1911: 130–1) asserts that he was appointed singingman at Christ Church in 1767, in place of Henry Church, deceased.

As a tenor soloist he not only appeared many times at the Music Meetings of Gloucester, Hereford, and Worcester, but also at the Handel Commemorations in Westminster Abbey. He sang at the Birmingham Music Meeting only a few days before his death at the home of Lord Dudley and Ward. In the course of a long obituary notice (under the mistaken name of Charles Norris), *GM* (1790, p. 862) says of him:

> This celebrated singer was originally a chorister in Salisbury Cathedral in which situation he attracted the notice of the learned author of 'Hermes' James Harris. Mr Harris, failing in his wish to fix him on the stage, advised him to settle at Oxford. . . . He soon after took the degree of bachelor of music in that University, was elected organist of St John's College [the notice says nothing about Christ Church], had a great many pupils among the students, and was a favourite singer at the weekly concerts in the Music Room. He was long and deservedly esteemed by the admirers of Handelian music. . . . He was an excellent musician and master of several instruments; but while academical indolence prevented his making any exertions on them, academical ale by degrees injured his voice, and he at last excited pity instead of applause. . . . His voice was a full fine tenor; and in pathetic passages he sang with so much manly dignity and unaffected tenderness, that it was impossible to hear him without being deeply interested . . . Numbers resorted from the country for the benefit of his instructions; but ease was so much dearer to Mr Norris than riches, that few returned the better for the journey.

His tomb at Himley had the following inscription, recorded by Bloxam (1853–7): 'In memory of Mr Thomas Norris, Bachelor of Music, who came to Himley Hall for the benefit of his health, and breathed his last there on the 3d of Sept. 1790 aged 50.' This evidence of Norris's age at death, coupled with the description of him on his admission as clerk of Magdalen as 'organicus de Mere, Wilton', leads us to an entry in the Parish Registers of Mere recording the baptism there of a Thomas Norris on 15 August 1741. At the same time, our present subject is usually identified with the 'Master Norris' from Salisbury who sang treble at Oxford in 1759 and 1760 (Mee 1911: 73) and at the Worcester Festival of 1761 (Lysons 1812: 191). This would have Norris singing treble at an incredibly late age, and one wonders whether there is some mistake about the age recorded on the tombstone at Himley, or whether two men with the same name, both boy singers in their day, have been confused. It also strikes one as curious that among the subscribers to the second edition of Boyce's *Cathedral Music* (1788), 'Mr Norris, M.B.', should have been described as organist of St John's College only, not of Christ Church as well, just as in *GM*.

William Crotch 1790–1807 (b. Norwich, 5 July 1775; d. Taunton, 29 Dec. 1847). Crotch showed exceptional musical gifts at an early age. His father, a carpenter, made a small organ on which, at the age of 2, Crotch taught himself to play 'God save the King' with a bass to the melody. When he was only 3 years old his mother took him to London, where he played at St James's Palace and Buckingham House (as the palace was then known). His precocity was celebrated by Burney (*Philosophical Transactions*, 69/1) and by Daines Barrington in his *Miscellanies* (London, 1781). Crotch's own manuscript memoirs are now in the Norfolk and Norwich Record Office (MS 11244).

Crotch was in Cambridge from 1786 to 1788, where he assisted *John Randall in his various appointments. Under the patronage of A. G. Schomberg, fellow of Magdalen College, he moved to Oxford with a view to entering the Church, but on Schomberg's death he adopted the musical profession. He was only 15 when he succeeded Norris as organist of Christ Church, drawing his first stipend for the quarter ending Christmas 1790. He matriculated at St Mary Hall in January 1791, and in 1794 he took the degree of B.Mus. (Foster 1887–92). On the death of *Philip Hayes in 1797, Crotch became professor of music in the University and organist of St John's College. In 1799 he proceeded to the degree of D.Mus. During the Napoleonic Wars he took a commission in the Oxford Loyal Volunteers, and was promoted ensign in 1893 (*Jackson's Oxford Journal*, 8 Oct. 1803).

Crotch appears to have withdrawn from Oxford at about the end of 1806 (see *Jackson's Oxford Journal*, 27 Dec. 1806 and 11 Apr. 1807). In 1805 and 1806 one Robert Bliss junior drew the Christ Church stipend 'for Dr Crotch', and Crotch himself signed the accounts for the last time at Midsummer 1807. It was at about this time that he settled in London, though he retained his Oxford professorship until his death. In 1822 he became the first principal of the Royal Academy of Music, retiring from this post in June 1832.

Besides his abilities as an executant and composer, Crotch had something of a scholar's interest in music, as shown by his lectures at the Oxford Music School and at the Royal Institution, London which he collected and published in 1831. The three volumes of *Specimens of various styles of music*, compiled in connection with these lectures and published in 1807–8, indicate the range of his interests; their contents were thought worth listing in *Grove*[1] and *Grove*[2], *sub* 'Specimens'. Crotch was also much interested in theology, and he was accomplished in drawing and painting. He is reputed to have been worth £18,000 on his death.

DNB.

William Cross 1807–25 (b. Oxford, 1777; d. Oxford, 20 June 1825). From an early age Cross was organist of St Martin's Church, Oxford, as was his father before him. Cross then succeeded Crotch at both St John's College (Dec. 1806) and Christ Church (1807). Stephens (1882) states that he took the Oxford degree of B.Mus. in 1823, but this is not mentioned in any official publication.

Stephens 1882.

William Marshall 1825–46 (b. Oxford; d. Handsworth, Birmingham, 17 Aug. 1875, aged 69). Mee (1911: 85) surmises that Marshall may have been the son of William Marshall, a prominent Oxford violinist, 1801–46. One of that name, 'musicae suppellectis venditor' ('seller of musical equipment'), was admitted to the privileges of the University in 1812 (Foster 1887–92). Our subject was a chorister in the Chapel Royal (see *Jackson's Oxford Journal*, 22 Apr. 1820). He followed Cross not only as organist of Christ Church but also of St John's College in 1825; his appointment to Christ Church was announced in *Jackson's Oxford Journal* for 2 July 1825. He took the Oxford degrees of B.Mus. and D.Mus. in 1826 and 1840 respectively (Foster 1887–92).

From 1839 he was also organist of All Saints' Church, Oxford. In 1846 he moved to Kidderminster as organist of the parish church there, and he remained in Kidderminster until 1867. In 1868 he was briefly organist of Christ Church, Hampstead, London (Stephens 1882).

Charles William Corfe 1846–82 (b. Salisbury, 13 July 1814; d. Oxford, 16 Dec. 1883). C. W. Corfe was among the younger of the fourteen children of *A. T. Corfe, organist of Salisbury Cathedral, and a brother of *J. D. Corfe, organist of Bristol Cathedral. He was taught by his father. He took the Oxford degrees of B.Mus. (1847) and D.Mus. (1852); he also held the University offices of coryphaeus (1856) and choragus (1860) under Ouseley. He resigned his post at Christ Church in 1882.

The story of his unvarying use of a certain group of stops, wittily named the 'Corfe-mixture', is well known (*MT*, 43 (1902), 521). He presented the Cathedral with a stained-glass window by Burne-Jones in the north aisle. His son, C. J. Corfe, became the pioneer missionary Bishop of Korea.

DNB.

Charles Harford Lloyd 1882–92 (b. Thornbury, Glos., 16 Oct. 1849; d. Slough, 16 Oct. 1919). The son of a solicitor, Lloyd was educated at Thornbury Grammar School, Rossall School, and Magdalen Hall, Oxford, where he held an open scholarship in classics. Intending to enter the Church, he read theology as well as taking a music degree (B.Mus., 1871; BA, 1872; MA, 1875). He therefore represents a new type of cathedral organist, with a resident university career and honours in an honour school. Lloyd did not take the D.Mus. degree until much later (1891). He also held the FRCO diploma.

He was appointed to Gloucester Cathedral in 1876 in succession to S. S. Wesley. He moved to Christ Church in September 1882, combining his post there with work on the staff of the Royal College of Music, 1887–92. In 1892 he became precentor of Eton College, where he remained until his retirement in 1914. He emerged from retirement, however, to become organist of the Chapel Royal in January 1917.

Lloyd seems to have been subject to odd nervous movements, giving rise to Arthur Benson's comment that 'of course we all of us have to struggle with the beast within us, but I think Lloyd has to struggle with the bird within him' (Denecke 1951: 45).

After his death, a volume of his organ accompaniments to unison hymn-singing was published by the Year Book Press. This sheds interesting light on the methods he used in Eton College Chapel. There is a memorial window to him in Gloucester Cathedral.

MT, 60 (1919) 621; *Grove*[3]; *WWW*, 1916–28.

Basil Harwood 1892–1909 (b. Woodhouse, Olveston, Glos., 11 Apr. 1859; d. London, 3 Apr. 1949). Harwood was the eldest son of Edward Harwood, a member of the Society of Friends. His early musical training was in the hands of *George Riseley, but he received his other education at Charterhouse and Trinity College, Oxford, which he entered in 1878. For a short time he studied composition with Jadassohn in Leipzig.

From 1883 to 1887 he was organist of St Barnabas's Church, Pimlico, London, moving to Ely Cathedral in 1887 (q.v.). He was organist of Christ Church from 1892 until his early retirement from professional life in 1909. He was the first conductor of the Oxford Bach Choir, 1896–1900, and from 1900 to 1909 he was choragus of the University.

Harwood took the Oxford degrees of B.Mus. and BA in 1880, MA in 1884, and D.Mus. in 1896. He also held the FRCO diploma.

There are very informative reminiscences about Harwood (by Henry Ley and Claude Williams) in *ECM* (19 (1949), 39); see also W. H. Harris, 'Basil Harwood—1859–1948' (*ECM*, 29 (1959), 43).

Grove[3]; *DNB*, 1941–50; *WWW*, 1941–50.

Henry (George) Ley 1909–26 (b. Chagford, Devon, 30 Dec. 1887; d. 24 Aug. 1962). The son of a clergyman, Ley was a chorister of St George's Chapel, Windsor under *Walter Parratt, and then went to Uppingham School and the Royal College of Music. He became organ scholar of Keble College, Oxford in 1906, after having been organist of St Mary's, Farnham Royal for a short time between 1905 and 1906. He became organist of Christ Church Cathedral before he had proceeded to any degrees. The appointment of so young and untried a man to such an important post, made on the personal responsibility of the dean, T. B. Strong, was at first viewed unfavourably by not a few established musicians.

Ley took the Oxford degree of B.Mus. in 1911, followed (not without difficulty, it was said) by those of BA and MA together in 1913; he proceeded D.Mus. in 1919. (As an amusing matter of academic protocol of those days, *Henry Havergal recounted how placing Ley at dinner in the hall of Christ Church posed a problem. He was certainly not a graduate; but, as organist, he was clearly distinguished from mere undergraduates. The matter was solved by introducing a small table for one, at which he sat in isolation.) He joined the staff of the Royal College of Music in 1919, and was made an honorary FRCO in 1920. He held office as choragus of the University, 1923–6. Like C. H. Lloyd, he left Oxford to become precentor of Eton College, a post he retained until his retirement in 1945. In 1941 he was elected an honorary fellow of Keble College.

He was a notable performer on the organ. In its obituary notice *The Times* said: 'Although he had a club foot, he showed exceptional executive skill and a lively style of playing that was criticized by some as being too pianistic. It is true that his organ technique was based on an excellent piano technique . . . Its corollary in his playing was clean phrasing and keen rhythm.' The *Keble College Record* quotes an Eton pupil as saying: 'He looked like Pickwick, but he was much more like Puck.'

MT, 63 (1922), 837; *Grove*[3]; *The Times*, 27 Aug. 1962; Drennan 1970; *Church Music Society Annual Report*, 70 (1976).

Noel Edward Ponsonby 1926–8.

See under Ely Cathedral.

Sir William (Henry) Harris, KCVO, 1929–32.

See under St George's Chapel, Windsor.

§**Sir Thomas (Henry Wait) Armstrong 1933–55** (b. Peterborough, 15 June 1898). Armstrong was a chorister in the Chapel Royal, subsequently serving his articles at Peterborough to *Haydn Keeton, whose sub-organist he became in 1915. Meanwhile, in 1914, he had become organist of Thorney Abbey. In 1916 he went to Oxford as organ scholar of Keble College, resuming his tenure there after war-service, and reading modern history. He became sub-organist of Manchester Cathedral in 1922, but moved to London in 1923 as organist of St Peter's, Eaton Square. While in London he undertook further study at the Royal College of Music.

Armstrong became organist of Exeter Cathedral in 1928, remaining there until his appointment to Christ Church in 1933. While at Christ Church he was choragus of the University (1937–54), and was made a student of Christ Church (the equivalent of a fellow of a college) in 1939, the first organist to be so distinguished.

In 1955 Armstrong resigned all his Oxford appointments on becoming principal of the Royal Academy of Music; he was elected an honorary fellow of Keble College the same year. He received a knighthood in 1958, and retired from the Royal Academy of Music in 1968. In 1981 he was elected an honorary student of Christ Church.

Armstrong took the following Oxford degrees: BA, 1922; B.Mus., 1923; MA,

1925; D.Mus., 1928. He received the honorary degree of D.Mus. from the University of Edinburgh in 1963, and he is an honorary FRCO. His son became secretary to the Cabinet, and was raised to the peerage as Lord Armstrong of Ilminster.

§**Sydney Watson, OBE, 1955–70** (b. Denton, Manchester, 3 Sept. 1903). After leaving Warwick School, Watson spent a year at the Royal College of Music (1921–2) and then went up to Oxford as organ scholar of Keble College (1922–5). He took the Oxford degrees of BA (1925), B.Mus. (1926), MA (1928), and D.Mus. (1932), and the FRCO diploma (1933, Lafontaine prize).

He was on the music staff of Stowe School, 1925–8, and then precentor (music master) of Radley, 1929–33. From 1933 to 1938 he was organist of New College, Oxford, succeeding *George Dyson at Winchester College (1938–45) before moving to Eton College as precentor (1946–55). On his appointment as organist of Christ Church he was made a student of the house.

From 1946 he taught at the Royal College of Music, and from 1956 he was also a University lecturer at Oxford, holding the office of choragus, 1963–8. In the Birthday Honours of 1970, shortly before his retirement that year, he was appointed OBE.

§**Simon (John) Preston 1970–81** (b. Bournemouth, Hants 4 Aug. 1938). Preston was educated at Canford School, the Royal Academy of Music (organ scholarship), and King's College, Cambridge, where he was organ student. He read music, taking the Cambridge degrees of BA (1961), Mus.B. (1962), and MA (1964). From 1962 to 1967 he was sub-organist of Westminster Abbey and then, for a year, acting organist of St Albans Cathedral. Concurrently with his appointment as organist and student of Christ Church, he was also tutor and lecturer in music there. He left Oxford to become organist of Westminster Abbey, a post from which he resigned at the end of 1987, thereafter devoting himself to free-lance work.

§**Francis (John Roy) Grier 1981–5** (b. Kotakinabalu, Sabah, 29 July 1955). From St George's Chapel, Windsor, where he was a chorister, 1963–8, Grier went to Eton College, 1969–73, and then to King's College, Cambridge, 1973–6, where, like his predecessor, he was organ student. After reading music he took the Cambridge degree of BA in 1976, having taken the FRCO diploma in 1972. He was assistant organist of Christ Church from 1977 until his appointment to the full post, when he also became student and tutor.

On leaving Oxford he travelled in India to study both Hinduism and the inculturation movement of the Catholic Church. Then, for more than two years, he shared the life of mentally handicapped persons in communities in London and Bangalore. In September 1989 he entered the Roman Catholic Benedictine abbey of Quarr on the Isle of Wight.

§**Stephen (Mark) Darlington, organist from 1985** (b. Lapworth, War., 21 Sept. 1952). On leaving King's School, Worcester, Darlington went up to Christ Church, Oxford as organ scholar, 1971–4, reading music and taking the degrees of BA (1974) and MA (1976). He holds the FRCO diploma (1972). From 1974 to 1978 he was assistant organist of Canterbury Cathedral, and then he became master of the music of St Albans Cathedral. On his return to Oxford as organist and student of Christ Church, he also became tutor and lecturer in music.

PETERBOROUGH

The Cathedral Church of St Peter, St Paul, and St Andrew

Main sources in this section (1963) (with Cambridge University Library (Cu) or Northamptonshire Record Office (NRO) references):

Chapter Acts
CA1 1585–1642 (Cu/P. MS 12)* (asterisk indicates microfilm in NRO).
CA2 1660–1814 (Cu/P. MS 54)*.

Accounts
Ac1 Receiver's and treasurer's accounts combined in one volume, 1541–1602, but no treasurer's accounts earlier than year ending October 1549 or later than year ending Michaelmas 1600; there are some gaps (Cu/P. MS 50)*.
Ac2 1611–71 (Cu/P. MS 52)*.
Ac3 1671–81 (Cu/P. MS 53)*.
Ac4 1680–1700 (NRO/ML 1030).
Ac5 1701–49 (NRO/ML 1032).
Ac6 1750–85 (NRO/ML 869–70).
Ac7 1786–1805 (Cu/P. MS 22).

Miscellaneous
LB Dean Fletcher's Ledger Book, 1587–1642, 1661 (Cu/P. MS 11).
PR Precentor's Registers of baptisms, marriages, and burials in the Cathedral (transcript, NRO/M(T) 51).

In connection with his new bishopric of Peterborough, Henry VIII founded Peterborough Cathedral in August 1541, taking over the buildings of the former Benedictine abbey of St Peter. Its choir included eight choristers under a master whose duties, as defined in the draft statutes, included the work of organist (see p. xix). From details given below, it will be seen how, from 1614 to 1714, the Peterborough authorities took it upon themselves to separate the two duties.

In interpreting the Peterborough records, it should be observed how frequently appointments appear to date from the Midsummer Chapter meeting. This can only mean that the formal record of these appointments was made then, and that the duties may have been taken up (or laid down) at any time during the preceding twelve months. Similarly, the seventeenth- and eighteenth-century accounts as far as 1807 (with one exception) appear to contain only the signatures of those officers in post at the end of the accounting year. Though seeming a little odd, the supposition must remain that a change may have taken place during the accounting year, for it cannot be thought that every change of appointment coincided with the beginning of such years. While very little of any significance may depend on this point, it should nevertheless be borne in mind. With regard to accounting procedure at Peterborough, the less usual practice was adopted from the 1640s until well into the nineteenth century of ending the accounting year at Lady Day (25 March) rather than Michaelmas (29 September).

Richard Storey 1541–9→. In 'The Booke of the Erection of the King's New College at Peterborough' (Mellows 1941: 71) 'Richard Story' is named as 'schoolmaster for the choristers' at a fee of £10 per annum. Storey's name is found in the accounts covering the period between the dissolution of the abbey and the founding of the Cathedral (Mellows 1940: 101). This creates a presumption that he had been a lay member of the monastic body, like Byrchley of Chester. In the earliest extant treasurer's account of the Cathedral (year ending 31 October 1549) he duly received his £2. 10*s*. per quarter as master of the choristers. There follows a gap in these accounts until the year 1582–3.

John Tyesdale ←1569→. In the list of organists carved on the back of the organ-loft in the Cathedral, there is the legend '*c*.1569 John Tyesdale'. This may well rest on the researches of W. T. Mellows, a learned and trustworthy antiquary, but I have failed to verify it in any documents I have seen. On the reverse of the flyleaf of LB is a reference to the appointment of one Richard Tyesdale as almsman, *temp*. Elizabeth I.

Richard Tiller ?–1583. As we have seen, the Cathedral statutes laid the duty of organ-playing on the officer whose title was master of the choristers. But when the accounts resume at the year ending Michaelmas 1583 the simple term 'organist' has come into use. This presumably reflects awareness, at quite an early date, of the growing importance of the organ in cathedral services. In that year Richard Tiller and John Mudd share the fee of £10, indicating that Tiller held the post for only part of the accounting year. The list of organists in the Cathedral gives *c*.1574 as the date of his appointment.

John Mudd 1583–1631 (d. Peterborough, Dec. 1631). The accounts which, with some gaps, run from 1582–3 to 1628–9 all show John Mudd consistently as organist. Latterly (at least from 1610–11) he also held the sinecure post of epistler. No later than April 1614 (CA1, f. 17^{v}) the duties of master of the choristers were divorced from that of organist, and Nicholas Byrne was appointed to teach the boys. Mudd resigned his place as organist in 1631 (see under Thomas Mudd below), by which time, having been in office for forty-seven years, he was perhaps feeling his age. A patent of 26 May 1630 (LB, f. 107), granting him the sinecure office of cook, may have been a way of providing for his retirement. He was buried in the Cathedral on 16 December 1631, described as 'organist of Peterborough' (PR). When a survey of houses in the precincts was made by the parliamentary commissioners in 1649, certain chambers were still in the occupation of John Mudd's representatives (Mellows 1941: p. xlix).

This John Mudd may well have been organist of Southwell Minster in 1582 (q.v.). It is asserted in *NG* that he was the son of Henry Mudd, mentioned above (p. 172) in connection with St Paul's Cathedral, and, further, that he is to be identified with 'John Mudde, son of Henry Mudde, citizen of London', who, according to the College records, was admitted pensioner of Gonville and Caius College, Cambridge at the age of 18 on 11 July 1573.

Thomas Mudd 1631–2. Although there are no baptisms in PR earlier than 1615 to clinch the matter, it seems reasonable to presume that Thomas is the son of the foregoing John, that same 'Mr Mudd's son' who was chosen chorister on 6 May 1619 (Mellows 1941: p. liii). The accounts for 1628–9 show a Thomas Mudd as chorister; assuming that this is the same person, he enjoyed a long tenure as a boy singer. The minute of Thomas Mudd's appointment reads: 'At the same Chapter [9 June 1631] Thomas Mudd was elected organist upon his father's resignation of that place' (CA1, f. 35). After no more than a year he ceased to be organist (see under David Standish below). The relevant accounts have not survived, so we do not know whether he was paid, or whether, as in the case of Richard Langdon (below), his election was inoperative. It seems a curiously short tenure.

The name Thomas Mudd crops up once more at Peterborough thirty years later, when it was resolved on 15 August 1662 'that Mr Thomas Mudd shall have a quarter['s] pay as petty canon at Michaelmas and after continue a petty canon if he shall do the duty of the place and procure Holy Orders' (CA2). He can be traced in this capacity up to Midsummer 1664 (Ac2). Can this be the same man, who, if he was the chorister of 1619, would by now be over 50? What did he go on to do immediately after 1632? Taking it on balance that the organist of 1631 and the minor canon of 1662 were one and the same man, a discussion of his conjectured career, taking in Lincoln, Exeter, and York, will be found under Exeter Cathedral (q.v.)

David Standish 1632–76 (b. *c.*1595; d. Peterborough, Dec. 1676). David Standish's election as organist is recorded on 1 June (1632) (CA1, f. 36). The year is omitted from the minute, but the sequence of entries establishes that it cannot be other than 1632. He had for some time been a lay clerk (accounts for 1628–9), and not later than 1642 he also became a minor canon (accounts for 1641–2, after a gap from 1629). In 1643–4 the accounts show him not only in both these capacities, but also as holding the sinecure appointment of gospeller. Bearing in mind that the Standish family included more than one David, it is important to note that the signatures for each of these three payments appear to be the same. When he was appointed gospeller on 22 November 1638 (CA1, f. 38^{v}), it was made a condition 'that he shall leave his curate's place at Paston and attend wholly upon the service of this church'. Perhaps one may conjecture, therefore, that the organist had taken holy orders and was trying to combine pastoral work with his Cathedral duties (already involving two capacities), and that the authorities tempted him back to full-time Cathedral work by the additional pay of gospeller.

The accounting year 1643–4 is the latest extant record to contain David Standish's signature in all capacities before the parliamentary edict disrupted the Prayer Book services. During the Interregnum he remained in the Close and rented the fourth prebendal house from the parliamentary commissioners (Mellows 1941: p. xlv). He survived to resume his posts, and in the accounts for the year to Lady Day 1662 he again signs for all three. He died in office in 1676, and was buried in the Cathedral on 7 December (PR). The inscription on his tomb is recorded thus by Willis (1742: ii. 554): 'David Standish, Deo in Ecclesia Petriburg Annos 50 serviens, & plusquam 80 Annorum taedio lassatus, attritas Mortalitatis exuvias deposuit. Dec. 6 1676.' ('David Standish, serving God for 50 years in the Church of Peterborough, and wearied by the weight of more than 80 years, relinquished his wasted remains of mortality Dec. 6, 1676.')

The Standishes were a large family connected with the Cathedral. From the time of Francis Standish (d. 1631, whose eldest child, Elizabeth, was baptized in 1625) and his brother David (our present subject, whose eldest child, Francis, was baptized in 1617) until the baptism of yet another David Standish in December 1723, there are between thirty and forty entries with that surname in PR. But the baptismal names Francis and David occur too frequently for relationships to be clear without further investigation. A much later David Standish, MA (d. Oct. 1720) was minor canon, 'head-schoolmaster' (headmaster of King's School, no doubt), and rector of Woodson. It may also be mentioned that one William Standish, MA, was admitted minor canon of St Paul's Cathedral in February 1687/8 (Lgh, MS 25,664/1).

As organist, David Standish had a close colleague in his brother Francis (see above), who was precentor and succeeded Nicholas Byrne as master of the choristers sometime before 1628–9 (Ac2). This relationship is disclosed by a Chapter minute of 12 May 1626 (CA1, f. 27[v]), when it was decided that 'David Standish should have the house wherein Francis Standish his brother now dwelleth'. David's own eldest son, also named Francis, was a chorister as late as 1642–3 (Ac1), and it could have been either he or his cousin (also Francis) who eventually became precentor and master of the choristers in June 1667 (CA2) and died in 1697 (PR).

William Standish 1677–86. William Standish was the grandson of his predecessor, as stated in the minute of his appointment, 21 June 1677 (CA2). He last received his stipend for the accounting year 1685–6 (Ac4). There seems to be no record of his death at Peterborough.

Roger Standish 1686–1713 (bap. Peterborough, 1 Nov. 1670; d. Peterborough, 12 July 1713). The exact relationship of Roger Standish to his two immediate predecessors has not yet been established. The son of one of the Francis Standishes, he was baptized in the Cathedral and eventually buried there. His appointment is not recorded in CA2, but Ac4 notes his first year's stipend in 1686–7. From the accounting year 1699–1700 he also held a minor canon's place. During Roger's time as organist, Francis Standish, master of the choristers died in 1697 and was succeeded by Roger's brother, a further David Standish. This David employed Roger as his deputy to teach the choristers, but it was not a happy arrangement. On 18 June 1711 (CA2) the Chapter noted with displeasure that the boys had been neglected, and it was determined not to reappoint David Standish (whose election was evidently regarded as annual) as master unless he provided a better deputy.

At the end of Roger Standish's time, the organ, built in 1680, fell into a bad state, and on 22 June 1713 (CA2) it was reported to be choked with dirt, out of repair with hundreds of pipes out of tune, and that the trumpet stop was useless.

James Hawkins (II) 1714–50 (d. 1750). There is no reason to doubt John Hawkins's statement (1853: 772) that this was the son of *James Hawkins, organist of Ely Cathedral. Following the state of affairs towards the end of Roger Standish's time, it is not surprising that he was appointed to the combined post of master of the choristers and organist (as under the draft statutes), and this is tacitly assumed in the case of all his successors. He received his first year's salary in 1714–15 (Ac5). Almost immediately, he complained that four of the boys, including one named Standish, were incompetent, and on 22 June 1714 the Chapter resolved that they should be dismissed. Hawkins himself was admonished for insolence on 17 June 1728 (CA2). In his later years he was not only master of the choristers and organist, but also surveyor of works (Ac5).

He was a subscriber to Croft's *Musica Sacra* (1724) and Greene's *Forty Select Anthems* (1743).

George Wright 1750–73. Wright was formally apointed to succeed Hawkins as organist and surveyor of works by Chapter minute of 18 June 1751, but he is named for a whole year's pay in the accounts ending Lady Day 1751. The end of his period of office (Lady Day 1773) is disclosed likewise in Ac6.

Carter Sharp 1773–7. Ac6 first names Sharp for the year ending Lady Day 1774. His dismissal 'for great neglect' was recorded at the July Chapter, 1777 (CA2).

James Rodgers 1777–84. Rodgers had been organist of Ely Cathedral, 1774–7 (q.v.). His appointment was formally recorded in Peterborough CA2 on 1 July 1777, and the accounts contain his signature for the last time for the year ending 25 March 1784 (Ac6). Among the subscribers to William Hayes's *Cathedral Music* (1795), there is listed 'Mr James Rodgers, late organist of Peterborough'.

A Chapter minute of 29 July 1784 records the appointment of *Richard Langdon to succeed Rodgers, and at the corresponding meeting next year, 28 June 1785, his resignation was minuted. Turning to the accounts, we find that John Calah (see below) signs for the whole stipend for the year ending 25 March 1785. The introductory remarks to this section will suggest why the Chapter minutes cannot necessarily be taken at face value. Langdon was organist of Armagh Cathedral from 1782 to 1794 (q.v.). The most that can be supposed is that, on some visit to England, he had considered, and indicated acceptance of, the post at Peterborough, but decided, before having time to notify Armagh Cathedral of his resignation, not to take it up. His resignation at Peterborough was then formally minuted in retrospect at the following Midsummer meeting. It certainly seems that he can hardly be regarded as in the effective succession of organists of Peterborough Cathedral. For his career as a whole, see under Exeter Cathedral.

John Calah 1784–98 (d. Peterborough, 4 Aug. 1798, aged 40). Calah's appointment was formally minuted at the same time as Langdon's resignation

(June 1785); but, as we have already noted, he signed for the organist's stipend for the whole accounting year ending March 1785. Before coming to Peterborough he had been organist of the parish church, Newark-on-Trent and master of the Magnus Song School there (Jackson 1964: 202). He may have been the 'John Calah or Calab, son of James Calab', who became a chorister of Southwell Minster on 26 October 1769 (James 1927: 103). He is buried in Peterborough Cathedral (PR).

The organ in which he acquiesced (or against which he rebelled) was in bad condition. It 'was some hundred years old; the keys were so worn that it was like putting your fingers into a row of ivory spoons. As to execution upon such an instrument, it was impossible.' (Gardiner 1838–53: iii.)

Samuel Spofforth 1798–1807. Spofforth is named in the accounts for the year ending Lady Day 1799 (Ac7), continuing to Lady Day 1807. For the year 1807–8 the stipend is divided between him and his successors.

See under Lichfield Cathedral.

Thomas Knight 1808–11 (b. 1789; d. 21 Nov. 1811). Knight took up duty during the accounting year 1807–8. *BMB* supplies his dates of birth and death.

Edmund Larkin 1812–36 (b. 1785; d. Stamford, Lincs., 9 Dec. 1838). Larkin is first credited with stipend for the year to Lady Day 1812, though Knight did not die until November 1811. *BMB*, giving Larkin's dates of birth and death, states that on leaving the Cathedral (Midsummer 1836) he became organist of Stamford Parish Church. West (1921) states that while at Peterborough Larkin was also organist of St John's Church there.

John Speechly 1836–69 (b. Peterborough, 1811; d. Peterborough, 7 Aug. 1869). Speechly's stipend ran from Midsummer 1836 to August 1869, when it was paid to his executors. There is a tablet to his memory in the south aisle of the Cathedral. *BMB* notes that, like his predecessor, he was also organist of St John's Church, Peterborough. Following his death, temporary arrangements were made until the arrival of his successor.

Haydn Keeton 1870–1921 (b. Mosborough, near Chesterfield, 26 Oct. 1847; d. ?Peterborough, 27 May 1921). Keeton's father, Edwin, was organist of Eckington Parish Church, Derbyshire from 1848. Haydn was a chorister in St George's Chapel, Windsor under *G. J. Elvey. He became organist of Datchet Parish Church, Berkshire in 1867, and was appointed to Peterborough Cathedral in March 1870 before he was 23. To this post he devoted himself for the rest of his life.

His personality and long tenure combined to forge an impression which was still strong in the minds of his pupils more than forty years after his death. Among those whom he taught and influenced were Malcolm Sargent and *Thomas Armstrong, articled pupils in 1911 and 1913 respectively. In 1903 his articled pupils presented him with a loving-cup.

He took the Oxford degree of B.Mus. in 1869, and proceeded D.Mus. in 1877. He was also the holder of the FRCO diploma.

MT, 62 (1921), 465.

§**(Richard) Henry (Pinwell) Coleman 1921–44** (b. Dartmouth, 3 Apr. 1888; d. 17 Feb. 1965). Coleman was a chorister in St George's Church, Ramsgate before going to Denstone College. He was then articled to *S. H. Nicholson, serving his articles at Carlisle and Manchester Cathedrals. While at Carlisle he was organist of St Stephen's Church. On completing his apprenticeship he was appointed sub-organist of Manchester Cathedral in 1908. He was then organist of Blackburn Parish Church (now the Cathedral), 1912, and of Derry Cathedral, Londonderry, 1914. He returned to England in 1920, and was for a short time organist of the Heritage Craft Schools, Chailey, Sussex before succeeding Keeton in 1921. During the brief vacancy following Keeton's death, *MT* (62 (1921), 718) had some wry comments on the conditions attached to the post of organist of Peterborough Cathedral.

After nearly twenty-five years of service, Coleman left Peterborough under unhappy domestic circumstances for which he could not be held responsible. Subsequently he was county music organiser for Staffordshire, 1944–7, organist of Hatfield Parish Church, Herts., 1947–8, organist of All Saints', Eastbourne, 1949–59, and then director of music at the Chapel Royal, Brighton.

He took the Dublin degree of Mus.B. in 1919, followed by that of Mus.D. in 1924, and he held the FRCO diploma. His book, *The Amateur Choir Trainer* (1932), reissued in 1964 as *The Church Choir Trainer*, exerted useful influence.

MT, 106 (1965), 290.

Charles Cooper Francis 1944–6 (b. Peterborough, 20 Dec. 1884; d. Stamford, Lincs., 29 Sept. 1956). After serving as a chorister in the Cathedral and attending King's School, Peterborough, Francis was articled to Haydn Keeton in 1899, and in 1905 became his assistant organist. He was then appointed organist of St Mark's Church, Harrogate, 1910–14, and of St Mary's Church, Peterborough, 1914–20. In the meantime, in 1916, he had joined the staff of the Royal College of Music. He took the Durham degree of B.Mus. in 1905, proceeding D.Mus. in 1916, and he also held the FRCO diploma (1906).

Information from Miss K. A. Francis.

Douglas (Edward) Hopkins 1946–53.

See under Canterbury Cathedral.

(William) Stanley Vann 1953–77.

See under Chelmsford Cathedral.

§**Christopher (Stainton) Gower, master of the music from 1977** (b. High Wycombe, Bucks., 15 Mar. 1939). Gower was educated at High Pavement School, Nottingham and Magdalen College, Oxford (organ scholar), where he read music, proceeding to the degrees of BA (1961) and MA (1965). He took the FRCO diploma in 1961.

His first appointment was as assistant organist of Exeter Cathedral, 1961–9, during which time he taught at the Cathedral School and was also, from 1967, lecturer in music at the University of Exeter. He also spent some time during 1965 as Ralph H. Lane Memorial scholar at the College of Church Musicians, Washington, USA. From 1969 until taking up his appointment at Peterborough towards the end of 1977, he was organist of Portsmouth Cathedral. In 1988 he became a Justice of the Peace.

PORTSMOUTH

The Cathedral Church of St Thomas of Canterbury

On the establishment of the diocese of Portsmouth in 1927, Old Portsmouth Parish Church was raised to cathedral status.

Hugh Ambrose Burry (1925) **1927–31** (b. 1871; d. 1939). Burry was a chorister of St Paul's Cathedral, London, and his first posts were as organist of St Augustine's and St Faith's in the City of London. In 1902 he became organist of St Mary's, Portsea, Hants, and he was appointed organist of St Thomas's, Portsmouth in 1925. He was in office when the church was raised to cathedral status. After his resignation he became voluntary organist at St Alban's, Copner, Portsmouth.

Thornsby 1912; *MT*, 80 (1939), 684.

Thomas Newboult 1931–44 (b. Silkstone, Yorks., 4 June 1889; d. Portsmouth, 25 June 1956). Newboult was a pupil of *E. C. Bairstow at York Minster, and took the FRCO diploma in 1913. Before becoming organist of Portsmouth Cathedral he held posts at St Leonard's, Newark-on-Trent, St James's, Whitehaven, All Saints', Scarborough, and St Paul's, King Cross, Halifax. While at Halifax he also taught at Crossley and Porter's School there. After leaving Portsmouth Cathedral he was organist of St Bartholomew's, Southsea, Hants, 1952–4.

Information from Mrs T. Newboult; *MT*, 97 (1956), 440.

John (Armitage) Davison 1945–59 (b. Kidderminster, Worcs., 23 Dec. 1898; d. Waltham Chase, Hants, 23 July 1972). Davison was educated at King Charles Grammar School, Kidderminster and Selwyn College, Cambridge, where he read history and won the John Stewart of Rannoch scholarship in sacred music, taking the degrees of BA (1920) and MA (1927). He was director of music at Dauntsey's School, Wiltshire (1923–8) and then Malvern College (1928–40). On his appointment to Portsmouth Cathedral in 1945 he also became director of music at Portsmouth Grammar School. After leaving these posts he became organist of Cirencester Parish Church, and in retirement he was organist of the village church of Shedfield.

Information from Mrs J. A. Davison.

§**Maxwell (Graham) Menzies 1959–64** (b. Liverpool, 19 Apr. 1912). Menzies was a chorister of St Michael's College, Tenbury, 1923–6, after which he went to St John's School, Leatherhead. Between leaving school and going up to Oxford he was a student at the Royal College of Music. He was organ exhibitioner of St John's College, Oxford, 1932–5. He then returned to St Michael's College in 1935 as choirmaster and organist. In 1952 he was appointed organist of Maidstone Parish Church, and moved to Portsmouth to the combined posts at the Cathedral and Grammar School in 1959. After leaving Portsmouth he joined the staff of the Birmingham School of Music, where he remained until retirement.

Menzies took the Oxford degrees of BA (1935), MA (1947), and B.Mus. (1956), and holds the diplomas of FRCO (1950) and ADCM (1951).

§**Peter (Anthony Stanley) Stevenson 1965–9** (b. Norwich, 28 Aug. 1928). Stevenson was educated at the City of Norwich School, Hatfield College, Durham, where he read music, and the Royal College of Music. He took the Durham degrees of BA (1951) and MA (1958), and holds the FRCO diploma. His first appointment was at Berkhamsted Parish Church, Hertfordshire, 1953–6. Then he was sub-organist of Ripon Cathedral for two years before becoming director of music at Wrekin College, Shropshire in 1958. He remained there until 1965, when he became organist of Portsmouth Cathedral. From 1966 he was also director of music at Portsmouth Grammar School. After leaving both these posts in 1969 he worked independently as lecturer, adjudicator, and examiner.

Christopher (Stainton) Gower 1969–77.

See under Peterborough Cathedral.

§**(James) Anthony Froggatt, organist and choirmaster from 1977** (b. Stockport, Cheshire, 16 Aug. 1946). Froggatt was educated at King's School, Macclesfield. He went to the University of Manchester and the Royal Manchester College of Music, taking the degree of Mus.B. in 1969, followed by some time at the University of Cambridge. From 1970 to 1977 he was assistant organist of Guildford Cathedral. Along with his post at Portsmouth Cathedral he is assistant music master at Portsmouth Grammar School.

RIPON

The Cathedral Church of St Peter and St Wilfred

(formerly a Collegiate Church, Ripon Minster)

Main sources in this section (1964):

Chapter Acts

Reg. A	Registrum A, 1626–89.
Reg. B	Registrum B, 1690–1718.
Reg. C	Registrum C, 1719–49.
Reg. D	Registrum D, 1749–75.
Reg. E	Registrum E, 1776–1800.
Reg. F	Registrum F, 1800–36.
Reg. G	Registrum G, 1836/7–62.
Reg. H	Registrum H, 1862/3–84.

Miscellaneous

PR	Registers of baptisms, marriages, and burials in the minster.

Ripon Minster was one of three collegiate churches of medieval foundation in the diocese of York, the others being Beverley and Southwell. All three were dissolved under the Chantries Act of 1547, and Beverley was never again to rise above parish-church status. Southwell was more fortunate (q.v.) though she was to suffer at the hands of reforming Victorians. Ripon was refounded as a collegiate church in 1604 by James I, whose endowment provided for seven 'vicars choral or singingmen', an organist, and eight choristers. It is clear, though the charter says nothing on the subject, that the organist was also to be master of the choristers. Thus, by Chapter Act (Registrum A) dated 13 June 1635, £16 was allotted to 'organistae qui et puerorum magister sit'; and it was also resolved that 'pueroru: choristaru: negligentias corrigat organista, qui eoru: magister est' ('the organist, who is their master, should correct the carelessness of the chorister boys').

Interesting light is shed on conditions at this period by the 'Orders for the Vicars and Organist' dated 25 May 1637 (Reg. A): 'That the sub-chanter and organist do agree about the Services and anthems to be sung (after Evening Prayer for the next morning, and after Morning Prayer for the evening) that the irreverent and indecent running to and fro of the boys in service time may be prevented.'

The earliest extant Register Book of the Jacobean foundation does not begin until 1626, and mentions no organist by name earlier than Henry Wanless (see below).

Henry Wanless ←**1662–74** (d. Ripon, Dec. 1674). One infers that Wanless was already in office by 1662 from an entry of a payment of 2*s*. on 4 October that year to 'Mr Wanlasse pro going to view the organs of Lord Darcy'—perhaps to obtain a temporary organ for the Minster (Ripon Minster Fabric Accounts, Yorkshire Archaeological Society Record Series, 118 (1953 for 1951), *Miscellanea*, vi). The same accounts reveal payments made to Preston, the organ-builder of York, for a new instrument at Ripon, 1663–4.

Wanless's only mention in the Chapter Acts occurs on 28 May 1670 (Reg. A), towards the end of his life:

It was then likewise consented and agreed before the said Chapter betwixt Mr Wanless Organist and Mr Wilson one of the singingmen that the said Mr Wilson should and would in consideration of the deafness and other impotency of the said Mr Wanless to perform the same both teach the chorister boys and play upon the organs for and instead of the said Mr Wanless if he the said Mr Wanless would sing in his room and stead in the choir and likewise allow him £4 per annum therefore, which he the said Mr Wanless then and there promised and agreed to do: and this agreement was to endure till midsummer come twelve-month and no longer.

This arrangement was renewed a year later, 'if the said Mr Wanlass shall so long live'. The burial, on 5 December 1674, of 'Henry Wanlass of Ripon Organist' is recorded in PR. Clearly he was an old man when he died; it is not impossible, therefore, that he had been organist of the Minster before the Interregnum. Two boys named 'Henry Wandless' were choristers of Durham Cathedral in 1609–10 and 1632–3 (Durham Ac). It could quite well be that the elder of these became the Ripon organist. (For a comment on the Wanless family, see under Lincoln Cathedral).

Wilson, whose Christian name is as yet unknown, seems to have given up before Wanless's death. The Fabric Roll already quoted contains the following entry dated 4 June 1674: 'Pro house organ bought of Mr Wilson late organist for the use of the next £7.' Notwithstanding the wording of this reference, Wilson appears only to have been acting organist; there is no minute of his appointment to the substantive post.

——**Shaw c.1674–7**. Shaw's tenure is inferred from a minute of 4 October 1677 (Reg. A) which ordered 'that Mr Shawe late organist be paid three pounds for his part of the last half year and that his bill for pricking be discharged by the Dean and brought into his accounts the next audit'. The Fabric Rolls record the payment of 9*s*. 6*d*. on 14 September 1674 to 'Mr Shaw pro pricking songbooks pro choristers'. He is not mentioned in PR, and his Christian name is nowhere to be found in the Ripon archives. Nevertheless, the appointment of an Alexander Shaw as organist of Durham Cathedral in 1677 makes it possible that this was the Shaw who left Ripon that same year.

See under Durham Cathedral.

William Sorrell 1677–82 (d. Ripon, Mar. 1682). The minute of Sorrell's appointment (Reg. A) is dated 26 May 1677. On 31 May 1679 he was granted an annual allowance of 5*s*. 'for wire and his pains in repairing the organ'. He was buried in the Minster on 15 March 1681/2 (PR).

John Hawkins 1682–90. Hawkins's formal admission is recorded thus under the date 27 May 1682 (Reg. A): 'At this Chapter Mr John Hawkins is admitted organist of this Church.' Nothing more is known of him. Perhaps he was the John Hawkins who was admitted singingman of York Minster on 2 August 1661 (York Minister CA18, p. 20).

Thomas Preston (I) 1690–1730 (d. Ripon, Oct. 1730). On 31 May 1690 Reg. B records: 'At this Chapter Mr Thomas Preston placed by Mr Dean as organist of this Church is confirmed in the same and is to receive his salary as organist from Ladyday last.' Soon afterwards, the baptism is recorded in PR, 23 August 1690, of 'Thomas and Mary, twins, son and daughter of Mr Thomas Preston, then organist of Ripon.'

By 1695 the organ, built thirty years ago, was no longer satisfactory, and in May of that year the Chapter decided to buy a new one, to which the dean and prebendaries all subscribed. The name of the builder is not mentioned. Preston himself later carried out some minor repairs (Reg. B, May 1706 and 1707); and on 29 May 1708 (Reg. B) the following minute was passed:

Whereas the organ of this Church hath been much damaged occasioned by the fall of the trumpet stop amongst the other small pipes which hath been repaired by Mr Thomas Preston the organist, for which this Chapter is well satisfied, that he deserves the sum of ten pounds; which sum is therefore ordered to be paid to him as followeth, vizt. five pounds, part thereof at Martinmas next and five pounds the remainder as soon as the same can be spared out of the Fabric money.

It seems obvious that Ripon, a poorly endowed college, was doing its best to maintain the music despite limited resources. A similar state of affairs is disclosed under the date 6 June 1696:

Forasmuch as Mr Preston, organist of this Church, having produced a note of eight song books by him pricked for the choir, and one for the organ, which amounteth to the sum of twelve pounds, and is content to be paid at three payments, to wit, one third part thereof at this Chapter, another third part at the next Grand Chapter, and thother third part at the Grand Chapter held in or about the month of May 1698, it is therefore ordered that he be paid out of the Fabric Rents accordingly.

Preston's burial is noted in PR on 15 October 1730 ('Mr Tho. Preston, Organist'). West (1921) states that Preston was born in 1662, the conjectured date in *DNB*. I have not myself seen any authority for this, except that Stephens (1882) says that Preston was 67 when he died.

Thomas Preston (II) 1730–48 (b. Ripon, Aug. 1690). At the Chapter held on 25 May 1731 it was recorded that (Reg. C): 'Mr Thomas Preston placed by Mr Dean as organist of this church is confirmed in the same'. This wording appears to imply that he took over soon after the death of his predecessor. One assumes that he was one of the twins born to Thomas Preston (I) in 1690. Such inspection of PR as I have been able to make does not disclose anything more about him.

William Ayrton 1748–99 (b. Ripon, Dec. 1726; d. Ripon, 2 Feb. 1799). The name of 'Airton' or 'Aerton' can be traced in Reg. B to 1691 and 1699 in connection with the supply by Edward Airton, 'clerk', of one of the vicar's places. William Ayrton was baptized in the Minster on 18 December (not November, as hitherto always stated) 1726, the son of Edward Ayrton, 'barber chirurgien'. The father (1698–1774), who may have been the son of the lay clerk, became an alderman of Ripon in 1758 and was mayor in 1760. William Ayrton's formal appointment as organist is entered in Reg. C under the date 7 June 1748. For his brother Edmund, see under Southwell Collegiate Church.

William Francis Morell Ayrton 1799–?1805 (d. Chester, 8 Nov. 1850, aged 72?) W. F. M. Ayrton is usually taken to be the elder son of his predecessor, though I have not myself been able to trace his baptism in PR. His appointment was minuted on 25 June 1799 (Reg. E). By implication (it would seem) from vaguely worded statements in *DNB*, it has generally been assumed that he retired as organist in 1802. This may be questioned, inasmuch as his successor's appointment was not formally minuted until 1805. *GM* (1850, ii: 673) records the death of 'W. F. M. Ayrton, Esq.' on 8 November 1850 at Abbott's Grange, Chester.

Nicholas Thomas Dall Ayrton 1805–22 (b. Ripon, Jan. 1782; d. Ripon, 24 Oct. 1822). The baptism in Ripon Minster of 'Nicholas Thomas Dall, son of Mr William Ayrton, organist, Ripon', is recorded in PR in January 1782. The minute of his appointment as organist is dated 2 June 1805 (Reg. F). The three Christian names are the Christian names and surname of his father's brother-in-law, the Danish painter (*DNB*). He is buried in the Minster yard, near the great east window.

John Henry Bond 1823–9. The precise date of Bond's appointment does not seem to have been recorded in the Chapter Register, but on 14 June 1823 the following minute was passed: 'Mr Bond, the organist, having given great attention to the improvement of the choir, particularly the boys, the Dean makes him a donation of £3 in addition to the usual extra donation of £2 in the accounts.' Spark (1892: 159) says that Bond was actually appointed on 26 June 1823, so he probably acted from N. T. D. Ayrton's death and was formally appointed on this date. He resigned his appointment at Ripon in June 1829. West (1921) states that he had earlier been organist of Portmouth Dockyard Chapel.

George Bates 1829–73 (b. Halifax, 6 July 1802; d. Ripon, 24 Jan. 1881). Bates's appointment was minuted at the same Chapter meeting as the formal receipt of Bond's resignation (30 June 1829, Reg. F). He is commemorated by a brass in the north aisle of the nave. Bates was in office when Ripon Minster became a cathedral. Reg. H has the following resolution, dated 8 July 1873: 'It was resolved and ordered that an annuity of £30 should be paid to Mr Bates for his life from the date of his retirement from the office of organist.' It is regrettable that the music seems to have been at a low ebb on his resignation. West (1899) makes the following observations: 'At the time of Dr Crow's appointment to Ripon there was no Cathedral Service. The canticles were merely chanted, and the priest's part was read. Dr E. G. Monk described the service as "so bad that it could not by any possibility be worse".'

Edwin John Crow 1874–1902 (b. Sittingbourne, 17 Sept. 1841; d. Harrogate, 6 Dec. 1908). I have given the month of birth as stated on the memorial inscription in the Cathedral; *Venn*, however, notes it as March 1841. Crow was a chorister in Rochester Cathedral, and a pupil there of *J. L. Hopkins and *John Hopkins. He then went to Leicester, where he was successively organist of Holy Trinity, St Andrew's, and St John's Churches. He was appointed organist of

Ripon Cathedral from 1 January 1874 by minute dated 22 January of that year. *Venn* states that he was choirmaster from 1873, but this may not be reliable. Crow was also music master of Ripon Grammar School and organist of Skelton-cum-Newby Church, 1876–81. He took the Cambridge degrees of Mus.B. (1872) and Mus.D. (1882), and also held the FRCO diploma (1868).

Stephens 1882; *Venn*.

Charles Harry Moody, CBE, 1902–54 (b. Stourbridge, Worcs., 22 Mar. 1874; d. Ripon, 10 May 1965). Moody was an articled pupil of *T. Westlake Morgan at Bangor Cathedral. He was organist, briefly, of St Michael's College, Tenbury, and then, from 1894, deputy (later acting) organist of Wells Cathedral. He was appointed organist of Wigan Parish Church in December 1895, moving to Holy Trinity, Coventry in January 1899. He took up his duties at Ripon Cathedral in January 1902, and retired in 1954.

In 1920 he was appointed CBE in recognition of his musical work for the troops in and around Ripon during World War I. In the same year he was made an honorary FRCO, and in 1923 he received the Lambeth degree of D.Mus. His antiquarian interests, especially in Fountains Abbey, were reflected in his fellowship of the Society of Antiquaries in 1927. On the completion of fifty years service at Ripon he was made a freeman of the borough.

In 1945 he instituted legal proceedings against the Dean and Chapter of Ripon in an effort to show that a reduction of the daily choral services was contrary to the statutes; but the court held that such a matter was outside its jurisdiction.

Moody 1926; *Grove*[5]; *WWW*, 1961–70.

Lionel Frederick Dakers, CBE, 1954–7.

See under Exeter Cathedral.

§(Joseph) Philip Marshall 1957–66 (b. Brighouse, Yorks., 24 June 1921). Before his appointment to Ripon, Marshall was organist of Boston Parish Church, Lincolnshire, 1951–7. He left Ripon to become organist of Lincoln Cathedral in 1966, and retired in 1986. He won three prizes with the FRCO diploma in 1946, and he took the Durham degrees of B.Mus. and D.Mus. in 1950 and 1955 respectively.

§Ronald (Edward) Perrin, organist and choirmaster from 1966 (b. Edmonton, London, 13 Apr. 1931). After attending Edmonton Grammar School, 1942–9, Perrin went up to Christ Church, Oxford as organ scholar, 1949–54. He read music, and took the degrees of BA (1953) and MA (1956), and the FRCO diploma (1951). In 1956–7 he was acting organist of Leeds Parish Church, and from 1958 to 1966 he was assistant organist of York Minster.

ROCHESTER

The Cathedral Church of Christ and the Blessed Virgin Mary

Main sources in this section (1963) (with Kent County Record Office references):

Registers of Patents, Indentures

Reg. 1	'Registrum Dict. Martini Cotes', 1574–1617 (DRc/E1b.1).
Reg. 1a	A single document, November 1560 (DRc/Aoo.1).

Chapter Acts

RB	'The Red Book', 3 vols., 1660–72, 1660–1737, 1756–1854 (DRb/Arb.1–3).
CA1	'Martin Cotes's Book', 1575–84 ('Liber Capitularis Roffensis') (DRc/Ac.1).
CA1a	A stray leaf, 1577 (DRc/Ac.1a).
CA2	1678–84 (DRc/Ac.2).
CA3	1684–95 (DRc/Ac.3).
CA4	1695–1706 (DRc/Ac.4).
CA5	1706–21 (DRc/Ac.5).
CA6	1721–43 (DRc/Ac.6).
CA7	1744–65 (DRc/Ac.7).
CA8	1766–88 (DRc/Ac.8).
CA9	1788–1808 (DRc/Ac.9).
CA10	1808–27 (DRc/Ac.10).
CA11	1827–39 (DRc/Ac.11).
CA12	1839–51 (DRc/Ac.12).

Treasurer's Accounts

1590–1, 1672–3, 1673–4 (DRc/FTb.4, 5, 6).

Registers of Baptisms, Marriages, and Burials

PR	*The Registers of the Cathedral Church of Rochester (1657–1837)*, ed. Thomas Shindler (privately printed, Canterbury 1892). This includes references to memorial inscriptions.

After the dissolution of the Benedictine cathedral priory of Rochester, Henry VIII refounded it in June 1541 to continue as the seat of the bishop. Provision was made for eight choristers with a master whose duties under the draft statutes, as in all of Henry's foundations, included playing the organ (see p. xix)

Of the first organists of the Henrician foundation we know nothing; but their earliest duties (before the Edwardine Prayer Books) are explained thus in the injunctions made for Rochester Cathedral by Bishop Heath in 1543 (Frere 1910: ii. 96):

> The master of the choristers shall be at Matins, Mass, and Evensong in all double feasts and nine lessons, and shall himself keep the organs at the same feasts. And also in Commemorations shall by him or by some other at his appointment cause the organs to be kept. And he shall cause the choristers to sing an anthem after Compline in every work-day.

James Plumley ←1560→. At the metropolitical visitation of the Cathedral in September 1560, negligence was alleged against Plumley, variously described as master of the choristers and 'the organ player' (Llp, Parker's Register, iii. 662). Later, in a patent of 27 November 1560 referring to Peter Rowle (see below), Plumley is named as one who 'hath by patent the mastership of the organs and teaching the choristers'.

Peter Rowle ?–1577. At the 1560 visitation, Rowle, then a singingman, succeeded in clearing himself of an accusation of adultery with a canon's wife. Very shortly afterwards, on 27 November 1560, he was assigned by patent the sum of £26. 13*s*. 4*d*. in consideration of his bearing the cost of boarding, lodging, and clothing the eight choristers, the Dean and Chapter providing each of them with a lined gown annually at Easter. At the same time he was given the reversion of the post of master of the choristers and organist on the death of James Plumley, when he would then receive an extra £5, but the authorities would no longer provide the eight gowns (Reg. 1a).

On 20 November 1576, described as 'one of the choir', he received formal admonition 'for divers faults and absences' (CA1, p. 4). However, this did not destroy confidence in him, because on 26 July 1577 he was allowed £14 a year 'in consideration of his well teaching, guiding, and furthering the choristers' (CA1a). It is not clear how this connects with the terms of the 1560 patent.

The records do not reveal at what point his reversion to the post of master of the choristers/organist became effective. The description of him as 'one of the choir' in 1576 does not rule this out, for even minor canons in those days were 'of the choir'; the likelihood that he did actually succeed to the post is strengthened by the fact that Rowle was dismissed from the choir on the same day, 25 November 1577, that Thomas Churchman was appointed master of the choristers (CA1, p. 9). As we have seen, he had been given a formal admonition just one year earlier.

Thomas Churchman 1577–?1579. The minute recording Rowle's dismissal from the choir (see above) also contains the following: 'it is agreed by the Dean and Chapter that Thomas Churchman shall henceforth have and enjoy the office of teaching the choristers of the said church according to the decree set down of 22 of July last under the hand of Mr Dean, Mr Woolward, and Mr Mapleson'. The decree referred to (found in CA1a) provided that he was to have an annual fee of £5 and the next vacant place of singingman.

Thomas Hillye 1579→. One cannot be quite sure that Hillye was ever formally appointed to the office of master of the choristers (and therefore organist). The entries relating to him are as follows: 'Also it is agreed that Thomas Hillye shall for this year have allowed unto him 20*s*. in consideration of his attendance to play on the organs' (CA1, p. 18, 25 November 1580); 'Also it is agreed that Thomas Hillye shall have yearly 20*s*. allowed him in consideration of his playing the organs so long as he useth himself well' (CA1, p. 24, 25 November 1582). The stipend of 20*s*. seems to suggest that he simply acted as organist without holding the office of master of the choristers in the strict sense of the statutes. He had been a singingman as far back as 1560.

Ropier Blundell 1588–99. Blundell's patent as 'master of the choristers or singing children and player upon the organs' is entered in Reg. 1 (f. 62b) with the marginal date 1588. From this it may be inferred that he was already a minor canon or lay clerk. In the treasurer's account for 1590–1 his stipend was the statutory £10 with 40*s*. augmentation. This is the earliest surviving Rochester amount to name the master of the choristers.

John Williams 1599–1609 (sole organist); **1609–?** (jointly with John Robinson). By patent dated 25 November 1599 (Reg. 1, f. 125b) 'John Williams the elder' was appointed both master of the choristers and minor canon in succession to Blundell, 'deceased'.

John Robinson 1609–? (jointly with John Williams). In July 1609 (Reg. 1, f. 205b) a patent was granted jointly to 'John Williams the elder, one of the ministers or company of the choir, and John Robinson the younger, one of the clerks or company of the choir, to be master of the choristers for the life of the longer liver'. There is nothing to show how long either of them lived.

John Heath ←1614–63 (perhaps for a short time jointly with his father, Philip Heath). In the survey of the parsonage of Chatham (on whose property the organist's stipend was charged), carried out in 1649 by order of the Long Parliament, it was deposed that in 1608:

> Thomas Blayne, then Dean of the foresaid Cathedral Church, granted unto Phillipp Heath and John Heath son of the said Philip Heath, the office of clerk and organist during the term of their natural lives and the longest liver of either of them with the annual fee or stipend of twelve pounds of lawful English money issuing and payable out of the foresaid parsonage of Chatham . . . Phillipp Heath is deceased, John Heath aged about sixty years. (Llp, Codex 915, f. 257.)

This reference to a grant in the year 1608 seems puzzling in relation to the known patent granted in 1609 to Williams and Robinson, but it may not be strictly reliable, coming as it does in a deposition of forty years later. Shindler (PR) notes that, on the evidence of an account-book which cannot now be traced, John Heath was in fact in office in 1614.

Heath survived the Interregnum, as we learn from this Chapter minute of 26 November 1661: 'Ordered that Mr Wm. Rothwell for the reversion of the organist's place after Mr Heath's death should have a patent' (RB2, f. 19). In March 1663 an arrangement was made to pension him off (RB2, f. 30): 'It was ordered that Mr John Heath the now organist shall have £20 per annum paid unto him during his life by the treasurer quarterly. Or the Dean and Chapter will otherwise provide for him by boarding of [him] out and a new organist elected.' From a further reference (f. 30^{v}) it appears that he became parish clerk of Rochester Parish Church. As late as Christmas 1672 the Cathedral accounts show John Heath as a lay clerk.

William Rothwell ?1663–72. There are no seventeenth-century accounts earlier than 1672–3, so it cannot be confirmed whether or not Rothwell actually succeeded Heath in accordance with the patent of 1661 (see above), but the presumption is strong. If he did, then he may have combined his post with a minor canon's appointment: a 'William Wrothwell' was granted a minor canonry in 1662, and 'William Rothwell' occupied such a post in 1673, after Wren's appointment as organist (RB).

Charles Wren 1672–3 (d. Gloucester, Dec. 1678). Certain knowledge of Wren begins with his receipt for a quarter's salary, Michaelmas to Christmas 1672. Although he is named as organist at the November audit of 1673 (RB), the accounts for the quarter ending at Christmas of that year name Henstridge as organist (see below). Presumably, therefore, Wren left Rochester in the later part of 1673.

Wren became organist of Gloucester Cathedral in January 1674 (q.v.). It almost looks as if an exchange of posts was arranged between him and Daniel Henstridge, his successor at Rochester—if he is the 'Mr Wren' referred to (as surely he must be) in the letter printed below, under Henstridge. He was buried at Gloucester on 5 December 1678 (Gloucester PR).

Daniel Henstridge 1673–98 (d. Canterbury, June 1736). It was for long assumed that there must have been two men called Daniel Henstridge, who between them held three posts as cathedral organist: Gloucester, 1666–73; Rochester, 1673–98; and Canterbury, 1698–1736. Indeed, in view of the seventy years covered by these appointments, such an assumption is not unreasonable. However, the Rochester and Canterbury organists were certainly one and the same man, for the Rochester Chapter Acts (CA4, 28 June 1699) speak of his removal 'to the Cathedral Church of Canterbury'. Moreover, there is no trace of the death of the Gloucester organist in the Gloucester PR; and the reference to the 'little ones' in the letter addressed to Henstridge (quoted below) suggests that the Rochester organist had previously served at Gloucester and that his children, born in Gloucester, were three years old and less at the time of the Rochester appointment. If, as these details seem to indicate, all three posts were held successively by one man, then he must have been some 90 years of age at his death.

On 26 March 1669 Elizabeth Waters was married in Gloucester Cathedral to Daniel Henstridge, 'organist of this church'. Three girls were born to them in Gloucester in March 1669/70, June 1671, and July 1673, and were baptized in the Cathedral. Henstridge (as we assume) moved to Rochester about Michaelmas 1673, for the accounts there show his stipend for the quarter ending Christmas of that year. His formal admission took place on 9 May 1674 (RB2). The following letter (Lbl, Add. MS 30933, f. 70, undated), addressed to Henstridge at Rochester, clearly implies his personal knowledge of affairs at Gloucester, and also illustrates how music circulated between one cathedral and another at that time.

Mr Henstridge. I have sent the 2 full anthems of Mr King's (which you desired in your letter dated Feb 2d). I put them in a score, because thus they take up less room, and so will make you less postage; I suppose they are altogether as fit for your use in a score. What words of the Psalms are repeated you are not unacquainted with. Notwithstanding, I have marked the repetitions so that any body may understand them with ease. I pray, send us the organ part of Behold thou hast made my days and Mr Wren's full anthem which is pricked in your books: or any thing else that you know we have not here; and I shall be ready to repay you in any services or anthems our church affords. If you will let me know in your next, where your Rochester carrier lies, I might send papers or anything else to you, at an easier rate, than I now do by post. Send the organ part as soon as you can; if it be large, direct it to be left at the Bull and Mouse . . . for the Gloucester carrier to convey it to me. You did not tell me in yours, whether mine came to your hands at all. I am glad Mrs Henstridge got safe to Rochester with your little ones. I wish you and yours all happiness. Edward Jackson.

Mrs Campion was buried Friday lst.

These for Mr Daniel Henstridge — To Lond, 3*d.*
Organist of Rochester at his — 5*d.* in all
house on Bulley Hill, in Rochester — forward 2*d.*

Judging from the enquiries about carriage and the references to Mrs Henstridge and the children (who perhaps had remained for a while in Gloucester), this letter was probably written not long after Henstridge had moved to Rochester.

While at Rochester, Henstridge had under him his own successor there, Robert Bowers, and also *William Popely. The unsatisfactory *Richard Henman may also have been one of his boys. His own son James entered the choir in 1681 (CA2); he was later a minor canon of Canterbury Cathedral, and sacrist there in 1704.

Henstridge himself departed for Canterbury late in 1698, where he was organist and master of the choristers until December 1718, and then (nominally) organist until his death (q.v.). His burial is entered in the Canterbury PR on 4 June 1736.

Several manuscript transcripts of church music made by him now form part of Lbl, Add. MS 30932. He was also interested in theoretical works, as evidenced by his transcripts of Bevin's *Brief . . . Introduction to the Art of Musicke*, and of the 'Rules for composition', which he misattributed to *John Blow in Lbl, Add. MS 30933.

Robert Bowers 1699–1704 (d. Rochester, Nov. 1704). Bowers's appointment was minuted thus on 28 June 1699 (CA4): 'Robert Bowers a lay clerk bred up in this Church is this day elected into the organist place of this Cathedral being vacant by the removal of Mr Daniel Henstridge the late organist to the Cathedral Church of Canterbury.' He was allowed £5 towards the repair of the organist's house.

In 1701 his health seems to have broken down, and on 4 July he was given leave to go into the country for a month (CA4). He is buried in the Cathedral yard (PR).

John Spain 1704–21 (d. Rochester, Nov. 1721). Like his predecessor, Spain had been brought up at Rochester Cathedral, appearing as a chorister at the November audit of 1689. At the time of his appointment as organist he was a lay clerk, and had been nominated to deputize for Bowers during the latter's absence in 1701. His formal appointment was minuted on 27 November 1704 (CA4).

In 1709 he was involved in some correspondence (printed in *MT*, 49 (1908), 155) with the representatives of 'Father' Smith who had maintained the Rochester Cathedral organ under contract (£4 a year) since 1668. On 12 July 1709 Spain wrote to say that the Dean and Chapter 'expect the Executrix to put the organ in order for the arrears which is [*sic*] due, and without she does, they won't pay a farthing'. During Spain's term of office the Chapter made an effort to place the lay clerks under him for training. On 6 July 1708 (CA5) it was resolved that 'the lay clerks do diligently and frequently attend the organist at such times in the choir as he shall appoint in order to improve themselves in the knowledge and practice of church music'. Further, on 2 December 1712 (CA5), it was resolved that 'the lay clerks and quiristers of this Church shall diligently and constantly repair to the organist for instruction as often as he shall appoint them'.

By present-day standards the musical repertory was somewhat confined at this time, as implied by a Chapter minute of 14 July 1713 (CA5) ordering 'that the treasurer do provide new books for the choir and that the organist transcribe therein six of the best services, twelve verse anthems, and six full anthems'.

Spain fell into debt at the end of his life, and in August 1721 the Cathedral treasurer paid some £60 to his various creditors (see the bundle of receipts, DRc/FTv/57). He was buried in the Cathedral on 16 November 1721 (PR).

Charles Peach 1721–53 (d. Rochester, 1753). Peach was admitted organist on 27 November 1721, 'the Dean having signified his consent and approbation' (CA6). In December 1728 he was paid £4 for music-copying at 3*d*. a page (CA6). His work with the choristers later gave dissatisfaction, and on 14 July 1737 (CA6) it was ordered 'that the payment of the organist's extraordinary salary [i.e., above the statutory provision] be suspended until the boys are to [*sic*] taught to sing so as to give better satisfaction'. At the roll-call in June 1753 (CA7) Peach was marked 'dead'. In 1724 he had been one of the subscribers to Croft's *Musica Sacra*.

Joseph Howe 1753–80 (d. Rochester, 1780). Howe's appointment was formally minuted in July 1753 (CA7). It appears from the following testimonial (Mee 1911: 68) that he had come from Oxford:

Music Room, Oxon. June 11, 1753

We, whose names are hereunto subscribed, do think the bearer, Mr Joseph Howe, in every respect qualified to undertake the office of a cathedral organist, and as such recommend him:

W. Hayes
G. Darch, A.M.
R. Cotes, A.M.
R. Church, Organist of Xt. Church

Jos. Jackson, First Violin
C. Orthman, Principal Violoncello
W. Walond, Assistant Organist

He was present at the audit in June 1780, but he must have died between then and the November audit.

Richard Howe 1780–92. Richard Howe was appointed organist on probation in the following terms on 28 November 1780 (CA8): 'Ordered that Mr Richard Howe be continued organist in the room of his late father deceased to Midsummer next and it is agreed . . . that if Mr Howe's behaviour be approved of . . . at Midsummer 1781 he shall then be nominated and appointed organist and shall be so continued during his good behaviour.' He was duly admitted formally on 28 June 1781.

Unhappily, Howe's work and conduct eventually proved unsatisfactory, and under the date 2 March 1790 (CA9) the Chapter minutes contain this entry:

Richard Howe, the organist, having for a long time past much neglected his duty in teaching the choir and otherwise misbehaved himself, ordered that from Christmas last the additional salary of £8 per annum hitherto allowed to the said Richard Howe be reduced to £3 per annum and resolved that Ralph Banks [*see below*] be and is hereby appointed teacher of the choir and that the treasurer do pay him a stipend of £10 per annum from Christmas last.

On 29 November 1791 the Chapter received notice of Howe's intention to resign at Lady Day 1792. An arrangement was approved whereby he and Banks were to exchange their respective posts of organist and lay clerk.

Ralph Banks 1792–1841 (d. Rochester, 20 Sept. 1841). Banks had been a chorister of Durham Cathedral under *Ebdon, whom he afterwards served as assistant while also being organist of Houghton-le-Spring Parish Church (Stephens 1882). As already noted (see above), he was given charge of the Rochester choir from Christmas 1789, the same time as he was appointed a lay clerk (CA9, 2 March 1790); he succeeded to the post of organist in 1792.

In an organ-book at Rochester he later recorded this memorandum, as transcribed by John Hopkins (see below), who communicated it to West (1921): 'When I came from Durham to this Cathedral in 1790, only one lay clerk attended during each week. The daily service was chanted. Two Services (Aldrich in G and Rogers in D) and seven Anthems had been in rotation on Sundays for twelve years.'

In June 1841 the Chapter approved a gratuity to him of 50 guineas for his 'long and meritorious' services (CA12). He is buried in the Cathedral yard.

For a few weeks until the appointment of a successor, *H. E. Ford acted as organist.

MT, 49 (1908), 159.

John Larkin Hopkins 1841–56. Hopkins's appointment, on the recommendation of *T. A. Walmisley, was minuted on 26 November 1841 (CA12).

See under Trinity College, Cambridge.

John Hopkins 1856–1900 (b. London (Westminster), 30 Apr. 1822; d. Rochester, 27 Aug. 1900). John Hopkins, a cousin of his predecessor, was a chorister of St Paul's Cathedral, 1831–8, and then succeeded his brother, E. J. Hopkins (1818–1901; organist of the Temple Church), as organist of Mitcham Parish Church, Surrey in 1838. His other posts before going to Rochester were as follows: St Stephens, Islington (1839), Holy Trinity, Islington (1843), St Mark's, Jersey (1845), St Michael's, Chester Square, London (1846), and Epsom Parish Church, Surrey (1854). He took the FRCO diploma in 1887.

He was appointed to Rochester after a competition judged by *John Goss in May 1856. It was presumably this competition which involved 'a very searching trial, for not only did the candidates play the organ, but they actually had to work a paper containing a chorale to harmonize, and a short subject on which to write a fugue' (J. F. Bridge 1918: 25, giving the date of 1855). The formal appointment was minuted on 25 June 1856, and the duties included tuning the organ. Among John Hopkins's former pupils, the following are mentioned in this book: J. C. Bridge, J. F. Bridge, E. J. Crow, and D. J. Wood.

BMB; *Grove*[2]; *MT*, 41 (1900), 684; 49 (1908), 158.

Bertram Luard Selby 1900–16.

See under Salisbury Cathedral.

(Arthur) Charles (Lestoc) Hylton Stewart 1916–30 (b. Chester, 21 (or 22) Mar. 1884; d. Windsor, 14 Nov. 1932). Stewart was the son of *C. H. H. Stewart, minor canon and precentor of Chester Cathedral and former organist of Chichester Cathedral. He was taught by *J. C. Bridge before going to Magdalen College, Oxford as a chorister. He went up to Peterhouse, Cambridge as organ scholar in 1903. While at Cambridge he held the John Stewart of Rannoch scholarship in sacred music, and acted for a year as assistant to *A. H. Mann at King's College. He took the Cambridge degrees of BA (1906), Mus.B. (1907), and MA (1910).

Stewart was music master at Sedbergh School (1907), organist of St Martin's, Scarborough (1908) and then of Blackburn Parish Church (now the Cathedral) (1914), where he succeeded *R. H. P. Coleman.

After fourteen years at Rochester Cathedral he returned to his birthplace as organist of Chester Cathedral. Following a brief tenure there (1930–2), he was appointed to succeed *H. W. Davies at St George's Chapel, Windsor. Having arrived in Windsor only at the beginning of September 1932, he died there on 14 November after less than twelve weeks in office. On 29 November 1932 the Dean and Canons of St George's Chapel passed the following minute, quoted by Fellowes (1940):

> Charles Hylton Stewart, MA, Mus. Bac., entered upon his duties as organist of this Chapel on the 1st of September last. His patience, tact, and singular charm of manner won the instant affection of all members of the Foundation. He was above all a devout Churchman and his reverent and dignified interpretation of the Services made a lasting impression upon all who worshipped here.

There are memorials to Stewart in both Rochester and Chester Cathedrals.

Grove[3]; *MT*, 73 (1932), 1137; *WWW*, 1929–40; Fellowes 1940.

§Harold Aubie Bennett 1930–56 (b. Eccles, Lancs., 30 July 1891; d. Rochester, 4 Feb. 1978). Bennett was educated at Leeds Central High School, and from 1913 to 1923 he was assistant organist to *E. C. Bairstow (whose pupil he had been) at York Minster, taking the FRCO diploma in 1914. While at York he was also, from 1915, organist of the priory church of Holy Trinity and lecturer at St John's College. In 1923 he became organist of Doncaster Parish Church, where he remained until his appointment to Rochester. In addition to his Cathedral post he was also director of music at King's School, Rochester.

§Robert James Ashfield 1956–77 (b. Chipstead, Surrey, 28 July 1911). Ashfield was educated at Tonbridge School, 1925–9, and then went to the Royal College of Music, 1929–36, as scholar and exhibitioner. He took the FRCO diploma in 1932, and the London degrees of B.Mus. and D.Mus. in 1936 and 1941 respectively. From 1934 to 1941 he was organist of St John's, Smith Square, Westminster. After the war he was appointed organist of Southwell Cathedral in 1946, remaining there until taking up his appointment at Rochester. In 1957 he joined the staff of the Royal College of Music.

§Barry (William Cammack) Ferguson, organist from 1977 (b. London, 18 July 1942). Having been a chorister of Exeter Cathedral, Ferguson went to Clifton College with a music scholarship, 1956–60, and then to Peterhouse, Cambridge, where he read music and took the degree of BA in 1963 (later MA). He took the FRCO diploma in 1962. His first appointment was as assistant organist of Peterborough Cathedral, 1964–71, after which, until moving to Rochester, he was organist and choirmaster of Wimborne Minster, Dorset.

ST ALBANS

The Cathedral and Abbey Church of St Alban

When the Benedictine abbey of St Alban was dissolved under Henry VIII, its great church was purchased by the citizens to be their parish church. On the foundation of the diocese of St Albans in 1877, it was raised to cathedral status.

John Stocks Booth (1858) **1877–9** (b. Sheffield, 1828; d. St Albans, 7 Dec. 1879). Booth is stated to have been a pupil of Gauntlett, Thalberg, Sterndale Bennett, and Molique. He was organist of Queen Street Chapel, Sheffield and then of Wortley Parish Church, near Sheffield, together with St Philip's, Sheffield. It was shortly after moving to Watford that he was appointed to St Albans Abbey in 1858. He is buried in the Cathedral yard.

At the time of his appointment in 1858, the services were of the old-fashioned parochial type, with metrical psalms and a parish clerk.

West 1921.

George Gaffe 1880–1907 (b. Cawston, Norfolk, 27 July 1849; d. 1907). Gaffe was one of *Zechariah Buck's choristers and articled pupils at Norwich. He was organist of Oswestry Parish Church from 1874, and held the FRCO diploma.

BMB; West 1921.

Willie Lewis Luttman 1907–30 (b. 20 Feb. 1874; d. 2 Feb. 1930). Luttman was educated at the Royal Grammar School, High Wycombe, Buckinghamshire, and studied music under J. G. Wrigley, organist of the parish church there, before proceeding to the Royal College of Music and then to Peterhouse, Cambridge as organ scholar in 1894. Between leaving Cambridge and his appointment to St Albans, he was organist of Hughenden Parish Church (1894) and Banbury Parish Church (1898). He took the Cambridge degrees of BA (1897), MA (1901), and Mus.B. (1903).

West 1921; *MT*, 71 (1930), 271; *Venn*.

Cuthbert Edward Osmond 1930–7 (b. Alderbury, Wilts., 1904; d. St Albans, 12 Jan. 1937). At the age of 12, Osmond was organist of Nunton Church, near Salisbury. After serving his articles to *W. G. Alcock, he became his assistant at Salisbury Cathedral, 1917–27. From 1928 to 1930 he was music master of Bryanston School. He took the Durham degree of B.Mus. in 1925, and 'to the feat of gaining both the RCO diplomas in the same year [1926] he added that of being awarded the highest marks in organ playing ever given at the College up to that time'.

During Osmond's illness in 1936, and until his successor arrived in 1937, *K. F. Malcolmson was temporary organist.

MT, 78 (1937), 176.

Albert Charles Tysoe 1937–47 (d. Chichester, 22 May 1962, aged 78). Before his appointment to St Albans, Tysoe had been organist of Leeds Parish Church from 1920. Before that he was organist of All Saints', Northampton. He took the Durham degrees of B.Mus. (1909) and D.Mus. (1915), and held the FRCO diploma. He conducted the Halifax Choral Society (in succession to *C. H. Moody) from 1922 to 1937.

WWM[2]; *MT*, 103 (1962), 784.

(Albert) Meredith Davies, CBE, 1947–9.

See under New College, Oxford.

(Claud) Peter (Primrose) Burton 1950–7 (d. Hemel Hempstead, Herts., 6 July 1957, aged 41). After war-service, Burton took up his first important post as organist of St Mary's, Warwick and music master of Warwick School in 1946, remaining there until 1950. He had been a pupil of *W. H. Harris before going up to St John's College, Oxford in 1933, and he took the degrees of BA, B.Mus. (1938), and MA (1943). He held the FRCO and CHM diplomas. His untimely death was due to an accident while swimming. A tribute to him, unfortunately devoid of biographical information, appeared in *ECM* (27 (1957), 76).

WWM[6]; *MT*, 98 (1957), 451.

§Peter (John) Hurford, OBE, 1958–78 (b. Minehead, Somerset, 22 Nov. 1930). After leaving Blundell's School in 1948, Hurford went to the Royal College of Music for a year, and then as organ scholar to Jesus College, Cambridge, 1949–53, where he read for part I of the music tripos and part II of the law tripos. He took the FRCO diploma in 1949, and the Cambridge degrees of BA (1953), MA (1956), and Mus.B. (1958). His first appointment was to succeed *Harold Dexter as organist of Holy Trinity Church, Leamington Spa (1956). He left Leamington at the end of 1957, and took up duties at St Albans in 1958. There he made a distinctive contribution by his foundation of the International Organ Festival in 1963, which has been continued by his successors at the Cathedral. In 1967–8 he was organist-in-residence at the University of Cincinnati, and was visiting professor at the University of Western Ontario, 1976–7. Since leaving St Albans Cathedral he has continued his activities as a recitalist in the UK, Europe, Japan, Australia, New Zealand, Canada, and the USA. In 1981 he was made an honorary doctor of Baldwin-Wallace College, Ohio (home of the Riemenschneider Bach Institute). He was appointed OBE in 1984, and is the author of *Making Music on the Organ* (1988).

Stephen (Mark) Darlington 1978–85.

See under Christ Church Cathedral, Oxford.

Colin (Stephen) Walsh 1985–8.

See under Lincoln Cathedral.

§Barry (Michael) Rose, master of the music from 1988 (b. Chingford, Essex, 24 May 1934). Though strongly attracted to music (especially the music of the Church of England) from an early age, Rose, after leaving Sir George Monoux Grammar School, Walthamstow, did not at first become a full-time professional musician. However, from boyhood he had held several posts in church music: organist of St Anne's, Chingford, 1946–56; choirman in Hampstead Parish Church, 1956–7; organist of St Andrew's, Kingsbury, London, 1957–60. But in 1958 he entered the Royal Academy of Music, studying there until 1960, with C. H. Trevor as his organ teacher. It was while he was a student there that he was appointed to Guildford Pro-Cathedral and Cathedral (q.v.).

While at Guildford he was also appointed to be music adviser to the head of religious broadcasting at the BBC, a post he has held continuously ever since 1971. He left Guildford in 1974 to become sub-organist of St Paul's Cathedral; a change in his responsibilities there was marked by his becoming master of the choir from 1977 to 1984. After leaving St Paul's he was master of choirs at King's School, Canterbury until taking up his appointment at St Albans Cathedral.

ST ASAPH

The Cathedral Church of St Asaph

Main sources in this section (1964) (with National Library of Wales references):

Chapter Acts	*Treasurer's Accounts*
1674–1754 (SA/CR/2).	1680–1755 (SA/CR/9).
1755–1847 (SA/CR/3).	1754–70 (SA/CR/10).
1847–87 (SA/CR/4).	1770–1824 (SA/CR/11).
1887–1911 (SA/CR/5).	1824–53 (SA/CR/12).

In view of the straightforward nature of these sources, and the ease with which each statement may be traced under the dates cited, it would be otiose to give detailed references in the text. I have used *Thomas* as a siglum for my citations of D. R. Thomas, *Esgobaeth Llanelwy: The History of the Diocese of St Asaph* (Oswestry, 1908–13).

As far back as 1296, when Bishop Llewellyn de Bromfield issued statutes for St Asaph Cathedral, provision was made for the appointment of an organist, who might be either a priest or a layman, 'bene cantantem et ad organa ludentem' (*Thomas*).

No original records have survived of the earliest post-Reformation organists. *Thomas* cites one John Day, 'Mr. of the Quire', who was buried on 26 April 1630, but I have been unable to obtain information about the original of this or the other burial records to which he refers. Day's successor as 'master of the choir' was Abednego Perkins, whose burial entry is quoted thus by *Thomas*: 'Choristaru[m] m[a]g[iste]r sepultus fuit in eccl[es]ia Cathedralis Asaphen 13° die Octobris 1631.' Perkins married John Day's widow. *Thomas* cites *Cwtta Cyfarwydd* for the following extract: 'upon Wednesday . . . the xxiv day of April 1639 . . . Anne Gruffith a John Grigor, widow, being the late wife of Abednago [*sic*] Perkins, Mr. of the Quire of the Cathedral Church of St Asaph, deceased, and former wife of John Day (being his predecessor there) buried'.

John Wilson ?–1641. *Thomas* specifically names Wilson as organist, stating that he was buried on 30 November 1641. The diary (or chronicle) of Peter (or Piers) Roberts, quoted by Bax (1904), states that it was in 1635 that 'the great and new organ . . . was set up and played upon, the same being first brought and carried thither from London'. Thenceforward we have no information about the organist until we reach the name of Thomas Ottey (see below).

Thomas Ottey ?–1671 (d. St Asaph, 19 Mar. 1671). The inscription on Ottey's tombstone in the choir of the Cathedral, as recorded in Willis (1720), reads thus: 'Here lyeth the Body of Thomas Ottey Vicar Precentor & Organist of this Cathedral who departed this Life March 19. Ao. Dom. 1670 [?1670/1].' *Thomas* states that he became organist in 1669, but cites no authority.

William Key(s) 1679–? Key(s) had been organist of Manchester Collegiate Church from 1669 (q.v.). The surviving Chapter Acts at St Asaph run from 1674. We know from the Manchester archives (CA1) that Key(s) moved to St Asaph no later than June 1679, but the first reference to him there is on 30 June 1680, when it was resolved 'That Mr Key, one of the vicars-choral and organist shall receive the sum of thirtyfive shillings for his care and charges in mending and setting in order the organ.' Somewhat later he received a further gratuity of £2 for attention to the organ as well as for 'other performance in the musical part of the service in the choir of this Cathedral'. However, on 10 July 1684: 'The Dean is requested to write to one Mr Smith an organmaker to come to St Asaph and view the organ of the Cathedral being out of order. And . . . two of the members of this Chapter are impowered hereby to treat conclude and agree with the said Mr Smith . . . (taking with them for their assistance the organist Mr Wm Key).'

In 1678 an Act of Parliament was passed (compare that of 1685 for Bangor Cathedral) allotting the tithes of Llanrayader for the upkeep of the fabric of the Cathedral and to augment the revenues of the choir, and providing that until these tithes became available, those of Skeivoig were to be used. Although the accounts of these tithes begin in July 1680, they do not mention the organist for the first ten years, from which it appears that he was not yet paid out of them. But in August 1690 'Mr Kay, Organist', was given £1 'by my Lord's order'. In the accounting year 1690–1 there is an entry of £4 per annum to 'the organist'; but *Thomas*, who states that Key was a vicar choral of St Asaph from 1680–6, assumes that he ceased to be organist in 1686. Unfortunately, he does not support his statement: if it derives from a presumption that this is the William Kay who was organist of Chester Cathedral, 1686–99, it might be treacherous; but if we could be sure that Key (Kay) left St Asaph then, it is by no means impossible that he was the Chester man.

Thomas Hughes 1692–3 (d. St Asaph, Sept. 1693). Hughes is mentioned by name in the accounts for the year 1692–3. According to *Thomas*, Hughes, 'Organist of the Cathedral Church of St Asaph', was buried on 6 September 1693.

Alexander Gerrard 1694–1738 (d. St Asaph Mar. 1738). Under the date 25 March 1698, the accounts note that Gerrard was paid arrears of three and a half years' salary at £4 a year. However, he was voted an additional £10 by Chapter minute of 25 August 1698, with a further £10 in 1705. On 9 August 1705 it was also ordered (somewhat curiously) 'that the organist for taking care to provide and fit boys for the choir shall upon the Bishop, Dean, or Chapter choosing any boy into the choir receive the first half year's salary when due for having taught him, if such boys' parents are poor'.

Thomas is our only authority for Gerrard's Christian name and date of death. Shortly after his death, at a Chapter meeting on 21 June 1738 attended by the dean alone (!), it was proposed to allow his widow one part of the salary due to him 'in consideration of his long services and her mean circumstance'; the other part was to go to John Gerrard for acting as organist during the vacancy. This was disallowed at the next regular Chapter meeting on 1 August 1738.

There is reasonable presumption that this was the Alexander Gerrard, a child of the Chapel Royal under *John Blow, whose voice had changed by December 1694 (Ashbee 1986–9: ii. 53).

John Gerrard 1738–79 (d. 1788). One takes for granted that the 'Mr Gerrard' found in the Chapter Acts is the John Gerrard mentioned above, doubtless Alexander's son, who became a supernumerary singingman on ceasing to be a singingboy in 1737. There is no formal minute of his appointment, but 'Mr Gerrard' is referred to as the organist on various occasions from 1738, and the Christian name John is found in the accounts at Michaelmas 1770.

On 6 March 1755 Gerrard was allowed 7*s*. for 'two anthems of Dr Boyce', and on 15 September 1756, at a meeting at which there was some complaint of neglect on the part of the choir, the dean was empowered to buy Boyce's *Cathedral Music*. On 26 July 1758 the Chapter accepted Gerrard's recommendation that the organ would sound better if the wainscotting on each side 'fronting the Broad Isle' [nave]' were removed.

Thomas states that Gerrard became organist of Wrexham Parish Church in 1779 and died in 1788.

John Jones 1782–5. The delay in appointing Gerrard's successor is likely to have been due to the building of a new organ. The minute of Jones's appointment, dated 31 July 1782, runs thus: 'Ordered that Mr John Jones be appointed organist and that he be allowed twenty pounds per annum provided he instructs a sufficient number of singing boys, not less than four in number, for the use of the choir till the organ be put up, and that afterwards he be allowed the same salary that was usually paid the organist heretofore.'

Edward Bailey 1785–91. The accounts show that Bailey was remunerated as both organist (£52) and singingman (£10). He was paid from Midsummer 1785 to Michaelmas 1791. There is no direct evidence to connect him with the Edward Bailey, organist of Chester Cathedral, 1803–23, although, of course, it is far from impossible that they were one and the same man.

Charles Spence 1791–3. Like Bailey, Spence also held a singingman's post. He was paid from March 1791 to Christmas 1793. On 31 July 1793 the Chapter voted him a gift of 50 guineas.

If *Thomas* (also West 1921) is correct in his surmise that this was a relative of a certain Thomas Spence, 'for seventy-nine years a member of the choir of Chester Cathedral', this constitutes one of several links between the personnel of St Asaph and Chester Cathedrals.

Henry Hayden 1794–?1828. According to West (1921) (who, however, believed Hayden to have remained at St Asaph until 1834), Hayden's Christian name, not mentioned in the Chapter Acts or accounts, was Henry. He states that Hayden had been a chorister under *John Beckwith at Norwich, and, furthermore, that he was aged 20 at the time of his appointment to St Asaph and was buried at Llanbelig in 1848.

William Hayden ?1828–33 (d. St Asaph, 20 Aug. 1833). From 1794 onwards, the Cathedral accounts refer simply to 'Mr Hayden' or 'the organist'. However, on 29 September 1829 'William' Hayden is specified (also in 1831 and 1832). He was doubtless the son of his predecessor, under whom he had been a chorister. On 29 September 1833 his widow was paid three months' salary outstanding. A plan of the Cathedral graveyard (Diocesan Registry) reveals that a William Hayden died on 20 August 1833; the grave is now built over.

Robert Augustus Atkins 1834–89 (b. Chichester, 2 Oct. 1811; d. St Asaph, 3 Aug. 1889). Atkins's appointment, to take effect from 1 March 1834, was minuted on 18 February 1834, and the Chapter Acts record his death in 1889, after fifty-five years' service. West (1921) gives the date of his birth, stating that he was the son of a lay vicar choral of Chichester Cathedral and that he was successively chorister and assistant organist there. *Thomas* (374) observes that from 1843 to 1862 there were daily choral services in the Cathedral.

Llewelyn Lloyd 1889–97. Lloyd was a chorister of the Cathedral under Atkins until 1869, and became assistant organist in 1875. He retired on account of ill health on 25 March 1897.

West. 1921.

Sir Hugh Percy Allen, GCVO, 1897–8. Allen's salary at St Asaph was £90 a year. Immediately on his appointment he reported the need for a better organ, and although his tenure was so brief, he was specially thanked for the improvement he had made in the choir's rendering of the services.

See under New College, Oxford.

Archibald Wayett Wilson 1898–1900.

See under Manchester Cathedral.

Cyril Bradley Rootham 1901.

See under St John's College, Cambridge.

William Edward Belcher 1901–17 (b. Handworth, Birmingham, 1864). Belcher was the son of a Birmingham musician, Thomas Belcher, D.Mus. (Oxon.). He was educated at King Edward's School, Birmingham, and in 1884 he became a choral scholar of King's College, Cambridge, taking the degrees of BA (1887) and MA (1891). After teaching music and mathematics for a time at Bromsgrove School (1889–91), he became organist of Kingston on Thames Parish Church, 1891–3, taking the FRCO diploma in 1892. He then moved to Leeds, where he was deputy organist of the town hall and organist of Headingley Parish Church, 1893–1901.

It is not surprising, in view of their recent experiences, that when appointing Belcher, the Dean and Chapter expressed the hope that he would stay for a minimum of two years. He resigned in 1917.

West 1921; *Venn*.

Harold Carpenter Lumb Stocks 1917–56 (b. Essendon, Herts., 21 Oct. 1884; d. St Asaph, 10 Feb. 1956). Stocks was educated at St Asaph Grammar School, and received his musical training under *A. W. Wilson, whose assistant he became at Ely Cathedral in 1906. He was organist of Yeovil Parish Church (1909) and Ludlow Parish Church (1911) before his appointment to St Asaph, where he remained until his death.

He took the Oxford degree of B.Mus. in 1911, and the Dublin degree of Mus.D. in 1921; he also held the FRCO diploma.

MT, 97 (1956), 156; *WWW*, 1951–60.

§Robert Duke Dickinson 1956–62 (b. Liverpool, 16 Nov. 1916). Dickinson, who was educated privately, took the Durham degree of B.Mus. in 1945, and also holds the FRCO and CHM diplomas. From 1944 to 1950 he was organist of Mold Parish Church, and then, from 1950 until his appointment to St Asaph, he was organist of Leamington Spa Parish Church. After leaving St Asaph he was director of music at St Catherine's School, Bramley, Guildford until his retirement.

§(James) Roland Middleton 1963–70 (b. Ringwood, Hants, 8 Mar. 1896; d. 13 Apr. 1983). Middleton's first organ appointment was at Mold Parish Church, 1922–44. From 1934 to 1944 he was also sub-organist of Chester Cathedral. In 1945 he became organist of Chelmsford Cathedral, returning to Chester as organist from 1949 to 1963, when he moved to St Asaph.

He held the FRCO diploma (1916), and took the Durham degrees of B.Mus. (1929) and D.Mus. (1935).

Graham (John) Elliott 1970–81.

See under Chelmsford Cathedral.

§John (Theodore) Belcher 1981–5 (b. Orpington, Kent, 3 Dec. 1937). After leaving Tonbridge School, Belcher spent two years at the Royal College of Music, where he won the Stewart prize, and then went to Trinity Hall, Cambridge, 1958–62, reading music and taking the degrees of BA (1961) and MA (1965). He holds the diplomas of FRCO (1962) and CHM (1964).

Before his appointment to St Asaph he was organist of Knockholt Parish Church, 1956–61, and Holy Trinity, Folkestone, 1963–7, assistant organist of Chester Cathedral, 1967–71, and organist of St Peter's, Bournemouth, 1971–81. He left St Asaph to become organist and master of the choristers of Tewkesbury Abbey. He is the author of a booklet on the organs of Chester Cathedral (1970).

§Hugh (Hooper) Davies, organist and master of the choristers from 1985 (b. Fishguard, Pembrokeshire, 17 Mar. 1952). Hooper was educated at Fishguard County Secondary School and St Catharine's College, Cambridge (choral scholar). He read music, and took the degrees of BA (1973), Mus.B. (1974), and MA (1977). He also holds the FRCO diploma (1974). From 1974 until his appointment to St Asaph he was assistant organist of Carlisle Cathedral.

ST DAVID'S

The Cathedral Church of St David

Main sources in this section (1964) (with National Library of Wales references):

Chapter Acts
CA1 1561–77 (SD/Ch/B1).
CA2 1578–99 (SD/Ch/B2).
CA3 1601–27 (SD/Ch/B3).
CA4 1621–60 (SD/Ch/B4).
CA5 1660–1709 (SD/Ch/B5).
CA6 1660–1722 (SD/Ch/B6).
CA7 1723–68 (SD/Ch/B7).
CA8 1768–1829 (SD/Ch/B8).
CA9 1830–79 (SD/Ch/B10).

Treasurer's Accounts
1384–1661 (SD/Ch/B13).
1669–92 (SD/Ch/B14).
1686–1724 (SD/Ch/B15).
1724–68 (SD/Ch/B16).
1768–1829 (SD/Ch/B17).
1830–79 (SD/Ch/B18).

Miscellaneous
Payne 'Collectanea Menevensia', two MS volumes compiled by H. T. Payne (SD/Ch/B27–8); particularly helpful in deciphering entries in the early CA.

Of the four cathedrals of ancient foundation in Wales, that of St David's was in fullest possession of the constitutional features of the Old Foundation by the close of the Middle Ages (see p. xxi), including a minor corporation of vicars choral. But in the earlier part of the period treated here, the title of the presiding officer was precentor (or chanter), only later changed to dean.

It has been stated that the organist at the time of the dissolution of the monasteries was Lewis Morris, *temp.* William Barlow, Bishop of St David's, 1536–47 (Yardley 1972: 89). But this seems to rest on some confusion. Close to the Cathedral yet distinct from it, there was formerly St Mary's College, a corporate body with its own choristers under a master. At the time of its abolition in 1549 under the Acts relating to chantries and colleges, a list of its members included 'Lewis Morres, master of the children, of the age of 34 years, having no other promotion'; he was given a pension of £6. 13*s.* 4*d.* as compensation (*Payne*, i. 185–6). The expression 'having no other promotion' rules out his having been concurrently organist of the Cathedral. West (1921) lists him as Cathedral organist in 1551, but I have not been able to find documentary confirmation of this. If he was organist, he probably did quite well if he retained his pension along with the Cathedral stipend. In the accounting year 1557–8 the Cathedral accounts note: 'To the master of the choristers for keeping of the organs and teaching of the choristers, £10', but they do not name the holder of the office.

Thomas Elliott 1563→. When Elliott was made a vicar choral on 8 September 1563, it was ordered that the

> said Thomas, besides his duty in the choir, shall teach the choristers their plainsong, pricksong, and descant, and shall play the organ when time requireth, upon such direction, order, and wages as the worshipful Mr Thomas Huet the Chanter at his next coming shall

take direction and order with the rest of his said brothers for his wages in doing yearly the same. (*Payne*, i, quoting CA1, p. 60.)

Extant accounts for the year 1565–6 give the wage of the master of the choristers as £6. 13*s*. 4*d*.

Thomas Tomkins (I) *c*.1570–*c*.1586 (b. near Lostwithiel; d. Gloucester, 1627). Tomkins was the sire of worthy progeny—*Thomas Tomkins (III), *John Tomkins, *Giles Tomkins (I), and, in the next generation, *Giles Tomkins (II). The clue to the connection between all of these and our present subject is the statement of Thomas Tomkins (III), in the preface to his *Songs of 3, 4, 5, and 6 parts* (1622), that he was born in Pembrokeshire. This, first followed up by E. H. Fellowes, taken in conjunction with genealogies preserved in the College of Arms, leads to the unmistakable inference that Thomas Tomkins, precentor of Gloucester Cathedral in the early seventeenth century and father of Thomas Tomkins (III), was the same man as Thomas Tomkins (I), our present subject, organist of St David's Cathedral in the late sixteenth century (Fellowes 1921: 293).

Having left his ancestral home in Cornwall, Thomas Tomkins is first heard of at St David's in 1565, when on 28 July he witnessed a deed (*West Wales Historical Records*, 1916, p. 11) as vicar choral of the Cathedral.

On 14 July 1571 (CA1, p. 236) the following scandalous entry was made concerning him:

Thomas Tomkins was monished by Mr Chanter . . . to procure and get home his wedded wife as is supposed betwixt this present day and one fortnight after Lammas day next: and for his sinful act committed with his maid servant etc. though he seem from the bottom of his heart to be sorry for his offence yet [he is ordered] to give to the poor namely to David Glover 3*s*. 4*d*. to pray for him upon pain of deprivation of his stall and living thereunto belonging, to which act he did assent.

The 'supposed' wife who was not allowed to live in the Cathedral Close (presumably according to the Queen's edict) must have been Margaret Poher or Pore, mother of Thomas Tomkins (III).

It is not until 1573 that Tomkins is named not only as vicar choral but also as master of the choristers or children (CA1, p. 253, 14 April 1573). But I am inclined to think that he held the latter post at least as early as 1571; for in a list dated 21 July 1571 (CA1, p. 237) his name comes in exactly the same position as in 1573, namely, after four vicars choral designated 'sir' (i.e., in holy orders), and first among the other nine vicars choral; no one else is named master of the choristers in this list, though the accounts for the year 1570–1 indicate the payment of such an officer at a salary of £6. 13*s*. 4*d*. a year. It is fairly evident that the master of the choristers at St David's was also the organist, not only because of the document of 1577 (see below), but because the accounts at this period do not allot payment to any organist as such. When they do so later (1618–42), the salary of the organist and the master of the choristers is only £3 each.

On 29 April 1577 Thomas Tomkins (II), though only a boy, was granted a place as vicar choral in order to increase the income of his father, 'master of the choristers and organ player in this church', who would otherwise be compelled to seek employment elsewhere (*Payne*, ii. 43, quoted *in extenso* by Atkins 1918: 39). This Thomas Tomkins (II) eventually went to sea and died in Sir Richard Grenville's famous ship *Revenge*, having been expelled from St David's Cathedral on 22 January 1586 (*Payne*, ii. 63) for gross misbehaviour.

On 27 July 1585 the Chapter resolved that 'the organ having been stated to be out of repair, the organist's salary is suspended' (*Payne*, ii); small wonder, then, that Tomkins did not remain at St David's. By 1594, evidently having acquired holy orders, he is found as a minor canon of Gloucester Cathedral (Gloucester CA1). He combined this post with that of vicar of St Mary-de-Lode Church and, for many years before 1625, the precentorship of the Cathedral. He made his will in March 1626/7, and it was proved at Gloucester on 19 April 1627. Its text is reproduced by Atkins (1918: 44).

He was apparently a man of antiquarian interests, and was the author of an 'Account of the Bishops of Gloucester', subsequently printed by Willis (1727: ii. 723). Atkins (1946) argues interestingly that Tomkins was also the anonymous author of the 'Description of St David's', used likewise by Willis in his *Survey of the Cathedral Church of St David's* (1717).

Marmaduke Pardo ←1617–19→. Following the disuse of the organ in 1585, the exact date of the next organist's appointment is uncertain, though it must have been some time before 1617, when we find the following (recorded by *Payne*, ii) under the date 24 July 1617: 'Divers articles were exhibited against Sir Marmaduke Pardo, vicar-choral, for sundry misdemeanours [and] he was censured by the said canons to stand suspended from his office in the said church vizt. from his place of vicar-choral, his room of organist and master of the children, and the curateship [of the parish of St David's].' Four days later, Sir Thomas Walters was given the curateship, Richard Marrock was made master of the choristers, and Marmaduke Pardo was allowed to keep his 'other places', as the record cites, in compassion for 'his poor estate'. It seems he had contracted a clandestine marriage. Later, on 24 July 1619, he was suspended for misdemeanours 'to the scandal of the whole society'.

From 1618–19 until 1642 the accounts show regular separate payments to an organist and an 'instructor of the children', but no names are given. After 1642 we lack evidence about an organist, named or unnamed, until the time of William Pardo.

William Pardo ←1672–97. In 1668 William Pardo was listed at a visitation as a vicar choral, but no one was specifically designated as organist or master of the choristers (CA5, p. 127). On 24 July 1672 (CA6) Pardo was dismissed as master of the choristers but retained the position of organist along with that of vicar choral (see stray list inserted on p. 312 of CA1, and dated 24 July 1673). A certain David George, also a vicar choral, was made master of the choristers, for which he received £3 a year, half the stipend formerly received by Pardo for the combined post.

During Pardo's time the organ again (as in Tomkins's day) became unusable, and in answer to visitation articles in 1691 the precentor stated: 'I answer that we have an organ, but out of order, for how long I do not remember.' Nevertheless, as the accounts of the master of the Fabric show, Pardo continued to receive the organist's stipend (£3), certainly to 1695–6, when he is named, and probably to 1696–7, when the stipend remained the same, though he is not mentioned by name. In the following year the stipend was doubled, and I take this to mark a new appointment.

Henry Mordant (I) 1697–1714. Although Mordant is not identified by name as organist until the accounting year 1704–5, it seems perfectly clear that he took up the post in 1697–8. Not only did the organist's stipend go up to £6 that year (see above), but in 1698–9, 1699–1700, 1702–3, and 1703–4 there are substantial payments, ranging from £5. 18*s*. 8*d*. to £3. 0*s*. 9*d*., to 'Mr Mordant' for copying music. Clearly he was the leading musician. Furthermore, the clerk setting out the accounts for 1704–5 took the opportunity to show how the £6 stipend was made up: 'To the organist (as Wm. Pardo) £3 & additional gift to Mr Mordant £3.' He was also paid £3 for his work as master of the choristers, together with 10*s*. 'for hearing the choristers read'. On 25 July 1713 the Chapter Acts noted (CA6): 'Henry Mordant to succeed to the next vacant vicar-choralship.' This was no doubt a means of enlarging his stipend; it would also secure his status.

When Mordant was appointed (on the assumption that this was in 1697), there was no organ fit to use, but a new one by 'Father' Smith was installed in 1705, and during 1704–5 Mordant was paid 'for getting it from Milford to St David's 14*s*.'.

By a minute dated 28 July 1697 (CA5) the Chapter decreed that the vicars choral should meet 'every week at the least and practise the anthems and services which are to be performed in the choir . . . and particularly Tallis his Service and Dr Blowe's Elami'. Ten years later (CA6, 27 July 1707), a fuller minute on the same subject recorded that the vicars and choristers were 'to practise singing together with the organ', and specified the following repertory:

> *Services*. Inglott, Tallis, Patrick and King Services and also Dr Blower's [*sic*] Service in Elami when there shall be voices that can reach it. Anthems. [*] Call to remembrance, [*] Hear my crying, Blessed be God, I will alway give thanks, O give thanks (Humphreys), Lift up your heads, Awake my glory, Rejoice in the Lord alway, Rejoice in the Lord, O ye righteous, [*] Praise God in his holiness.

The anthems marked with an asterisk were copied out by Mordant in 1704–5, together with 'O praise the Lord, for it is a good thing' and—especially interesting—'Dr Gibbons Responses'. This particular copying-bill came to 16*s*. Mordant did further copying 1707–8, 1708–9, and 1710–11. Clearly, a sustained effort was being made to keep up the choral services of the Cathedral.

The accounts in the time of both Henry Mordant (I) and Henry Mordant (II) (see below) contain some intriguing but not self-explanatory entries. In 1706–7 and 1712–13 respectively we find 'Entertainment at St David's as per Mr Mordant and butcher's bill, £20. 9*s*. 2*d*.', and 'For entertaining my Lord Bishop at St David's, 1711, Mr Mordant's bill, £10, Mr Ford's, £7. 7*s*. 6*d*.' In both 1714–15 and 1715–16 we find 'Mr Mordant's bill for entertainment' and 'the butcher's bill' in association, while in 1716–17 there is 'to Mr Mordant's servant for artichokes, 1*s*.'.

Henry Mordant (II) 1714–?1719. Henry Mordant (I) did not enjoy his post of lay vicar choral for long. At the annual July Chapter on 24 July 1714 it was ordered that 'Henry Mordant the younger to be organist in room of his father Henry Mordant the elder and elect Henry Harries to be a chorister in the room of Mordant.' Though evidently young at the time of his appointment, Henry Mordant (II) had only a short tenure, about which nothing is known.

Richard Tomkins ?1719–20. On 24 July 1719 the Chapter resolved permanently to annex one of the posts of vicar choral to that of organist, but there was an express proviso that 'Richard Tomkins, the organist', was to be vicar choral 'so long and no longer as he shall hold the situation and perform the duties of organist' (CA6). This provision was recalled in 1870 in the dispute between the Cathedral and W. P. Propert (see below).

A year later, on 23 July 1720, the office of organist was declared vacant, 'in consequence of the dereliction of the same by Richard Tomkins', and the joint appointment of organist and lay vicar choral was given (the precentor dissenting) to William Bishop.

William Bishop 1720–7 (suspended 1725–7). Bishop ran into trouble early, and on 24 July 1722, after a period of suspension, he was restored for one year 'by way of probation'. In 1725 he was suspended for two years 'for his stupid and notorious neglect of duty and intemperance and more especially for his drunkenness'. Matthew Madox was appointed vicar choral and organist for these two years. As it turned out, Bishop never resumed duty.

Henry Williams 1727–34. Williams was appointed (for one year in the first instance) on 26 July 1727. It must be borne in mind when interpreting the Midsummer Chapter Acts that they may have regularized events which had taken place some months earlier.

Matthew Philpott (alias Phillips) 1734–?1775. It might seem that there were two men involved here: Matthew Philpott and Matthew Phillips; but in fact the surnames were loosely applied to a single individual who was appointed organist and vicar choral on 24 July 1734. This could have been the Phillips who briefly acted as organist of Magdalen College, Oxford in 1734 (Bloxam 1853–7: ii. 210).

In 1736, when ordered to teach the choristers for two hours daily, Philpott was given James Roberts and Robert Hughes as assistants. In 1753 the vicars were ordered to rehearse anthems with the organist twice a week. In 1755 the Chapter voted a guinea to Nicholas Roberts for helping the organist to teach the choristers, and 5*s*. for music-copying. Some years later, in 1761, they ordered the sum of £2. 2*s*. to be given 'to the Revd Nicholas Roberts for his extraordinary performance in singing anthems'.

On 24 July 1775 Philpott's post of vicar choral was conferred on John Bowen, who was in holy orders. Bowen did not serve as organist, and the fact that the vicar choralship was filled in such a way seems to indicate that no appointment as organist was made for the time being.

John Day 1782–7. It is significant (for the reasons discussed above, under Philpott) that when Day was elected vicar choral on 24 July 1782, he was given a place vacated by a priest-vicar choral, thus restoring the balance. On 24 July 1783 Day was given £10. 10*s*. for his trouble in instructing the choristers, and was specifically given 'the sole care' of the choir. On that account he was excused the normal duty of a lay vicar choral of reading the First Lesson (the practice of having a lay vicar read the First Lesson ceased at St David's only in 1804). His resignation is recorded on 24 July 1787. The records do not use the term 'organist' in relation to him or his post in charge of the choir. Though not conclusive, this may indicate that he was master of the choristers only. If so, then there was no organist for some twelve years.

Arthur Richardson 1787–1826 (informally until 1792) (d. St David's 1826). Richardson, 'from the Cathedral Church of Armagh in Ireland', was formally appointed vicar choral on the day that John Day resigned. A year later he was given a gratuity 'for his attention to the music of the church', and it was ordered that the organ should be repaired. Richardson, 'vicar choral and organist', gave £5. 5*s*. towards this (*Payne*, ii. 447); he was also described as organist at the episcopal visitation of 1790. Nevertheless, this appears to have been an informal status, since he was not specifically appointed organist until 24 July 1792, when the 'Chapter gift' (by way of addition to the £6 basic stipend) was increased from £9 to £20, 'during the pleasure of the Chapter'. In 1821, in reply to the articles of enquiry of the Ecclesiastical Commissioners, the emoluments were stated to be £31 as organist (£6 plus £25) and £68 as a member of the College of Vicars Choral.

Three of Richardson's sons were choristers under him: John, William, and Peter. Peter became perpetual curate of Henfynyw, Cardiganshire in 1824.

At the end of his period of office, things appear to have grown slack, and on 23 July 1825 it was found necessary to order 'that the Chapter gift of six guineas to the lay vicars for anthems on Sundays be withdrawn, no anthem having been sung for the last two years; and that the organist be admonished to pay more attention to the instruction of the choir than he has lately done'.

John Barrett 1826–51 (d. 1851). Barrett's election as a lay vicar choral and his appointment as organist were minuted on 24 July 1826. At the same time, his son Arthur was also elected lay vicar choral. No details of Barrett's biography or tenure are known, beyond the fact that he died in office.

William Peregrine Propert 1851–72 (b. Milford, 24 Feb. 1831; d. St David's, 3 Oct. 1906). William was the eldest son of David and Ann Propert of Milford. His father at one time commanded one of HM Irish packets, and afterwards his own ship, the *Peregrine*. He was influential in securing the erection of the South Bishop Rock lighthouse in 1839.

On William's admission to St David's College, Lampeter in Michaelmas term 1848, it was recorded that for five years he had attended 'St David's Collegiate School'—presumably an institution connected with St David's, certainly not Lampeter. He won an organ scholarship to Lampeter in October 1848, and took two prizes in 1849, after which his record there ceases. In November 1849 he matriculated at Jesus College, Oxford, and took the B.Mus. degree as a non-resident in 1850. Such a step was exceptional at the time for so young a man, and it argues unusual aspiration. When he died in 1906 he must have been one of the last surviving holders of the Oxford B.Mus. as it was before the institution of examinations prior to submission of an exercise.

At the annual Chapter on 24 July 1851, his appointment as organist of St David's Cathedral was minuted thus: 'Ordered and decreed that William Peregrine Propert Bachelor of Music be appointed Junior Lay Vicar and Organist of this Cathedral Church vacant by the death of John Barrett Organist thereof.' Some kind of arrangement, which was not recorded, appears to have made it possible for Propert to continue to hold his organist's post while keeping terms at Cambridge, for he matriculated at Trinity Hall during Lent term 1852; he was also incorporated as Mus.B. on 24 November 1852 in virtue of his Oxford degree. He took the Cambridge degree of BA in 1856, having read mathematics and theology. Two of his letters to the Chapter of St David's have survived. The first is dated 24 July 1853, and gives an account of the choristers' work during the preceding year ('seventeen anthems have been learnt by them, and committed to memory, together with fifty chants and sixteen psalm tunes. The rudiments of music have not been neglected . . .'); it also propounds a scheme for improving the choir by raising three adult singers locally for £45–50 a year. In the second, written on 24 July 1855, Propert asks to be considered for the post of 'minor canon' (priest-vicar choral), in which case he would seek holy orders and resign as organist; but nothing came of this (SD/Ch/Let/320, 331).

In 1864, because of restoration work in the Cathederal, the organ was dismantled. At this point the Chapter stopped paying Propert the annual Chapter gift of £20 (see above under Richardson) together with £5 for tuning, leaving him (as organist) with no more than the basic stipend of £6 paid to Henry Mordant (I) in 1697–8—though, of course, he continued to receive the much larger emoluments of the lay vicar choral's post attached to that of organist. In 1870, after five years had elapsed, Propert sued the Chapter for £125 (SD/Ch/Misc/162; Let/577). How the matter was decided, or whether it was settled out of court, I have not been able to discover; however, Propert was paid the basic £6 for the last time on St James's Day 1870, and on 25 July 1871 it was resolved that he be paid £40 and given six months' notice. The accounts for 1872–3 include his 'final payment in full of all demands: £52. 10*s*.'.

There was much discussion about Propert's post as lay vicar choral, and whether he was free to retain this when the intention had been to attach it to the post of organist. I have not been able to trace any documents proving what happened, but West (1921), whose first edition appeared while Propert was still alive, stated that he remained a vicar choral for life. On the other hand, Stephens (1882), also writing during Propert's life, says that he became a vicar choral in 1875. I have not been able to get to the bottom of this; but Stephens's account of

Propert contains a couple of inaccuracies. However, *W. H. Harris recollected his singing in St David's Cathedral choir in 1897, looking 'very imposing' in his Cambridge LL D hood.

After ceasing to be organist, Propert embarked on a new career. Having been admitted to the Inner Temple in December 1871 and having proceeded to the Cambridge degree of LL M in 1872, he was called to the Bar in January 1875 and took the LL D degree in 1878. Some interests outside music and law are reflected in his fellowships of the Royal Meteorological Society and the Royal Geographical Society. He died at Manor House, St David's on 3 October 1906. He was buried in the Cathedral cemetery, where his tombstone describes him erroneously as MA, and cites the year of his birth as 1836. It makes no mention of his degree of B.Mus. It is noteworthy that neither this inscription nor the obituary notice in the *Haverfordwest and Milford Haven Telegraph* (10 October 1906) so much as hints at his connection with St David's Cathedral.

Records of St David's College, Lampeter, Jesus College, Oxford, and Trinity Hall, Cambridge; Cambridge University *Subscriptiones* Book; *MT*, 47 (1906); *Venn*; personal communication from Sir William Harris, Oct. 1964.

Robert Ellis 1874→. What happened to the Cathedral music following Propert's dismissal is obscure. On 27 July 1874 the Chapter minuted the appointment of Robert Ellis, 'organist of St. Mary's Church, Tenby', as lay vicar choral and organist. There was still no organ, however, and it was not until 1879 that steps were taken to approach Henry Willis about a new instrument. The available Chapter Acts end at 1879, and Ellis's history is unknown. The accounts for 1877–8 and 1878–9 (the latest available) note the payment to William Appleby of £31 (the sum for which Propert had contended) for 'playing harmonium and teaching boys of the choir'.

Frederick S. Garton 1883–94. Garton appears to have been appointed at the time of the opening of the new Willis organ. According to West (1921) Garton had been a pupil of *William Done, and assistant organist of Worcester Cathedral before being appointed to Dudley Parish Church, from where he moved to St David's. On leaving there, he became organist of St Martin's, Haverfordwest.

West 1921.

D. John D. Codner 1894–6 (b. 1851). Prior to his appointment to St David's, Codner had been organist of St Bride's Church, Fleet Street, London for some years up to 1888. He resigned his post at the Cathedral on account of ill health.

C. W. Pearce 1909; West 1921.

Herbert Charles Morris 1896–1921 (b. Coventry, 18 June 1873; d. Wolverhampton, 15 Jan. 1940). At an early age Morris had lessons from *A. H. Brewer, then at Coventry. At a later date he was pupil-assistant to E. H. Lemare at Holy Trinity, Sloane Square, London, and he also studied at the Royal College of Music. His early organ appointments were at Kenilworth Parish Church, at various London churches, and at Boscombe Pavilion. He was assistant organist at Manchester

Cathedral under *J. K. Pyne, and was then briefly organist of St Andrew's, Bath in 1896, the year of his appointment as organist and lay vicar choral of St David's Cathedral.

In 1904 he matriculated at Cambridge as a non-collegiate student, taking the degrees of BA and MA in 1908 and 1911 respectively. He also held the FRCO diploma.

Shortly after the disestablishment of the Church in Wales (1920), Morris left St David's to become organist of Queen Street Congregational Church, Wolverhampton, where he remained from 1921 until his retirement in 1938.

Book of Matriculations . . . in the University of Cambridge, 1901–12 (Cambridge, 1915); West 1921; *Wolverhampton Express and Star*, 10 Oct. 1921, 7 Feb. 1938, 16 Jan. 1940.

§**Joseph Soar, MBE, DL, 1922–54** (b. Sheffield, 9 Oct. 1878; d. 9 June 1971). Soar studied at the Royal College of Music, where he was an exhibitioner, and he also worked at the Temple Church under *H. W. Davies. By the time he was 14 he had already become organist of Chapeltown Parish Church, Sheffield (1892). After completing his studies in London, where he held an appointment at St John's Church, Clapham, he was appointed organist of All Saints', Derby (now Derby Cathedral) from 1901, and of the parish churches of Barnsley (1904), Halifax (1912), and Burnham-on-Sea (1921). He retired from his post at St David's with the title of organist emeritus in 1954.

While he was at St David's, not only was Soar honorary secretary of the lifeboat station from 1926, but he was also an active member of the lifeboat crew. In 1943 he received the bronze medal for gallantry from the Royal National Lifeboat Institution (the citation of which is printed in *MT*, 84 (1943), 154). He was appointed MBE in 1947, and in 1960 he was elected an honorary life governor of the RNLI. He became a deputy-lieutenant for the County of Pembroke in 1950.

Soar took the FRCO diploma in 1900, and the Durham degree of B.Mus. in 1910. He received the Lambeth degree of D.Mus. in 1934.

Peter Boorman 1954–77.

See p. ix.

§**Sir Nicholas (Fane St George) Jackson, Bt., 1977–84** (b. 4 Sept. 1934). The grandson of Sir Thomas Graham Jackson, Bt., the noted architect, Jackson was educated at Radley College, and in 1955 he went up to Wadham College, Oxford. For personal reasons, however, he did not complete his course there, but moved to the Royal Academy of Music, where he was an organ pupil of C. H. Trevor, 1956–9. Afterwards he studied the harpsichord under George Malcolm and Gustav Leonhardt.

Before his appointment to St David's he held three London organ posts: St Anne's, Soho (1963–8), St James's, Piccadilly (1971–4), and St Lawrence Jewry (1974–7). He succeeded to the family baronetcy in 1979. After leaving St David's he settled in London as a free-lance musician, and among his other activities he became director of the Festival-Bach at the monastery of Santes Creus, Spain.

§Malcolm (Gruffydd) Watts, organist and master of the choristers from 1984 (b. Cardigan, 6 May 1947). Watts was educated at University College, Cardiff, and took the degree of B.Mus. (Wales), afterwards qualifying as a teacher. He succeeded to the full post at St David's Cathedral in November 1984, after having been assistant organist from 1977.

SALISBURY

The Cathedral Church of the Blessed Virgin Mary

Main sources in this section (1967):

Chapter Acts

CA14	Harwood's Memorials (1499–1538), Holte and Blacker Registrum (1538–63); bound together as 'No. 14'.
CA15	Blacker (1563–88), Mortimer (1603–6); bound together as 'No. 15'.
CA16	Penrudocke (1588–99), 'No. 16'.
CA16b	Unbound draft Chapter Acts surviving with the records of the peculiar jurisdiction of the dean.
CA17	Shuter's Memorials (1623–42), 'No. 17'; a scribbled book of notes used by the Chapter clerk to make up his fair-copy Acts. This fair copy is no longer extant; but Canon Isaac Walton (d. 1719) left transcripts of various Cathedral documents, among them the index to this missing Act book, which he termed 'Shuter's Register, 1621'. Shuter's Memorials are almost impossible to decipher, and Walton's transcript of this index is of much help.
CA18	Greenhill–Butler (1660–75), 'No. 18'.
CA19	Frome–Prince (1675–96), 'No. 19'.
CA20	Frome alone (1696–1741), 'No. 20'.
CA21	1741–96, 'No. 21'.
CA22	1796–1813.
CA23	1813–34.
CA24	1834–51.
CA25	1851–63.

Details from later Act Books kindly communicated by the Revd Canon Cyril Taylor.

Accounts

Ac1	Fabric (clerk of works) Accounts Box labelled '16th century'; 1539–40 to 1597–8, with gaps. 1597–8 to 1695–6, with gaps.

Miscellaneous

CB	Box of indentures and other documents labelled 'Choristers Box' (Press 3).
L&P	Folder headed 'Letters and Petitions to the Dean and Chapter'.
DCAB2	Dean's Court Act Book 2.
PR	Registers of baptisms, marriages, and burials in the Cathedral Close (in care of head virger).

Salisbury Cathedral was consecrated in 1225. Its body of vicars choral was incorporated in 1409, and laymen began to be admitted as vicars later in the century. Post-Reformation documents at Salisbury generally (though not entirely consistently) speak of 'vicars choral' (i.e., priest-vicars choral) for those in holy orders, and 'lay vicars' (i.e., lay vicars choral) or, more simply, 'laymen' for those not ordained.

The choristers were given an endowment for maintenance and education in the reign of Edward II, and the statutes of Bishop Roger de Mortival, dated 1319–24, placed them under the surveillance of a *custos*, or warden, one of the canons. This officer was often known as master of the choristers (see also under Lincoln Cathedral); and though the person who actually trained them in music was sometimes loosely described thus at Salisbury, the title was mainly reserved there for the *custos*, with 'teacher' or 'instructor' of the choristers generally being used for whomever undertook their direct musical teaching. Details given below will indicate those occasions on which the organist also filled this latter post, and also the large extent to which it was usual to appoint him a lay vicar. As late as the Cathedrals Commission of 1927 (Report, Church Assembly, London, 1927) it was stated that the seven lay clerks (*recte*: lay vicars) included the organist.

At the time of the dissolution of the monasteries, the organist of Salisbury Cathedral was Thomas Knyght (see below).

Thomas Knyght ←1538→. Knyght's agreement, dated 30 April 1538, is to be found in a lease-book, 25 Henry VIII–4 Elizabeth I, no. 136777, in the keeping of the Church Commissioners. It describes him as 'singingman', and appoints him to the 'office of organ playing' and 'schoolmaster of the choristers'. His salary was to be £6. 11*s*. 8*d*. a year, and he was entitled to claim dinner and supper every day from the resident canons, starting with the most important and senior and working downwards. Some one of this name became sub-treasurer of the Cathedral in December 1537 (CA14, p. 49).

——**Beckwyth ←1558–9→**. Ac1 has the entry for the year 1558–9: 'Also paid to Sir Beckwyth playing on the organs for the whole year 26*s*. 8*d*.' The previous extant account (1539–40) does not mention an organist. The designation 'Sir' indicates a clergyman of inferior social status, such as that of vicar choral.

Robert Chamberlayne ←1561–2→. The next available account in Ac1 has the entry for the year 1561–2: 'Also paid to Mr Chamberlayne for the organs for the whole year, 26*s*. 8*d*.' He can therefore be identified as the Robert Chamberlayne, vicar choral, who on 13 December 1563 was summoned before the Chapter on account of scandalous and disgraceful words ('verba opprobiosa vilipendiosa') spoken against Thomas Smith, also a vicar choral (CA15, f. 5^{v}).

Thomas Smith ←1566–87. 'Mr Smythe' was paid the fee of 26*s*. 8*d*. for organ-playing, according to the next available account, 1566–7, and he continues to be paid thus in all other such accounts up to and including 1586–7. He is sometimes entered as 'Mr Smith'. His Christian name is disclosed in John Farrant's indenture of 1580. Maybe he was the Thomas Smith of whom Chamberlayne spoke so ill in 1563. In 1566 (DCAB2) he threw stones (while wearing his surplice) at Agnes, wife of one Richard Chamberlain. In 1568 his conduct came officially to the notice of the bishop (Jewel), when he was accused of twofold adultery and an earlier offence, dreadful to speak of ('dictu horrend: est'); he was also named as quarrelsome in choir, one who brawled with other vicars, swore, drank, and played at dice in public. The bishop ordered him to be removed from his post as instructor of the choristers (the only mention we have of his being such). From the Chapter Acts dealing with the bishop's censure it transpires that Smith came to Salisbury with a recommendation from the mayor of Lyme, where he had lived for two years (CA15, ff. 20ᵛ–21ᵛ). He was succeeded as instructor of the choristers from Michaelmas 1569 by John Taylor (CB). Retaining his post of organist Smith did not forget Bishop Jewel: on 28 September 1574 (CA15, f. 38) he was hauled up before the Chapter for having said that the late bishop was 'an angel in the pulpit, but a devil abroad'. The burial of a Thomas Smith on 21 February 1587/8, as noted in PR, may be relevant.

John Farrant (I) 1587–92. John Taylor died in 1571 (CA15, f. 27ᵛ), and on 20 October 1571 John Farrant was admitted lay vicar choral (CA15, f. 30). Already, on 4 October 1571, 1*s*. 8*d*. had been laid out on a psalter for 'Mr Farrant, master of the children' (Ac1). A finely written indenture (now in CB), dated 31 May 1580 and bearing a splendid specimen of his signature, committed him to provide, train, and board eight choristers. He is described as 'John Farrant the elder of the close of Sarum', and the express statement that the choristers had to have 'good and commendable voices for trebles and means'—note this important technical distinction—is particularly interesting. Although the terms of his appointment included the duty of playing the organ, they also provided that he should have 'the reversion of the place of organist whenever, and in whatever manner, it shall be avoided by Thomas Smyth'. In due course, from Michaelmas 1587, the accounts show payments to Farrant as organist. He had already been given a degree of authority over his fellow vicars in choir when it was decreed, on 24 March 1585/6 (CA15, f. 65), that he should be 'moderator temporum et tonorum in cantu chori'—a sort of choirmaster.

John Farrant is almost certainly the only cathedral organist actually to have threatened to murder his dean—who, in Farrant's case, was also his wife's uncle. He had displayed signs of turbulence by fighting with a lay vicar named Cranborne in September 1575 (CA15, f. 39), but that was nothing to what happened later. At a Chapter meeting on 7 February 1591/2 the dean gave some account of how he had had to speak to Farrant about his ill-use of his wife, to which remonstrance Farrant had replied threateningly. The following day Farrant suddenly left the Cathedral during Evensong, and, still wearing his surplice, went to the deanery and threatened the dean with an unsheathed knife, saying: 'Durst thou seek to take away my living . . . by God's wounds I will cut thy throat.' In attempting to escape his clutches, the dean's gown was torn off, but he managed to reach his bedroom and shut the door—whereupon Farrant went back to the Cathedral and took his part in the anthem! On 9 February 1592[1] the Chapter summoned Farrant to appear, but he had already made off; he was therefore deprived of all his offices in the Cathedral, 'never henceforth [to] be admitted to the said church or officiate therein' (CA16, modern foliation, 20ᵛ–23ᵛ).

[1] Here the Chapter clerk, exceptionally, used the modern form of the date, not 1591, as he should have done to be consistent. His preceding entry is dated 7 February, 34 Elizabeth—that is, 1591/2—and the next entry is in October 1592.

While at Salisbury, Farrant had four children, one of whom, John, baptized on 28 September 1575 (PR), was a chorister of the Cathedral in 1585 (CA15, f. 63[v]).

A curious item, known to me only at second hand, is an entry in the Parish Registers of Cheriton, Wiltshire, dated 8 April 1589, of the marriage of 'John Farrant of the Close, Salisbury' to one Mary Bird. But our subject's wife Margaret (the dean's niece) was still alive at the time, and the living of Cheriton was then held in plurality by none other than that dean. One can do no more than record this puzzling piece of information.

For discussion of the presumed identity of John Farrant (I), see under Bristol Cathedral.

Richard Fuller 1592–?1600. The accounts for 1591–2 show a payment to Farrant up to Christmas, then for one quarter to 'Mr Lambert', and lastly, for the half-year from March 1592, to 'Fuller' as organist. Later accounts supply the Christian name. He is last mentioned in the accounting year 1597–8, after which accounts fail until 1600–1. Robertson (1938: 166) refers to his agreement or indenture, but I have not traced this myself. He was lay vicar choral and instructor of the choristers. At the episcopal visitation of 1592 the vicars were asked (article 27) whether any of their number had any other appointment in the Cathedral, and they replied (CA16, modern foliation, 30[v]–31[v]): 'We say that Richard Fuller being layman [lay vicar choral] organist and master of the choristers cannot discharge his duties in all those offices in their several places.' By this, they no doubt meant that he could not sing in the choir while playing the organ. Under another article (31) they complained that Fuller had not been lawfully admitted, inasmuch as they had not been consulted about him. His indenture as teacher of the choristers was formally issued on 21 April 1595 and is recorded in Chapter Lease Book 2 (1563–1609) (temporarily designated now as 'Church Commissioners: Bishoprick 136778').

John Farrant (II) 1600–18 (?bap. Salisbury, 28 Sept. 1575; bur. Salisbury, 30 Sept. 1618). This John Farrant was admitted vicar choral (the word 'laicus' is crossed out, so he was doubtless in holy orders) and organist (not instructor of the choristers) on 8 October 1600 (CA16b). The minute of his appointment makes the curious proviso that it was to be understood that he was to be junior to his brethren. It may be somewhat bold to assume that he was the son of John Farrant (I) who was born at Salisbury in 1575, but I do so provisionally. Two of his daughters, Anne (1606) and Lucie (March 1610/11), were baptized at Salisbury, but there is no record of his marriage there (PR).

Fuller's successor as instructor of the choristers appears to have been John Bartlett, concerning whom there is an undated set of articles objecting to his ill-usage of the boys (CB).

Edward (or Edmund) Tucker 1618–? The accounts of the clerk of the works record payment of a stipend of 26*s*. 8*d*. to 'Edward Tooker the organist' for the year Michaelmas to Michaelmas 1618–19 in succession to John Farrant, who received a similar payment for 1617–18. Thereafter these accounts are as follows:

1619–20	Rough cashbook only.
1620–1	Edward Tooker 26*s*. 8*d*.
1621–2	Edward Tooker 26*s*. 8*d*.
1622–9	No accounts extant.
1629–30 } 1630–1 }	To the organist for his fee 26*s*. 8*d*.
1631–2	No accounts extant.
1632–3 } 1633–4 }	To the organist for his fee 26*s*. 8*d*.
1634–5	No accounts extant.
1635–6	To the organist for his fee 26*s*. 8*d*.
1636–7	No accounts extant.
1637–8	To the organist for his fee 26*s*. 8*d*. 'Addition money' to the organist 6*s*. 8*d*.

There are no further accounts until after the Restoration.

The cessation of names from 1622 is tantalizing, in view of an undated petition from 'Edmund Tucker, organist', which states that 'times are hard, his means small and scholars failing him' (L&P). He therefore asks that he may take a lay vicar's place now vacant, so that 'Mr Holmes' may become organist: 'who is fit for it because of his boys and I may perform the better service below in the choir'. As an alternative, he asks that he might be given £4 a year more by being appointed altarist (26*s*. 8*d*.), a grace (20*s*.), and a pricker of church books [music-copyist] (5 nobles). This petition probably relates to a minute in CA17 (p. 5) dated 26 March 1623: 'Mr Tooker to have the next altarist place and playing on the sackbutts [*illegible*] and a grace until an altarist's place fall in.'

John Holmes had succeeded Bartlett as teacher of the choristers *c*. 1621, so far as may be judged from the position of a note about this in Isaac Walton's transcript of items from a missing register (see p. 257). (For Holmes's earlier career, see Winchester Cathedral.) It is not possible to say whether or not any arrangement was concluded with him to do duty as organist, as Tucker suggested.

The next item to shed any light on Tucker's position is found in CA17 (p. 127), dated 19 October 1631: 'Mr Tucker admitted to perform his office of pricker &c., provide books, &c. Mr Tomkins to go to the organ when he will, saving Mr Tucker's place's right and so as he do not wholly take up the organs to the prejudice of Mr Tucker's practice and take away his [hands?].' Walton summarizes the lost minute derived from this rough note as: 'Potestas organizandi concess: Egidio Tomkins, salvo jure Ed. Tucker organistae.' Whether this means that Giles Tomkins was simply allowed access to the organ for private purposes, or that he became *de facto* organist without the formal appointment, is not clear, though the latter is the more probable. The minute certainly does make clear that Tucker remained in possession of his rights as organist of the Cathedral.

See the reference to an Edmund Tucker under Wells Cathedral.

Giles Tomkins (I) 1630–68 (bur. Salisbury, 4 Apr. 1668). Giles Tomkins was the fourth son of Thomas Tomkins (I) by his second wife, Anne. From December 1624 to June 1626 he was organist of King's College, Cambridge (q.v.).

John Holmes's death in Salisbury in January 1628/9 was followed by a dispute about who should succeed him as instructor of the choristers. The dean supported Giles Tomkins, while the master or *custos* of the choristers supported Holmes's son, Thomas. Matters were much complicated by the intervention of the bishop on the side of Thomas Holmes, and the resulting arguments about the constitutional position of the bishop in the Chapter. In the event, the dean forced through Tomkins's appointment as lay vicar, and the questions of his appointment as instructor of the choristers and the bishop's standing in the affair were remitted for royal decision. On 28 June 1629 the King issued the following indecisive ruling: 'Giles Tomkins be admitted by way of provision', while 'for the validity of the election [the question of the bishop's vote] His Majesty leaves the same to a trial at law'. There still remained the difficult problem of securing possession of the choristers' house from John Holmes's widow and his son Thomas, which required an order of the Court of Chancery, 5 November 1629, at which point the dispute seems to have been laid to rest. (See CA17, many entries between pp. 76 and 115; *CSPD*, Charles I, 1628–9: 586, 593; 1629–31: 13; the story is told in lively fashion by Robertson 1938: chap. 11; see also Stevens 1957: 16–18.) For Thomas Holmes's subsequent history, see under Winchester Cathedral.

However, into all of this, which had as much to do with constitutional rights as musical fitness, the explicit term 'organist' does not enter. According to a note in the *Bulletin of New York Public Library* (80/4 (Summer 1977)), Tomkins was installed as both organist and teacher of the choristers in December 1630. But, as we have seen (above), Edmund Tucker still enjoyed certain rights as organist in October 1631. It may be that Tomkins acted for him in a gradually increasing capacity, and that, on Tucker's death or incapacity, he simply slipped into the post. However this may be, Tomkins was described as 'Organist of this church' (PR, 4 April 1668) when he was buried.

Tomkins combined his work at Salisbury with a Court appointment in London, having been made a 'musician for the virginals' on 2 April 1630 (Ashbee 1986–9: iii. 51). At Archbishop Laud's visitation of Salisbury Cathedral in 1634, reference was made to his periodic absences at Court:

> One Giles Tomkins hath the charge of instructing [the choristers] in the art of singing, which he protesteth he doth carefully, and I believe he doth. He hath been blamed lately for leaving them without a guide and teacher once or twice when he went to wait at court, but he promiseth he will do no more so, yet protesteth that they all save two sing their parts perfectly, and need no teacher in his absence. (Stevens 1957: 19.)

After the Restoration he resumed his Court appointment (Ashbee 1986–9: i. 68). (For his second son, Giles Tomkins (II), see under Worcester Cathedral.)

Michael Wise 1668–87 (d. Salisbury, 24 Aug. 1687). Wise, 'formerly of Windsor in the County of Berks', was admitted organist and instructor of the choristers on 2 April 1668 (CA18). This identifies him with the Michael Wise who, by May 1666, was a lay clerk of St George's Chapel, Windsor (Windsor CA, 1660–72), and, surely, with the 'Mr Wise' who was a clerk of Eton College, 1666–8 (Eton College Audit Book, 1666–7 to 1676–7); there can be no doubt that he was the Michael Wise who was one of the children of the Chapel Royal under Henry Cooke immediately following the Restoration, and whose voice had changed by the end of 1663 (Ashbee 1986–9: i. 54). Hawkins (1853: ii. 719) asserts that Wise was born in Wiltshire; Burney (1776–89: iv. 457) narrows his birthplace down to Salisbury.

Hardly had he begun his duties at Salisbury when Wise complained of violence threatened to him in the Close by John Smedmore, a lay vicar: Smedmore was found to be in the wrong, but Wise was told to watch his tongue in future (CA18, 1 and 13 Aug. 1668). In May 1670 an arrangement was approved whereby a lay vicar named Thomas Smith was deputed to teach the choristers, in return for which Wise promised to teach Smith to play the organ. As early as August of that same year, Wise had to be warned to be more diligent in carrying out his side of the bargain (CA18, 6 May, 17 August 1670). The minute of his appointment in 1668 does not specifically say that he was to be a lay vicar, but on 3 October 1672 he was ordered to be present in the choir, wearing his surplice, on Wednesdays, Fridays, and other days when the organ was not used (CA18). Later, in an unguarded moment, he was heard to say 'that the Chapter within these seven years last past have received of the choristers' rents [endowments] above the sum of three hundred pounds, more than ever they paid to him or the choristers', which statement he was obliged to retract and apologize for (CA18, 11 and 23 May 1674). None the less, in April 1675 he was perpetuated as organist (CA18).

On 6 January 1675/6 Wise, described as a 'countertenor from Salisbury', was sworn as a gentleman of the Chapel Royal (Rimbault 1872: 16); he was then in trouble on at least five occasions for absence from duty at Salisbury (CA19, pp. 24, 57, 63, 69, 92).

On 22 September 1677 his former adversary, John Smedmore, was elected instructor of the choristers in place of Wise, who complained of bodily infirmity; but he was generously allowed to retain his stipend in recognition of his outstanding musical skill and his various sacred compositions ('propter eximiam in musica peritiam et hymnorum variorum compositionem honorem illum deferendum esse')—an interesting tribute to him as a composer (CA19). Because he was away so much, it was arranged that Stephen Jeffreys should be allowed 10*s*. a week as deputy organist during Wise's absence, with this amount being deducted from Wise's pay (CA19, 7 November 1677). It could well be that this was the Stephen Jefferies who became organist of Gloucester Cathedral in 1682 (q.v.). Later, Joachim Jeremiah Mitternacht—himself to be dismissed as lay vicar in March 1681/2—was paid for playing the organ for six weeks during Wise's absence (CA19, 23 April 1679).

At the episcopal visitation of the Cathedral in 1683, the Dean and Chapter of Salisbury did not mince words. Replying to article 44 of the visitation enquiries, they said:

> Mr Michael Wise the organist of this church is very shamefully and contemptuously negligent in the performance of his duty in this church, and that he, the said Wise, doth lie and labour under a notorious fame of profaneness [*sic*], intemperate drinking, and other excesses in his life and conversation to the great scandal of religion and the government of this church. (Seth Ward's Visitation Papers, 1683, Diocesan Record Office.)

On 30 October 1684 Wise petitioned the Dean and Chapter to be allowed to resume his office as instructor of the choristers, but no action was decided upon

(CA19). He was also under some kind of cloud at the Chapel Royal at the time of the Coronation of James II in 1685, when he was noted 'suspended and did not appear' (Rimbault 1872: 129), but he was not permanently out of favour, for the King brought influence to bear to secure his return to London, as revealed by the following minute of the Dean and Chapter of St Paul's Cathedral, 24 January 1686/7 (Lgh, MS 25,738/3, p. 1): 'Mr Wise who hath obtained His Majesty's letter for the Almoner's place vacant by the death of Mr Jewett [*Randolph Jewett] appearing, the Chapter declared that they did receive the King's letter, and in obedience thereunto they ordered that Mr Wise be admitted into the said place.' He was admitted and granted his indenture as 'Michael Wise of Salisbury' at St Paul's on 27 January 1686/7 (Lgh, MSS 25,664/1, f. 195; 25,630/13, f. 202[v]).

What steps, if any, he had taken to resign his post at Salisbury when he died a few months later, we do not know. Wood (MS Notes) relates that 'He was knocked on the head and killed downright by the night watch at Salisbury for giving stubborn and refractory language to them, on St Bartholomew's day at night, anno 1687.' Hawkins (1853) says that Wise had rushed out of the house in a passion after quarrelling with his wife. It must be noted that Wise's burial does not figure in PR.

Peter Isaac 1687–92. Described as 'nuper de civitate Dublin . . . generosus', Isaac was appointed organist and lay vicar on 13 September 1687, and was made instructor of the choristers on 9 February 1687/8 (CA19).

See under St Patrick's Cathedral, Dublin.

Daniel Roseingrave 1692–98. When Isaac indicated his wish to return to Ireland, the Chapter considered four candidates to replace him: Roseingrave 'of Winchester', *Stephen Jefferies 'of Gloucester', and *Vaughan Richardson and John Freeman 'of London', and the opinion of the vicars choral, both ordained and lay, was sought. Roseingrave was chosen and admitted organist, instructor of the choristers, and lay vicar on 19 April 1692 (CA19, pp. 125–7).

See under St Patrick's Cathedral, Dublin.

Anthony Walkeley 1700–18 (d. Salisbury, 16 Jan. 1718, aged 45). Walkeley probably came from Wells. There are references to an Anthony Walkeley of a previous generation there in 1632, and to another, who may possibly be our subject, in 1690–1, when he was paid for music-books, in 1705–6, when he was paid for an anthem, and in 1707–8, when he was paid for a Service (HMC, *Manuscripts of the Dean and Chapter of Wells*, ii (1914), 395, 470, 487, 490). Anthony Walkeley was admitted organist, instructor of the choristers, and lay vicar of Salisbury on 1 August 1700 (CA20). His salary was increased on 8 February 1711/12, and on 14 September 1713 he was made a present 'in consideration of his extraordinary care and diligence in teaching and preparing them [the choristers] for the service of the church' (CA20).

He is buried in the centre of the nave, second bay from the west, and the slab reads: 'Here lyeth the Body of Anthony Walkeley Gent late Organist of this Cathedral who died Jan. 16 1717 [1717–18] Aged 45 years.'

Edward Thompson 1718–46 (d. Salisbury, July 1746). On Walkeley's death the Chapter elected Edward Thompson, 'organistam modo Herefordiensem', as organist and instructor of the choristers on condition that he would leave Hereford within three months (CA20, 3 April 1718). Thompson had been organist of Hereford Cathedral from 1714 (q.v.). He was not explicitly designated a lay vicar of Salisbury, though that may have been an implied intention.

An interesting minute of 3 July 1729 orders that 'the organ shall for the future every morning and evening be played while the psalms are chanting' (CA20).

The will of *Thomas Hecht of Magdalen College, Oxford, dated 1734, names 'my cousin, Edward Thompson, now organist of the Cathedral Church of Salisbury', as executor and beneficiary, while releasing him 'from all claims and demands whatsoever, which I [Hecht] now have or shall have on him by bonds, judgements, execution, or by any other ways whatsoever he shall stand indebted to me at the time of my decease' (Bloxam 1853–7: ii. 209). It is therefore possible that he was the Edward Thompson who was admitted chorister of Magdalen College in 1700 (ibid. i. 126).

A much-worn slab at the foot of the lectern in Salisbury Cathedral is inscribed: 'Here lyeth the Body of Edward Thompson Gent Late Organist of this Cathedral who died July [*illegible*] 1746 Aged [*illegible*].'

John Stephens 1746–80 (d. Salisbury, 15 Dec. 1780, aged 60). Stephens, as it appears from his recommendation by the Bishop of Gloucester (see memorial inscription below), came from Gloucester, where he was very probably a chorister in the Cathedral. He renewed his connection with Gloucester in later life by conducting the Gloucester Music Meeting of 1766 (Lysons 1812). One of the chimes still played by the Gloucester Cathedral bells was composed by him. Before moving to Salisbury he was organist of St James's Church, Bristol, as the minute recording his nomination at Salisbury (CA21, 1 October 1746) recites. He was formally elected and admitted organist, instructor of the choristers, and lay vicar on 8 October 1746, the other candidates having been *John Merifield and one Snow, organist of St John's College, Oxford.

The *Salisbury Journal* reports his taking the Cambridge degree of Mus. D. in 1763, though *Venn* does not record this. However, the initials 'M.D.' on his memorial indicate a doctorate of music; and when, on 23 December 1773, his salary was increased by £20 'in consideration of his long and useful services in the choir, particularly for his great care and assiduity in instructing the choristers', he was called 'Dr Stephens' (CA21).

He is buried near to the eastern end of the north nave aisle. A long tribute on a mural tablet tells how he was appointed not only on the recommendation of the then Bishop of Gloucester, but on that of other well-disposed persons; that he discharged his duties honourably and conscientiously until his sudden death, and that he was esteemed by the Dean and Chapter; that he taught many of the gentry and nobility of the city and its surroundings; that as a teacher he was kindly, courteous, and gentle ('a father rather than a teacher'); and that his many friends revered the memory of one who was upright and utterly trustworthy. The full text is as follows:

M.S. Johannis Stephens M.D. et Mariae Uxoris ejus dilectae Ille A.D. 1746 Edvardo Thompson Ecclesiae hujus Cathedralis Organico et Chorodidascalo, successit (a Prestule vere bono et sapiente Martino Benson, Episcopo tunc Glocestriense nec non Testimoniis liberalium haud paucorum commendatus) quae Munera sedulo et honorifice explevit, dum Mors inopina Artus Artemque dissolverit Die Decembris decimo quinto A.D. 1780 Aetatis 60.

Beneficia in illum a Decano et Capitulo, Collata, eorum Existimationem satis indicavere. Plurimos hujusce Civitatis Generosorum, et Regionis adjacentis Nobilium, Artem musicam edocuit, qua Scientia, et Felicitate, Discipuli clarissima et gratissima praebuerunt Argumenta; Qua Comitate Urbanitate, Lenitate, (Patris potius quam Magistri) intima Consuetudo Discipulos inter Magistrumque, non nisi cum Vita dirupta testaetur. Multorum bonorum Familiaritate vivus plene usus est; qui defuncti Memoriam Reverentia, ut probi, et sine fuco integri, prosequuntur.

The rest of the inscription relates to his wife, who died in 1779.

Robert Parry 1781–92 (d. 1792). Parry had been a chorister under Stephens from 1761, and CA21 records the grant to him, in the years 1771, 1772, and 1773, of £5. 5*s*. 'for his extraordinary services in the choir'—possibly a way of encouraging the abilities of a promising ex-chorister. On 1 July 1773 he was appointed organist and master of the choristers of Wells Cathedral (q.v.). On 1 January 1781 he was elected organist, instructor of the choristers, and 'layman' (lay vicar) at Salisbury (CA21). Unfortunately, the election was disputed, with a majority voting for Parry while the dean supported Joseph Corfe (see below). Parry and Corfe were both ex-choristers, and their rivalry was carried into the musical affairs of the town, freely reported in the pages of the *Salisbury Journal* (22 June, 20 August, 8 October 1781, and 4 November 1782).

Parry was a singer of some note, and was engaged as the solo bass by the Antient Concert in London in 1787. His mind became unbalanced towards the end of his life (Robertson 1938: 247).

Joseph Corfe 1792–1804 (b. Salisbury, 25 Dec. 1740; d. Salisbury, 29 July 1820). The Corfe family was connected with Salisbury Cathedral for 170 years. John Corfe (d. 1743), who seems to have come from Winchester, was admitted as a lay vicar (countertenor) on 24 June 1692 (CA19). He had a recognized agreement with Edward Thompson whereby he also taught the choristers for some years before August 1720, when he came under suspicion of being a Roman Catholic, and Thompson indicated that he would like to teach the boys himself. John Corfe then took oaths clearing himself of suspicion, but Thompson took over the choristers, and Corfe was admonished to execute his post of clerk of the Close in person (CA20). Even so, on 11 September 1721, after three admonitions, he was removed from this post also (CA20). Several members of the family became choristers and lay vicars choral between 1710 and 1759.

Our present subject was the grandson of this John Corfe. He was a chorister under Stephens, and then a lay vicar (1759), and, like Parry, he was paid extra 'upon account of his particular use and service in the choir'. He also enjoyed the patronage of James ('Hermes') Harris. No doubt he is the 'Mr Corfe, Salisbury', mentioned among the subscribers to Burney's *History of Music* in 1776.

As we have already noted (see above under Parry), Corfe was passed over in favour of Parry for the post of organist in 1781. Corfe, however, was appointed a gentleman of the Chapel Royal in February 1781 (CB2), and it was as a 'Gentleman of his Majesty's Chapel and Lay Vicar of Salisbury' that he subscribed to Arnold's *Cathedral Music* (1790). On Parry's death he was appointed organist and instructor of the choristers at Salisbury on 26 July 1792 (CA21), resigning this position in 1804. He is buried in the north-west transept of the Cathedral, and over his tomb (in front of the chapel of St Edmund Rich) there is the following inscription: 'Sacred to the memory of Joseph Corfe Senior Gentleman of his Majesty's Chapel Royal and Organist of this Cathedral. He died July 29th 1820 aged 79 years.'

Corfe was the author of a *Treatise on Singing* (1799) and *Thorough-bass simplified* (1805?).

Arthur Thomas Corfe 1804–63 (b. Salisbury, 9 Apr. 1773; d. Salisbury, 28 Jan. 1863). The third son of his predecessor, A. T. Corfe was a chorister of Westminster Abbey from 1783 under Benjamin Cooke, and had piano lessons from Clementi (autobiographical notes, Gu, MS R.d. 85). He was appointed to succeed his father as organist and 'layman' at Salisbury on 15 November 1804 (CA22). A tribute to his work appeared in *GM* (1813, p. 394). Some very readable reminiscences by John Harding, a Salisbury chorister at the time of Corfe, will be found in Robertson (1938: chap. 14).

Corfe was buried in the southern walk of the Cathedral cloisters; the memorial inscription on the wall recounts how he died while kneeling in prayer. Of his fourteen children, the eldest son, *John Davies Corfe, became organist of Bristol Cathedral; Joseph, his second son, became a chorister of Magdalen College, Oxford, took a first class in mathematics and physics, and went on to become chaplain of New College and priest-vicar choral of Exeter Cathedral; George, the fourth son, was likewise a chorister of Magdalen and then became a physician; and *Charles William Corfe, a much younger son, became organist of Christ Church, Oxford.

John Elliott Richardson 1863–81 (b. Salisbury). Richardson was a pupil of A. T. Corfe, and then his assistant organist for eighteen years. His appointment to succeed his master as organist was minuted on 5 March 1863 (CA25). His resignation in 1881 was on account of ill health. According to West (1921), he subsequently became organist of a Roman Catholic church in Bognor, Sussex. He was the author of *The Tour of a Cathedral Organist* (Salisbury, 1870).

BMB; West 1921.

Bertram Luard Selby 1881–3 (b. Ightham, Kent, 12 Feb. 1853; d. Glenford Brigg, Lincs., 26 Dec. 1918). Selby (usually referred to by the compound surname 'Luard Selby', with or without a hyphen) studied at the Leipzig Conservatory under Reinecke and Jadassohn. His first appointments were as organist of Highgate School and St Barnabas's Church, Marylebone, London in 1876. His appointment to Salisbury Cathedral was minuted on 20 April 1881.

After leaving Salisbury in 1883, he became organist of St John's Church, Torquay (1884) and then of St Barnabas's, Pimlico, London in 1886. He returned to cathedral work as organist of Rochester Cathedral in 1900, where he remained until his appointment as director of music at Bradfield College, Berkshire in 1916. He was the music editor of the 1904 edition of *Hymns Ancient and Modern*.

Grove[2]; *MT*, 46 (1908), 159; 60 (1919), 74.

Charles Frederick South 1883–1916 (b. London, 6 Feb. 1850; d. Salisbury, 12 Aug. 1916). South was a pupil in London of *George Cooper, and he was appointed organist of Aske's Hospital, Hoxton, London at the age of 16. In 1868 he became organist of St Augustine-with-St-Faith's Church (under the shadow of St Paul's Cathedral), where he remained until his appointment to Salisbury Cathedral, minuted on 9 July 1883. There is a memorial to him on the organ-case in the north choir aisle.

BMB; *MT*, 57 (1916), 412.

Sir Walter (Galpin) Alcock, MVO, 1917–47 (b. Edenbridge, Kent, 29 Dec. 1861; d. Salisbury, 11 Sept. 1947). Alcock was the son of a village schoolmaster who later became superintendent of the Metropolitan and City Police Orphanage, Twickenham, Middlesex. In 1875 he won a scholarship to the National Training School for Music (the precursor of the Royal College of Music), of which he was one of the first students, and where he studied under Sullivan and *John Stainer. In 1880 he became organist of St Mary's, Twickenham, and in 1886 he began to work as one of *J. F. Bridge's assistants at Westminster Abbey. From 1887 he combined this work with the post of organist of Quebec Chapel (now the church of the Annunciation, Bryanston Street), moving in 1895 to Holy Trinity, Sloane Street, and from there in 1902 to the Chapel Royal. He continued his work at the Abbey during all this time, and in 1896 he was appointed official assistant organist there by the Dean and Chapter. Meanwhile, from 1893, he had been on the staff of the Royal College of Music.

He played the organ at the Coronations of King Edward VII (1902) and King George V (1911), and took part again, by invitation, at that of King George VI (1937), when he contributed improvisations before, during, and after Parry's anthem 'I was glad', and again before and after the National Anthem.

At the end of 1916, possibly following some hint that he was not likely eventually to succeed Bridge as organist of Westminster Abbey, Alcock left London, and in January 1917 he became organist of Salisbury Cathedral, where he remained until his death. He retained his position at the Royal College of Music.

He took the FRCO diploma (1881) and the Durham degrees of B.Mus. (1896) and D.Mus. (1905). He was appointed MVO (5th class) following the Coronation of 1911, was promoted to the 4th class in 1917, and received a knighthood in the New Year Honours of 1933. He was one of the pre-eminent organ recitalists of his day. Like certain other organists (e.g., *J. C. Beckwith and *S. S. Wesley), he enjoyed a reputation for his improvisations, but he is perhaps unique in that some of these—namely, for the Coronation of King George VI—were recorded. He was an enthusiastic amateur engineer who built himself a primitive motor car and a model railway for his garden at Salisbury. His textbook, *The Organ* (1913), achieved a standard reputation.

Alcock submitted his resignation in June 1947 (CA35), and died three months later. He is buried in the Cathedral garth.

West 1921; *Grove*[3]; *MT*, 88 (1947), 317, 334; *Alcock of Salisbury* (privately printed family memoir, 1949); *WWW*, 1941–50.

Sir David (Valentine) Willcocks, CBE, MC, 1947–50. The minute appointing Willcocks as Alcock's successor is dated 29 July 1947.

See under King's College, Cambridge.

Douglas (Albert) Guest, CVO, 1950–7.

See under Westminster Abbey.

Christopher (Hugh) Dearnley 1957–68.

See under St Paul's Cathedral.

§Richard Godfrey) Seal, choirmaster and organist from 1968 (b. Banstead, Surrey, 4 Dec. 1935). Seal was a chorister of New College, Oxford under *H. K. Andrews, and then won a music scholarship to Cranleigh School. From 1954 to 1957 he was organ scholar of Christ's College, Cambridge, following which he studied for a year with a scholarship at the Royal College of Music. He took the Cambridge degrees of BA (1957) and MA (1961), having read music, and the FRCO diploma (1958). During his year at the Royal College of Music he was assistant organist at the Kingsway Hall, London, and from 1960 to 1961 he was assistant organist at St Bartholomew the Great, London. Immediately before his appointment to Salisbury Cathedral he was assistant organist of Chichester Cathedral, 1961–8.

SHEFFIELD

The Cathedral Church of St Peter and St Paul

On the establishment of the diocese of Sheffield in 1914, the ancient parish church of the city became the Cathedral. Among the earlier organists of Sheffield Parish Church of any note are **Robert Bennett** (d. 1819), father of Sir William Sterndale Bennett, ***John Camidge** (only briefly), **Joseph Bottomley**, who was appointed, in his own words, with 'a liberal salary' (Gu, MS R.d. 85), and **E. H. Lemare**, who was organist from 1886 to 1892. By a fascinating incident of history, the organists of Sheffield Parish Church and Cathedral are unique in being appointed by a corporate body, the Twelve Capital Burgesses, which is distinct from that of the Cathedral, though in this matter acting in consultation with it.

In the late Middle Ages the income from certain property was used to repair the church, to care for bridges and ways, and to relieve poverty in the town of Sheffield, and by 1538 or 1539 part of it began to be used to sustain three priests to assist the vicar of Sheffield. This caused the endowment to be deemed within the provisions of the Chantries Act of 1547, and it was therefore forfeit to the Crown under Edward VI. But, following a petition, it was restored by Mary I, who went so far as to place it on a formal and permanent footing in letters patent of 8 June 1554 (Hunter 1819: 239–43). This vested it in a body created for the purpose and entitled 'Duodecim Capitales Burgenses et Communitas villae et parochiae de Sheffield', who were to apply the income in maintaining three priests to conduct divine worship, celebrate the Sacrament, 'aliaque ad divinum cultum necessaria in ecclesia parochiali'. Any surplus was to go towards repairs to the church, care of bridges and ways, and relief of poverty.

In changed conditions, the present income, administered under a scheme made by the Charity Commission, is applied in three ways: a fixed annual sum helps to maintain the fabric of the Cathedral; a contribution is made towards the stipend of the assistant clergy; and the organist is paid by the Capital Burgesses, in whose hands his appointment and, if necessary, his dismissal lie. One supposes this provision is an echo of the phrase 'other things necessary' for divine worship.

Thomas William Hanforth (1892) **1914–37** (b. Hunslet, Leeds, 6 Mar. 1867; d. Sheffield, 1948). Hanforth was a chorister in York Minster and a pupil of *W. H. Garland and *John Naylor. He was private organist to Archbishop Thomson of York, 1885–8, and became assistant organist of York Minster in 1891. He was appointed organist of Sheffield Parish Church in 1892, thus becoming the first organist of the Cathedral. At various times he was music master of the Yorkshire School for the Blind, York and bandmaster of the Sheffield Artillery Brigade. He took the Durham degree of B.Mus. in 1892, and the FRCO diploma in 1897. He was also Sheffield City organist, continuing in that post after retirement from the Cathedral.

West 1921; *MT*, 78 (1937), 635; Thornsby 1912.

(Reginald) Tustin Baker 1937–66 (b. Gloucester, 4 July 1900; d. near Sheffield, Dec. 1966). Baker was a chorister of Gloucester Cathedral, and then served his articles to *A. H. Brewer, whose assistant he became from 1920 to 1926. He then spent two years in the USA as organist of St Luke's Church, San Francisco before he succeeded *N. S. Wallbank as organist of Hexham Abbey in 1928. A year later he became organist of Halifax Parish Church, where he remained until his appointment to Sheffield Cathedral in 1937. He took the Durham degrees of B.Mus. (1924) and D.Mus. (1934), and held the FRCO diploma (1920). He died only a few days before his intended retirement, announced for the end of December 1966.

Information from Mrs R. Tustin Baker.

§Graham (Hedley) Matthews, organist and choirmaster from 1967 (informally known as master of the music) (b. London, 17 Oct. 1935). Matthews went to the Royal Academy of Music with a county scholarship in 1954, and completed his studies in 1961 after an interruption for National Service. He took the FRCO diploma in 1961, that of CHM (with the Brook prize) in 1962, and the London degree of B.Mus. in 1963. From 1958 to 1967 he was sub-organist of Winchester Cathedral, combining this work with teaching at Pilgrim's School, Winchester and elsewhere. Following his appointment to Sheffield Cathedral he was also city organist until that post fell into desuetude.

SOUTHWARK

The Cathedral and Collegiate Church of St Saviour and St Mary Overie

Before the Reformation, Southwark Cathedral was the collegiate church of the Augustinian priory of St Mary Overie. Following the dissolution of the monasteries, it became a parish church from 1541. After 1611 it had a complex history under the government of a body of trustees, but in 1898 it was raised to the status of a collegiate church in the diocese of Rochester. In 1905 it was inaugurated as the Cathedral of the new diocese of Southwark.

Alfred Madeley Richardson (1897) **1898–1908** (b. Southend-on-Sea, Essex, 1 June 1868; d. New York, 23 July 1949). After some time at the Royal College of Music, Richardson went up to Oxford as organ scholar of Keble College in 1886. He took the Oxford degrees of B.Mus. (1888), BA (1890), MA (1892), and D.Mus. (1896), and he also held the FRCO diploma. On coming down from Oxford he was appointed organist of Hindlip Church, near Worcester in 1889, moving from there to London, first as organist of Holy Trinity, Sloane Street (1891), and then of St Jude's, Gray's Inn Road (1892). In 1892 he became organist of All Saints', Scarborough, where he remained until his appointment to Southwark a year before the church was granted collegiate status.

An interesting feature of his regime at Southwark was his idea of illustrating the various moods in the Psalms by means of organ interludes played between verses as appropriate (see his *Southwark Psalter*). He left Southwark to become organist of St Paul's Church, Baltimore, USA, in 1909, and moved to Trinity Church, Rhode Island a year later. From 1912 he taught at the Juilliard School of Music, New York.

BMB; West 1921; *Grove*[3]; *MT*, 90 (1949), 291; Drennan 1970.

Edgar Tom Cook, CBE, 1909–53 (b. Worcester, 18 Mar. 1880; d. Chipstead, Surrey, 5 Mar. 1953). Cook was educated at the Royal Grammar School,

Worcester, and was a pupil of *Hugh Blair and *Ivor Atkins at Worcester Cathedral. His first organ post was at St Oswald's, Worcester (1893), followed by St Leonard's, Newland, near Malvern (1897); at that time St Leonard's, which had a strong plainsong tradition, had its own choir school. From 1904 Cook was also assistant organist of Worcester Cathedral. He left both these posts when he was appointed to Southwark Cathedral in 1909, remaining there until his death.

He took the Oxford degree of B.Mus. in 1905, and held the FRCO diploma. He taught for many years at the Royal College of Music, where he was in charge of the choir-training class. After twenty-five years at Southwark he received the Lambeth degree of D.Mus. in 1934, and in 1949 he was appointed CBE. Even in the crowded musical life of London he achieved a place for the performances of his Special Choir in the Cathedral. He occupies a small niche in the early history of sound broadcasting: in the late 1920s and early 1930s his weekly midday organ recitals were the first extended series to make organ music known through the BBC. He wrote a useful small book, *The Use of Plainsong*.

Grove[3]; *MT*, 94 (1953), 185; *WWW*, 1951–60.

Sidney (Scholfield) Campbell, MVO, 1953–6.

See under St George's Chapel, Windsor.

§**Harold Dexter 1956–68** (b. Leicester, 7 Oct. 1920). Dexter went to Corpus Christi College, Cambridge in 1939 from Wyggeston Grammar School, Leicester. He had been a chorister in Leicester Cathedral, and a pupil there of *G. C. Gray. At Cambridge he was John Stewart of Rannoch scholar in sacred music, taking the degrees of BA and Mus.B. in 1942, and proceeding MA in 1946. He holds the diplomas of FRCO (1940) and ADCM (1948).

Dexter was organist of Louth Parish Church, Lincolnshire, 1946–9, and then of Holy Trinity, Leamington Spa (in succession to *W. Stanley Vann) from 1949 to 1956. While at Southwark he joined the staff of the Guildhall School of Music, becoming head of the general musicianship department. He continued in this post after leaving the Cathedral.

§**Ernest Herbert Warrell 1968–75** (b. London, 23 June 1915). Warrell attended Loughborough School, London, 1927–31, and was meanwhile a junior exhibitioner of Trinity College of Music, 1927–9. He did not enter the musical profession immediately, but in 1938 he became articled assistant to E. T. Cook at Southwark Cathedral. He was sub-organist there from 1946 to 1954, and then became organist of St Mary's, Primrose Hill, London (1954–9) and St John the Divine, Kennington (1961–8). From 1953 he has been organist of King's College, London and lecturer in music in its theological department. He was made a fellow of the College in 1979. (See Addenda, p. 434.)

§**Harry (Wakefield) Bramma 1976–89** (b. Shipley, Yorks., 11 Nov. 1936). From Bradford Grammar School, and after organ lessons from *Melville Cook, Bramma went up to Pembroke College, Oxford as organ scholar, 1955–60. There he took the honour school of music and the degree of BA in 1958 (later

MA), followed by the honour school of theology in 1960. In 1958 he took the FRCO diploma with the Harding prize. His first post was as director of music at King Edward VI Grammar School, Retford, and then from 1963 to 1976 he was assistant organist of Worcester Cathedral and director of music at King's School there. He left Southwark Cathedral in March 1989 to succeed *Lionel Dakers as director of the Royal School of Church Music.

§**Peter (Michael) Wright, organist from 1989** (b. Barnet, Herts., 6 Mar. 1954). From Highgate School, where he was a music scholar, Wright won an organ exhibition to the Royal College of Music, and afterwards became organ scholar of Emmanuel College, Cambridge (1973–6), where he read music and took the degree of BA (subsequently MA) followed by the postgraduate certificate in education. He holds the FRCO and CHM diplomas (1972, 1973). From 1977 until taking up his post at Southwark he was sub-organist of Guildford Cathedral and also taught at Guildford Royal Grammar School.

SOUTHWELL

The Cathedral Church of St Mary the Virgin

(formerly a Collegiate Church, Southwell Minster)

Main sources in this section (1965):

CA9	Chapter Register 1558–90 (MS 9).
CA10	Chapter Register 1590–1616 (MS 10).
CA11a	Chapter Book, 1660–1727 (MS 11a, formerly 6).
CA11	Chapter Minute Book, 1671–94 (MS 11).
CA12	Decree Book, 1727–84 (MS 12, formerly 7).
CA13	Decree Book, 1784–1814 (MS 13).
CA14	Decree Book, 1814–38 (MS 14).
CA15	Decree Book, 1838–72 (MS 15).
PR	Registers of baptisms, marriages, and burials (some printed in Phillimore's Parish Register Series).

St Mary's Collegiate Church, Southwell was one of three such medieval foundations in the diocese of York, having been founded during the tenth century by Archbishop Oskytel. For some reason the College surrendered unnecessarily to Henry VIII in August 1540, but this seems to have been recognized as a mistake, and it was refounded in 1543 by Act of Parliament, and Henry acquired credit as its founder. However, like its sisters of Beverley and Ripon, it fell again during the first year of King Edward VI under the Chantries Act of 1547, and the building was secured by the citizens as a parish church. Under Philip and Mary it was for a second time restored by Act of Parliament (1557), and statutes were promulgated by Elizabeth I on 2 April 1585. In 1841, by a deplorable decision ostensibly based on the need to provide finance for the new dioceses of Manchester and Ripon, it was decreed that the College should expire on the death of its last surviving prebendary, which took place in 1873. No part of its funds was, in fact, transferred to Manchester or Ripon, though Southwell retained nothing. By the time the diocese of Southwell was created in 1884, the church had become simply parochial on the expiry of the College, and, notwithstanding its history it now ranks as a 'parish-church cathedral' under a provost rather than a dean. Nevertheless, for present purposes I have ignored the short break in its constitutional history, 1873–84, and have treated it on the same footing as Manchester and Ripon, that is to say, as a collegiate church refounded after the dissolution of the chantries and eventually becoming a bishop's see.

The Elizabethan statutes, which held good until 1873, are recorded by Dickinson (1787). The choral foundation included six choristers under a master designated 'magister et rector chori', who was also to play the organ. We can thus assume that, from the time of the post-Reformation refoundation, the masters of the choristers were also organists. A former honorary librarian of the Minster, Mr R. M. Beaumont, has noted, unfortunately without references, that in 1540 the organist was **John Hutchinson**. The earliest mention of an organist in the records, however, is that of George Thetford (see below).

George Thetford 1568–? On 28 December 1568 (CA9) George Thetford, master of the choristers, was granted an annuity of £15 for life in consideration of his faithful service 'already done and to be done in future'. On 26 June 1577 he was admitted as vicar choral.

John Mud(d) 1582–?1583. 'John Mud laicus' was formally admitted master of the choristers on 7 July 1582 (CA9). There are no signatures in the records, or entries in PR, which can help to establish his relationship to the other Mudds in this book; but it could well be that he was the John Mudd who became organist of Peterborough Cathedral in the last quarter of 1583 (q.v.).

Thomas Foster 1584–?1586. 'Thomas Foster laicus' was formally admitted both singingman and master of the choristers on 18 July 1584 (CA9).

William Colberke 1586–?. Colberke, who was also described as 'laicus', was similarly admitted on 20 December 1586 (CA9). A. Smith (1964), who uses the form 'Colbeck', says that someone with this name was a lay clerk of Norwich Cathedral in 1581.

John Beeston ←1594–c.1595. When Beeston was admitted singingman on 2 January 1589/90 (CA9), there was no mention of his appointment as master of the choristers. However, on 28 January 1594/5 (CA10), when he was described as 'one of the singers and master of the choristers', he was admonished 'that he do from henceforth order and teach and instruct the choristers in his charge more diligently that he hath done upon pain to be removed from the charge of them'. A. Smith (1964) notes that a man of this name was a singingman of King's College, Cambridge, 1580–8.

Edward Manestie 1596–1617 (d. Southwell, Aug. 1617). Manestie had previously been master of the Magnus Song School at Newark-on-Trent (Jackson 1964: 72).

On Manestie's appointment to Southwell, the work of organist (combined with that of singingman) was treated as independent of that of master of the choristers, and he was admitted to each separately on 6 April 1596, with a salary of £10 for each post (CA10). Three years later he was appointed receiver-general of the College, but trouble arose, and on 27 November 1604 he was dismissed from that post. A Chapter minute dated 7 January 1604/5 recounts not only how he had been absent and inefficient in teaching the boys, but also that he had embezzled Chapter funds. In the absence of further records, one assumes that he continued in office until his death. He was buried on 21 August 1617 (PR).

Francis Dodgson ?1617–22 (d. Southwell, Dec. 1622). After 1616 there is a break in the Chapter Acts. All we know about Dodgson is an entry in PR of the interment of 'Francis Dodgson, organist of Southwell', on 7 December 1622. Note the similarity of surname to that of one who briefly officiated as organist of Durham Cathedral *c.*1612–13 (q.v.).

John Hutchinson ?1622–?1634. For the same reason, all we know of Hutchinson is that on 23 November 1628 'John Hutchinson, organist', married Anne Tytan (PR). He was still at Southwell in January 1633/4, for the 18th of that month his daughter Bridget was baptized. This is compatible with, if short of proof of, his having been the same man as the John Hutchinson who was appointed organist of York Minster in March 1634 (q.v.).

Edward Chappell ?1661–?1689. James (1927: 60) cites a payment to Edward Chappell, 'organist', on 31 May 1661, but I have not found the source of this statement. Note, however, that CA11a, which is silent about the post of organist at this period, records the appointment on 20 July 1661 of Edward Chappell, *clericus*, as vicar choral. On 12 March 1657/8, during the Interregnum, an E. Chappell and a G. Chappell had received 27*s.* 6*d.* and 25*s.* respectively from the Trustees for the Maintenance of Ministers (Matthews 1948).

George Chappell 1689–96. Chappell is a common surname in the Southwell records at this time. There is one George Chappell, *clericus*, who became a vicar choral on 10 October 1663, and another George Chappell, *literatum*, son of Edward Chappell, *clericus*, who was admitted singingman on 13 August 1664 (CA11a). Probably it was that second George who, by Chapter decree of 15 August 1689, was appointed organist, master, and *rector chori* (CA11). On 14 November 1695 (CA11a) it was arranged that he should give up his post because of ill health, but 'in consideration of his former good service to this church' he was granted the pay of a singingman (£10) for life. Meanwhile, one William Clay, 'an assistant in the choir', was made acting organist. A little later, on 31 January 1695/6 (CA11a), it was decided that 'if Mr Chappell the organist chance to die', his singingman's place should go to the new organist.

William Popely (I) 1696–1718 (d. Southwell, May 1718). A Chapter minute of 11 June 1696 (CA11a) decreed that 'Mr William Popely succeed Mr George Chappell in his organist's, rector chori and singingman's place . . . paying to William Clay five pounds per annum as his assistant'. Popely apparently came from Rochester, where the Chapter had made him a present of 10*s*. to encourage him 'in his learning to play on the organs' (Rochester CA2, 10 October 1679), and subsequently apprenticed him to *Daniel Henstridge (ibid., ff. 14, 40). His apprenticeship expired at Christmas 1683, and he is last mentioned at Rochester at the November audit in 1684.

William Clay was probably not so much assistant organist as a deputy in the choir, for on 10 October 1716 (CA11a) it was ordered that Cornelius Neep should be 'Mr Popely's substitute as to his singingman's place' for the sum of £5.

Popely was buried in the Minster, where the south aisle merges into the transept, on 30 May 1718 (PR).

William Popely (II) 1718–21 (d. Southwell, Oct. 1722). William Popely 'junior' was admitted a singingman on 10 October 1716 (CA11a). New dispositions were made on his father's death: Cornelius Neep succeeded the elder Popely as singingman; Robert Dring became *rector chori* and master of the organists; and the younger Popely was appointed organist, retaining his singingman's place but paying Robert Clay £5 per annum to deputize for him (CA11a). William Popely (II) was buried at Southwell on 21 October 1722 (PR).

There was another son of the elder Popely, Joseph by name, who was admitted chorister of Southwell on 24 April 1712. It may have been he who, as 'Mr Popely, organist at Bishop's Stortford', subscribed for two copies of A. Scarlatti's *Thirty Six Ariettas*, published in London *c.*1755.

William Lee 1721–54 (d. Southwell, Jan. 1754). Lee's appointment (CA11a, 20 April 1721) was initially on the same terms as that of William Popely (II). But on 22 July 1725 it was arranged that he should have the full pay of his singingman's place, the Chapter henceforth paying the deputy. He was a subscriber to Croft's *Musica Sacra* in 1724. On 21 October 1725 Lee was chosen as auditor of the church, but it was decided that the extra £5 accruing from the July 1725 arrangement should be reduced to £3. In April 1733 Dring, who had been *rector chori* since 1718, gave up his post, and the office was once more united with that of organist (CA12).

Lee was buried in the north transept of the Minster on 10 January 1754 (PR).

Samuel Wise 1754–5. The minute of Wise's appointment as organist, *rector chori*, auditor, and probationer singingman is dated 24 January 1754 (CA12). Like Edward Manestie, he had been master of the Magnus Song School (Jackson 1964: 199). It has been stated that after leaving Southwell he became organist of

St Mary's Church, Nottingham; certainly a 'Mr Sam. Wise, Organist, Nottingham', was among the subscribers to Burney's *History of Music* (1776). A Mr Wise had also been a junior vicar and temporary organist of Lincoln Cathedral in 1733 (q.v.).

Edmund Ayrton 1755–64 (bapt. Ripon, 19 Nov. 1734; d. Westminster, 22 May 1808). Edmund was the younger brother of *William Ayrton, organist of Ripon Minster. When he was appointed organist and *rector chori* of Southwell on 23 October 1755, the curious provision was made that 'he get [*sic*] all the services and anthems usually sung in this church before this time twelve months'. Like his recent predecessors, he was also auditor and singingman (CA12). On 22 April 1756 the Chapter granted him leave to go to London 'for three months for further instructions by Mr Nares the organist'. While at Southwell he married Ann Clay on 20 September 1762, and Elizabeth, the first of their fourteen children, was born there in July 1763 (PR). Their son William Ayrton (FRS and FSA, 1777–1858) became a well-known writer on music, and their grandson Dr John Ayrton Paris (1785–1856) was president of the Royal College of Physicians of England.

Ayrton moved to London on his appointment as gentleman of the Chapel Royal in 1764. He combined this post with that of vicar choral of St Paul's Cathedral (1767) and then with that of lay vicar of Westminster Abbey (1780). From 1780 to 1805 he was master of the children of the Chapel Royal in succession to James Nares. J. S. Bumpus (1972: ii. 568) refers to certain memoranda, *c.*1785 (at one time belonging to W. H. Cummings), which state that the boys of the Chapel Royal complained that Ayrton (with whom they boarded) starved them: 'The parents took it up, and complained by petition to the Bishop of London, and said that if he did not redress them they would go to the king. The Bishop made enquiry, and found, on Dr Ayrton's bringing the weekly accounts of meat, that they had very sufficient provision.' Ayrton took the Cambridge degree of Mus.D. in 1784 (*Venn*). He subscribed to the second edition (1788) of Boyce's *Cathedral Music*, to Arnold's *Cathedral Music* (1790), and to the collections of W. Hayes (1795) and Dupuis (1797). He died on 22 May 1808, and was buried in the cloisters of Westminster Abbey.

GM, 1800, i. 470; Chester 1876.

Thomas Spofforth 1764–1818 (d. Southwell, May 1826, aged 84). Spofforth's appointment as organist, *rector chori*, singingman, and auditor was minuted on 12 April 1764 (CA12). When he retired in July 1818 he was allowed £25 per annum 'in consequence of his long and faithful services in the choir' (CA14). A board in the south transept of the Minster records his considerable benefactions for educating and clothing children, for bread for the poor at Christmas and Easter, and for coals for the poor at Christmas. He was buried in the Minster yard on 16 May 1826. His two nephews, Reginald and *Samuel Spofforth, were choristers under him.

Edward Heathcote 1818–35 (d. Southwell, Jan. 1835, aged 38). Heathcote was appointed organist, *rector chori*, and singingman on the same day as Spofforth's pension was granted; the minute does not mention the auditorship. At the same time it was ordered 'that the organist be authorized to require the attendance of the singingmen for their instruction and improvement in music once at least in every week for one hour immediately after morning service'.

Heathcote was buried on 28 January 1835. When his successor was appointed on 23 April 1835, Heathcote was referred to as 'our late highly respected and lamented organist' (CA14).

Frederick Gunton 1835–40 (b. Norwich, 1813; d. Chester, 1888). West (1921) notes that Gunton was a pupil of Alfred Pellet, organist of St Peter Mancroft, Norwich. Gunton was appointed organist of Southwell Minster in April 1835, and moved to Chester Cathedral at Michaelmas 1840 (q.v.) at the instance, it has been stated, of Anson, prebendary of Southwell, who became Dean of Chester in 1839. On his retirement from Chester in 1877 Gunton was granted the title of honorary organist (Chester CA6).

Dickson (1894) described him as 'a good musician and sound player of the "middle period" between manual organs and pedal organs', and stated that 'under his management the Chester services were orderly and careful; the choir, though numerically weak, was of good quality'.

Chappell Batchelor 1841–57 (b. Southwell, June 1822; d. Derby, 11 Jan. 1884). Batchelor was baptized in Southwell Minster on 1 July 1822; his father was an apothecary (PR). During the three months between Heathcote's death and Gunton's appointment he had acted as organist, and the Chapter ordered that the pay for that period should be granted to 'Chappell Batchelor, aged 12 years, for his exemplary conduct, as well as for the singular musical talent with which he has . . . supplied the vacancy'. He went to the Royal Academy of Music as a scholar in 1838. Stephens (1882) informs us that Batchelor also studied under Vincent Novello.

His appointment as organist, *rector chori*, and auditor was minuted on 21 January 1841. He resigned in 1857 and (according to Stephens) moved to Belper and Derby. James (1927: 74) notes that his name is cut into the stone parapet of the pulpitum at Southwell.

By the time of Batchelor's departure, the Collegiate Church was already running out its appointed time (see the introductory notes to this section). Though the Chapter records continue to 1872, no further appointments as organist were recorded by capitular minute, and other written records, so far as I have been able to discover, fail us. Batchelor was followed, it seems, by **Herbert Stephens Irons**, the last organist of the College, who held office (according to James 1927) from 1864 to 1875, though Stephens and *BMB* give 1857–72. Details about him will be found in *MT* (46 (1905), 534, 596). After leaving Southwell he was assistant organist of Chester Cathedral, 1873–5, and from then until his death in 1905, organist of St Andrew's, Nottingham. He was followed as parish organist by Cedric Bucknall, B.Mus. (Oxon.) (1872–6, according to West 1921; 1875–7, according to W. A. James), and William Weaver Ringrose, B.Mus. (Oxon.) (1876–9, according to West 1921; 1877–81, according to James).

Arthur (or W.) Marriott 1879 or 1881–8. West (1921) states that Arthur Marriott was appointed organist in 1879; James (1927) speaks of 'W. Marriott', appointed in 1881. Both agree that he resigned in 1888 and went to North America. On the establishment of the see of Southwell, he became the first organist of the Cathedral.

Robert William Liddle 1888–1917 (b. Durham, 14 Mar. 1864; d. Southwell, 23 Dec. 1917). Liddle was a chorister in Durham Cathedral and a pupil of *Philip Armes. Before his appointment to Southwell he was organist of St Baldred's Church, North Berwick.

BMB; West 1921.

Harry William Tupper 1918–29 (b. Dartford, Kent; d. 1929). Tupper's earliest appointments were as organist of St Peter's Church, Staines (1889) and the parish churches of Bishop's Stortford (1891) and Burton-on-Trent (1898). In 1904 he became acting organist and master of the choristers of Lichfield Cathedral. In 1917 he was appointed organist of Hexham Abbey. He held the FRCO diploma, and took the Oxford degree of B. Mus. in 1899.

Thornsby 1912; West 1921.

George Thomas Francis 1929–46 (d. Southwell, June 1946). Francis was pupil and assistant under *E. C. Bairstow at Wigan, Leeds, and York. He was organist to the Cowley Fathers, Oxford and music master of Ardingly College, Sussex before his appointment to Southwell. He held the FRCO diploma.

MT, 87 (1946), 289.

Robert James Ashfield 1946–56.

See under Rochester Cathedral.

Sir David (John) Lumsden 1956–9.

See under New College, Oxford.

§Kenneth (Bernard) Beard 1959–88 (b. Royton, Lancs., 9 June 1927). After attending Kingswood School, Bath, Beard studied at the University of Manchester and the Royal Manchester College of Music, 1946–9, taking the degree of Mus.B. in 1949. He then went to Cambridge as organ scholar of Emmanuel College, 1949–52, and read for part II of the music tripos. He took the Cambridge degrees of BA (1951) and MA (1955). He also holds the FRCO (1948) and CHM (1954) diplomas.

His first appointment was as choirmaster and organist of St Michael's College, Tenbury Wells, Worcestershire, 1952–9, where he had charge of the music at the time of the College's centenary celebrations. On retirement from Southwell at the end of December 1988 he accepted the post of organist of Mold Parish Church, Cheshire.

§Paul (Robert) Hale, organist and *rector chori* from 1989 (b. Crouch End, Hornsey, London, 4 Mar. 1952). After holding a music scholarship at Solihull School, Hale became organ scholar of New College, Oxford, 1971–4, reading music and taking the degrees of BA (1974) and MA (1979). He took the postgraduate certificate in education from Westminster College, Oxford in 1975. He then taught at Tonbridge School and, while there, obtained the FRCO diploma (1979). From 1982 until taking up his post at Southwell he was assistant organist of Rochester Cathedral and assistant director of music at King's School. He contributed the section on the College music in J. Buxton and P. Williams (eds.), *New College, Oxford, 1379–1979* (Oxford, 1979).

TRURO

The Cathedral Church of St Mary

The diocese of Truro was established in 1877. A new cathedral was built, incorporating an aisle of St Mary's Parish Church, which was consecrated in 1887. The first organist appears to have been appointed in 1880, but Chapter minutes and the register of appointments to offices exist only from the year 1888.

George Robertson Sinclair 1880–9.

See under Hereford Cathedral.

Mark James Monk 1890–1920 (b. Hunmanby, Yorks., 16 Mar. 1858; d. Blackheath, Kent, 5 May 1929). M. J. Monk was a chorister and pupil at York Minster under *E. G. Monk. He was not related to his master, whose niece, however, he married. In 1879 he became organist of St John's Church, Ladywood, Birmingham; he then moved to Ashby de la Zouch Parish Church (1880) and Banbury Parish Church before his appointment to Truro. He took the Oxford degrees of B.Mus. (1878) and D.Mus. (1888), and held the FRCO diploma.

BMB; *MT*, 70 (1929), 559.

Hubert Stanley Middleton 1920–6.

See under Trinity College, Cambridge.

Sir John Dykes Bower, CVO, 1926–9.

See under St Paul's Cathedral, London.

§(Francis) Guillaume Ormond 1929–70 (b. San Remo, Italy, 27 Jan. 1896; d. Truro, Feb. 1971). Ormond was born of Swiss and American parentage; his mother was the sister of John Singer Sargent, RA. From an early age, however, his home was in London. He was educated at Westminster School, and then, after studying for a time at the Royal College of Music, he went up to Exeter College, Oxford in 1915. Before his own career was interrupted by war-service, he acted as College organist while the organ scholar was in the services. He became a naturalized British citizen in 1916, with Robert Erskine Childers, the Irish patriot, as one of the sponsors for his application. He took the Oxford degrees of BA (1922) and MA (1964).

While a student at the Royal College of Music, he was for a short time organist of Beaconsfield Parish Church and also assistant at St Michael's, Cornhill, London. After leaving Oxford he became organist and choirmaster of Lady Craven's Choir School, Ashdown, Shrivenham (1923–4). He was then assistant organist at Chester Cathedral (1925–6) and at Ely Cathedral (1927–9). He took up his post at Truro in September 1929, and retired at the end of 1970.

John (Charles) Winter 1971–88 (b. Bungay, Suffolk, 19 June 1923). Winter was educated at Bungay Grammar School and the Royal College of Music. In 1949 he became director of music at Truro Cathedral School, becoming also assistant organist of the Cathedral slightly later. He took up duty as Cathedral organist in January 1971, and retired at the end of 1988.

§David (John) Briggs, master of the choristers and organist from 1989 (b. Bromsgrove, Worcs., 1 Nov. 1962). Before leaving Solihull School, Briggs had obtained the FRCO diploma with the Limpus and four other prizes (1980). He was then organ student at King's College, Cambridge, 1981–4, holding also the John Stewart of Rannoch scholarship in sacred music from 1982. He read music and took the degrees of BA (1984) and MA (1988). From 1985 to the end of 1988 he was assistant organist of Hereford Cathedral.

WAKEFIELD

The Cathedral Church of All Saints

All Saints' Parish Church became a cathedral when the diocese of Wakefield was founded in 1888.

Joseph Naylor Hardy (1886) **1888–1930**. Hardy was a pupil of J. Emmerson, his predecessor at Wakefield Parish Church, and he also studied under *William Creser. He was appointed organist of Wakefield Parish Church in 1886, so he also became the first organist of the Cathedral. He had held earlier posts at the Roman Catholic Church, Wakefield (1875) and West Parade Chapel, Wakefield

(1878). He was organist only at the Cathedral; Matthew Henry Peacock, MA, D.Mus. (Oxon.) was the choirmaster.

West 1921.

Newell Smith Wallbank 1930–45 (b. Oakworth, Yorks., 26 Apr. 1875; d. Wakefield, 23 June 1945). Wallbank was an articled pupil of *E. J. Crow at Ripon Cathedral. He was organist of All Souls' Church, Leeds from some date before 1911, Hexham Abbey, 1911–17, St Margaret's, Alttingham, 1917–18, Hexham Abbey again, 1918–26, Lancaster Priory, 1926–8, and Scarborough Parish Church, 1928–30, before his appointment as both organist and choirmaster of Wakefield Cathedral. He held these latter posts from 1930 until his death.

Information from the Revd Dr N. S. Wallbank.

§Percy (George) Saunders 1946–70 (b. London, 17 Feb. 1902; d. Wakefield, 18 Apr. 1970). Saunders was educated at the County High School, Ilford, Essex and the Royal College of Music. After posts at St Mary's, Ilford (1920–3), Ilford Parish Church (1923–8), and Melton Mowbray Parish Church (1928–30), he moved to Doncaster Parish Church to succeed *H. A. Bennett. He was appointed to Wakefield Cathedral in 1946. Together with his organ posts at Doncaster and Wakefield, he was director of music at Silcoates School, Wakefield.

Saunders took the FRCO diploma and the London degree of B.Mus. in 1923, proceeding to the D.Mus. degree in 1928.

§Jonathan (Leonard) Bielby, organist from 1970 (b. Oxford, 23 Nov. 1944). Bielby attended Magdalen College School, Oxford and then went up to St John's College, Cambridge as organ student, 1963–7. At Cambridge he read music and took the degrees of BA (1966), Mus.B. (1967, with distinction in organ performance), and MA (1970). He took the FRCO diploma in 1963. After leaving Cambridge he was assistant organist of Manchester Cathedral, 1968–70. Concurrently with his present post he was borough organist of Kirklees (Huddersfield Town Hall), 1974–88, and from 1979 he has been lecturer at the City of Leeds College of Music.

WELLS

The Cathedral Church of St Andrew

(Diocese of Bath and Wells)

Main sources in this section (1965):

Chapter Acts

CA1	1571–99 (Letter 'H').
CA2	1591–1607 (drafts).
CA3	1608–22.
CA4	1622–35.
CA5	1635–45.
CA6	1664–6.
CA7	1666–83; Bailey, D. S. (ed.), *Wells Cathedral Chapter Act Book 1666–83* (Somerset Record Society, 1973).
CA8	1683–1705.
CA9	1705–25.
CA10	1726–44.
CA11	1744–60.
CA12	1761–77.
CA13	1777–92.
CA14	1792–1817.
CA15	1817–32.

Chapter Minutes

1831–7, 1837–49, 1849–59, 1860–72, 1873–86, 1886–92, 1893–1909.

Vicars Choral Acts

VCA	1541–93; calendared by L. S. Colchester (privately printed, Wells, 1986).

Accounts

Communar's accounts for years ending at Michaelmas are extant from 1327–8. Those consulted for present purposes run from 1537–8 to 1680–1. They survive in three forms, each of them with sundry gaps, and do not form a single series. In both the rolls and books, references to the organist are usually to be traced in the sections devoted to the revenues of Biddisham.

Ac(r)	Fair copies in roll-form.
Ac(b)	Fair copies in book-form.
Ac(nb)	Rough notebooks.

Miscellaneous

Cal.	Various documents as quoted in Baildon, W. P., *Calendar of the Manuscripts of the Dean and Chapter of Wells*, ii (Historical Manuscripts Commission, 1914).
PS	Parliamentary survey of Cathedral property, 1649 (DD/CC, 111733 (Chapter records), Somerset County Record Office, Taunton).

The first Bishop of Wells was consecrated in 909. In 1090 the see was transferred to Bath, but from 1136 the church of Wells was recognized jointly with the cathedral priory of Bath, and from 1245 the Chapters of Bath and Wells alternately exercised the right to elect the bishop. The priory of Bath was dissolved in 1539, from which time Wells Cathedral has been the sole see of the Bishops of Bath and Wells.

Wells Cathedral had its College of Vicars Choral, the former residences of which, with hall and chapel, survive today as the most picturesque example of buildings associated with such a college. A charter of incorporation was secured in the fourteenth century, but for the removal of doubts, a confirmatory charter was granted by Elizabeth I in 1592. There was no requirement that vicars must be ordained (though for practical purposes some must have been in holy orders), only that they were to be 'sufficient, skilful, and suitable'. So, as at Exeter, laymen could be, and were, full members of the College.

At Wells, a cathedral of the Old Foundation, the post of organist developed out of practical requirements, without resting on any charter or foundation. Even in the post-Reformation charter granted to the Cathedral in 1591 by Elizabeth I (Reynolds 1881: 243–78) nothing was specified about either an organist or a master of the choristers. Very probably, the earliest organists were found within the existing ranks of the vicars choral. Later, although one or two of the organists were already vicars choral, it became usual for the organist to be made a member of the College of Vicars Choral, so acquiring a freehold and some remuneration from that status. This arrangement was maintained until the death of William Perkins in 1860.

Under the charter of incorporation, all vicars choral were to be admitted in the first place on a year's probation; and though the Dean and Chapter nominated the vicars, the College had the right of rejection both at the point of probation and that of 'perpetuation' a year later. In certain circumstances this gave the College an indirect veto on the appointment of an organist, but there is no instance of the rejection of a Chapter nominee, apart from an ineffectual individual protest in 1781.

For a long time Wells Cathedral continued to use the old terms (in Latin) of 'keeper of the organs' and 'keeping the organs' (derived from *custos organorum*) for organist and organ-playing.

Nicholas Prynne 1547–54. Prynne, a vicar choral who in 1550 was receiver-general of the College (VCA, f. 9), received remuneration 'pro custod: organ:' at the rate of 13*s.* 4*d.* a year in Ac(r) 1547–8, and Ac(b) 1549–50, 1550–1, and 1553–4, after which these records fail until 1556–7.

John Marker 1556–7. Payment to Marker as organist is found in Ac(b) 1556–7. He had been a vicar choral from January 1542/3 (VCA).

Robert Awman 1557–? In a notebook kept by the communar and marked on the cover '1556', there is a memorandum (f. 5ᵛ) stating that Robert Awman was admitted a vicar choral on 11 October 1557 and was allotted an inclusive stipend of £12 to cover his post as vicar, playing the organ, and instructing the choristers; in the same book (f. 7ᵛ), among a number of miscellaneous payments, there is a note of 20*s.* paid to Awman on that date for his expenses in coming to Wells ('pro expens: suis versus Well: ad mandat: decani et cap:'). This appears to reflect some decision to improve the remuneration of the organist and master of the choristers and to bring in a man from outside. But apart from a passing reference to Awman as an intermediary among a note of expenses incurred in 1558 (f. 8), his name is not found anywhere else, and there is no record of his admission or perpetuation as vicar choral in VCA. Ac(r) 1557–8 is imperfect.

William Lyde 1559–62. No accounts survive for 1558–9, but Ac(r) 1559–60 records payments to Lyde both for 'keeping' the organ and as Cathedral schoolmaster. Ac(r) 1560–1 shows payment to him for one quarter only as schoolmaster (in which office he was succeeded by Thomas Ellis) but he continued to be paid as organist up to Michaelmas 1562 (Ac(b) 1561–2). During his time as organist the repertory was extended. Ac(nb) 1559–61 records that in 1560–1 he was paid 1*s.* 1½*d.* 'for a good song, viz. Te Deum in English which he brought from Harforde [Hereford?]'; Alexander Ward, a vicar choral, received

3*s.* 4*d.* 'for songs which he brought from Gloucester and from Bristol'; while Lyde had eight quires of paper delivered 'to make books for to prick the same songs and others'.

Thomas Tanner 1562–? Tanner was admitted to probation as vicar choral on 29 November 1562, and is last mentioned as a vicar on 30 July 1564 (VCA). His inclusion in the list of organists rests on references in *Cal.* to accounts for 1562–3 and 1563–4 which I have been unable to verify. Ac(nb), labelled '1562', contains notes (ff. 21, 42) of gratuities to Thomas Tanner for unspecified purposes in those years, as well as of the cost of paper supplied to him, perhaps for music-copying.

Matthew Nailer 1568–? After a gap in the accounts, Ac(b) 1568–9 records payment to Nailer 'pro custod: organ:'. He had been a vicar choral from 6 November 1563 (VCA), and as he remained such until at least 1578, he may well have continued as organist also.

John Clerke 1587–91. The next available accounts are in Ac(r) 1587–8, which name Clerke (Clark) as keeper of the organ at £2 a year, along with Matthew Jefferies (a vicar choral) as master of the choristers at £20. He himself had been admitted vicar choral on 1 October 1585 (CA1, f. 32). He is named as organist in Ac(nb), labelled '1591', for the years 1590–1 and 1591–2, receiving an extra 6*s.* 8*d.* per quarter *ex gratia*. On 12 October 1591 he refused, under penalty, the office of escheator (CA2, ff. 85ᵛ, 86). He may well have continued as organist throughout the rest of his time as vicar choral, though we have no accounts to verify this. He was one of the vicars choral who voted for *John Farrant (I) in the dispute about Farrant's admission as perpetual vicar choral of Wells in 1595 (see p. 34). He is last heard of in 1606, when, as one of the principal vicars, he was suspended from his emoluments for refusing to admit *John Fido into the College of Vicars Choral; at the same time he was ordered to procure deacon's orders for himself (CA2, f. 193).

As both Farrant and Fido are known to have been organists at other cathedrals, and in the absence of evidence one way or another, one may speculate in passing whether their appearance among the vicars of Wells was connected in some way with the post of organist there.

James Weare 1608–?1613. Although Chapter Acts exist from 1577 onwards, Weare is the first organist of Wells Cathedral whose appointment is noted in them. He was admitted organist and began his year's probation as vicar choral on 1 October 1608, and was perpetuated as vicar on 2 October 1609 (CA3, ff. 12, 27).

Edmund Tucker 1613–14. Tucker was admitted vicar choral for the customary year's probation on 1 April 1613, when he was also appointed organist (CA3, f. 66ᵛ), but before the twelve months had expired, his successor in both capacities had been appointed. It is possible that he was the Edward (or Edmund) Tucker who became organist of Salisbury Cathedral in 1618 (q.v.).

Richard Browne 1614–?1620. Browne's admission as vicar choral and organist was minuted on 26 March 1614, and he was duly perpetuated one year later (CA3, ff. 84ᵛ, 103ᵛ).

John Okeover (or Oker) (1st tenure) **1620–42**; (2nd tenure) **1661–c.1662**. The surname of this musician takes two forms, apparently quite interchangeable. While the form 'Oker' predominates in clerks' and treasurers' documents at both Gloucester and Wells, his own numerous signatures at Wells (see Ac(nb) 1638–42) are invariably in the form of 'Okeover'. Is it possible that 'Oker' is a phonetic rendering?

This is presumably the John Okeover who had been in service as a domestic musician at Ingatestone Hall, Essex from 1616. (For a suggestion that before then he may have been organist of Winchester College, see p. 398.)

He was admitted vicar choral on probation and also organist of Wells Cathedral on 16 February 1619/20, and exactly a year later he was duly perpetuated as a vicar. As early as 12 February 1622/3 the precentor had complained to the dean that the choristers were not being taught properly, and in June 1625 Okeover was made master of the choristers in place of Walter Tailer (Ledger G, *Cal.*, 383). In 1633, described by Wood (1815–20: i. 468) as 'organist and vicar choral of the church of Wells', he took the Oxford degree of B.Mus. There is a faint suggestion that he was married by 1634, when the will of John Beaumont of Wells speaks of 'my daughter Elizabeth and her husband John Oker'. This is not necessarily our present subject, but, if it is, he had presumably been widowed by the time he married Mary Mills in 1642 (see below). Early in 1635 he was involved in a curious matter of liturgical observance, when he was charged with having given notice to the vicars choral, without first consulting the resident canons, that 'there should be no anthem sung instead of Nunc Dimittis or Benedictus but only according to the form of Common Prayer'. To this he replied that he had acted on the instruction of the bishop, given in the presence of 'Mr Doctor Wood'. Nevertheless, he was suspended as a vicar for a week (CA4, f. 168, 2 January 1634/5, endorsed in the margin on 20 March: 'Hoc actum delendum est de mandato domini decani' ('this act was expunged by order of the dean'))

He can be traced in the Wells CA and accounts up to 1641–2 (Ac(nb) 1638–42), when his quarterly stipends of 15*s*. as vicar choral and 10*s*. as organist are recorded. Ford (1957–8) notes that he signed for his dividend as a vicar choral as late as December 1642. At that point the name disappears from the Cathedral documents at Wells, which then fall silent early in 1645 until after the Restoration. But when the parliamentary commissioners made their survey of Cathedral property in 1649, they noted that the choristers' house was 'now in the occupation of the widow Oker'.

However, a certain John Okeover became organist of Gloucester Cathedral in April 1640, and archival records present an unresolved problem of identity. Further Gloucester detail (fully cited on p. 119) can be summarized thus: married Mary Mills in Gloucester, 1642, and had a son by her (John) baptized in Gloucester; joined the parliamentary army during the Civil War, and subsequently claimed some favourable consideration on that account; was resident in

Gloucester from 1649 up to at least 1659; shadowy hints that the Gloucester Cathedral authorities may have thought of him as still being their organist when services were resumed after the Restoration, though he did not in fact resume his duty; paid by Gloucester Cathedral in 1661–2 for writing out some organ-parts. This Gloucester episode, then, overlaps with Okeover's tenure as organist of Wells up to Michaelmas 1642.

Returning now to the archives at Wells, we find that from one quarter (presumably Midsummer to Michaelmas) of the accounting year 1660–1 (Ac(nb), *Cal.*, 431), Okeover was once again paid as organist of the Cathedral, and about two years later, in 'the humble petition of John Oker, organist' for arrears of certain monies, which speaks of a 'long and tedious sickness' (Deeds, 3rd series, *Cal.*, 433), he referred to his 'happy restoration' to his post there—a significant remark, unmistakably referring to a pre-Civil War tenure. There are no available accounts at Wells for 1661–2 and 1662–3, but, according to Ford (1957–8), his name is not on the list for vicars' dividend distribution in July 1663, and it is reasonable to assume that he was dead by then. In 1664–5 the accounts disclose a payment to Mary Oker (who signs thus) of £3. 15*s*. for her son John, one of the Wells choristers.

In attempting a speculative reconstruction from all this, it is possible to suppose, but not to prove, that we are dealing with one man only. For reasons unknown, he moved from Wells to Gloucester in 1640, perhaps, like Mudd at Peterborough and Lincoln (q.v.), making the best of two worlds—still qualifying, by virtue of his life tenure, for his dividend as a vicar choral of Wells, and leaving his widowed mother in occupation of the choristers' house. Given the imminent destruction of the organ and the suppression of Prayer Book worship, Wells Cathedral would not miss an organist. Meanwhile, he marries in Gloucester, goes off to the war, and resettles there until the Restoration. But instead of fulfilling Gloucester's expectation that he would resume office there at that point, he returns to Wells, where, covered by the confusion concerning cathedral bodies between 1645 and 1660, he succeeds in securing recognition of his entitlement to his former status, some part of which gave him a freehold. It is known that after his death, his widow, presumably the Mary whom he married at Gloucester (see above), remained at Wells with her son.

More evidence is needed, perhaps from signatures, wills, and Parish Registers, to confirm this. But Okeover's own petition establishes a link between the two periods at Wells, while the wife Mary represents a link between Gloucester and the second of these.

John Browne *c.*1662–74. Browne is named in accounts of one kind or another (*Cal.*, 434–43) from 1663–4 until 1673–4, when payment is shared between him and his successor. He was a vicar choral by April 1664 at the latest, when he was named as such in a roll-call (CA6).

West (1921) states that Browne was buried on 7 May 1674. Ac(nb) 1675–6 notes a payment of £11. 14*s*. as a gift to his widow Mary, together with £2. 10*s*. for the rent of her house.

John Jackson 1674–88 (d. Wells, 1688). Although the accounts for 1673–4 show the stipend of organist divided between Browne and Jackson, there was evidently a short gap before Jackson took over, as we gather from a belated entry in Ac(nb) 1677–8: '£5 to Mr Hall, late organist, for two months allowed him in the accounts for 1674'. This may indicate that Henry Hall (I), afterwards of Exeter and Hereford, was employed here briefly as acting organist.

Jackson himself was admitted as organist and vicar choral on 9 September 1674 (CA7). Various forms of accounts (*Cal.*, 444) from 1677–8 until 1680–1 show that for a time he was also master of the choristers. However, from a reference to 'Mr Gabriel Green, master of the boys' (CA8, 4 October 1683), it appears that he relinquished this part of his work. Ac(nb) 1680–1 shows that on 13 April 1681 the Chapter was pleased to give Jackson £1 for composing a Service and £1 as a reward, while on 22 October 1682 he was voted 40*s*. for his pains in securing Services for the choir (CA7).

He died in office. It should be noted that someone of the same name was master of the choristers of Ely Cathedral, 1669–70 (q.v.).

Robert Hodge 1688–90. Hodge's history before his appointment to Wells is of some interest. He had been a chorister of Exeter Cathedral, and on 6 October 1683 (Exeter CA8) the Dean and Chapter there approved an arrangement whereby he was to go to London to be taught 'by Dr [*John] Blow or some other person of the King's Chapel as Mr Dean shall think fit'. In the event, he worked under Henry Purcell, who (ibid., 13 December 1684) was allowed 30*s*. to buy a winter coat for his pupil. Later, while tactfully drawing attention to arrears of fees and expenses due to him, Purcell was to write to the Dean of Exeter on 2 November 1686: 'Compassion moves me to acquaint you of a great many debts Mr Hodge contracted whilst in London and to some who are so poor 'twere an act of charity as well as justice to pay them.' (Exeter Cathedral, Misc. Letters, 1; a photographic reproduction of Purcell's letter will be found in Westrup 1968.) As it happens, the Exeter authorities had dealt with this matter a few days earlier, and on 9 July 1687 they also 'ordered a debt of Robert Hodge's of forty shillings, at Wells, to be paid'. But they were ill requited for their generosity: on 3 March 1687/8 it was recorded that Hodge had 'deserted the service of the choir' (Exeter CA9).

Hodge's name first occurs at Wells on his admission as vicar choral on probation on 13 January 1686/7, while Jackson was still organist, and on 7 April 1688 he was appointed organist of the Cathedral on Jackson's death (CA8). There is, however, a supplementary minute of 1 August 1688 appointing him during pleasure of the Chapter and naming his stipend as £5 a quarter (CA8). Between the two comes a minute of 5 July 1688 admonishing him for breaking windows during his probationary year as vicar choral. He was named in the roll-call of April 1690, but the end of his Wells career is recorded in a minute of 1 July 1690 disposing of his stall as vicar choral, vacant 'by the going off of Mr Robert Hodge, late vicar and organist'. Throughout Hodge's time at Wells, Gabriel Greene continued as master of the choristers.

Hodge soon makes an appearance as lay clerk (countertenor) of Durham Cathedral in April 1691, from where he set out for 'Hibernia' in April 1692 (Durham Cathedral Mickleton MS).

See under St Patrick's Cathedral, Dublin.

John George 1690–1712. George, already a vicar choral (admitted on probation, 9 May 1688), was granted the salary of organist from Michaelmas 1690 by a minute dated 24 October 1690 which contained a proviso about good behaviour (CA8). In July 1709 it was necessary to warn him that in future he was not to withdraw before the end of the services. He died in office as organist late in 1712. In October 1694 (CA8) Greene resigned as master of the choristers on account of age and infirmity, and was succeeded in that capacity by Thomas Webb.

William Broderip 1713–26 (d. Wells, 31 Jan. 1727, aged 43). Broderip had been a vicar choral since April 1701 (CA8), and became sub-treasurer of the Cathedral on 1 October 1706. He was admitted organist on 2 January 1712/13, 'per mortem magistri Johannis George' (CA9). On Thomas Webb's death in 1716 Broderip became also master of the choristers. He is buried in the nave of the Cathedral. By resolution of 17 April 1727 the Chapter allowed his widow 10*s*. a week for the support of herself and her ten children.

William Evans 1727–40 (d. 22 Sept. 1740, aged 47). On Broderip's illness at Christmas 1726 Joseph Millard played the organ, and was paid £2. 2*s*. for continuing to do so until a new organist was elected (Accounts, 1726–7).

William Evans was chosen to fill the vacancy 'per mortem magistri Willelmi Broderip', and was admitted vicar choral on probation, organist, and master of the choristers on 27 April 1726/7 (CA10). The accounts for 1730–1 note that he was paid £3. 9*s*. 6*d*. for the composition of a Service (after it had been approved by the precentor, Robert Creighton, as current regulations required), the odd sum no doubt including the cost of transcription. Evans is buried at the eastern end of the south nave aisle.

John Broderip 1741–70 (bur. Wells, 30 Dec. 1770). Broderip was admitted vicar choral on probation on 2 December 1740, and on 1 April 1741 he was formally appointed organist and master of the choristers, 'having supplied the place from the death of Mr Evans' (CA10). Perhaps he was the son of William Broderip (see above).

Peter Parfitt 1771–3. Parfitt's admission as vicar choral on probation, 'in the room of John Broderip, deceased', took place on 26 April 1771, and the following day he was elected organist and master of the choristers (CA12).

Robert Parry 1773–80. Parry began his probationary year as vicar choral on 1 July 1773, and was appointed organist and master of the choristers on the same day (CA12).

See under Salisbury Cathedral.

Dodd Perkins 1781–1820 (d. Wells, 9 Apr. 1820). According to a note in volume 2 of Clarke-Whitfeld's *Cathedral Music* (1805), Perkins had been a pupil of *Philip Hayes. On 2 July 1781, when he was being admitted vicar choral of Wells on the resignation of his predecessor, the senior vicar in holy orders, Aaron Foster, exercised his right of dissent (see introductory notes to this section), but to no avail. At the same time Perkins was made organist and master of the choristers (CA13). When the time came for him to be perpetuated as a vicar choral, no further protest was heard. 'Mr Perkins, Organist, Wells, Somersetshire', was one of the subscribers to the second edition of Boyce's *Cathedral Music* in 1788, and he also subscribed to Arnold's and William Hayes's publications of 1790 and 1795 respectively. He died on 9 April 1820, and was buried in the Cathedral garth.

William Perkins 1820–60. The date of William Perkins's election and admission as organist and master of the choristers was 1 July 1820 (CA15). He was already a vicar choral, having been admitted on probation on 14 February 1804 and perpetuated on 18 February 1805 (CA14). In 1831 and 1832 the Chapter minutes indicate some dissatisfaction with him: he had to be reminded to have an anthem every Wednesday and Friday afternoon; to get a better assistant; and to attend personally to the instruction of the choristers. Having been ill for some time, he resigned in 1859 (Chapter minutes, 1 July) with a small allowance (see below). He died on 11 November 1860, and was buried by the side of his predecessor, whose son he was.

Charles Williams Lavington 1859–95 (b. 20 Feb. 1819; d. 27 Oct. 1895). Lavington had been a chorister of the Cathedral, and was subsequently a pupil of *James Turle, himself a former Wells chorister. Apparently he had been acting organist for Perkins, and was appointed to the full post on 1 July 1859, the first organist of Wells Cathedral not to have been also a member of the College of Vicars Choral. The Chapter minutes note a curious arrangement whereby £28 was to be deducted from Lavington's stipend, along with 'customary fees', as an allowance to his predecessor on retirement, while on the other hand he was to receive, in addition to his own salary, the stipend (£20) of deputy organist. The tablet to his memory in the south transept of the Cathedral states that he was organist for fifty-three years, but probably only some thirty-five of these were in his own right. He is buried in the Cathedral garth.

BMB.

Sir Percy (Carter) Buck 1896–9 (b. London (West Ham), 25 Mar. 1871; d. Hindhead, Surrey, 3 Oct. 1947). Buck attended the Merchant Taylors' School, London, 1881–8, and then studied at the Guildhall School of Music, moving to the Royal College of Music with a scholarship, and from there to Worcester College, Oxford in 1891, taking the Oxford degree of B.Mus. in 1892. While still *in statu pupillari* he qualified for the D.Mus. degree (1893), but, not yet having entered on the ninth term from his B.Mus., he was not actually eligible to take the degree. In fact he did not do so until 1897, when he also took the MA degree. He also held the FRCO diploma.

On leaving Oxford he was for a short time on the staff of Rugby School, but in December 1895 he was offered the post at Wells (for which *A. H. Brewer and *M. J. Monk were also candidates). He took up duties in February 1896. It is pleasing to note that the Dean and Chapter voted him £12. 10*s*. towards his expenses in taking his doctor's degree in 1897 (Chapter minutes). He was subsequently organist of Bristol Cathedral, 1899–1901 (q.v.).

His subsequent career lay in the field of education: as director of music at Harrow School, 1901–17 and as an influential member of the staff of the Royal College of Music. He combined these posts with a number of part-time appointments: professor of music, Trinity College, Dublin, 1910–20; King Edward professor of music, University of London, 1925–37 (subsequently professor emeritus); professor of music, University of Sheffield, 1927–8; music adviser, London County Council, 1927–36. He became an honorary fellow of Worcester College, Oxford in 1920, and received a knighthood in 1937.

Among his various writings, *Unfigured Harmony* (1911) took an independent line for the time, while the handbook *Psychology for Musicians* (1944), though not original, gives some idea of the clarity of his teaching. He was a member of the editorial committee of *Tudor Church Music*, the only one of the four to have been a cathedral organist.

Grove[3]; *MT*, 88 (1947), 366; *WWW*, 1941–50; personal knowledge.

Thomas Henry Davis 1899–1933 (b. Birmingham, 25 Sept. 1867; d. Wells, Oct. 1947). Davis was educated at King Edward's School, Birmingham, to which he returned as mathematics master after taking the London degree of BA in 1887. He studied music under W. T. Belcher (father of *W. E. Belcher), and was for a time organist of St Matthew's Church, Birmingham. On taking holy orders he became curate of St Mary's, Warwick in 1892. He was appointed a vicar choral of Wells Cathedral in 1895, but resigned when, on Buck's recommendation, he became Cathedral organist in 1899. He had already taken the London degree of B.Mus. (1889), and followed this with the D.Mus. degree in 1900.

In 1912 he was collated to a prebendal stall in the Cathedral, and in 1920 he became precentor and canon residentiary (see p. xxiv). He retired as organist in 1933, retaining the canonry and precentorship until his death.

Crockford's Clerical Directory, 1921; *WWW*, 1931–40.

Conrad (William) Eden 1933–6.

See under Durham Cathedral.

§Denys (Duncan Rivers) Pouncey 1936–70 (b. Midsomer Norton, Somerset, 23 Dec. 1906). Pouncey was educated at Marlborough College, 1920–5, and Queens' College, Cambridge, 1926–9. He took the Cambridge degrees of BA (1929), Mus.B. (1932), and MA (1933), and holds the FRCO diploma (1934). From 1929 to 1934 he was honorary assistant to *C. B. Rootham at St John's College, Cambridge. In 1934 he became organist of St Matthew's Church, Northampton, moving from there to Wells Cathedral in 1936. He retired at the end of December 1970.

§Anthony Crossland, organist from 1971 (b. Nottingham, 4 Aug. 1931). Crossland was educated at High Pavement School, Nottingham and at Christ

Church, Oxford (1957–61), where he read music and took the degrees of BA (1960), B.Mus. (1961), and MA (1963). He holds the diplomas of FRCO (1957) and CHM (1958). He was assistant organist of Wells Cathedral, 1961–70.

WINCHESTER

The Cathedral Church of the Holy Trinity, St Peter, St Paul, and St Swithun

Main sources in this section (1962):

Chapter Acts

CA1 1553–1600.
CA2 1622–45.
CA3 1660–95.
CA4 1696–1739.
CA5 1739–76.
CA6 1776–1803.
CA7 1802–4.
CA8 1804–24.
CA9 1824–50.
CA10 1850–76.
CA11 1876–96.
CA12 1896–1914.
CA13 1915–29.

Accounts

Ac1 1541, 1542, 1566, 1625.
Ac2 1562.
Ac3 1618–40 (with some gaps).
Ac4 1614–63 (actually to 1665).

Registers of Baptisms, Marriages, Burials

PR Phillimore's Parish Register Series, 1905.

Winchester Cathedral was formerly a Benedictine cathedral priory. After its surrender to the royal commissioners it was refounded by Henry VIII in 1541 as the cathedral church of the Holy Trinity. As at Canterbury Cathedral, the choral foundation was on a generous scale, including twelve choristers under a master who, as usual in Henry's foundations (see p. xix), also had the duty of playing the organ. Revised statutes of Charles I later permitted separate posts of master of the choristers and organist (see also Canterbury, Ely, Norwich, and Worcester for corresponding revisions relating to other New Foundations).

Despite the common form for cathedrals of the New Foundation, and, specifically, its own statutes, Winchester Cathedral used the term 'lay vicar' instead of 'lay clerk' for its adult singers. As the term 'vicar', whether lay or otherwise, in choral foundations is distinctive of cathedrals of the Old Foundation, 'lay vicar' is enclosed in inverted commas when citing from Winchester Cathedral documents.

From the earliest date, the annual accounts and roll-calls of Winchester Cathedral exhibit an apparently misleading peculiarity. Normally these should have included a heading, 'Magister choristarum', with the name of the officer beneath, and, in the accounts, the amount of his stipend; followed by another heading, 'Clerici laici' (at Winchester, 'Vicarii laici'), listing the twelve men. If, perhaps for reasons of extra remuneration, the master of the choristers was also given a lay clerk's place, he would then be shown twice. But at Winchester there is no heading for the master of the choristers. Instead, under the heading for 'lay vicars', there are thirteen names instead of twelve, with the first one, sometimes described as master of the choristers, sometimes not, having the higher stipend (£10 as against £6. 13*s*. 4*d*.), or at any rate some allowance connected with the choristers. This matter is alluded to in detail in connection with Richard Winslade (see below).

To begin with, this may have been nothing but clerical practice. But there was certainly some intertwining at Winchester of the office of master of the choristers/ organist and that of a 'lay vicar'. How far this was merely clerical confusion, how far an attempt to get the work of two men out of one, or how far it reflected a means of adding something extra to a man's salary (and it may have been any of these things at different times), would require more investigation to discover than I have been able to undertake. At one point Winslade received only the stipend of a 'lay vicar'; George Bath, on the other hand, had three separate stipends: £6. 13*s*. 4*d*. (obviously as a 'lay vicar'), £3. 6*s*. 8*d*. 'pro informatione [choristarum]', and further payment 'pro pulsandis organis'.

Richard Winslade 1541–72. On the refoundation of the Cathedral in 1541, the last monastic organist and teacher of the singingboys, Matthew Fuller (*VCH Hampshire*, ii. 159–60), was passed over to become simply a lay clerk (contrast Storey of Peterborough). In the 'Book of Portions' setting out the amounts it was intended that the endowments should yield for each proposed post, Richard Winslade is named as master of the choristers at £10 per annum (Kitchin and Madge 1889: 55). Doubtless he was connected in some way to Thomas Windslade, one of the original minor canons of the Cathedral. Perhaps also he was the Richard Wynslate who was a conduct of St Mary-at-Hill, London from 1537 to 1540 (Baillie 1962).

The accounts for the first year of the Cathedral's new life have survived (Ac1) and show Winslade at the head of the list of singingmen at Christmas, but he is not actually named as master of the choristers. His quarterly stipend, however, was 50*s*., as against 33*s*. 4*d*. to each of the others in the list. As there are only eleven of these (apart from William Kay, evidently some kind of probationer, who was given 6*s*. 8*d*. 'for repeating in the quire') instead of the full complement of twelve, one wonders whether there was some economy here. However, at the other quarter-days of the year there is the full number of 'lay vicars' besides Winslade, who is then explicitly described as master of the choristers. Nevertheless, the practice thus begun of listing the master of the choristers among the 'lay vicars' persisted until the roll-call of November 1906.

These early accounts reveal something of what the work of a man like Winslade involved. Each quarter-day in the financial year 1541–2 he received £8. 6*s*. 8*d*. for the choristers' food and clothing, and 20*s*. for the cook's wages. At the end of the whole year he was recompensed for 'charges and expenses laid out', covering fines, rent, and a payment to secure possession for the choristers' house; a mantel and a chimney; reparations to the house; one bed and coverlet with five blankets and six pairs of sheets; and charges of the chorister coming from 'Guylford', all adding up to £6.19*s*. but wrongly totalled as £5. 19*s*.

The next extant accounts are for the years ending 1562 (Ac1) and 1566 (Ac2, now undated, but corresponding to the roll-call for that year in CA1). In these

Winslade receives no more than 33*s*. 4*d*. per quarter, like the other 'lay vicars', but he also receives £10. 3*s*. 4*d*. each quarter 'pro hospitio choristarum'. Turning to the roll-calls of General Chapters held in June and November each year (of which there is a continuous series in CA1 from June 1553 to November 1600), Richard Winslade's name occurs at the head of the list of 'lay vicars' from 1553 to November 1572 (ff. 2[v], 71). The description 'master of the choristers' is found only in 1553, 1554, and 1555. The omission of that title in other years is not necessarily significant, for, as we have seen, he was paid 'pro hospitio choristarum' in 1562 and 1566, and no one else is named as master. After November 1572 Winslade's name drops out of the documents, probably on his death.

William Bath ?1595–9. From June 1573 to November 1600 none of the 'lay vicars' is described in the roll-calls as master of the choristers, and there are no accounts to help with evidence for these years. However, someone must have done the work, and it seems sensible to look for clues among the singingman. Hence, William Bath, a 'lay vicar', 1595–9, who had been a chorister from 1583 to 1587, is included here speculatively. John Holmes (see below) succeeded Bath in his capacity as 'lay vicar' in 1599, and as there are good grounds for believing that Holmes became master of the choristers in that year, there is some presumption that Bath may have been his predecessor as such. PR notes Bath's death in November 1599.

John Holmes 1599–1621 (d. Salisbury, Jan. 1629). Although Holmes's connection with Winchester Cathedral lacks full documentation, there is no doubt at all about it, and very little that he was master of the choristers/organist. Information must be assembled from various scattered indications.

Officially, the only real evidence of his tenure is the minute of his admission as a 'lay vicar' on 18 December 1599 (CA1, f. 147). This does not make itself completely clear, but it seems to indicate that he was given some special treatment. It recites first that he was granted the place of a 'lay vicar' on the death of William Bath, and then goes on to say that he was also to be granted the next place of 'lay vicar' to fall vacant. But it is curious that he did not answer his name at the roll-call for June 1600 (the last in CA1), after which this source of information fails us for more than twenty years.

However, the Ledger Book of Thomas Bilson, Bishop of Winchester, notes that Holmes was the organist at installation ceremonies in January 1610/11, June 1613, and August 1621. In 1613 he took some Winchester choristers to Salisbury to sing on the occasion of a visit from James I (Robertson 1938: 149). He is termed 'organist' in an indenture dated 20 January 1615/16 between himself and the Dean and Chapter of Winchester for the lease of his house in the parish of Kingsgate. A manuscript in the Bodleian Library (Tenbury MS 791) indicates that he taught Adrian Batten: and the carving 'ADRIAN BATTIN: 1608' is found on the eastern end of Bishop Gardner's Chantry in the Cathedral. Finally, the same manuscript describes him as 'organist of Winchester and afterwards of Salisbury', though it must be said that the second part of that assertion is wrong, though perhaps pardonably.

He left Winchester for Salisbury Cathedral, where he was admitted lay vicar on probation in 1621 (q.v.) succeeding John Bartlett as master of the choristers (not organist). It was in Salisbury that he died (Salisbury PR).

In his book *La Musa madrigalesca* (1837) Thomas Oliphant refers to catches collected by John Lant, 'organist of Winchester Cathedral, d.1615'. One John Lant was in fact buried in Winchester Cathedral in that year, but he was not described, as was then customary, as 'lay vicar' or master of the choristers, etc. The dates given for John Holmes (above) make it difficult to fit Lant into the sequence at Winchester, and any claim for his inclusion seems slender indeed.

George Bath 1622–31 (bap. Winchester, 23 July 1596; bur. Winchester, 11 Feb. 1631). The Chapter Books containing roll-calls resume again in 1622 (CA2). The first list (f.1^{v}, November 1622) describes George Bath as a 'lay vicar', and it is not until June 1626 (f. 11^{v}) that he is noted as master of the choristers. However, Dean Young's diary for 26 June 1622 contains the following: 'George Bath admitted master of the choristers and organist.' Bath's remuneration is detailed thus in stray surviving accounts for the years ending 1625, 1627, and 1629 (Ac3) where he is described in the list of 'lay vicars' as *informator choristarum*:

pro stipendio	£6. 13*s*. 4*d*.
pro hospitio choristarum	£10. 13*s*. 4*d*.
pro informatione	£3. 6*s*. 8*d*.
pro pulsandis organis	£10 (£2 only in 1627).

Bath last appears in the roll-call for November 1630. His family was closely connected with the Cathedral choir: John Holmes had been appointed 'lay vicar' on the death of William Bath (see above); a Thomas Bath, no doubt the father of George and possibly also of William, was 'lay vicar' from 1579 until at least 1600; he would have been the 'Thomas Bath, singingman', who in 1584 leased property in Kingsgate parish (described in Stephens and Madge 1897: 67). The memorial in the Cathedral to George Bath's wife has the following inscription: '1625—Feb: 8. Organa qui Tepli pulto, deccog Choristas, Isthic Sepultam lugeo Uxorem bonam Marriam Georgius Bath F: Thomas Bath Juxta Sepulti.' (Except for his use of the word 'also', Vaughan's (1919) translation of this curious Latin may suffice: 'I, George Bath, son of Thomas Bath, Also play the organ and teach the choristers, Lament a good wife, Mary, Buried here 1625, February 8.' George Bath himself, described as master of the choristers and organist, was buried in the Cathedral on 11 February 1630/31 (PR).

Thomas Holmes 1631–8 (bap. Winchester, 11 Apr. 1606; d. 25 Mar. 1638). Thomas Holmes, 'generosus', was admitted organist and lay vicar on the death of George Bath on 5 April 1631 (CA2). His appointment seems to have been at the particular wish of Dean Young, who noted in his diary for 2 April 1631:

> I acquainted them [the prebendaries] that I had brought Th. Holmes with me (as some of them present, Dr Kercher and Dr Alexander had desired me) for our organist; and I hoped they all would like well of him. Dr Kercher only spoke that he liked him well; the rest gave a

tacit assent. Dr K. spoke to me to put it to voices [i.e., to a vote]; I said that I should not need.

This can hardly be other than the son of John Holmes (above) who was baptized at St Swithun's, Winchester in 1606. It must also have been this Thomas Holmes who was involved in the protracted dispute (recounted on p. 262) leading to the appointment of Giles Tomkins (I) to succeed John Holmes at Salisbury in 1629.

On 17 September 1633 Thomas Holmes became a gentleman of the Chapel Royal (Rimbault 1872: 12), and, beginning with the roll-call for November 1633, he is carefully noted as such at Winchester (CA2, f. 39). In October of the same year some question concerning Holmes seems to have arisen between the King and the Winchester Chapter (whether in connection with his appointment to the Chapel Royal or otherwise does not appear). The following extract from Dean Young's diary, 8 October 1633, refers to the matter:

I acquainted the company [i.e., the prebendaries] with the Archbishop's letter in behalf of Thom. Holmes. They all resolved to write to his Grace and to represent the necessity our church had of his presence: which I promised to deliver; but did not, because the King's majesty had laid his command upon me, and it had not then been fit to join in a petition to have it taken off.

Holmes died in Salisbury on Lady Day 1638 (Rimbault 1872: 12); the year remains the same whether one uses OS or NS reckoning, though it has been cited as 1639 (Robertson 1938: 185). He was buried at Salisbury (PR).

Christopher Gibbons 1638–*c.*1660 (b. Westminster, Aug. 1615; d. Westminster, 20 Oct. 1676). The revised statutes of Charles I, dated October 1638, were anticipated in June 1638 with the appointment of an organist who was not also master of the choristers. The King himself appears to have been interested in the appointment, for Dean Young wrote in his diary for 23 June 1638 that at a Chapter meeting 'My Lord Chamberlain's letter was read in the behalf of Mr Gibbons to be our organist'. He was formally admitted as 'lay vicar' and organist on 26 June (CA2, f. 56).

The division of the two posts and the King's wishes involved some financial rearrangement. Part of the emoluments of the master of the choristers was now to go to the organist; but it seems that the Cathedral was anxious for the former officer to receive more than the latter, so John Silver (who at this point became master of the choristers) was allowed to draw the salary of a lay clerk over and above what he earned as master. Young's diary for 25 June 1638 reads:

I admitted Jo: Silver master of the choristers and singingman, and Ch: Gibbons organist and singingman. His place is to be made to him worth £30 per annum at my Lord Chamberlain's command, and because the master of the choristers is allowed £40 whereof Gibbons hath £10, we added to Jo: Silver the other singingman's place to make his up.

The accounts for 1640 (Ac3), the only complete extant accounts covering Gibbons's tenure, do not exactly bear this out, but at least the master of the choristers gets the larger sum: 'Silver, master of the choristers, £35; Gibbons, organist, £30.'

Christopher Gibbons, second and elder surviving son of Orlando Gibbons, was born at Westminster and baptized in St Margaret's Church on 22 August 1615. He was a chorister in the Chapel Royal. He married his first wife, Mary, daughter of Dr Robert Kercher (successively canon of Winchester and St Paul's Cathedral), in 1646, by which time he is likely to have joined the royalist army in the Civil War (petition of 28 February 1660/1, *CSPD*, Charles II, 1660–1: 518). The Winchester Chapter Books break off after June 1645, when Gibbons was still nominally organist. On 2 June 1648 the Committee for Sequestrations ordered that he should be paid his dues as organist, with arrears; and the Trustees for the Maintenance of Ministers granted him £5 in 1655. He had no share in a further distribution to Winchester Cathedral officers in 1657 (Matthews 1948). When the Chapter Books resume in 1660, after the Interregnum, Gibbons is entered as organist in November, but against his name for Midsummer 1661 is written the note 'resignavit'. By 1660 he had already been appointed organist of Westminster Abbey (q.v.) and one of the organists of the Chapel Royal, as well as a household musician to Charles II (see p. 8). He ceased to be organist of the Abbey after March 1666, but he retained his royal appointments until his death.

A conspicuous mark of royal favour is found in a letter, dated 2 July 1663 (summarized in *CSPD*, Charles II, 1663–4: 191), from the King to the University of Oxford recommending that Gibbons should be admitted to the degree of D.Mus. Perhaps this recognized his loyalty during the Civil War. The letter reads:

> Whereas the bearer, Christopher Gibbons, one of the organists of our Chapel Royal, hath from his youth, served our royal Father and ourselves, and hath so well improved himself in music as well in our judgment as the judgment of all men well skilled in the science, as that he may worthily receive the honour and degree of doctor therein. We in consideration of his merit and fitness thereunto have thought fit by these our letters to recommend him unto you, and to signify our gracious pleasure to you that he be forthwith admitted and created doctor in music.

The degree was duly granted, and the Westminster Abbey accounts for the year ending Michaelmas 1664 (Lbl, Harl. MS 4184) contain the entry: 'Given to the organist at the taking of his degree, £5.'

Gibbons died on 20 October 1676, and was buried in the cloisters of Westminster Abbey (Chester 1876). There is a portrait of him by Van Dyck among the Music School collection at Oxford (Poole 1912–25: i. 155).

Fellowes 1951.

John Silver 1661–6. John Silver, 'etat 32', was made 'lay vicar' and master of the choristers on 26 June 1638, following the death of Thomas Holmes (CA2, f. 56). This means he was the right age to be the John Silver who was admitted 'lay vicar' in 1626 and whose name is struck through in the roll-call for November 1627; but unless his voice broke unusually late, he could hardly be the John Silver whose name as chorister occurs for the last time in November 1624. The lay clerk who departed in 1627 is mentioned in the Mundum Books of King's College, Cambridge, where, at Michaelmas 1627, he was paid 30*s*. 'pro expensis in itinere de Winton', possibly with a view to becoming organist there, a vacancy to which

Henry Loosemore was actually appointed. Betty Matthews (the *Organ*, 51 (1971–2), 151) has traced him next to Dulwich College, where he was organist between 1 September 1627 and 26 March 1631. On 25 June 1638 he was made master of the choristers of Winchester Cathedral (Dean Young's diary). He appears to have remained in Winchester throughout the Civil War, and the parliamentary survey of houses in the Close includes the following entries (recorded in Stephens and Madge 1897: 87):

> A house in the possession of one Mr Silver formerly organist [*sic*] of the Cathedral Church, and did hold the same in right of his place. The said house consisting of three chambers and three small rooms all above stairs valued at forty shillings per annum.
>
> Under the said house is the porter's lodge that keeps the gates of the said close [the porter's lodge was at the exit from the close into St Swithun's Street].

In 1655 and 1657 Silver received small payments from the Trustees for the Maintenance of Ministers (Matthews 1948).

When Christopher Gibbons finally resigned after the Civil War (see above), Silver was admitted organist in June 1661 (CA3), thus reuniting the tenure of the two chief musical posts. His name appears in the roll-call for the last time in June 1666, and when his successor was admitted, Silver was described as 'defunct'.

The organist/master of the choristers was already well remunerated at Winchester by Silver's time. In 1663 and again in 1665 (Ac4) Silver received rather more than £57, compared with a typical prebendarial stipend of £31. This state of affairs was in marked contrast to most other cathedrals, where, even with augmentations to the basic salary, the stipend remained well below £50 even in the eighteenth century. As late as 1824 the organist of Chester Cathedral received no more than £10 plus £12 augmentation per annum, and it was only in 1848 that the augmentation there was raised to £38.

Randolph Jewett 1666–75. Jewett, described as 'gen[erosus]', was admitted 'lay vicar', master of the choristers, and organist on 25 November 1666 (CA3). This was in fact the annual roll-call day, and he may have been doing the work for a short time before. He is buried in the north transept of the Cathedral.

See under St Patrick's Cathedral, Dublin.

John Reading 1675–81 (d. Winchester, 1692). Our present subject, who may just possibly have been the John Reading who was both organist and master of the choristers at Chichester (q.v.) seems to have been a junior vicar and poor clerk of Lincoln Cathedral in 1667, and master of the choristers there from June 1670 (Lincoln CA6). His departure from Lincoln would appear to have been in 1675, when William Holder took charge of the choristers and was admitted junior vicar there (ibid.); this coincides with Reading's appearance at Winchester, where he was admitted 'lay vicar', master of the choristers, and organist on 25 November 1675 (CA3).

Not long after Reading's arrival, some trouble arose in connection with the arrangement, dating from Jewett's time, necessitated by the practice at Winchester of regarding the organist as a lay clerk. What seems to have happened is that, in Jewett's time, the organist's turn of duty in the choir as a lay clerk had been undertaken, by order of the dean, by another lay clerk called Thomas Webb. After Jewett's death, Webb refused to continue with this arrangement, whereupon he was penalized. He then appealed to the dean in a letter dated 2 July 1676 (Stephens and Madge 1897: 177). There is nothing to show how the matter was resolved, but it was obviously impossible for the organist also to sing in the choir. (At about this time, Peter Pasmore of Exeter Cathedral was allowed a deputy to act for him in his capacity as lay vicar choral.) The Winchester episode should be compared with the incident involving Edmund Baker at Chester Cathedral almost sixty years later (q.v.) and with further trouble at Winchester in S. S. Wesley's time.

Reading gave up his post at the Cathedral in 1681 to become organist of Winchester College, a position he held until his death in 1692 (q.v.).

Daniel Roseingrave 1681–92. Under the date 25 November 1681, CA3 contains the following entry: 'At this Chapter . . . Mr Daniel Roseingrave was chosen organist and master of the choristers in place of Mr Reading (his place to continue at St Thomas Day [21 December]) in the meantime Mr Reading to continue.' Roseingrave was also made a 'lay vicar'.

See under St Patrick's Cathedral, Dublin.

Vaughan Richardson 1692–1729 (d. Winchester, May 1729). Richardson was a chorister in the Chapel Royal under *John Blow, and he sang at the Coronation of James II in 1685 (Sandford 1687). Since he was already in the Chapel Royal choir by 1678, then the order for his allowance of clothing after the breaking of his voice, dated June 1688 (recorded by Ashbee 1986–9: ii. 19), must surely have been delayed; that being so, he may well have been the Vaughan Richardson who acted as organist of Worcester Cathedral from December 1686 to May 1688 during the last years of Richard Davis's tenure (q.v.). He was not, however, appointed to the vacant post on Davis's death in April 1688.

He was admitted at Winchester, 'loco Mr Rosingrave', on 7 December 1692 (CA3), and the roll-calls (see that for Midsummer 1693) include him in the list of 'lay vicars', with the added designation of organist and master of the choristers. The marriage of 'Mr Richardson, organist, and Mrs Apleford, of College Street', is noted in PR on 5 October 1710; the burial of 'Mr Richardson the organist' is recorded on 9 May 1729. In 1724 he subscribed to Croft's *Musica Sacra.*

John Bishop 1729–37. Bishop was appointed organist and master of the choristers on 30 June 1729 (CA4). He had been a 'lay vicar' of the Cathedral from June 1697 (CA4).

See under Winchester College.

James Kent 1738–74 (b. Winchester, 13 Mar. 1700; d. Winchester, 6 May 1776). Kent was admitted as organist on 13 January 1737/8 (CA4). On the Midsummer roll-call for 1738 he is entered as master of the choristers and organist in the list of 'lay vicars'. PR notes his interment at Winchester College on 10 May 1776; his wife Elizabeth was buried less than a month later, on 4 June 1776.

The following account of Kent is given in Arnold's *Cathedral Music* (i. 82):

Mr James Kent was born in Winchester, March the 13th 1700, his father being a glazier, in very good circumstances, placed him at an early age a chorister in the Cathedral of that place under Mr Richardson, where he did not continue long [CA4 shows that he was a chorister from November 1711 for two years], but was soon after admitted one of the children of the Chapel Royal, under Dr [*William] Croft, then master of the boys, and organist to the king, where he remained, till his patron the Rev. Sir John Dolben, Bart. took him to his seat in Northamptonshire, and by whose interest he was appointed organist of Findon [Finedon] in that county, from which place he was chosen organist of Trinity College, Cambridge, [1731] and continued there till about the year 1737, when he succeeded Mr Bishop, to the Cathedral and College at Winchester, which place he held till the year 1774, when he resigned in favour of his pupil Mr Peter Fussell, the present organist. Mr Kent died at Winchester the 6th of May, 1776, aged 76 years, and was buried in the north aisle of that Cathedral.

A few years before he died, he presented some of his compositions to Trinity College, Cambridge, for which he received the thanks of that body, from the Master, informing him at the same time that the College has voted him a piece of plate, value ten pounds, and desiring to know in what form it should be presented, Mr Kent chose a tankard [in fact a coffee-pot was sent (College Conclusion Book, May 1763)].

An interesting tribute to Kent from George Isaac Huntingdon, warden of Winchester College, contained in Kent's posthumous *Morning & Evening Service with Eight Anthems*, says that 'he was conscientiously diligent, not only in punctual attendance at times of choral prayers, but also in the more laborious and indispensably requisite part of an organist's duty, the teaching of the boys'.

Kent was named by Boyce as one of those who had helped him in connection with his *Cathedral Music*, and when that work appeared, Kent was one of the subscribers. While he was still at Finedon he had taken a copy of Croft's *Musica Sacra* (1724), and in 1743 he subscribed to Greene's *Forty Select Anthems*. He was interested in the music of the Italian composer Bassani (*c.*1657–1716), from which he borrowed in his anthems 'Lord, what love hath the Father' and 'Hearken unto this'. An interesting volume of Bassani's music (in manuscript full score) which was once Kent's property is now in the Bodleian Library (Tenbury MS 920).

There is a portrait of Kent in the warden's house at Winchester College, paying tribute to him as gentle, benevolent, honourable, and pious in the following inscription: 'Hujusce Collegii ab anno 1737 per annos 36 deinde sequentes, Organista; Vir mitis, benevolus, probus, pius.'

Peter Fussell 1774–1802 (d. Winchester, July 1802). Fussell was a chorister in Winchester Cathedral under Kent, and was named as such for the last time in the roll-call for November 1744 (CA5). He was admitted 'lay vicar' on 11 February 1752, the clerk writing 'New Clock' after the date, meaning 'New Style' as adopted in that year. He became organist and master of the choristers, replacing Kent, who had resigned, on 8 July 1774 (CA5) and was also organist of the College. In 1788 Fussell subscribed to the second edition of Boyce's *Cathedral Music*, and in 1790 he did likewise to Arnold's *Cathedral Music*. He was buried on 1 August 1802 in the north transept of the Cathedral (PR).

George William Chard 1802–49 (b. Winchester, 1765; d. Winchester, 23 May 1849). Chard was a chorister in St Paul's Cathedral (see letter from A. T. Corfe, quoted by Jebb 1847–57: ii. 13). He returned to Winchester, and on 23 June 1791 he was admitted 'lay vicar'. This office was clearly meant to cover his appointment as assistant organist, for his promise 'to quit the office of a lay vicar whenever I resign my employment as deputy organist of the Cathedral' is recorded in CA6. He was described as Mr Chard 'of Winchester' when he subscribed to the second edition of Boyce's *Cathedral Music* in 1788. On 14 September 1802 he was admitted organist and master of the choristers (CA6), and he also succeeded Fussell at Winchester College (q.v.). In 1812 he took the degree of Mus.D. at Cambridge (*Venn*). He was buried in the cloisters of the College. For many years up to his death he was also organist of St Maurice's Church, Winchester (Stephens 1882).

West (1921) remarks that Chard 'gained some reputation as a trainer of boys' voices'. If so, it must have been in his later years, for on February 1815 (CA8) the Chapter resolved that Chard be

> desired to instruct the choristers regularly and systematically in their duty and teach them by note and that he be particularly impresssed with the necessity of instructing them to make the responses etc. in a decent uniform manner and not at the highest pitch of their voices as at present which resembles a street cry rather than a religious rite.

Chard was at one time the owner of the Andreis Ruckers harpsichord, dated 1651, now in the Victoria and Albert Museum as 'Handel's harpsichord'. This came to him by two removes from Lady Rivers, who had it from J. C. Smith the younger, Handel's pupil (see Russell 1959: 167, for Chard's correspondence on the subject.) Chard was mayor of Winchester for the year beginning September 1832.

Samuel Sebastian Wesley 1849–65. Wesley was appointed organist on 21 August 1849 (CA9), when the statute relating to his post was read over to him. He was formally sworn as organist and master of the choristers on 5 October 1849. In the roll-calls his name was listed at the head of the 'lay vicars', though he was never appointed as such. His salary was £150 a year, with an allowance of £20 towards the remuneration of an assistant, if desired, to be approved by the Dean and Chapter. Within a short time of his arrival at Winchester Wesley was also appointed organist of Winchester College, and in 1850 he began to teach the organ at the Royal Academy of Music.

There was a good deal of friction between Wesley and his superiors at Winchester Cathedral, the details of which are to be found in CA10. On 28 June 1854 the Chapter passed a minute supporting the precentor's efforts to get Wesley to attend rehearsals. In November 1858 he was requested to give more attention to training the boys, and at the same time it was considerately proposed that if he needed an assistant teacher (in addition to his assistant as organist), the Chapter would pay half the stipend. This was actually done, and a lay clerk named Wylie was appointed. Wesley was also asked to introduce new chants and services. Matters did not improve, and on 25 November 1859 it was 'the painful duty' of the Chapter to administer a formal admonition to Wesley, who had made only 383 attendances in the year out of a possible 780, had left the duty of organ-playing to a boy of 14, was accused of discourtesy to the Dean and Chapter, and had threatened to place a letter from one of the canons in the hands of a solicitor. At the same time it was stated that only two of the boys were capable of singing solos. A second admonition took place on 28 September 1861 because he had been absent without leave and had also refused to attend the voice trial of a lay clerk. Wesley eventually agreed to attend the latter, but he refused to give an opinion on the ground that it would be used to the injury of whatever candidate he favoured. Though in the end he apologized, the Chapter recorded that 'they could not efface from their minds his behaviour'. Wesley was now on thin ice, since by statute a third admonition would remove him from office. Even so, in February 1864 he refused to attend a voice trial unless he was paid a fee, but once more he climbed down. Lastly, in 29 September 1864 complaints were made about his neglect of the weekly full choir practice and also about 'his leaving the choir for the organ loft'. However awkward Wesley may have been, the Chapter was wrong to make an issue of the latter, for Wesley was not a 'lay vicar' under the terms of his appointment and admission in 1849, even though he was always included as such in the twice yearly roll-calls.

For the rest of his career, see under Gloucester Cathedral.

George Benjamin Arnold 1865–1902 (b. Petworth, 22 Dec. 1832; d. Winchester, 31 Jan. 1902). Arnold was a pupil at Winchester of Chard and then of S. S. Wesley. His early appointments were as organist of St Columba's College, Rathfarnham, near Dublin (1853) and of St Mary's Church, Torquay (1856). He became organist of New College, Oxford in 1860, before moving to Winchester in 1865. He was appointed organist and master of the choristers of Winchester Cathedral by minute dated 23 February 1865, but he was not included in the Midsummer roll-call of that year (CA10). He is first named in the roll-calls at November 1865, when, like Wesley, he was listed among the 'lay vicars' even though he was not appointed as such. His appointment represented a break in the association between the post of College organist and that of the Cathedral, an association going back to Bishop's appointment in 1695 and interrupted only briefly between Chard's death and Wesley's appointment to the College.

Arnold took the Oxford degree of B.Mus. in 1855, proceeding D.Mus. in 1861 while organist of New College. He also held the FRCO diploma (1865).

My late venerable friend Canon M. F. Alderson (1869–1962), who, on Ouseley's advice, was an organ pupil of Arnold's while a boy at Winchester College (in preference to Hutt, who was rated rather poorly), used to say that, as a player, Arnold was 'very rough'. There is a tablet to Arnold's memory in the north transept of the Cathedral.

DNB; Stephens 1882.

William Prendergast 1902–33 (b. Burneston, Yorks., 4 Nov. 1868; d. 20 Feb. 1933). Prendergast's father became organist of the parish church, Wem, Shropshire, and William received his education at Wem Grammar School. He then became a pupil of G. B. Arnold, and was afterwards his assistant at

Winchester Cathedral as well as organist of St Laurence's Church, Winchester. He became organist of St Baldred's Episcopal Church, North Berwick and of St Paul's Church, York Place, Edinburgh (1891). During his time at Edinburgh he taught at Fettes College. He was appointed organist of Winchester Cathedral by minute dated 25 February 1902 (CA12), and was listed (erroneously, as with Wesley and Arnold) in the roll-call for June 1902 among the 'lay vicars'. The Chapter clerk corrected this long-standing anomaly, going back to Winslade, in June 1907.

Prendergast took the Oxford degrees of B.Mus. (1898) and D.Mus. (1904). He is commemorated by a memorial in the north transept of the Cathedral. In a tribute to him, a pupil said 'Dr Prendergast taught us not only how to play, but how to live!'

MT, 74 (1933), 370; *WWW*, 1929–40.

Harold (William) Rhodes 1933–49. Rhodes was appointed by minute dated 20 April 1933 (CA13), the appointment to run from a date to be fixed. He was listed in the roll-call for November of that year.

See under Coventry Cathedral.

§(Reginald) Alwyn Surplice 1949–71 (b. Pangbourne, Berks., 20 Aug. 1906; d. Winchester, 21 April 1977). Surplice attended Reading Collegiate School. In addition to musical studies at Reading University, he also worked privately at various times under *Malcolm Boyle, Harold Darke, and *Ernest Bullock. He was assistant organist at St George's Chapel, Windsor, 1927–32, and sub-organist there from 1932 to 1945. Throughout this time (1927–45) he was also organist of Holy Trinity Church, Windsor.

After World War II he was appointed organist of Bristol Cathedral (1946), where he remained until his move to Winchester. From 1951 he was also on the staff of King Alfred's College, Winchester.

Surplice held the FRCO diploma (1932), and took the Durham degree of B.Mus. in 1938. In 1971, the year of his resignation as Cathedral organist, he received the Lambeth degree of Mus.D.

Martin (Gerard James) Neary 1972–87.

See under Westminster Abbey.

§David Hill, organist and master of the music from 1988 (b. Carlisle, 13 May 1957). Hill was educated at Chetham's School of Music, Manchester (1969–76; organ scholar, Manchester Cathedral, 1971–6) and at St John's College, Cambridge (organ student, 1976–80). He took the FRCO diploma in 1974 with four prizes and the silver medal of the Worshipful Company of Musicians. At Cambridge he read music, taking the degree of BA (subsequently MA). On leaving Cambridge he became sub-organist of Durham Cathedral for two years, after which he was master of the music of Westminster Cathedral from 1982 until his appointment to Winchester.

WORCESTER

The Cathedral Church of Christ and the Blessed Virgin Mary

Main sources in this section (1967) (with Cathedral library references):

Ledger Books

LB1	1543–59 (A.vii. 2).
LB2	1616–20 (A. vi.9).

Chapter Acts

CA ex.	'Excerpta ex acti' (from 1555) (A.lxxiv).
CA1	1605–45 (A.lxxv).
CA2	1660–1701 (A.lxxvi).
CA2*	Fair copy, 1660–79.
CA3	1702–47 (A. lxxvii).
CA4	1747–79 (A.lxxviii).
CA5	1780–1815 (A.lxxx).
CA6	1816–48 (A.lxxxi).
CA7	1848–69 (A.lxxxii).
CA8	1862–73 (Order Book) (A.297).
CA9	1873–95 (A.298).
CA10	1895–1918 (A.299).

Accounts

Ac1	1543–4 (A.cciii).
Ac2	1568–9 (A.ccxvi).
Ac3	1580–1 (Accxxi).
Ac4	1584–5 (Accxxv).
Ac5	1589–90 (A.ccxxvi).
Ac6	1590–1 (A.ccxxvii).
Ac7	1594–5 (A.ccxxxi).
Ac8	1595–6 (A.ccxxxii).
Ac9	1596–7 (A.ccxxxiii).

Miscellaneous

LC	'Liber Canonum' (A.xiv).
LI	'Liber Install.', 1660–71 (A.lxix).
PR	Registers of baptisms, marriages, and burials (printed as *The Registers of Worcester Cathedral, 1693–1811*, Worcestershire Parish Register Society, 1913).

After the dissolution of the Benedictine cathedral priory, Worcester Cathedral was refounded by Henry VIII in January 1541/2. There was provision in the musical establishment for ten choristers under a master whose duties, under the draft statutes, included those of organist (see p. xix). Further statutes of Charles II reflected the increased importance of organ-playing by speaking of the 'magister choristarum sive organista' (Cap.xxi), and by saying of him who should teach the choristers to sing and to play instruments, 'et hic vocabitur organista' (Cap. xxvi). At the same time it was made possible, if desired, for the master of the choristers and the organist to be two different persons. The first master of the choristers (and therefore organist) of the new foundation appears to have been Richard Fisher (see below).

Richard Fisher ←1543–69 (d. Worcester, Jan. 1569). The earliest extant treasurer's account (Ac1, f. 9^{v}) is for the financial year 1543–4, and records 'Ricardus Fyssher' as 'preceptor corustarum ad cantandum, vulgariter vocatus the Master of the Querestershe'.

Early in the reign of Elizabeth I, Fisher was granted a patent, dated 3 April 1559, of the office of *magister choristarum*. This can only be explained as a way of clearing up any doubt about his title in a new reign (cf., Edmund Inglott of Norwich). The document (LB1, f. 53, printed *in extenso* by Atkins 1918: 23) gave Fisher power of distraint on the manor of Himbleton. The registers of St

Michael's, Worcester record his burial on 23 January 1568/9, but he may well have been buried in the Cathedral, for such burials were entered in these registers. According to Atkins (1918), Fisher died much in debt.

John Colden 1569–81 (d. Worcester, Apr. 1581). The accounts for 1568–9 (Ac2, f. 4) name Colden as master of the choristers, but we can assume that he served only from Fisher's death. He had been a lay clerk. The year of his death is settled by the date of his will (2 April 1581) and the date of its probate (11 April 1581). He bequeathed his clavichords and all his song-books to Nathaniel Giles, his successor and a witness to the will, which is printed in Atkins (1918: 25).

Nathaniel Giles 1581–5. The accounts for 1580–1 (Ac3, f. 3ᵛ) name Giles as master of the choristers, but he can only have served from April 1581 at the earliest, as Colden described himself as master of the choristers in his will dated that month.

See under St George's Chapel, Windsor.

Robert Cotterell 1586–90. Giles left for Windsor in 1585, and Cotterell was appointed by the vice-dean (in the absence of the dean) on 28 March 1586, after Giles had enquired whether he could make over his post as master of the choristers to Cotterell (LC, f. 66ᵛ). Atkins (1918) pertinently suggests that Giles, on his appointment to Windsor, may have handed over to Cotterell without formally resigning himself. The somewhat similar instance of William Byrd and Thomas Butler at Lincoln (q.v.) comes to mind.

There is a gap in the treasurer's accounts after 1584–5 (Ac4), but Cotterell is duly named in the next extant account 1589–90 (Ac5). He had, however, ceased to hold office before Michaelmas 1591.

Nathaniel Patrick 1590–5 (bap. Worcester, 9 Mar. 1569; d. Worcester, Mar. 1595). Patrick is named for the first time as master of the choristers in the treasurer's account for 1590–1 (Ac6). Atkins (1918) suggests that one John Tomkins may have been in office in 1590, but this is not so. Atkins writes: 'Noake, in his *Monastery*, p. 476, apparently quoting from the Cathedral Records, has the following passage: "In 1590, it is said, Dean Willis, on the motion of John Tomkins, organist, gave £4 for the old organ of St Mary's, Shrewsbury."' The explanation is that Noake was mistaken. The organ of St Mary's, Shrewsbury was sold in 1590 to the Dean of Worcester, likewise also 'at the motion of Mr Jhon Tomkis and us the churchwardens a communion book worth 7*s*. 4*d*.'. Tomkis was the parish minister of St Mary's, Shrewsbury (Owen and Blakeway 1825: ii. 358–60).

Nathaniel Patrick, son of William Patrick, weaver, was baptized at St Swithun's Church, Worcester on 9 March 1568/9. Following the episcopal visitation of the Cathedral in 1593, he was admonished to be more diligent in teaching the choristers (LC, f. 77). On 23 September 1593 he married Alice Hassard (St Michael's Registers), and he died in March 1595 (buried 23 March 1594/5, ibid.). His will (12 March 1594/5, printed in Atkins 1918) mentions 'an old virginal and an old recorder' valued together for probate at 10*s*.

John Fido 1595–6. The treasurer's accounts for 1594–5 and 1595–6 (Ac7, 8) show Fido as Patrick's successor. He had already been organist of Hereford Cathedral for two spells, and returned there for yet a third following his tenure at Worcester.

See under Hereford Cathedral.

Thomas Tomkins (III) 1596–1656 (b. St David's, Pembrokeshire; d. Martin Hussingtree, near Worcester, June 1656). Tomkins was the third son of Thomas Tomkins (I) (see p. 249) by his first marriage, and was the half-brother of *John Tomkins and *Giles Tomkins (I). Tomkins is first mentioned (without Christian name) as master of the choristers at Worcester in the treasurer's account for 1596–7 (Ac9). In the heraldic visitations of Worcestershire (1634) and of Herefordshire and Monmouth (1683), Tomkins is said to have married Alice Hassard, presumably the widow of Nathaniel Patrick (see above). They had a son Nathaniel, afterwards chorister, minor canon, and canon of Worcester Cathedral, in 1599.

In 1607, described as '14 years student in music', Tomkins took the Oxford degree of B.Mus. as a member of Magdalen College (Wood 1815–20: i. 320). In August 1621 he was sworn as one of the organists of the Chapel Royal (Rimbault 1872: 10), and in 1622 he published his *Songs of 3. 4. 5. and 6. parts*, describing himself as 'organist of His Majesty's Chapel Royal in Ordinary', without mentioning Worcester. In 1625 he was organist at the funeral of James I (Ashbee 1986–9: iii. 1), and later received 40*s*. 'for composing of many songs against the Coronation of King Charles' (Rimbault 1872: 58). In 1628 he was appointed composer in ordinary to Charles I (the royal warrant is reproduced in facsimile by Stevens, 1957), but this had to be revoked because the place had already been promised to Henry Ferrabosco.

In 1636 he was moved to make a generous present to the City of Worcester, the intention of which is unknown. On 16 December 1636 the City Chamber Order Book (1602–50) records that 'At this Chamber it is likewise agreed that the gift of Thomas Tompkins, gent., organist of the Cathedral Church of Worcester, being the sum of fifty pounds in such manner and form as he hath proposed the same to this house, shall be accepted of and that the City shall acknowledge the receipt thereof under the common seal.' The income was to be disposed of 'according to the meaning of the said Mr Tomkins'.

He was still in office at Worcester when the Prayer Book services had to be abandoned at the Cathedral in July 1646. Somewhat later he appears to have gone to live with his son Nathaniel at nearby Martin Hussingtree, where Nathaniel's wife was patron of the living. There, according to the Parish Register, 'Mr Thomas Tomkins organist of the King's Chapel and of the Cathedral Church of Worcester was buried the 9th day of June 1656.' His age can be reckoned from a certificate of the mayor and aldermen of Worcester stating that in June 1650 he was 78 years old (see facsimile in Stevens 1957).

Giles Tomkins (II) 1661–2 (bap. Salisbury, 3 Sept. 1633; d. Martin Hussingtree, near Worcester, 20 July 1725). Giles Tomkins was the second son of *Giles

Tomkins (I) (see p. 261), and the nephew of Thomas Tomkins (III). He was admitted as organist and master of the choristers (the earliest use of the joint title at Worcester) on 28 August 1661 (LI, p. 84), and was granted letters patent of appointment. But as early as 24 March 1661/2 he was pronounced 'contumacious for absence', and his post was declared void (CA2). He was subsequently ordained, however, becoming rector of Martin Hussingtree, near Worcester in 1672 and of Hindlip in 1673, retaining both these livings until his death (Atkins 1918: 69).

Richard Browne 1662–4 (bur. Worcester, 27 Aug. 1664). Browne, already one of the minor canons, was appointed organist and master of the choristers by Chapter minute dated 26 April 1662 (CA2). Atkins (1918: 70) states that he had been a chorister of the Cathedral and then a lay clerk (1642), becoming a minor canon in 1644. In 1655 and again in 1658 he received small sums from the Trustees for the Maintenance of Ministers (Matthews 1948). He was one of the very few members of the Cathedral body to survive the Interregnum. On 7 November 1660 (CA2*) he was allotted the house over the Cathedral water-gate and was presented to the rectory of St Clement's, Worcester. He gave up his parish on becoming organist. His burial, as 'organist of the College', is entered in the register of St Michael's Church.

Richard Davis 1664–88 (d. Worcester, Apr. 1688). Davis was formally admitted on 14 December 1664 (LI). He had been both chorister and king's scholar of the Cathedral (Atkins 1918: 70). Evidently in Davis's time it was already the custom for the adult members of the choir to rehearse together, for a Chapter minute of 25 November 1671 ordered 'that the lay members of the choir shall in a respective [*sic*] grateful acknowledgment of their obligation to the minor canons provide three tons of coal and a sufficient proportion of candles for the winter preparatory musical exercises in the lodgings of Mr Davis the organist' (CA ex.). The nature of the obligation mentioned is unknown.

On 23 June 1673 the Chapter resolved that one of the choristers, Charles Hopkins, should be paid £2 per annum 'for his playing the organs in the church over and besides his salary as chorister' (CA2*). On 23 June 1674 it was decided that Davis should be allowed £2 'for his pains and care (as organist) in setting the lesser organ in order in the body of the church' (CA2*).

Davis is buried in the north cloister of the Cathedral. It appears from the fact that Vaughan Richardson (see under Winchester Cathedral) acted as deputy organist from Christmas 1686 to May 1688 that Davis was infirm in his last months. At the Chapter meeting on 25 November 1689 the sum of £2 was granted 'to the son of Mr Richard Davys the organist deceased, to assist in the setting of him forth to service; and £10 yearly . . . to the widow of the said Mr Davys deceased'.

Richard Cherrington 1688–1724. Nothing is certainly known of Cherrington's earlier history, but it seems likely that he was the Chapel Royal chorister under *John Blow who broke his leg in 1677 (Ashbee 1986–9: i. 176). He was elected organist and master of the choristers at Worcester on 17 May 1688, and formally admitted on 30 June 1690 (CA2). While Davis was still alive the Chapter had resolved on 23 June 1684 that no 'inferior office' (e.g., the post of organist and master of the choristers) should be granted otherwise than 'durante bene placito', and Cherrington was the first organist to be appointed under that ruling. On 8 October 1697 'Richard Cherrington, organist of this church and master of the choristers, and John Thatcher, one of the lay clerks (being excommunicated by the Chancellor of the Diocese for brawling and fighting in the Cathedral Church and Churchyard, and having stood so for the space of seven weeks or thereabouts) did submissively appear before the Dean and Chapter' and were admonished 'to avoid the frequenting of public alehouses and taverns' (CA2).

A minute of 5 April 1715 (CA3) sheds some light on the condition of the 'lesser organ' referred to above under Richard Davis: 'That the little organ not having been used for some time past, and having been shamefully neglected when it was used, it is ordered that the salary of three pounds per annum which has hitherto been allowed for the playing upon it be stopped at the expiration of this quarter.'

It was during Cherrington's time as organist that the earliest Worcester Music Meetings (the Three Choirs Festivals) were held, but there is no evidence that he played any part in connection with them.

John Hoddinott 1724–31 (d. Worcester, 23 Aug. 1731). After having been a chorister in the Cathedral (Atkins 1918: 70), Hoddinott (or Hodynott) became a lay clerk on 27 June 1711 (CA3), but he was expelled on 25 November 1713 for having led 'a loose, immoral, and profane life'. However, this did not preclude his admission as organist on 25 November 1725 (CA3). He is buried in the north cloister of the Cathedral (PR).

With some regularity between 1731 and 1746 his widow and children received grants from the Three Choirs charity (Shaw 1954: 4).

William Hayes 1731–4. 'Mr William Hayes of Shrewsbury' was elected organist on 25 November 1731 (CA3).

See under Magdalen College, Oxford.

John Merifield 1734–47 (d. 13 Oct. 1747). Merifield was elected organist on a year's probation on 25 November 1734, and he was admitted to the full post a year later (CA3). Atkins (1918) states that he took up his duties in March 1735. On 24 June 1745 it was ordered that 'Mr Merifield's salary for playing on the little organ [see under Richard Cherrington above] be augmented to six pounds yearly'. He is buried in the north cloister of the Cathedral (PR).

Elias Isaac 1747–93 (d. Worcester, 14 July 1793, aged 68). Isaac came from Gloucester Cathedral, where he had been a lay clerk from 1743 (Gloucester CA3). He is said to have been a pupil of Maurice Greene (West 1921). He was elected organist of Worcester Cathedral on 25 November 1747 (CA3), and was 'fully admitted' on 25 November 1748 (CA4). A minute of 23 June 1777 (CA4) reads:

The profits of one of the chorister's places having for several years past been received and enjoyed by Mr Elias Isaac organist, he surrendered and gave up his interest in and to the same in consideration whereof and of his punctual attendance and services for near thirty years past it was ordered that from this day the profits of a lay clerk's place now vacant . . . be received by the said Elias Isaac and he was elected and appointed to the said vacant place.

Isaac conducted the Worcester Music Meetings from 1761, the Gloucester Meetings from 1769 to 1787, and the Hereford Meeting in 1777 (Shaw 1954: 23). He was a subscriber to the first edition of Boyce's *Cathedral Music* (1760–73) and to the second (1788), as well as to Arnold's in 1790.

He is buried in the north cloister of the Cathedral (PR). *GM* (1793, p. 677) recorded his death: 'At his home in Edgar-street, Worcester, in his 69th year, Mr Elias Isaac . . . many years organist of the cathedral . . . To his professional skill, which, by the cognoscenti, was rated highly, he added the qualities, of still higher value, that characterize an honest man.' The Cathedral music library contains a reputed portrait of Isaac. A footnote in the *Registers of Worcester Cathedral, 1693–1811* states that he was born in 1725 at Tormanton, Gloucestershire.

Thomas Pitt 1793–1806 (d. Worcester, 21 Apr. 1806). Pitt became a chorister of the Cathedral in 1754 under Isaac (CA4), whom he succeeded as master of the choristers on 10 December 1790 (CA5). In 1788 he subscribed to the second edition of Boyce's *Cathedral Music.* On 25 November 1793 he was appointed organist, 'as also a lay clerk', on a year's probation from the time of Isaac's death (CA5). He resigned all three of his posts (organist, master of the choristers, lay clerk) on 19 April 1806, and died two days later, during his year of office as sheriff of the City of Worcester (PR). He compiled an interesting manuscript account, now in the Cathedral music library, of the visit of George III to the Worcester Music Meeting of 1788.

Berrow's Worcester Journal, 24 April 1806.

Jeremiah Clark(e) 1806–7 (d. Bromsgrove, 11 May 1809, aged 66). Clarke, the son of a Worcester Cathedral lay clerk who organized concerts in the city, was elected organist, 'as also a lay clerk', on 5 May 1806 (CA5). The Chapter Acts contain this note: '*NB.* The lay clerk's place given with the place of organist was mentioned to the Bishop of Worcester and from the necessity of the case owing to the insufficiency of the office of organist it was approved by the Bishop.'

Clarke resigned on 23 June 1807 (CA5). In reporting his death, *Berrow's Worcester Journal* for 18 May 1809 described him as 'Jeremiah Clarke, B.M. [Bachelor of Music] of High-street in this city, and late organist of our Cathedral', giving his age as 66.

All the foregoing references spell his name as 'Clarke'. The university degree links him to the Jeremiah Clark (no 'e') who matriculated at Oxford (Magdalen Hall) on 20 February 1799, aged 49, but Foster (1887–92) contains no record of this. However, as with *Thomas Norris and others, it could well be that, though care was taken with the Matriculation Register, the recording of mere music degrees was casual, and Clark(e) may indeed have received one. But the stated age at matriculation, if correct, raises a problem of identification.

There was a Jeremiah Clark (no 'e') 'of Worcester' who published *Eight Songs with the Instrumental Parts* (announced in *Berrow's Worcester Journal* for 21 July 1763); and also a Jeremiah Clark, 'organist in Birmingham', who published his Opp. 2 and 3 about 1775 and (as 'Organist, Birmingham') his Op. 4, dedicated to the Marquess of Donegal, in 1791. These opus numbers make sense if the 1763 publication is regarded as Op. 1, and the whole series as the work of the same man. Chambers (1820: 468), spelling the name as 'Clarke', definitely identifies the Worcester Cathedral organist with the composer of Op. 4, and says that he settled in Birmingham for some time. As Chambers's book is dated 1820, this appears to settle the matter—the Jeremiah Clarke who was briefly organist of Worcester Cathedral was evidently the same Jeremiah Clarke who was organist of St Philip's Church, Birmingham from 1765 to 1803 (information from Mr Roy Massey) and the composer of the works mentioned. Langford (1868: i. 337, ii. 118, 128) notes that he played the violin at the Birmingham Musical Festival of 1778, and the harpsichord at the Birmingham Theatre in the season advertised in 1795.

DNB, *sub* 'Clark'.

William Kenge 1807–13. Kenge had been Clarke's deputy, and was appointed his immediate successor as organist and lay clerk (CA5). He was statutably admonished 'prima vice' on 11 May 1811, and submitted his resignation on 4 January 1813.

Charles Erlin Jackson Clarke 1814–44 (b. Worcester, 19 Dec. 1795; d. Worcester, 28 Apr. 1844). This is no doubt the Charles Clarke who was admitted a chorister of Worcester Cathedral on 24 November 1804 (CA5). He was appointed organist of Durham Cathedral in 1811, while still in his sixteenth year. He was elected organist of Worcester Cathedral on 19 November 1813 (CA5), and returned to Worcester in 1814; but no mention was made of his holding a lay clerkship like his three predecessors. Nevertheless, on 24 November 1824 it was ordered (CA6) that 'the allowance to the organist as lay clerk [was] not to be paid to him without attendance in person'—whatever that may mean.

The Cathedral records of both Durham and Worcester always refer to him simply as 'Charles Clarke'; and Bentley's *Directory . . . of Worcester* (1840–1) records a Charles Clarke, 'music-professor, Britannia Square'. His death was announced in *Berrow's Worcester Journal* for 2 May 1844: 'April 28, aged 49, at his residence in Britannia Square, after a few days' illness, Charles Clarke, Esq., organist of Worcester Cathedral.' However, the burial register of St Michael's Church refers to him as 'C. E. J. Clarke' of Britannia Square, aged 48, and this identifies him as the Charles Erlin Jackson Clarke, son of Thomas Clarke, sacrist of the Cathedral, who was born on 19 December 1795 and baptized in the Cathedral on 1 January 1796 (PR). His own letter, dated December 1823, in which he describes himself as 'Charles E. J. Clarke' (Gu, R.d.85), establishes that the Durham and Worcester organists were in fact the same man.

Noake (1866: 489) says that he 'was distinguished in his youth by a charming voice', and praises the 'beauty and refined taste' of his extemporizations, adding that 'Mr Clarke, however, shrank from display, and could not be got to publish'.

William Done 1844–95 (b. Worcester, 4 Oct. 1815; d. Worcester, 17 Aug. 1895). According to his own account, Done was articled to C. E. J. Clarke for seven years from 1 March 1828, and then became deputy organist. Recording this in its obituary notice of Done, the local newspaper recalled how in 1841, when Clarke was ill, Joseph Surman, conductor of the Sacred Harmonic Society of London, took his place as conductor of the Worcester Festival, 'to the intense disgust of Done, who, however, revenged himself by such a performance of one of Bach's fugues on the organ as to fully establish his position as an executant'. One wonders whether this was one of the '48' rather than one of the 'pedal fugues', as the organ-works of Bach were then known in England. The organ of Worcester Cathedral was not equipped with a full compass pedal department of 'non-returnable' pipes until 1842.

Done was elected organist of the Cathedral on a year's probation on 25 June 1844, at a salary increased by £50 but without a lay clerkship (CA6). To mark the jubilee of his appointment he was awarded the Lambeth degree of D.Mus. in 1894.

As conductor of the Worcester Three Choirs Festivals during his long term as organist, Done saw great changes: in 1845 Mendelssohn's *Walpurgis Night* was thought progressive in idiom; later, in 1884, Done brought Dvořák to conduct his own works in person; in 1887 young Edward Elgar was among the violinists in the orchestra. Done resigned from the Festival conductorship in 1890 (Shaw 1954: *passim*).

There is a memorial to him in the north choir aisle of the Cathedral.

Berrow's Worcester Journal, 24 Aug. 1895.

Hugh Blair 1895–7 (b. Worcester, 25 May 1864; d. Worthing, 22 July 1932). Blair's father was vicar of St Martin's, Worcester and the founder of Worcester College for the Blind. Hugh attended King's School, Worcester, and had lessons from Done before going up to Christ's College, Cambridge as choral scholar (1883) and *H. P. Allen's successor as organ scholar (1884–6). He took the Cambridge degrees of BA (1886), Mus.B. (1887), MA (1896), and Mus.D. (1906). From 1866 he was assistant organist of Worcester Cathedral, and in that capacity he conducted the Worcester Three Choirs Festival of 1893.

On 19 November 1895 he was admitted as organist with effect from 29 September 1895 (CA9), and it was agreed that, as he had been assistant organist for nine years, the term of probation should be dispensed with. On 12 July 1897 (CA10) he submitted his resignation from 19 September, but in the meantime, from 23 July, the Dean and Chapter considered it necessary to suspend him from duty.

Blair gave the first performance of Elgar's Organ Sonata in G, which is dedicated to him, and Elgar's *The Light of Life* was first performed at the 1896 Three Choirs Festival, for which Blair was responsible.

After leaving Worcester he moved to London and became organist of Holy Trinity, Marylebone, and organist and musical director for the borough of Battersea.

Venn; *MT*. 73 (1932) 848.

Sir Ivor (Algernon) Atkins 1897–1950 (b. Llandaff, near Cardiff, 29 Nov. 1869; d. Worcester, 26 Nov. 1953). Atkins's father was organist of St John's Church, Cardiff. He himself was a pupil of, and assistant to, *G. R. Sinclair at Truro Cathedral (1885–6) and Hereford Cathedral (1890–3) before becoming organist of Ludlow Parish Church, 1893–7. He was elected organist of Worcester Cathedral on 4 August 1897 and formally admitted on 20 November.

Atkins took the Oxford degrees of B.Mus. (1892) and D.Mus. (1920), and held the FRCO diploma. In 1921, in recognition of his achievement in reviving the Three Choirs Festival after World War I, he received a knighthood. He was elected a fellow of the Society of Antiquaries in 1921.

He resigned as Cathedral organist at Easter 1950, after what the *Birmingham Post* (5 September 1951) called his '52 noble years in office', but he continued to serve as librarian of the Cathedral until his death. He is buried in the Cathedral.

His thoughtful editions of Bach's *St Matthew Passion* (1911), *St John Passion* (1929), and *Orgelbüchlein* (1916) were of significant influence. In the first of these, Elgar's name was joined as editor, but it may well be supposed that the impulse and main burden were Atkins's. His characteristically careful book on the earlier organists and masters of the choristers of Worcester Cathedral has been cited frequently in these pages. Jointly with Neil Ker he published *Catalogus Librorum Manuscriptorum Bibliothecae Wigorniensis, 1622–33* (Cambridge, 1944), a scholarly work dealing with the early holdings of the Cathedral library.

MT, 95 (1954), 38; *DNB*, 1951–60; *WWW*, 1951–60; personal knowledge.

Sir David (Valentine) Willcocks, CBE, MC, 1950–7.

See under King's College, Cambridge.

Douglas (Albert) Guest, CVO, 1957–63.

See under Westminster Abbey.

Christopher (John) Robinson, LVO, 1963–74.

See under St George's Chapel, Windsor.

§Donald Hunt, master of the choristers and organist from 1975 (b. Gloucester, 26 July 1930). Hunt was a chorister in Gloucester Cathedral choir. After leaving King's School he became an articled pupil of *H. W. Sumsion, and then, from 1947 to 1954, he was assistant organist of the Cathedral. He took the FRCO diploma in 1951. After experience as organist of St John's Church, Torquay, he succeeded *Melville Cook as organist of Leeds Parish Church in 1957. While at Leeds he was active in the musical affairs of what was then the West Riding of Yorkshire, particularly as conductor of the Halifax Choral Society from 1957 and chorus-master of the Leeds Festival Chorus, in recognition of which he received the honorary degree of D.Mus. from the University of Leeds in 1975 on taking up his appointment at Worcester.

YORK

The Cathedral and Metropolitical Church of St Peter (York Minster)

Main sources in this section (1964):

Registers of Patents, etc.
Reg. 1 1508–43 (Wa).

Chapter Acts

CA16	1543–58.
CA17	1565–1634.
CA18	1634–1700.
CA19	1700–1728.
CA20	1728–47.
CA21	1747–56.
CA22	1756–71.
—	No CA known, 1772–83.
CA24	1784–1807.
CA25	1807–30.
CA26	1830–42.
CA27	1842–73.
CA28	1873–90.

Accounts

ChR	Chamberlain's Rolls; a broken series (E1/72–107) from 1537–8 to 1603–4. Each roll covers an unequal part of a year, Martinmas (11 November) to Whitsun, and Whitsun to Martinmas.
ChAc	Chamberlain's Account Book, 1599–1613 (E2/2).
Ac1	St Peter's Accounts, 1572–1600 (E2/21).
Ac2	St Peter's Accounts, 1667–1720 (E2/22).
Ac3	St Peter's Accounts, 1720–69 (E2/23).

The ecclesiastical history of York begins with the consecration of Paulinus as bishop in 625, and the building of the first Cathedral in 627. The capitular constitution as a college of secular clergy can be traced back to early Norman times. The subsidiary College of Vicars Choral was founded in 1252. As at Hereford Cathedral (but unlike Salisbury, for example), laymen were not admitted to the College; but, unlike Hereford, no post-Reformation organist of York was ever a vicar choral; nor, with one very vague possible exception, was any one of them at any time a 'songman', as the lay adult singers at York were (and still are) known.

Thomas Kirkby 1531–40 (d. York, 1540). Kirkby's patent as master of the choristers, dated 3 June 1531, is recorded in English in Reg. 1 (ff. 50v–51). Its early date makes the terms of appointment worth noting in summary:

(*a*) He was to teach the choristers plainsong, pricksong, 'figuration', and descant. So far as the wording can be understood, he was to 'take for the teaching of descant' (i.e., receive payment of) such sums 'as he and the friends of the said children can agree for the same'.

(*b*) The appointment was to be for life, a deputy being permitted during illness.

(*c*) He was to 'keep the Lady Mass at all times accustomed with the said quiristers or children within the chapel of our Lady in the same church. And also keep and play of the organs within the said chapel during the said mass. And also shall play of the organs in the high quire of the said church at such times as shall be convenient and requisite within the same.'

(*d*) No boy was to be elected chorister unless considered 'apt and able' by Kirkby.

(*e*) The yearly stipend was to be 20 marks (£13. 6*s*. 8*d*.).

(*f*) He was to provide meat and drink for the choristers, and was allowed £18. 4*s*. per annum for this purpose.

(*g*) Further, he was to have a 'reward' of £5 yearly.

(*h*) He was to have a house for himself and the choristers.

(*i*) He was to have twenty loads of wood in exchange for the sum of £4 formerly paid to the master of the choristers by the chantry priest of Our Lady's Chantry.

(*j*) He might be allowed eight weeks' leave of absence a year (so far as I know, a unique provision at this date), but must not be away at Christmas, Easter, Whitsun, or the feast of SS Peter and Paul without special leave. He was to arrange for a deputy during his absence.

(*k*) If he did not carry out the terms of the agreement, then, after 'reasonable monitions', the patent was to be void.

It is clear that his remuneration must have been classified under more than one account, for the only references in extant accounts (ChR 73 and 72, Martinmas to Whitsun 1537–8 and 1539–40 respectively) are as follows: 'Thome Kirkbye organizanti infra choru: 6*s*. 8*d*.'.

Kirkby's death in 1540 is attested by the grant of letters of administration of his estate on 13 September 1540 (Yorkshire Archaeological Society, *Index of York Wills 1514–53*). He was buried in the Minster. Torre (Y, MS L7(7): 179), records the following epitaph:

Hic cubat egregius cantor Kirkbeius in urne
  Organa qui scite tangeret unus erat.
Edidit insignes cantus modulamine dulci,
  Hujus erat templi gloria, splendor, honor.
Magna hujus fuerat probitas, sapientia, virtus,
  Consilio enituit, moribus, ingenio.

With slight freedom, this may be rendered thus: 'Here in his grave reposes Kirkby, an excellent singer, one who played the organ skilfully. He brought forth distinguished songs, sweetly melodious. He was the glory, lustre, and honour of this sanctuary. Great was his integrity, his wisdom, his virtue; he shone by his understanding, character, and talents.' Willis (1727: i. 12) renders Kirkbeius as 'Kubeus'. The epitaph is also printed by Drake (1736: 495).

Kirkby's immediate successor has not been identified. The name of the organist given in ChR 77, Martinmas 1540–Whitsun 1541, though illegible, is certainly not that of John Thorne, the next known organist. Whoever he may have been, his tenure was so short as to justify his being regarded as no more than a stopgap.

John Thorne 1541–73 (d. York, 7 Dec. 1573, aged about 59). Thorne's patent (Reg. 1, ff. 157^{v}–158^{v}) was not granted until July 1542, in broadly similar terms to that of Kirkby (see above), and with the same remuneration of 20 marks together with £18. 4*s*. for the choristers' subsistence, but with an increased 'reward' of

£6. 13*s*. 4*d*. His entry in Chr 79, Whitsun–Martinmas 1541, however, is the same as Kirkby's. Later rolls not only use English instead of Latin, so that he is described as 'organ player', but they record payments to him for boarding the twelve choristers at a weekly rate of 1*d*. each. Someone of the same name has been traced as a conduct of St Mary-at-Hill, London in 1539–40 (Baillie 1962).

It was during John Thorne's time that Archbishop Holgate, in his injunctions for York Cathedral dated 1552, ordered:

Item 24. That there be no more playing of the organs . . . but that the said playing do utterly cease and be left the time of Divine Service within the said Church.

Item 25. Also, forsomuch as playing of the organs ought and must be ceased . . . we think it meet that the Master of the Choristers for the time being who ought to play the same organs in time past . . . we will and command that the said Master of the Choristers for the time being help to sing Divine Service to the uttermost of his power within the quire of the Church of York, specially of the Sundays and other Holy-days. (Frere 1910: ii. 316.)

Thorne's burial on 8 December 1573 is entered in the registers of St Michael-le-Belfry, York, together with his age. He lies buried in the Minster. Drake (1736: 500) and Willis (1727: i. 11) record the following inscription:

Here lyeth Thorne, Musitian most perfitt in art,
In Logick's lore who did excell, all vice who set apart,
Whose lief and conversation did all men's love allure,
And now doth reign above the skyes in joyes most firm and pure.
Who dyed Decemb. 7, 1573.

Thorne's inclusion in a list of musicians (1571) who suffered for loyalty to the old religion (*MT*, 61 (1925), 28) may have some relevance to Holgate's injunctions above, though he held the position of clerk of the fabric between 1567 and 1571. Though now obscure, he may well be the 'Thorne' cited by *Thomas Morley on the last page of his *Plaine and Easie Introduction* (1597) among the 'practitioners' whose works he had 'diligently perused' for purposes of his book. Thorne was also a versifier, three of whose poems are included in Lbl, Add. MS 15233 (a reference owed to Peter Aston).

Henry Thorne 1573–97 (d. York, Mar. 1597). Henry Thorne's appointment is entered in CA16 (f. 115^{v}) under the date 17 December 1573. He was appointed initially for one year, subject to 'good conversation', but he was confirmed at the end of it. As he is described as master and instructor of the choristers and keeper of the organs ('custodem organorum'), it appears that the organ was again in use by the time he took up his post. The intermittent ChRs mention him up to Whitsun 1597, and the registers of St Michael-le-Belfry note his burial in the Minster on 28 March 1597.

Cuthbert Byas 1597–1604. Byas can be traced in Ac1 from the time of Thorne's death, and in ChR for the part-year ending Whitsun 1604. From then until Martinmas 1604 ChR speaks only of 'the organist'. Someone named Cuthbert Byers had been a chorister of Durham Cathedral.

Henry Farrande 1604–7. Farrande is named for the first time in ChAc for the part-year Martinmas 1604 to Whitsun 1605, and CA17 (f. 395) records his formal admission as organist and master of the choristers on 22 November 1605. His tenure was cut short by his dismissal (CA17, f. 422) on 22 December 1607 for negligence, fraud, and stirring up trouble among the vicars choral. Whether there was any connection between him and the other Farrants named in this book is a matter for speculation.

——**Browne** ***c.*****1607–?1616**. Following Farrande's dismissal, there is a gap in the series of organists disclosed in the Chapter Acts, while the record of stipends in the accounts speaks only of 'the organist' without mentioning a name. But when examining a Fabric Roll for the year beginning 1 January 1607 (NS), Mr Bernard Barr found a hint in the form of a payment of 20*s*. to a vicar choral named Barton for playing the organ in the absence of 'Mr Browne'. There was a songman of York named Browne, whose stipend as such may be traced for the years 1608–15. If Browne the putative organist was the same as Browne the songman, then this constitutes the sole instance in the post-Reformation period of an organist who was also a songman. The same Fabric Roll also notes a payment to another of the songmen, Morley by name, for his journey to Durham 'for the organist there'. This draws our attention to William Browne of Durham, who ceased to be organist there some time after September 1607 and certainly before October 1608 (q.v.). Can it be he whom Morley was sent to see? Did he go on to conclude his career by becoming organist of York Minster between 1607 and 1616, a period not otherwise accounted for? The words 'for the organist there' are uncertain in meaning, while the slender nature of these documentary allusions, the not uncommon surname, and the lack of a Christian name all make a tempting identification necessarily tentative.

Thomas Kingston 1616–29→. Kingston, 'in musicis expertus', was admitted organist, 'so long as he conducts himself laudably', on 30 August 1616, and on 24 September he was also admitted master of the choristers (CA17). The dates strongly suggest that he was the Thomas Kingston who left Lincoln in 1616. On 12 November 1618 he was allowed £5 for a set of viols ('cohorte fidium'), no doubt for the choristers to learn, and was made financially responsible for any damage to them.

He then fell from favour and was expelled as master of the choristers on 4 February 1618/19, to be followed in that office first by Christopher Spenceley and then (from Martinmas 1619) by John Norwood. He remained organist, however, and ten years later (as noted in CA17, 11 August 1629) he was admonished for drunkenness. Just as he appears to be Thomas Kingston who came from Lincoln, so he also appears to be the Thomas Kingstone who became master of the Magnus Song School, Newark in 1633 (Jackson 1964: 72).

See also under Lincoln Cathedral.

John Hutchinson 1634–Interregnum (d. York, Jan. 1658). Hutchinson's appointment as organist 'during good behaviour' was formally recorded in CA17 on 24 March 1633/4. There is no mention of the master of the choristers, and we do not know whether he, Norwood (see above), or someone else performed this duty. Hutchinson came into office shortly after the building of a new organ by Dallam (1632–3). Possibly this circumstance gave rise, in a confused way, to the legend, stated to be found in William Mason's *Cathedral Music* (1782), that he played for the first time in York Minster on 24 May 1636, when King Charles I attended. It may very well be that he was the John Hutchinson who was organist of Southwell Collegiate Church in 1628 (q.v.); alternatively, though less likely, he may have been the son of Richard Hutchinson of Durham, baptized in Durham Cathedral on 2 July 1615.

The abolition of cathedral worship under Puritan rule bore hardly on Hutchinson. In common with others, he found his work and stipend at an end, and he appealed to the Commonwealth Committee for York and the Ainsty, which was empowered to deal with hardship thus caused. But its 'Proceedings' reveal the weak position of a cathedral musician without a freehold or endowed office: '9 March 1647/8. Upon petition of John Hutchinson, organist, for that it appeareth that the petitioner was only a servant at pleasure to the Dean and Chapter, therefore this Committee contendeth that they have not any means or power to relieve the petitioner herein.' (Yorkshire Archaeological Society Record Series, 118 (1953 for 1951), *Miscellanea*, vi.) Eventually, however, something was done for him, and on 10 November 1657 he was granted £4 by the Trustees for the Maintenance of Ministers (Matthews 1948).

Hutchinson's burial is recorded in the registers of St Michael-le-Belfry, 6 January 1657/8.

For some years after the Restoration the identity of the organist and master of the choristers at York is uncertain. The ChRs no longer cover these officers, who are now dealt with in the accounts, but there are none of these extant before 1667. In a volume headed 'Chapter Minutes and Drafts, 1661–3', Mr David Griffiths has noticed two references to the organist, but in each case the name is far from clear, though it may be 'Hawkswell'. The organ is mentioned in CA18, when, on 31 October 1663, Edward Preston was allowed 40*s*. for looking after it for three years. This must be the 'great organ' which Archbishop Frewen directed to be set up 'before Michaelmas next' by an injunction dated 20 February 1662/3 (Raine 1900: 97).

Thomas Mudd 1666 (d. Durham, July/Aug. 1667). The Chapter Act recording Mudd's appointment (CA18, 20 August 1666) speaks of him as master of the choristers. He may well have been intended to be organist also—or at least, he must have permitted it to be thought that he held such a post, even after he had left York—for on 2 August 1667 the burial of 'Thomas Mudd, Ecclesiae Cathedralis Eboracensis Organista', was entered in the Durham Cathedral PR.

See also under Exeter Cathedral.

Thomas Preston 1666–91 (d. York, Mar./Apr. 1691). Thomas Preston was appointed master of the choristers and organist by Chapter Act dated

6 September 1666 (CA18). In 1675, however, he relinquished the former duty, and Ac2 names 'Mr Tong' (Thomas Tong, a vicar choral) as 'Master of the Singing Boys'. From Candlemas 1676 the duty devolved on William Greggs (see under Durham Cathedral) until Preston himself resumed office for the year Whitsun to Whitsun 1681–2. At that point John Blundeville became master of the choristers until the end of Preston's time as organist. Some one of that name had been master of the choristers at Lincoln, 1661–7, and at Ely, 1670–4 (q.v.), and had also been a Chapel Royal chorister, 1661–4 (Ashbee 1986–9: i. 63).

The registers of St Michael-le-Belfry, York record the burial on 2 April 1691 of 'Mr Thomas Preston, Organist of the Minster'. It seems likely that there was some family connection between Thomas, William the organ-builder, Edward Preston (see above), and the Prestons (father and son) who were organists of Ripon Collegiate Church. The precise relationship between the various Prestons mentioned in the York Parish Registers at this time cannot be firmly established. One possible reading is that this was the Thomas Preston who married Mrs Elizabeth Harryson, a widow, at Holy Trinity Church, Goodramgate on 30 March 1675 and was the father of Darcy Preton (baptized at St Michael-le-Belfry, 13 January 1680/1), who later became town clerk and bailiff of the Liberty of St Peter. On the other hand, Knowles (Y, MS Add. 157/1–5) says that Thomas Preston's *son* married the daughter and heiress of Darcy Conyers, Esq. of Holtby, widow of Henry Harrison, and refers to an undated registration of marriage which reads: 'Thos Preston late organist of the Cathedral to Mary the widow of Mr Wanless' in St Michael-le-Belfry Church. I have not been able to detect this entry. There is obviously a good deal of confusion here. (See below under Wanless, for his alleged marriage to a daughter of Henry Harrison of Holtby.)

Thomas Wanless 1691–1712 (d. York, Feb. 1712). Wanless was appointed organist by Chapter Act dated 18 April 1691 (CA18). His name is there spelt 'Wandlas' and 'Wandlesse'; Ac2 generally uses the form 'Wanless' as he himself signed.

John Blundeville (see above) retained charge of the choristers until Whitsun 1692, when Wanless himself, as the accounts show, took over until 1698. At that point a certain Mr (Thomas) Benson assumed this duty.

According to Dugdale (1917: iii. 270), Wanless married Mary, daughter of Henry Harrison of Holtby, Yorkshire on 10 February 1697/8. Later that year he took the Cambridge degree of Mus.B. (*Venn*). He clearly gave good service at York; a loose piece of paper, now inserted in the accounts, contains the following note from the dean:

8 Octr: 1706

Mr Squire

Pray pay to Mr Wanless the Sun of Fifty Shillings which the Residentiaries agree with me to give him as an Encouragement for his diligent Attending the Service of the Church.

Henry Finch

His burial on 2 February 1711/12 is entered in the register of St Michael-le-Belfry. He was the editor of a volume entitled *Full Anthems and Verse Anthems as they are ordered by the Dean and Chapter to be sung in the Cathedral and Metropoliticall Church of St Peters in York. Collected by Thomas Wanless Batchelor of Music and Organist there.* This collection of words was published at York *c.*1703.

For a discussion of the Wanless family, see under Lincoln Cathedral.

Charles Murgatroyd 1712–21. Murgatroyd was elected organist on 10 November 1712 (CA19). As his successor was appointed in November 1721, there seems little room for doubt that this was the Charles Murgatroyd who was admitted organist of Lincoln Cathedral on 31 July 1721.

See under Lincoln Cathedral.

William Davis 1721–2. Davis's appointment is registered in the Chapter Acts dated 27 November 1721 (CA19). He disgraced himself early on in his tenure, and on 2 March 1721/2 he was dismissed for 'quitting the city and absenting himself without leave and against the orders of the dean'.

These dates suggest that he may have been the William Davis, master of the choristers of Worcester Cathedral (1721–45) who, very soon after he had received his formal appointment at York, took himself back to Worcester. During the ensuing interregnum Thomas Benson, master of the boys, acted as organist, and was paid £4. 7*s.* 6*d.* for doing so (Ac3, 4 July 1722).

Charles Quarles 1722–7. Quarles's appointment to York is dated 30 June 1722 (CA19). *Grove*[3] states that he died in 1727. The third volume of the *Cathedral Magazine* (1775) ascribes an anthem, 'Out of the deep', to 'Mr Charles, late Organist at York'; it seems extremely likely that this was really Charles Quarles. The uncommon surname strongly suggests a family relationship between Charles Quarles of Trinity College, Cambridge, and Charles Quarles of York, perhaps that of father and son.

Edward Salisbury 1728–35. Salisbury was appointed organist on 13 February 1727/8 (CA19), with Benson (see above) still continuing as master of the choristers. This was probably the Edward Salisbury who had been *Maurice Greene's apprentice in 1718, and who had become organist of All Hallows, Bread Street, London in March 1726/7 (Dawe 1983).

As early as February 1730/1 (CA20) Salisbury was admonished for taking absence without leave. In 1735 he offended again, and matters took a serious turn at the Chapter meeting of 12 April:

> Edward Salisbury the organist being called in . . . the Dean objected that notwithstanding the monition he was laid under in . . . 1730 not to go out of or absent himself from this City without leave of the Dean . . . he the said Edward Salisbury had lately absented himself . . . without such leave for ten days or upwards that it was the duty of the organist to attend the Church at other times besides those appointed for Divine Service in order to play upon the organ and instruct the singing boys and others of the choir . . . and . . . that he the said Dean had several times within the space of two years last past privately admonished the said Salisbury to receive the Sacrament at the said Cathedral yet he . . . had never received the same thereupon the said Salisbury confessed that he had lately been absent from this City

nine days without leave but said he was used with severity and that he believed that they . . . wanted to put another in his place . . . and as to his receiving the Sacrament at the Cathedral he said he thought it looked like hypocrisy in him to come there on that occasion but that he would receive the Sacrament there tomorrow. Whereupon the said Dean admonished him to observe his duty as organist in attending the Church and not to go out of town without leave first obtained and to instruct the singing boys in singing to the organ and especially the new anthems and the said Dean and Chapter assigned to deliberate further as to the late absence of the said organist and as to his insolent behaviour at this Chapter.

Finally, on Monday 21 April 1735, Salisbury was formally asked to submit; upon his refusal, he was expelled. It is interesting to note that although Salisbury was not master of the choristers, this citation implies that he had to rehearse the boys in the Cathedral.

This is presumably the Edward Salisbury who became organist of Trinity College, Cambridge in 1738 (q.v.).

James Nares 1735–56 (b. Stanwell, Middlesex, 19 Apr. 1715; d. Westminister, 10 Feb. 1783). During the short interregnum following Salisbury's dismissal (25 April to the end of July) Thomas Benson was again appointed acting organist (see above under Davis). Nares's appointment was formally minuted (CA20) on 8 November 1735, though he actually entered on his duties at the beginning of August. His salary was £40.

A son of the steward of the Earl of Abingdon, Nares had been educated as a chorister in the Chapel Royal under Bernard Gates, and was also a pupil of Pepusch. When Nares took up his appointment at York, Benson was still master of the choristers, but from 1739 onwards Nares himself took over that post, from which time it has always been combined with that of organist. This makes it necessary to refer to Thomas Ellway, who, in 1736, published a collection of words of *Anthems . . . as they are now performed in the Cathedral Church of St Peter in York . . . in . . . Durham and . . . in Lincoln* in which he described himself (2nd edition, 1756) as 'Master of the Children of the Cathedral at York'. At no time did Ellway receive payment as such: the accounts show a continuous and regular sequence of payment to Benson and then to Nares. Ellway did receive periodic sums for copying music; and from May 1748 until January 1750/1 he regularly received a small stipend for some unnamed function. He died on 18 January 1750/1, and was buried at St Michael-le-Belfry, where he was parish clerk. One can only suppose that he actually did the work of teaching the boys and was paid privately by Benson and Nares until 1748, when an official allowance (in effect, an increase in Nares's salary) was arranged.

In 1743 Nares subscribed to Greene's *Forty Select Anthems*, and in 1760 he subscribed to the first edition of Boyce's *Cathedral Music*.

Nares succeeded Maurice Greene as one of the two organists and composers of the Chapel Royal in January 1756 (q.v.), on the commendation of John Fountayne, Dean of York from 1747. In 1757 he took the Cambridge degree of Mus.D. (*Venn*), and on 18 March that year he succeeded his old teacher, Gates, as master of the children of the Chapel Royal (CB2). He gave up this last appointment in July 1780, but retained the others until his death. Before he died he had subscribed to Arnold's *Cathedral Music*, which did not appear until 1795. He is buried in St Margaret's Church, Westminster. According to the memoir by his son Robert (prefixed to Nares's *Morning and Evening Service, etc.*, 1788), 'his constitution was never strong'. His brother Sir George Nares was a judge of the Court of Common Pleas; his son Robert (FRS and FSA), who became Archdeacon of Stafford and a canon of Lichfield, was one of the founders of the Royal Society of Literature; and it was his nephew Edward, Regius professor of modern history at Oxford, who was the subject of excoriation by Macaulay in a review (1832) of his *Memoirs of Lord Burghley*.

Besides his musical compositions, Nares wrote two books on singing, with useful accounts of singers' ornaments, and a harpsichord instruction book.

GM, 1783, i. 182.

John Camidge (I) 1756–99 (bap. York, 8 Dec. 1734; d. York, 25 Apr. 1803). There is no doubt that this is John, the son of Robert Camidge, who was baptized at Holy Trinity Church, Goodramgate, York. *DNB* records that John Camidge was articled to Nares at York and afterwards had lessons from Greene and Handel in London. He was appointed organist of Doncaster Parish Church in August 1755, but almost immediately succeeded Nares at York, where he began work on 31 January 1756 (CA21). It has been stated that he introduced Handel's music into the Minster services.

On 11 November 1799 he appeared personally before the Dean and Chapter to beg leave to resign as organist and master of the boys (CA24). A portrait of him by an unknown artist hangs in the York City Art Gallery.

GM, 1803, i. 484.

Matthew Camidge 1799–1842 (b. York, 25 May 1764; d. York, 23 Oct. 1844). Matthew Camidge, who was baptized at Holy Trinity, Goodramgate, York, became a Chapel Royal chorister under Nares. On the same day as his father resigned his positions at York, Matthew successfully petitioned to succeed him. *DNB* makes particular mention of the fact that he taught his choristers to read music, a thing apparently not done under his more recent predecessors. On 21 June 1803 (CA24) his salary was raised from £48 to £60 'in consideration of the great attention necessary to be paid by him in instructing the choristers in church music'. He resigned his appointment on 8 October 1842 (CA26).

John Camidge (II) 1842–59 (d. York, 21 Sept. 1859, aged 69). John Camidge (II) succeeded his father in 1842, having already (according to *DNB*) been 'retained at a high salary from the Dean and Chapter as assistant to his father', whose pupil he had been. His appointment is dated 15 October 1842 (CA26). In 1812 and 1819 he had taken the Cambridge degrees of Mus.B. and Mus.D. from St Catharine's College (*Venn*).

In November 1848 he was stricken with paralysis, and his son, Thomas Simpson Camidge, carried out his father's duties. This arrangement does not seem to have satisfied the authorities, though so long as John Camidge retained his office it may have been difficult to interfere. Eventually, on 10 September

1858 (CA27), a way was found, in effect, of giving T. S. Camidge six months' notice:

The Chapter having deliberated upon the present state of the choir and recognizing the long and valuable services of Dr Camidge, Resolved that in consequence of Dr Camidge's continued illness a pension of one hundred pounds per annum be granted for the rest of his life commencing from the first day of May next. His present salary to be paid in the interim, Dr Camidge continuing to provide for the services of the acting organist during the latter period of six months. The Dean was then requested to make enquiries for a qualified successor to Dr Camidge and it was resolved that the salary of the organist in future be one hundred and fifty pounds per annum.

In 1855 Archbishop Sumner granted John Camidge (II) the Lambeth degree of Mus.D., one of the rare instances of this award being made to someone who already held a university doctorate. The *York Gazette* for 24 September 1859 records his death thus: 'On Wednesday, the 21st inst., aged 69, John Camidge Esq., of this city, Mus. Doc. Cantab.' There is a portrait of him by William Etty in the Fitzwilliam Museum, Cambridge.

The reign of the three Camidges at York extended from 1756 to 1859. The dynasty was further represented by T. S. Camidge, 1828–1912 (see above), and his son John Camidge (III), 1853–1929, organist of Beverley Minster from 1876. *MT* (44 (1903), 300) contains reproductions of portraits of John, Matthew, and Dr John Camidge which at that time belonged to T. S. Camidge.

Edwin George Monk 1859–83 (b. Frome, Somerset, 13 Dec. 1819; d. Radley, 3 Jan. 1900). After early appointments at Midsomer Norton and Frome, Monk became the first organist and music master of St Columba's College, Rathfarnham, near Dublin in 1844. He came back to England in 1847, and was appointed organist and music master of St Peter's College, Radley in 1848. He took the Oxford degrees of B. Mus. (1848) and D.Mus. (1856). His appointment at York is minuted in CA27. He took the FRCO diploma in 1866. From 1871 to 1883 Monk was an examiner for Oxford degrees in music. In 1872 he became a fellow of the Royal Astronomical Society. On his retirement from York in 1883, with a pension of £150 (CA28), he settled at Radley.

Grove[2]; West 1921.

John Naylor 1883–97 (b. Stanningley, near Leeds, 8 June 1838; d. at sea, 15 May 1897). Naylor was a chorister of Leeds Parish Church under R. S. Burton. He held two organist's posts in Scarborough—St Mary's (1856) and All Saints' (1873). His appointment at York was minuted in October 1883 (CA28). He was to receive £300 a year, plus a further £100 after Monk's death. He resigned his post at York in April 1897 on account of ill health, and died while on a voyage to Australia. There is a memorial to him in the north transept of the Minster.

E. W. Naylor (1867–1934), organist of Emmanuel College, Cambridge, was John Naylor's son; he was the author of *Shakespeare and Music* (London, 1896) and a commentary on the Fitzwilliam Virginal Book (London, 1905). A third generation of this musical dynasty is represented by E. W. Naylor's son Bernard (b. 1907). *H. W. Hunt was John Naylor's nephew.

Grove[2]; West 1921.

Thomas Tertius Noble 1898–1912.

See under Ely Cathedral.

Sir Edward (Cuthbert) Bairstow 1913–46 (b. Huddersfield, 22 Aug. 1874; d. York, 1 May 1946). As a boy, Bairstow attended Nottingham High School and the Grocers' Company School, Hackney Downs, London. He studied music under John Farmer and then under *J. F. Bridge, to whom he was articled in 1893. From 1894 to 1899 he was organist of All Saints' Church, Norfolk Square, Paddington, London, before moving to Wigan Parish Church (1899–1906) and then to Leeds Parish Church (1906–13). He left Leeds for York in 1913.

In 1929 he succeeded *J. C. Bridge as (non-resident) professor of music in the University of Durham. He was Ferens fine art lecturer at University College, Hull in 1940, and his lectures were published as *The Evolution of Musical Form* (London, 1943). Bairstow also wrote a substantial volume, *Counterpoint and Harmony* (London, 1937), and collaborated with H. Plunket Greene in *Singing Learned from Speech* (London, 1945).

He took the Durham degrees of B.Mus. (1894) and D.Mus. (1901), and held the FRCO diploma. In 1932 he received a knighthood, and he received the honorary degrees of Litt.D. from the University of Leeds in 1936 and D.Mus. from the University of Oxford in 1945.

Grove[3]; *MT*, 87 (1946), 186; *ECM*, 16 (1946), 18; *DNB*, 1941–50; *WWW*, 1941–50.

§Francis (Alan) Jackson 1946–82 (b. Malton, Yorks., 2 Oct. 1917). Jackson was a chorister of York Minster, 1929–33, under Bairstow. From 1933 to 1940 he was organist of Malton Parish Church. He was appointed assistant organist of York Minster in 1946, succeeding his old master in the full post almost immediately.

Jackson, who holds the FRCO diploma (Limpus prize, 1937), took the Durham degrees of B.Mus. in 1937 and D.Mus. in 1957. He was appointed OBE in 1978, and received the honorary degree of D.Univ. from the University of York in 1983.

§Philip (John) Moore, organist and master of the music from 1983 (b. 30 Sept. 1943). Moore was educated at Maidstone Grammar School and the Royal College of Music, 1962–5, where he won the Walford Davies prize for organ. On taking the FRCO diploma in 1965 he was awarded the Limpus, Turpin, and Read prizes, and he holds the Durham degree of B.Mus. On leaving the Royal College of Music he was assistant music master at Eton College and then assistant organist of Canterbury Cathedral. From 1974 to 1982 he was organist of Guildford Cathedral.

3

Collegiate Churches

WESTMINSTER

The Collegiate Church of St Peter (Westminster Abbey)

(formerly a Cathedral Church, 1540–50)

The primary sources for early appointments at Westminster are Chapter Books, accounts, and such miscellaneous documents as patents, petitions, etc.

With breaks for the restored Marian monastery and the Commonwealth period, the Chapter Books run continuously from 1542 and have been consulted down to 1875. For the greater part of our period, the appointment of the organist or the master of the choristers was considered a matter for the dean alone, so these books do not yield a great deal of information, though a little may be gleaned from those for 1542–1609, 1609–42, and 1683–1714 (herein CA1, CA2, and CA5 respectively).

There is a long series of extant accounts, with a few gaps, nearly all of which are for complete years running from Michaelmas to Michaelmas, beginning with the accounting year 1542–3. Though these constitute our most substantial source, they need circumspect interpretation. They are simply summaries or 'views' of the annual finances, presumably resting on more detailed documents which have not survived. For the most part they are content to name the officer in post at the end of the year, irrespective of any change which may have taken place during that year; it was apparently sufficient merely for the right number of people to be named and the correct amount of money be accounted for. Thus, Hooper, though he was organist only, was entered as master of the choristers, while Gibbs, who was master of the choristers, was entered under a section for casual payments. Sometimes, even, as now and again can be verified from other information, the name of someone recently dead might be copied from an old list instead of the current man's name: but the number and the money would be right.

The accounts and the miscellaneous documents are catalogued with WAM (Westminster Abbey Muniment) numbers, so it is unnecessary to devise any ad hoc system of references here.

The Benedictine abbey of Westminster surrendered to the commissioners of Henry VIII in January 1539/40. In December 1540 the King replaced the abbey with a cathedral, with a dean and prebendaries, to serve a new, short-lived diocese of Westminster. Ten years later its cathedral status was taken away (though the informal title tended to remain in use), while the dean and other personnel remained. In 1556 Mary I dissolved this body and re-established a Benedictine abbey. Elizabeth I reversed her sister's act soon after her accession, and on 21 May 1560 founded by royal charter the collegiate church of St Peter as it is today, the institution widely known as Westminster Abbey, one of only two collegiate churches now in the provinces of Canterbury and York which are not the sees of bishops.

There are no statutes for Henry's foundation of 1540, but the list of its original officers (see below under Green) includes a master of the choristers. By statutes drafted under Elizabeth (but never enacted), there was to be a master of the choristers, but no mention was made of organ-playing among his duties. However, there is a strong enough parallel with other cathedrals of Henry's foundation to make it reasonably certain that the master of the choristers was intended to play the organ, and it would not be hazardous to suppose that arrangements for the Elizabethan collegiate church were similar. Until the year 1606, therefore, our discussion proceeds on the assumption that the officer entitled master of the choristers was also the organist. Be that as it may, however, from that year the Westminster authorities began to treat the duties of organist as separable from those of master of the choristers, so creating two posts which they either fused or separated as convenient. The financial officers seem to have found this puzzling, sometimes putting the name of the organist against the office and stipend (£10) of the master of the choristers, while dealing with the actual master of the choristers by way of 'regard', or supplementary payment. It will be necessary to comment below on some instances of confusion on this point in the early seventeenth century before steps were taken to regularize things. From 1660 until the nineteenth century the two posts were nearly always distinct, but from 1804 (WAM 33836) onwards they have been combined in one office. On the subject of distinctive terminology, it should be noted that the adult members of the choir of Westminster were (and are) termed lay vicars, and not, as in cathedrals of the New Foundation, lay clerks.

The first three men named below held office under the Henrician foundation.

William Green 1541–3 (d. Jan. 1547). Green was the first master of the choristers (and we assume, therefore, organist also) under the foundation of Henry VIII, and was named as such in the 'Book of Erection of the King's New College at Westminster' (WAM 6478). This document notes that Green was to surrender some existing patent, which suggests that he may have held this or some similar post in the former abbey. His will was made in January 1546/7, and was proved later in the same month (Pine 1953: 38–41).

Robert Fox 1543–6. The accounts up to Michaelmas 1543 name Fox as Green's deputy in March, and as 'Mr of the chyldern queresters' in June (WAM 37045). In CA1 there is a resolution of 26 January 1543/4 granting him

> the whole governing of the choristers, to teach them, to provide for meat and drink and to see them cleanly and honestly apparelled in all things . . . also that the said Master of the Choristers shall have the house over the gate going in to the Almonry for himself and the said choristers rent free, he repairing it sufficiently before Easter next coming.

The official accommodation was a poor bargain for him. The same minute proceeds to say: 'And because the house is now in great ruin, agreed that the said Fox shall only have 40 shillings towards the charges of the said reparations.' Two years later the question of his accommodation was still a troublesome affair: as far as one can make out from a Chapter minute of February 1545/6, he was not yet in his official house: 'It is also agreed by the parties aforesaid that Fox, Master of the Choristers, shall dwell in the house, and the house that he lieth in now to be a house for the audit and to keep the evidence [muniments] in.'

Nothing more is known of Fox, but it appears that he had ceased to be master of the choristers before the death of Edward VI in 1553. Baillie (1962) notes a Robert or Richard Fox who was a conduct of St Mary-at-Hill, London in 1537–40.

Thomas Heath ←**1553–6**→. The accounts for the year ending Michaelmas 1554 (WAM 33604) cite Heath as master of the choristers, and Pine (1953: 62) thinks he was in office before Michaelmas 1553. He had been a lay vicar from 1541 (WAM 6478). He can be traced as master of the choristers to Michaelmas 1556 (WAM 37713), but no further documents relating to him have survived at Westminster. It is possible that he was disturbed by the Marian refoundation of the abbey in November 1556. It could quite well be that he was the Thomas Heath who became organist of Exeter Cathedral in 1558 (q.v.), and I have provisionally assumed this.

With the re-establishment of the Benedictine abbey late in 1556, under the abbacy of John de Feckenham, we enter an obscure period. However, in his summary of accounts for October 1558 to September 1559 (WAM 33198E) the receiver-general recorded that on 22 March 1558/9 'John, former Abbot', appointed **Robert Lamkyn** as master of the choristers, and his accounts for July–September 1559 (WAM 37931) note a quarter's payment of 50*s.* Queen Elizabeth had come to the throne in November 1558, and these were uncertain times for the monastery. How long Lamkyn continued as master of the choristers is not known; he does not appear to have been appointed as such under Elizabeth's new foundation, but he was still about for many years, being a witness to the wills of *Robert White and his wife Ellen in November 1574 (Arkwright 1898: 5–9).

We now pass to the Collegiate Church of Elizabeth I, established in 1560.

John Taylor ←**1561–9**. Taylor is the first known master of the choristers (and we assume, therefore, organist) of Westminster Abbey on its present foundation. Accounts ending at Michaelmas 1560 and 1561 (WAM 33617–8) speak only of 'the schoolmaster of the choristers', but Taylor is mentioned regularly by name from the quarter ending Christmas 1561 to that ending Michaelmas 1569 (WAM 33619–28). Baillie (1962) suggests that he was probably master of the choristers of St Anthony's Hospital, London in 1556–7. It is generally assumed that he died in 1569.

Robert White 1570–4. CA1 (f. 137) records the sealing of White's indenture as master of the choristers on 3 February 1569/70. Correspondingly, in the accounts for the year ending Michaelmas 1570 (WAM 33629) Taylor's name is struck out and White's inserted. During his tenure White received not only the stipend of the master of the choristers together with the annual allowance for each boy, but a supplementary payment or 'regard' for teaching the choristers. The patent of John Parsons's appointment explicitly as organist in 1621 (see below) names White as one of his predecessors in such a post. In his will White describes himself as 'master of the queristers of the Cathedral Church of St Peter's'.

See under Ely Cathedral.

Henry Leeve 1574–85. The accounts for the years 1574–5 up to and including 1584–5 (WAM 33635–42) disclose Leeve's name as master of the choristers. His remuneration was the same as White's had been (see above).

Edmund Hooper (master of the choristers [/organist]) **1585–1606** (organist) **1606–21** (b. Halberton, Devon, ?1563; d. London (Westminster), 14 July 1621). For the years ending Michaelmas 1586 to 1605 inclusive the accounts show Hooper on exactly the same footing as Leeve and White had been (see above). On 3 December 1588 he was given security of tenure by the grant of 'the mastership of the children for term of his life' (CA1). Some documents speak of him as 'Hoop'.

On 1 March 1603/4 (Rimbault 1872: 6) he was appointed a gentleman of the Chapel Royal and, by inference (see p. 6), organist also, in spite of the fact that there had been some difficulty about his management of the Westminster choristers. In December 1603 there is a reference in CA1 to 'many disorders in the choristers', and it was decided that Hooper should be called before the Chapter, bringing with him the patent of his appointment. At some date, perhaps 1603–4, a complaint was also made that certain payments which it was his obligation to disburse to the minor canons and lay vicars had fallen short. Consequently, the dean (Lancelot Andrewes) ordered (WAM 65886) that 'Mr Treasurer do make stay in his hand of so much of Mr Hooper's wages as doth amount to this sum until Mr Hooper's answer be heard concerning this demand, which if it be not liked then may they receive their several sums according to their desires.' We do not know the outcome of this.

In spite of such matters, a Chapter resolution of 19 May 1606 (CA1) granted Hooper a patent as 'organist of the church' with fee of £16. From this point the annual accounts record John Gibbs as receiving the allowance for each chorister and the 'regard' for teaching them which Hooper, Leeve, and White had formerly received. Gibbs was paid these sums regularly until, in the course of the accounting year 1612–13, he was succeeded by John Parsons, who continued in a similar capacity until Hooper's death. Gibbs, then, was effectively master of the choristers and was regarded as such by the Chapter; but the treasurer confused things by entering Hooper (who was now simply the organist) under the old heading of master of the choristers at the old fee of £10. Formal recognition of the separate posts is found in CA2 under the date 7 May 1610, which records that:

> upon due consideration of the good service which Mr Hooper our organist hath and doth continually perform in the service of the church it is decreed by us that the said Mr Hooper shall peaceably enjoy that part of the house allotted for the master of the choristers and the children themselves the said choristers which he now dwelleth in and enjoyeth, howsoever the now master of the choristers or any other shall impugn the same.

One scents in this some dispute about whether Gibbs or Hooper was technically master of the choristers and so entitled to the official house. At the same time, the opportunity was taken to grant Hooper a new patent as organist, free from some unspecified defect (possibly relating to this very point) perceived in that of 1606.

Yet another patent of the post of organist was issued on 17 December 1616. In this case the document has survived (WAM 9835). It refers to Hooper's 'good and faithful service . . . heretofore of long time in the said church'. His emolument was to be £16, made up of two yearly annuities or rents of £14 and £2 each, with the addition of his share of the annual dividends of the church. He was to retain the chambers which he was at that time occupying. The patent also mentions 'the tenement wherein John Parsons, master of the choristers of the said collegiate church now dwelleth'. Another document (WAM 9836) appears to be a scribbled memorandum surrendering the patent which this replaced.

Not long before his death, Hooper and his wife were jointly granted what appears to have been a very favourable lease of property by the Chapter (WAM 35549, 23 May 1620). The document in question calls him 'organist' and speaks of his service 'in the said church for 33 years', a reckoning going back to the patent of 1588.

Hooper died on 14 July 1621 (Rimbault 1872: 10), and was buried in the Abbey cloisters on 16 July (Cheter 1876).

His will (Chester 1876: 118), drawn up in 1620, is of much interest. It alludes to his having served the Abbey for thirty-eight years or more, that is, before his appointment as master of the choristers/organist in 1585. He left bequests to the poor at Halberton, Devon, which he named as his birthplace; at Bradninch, Devon, where he was brought up; and at Greenwich, where he was put to school by Sir James Dyer. A legacy of 1*s.* each to sixty-seven poor men and women suggests his age at the time the will was made.

John Parsons 1621–3 (d. London (Westminster), Aug. 1623). At the time of Hooper's death Parsons was already master of the choristers, having taken over from John Gibbs during the accounting year 1612–13. By patent dated December 1621 (WAM 9837), endorsed 'John Parsons, organist and master of the choristers', he was granted these combined offices for life, and was required to carry out his duties 'in as large and ample a manner as our Master White or our Edmund Hooper' had done. As well as the £16 per annum and the official house allotted to Hooper, Parsons also received ('towards the finding of the said choristers' bread and board') regular annual allowances totalling £36. 13*s.* 4*d.*, together with 1½ bushels of 'good and seasonable wheat' weekly. During his tenure, therefore, there were no problems of apportioning salary and accommodation between an organist and a master of the choristers.

One observes that the accounts for the years ending Michaelmas 1622 and 1623 (WAM 33679–80) show Hooper and Parsons as sharing the stipend (entered under 'master of the choristers', but clearly referring to the organist). This is obviously a clerical error, a mechanical carrying-forward of the entry for the year ending Michaelmas 1621 (WAM 33678) during which Parsons succeeded Hooper as organist.

Parsons was buried in the Abbey cloisters on 3 August 1623 (Chester 1876). Camden's *Remains concerning Britain* (1657) contains verses which are generally taken to refer to Parsons:

> Death passing by and hearing Parsons play
> Stood much amazed at his depth of skill,
> And said, 'This artist must with me away',
> For death bereaves us of the better still;

But let the quire, while he keeps time, sing on,
For Parsons rests, his service being done.

Orlando Gibbons 1623–5. In the accounts for the two years ending Michaelmas 1624 and 1625 (covering Gibbons's tenure) the stipend of the master of the choristers has the names of both Gibbons and Thomas Day entered against it (WAM 33681–2); Day, however, is credited with the allowances for the choristers and the 'regard' for teaching them. One cannot believe that Gibbons shared a stipend with Day; clearly, he succeeded Parsons in his capacity as organist, and what we see in the accounts is the continuing inability of the treasurer to express how matters stood since the division of the two offices under Hooper, their reunion under Parsons, and now their separation once again.

See under the Chapel Royal.

Richard Portman 1625–Interregnum (d. ?1655). In the first accounting year to mention Portman (ending Michaelmas 1626, WAM 33682), his name, like that of Gibbons before him, was perversely bracketed with Day against the entry of the stipend of the master of the choristers. (Day, however, received the other emoluments connected with the choristers.) But, beginning with the year ending Michaelmas 1627 (WAM 33683), some steps were taken to adjust this by entering only Day's name against the regular stipend of master of the choristers together with the choristers' allowances; to confuse things, however, Portman's name was put against the 'regard' for teaching the choristers. After some years it seems to have occurred to the treasurer that he had still not got things right, and so in the year ending Michaelmas 1638 (WAM 33688) the clerk wrote firmly against this 'regard' the word 'Organist'. Portman's name remains thus in the accounts until Michaelmas 1644, the last account before the Restoration.

On 25 January 1640/1 the problem of how to deal with the two officers' salaries was brought to the attention of the Chapter, and an attempt was made to clarify things with a minute reading thus (CA2):

> Whereas there was a difference between the organist and the master of the choristers about a stipend of ten pounds per annum [the regular fee attached to the post of master of the choristers in the accounts] as to whether of them it should be paid, and it appeared to us that the organist hath been in possession of the said stipend for many years together, but that the right was and is in the master of the choristers. It is therefore thought fit and ordered by the Dean and Chapter, that in respect of both their interests and pains, that the said ten pounds shall be continued to the organist and that ten pounds more shall be paid by the treasurer to the master of the choristers yearly.

Meanwhile, Day continued as master of the choristers until Michaelmas 1632, when the accounts fail us until the year 1637–8, when James Trye is found. During 1638–9 Walter Porter follows Trye, and he remains as master of the choristers until the break in the series of accounts after Michaelmas 1644. But as late as 1657 Porter (who died in 1659) described himself thus on the title-page of his *Mottets of Two Voyces*.

Portman became a gentleman of the Chapel Royal in September 1638, on the death of *John Tomkins (Rimbault 1872: 12). During the Commonwealth he had difficulty paying the rent for a lease, which he had obtained from the Chapter in 1640, because he had lost his livelihood (WAM 65899). He was threatened with imprisonment, and had to petition for relief from paying arrears—with what result we do not know. On 19 April 1655 he was allowed £5 by the Trustees for the Maintenance of Ministers (Matthews 1948), and in 1651 he was among those mentioned in Playford's *Musical Banquet* as being available in London to teach the organ or virginals.

Wood (MS Notes) contains the following observations about him: 'He was bred up under Orlando Gibbons, then travelled in France with Dr John Williams, Dean of Westminster, by whose favour he became organist of Westminster and to K. Cha. I—a little obliging man, a sober religious man.' There is no corroborative evidence that Portman was organist to Charles I. He is generally thought to be the Richard Portman who in 1645 published a devotional work entitled *The Soules Life*.

Christopher Gibbons 1660–6. After the Restoration, the Abbey accounts do not record any payments to either an organist or a master of the choristers in the year ending Michaelmas 1660, but at Michaelmas 1661 they disclose a year's stipend as organist to Christopher Gibbons, and a payment for the last three quarters of the year to Henry Purcell the elder as master of the choristers (WAM 33695). Purcell died in August 1664 (Chester 1876), but the account for the year ending Michaelmas 1664 (Lbl, Harl. MS 4184) ascribes the whole year's stipend to him. However, in the year ending 1665 (WAM 33698) Gibbons is entered not only as organist but as master of the choristers also, no doubt having succeeded Purcell on his death. With unusual precision, the accounts for the following year (WAM 33699) show Gibbons as having been paid half a year's stipend, i.e., to 25 March 1666, in both capacities.

See under Winchester Cathedral.

Albertus Bryne 1666–8. The accounts for the year ending Michaelmas 1666 (WAM 33699) cite Bryne as organist from 25 March 1666. Gibbons was succeeded as master of the choristers by Thomas Blagrave, who held the post until 1670. The accounts show Bryne as organist up to Michaelmas 1668 (WAM 33701). That was not quite the end of his time, however, for at the end of the next three months his share of the money collected for showing the Abbey monuments to sightseers was 'allowed to Mr Bryan's executor' (WAM 61228A).

See under St Paul's Cathedral, London.

John Blow (1st tenure) **1668–79**. The accounts attribute a complete year's salary to Blow in the year ending Michaelmas 1669 (WAM 33702), but it is probable that he did not become organist until towards the end of 1668. He made his formal declaration on taking office before the precentor on 3 December 1668 (WAM 61228A). In March 1670 (WAM 33703) Blagrave was succeeded as master of the choristers by Edward Braddock, whose daughter Blow was to marry. The organist's stipend is attributed to Blow up to Michaelmas 1679 (WAM 33714), but he may have handed over to Purcell in the course of the ensuing financial year.

See under the Chapel Royal (and below, for his second tenure).

Henry Purcell 1679–95 (b. London (Westminster), 1659; d. London, 21 Nov. 1695). Purcell was the son either of Thomas Purcell, gentleman of the Chapel Royal, or of Henry Purcell the elder, gentleman of the Chapel Royal and master of the choristers of Westminster Abbey. He was brought up in the choir of the Chapel Royal. His voice had broken by the end of 1673, when he was made assistant to John Hingston, the keeper of the king's wind instruments (including organs), with reversion to the full post, to which he succeeded in 1683; from 1677 he was also 'composer for the violins' in the royal household (Ashbee 1986–9: i. 126, 131, 173, 208). Meanwhile, between 1674 and 1677 he obtained casual employment by tuning the Abbey organ and copying music there (WAM 33709–13).

He became organist of the Abbey at some point in the accounting year ending Michaelmas 1680 (WAM 33715), when the accounts attribute the year's stipend to him. From 1682 he combined this post with that of one of the three organists of the Chapel Royal (q.v.), and from the accession of James II in 1685 he added the further appointment of royal harpsichordist to his many other duties (Ashbee 1986–9: ii. 3).

One incident marred his relations with the Abbey. At the Coronation of William and Mary in 1689 he admitted visitors to the organ-loft and took payment from them, perhaps regarding this as a perquisite. On 18 April 1689 he was called upon to hand over 'all such money as was received by him for places in the organ loft at the coronation of King William and Queen Mary by and before Saturday next' on pain of forfeiting his post (CA5, f. 25).

Purcell died on the eve of St Cecilia's Day 1695, having made his will that day. He was buried in the north choir aisle of the Abbey at the expense of the Dean and Canons (Chester 1876). The inscription over his grave reads: 'Hic requiescit Henricus Purcell hujus ecclesiae collegiatae organista ob. XXI Nov. an. aetat. suae XXXVII A.D. MDCXCV', followed by the verses:

Plaudite, felices superi, tanto hospite; nostris
  Praefuerat, vestris additur ille choris:
Invidia nec vobis Purcellum terra reposcat,
  Questa decus secli deliciasque breves
Tam cito decessisse, modos cui singula debet
  Musa prophana suos, religiosa suos.
Vivit, io et vivat, dum vicina organa spirant,
  Dumque colet numeris turba canora deum.

Hawkins (1853: 748), who prints 'seeli' for 'secli' (which is perhaps a contraction for 'seculi'), gives a free translation of this as follows:

Applaud so great a guest, celestial pow'rs,
Who now resides with you, but once was ours;
Yet let invidious earth no more reclaim
Her short-liv'd fav'rite and her chiefest fame;

Complaining that so prematurely dy'd
Good-nature's pleasure and devotion's pride.
Dy'd? no he lives while yonder organs sound,
And sacred echos to the choir rebound.

On a pillar near the grave is a tablet stating that he 'is gone to that Blessed Place Where only his Harmony can be exceeded'.

One of his sons, Edward (d. 1740), became organist of St Clement's, Eastcheap, London in 1711, and of St Margaret's, Westminster in 1726, both of which posts he held until his death. Edward's son, Edward Henry (d. 1765), was organist of St Clement's, Eastcheap, 1740–65; of St Edmund, King and Martyr, London, 1747–53; and of St John's, Hackney, 1753–65 (Dawe 1983).

John Blow (2nd tenure) **1695–1708**. Blow was reappointed without the slightest delay. Announcing Purcell's death, the *Post Boy* for 28 November 1695 added that 'his place of organist is disposed of to that other great master Dr Blow'. Although Purcell did not die until November 1695, the Abbey accounts, conforming to general practice, attribute a full year's salary to Blow at Michaelmas 1696 (WAM 33729). He remained in office until his death. Meanwhile, his father-in-law, Edward Braddock, had remained master of the choristers until he died in June 1708 (Chester 1876), when he was succeeded by John Church, who retained the post until 1741.

See under the Chapel Royal.

William Croft 1708–27. Croft's name is attached to the post of organist in the accounts from the year ending Michaelmas 1709 to Michaelmas 1727 (WAM 33741–59). During his tenure the pitch of the Abbey organ was lowered a semitone to bring it into line with St Paul's Cathedral and the Chapel Royal, 'whereby the service of the church will be performed with much more ease and decency by the whole choir' (CA2, 11 May 1710).

See under the Chapel Royal.

John Robinson (II) 1727–62 (d. London (Westminster), 30 Apr. 1762, aged 80). Croft died in August 1727, but the accounts do not name Robinson as organist until the year ending Michaelmas 1728; he is last mentioned at Michaelmas 1761 (WAM 33760, 33792). According to Boyce's *Cathedral Music* (iii. p. x), he had been a Chapel Royal boy under Blow; he must therefore be the John Robinson whose voice had broken by May 1705 (Ashbee 1986–9: ii. 80). Stephens (1882) asserts, and this is quite probable, that he was Croft's deputy for many years. His first wife was Anne, daughter of William Turner, a contemporary and colleague of Blow. Mrs Robinson sang for Handel. Robinson was buried in the north aisle of the Abbey on 13 May 1762 (Chester 1876).

Meanwhile, in 1741 Bernard Gates, a contemporary of Robinson in the Chapel Royal, succeeded John Church as master of the Abbey choristers. He retired in 1757.

Robinson was organist of St Lawrence Jewry, London from 1710, and also of St Magnus the Martyr, London Bridge from 1712 (Dawe 1983); he continued to hold both these posts, along with that at the Abbey, until his death. It was as 'Organist of St Laurence, Guildhall' that he subscribed to Croft's *Musica Sacra* in 1724. Hawkins (1853: ii. 827) says of Robinson that 'Being a very active and industrious man, and highly cultivated as a master of the harpsichord, he was in full employment for many years of his life', having 'a greater number of scholars than any one of his time.'

Boyce (*Cathedral Music*) observed that he was 'a most excellent performer on the organ', and Hawkins (1853: ii. 827) remarks that he was 'a very florid and elegant performer on the organ, insomuch that crowds resorted to hear him'. But under the initials 'J. H.' in the second edition of Boyce's *Cathedral Music* (1788), the same writer gives a less urbane account of Robinson's playing:

> In parish churches the voluntary between the psalms and the first lesson was anciently a slow solemn movement, tending like the Sanctus in choral service, to compose the minds of the hearers, and to excite sentiments of piety and devotion. Mr Robinson introduced a different practice, calculated to display the agility of his fingers in Allegro movements on the Cornet, Trumpet, Sesquialtera, and other noisy stops, degrading the instrument, and instead of the full and noble harmony with which it was designed to gratify the ear, tickling it with mere airs in two parts, in fact solos for a flute and a bass.

When Abraham Jordan first devised an organ manual 'adapted to the art of emitting sounds by swelling the notes' in a four-manual organ at St Magnus the Martyr, it fell to Robinson to be the first person publicly to play on it (*Spectator*, 8 February 1712/13). Some years later, Jordan made an addition to the Abbey organ, presumably in the form of a Swell manual, and this was opened by Robinson on 1 August 1730.

Benjamin Cooke 1762–93 (d. London (Westminster), 14 Sept. 1793, aged 58). Chester (1876) notes that Cooke is 'said to have been the son of Benjamin Cooke, a music-seller in New Street, Covent Garden'. He is also stated to have been a pupil of J. C. Pepusch, and Robinson's assistant organist from the age of 12. He became a lay vicar of the Abbey in 1752, and on the retirement of Bernard Gates he became master of the choristers in 1757 (WAM 33789). Although Robinson did not die until the end of April 1762, Cooke's name is given as organist in the accounts for the full year 1761–2 (WAM 33793). From 1752 to 1789 he was Pepusch's successor as conductor of the Academy of Ancient Music. While organist of the Abbey he applied (unsuccessfully) to become organist of St Michael's, Cornhill, London in 1781 (Dawe 1983); and from 1782 he was in fact organist of St Martin-in-the-Fields. He took the Cambridge degree of Mus.D. in 1775 (*Venn*) and, though not officially listed, he clearly incorporated as D.Mus. of Oxford, perhaps in 1782.

Laetitia, daughter of Hawkins, the historian of music, recorded some reminiscences of Cooke, quoted here from Scholes (1953: 157–8):

> Every thing agreeable is connected with the remembrance of Dr Cooke. He was one of the worthiest and best-tempered men that ever existed . . . [and] had escaped all the ills connected with music and prosperity. Being of a rather taciturn disposition . . . his peculiar talent for humour was not generally known, but it was genuine and of the best description.

> No one was ever less vain of superior excellence in an art . . . he certainly supposed that every body could do what he did, 'if they would but try'; when seated at the organ of Westminster Abbey . . . no one ever excelled him in accompanying an anthem. He would press every hand that could be useful, into his service; and even at the risk of addressing himself to persons ignorant of the first principles of music, he would say to any lad who . . . found his way up to the organ, 'Young gentleman, can't you lend a hand here?' To his boys he would say, 'Come, come, don't stand idle, put in one hand here, under my arm.'

The lengthy inscription on his grave in the west cloister of the Abbey records that 'His professional knowledge, talents, and skill were profound', and speaks of the 'simplicity of his manners, the integrity of his heart, and the innocency of his life'.

It was during Cooke's time as organist that the Abbey organ was first fitted with pedals, and he composed a part for them in his well-known Service in G. He was among the subscribers to the second and third volumes of the first edition of Boyce's *Cathedral Music* (1768–73) and to the complete second edition (1788). In 1776 he subscribed to Burney's *History of Music*, and when William Hayes's *Cathedral Music* came out in 1795, he was entered in the subscribers' list as 'late Organist of Westminster Abbey'.

GM (1793), 870; Henry Cooke.

Samuel Arnold 1793–1802 (b. London, 30 July 1740; d. London, 22 Oct. 1802). Arnold was educated as a chorister of the Chapel Royal under Gates, and later studied under *James Nares. In the course of an exceptionally long obituary notice, *GM* states that he was also 'originally under the superintendence of the immortal Handel'. He was chiefly active as a composer for the London stage, and from 1769 to 1776 he was proprietor of Marylebone Gardens. Nevertheless, he succeeded Nares as both organist and composer to the Chapel Royal in 1783 (q.v.). In 1773 he took the Oxford degrees of B.Mus. and D.Mus. by accumulation. He was appointed organist of Westminster Abbey on 29 September 1793 (*GM* (1831), 280). When he was offered the appointment, Arnold stated that his extensive professional commitments would hardly permit him to fulfil its duties, but the dean, anxious to obtain his services, allowed him the requisite freedom to accept. The post of master of the choristers was now assumed by Richard Guise.

Arnold was a subscriber to Burney's *History of Music* (1776), and in 1790 he published his own three-volume anthology of *Cathedral Music*, on the lines of Boyce's celebrated volumes and by way of supplement to them. But his chief claim to fame is his edition in full score (forty volumes, completed in 1797) of the works of Handel, the earliest instance of a collected edition in musical history.

He is buried in the north choir aisle of the Abbey, and at the funeral it was 'observed that the lead of Purcell's coffin was visible'. The slab over the grave gives the date of his appointment to the Abbey, wrongly, as 1789. Nearby is a mural monument erected by his widow, with some verses by Samuel James Arnold, his son. It gives the date of birth as above, i.e., Old Style. Some works of reference adjust this to 10 August, NS, maybe because he did not die until long after the change of calendar; but in accordance with what is said above (p. xxx), it is not usual to make such adjustments.

GM (1802), 1069; *Harmonicon* (1830), 137.

Robert Cooke 1802–14 (d. London (Westminster), 23 Aug. 1814, aged 46). Robert was the son of *Benjamin Cooke, and succeeded his father as organist of St Martin-in-the-Fields in 1793 (*GM* (1793), 1062). The Dean of Westminster, quite exceptionally, reported his appointment as Abbey organist at a Chapter meeting on 7 December 1802. The appointment had already been announced in the *Morning Chronicle* on 15 November, which said: 'There were a number of applications, but the contest was between the successful candidate and Mr Wm. Ayrton, son of Dr [*Edmund] Ayrton.' (Lbl, Add MS 27693, f. 3.)

At some point after Michaelmas 1804 he succeeded Guise as master of the choristers, being named thus in the accounts for the year ending 1805 (WAM 33836). From that time to this, the posts of organist and of master of the choristers have been conjoint.

The Abbey Funeral Book notes that he was drowned in the Thames, and it is usually stated that he took his own life. He was buried in his father's grave (Chester 1876), where the tombstone gives the date of death as 22 August, though the burial register records it as 23 August.

George Ebenezer Williams 1814–19 (b. London (Clerkenwell Green), 30 Aug. 1783; d. Westminster, 17 Apr. 1819). In its obituary notice, *GM* (1819, p. 487) set out Williams's career as follows:

> This gentleman received his musical education in St Paul's [Cathedral] Choir under Mr Richard Bellamy. After he left school he officiated for some years at Westminster Abbey as Dr Arnold's deputy; he was appointed organist of the Philanthropic at the opening of the Chapel, and of Westminster on the death of Mr Cooke in 1814. At the Philanthropic he is succeeded by his pupil, Mr James Turle; and by Mr Greatorex, as organist and music-master of Westminster Abbey.

Stephens (1882), our authority for the date and place of birth, says that Williams was also deputy to R. J. S. Stevens at the Temple Church.

GM (1831, p. 280) gives the formal date of his appointment to the Abbey as 1 October 1814. He is buried in the cloister (Chester 1876). On 19 April 1819 the Chapter minuted that he died 'very much distressed', and made a gift of £40 to his family.

Thomas Greatorex 1819–31. *GM* (1831, p. 280) gives the formal date of Greatorex's appointment to the Abbey as 30 December 1819, some nine months after his predecessor's death. Nevertheless, the accounts for the year ending Michaelmas 1819 (WAM 33850) name him as recipient of the stipend. Greatorex is buried in the west cloister.

See under Carlisle Cathedral.

James Turle 1831–82 (nominally only from 1875) (b. Taunton, 5 Mar. 1802; d. London, 28 June 1882). Turle was a chorister of Wells Cathedral under *Dodd Perkins. He became a pupil of G. E. Williams, whom he succeeded as organist of the Philanthropic Chapel, London in 1819, the same year as he became organist of Christ Church, Southwark. In 1829 he was appointed to St James's, Bermondsey as well as becoming music master for the School for the Indigent

Blind. The Chapter minute of his appointment as organist and master of the choristers of the Abbey, where he had already assisted Greatorex, is dated 15 December 1831.

In 1866 he became an honorary FRCO. As an organ accompanist he appears to have had skill and taste. Dickson, writing in 1894 of his playing on the Schreider/Jordan organ at the Abbey, says:

> The combination 'full without reeds' was of a silvery sweetness never heard in organs of the present day; I imagine that the Mixtures were of a small scale, and they invariably included the Tierce and its octave, now generally omitted. Mr Turle was in the habit of using this combination freely in the accompaniment of the voices, and it suited admirably the style of music exclusively in use at the Abbey, i.e., Services of Aldrich, Gibbons, and Rogers; anthems of Boyce, Croft, Greene, and Purcell.

Bumpus (1972: 156) quotes the *Atlas* for 1848 (reporting the reopening of the choir of the Abbey) as follows: 'Mr Turle employed it [the organ enlarged by Hill] with the greatest taste and address; without overdoing his part—interfering with or covering the choir, he found an opportunity to let all the finest effects of his instrument be heard'. And yet, when the Chapter increased Turle's salary by £50 a year in August 1869, they did not omit to ask him 'to improve the condition of performance of voluntary at end of services'.

Turle had exceptionally large hands, the subject of the following anecdote (*MT*, 48 (1907), 448):

> On one occasion, at the Prussian Embassy, he met the Chevalier Neukomm, who boasted that he could extend his hand on the keyboard over an octave and three notes. Turle quietly approached the pianoforte, and taking an octave and a half into his enormous hand, exclaimed, 'One more for luck!'. No wonder that a roar of laughter greeted the triumph of the English organist over the German composer.

Turle retired from active duty at the Abbey in September 1875, but retained his office until his death. There is a memorial window to him in the north choir aisle, and a tablet in the west cloister.

Grove[2].

Sir (John) Frederick Bridge, CVO, 1882–1918 (permanent deputy from 1875) (b. Oldbury, Worcs., 5 Dec. 1844; d. London, 18 Mar. 1924). Bridge, elder brother of *J. C. Bridge, was a chorister of Rochester Cathedral (where his father was a lay clerk) under *J. L. Hopkins, to whom he was later articled. He became organist of Shorne Parish Church (1861) and then of Strood Parish Church (1862), both near Rochester. He moved to Windsor as organist of Holy Trinity Church in 1865, and studied under *John Goss and *G. J. Elvey. In 1869 he was appointed organist of Manchester Cathedral (q.v.), and in the autumn of 1875 he took up duty as permanent deputy organist of Westminster Abbey (Chapter minute, 27 July 1875), formally succeeding Turle as organist in 1882 (Chapter minute, 10 July).

While in Manchester, Bridge taught harmony at Owen's College (now the University). After his move to Westminster he joined the staff of the National Training School for Music in 1876, and became one of the original professors of the Royal College of Music on its foundation in 1883. In 1890 he became Gresham professor of music, and after the establishment of the King Edward chair of music in the University of London in 1902, he became its first occupant.

Bridge directed the music at Queen Victoria's Jubilee Thanksgiving Service at the Abbey in 1887, and was in charge of the music at the Coronations of 1902 and 1911. From 1896 he conducted the Royal Choral Society.

He took the FRCO diploma in 1867; he held the Oxford degrees of B.Mus. (1868) and D.Mus. (1874); and was granted the MA degree of the University of Durham in 1905 by decree. He received the Jubilee Medal in 1887, was knighted in 1897, appointed MVO (4th class) in 1902, and advanced to CVO in 1911.

He retired from the Abbey at the end of 1918, and was accorded the title of organist emeritus. There is a memorial to him on the west cloister wall. His mild antiquarian interests are reflected in two books, *Samuel Pepys: Lover of Musique* (1903) and *Twelve Good Musicians* (1920).

Grove[2]; J. F. Bridge; *MT*, 65 (1924), 305; *WWW*, 1916–28; *DNB*, 1922–30.

Sir Sydney (Hugo) Nicholson, MVO, 1919–28 (b. London, 9 Feb. 1875; d. Ashford, Kent, 30 May 1947). Nicholson was the youngest son of Sir Charles Nicholson, 1st baronet, MD, the first president of the Legislative Council of Queensland, Australia, and he was brother to Sir Charles Nicholson, 2nd baronet, FRIBA, and A. K. Nicholson, stained-glass artist.

S. H. Nicholson was educated at Rugby School, New College, Oxford (where he read English), and the Royal College of Music. After a brief period as organist of the Lower Chapel, Eton College (1903), he became acting organist of Carlisle Cathedral in 1904 (q.v.). In 1908 he was appointed organist of Canterbury Cathedral, but he withdrew his acceptance on being offered the post at Mancheter Cathedral (q.v.). He left Manchester for Westminster Abbey. In 1928 he gave up his Westminster appointment to devote himself to the work which is his memorial—that of directing the School of English Church Music (since 1945 the Royal School of Church Music), which he founded in 1927. He was the music editor of the 1916 Supplement to *Hymns Ancient & Modern*, and was chiefly responsible for the musical editorial work on *Hymns Ancient & Modern Revised* (1950).

He took the Oxford degrees of BA (1897), MA (1900), and B.Mus. (1902), and held the FRCO diploma. He received the Lambeth degree of D.Mus. in 1928. He was made MVO (4th class) in 1926, and received a knighthood in 1938. He is buried in the cloisters of the Abbey.

MT, 88 (1947), 235; *ECM*, 17 (1947), 26; *DNB* 1941–50; *WWW*, 1941–50; *Grove*[5].

§**Sir Ernest Bullock, CVO, 1928–41** (b. Wigan, 15 Sept. 1890; d. near Aylesbury, Bucks., 23 May 1979). Bullock was educated at Wigan Grammar School and under *E. C. Bairstow at Leeds. From 1907 he was assistant to Bairstow at Leeds Parish Church, and from 1912 he was sub-organist of Manchester Cathedral. He took the Durham degrees of B.Mus. (1908) and D.Mus. (1914), and held the FRCO diploma (1913). On return from war-service in 1919 he was briefly organist of St Michael's College, Tenbury, but before the end of that year he was appointed to Exeter Cathedral, where he remained until becoming organist of Westminster Abbey.

Bullock was director of music at the Coronation of George VI in 1937, but his appointment was not a foregone conclusion. He was hardly known to the public at large, and there were those who thought that, as master of the king's music, *H. W. (Sir Walford) Davies should be in charge. (Davies was, of course, extremely well known (see p. 351).) The Archbishop of Canterbury asked the keeper of the Muniments of Westminster Abbey to examine precedents and write a memorandum on the subject. As a result, Bullock, in his capacity as organist of the Abbey, was appointed, with the proviso that he was to take the master of the king's music into consultation. Unfortunately, the preface to the official musical edition of the *Form and Order of Service* for the Coronation gives the impression that they were jointly responsible, and this was not so. These arrangements were followed in 1953 for the Coronation of Queen Elizabeth II, when the Abbey organist (McKie) was again appointed director of music, responsible for both its selection and performance. On that occasion the archbishop wrote to McKie to say that 'According to precedent the Master of the Queen's Music is associated with you in the discharge of your responsibility, but the chief responsibility and final voice is with you and not with him.' (This matter is alluded to here as relevant to the status of the organist of Westminster Abbey; see Tanner 1969: 145, and letters to me from Sir Ernest Bullock and Sir William McKie, now part of Lcm, MS 6068.) The question of whether Bullock wrote all, or merely some, of the fanfares used in 1937 seems indeterminate (see *MT*, 94 (1953), 273).

The outbreak of war in 1939 caused the Westminster Abbey choir to be disbanded for the time being, and in 1941 Bullock accepted the combined posts of professor of music in the University of Glasgow and principal of the Royal Scottish Academy of Music. In January 1953 he returned to London as director of the Royal College of Music, retiring in 1960.

He was appointed CVO in the Coronation Honours of 1937, and received a knighthood in 1951. In 1955 the University of Glasgow conferred on him the honorary degree of LL D. There is a portrait of him by J. S. Ward in the Royal College of Music.

Grove[5]; *WWW*, 1971–80.

§**Sir William (Neil) McKie, MVO, 1941–63** (b. Melbourne, 22 May 1901; d. Ottawa, 1 Dec. 1984). McKie, the son of a clergyman was educated in Melbourne, and came to England in 1919 to study at the Royal College of Music. In 1921 he went up to Worcester College, Oxford as organ scholar, and took the Oxford degrees of BA with B.Mus. (1924) and MA (1930). From 1923 to 1926 he was on the staff of Radley College, and from 1926 to 1930 he was director of music at Clifton College. He then returned to Australia as city organist of Melbourne, and later became director of music at Geelong Grammar School.

McKie came back to England in 1938 as organist of Magdalen College, Oxford. He was appointed to succeed Bullock at the Abbey in 1941, but since he was in the RAF at the time and unable to take up the post, **Dr Osborne H. Peasgood** acted as organist. On coming to Westminster McKie also joined the staff of the Royal Academy of Music.

He was director of music at the Coronation of 1953 (see above under Bullock), and received a knighthood in the Coronation Honours, having already been appointed MVO (4th class) after the wedding of Princess Elizabeth in 1947.

He received the Oxford honorary degree of D.Mus. in 1944, and was an honorary FRCO and an honorary fellow of Worcester College, Oxford (1954). In 1961 he received the honorary degree of D.Mus. from the University of Melbourne, and he became a Commander of the Norwegian Order of St Olav, with star, in 1964.

WWW, 1984.

§**Douglas (Albert) Guest, CVO, 1963–81** (b. Mortomley, Yorks., 9 May 1916). Guest was educated at Reading School, the Royal College of Music, and King's College, Cambridge, where he was organ student and held the John Stewart of Rannoch scholarship in sacred music. He took the Cambridge degrees of Mus.B. (1938), BA (1939), and MA (1942; *ad eundem* Oxon., 1947). In 1965 he was made an honorary FRCO.

From 1945 to 1950 he was director of music at Uppingham School; he then became organist of Salisbury Cathedral, 1950–7, and Worcester Cathedral, 1957–63, before his appointment to Westminster Abbey. When he came to London he also joined the staff of the Royal College of Music.

He was appointed CVO in 1975, and received the Lambeth doctorate of music in 1977. On retirement from the Abbey he was complimented by the title of organist emeritus.

Simon (John) Preston 1981–7.

See under Christ Church Cathedral, Oxford.

§**Martin (Gerard James) Neary, organist and master of the choristers from 1988** (b. London, 28 Mar. 1940). Neary, who as a boy was one of the children of the Chapel Royal, was educated at the City of London School and then at Gonville and Caius College, Cambridge, where he was organ scholar, 1958–63. He read for part I of the theological tripos and part I of the music tripos, taking the degrees of BA and MA in 1962 and 1964 respectively. He also holds the FRCO diploma, and in 1963 he won both the second prize at the St Albans International Organ Festival and a conducting scholarship at the Berkshire Music Center, USA. He received a diploma at the J. S. Bach Competition in Leipzig in 1968. In 1971 he was made an honorary citizen of Texas, USA.

His first appointment was as organist of St Mary's, Hornsey Rise, London in 1958. From 1963 to 1965 he was assistant organist of St Margaret's, Westminster, where he was subsequently organist and choirmaster from 1965 until taking up the post of organist of Winchester Cathedral in January 1972. He began his duties at Westminster Abbey in January 1988.

WINDSOR

The Royal Free Chapel of St George in Windsor Castle

(St George's Chapel, Windsor)

Main sources in this section (1972):

Chapter Acts

CA2	1596–1641 (WR/VI.B.2).
CA3	1660–72 (WR/VI.B.3); CA2, 3 are calendared in *Historical Monographs relating to St George's Chapel*, xiii, ed. S. Bond (Windsor, for the Dean and Canons, 1966).
CA4	1672–84 (WR/VI.B.4).
CA5	1684–1717 (WR/VI.B.5).
CA6	1717–48 (WR/VI.B.6).
CA7	1748–73 (WR/VI.B.7).
CA8	1773–1814 (WR/VI.B.8).
CA9	1815–40 (WR/VI.B.9).
CA10	1840–66 (WR/VI.B.10).
CA11	1866–95 (WR/VI.B.11).

Accounts

A series of treasurer's computa: 1541–2, 1558–9, 1562–3 to 1631–2, with gaps. WR references for these cited individually are: 1541–2, XV.59.3; Oct. 1558–June 1559, with some jottings for 1563–4, XV.56.78; 1562–3, XV.59.5; 1563–4, XV.59.6; 1566–7, XV.59.7; 1568–9, XV.59.8–9; 1571–2, XV.59.11; 1575–6, XV.59.12; 1586–7, XV.59.13; 1628–9, XV.59.39.

Registers of Baptisms, Marriages, and Burials

Published in *Historical Monographs relating to St George's Chapel*, x, ed. E. H. Fellowes and E. R. Poyser (Windsor, for the Dean and Canons, 1957).

'The Royal Free Chapel of Our Lady, St George, and St Edward' was founded by Edward III in 1348. Almost immediately thereafter, in his statutes for the Order of the Garter (1349), the King made the clergy of the Chapel members of the establishment of that Order, so forging the enduring link between the Chapel and the Knights of the Garter. The statutes governing the Chapel, dated 1352, prescribed, *inter alia*, for priest-vicars (precursors of the minor canons), clerks in minor orders (precursors of the lay clerks), and six choristers under the instruction of one of the vicars. By the time our period is reached, this master of the choristers had ceased to be one of the vicars, and was a layman. The statutes do not specifically provide for an organist; as in other such early foundations, the post arose in response to later needs.

John Merbecke ←1541–?1585 (jointly at various times with George Thaxton, Preston, Robert Golder, and Richard Farrant). In the dedicatory address to the King prefixed to his *Concordance* of 1550 (reprinted as part of a valuable biographical note by Hunt) Merbecke stated that he was 'altogether brought up in your highness' College at Windsor, in the study of music and playing on organs, wherein I consumed vainly the greatest part of my life'. He was associated with St George's Chapel in some adult capacity by 1 May 1531 at the latest, when an inventory of the property of the minor canons included 'one silver spoon written thereon John Merbeke' (WR/XI.B.40). The earliest surviving treasurer's account to name him as organist is that for 1541–2, when he received 40*s*. 'pro modulatione organorum' and 13*s*. 4*d*. 'pro sufflatione organorum'; at the same time he was also one of the lay clerks. John Hake was paid 'pro informatione puerorum in cantu' in that year.

In the accounts for 1558–9, the next available record, Merbecke continues to be paid as both clerk and organist. In the first quarter, Hake and one Watson share the payment for teaching the boys; in the second and third quarters, both Merbecke and Preston (see below) are remunerated as organists, while (curiously) Merbecke is paid as 'master' of the choristers and Preston as 'instructor' of them. This account does not cover the full year.

In 1562–3 Merbecke and Golder (see below) are designated, delightfully, 'agitatores organorum'. The next extant accounts to mention Merbecke (1563–4, 1566–7, 1568–9, 1571–2) indicate that he was clerk and sole organist, but Golder probably remained his colleague for part of 1563–4, and Richard Farrant thereafter (see below).

Accounts from 1571–2 imply that Merbecke held a sinecure chaplaincy to the Lord Hastings Chantry in St George's Chapel, a point fully discussed by Fellowes (1940: 14). Standard works of reference accept the date of his death as *c.*1585, but it is not clear upon what this is based, though his latest published work appeared in 1584. His son Roger (1536–1605) became provost of Oriel College, Oxford and physician to Elizabeth I.

In the dedicatory address to the *Concordance* (see above) Merbecke recounts how, on 16 March 1543/4, his house at Windsor was searched, and as a result of the discovery of his Calvinistic sympathies, he was condemned to death at the stake, and the manuscript of the *Concordance* was destroyed. He was reprieved in the following October and undertook the labour of rewriting his work. When this proved too large for printing, he set himself to write out a shorter version, but, even then, this ran to more than 900 leaves when published. This was the first concordance of the Bible to be produced. Meanwhile, he had supplicated for the Oxford degree of B.Mus. (Wood 1815–20: i. 130), which he presumably received, and his renowned *The booke of Common praier noted* appeared in 1550. He was a considerable author on religious and theological subjects, beginning with *The Lyves of the Holy Sainctes, Prophets, Patriarches* in 1574.

George Thaxton ←1550→ (jointly with John Merbecke). The royal injunctions of Edward VI, dated 26 October 1550 (Frere 1910: ii. 258), which decreed the suspension of organ-playing in St George's Chapel during divine service, spoke of Merbecke and George Thaxton as having had 'fees appointed them severally for playing upon organs', and allowed them to keep these emoluments. Within a few years, however, the prohibition of organ-playing became a dead letter.

——**Preston ←1559→** (jointly with John Merbecke). From January 1559 (see above under Merbecke) the accounts show that Preston was paid as instructor of the choristers and as organist along with Merbecke.

Robert Golder ←1562–3 (jointly with John Merbecke). Under the name of 'Coulder' in the accounts for 1562–3, Golder and Merbecke were both paid as 'agitatores organorum'. In some jottings for 1563–4 found with the accounts for 1558–9 it is stated that Golder died 'in the end of November', having been paid as master of the choristers and organist to the end of November 1563. His will, dated 28 November 1563, described him as 'one of the players of the organ within the Queen's Majesty's Free Chapel within her castle of Windsor' (Fellowes 1940: 23).

Richard Farrant 1564–80 (jointly with John Merbecke) (d. 30 Nov. 1580). Farrant was appointed by indenture dated 24 April 1564. This has not survived, but according to a memorandum (WR/IV.B.16) it referred to him as 'one of the Queen's Chapel' (i.e., the Chapel Royal), and appointed him to be 'master of the choristers of this Church, and to have a clerk's place and to be one of the organists in this chapel: he to have the boarding, clothing, lodging and finding of the ten choristers'. Even though the accounts only mention him as master of the choristers, it is plain that he rates as one of the organists.

According to an establishment list (Lbl, Stowe MS 571, f. 36), Farrant was a gentleman of the Chapel Royal by the year 1552. He took part in the funeral of Edward VI, the Coronation and funeral of Mary I, and the Coronation of Elizabeth I (PRO, E101/427/6; LC2, 4/2; LC2, 4/3). He relinquished this position on the date of his indenture at Windsor, but he was reappointed on 5 November 1569 or 1570 (Rimbault 1872: 1, 2; see observations on p. 3 concerning the dates in the Chapel Royal Cheque Book about the time of this reappointment), and thereafter held the two posts concurrently. From 1567 he was closely involved in the production of choirboy plays before the Queen (Arkwright 1913–14), and his will (PRO, PCC 9, Darcy) tells us that he had a house in Blackfriars, London.

John Mundy ←1585–1630 (jointly with Nathaniel Giles) (d. Windsor, 29 June 1630). After Michaelmas 1576 there is no account until 1586–7, when, in the place where Merbecke's name was entered as clerk and organist we now find Mundy. We know from Giles's indenture, however (see below), that Mundy was already living in the Windsor cloisters by June 1585. All available accounts show him as clerk and organist up to 1628–9, but there is no extant account for the year of his death, 1629–30.

He was the elder son of William Mundy (d. 1591), vicar choral of St Paul's Cathedral and gentleman of the Chapel Royal (Lbl, Harl. MS 5580, f. 20). In 1586 he took the Oxford degree of B.Mus., and proceeded D.Mus. in 1624 (Wood 1815–20: i, 235, 416). He was buried at St George's.

Nathaniel Giles 1585–1634 (jointly with John Mundy and then William Child) (b. Worcester; d. Windsor, 24 Jan. 1634, aged 75). Born 'about the city of Worcester' (Wood MS Notes), Giles was organist of Worcester Cathedral, 1581–5 (q.v.). His indenture as organist and master of the choristers of St George's Chapel (WR/XI.B.30) is dated 8 June 1585. He was to have

> the room and place of a clerk . . . and to be one of the players of the organs there and also the office of instructor and master of the choristers . . . and the office of tutor, creansor, or governor of the same ten children . . . to be instructed . . . in the knowledge of music, that is to say in singing, pricksong, descant, and such as be apt to the instruments.

He was to lodge, feed, and clothe the boys, and was granted 'one dwelling house in the said castle [of Windsor] commonly called the old commons [the house of the present organist] wherein John Mundy doth now inhabit . . . in such wise as one Richard Farrant lately enjoyed the same'.

In 1597 Giles added the duties of a gentleman and master of the children of the Chapel Royal to his other commitments (Rimbault 1872: 5), and, undoubtedly, it was this that led to an arrangement whereby *Leonard Woodson of Eton College, who was also a lay clerk of St George's, did duty as acting master of the choristers (CA2, 8 April 1605). This was at Giles's own request, and it was on the understanding that he himself would resume the work at three months' notice whenever the Dean and Chapter should wish. Woodson lived until 1647, but he had ceased to have charge of the Windsor choristers by April 1633 at the latest (see below under Child), and in November 1633 one Wenceslow by name was allotted the duty (CA2, f. 112). It was in his capacity as a member of the Chapel Royal that Giles accompanied Charles I to Canterbury in 1625 to await the arrival of the King's bride from France. He had been given special leave from Windsor (CA2, f. 125).

His early connection with Worcester was renewed when he married Anne Stainer ('an Alderman's daughter who had a good fortune', according to Wood MS Notes) at St Helen's Church there on 14 June 1587. One son of this marriage, also called Nathaniel, became a canon of St George's Chapel in 1624, and a daughter, Margaret, married a future Bishop of Hereford, Herbert Croft. Giles is buried in St George's Chapel, where the memorial to him erected by his son Nathaniel describes him as master of the children rather than as organist. The year of death inscribed on the memorial, 1633, is of course OS. Giles took the Oxford degrees of B.Mus. in 1585 and D.Mus. in 1622 (Wood 1815–20: i. 229, 405).

No successor was appointed to Giles as organist. The work of master of the choristers was carried on by a number of persons in succession (notably Matthew Green, who held the post from the Restoration until January 1703/4) until the office was reunited with that of organist under John Golding (see below).

William Child ?1630–4 (jointly with Nathaniel Giles) **1634–97** (sole organist) (b. Bristol; d. Windsor, 23 Mar. 1697, aged 90). Wood (1815–20: ii. 265) is in error in asserting that Child was a pupil of Elway Bevin. Hudson and Large (1970) have established that in 1620 he was apprenticed to a singingman of Bristol Cathedral named Thomas Prince. The lists of choristers of that Cathedral are complete for the period, but do not include Child.

Child's connection with Windsor began on 19 April 1630, when he was elected to the next vacant post of lay clerk (CA2, f. 106); on 26 July 1632, when he was assigned a 'St Anthony' exhibition, he was described as organist (f. 117). It is fairly clear, therefore, that he was John Mundy's successor. Meanwhile, on 8 July 1631 he had taken the Oxford degree of B.Mus. (Wood 1815–20: i. 459).

For a short time in 1633 Child took over the teaching of the choristers, but otherwise he was never master of the choristers. When Nathaniel Giles died and his post as organist remained unfilled, it was arranged that Child should receive double stipend but be responsible for a deputy when necessary. The minute recording this (CA2, f. 123) reveals that Child had actually been doing the duty of two organists efficiently for some time ('per longum tempus . . . non sine sua laude').

In the prefatory notes to volume 1 of his *Cathedral Music* (1790) *Samuel Arnold records a tradition that, during the Interregnum, Child 'retired to a small farm which he then occupied' and busied himself composing church music, convinced that the King was sure to be restored. The House of Lords granted him seven months' arrears of pay in January 1645/6, and the Trustees for the Maintenance of Ministers awarded him £5 in February 1657/8 'provided he show what office he hold' (Matthews 1948).

After the Restoration, Child not only resumed his post as organist of St George's but received appointments in the royal household in London. In June 1660 he became one of the musicians in ordinary for wind instruments (Ashbee 1986–9: i. 3). He also became one of the three organists of the Chapel Royal (q.v.). In July 1663 he was licensed to proceed D.Mus. at Oxford (Wood 1815–20: ii. 265).

Difficulties arose at Windsor, partly because of his work at Court, partly because he was receiving pay for double duty as organist. In May 1666 there was uncertainty about whether he should be given two portions of burial fees and of the dividend from the offerings from the Knights of the Garter. In 1672 he claimed a double fee for the installations of Knights, adding that he took 'extraordinary pains' on such occasions. As to the former, the decision went against him; but in the latter instance he received double pay on the one occasion. Earlier, on 1 September 1662, Child's poor attendance led the Dean and Chapter to consider engaging another organist and dividing the pay, 'unless Mr Child shall give assurance of better attendance'. In October 1662 *Benjamin Rogers was appointed as lay clerk, with extra pay (deductible from Child's stipend) of £1 for every month he played in Child's absence. What happened on Rogers's departure for Oxford in 1665 is not disclosed; but the Dean and Chapter were evidently not displeased with Child, allowing him his house rent-free from May 1675.

On 1 August 1668 the Chapter Acts record how Child was the subject of a disgraceful attack from Matthew Green, master of the choristers: '[he] did hastily and irreverently go out of the Chapel in time of Divine Service and gave Dr Child uncivil and rude language while he was doing his duty in playing upon the organ, and after the ending of the Divine Service did trip up his heels, and when down did unhumanly beat him'. (All the foregoing matters from 1662 may easily be traced in CA3.)

Child was buried in St George's Chapel, where the gravestone records his death on 23 March 1696/7 in the 91st year of his age, and states that he was born in Bristol. His will, dated 9 February of that year (WR/XIII.B.2), bequeathed £20 towards the building of Windsor Town Hall. Earlier he had given the town £50 to be distributed to the poor.

There is a curious note on Child's gravestone which reads: 'He paved the body of the choir.' This is explained in a memorandum written in 1717 by one of the canons (WR/IV.B.18): at a time when Child had some £500 arrears of salary due to him from Charles II, he jokingly said that he would gladly exchange his right to these arrears for £5 and some bottles of wine. Some of the canons accepted this proposal, but later, to Child's embarrassment, these arrears were paid off. The canons considerately released him from his bargain, with the proviso that he should pay for the marble paving of the choir. The black marble paving is still there.

There are numerous references to Child in Pepys's *Diary*. A painting of him in his doctor's robe is among the Music School collection at Oxford (Poole 1912–25: i. 157).

John Golding 1697–1719 (b. Windsor; d. Windsor, 7 Nov. 1719). On 2 May 1677 Golding was promoted from half to full pay as a chorister of St George's Chapel; and on 14 April 1684 he received a gratuity of £5 on the breaking of his voice (CA4). The following minute was passed on 24 July 1685 (CA5):

> Whereas John Golding, formerly a chorister of this Church, hath attained sufficient skill in music to be capable of performing the duties of organist as well as the master of the choristers [N.B., less than a year after his voice broke]; the Chapter having had the judgment of all the petticanons herein; and whereas Dr Child, the present organist, and Mr Green, the master of the choristers, have with great diligence performed their duties for many years past, 'tis now agreed for their ease that the said Golding shall receive monthly from the Treasurer half a clerk's pay, provided he assist the organist upon all necessary occasions and diligently instruct the choristers in the art of singing.

Golding received a half place as lay clerk on 15 April 1687 and a full place on 5 August 1689, while on 7 May 1691 he was awarded £5 (with a promise of more) for his 'extraordinary pains in instructing the choristers'. Having been granted the reversion of their posts on 10 December 1694, he duly succeeded Child as organist on 12 April 1697 and Green as master of the choristers on 4 January 1703/4 (CA5).

Boyce's *Cathedral Music*, which, echoed by Hawkins (1853: ii. 798), calls him 'Goldwin' or 'Golding', is the authority for the date of his death. All the St George's records refer to him as Golding.

John Pigott 1719–56 (d. 24 Nov. 1762). Pigott was the son of *Francis Pigott, and, on his mother's side, the nephew of John Pelling, canon of St George's Chapel and of St Paul's Cathedral. In 1704 he succeeded his father as organist for both the Inner and Middle Temple at the Temple Church, London. He continued as the Inner Temple organist until February 1728/9, and for the Middle Temple until 1736 (Dawe 1983).

Meanwhile, he was appointed organist of St George's Chapel by minute dated 3 December 1719 (CA6); on account of his uncle's interest he was preferred to *Nathaniel Priest. Furthermore, Pigott was allowed the special favour of leave on fifteen Sundays a year to enable him to retain his position at the Temple Church. It was arranged that *Benjamin Lamb of Eton, who was already receiving half pay as master of the choristers, should now receive full pay in return for his assistance when Pigott was absent at the Temple (WR/IV.B., f. 110). But the position was complicated because the Chapter did not wish to divorce the mastership of the choristers from the post of organist should Pigott resign at any time. On 25 April 1726 Pigott was expressly and formally appointed master of the choristers (CA6), and Lamb continued to have the stipend until such time as Pigott might leave the Temple, when Lamb would revert to half pay and continue to play for Pigott on occasion. But, as things turned out, Pigott himself became organist of Eton College in succession to Lamb in 1733 (q.v.). From 1733 to 1736, then, he was organist to the Middle Temple, organist of St George's Chapel, and organist of Eton College in plurality.

On the death of his uncle, John Pelling, Pigott received a legacy of £1,000, and he resigned from both St George's Chapel and Eton in 1756. On his death some six years later he was buried at St George's.

Edward Webb 1756–88 (bap. Windsor, 28 Sept. 1725; d. 3 Mar. 1788). Webb, whose father had been a lay clerk of St George's, and who himself had been a chorister and lay clerk, was appointed organist on Pigott's resignation by minute dated 11 May 1756 (CA7). He was further appointed succentor on 6 December 1764; Fellowes (1940) remarks that although seven of Webb's successors were similarly appointed, it is doubtful whether such appointments of laymen were lawful at St George's. (At Exeter Cathedral, William Jackson, Paddon, and S. S. Wesley, all laymen, were succentors as well as organists; but membership of the College of Vicars Choral was open to laymen there.)

From 1756 Webb was also organist of Eton College (q.v.). According to one of his pupils, William Sexton, he was brother-in-law to Dr T. Davis, provost of Eton and canon of St George's (Gu, MS R.d.85).

BMB (using the Christian name William) says that Webb died 'from loss of blood, after undergoing an operation for removal of a wen in the nostril'.

Theodore Aylward 1788–1801 (d. London, 27 Feb. 1801, aged 70). On matriculating at Oxford in 1791 Aylward described himself as 'son of Henry Aylward of Chichester, gentleman' (Foster 1887–92). *DNB* notes that he seems to have sung as a boy in Drury Lane Theatre. At about 1760 he was organist of Oxford Chapel, London (Stephens 1882) and then of St Lawrence Jewry (1762–88), resigning from Oxford Chapel on his appointment to St Michael's, Cornhill (1768–81) (Dawe 1983). He was appointed Gresham professor of music in 1771, and retained this part-time lectureship after his move to Windsor. He was among the subscribers to volume 3 of the first edition of Boyce's *Cathedral Music* in 1773, to the complete second edition in 1788, and to William Hayes's *Cathedral Music* in 1795.

He was appointed organist, master of the choristers, and succentor of St George's Chapel on probation by minute dated 10 May 1788 (CA8). He took the Oxford degrees of B.Mus. and D.Mus. within a couple of days of each other in 1791. On his death he left a bequest to the Royal Society of Musicians and was buried at St George's, where there is a tablet to his memory with some verses by the poet William Hayley. These speak of 'my pleasing gentle Friend' to whom 'Heaven most freely to thy Life assign'd Benevolence, the Music of the Mind!'

William Ayrton, writing on 16 November 1837 (Lcm, MS 2170), said: 'I perfectly remember him—a stout Dutch-built man, whose features were anything but an index to intellectual powers . . . Dr A. lived at Windsor, but came to town twice a week, to teach at a very good school in Queen Square, if I am not mistaken.' W. H. Husk (*Grove*[1]) stated that 'Aylward is said (on the authority of Bowles, the poet) to have been a good scholar, and possessed of considerable literary attainments.'

William Sexton 1801–24 (b. 1764; d. Windsor, 27 Apr. 1824). Sexton was appointed probationer singingboy of St George's Chapel on 23 February 1773 (CA7), and at the same time he joined the choir of Eton College. On 13 April 1801 (CA8) he was appointed 'probationer organist in the room of Dr Aylward, deceased'. A Chapter minute of 30 June 1824, referring to Sexton's death and the appointment of his successor, discloses that he also held the office of succentor. In some autobiographical notes (Gu, MS R.d.85) he describes himself as 'organist, sub-precentor, and master of the choristers' of St George's Chapel and as 'lay clerk etc.' of Eton College, implying that he also acted as organist at Eton, where the holder of the post was 'yet living but past duty'.

On 16 April 1822 he was admonished by the Chapter for having insulted the precentor, to whom he had written 'an extremely intemperate letter' (CA9). He was buried at St George's.

Karl Friedrich Horn 1824–30 (b. Nordhausen, Saxony, 1762; d. Windsor, 5 Aug. 1830). It seems that Horn came to England in 1782 and, through the patronage of the Saxony ambassador, presently became a fashionable music teacher. The memorial to him in the Dean's Cloister of St George's Chapel records that he was 'Tutor in Music to her late Majesty Queen Charlotte [consort of George III] and the Princesses'. He collaborated with Samuel Wesley in the production of an early English edition of Bach's *Wohltemperierte Clavier* (1810).

It was at the late age of 62 that he was appointed probationer organist and master of the choristers of St George's Chapel on 30 June 1824. He was confirmed in office on 30 September 1825 (CA9). The memorial referred to above was erected by 'An affectionate son', that is, Charles Edward Horn (1786–1849), composer of the air 'Cherry Ripe'; it gives the date of death (slightly wrongly) as 3 August.

Grove[1].

Highmore Skeats (II) 1830–5 (b. ?Ely; d. Windsor, 24 Feb. 1835, aged 48). Pending the appointment of a successor to Horn, John Mitchell (see p. 376) became acting organist at St George's. There were seven candidates for the post (see flyleaf of Lbl copy of John Alcock, *Twentysix select anthems*), including Mitchell, *Robert Janes, and *John Speechly.

Skeats's father, *Highmore Skeats (I), was successively organist of Ely and Canterbury Cathedrals; following the father's move to Canterbury in 1803 the son succeeded him at Ely (q.v.). His appointment as probationer organist and master of the boys at St George's Chapel was minuted on 8 November 1830 (CA9). He died at Windsor, and there is a memorial to him in the Dean's Cloister. This gives his age at death as 48, whereas *GM* says he died 'in his 50th year'. His daughter Harriet became the first wife of his successor.

GM, 1835, i. 443.

Sir George (Job) Elvey 1835–82 (b. Canterbury, 27 Mar. 1816; d. near Windsor, 9 Dec. 1893). G. J. Elvey, brother of *Stephen Elvey, was a chorister of Canterbury Cathedral under *Highmore Skeats (I). On his brother's appointment as organist of New College, Oxford, George also moved to Oxford as his pupil and began to deputize at the organs of New College, Magdalen, and Christ Church. When, at the age of only 19, he was considered for appointment to St George's Chapel in competition with *George Smart, Henry Bishop, and *S. S. Wesley, William IV made his views known: 'In the evening after the trial, the Dean and some of the Chapter were dining with the King (who claimed the final vote respecting the appointment), and he enquired about the candidates. On being told that Elvey was the best, but was too young, he replied, "The best man is to have it."' (Elvey 1894.)

His appointment on probation was minuted on 27 April 1835 and confirmed on 15 June 1836 (CA9). He subsequently became private organist to Queen Adelaide and, by royal warrant, to Queen Victoria. He took the Oxford degrees of B.Mus. and D.Mus. in 1838 and 1840 respectively, receiving a dispensation to proceed to the latter degree in less than the statutory four years after the first.

At the time of his trial for the appointment at St George's, Elvey found the organ pedals (doubtless of only one octave in compass) covered by a board. When, in 1843, the organ was enlarged and the pedal compass extended so that 'the difficult fugues of the great Sebastian Bach can now be executed with ease' (Elvey 1894: 71), the compass of the Great and Choir manuals remained the old extended one down to F, which Elvey preferred to the end of his life. In letters written after his retirement (quoted in Elvey 1894: 316, 318), he said:

> Probably I stand alone, but I prefer the old G or F organs . . . they are, in my opinion, more suitable for Church music. Gibbons in F, that service of services, on my old instrument where every stop went down to F, will not be forgotten by me, and possibly by others. I am fully aware that Bach's pedal fugues cannot be played on G organs, but there are many grand compositions which can be better performed on G than on CC organs, and Handel's six organ fugues were written for the G organs.

Elvey also played the violin, and, along with *W. H. Longhurst, he was a member of the orchestra at the Handel Festival of 1888. He insisted that all his articled pupils should learn the instrument.

In 1842 or 1843, seeking an increase in stipend, Elvey applied for, and was offered, the post of organist of Exeter Cathedral, but he remained at Windsor when the Chapter agreed to increase his salary from £135 to £200 a year. *S. S. Wesley was then appointed to Exeter.

Prior to 1849, the music at all royal funerals in St George's Chapel had been the responsibility of the organist of the Chapel Royal. Fellowes (1940: 76) explains that, on the occasion of the funeral of Queen Adelaide in that year, 'Elvey succeeded in overthrowing the custom . . . and since that date he, and all his successors at St George's Chapel, enjoyed the sole and undisputed right to conduct the musical arrangements at all State ceremonies in the Chapel.'

Elvey received a knighthood following the wedding of Princess Louise, daughter of Queen Victoria, in 1871. His widow hints at some unhappiness behind her husband's retirement in 1882, saying that the reasons for this 'are well known to those who created them, and must, or at least should, fill them with lifelong pain and remorse' (Elvey 1894: 261). Nevertheless, he was granted 'a liberal pension' (Fellowes 1940: 77). He is buried outside the Chapel and is commemorated by a brass and a window within it. He was married four times; his first wife was the daughter of his predecessor.

Sir Walter Parratt, KCVO, 1882–1924 (b. Huddersfield, 10 Feb. 1841; d. Windsor, 27 Mar. 1924). Parratt's father, Thomas, was organist of Huddersfield Parish Church, and it is related that at the age of 10 the boy could play the whole of Bach's '48' by heart. When he was only 11 he succeeded his elder brother as organist of Armitage Bridge Church, near Huddersfield, but later that year (1852) he went to the choir school of St Peter's Chapel, Palace Street, London. While there he had lessons from *George Cooper. In 1854 he returned to Huddersfield as organist of St Paul's Church.

Wider opportunity came with his appointment as private organist to the Earl of Dudley at Witley Court, Worcestershire in 1861; there he came to the notice of Sir Frederick Ouseley, and he often walked the twelve miles to St Michael's College, Tenbury, sometimes before breakfast (personal reminiscence from E. H. Fellowes). From Great Witley he returned to the north of England as organist of Wigan Parish Church in 1868. Then, from 1872 to 1882, he was organist of Magdalen College, Oxford (q.v.), taking the Oxford degree of B.Mus. in 1873.

The Dean and Chapter of St George's Chapel resolved to offer him the post of organist by minute dated 6 July 1882 (CA11). He received a knighthood in 1892, and was appointed master of the queen's music in 1893 (he was also master of the king's music under Edward VII and George V). His successive appointments in the Royal Victorian Order were as follows: MVO (4th class), 1901; CVO, 1917; KCVO, 1921. He received the honorary degree of D.Mus. from Oxford (at the Encaenia, 1894) and Durham (1912), and of Mus.D. from Cambridge (1910).

On the establishment of the Royal College of Music in 1883 Parratt became the principal professor of the organ; through a number of unusually illustrious pupils, both there and at Windsor, he was to found a distinctive school of organ-playing. From 1908 to 1918 he was professor of music at Oxford, being thereupon created MA and D.Mus. by decree.

Parratt was a skilled chess-player. Among the many stories told of his prowess, Ponsonby (1951: 353–4) recounts a particularly interesting one about a game at Windsor Castle with the prime minister, Bonar Law. His account differs slightly from the version in Tovey and Parratt (1941), but Ponsonby was an eyewitness, and repeats George V's remark to the discomfitted Law: 'I hear old Parratt beat your head off!'

There is a small portrait of Parratt in Magdalen College, Oxford. His ashes are buried close to the organ-loft of St George's Chapel.

Grove[1]: *DNB*, 1922–30; *WWW*, 1916–28; Tovey and Parratt 1941.

On Parratt's death, the appointment was offered to H. W. (Sir Walford) Davies, but at that time he felt unable to accept. Restoration work had begun in the Chapel in 1921, and since then there had been only a small temporary organ. For the time being, therefore, the post of organist was left vacant. ***M. C. Boyle** was appointed acting organist, and E. H. Fellowes (1870–1951) became master of the choristers with responsibility for the full choir. Fellowes, already by that time distinguished as a scholar and editor of late Tudor and early Stuart music, both sacred and secular, had been a minor canon of the Chapel since 1900, and was to serve as such in five reigns.

Sir (Henry) Walford Davies, KCVO, OBE, 1927–32 (b. Oswestry, Shropshire, 6 Sept. 1869; d. Wrington, Somerset, 11 Mar. 1941). Davies was born into an Independent (Congregationalist) family, but he became a chorister of St George's Chapel in 1882. He learnt the organ as Parratt's pupil-assistant, and from 1883 (before the breaking of his voice) to 1890 he was organist of the private chapel in Windsor Great Park. He went to the Royal College of Music in 1890, when he became organist of St Anne's, Soho, Westminster, a post which he soon exchanged for that of Christ Church, Hampstead (1891–8). From 1895 to 1903 he was on the staff of the Royal College of Music. Meanwhile, in 1898 he became organist of the Temple Church, a post distinguished by his predecessor, E. J. Hopkins. During this period he conducted the (London) Bach Choir, 1902–7. In 1917 he was appointed director of music to the Royal Air Force, and for his services was made an OBE in 1919.

He became professor of music at the University College of Wales, Aberystwyth in 1919, and also chairman of the National Council of Music for the University of Wales. At this point he became merely titular and honorary organist of the Temple Church until he resigned in 1923. He relinquished his chair at Aberystwyth in 1926, but continued as chairman of the National Council until his death. In 1924 he succeeded *J. F. Bridge as Gresham professor of music.

Following the offer of the post at St George's in 1924 (see above), there is no actual minute relating to his eventual appointment from Michaelmas 1927. His tenure was relatively short. One gathered, from some of those who had been alive at the time, that although he had been a chorister there, his subsequent experience in the different atmosphere of the Temple Church, and the influence of his posts outside church music, made him, though far from an iconoclast, somewhat less than completely at home in the more reserved, central tradition of cathedral music appropriate to St George's.

In the early 1920s, when sound broadcasting began to establish itself, the amount of serious music thus disseminated caused no small bewilderment, even irritation, to a very large section of the public, outside whose experience it had hitherto lain. Davies achieved a pre-eminent reputation among those who attempted to meet the educational need thus revealed. From his Aberystwyth days to the end of his life he contributed many series of 'wireless' talks under such headings as 'Music and the Ordinary Listener' and 'The Melodies of Christendom'. The characteristic tones of his voice and his highly personal choice of utterance became known and loved in themselves, independent of his musical exposition. This, combined with his long series of broadcast lessons to schools, gave him a unique place in public esteem, making him, in his day, far more widely known than any other figure in this book.

While at the Royal College of Music Davies took the Cambridge degree of

Mus.B. in 1892, followed by that of Mus.D. in 1898. In 1904 he was elected honorary FRCO, and he received honorary degrees of LLD (Leeds, 1904; Glasgow, 1926), Mus.D. (Dublin, 1930), and D.Mus. (Oxford, 1935, at the Encaenia). He received a knighthood in 1922, and was appointed CVO on his retirement from Windsor. He succeeded Elgar as master of the king's music in 1934, and was promoted to KCVO in the Coronation Honours of 1937.

Grove[3]; Colles 1942; *DNB*, 1941–50; *WWW*, 1941–50; *Venn*.

(Arthur) Charles (Lestoc) Hylton Stewart 1932.
See under Rochester Cathedral.

§Sir William (Henry) Harris, KCVO, 1933–61 (b. London (Tulse Hill), 28 Mar. 1883; d. 6 Sept. 1973). Harris was a chorister of Holy Trinity, Tulse Hill, London, and then for a time he was pupil and assistant to *H. C. Morris at St David's. He took the FRCO diploma in 1899, when he went to the Royal College of Music with an organ scholarship as a pupil of Parratt. As a young man he held several organ appointments in or near London (St John the Baptist, Kensington; Wimbledon Parish Church; Ewell Parish Church; assistant organist, the Temple Church). In 1911 he became assistant organist of Lichfield Cathedral and also organist of St Augustine's, Edgbaston, Birmingham.

In 1919 he became organist of New College, Oxford, and ten years later he moved to Christ Church Cathedral. He retired from St George's Chapel in 1961.

Harris took the Oxford degrees of B.Mus. (1904) and D.Mus. (1910). Following his move to New College he qualified as a full member of the University by taking the degrees of BA and MA together in 1923. In 1942 he was appointed CVO, and was promoted to KCVO in 1954.

West 1921; *Grove*[5]; *WWW*, 1971–80.

§Sidney (Scholfield) Campbell, MVO, 1961–74 (b. London, 1909; d. Windsor, 4 June 1974). Campbell did not at first intend to follow a musical career, but worked in local government. Later he studied the organ under *Ernest Bullock and Harold Darke. In 1927 he became organist of St Margaret's Church, Leytonstone, London. Two years later he moved to Chigwell Parish Church, Essex, and then to West Ham Parish Church, where he was organist from 1931 to 1937. His next appointment (1937–43) was at St Peter's, Croydon, followed by four years at St Peter's, Wolverhampton, 1943–7.

He was sub-warden of the College of St Nicolas (Royal School of Church Music), Canterbury, 1947–9. Then he was organist of Ely Cathedral (1949), Southwark Cathedral (1953), and Canterbury Cathedral (1956) before his appointment to St George's Chapel.

Campbell took the Durham degrees of B.Mus. (1940) and D.Mus. (1946), and held the FRCO diploma (1931). In 1972 he was appointed MVO (4th class).

§Christopher (John) Robinson, LVO, organist and master of the choristers from 1975 (b. Peterborough, 20 Apr. 1936). Robinson was a chorister of St Michael's College, Tenbury and music scholar of Rugby School before going up to Christ Church, Oxford as organ scholar in 1954. At Oxford he read music and was assistant organist of Christ Church Cathedral and New College. He took the FRCO diploma in 1954, and the Oxford degrees of BA (1957), B.Mus. (1958), and MA (1964).

His first post was on the music staff of Oundle School, 1959–62, before becoming assistant organist of Worcester Cathedral one year prior to his appointment as the Cathedral organist. He has been conductor of the City of Birmingham Choir from 1964 and of the Oxford Bach Choir from 1977. In 1986 he was appointed LVO, and in 1988 he received the honorary degree of M.Mus. from the University of Birmingham. (See Addenda, p. 434.)

4

Academic Choral Foundations

CAMBRIDGE

The King's College of Our Lady and St Nicholas in Cambridge (King's College)

The main source of information about the organists of King's College is the series of annual Mundum Books (hereinafter MunB), contemporary compilations showing payments term by term to all members of the foundation. These are now bound into volumes, and those consulted extend from volume 11 (1536–46) to volume 64 (1799–1802). The years, running from Michaelmas to Michaelmas, are divided into four terms: Michaelmas to Nativity; Nativity to Annunciation (25 March); Annunciation to St John the Baptist's Day (24 June); St John the Baptist's Day to Michaelmas. Each term is named by its opening, so that Nativity (or Christmas) term runs up to 25 March.

A convenient guide to the Mundum Books is a series of manuscript 'Year Lists of Members of the Foundation . . . of King's College, Cambridge', compiled with great care by F. L. Clarke, formerly bursar's clerk, and including a little supplementary material.

King's College was founded by Henry VI in 1443. Among other provisions for the services of the chapel, the original statutes ordained that one of the ten chaplains and six clerks was to be able to play the organ ('quorum . . . unus sciat jubilare in organis') (Heywood and Wright 1850).

It is striking to find, before the middle of the fifteenth century, this explicit provision for an organist in both of Henry VI's foundations at Eton and Cambridge, in contrast to Magdalen College, Oxford, where the founder, William of Waynflete, made no such arrangement in 1448.

Nevertheless, with one slight exception, there is no trace at King's College of any organist within our period until the beginning of the seventeenth century, though many names of teachers of the choristers can be found. Is it possible, therefore, that the early clerks who 'knew how to play the organs' were expected to do this as part of their normal duties, while the doubtless more exacting task of instructing the choristers attracted extra remuneration?

The slight exception referred to occurs in the St John the Baptist term ending Michaelmas 1545, when, under the name of **Henry Cool** (a clerk since 1536, if not earlier), with his clerk's stipend of 18*s.* 4*d.*, MunB records: 'Idem jubilante org:' but the sum of money is not readable.

It may be useful to provide a list of the instructors of the choristers from Cool's time to the end of the sixteenth century: 1555–8, Henry Cool; 1559–?1560, Richard Brameley; 1560–73, Richard Pollye; 1573–?1578, Richard Gomester; 1578–86, Nicholas Rookes; 1586–8, Richard Burton; 1588–92, Thomas Hamond; 1592–8, Edward Gibbons; 1598–?1605, Thomas Hamond.

Leaving on one side the vague reference to Cool in 1545, the earliest distinctively named organist of King's College is John Tomkins (see below).

John Tomkins 1606–19→. (b. St David's, Pembrokeshire, 1586; d. London, 1638). Tomkins was the third son of *Thomas Tomkins (I), the half-brother of *Thomas Tomkins (III), and the brother of *Giles Tomkins (I). Nothing is known of his early life. His appointment at King's may well have been connected with a new organ built by Dallam in 1605–6. MunB (22) shows that he became organist and master (or teacher) of the choristers from March 1606, and he can be traced continuously as such up to 25 March 1619. No payment to any organist is recorded for the next two terms up to Michaelmas 1619, though Clarke's Year Lists show that Tomkins remained in the 'Liber Communarum' as drawing commons for them. In 1608 he took the Cambridge degree of Mus.B. (*Venn*). As late as the quarter ending Michaelmas 1627 there is a payment of £10 'in full payment of all arrears' to 'Mro Johani Tompkins nuper organistae', but this is conceivably a slip for Giles Tomkins (I) (see below). (For the connection of John Tomkins with St Paul's Cathedral, London, see p. 172).

Matthew Barton 1622–3→. No MunB has survived for either 1619–20 or 1620–1. In that for 1621–2 no organist is mentioned until the quarter ending Michaelmas, when the name of Matthew Barton appears. He continued throughout the year 1622–3, but the MunB for 1623–4 has not survived.

Giles Tomkins (I) 1624–6. There is no entry in MunB for an organist in the term ending Christmas 1624, but Giles Tomkins is named thereafter, with Laurence Eusden as instructor of the choristers. He received his last payment as organist for the quarter ending June 1626, but a casual payment of 30*s*. to Giles Tomkins, 'nuper organistae', was made in the quarter ending Christmas 1626.

See under Salisbury Cathedral.

Henry Loosemore 1627–70. After the departure of Giles Tomkins (I), it was some little time before the College was again settled with an organist. The Earl of Sheffield recommended one **George Marshall**, a pupil of *John Bull, for a trial period (letter of 29 September 1626, King's College Letter Book, ii/2), and for the quarter ending Christmas 1626 Marshall accordingly received 10*s*. Though he was no more than a bird of passage, the following copy-letter has its own interest:

> This bearer, [*blank*] Marshall, being entertained to probation here accordingly, and having present necessary occasion to travel abroad, but hearing of a press for the wars now coming forth, hath thought it meet before his departure hence to desire my certificate as touching his immunity and privilege in that kind. These are therefore to certify all whom it may concern that by our College Charter he is and ought to be freed from that and all such kinds of service, and do therefore hereby desire all his majesty's loving subjects to permit and suffer him quietly to pass about his business that he may in due time return hither again to his service which is daily and of no small use and behoof unto our College. Given in the King's College in Cambridge this 8th day of October 1626.

But he did not 'in due time return'; and it is not until the quarter ending Michaelmas 1627 that there is any sign of a permanent successor to John Tomkins. In that quarter MunB records payment of 30*s*. to 'Mro Silver organistae pro expensis in itinere de Winton' (*John Silver of Winchester was apparently a candidate for the post), and 25*s*. to 'Mro Loosmore organistae' for half the quarter. Gradually, Loosemore's stipend rose from 50*s*. a quarter to £5; but he received no less than £5 'in considerationi novi organ book' in the quarter ending Christmas 1627. In 1640–1 he succeeded Laurence Eusden as teacher of the choristers, and he regularly received the stipend of both posts throughout the Interregnum. In the term beginning June 1669 Matthew Eusden took over the teaching of the choristers, and Loosemore himself was paid as organist for the last time in June 1670. Wood (MS Notes), leaving a blank for the year, notes that Henry Loosemore 'died suddenly in a privy house about the time of a certain commencement'.

In 1640 Loosemore took the Cambridge degree of Mus.B. (*Venn*), and in a letter written in 1658 (Wilson 1959: 4) Dudley, Lord North, made a pleasant reference to his graduate status:

> Good M[aste]r Henry Loosemore!
>
> For more than bachelor belongs unto you, so excellent have you showed yourself in what you favoured me, to leave with me such good, such sweetness. Art and Air come seldom from under a gown . . . [I desire] to compliment with your brother George, and take in the pleasures of his Fancies, gave the occasion.

Thomas Tudway 1670–1726 (d. 23 Nov. 1726). An older Thomas Tudway was a lay clerk of St George's Chapel, Windsor from at least April 1631. He survived the Interregnum, but on 2 October 1665 the St George's CA3 record that 'by common consent the pay of Tudway the chorister was taken away, and he dismissed his place. The sub-chanter ordered to give notice to his father of it; he being superannuated and having done no service to the Church this twelve month and more.' It is possible that our present subject was connected with this older Tudway, and was perhaps a brother of 'Tudway the chorister'. There can be no doubt that he was the Thomas Tedway, one of the children of the Chapel Royal, whose allowance payable on the breaking of his voice was dated Michaelmas 1668 (Ashbee 1986–9: i. 89). In stating that Tudway was appointed a tenor lay clerk of St George's on 22 April 1664, Hawkins (1853: ii. 795) has perhaps fallen into the trap of identifying him with the older man who on that day was ordered 'to sing a tenor in the quire and to help the countertenors upon occasion'.

Tudway began duty as organist of King's College in the quarter beginning Michaelmas 1670, and he took over the work of teaching the choristers from Matthew Eusden the following quarter. He relinquished the teaching of the choristers after the summer quarter of 1680. According to his own account, he took the Cambridge degree of Mus.B. in 1681 (Lbl, Harl. MS 7338, f. 238); he proceeded Mus.D. in January 1704/5 (*Venn*; Corrie 1864), when the University complimented him by reviving in his favour the title of professor of music which had lapsed since the death of Nicholas Staggins in 1700.

Meanwhile, he had been petitioning unsuccessfully for a place at Court (*CSPD*, 6 July 1702), seeking appointment as one of the three organists of the

Chapel Royal, stating that in 1682 he had actually been promised the next vacant place by Charles II, and pointing out that Henry Purcell's place had never been filled. Nothing came of this; and although his compositions include a number of anthems stated by him to have been composed specially for Queen Anne, nevertheless he was accused of 'speaking words highly reflecting upon Her Majesty and her administration'. In July 1706 he was therefore suspended from his College and University offices (by this time he was organist of St Mary's Church and Pembroke College also) and deprived of his degree. But on 10 March 1706/7 he was restored to his posts and dignity, after having publicly admitted in the Regent House that he had 'rashly and unadvisedly' uttered words uncomplimentary to Her Majesty (see HMC, Appendix to 4th Report, 1874, p. 419; King's College, 'Liber Protocoll', 1678–1728, p. 252). His suspension is reflected in MunB, in which a stipend of 33*s*. 4*d*. only is entered for him in the quarter ending Michaelmas 1706, and nothing at all for the quarter ending at Christmas.

In his later years Tudway was paid £1 extra each quarter 'pro opere extraordinario', and in March 1726 he was given 10 guineas 'for extra work'. He received his final quarterly stipend at Christmas 1726, and for the same quarter there is the entry in MunB: 'elargit Mro Tudway £10'.

Between 1715 and 1720 he carried out the work by which he is now chiefly remembered, namely, the six substantial manuscript volumes of English church music in score from Tallis to Handel (not forgetting Tudway) which he compiled for Edward, Lord Harley (Lbl. Harl. MSS 7337–42). In Lbl, Add. MS 36268 he describes himself (perhaps more hopefully than accurately) in 1721 as 'Master of the Music' in Harley's chapel.

He subscribed to Croft's *Musica Sacra* in 1724. There is a portrait of him in the Oxford Music School collection (Poole 1912–25: i. 158).

Robert Fuller 1726–42 (d. Cambridge, 1743). This is no doubt the 'Mr Fuller' who, as one of the clerks, had filled Tudway's place as organist during his suspension in the second part of 1706, receiving £1 'pro jubiland: in org:' for the two quarters ending Michaelmas and Christmas 1706. Though not described in MunB as organist, he succeeded to Tudway's quarterly stipend of £5 from Christmas 1706, and must therefore have been organist from that time. After Tudway gave up the teaching of the choristers in 1680, there had been some ten short-lived appointments to the post, but from Michaelmas 1730 Fuller assumed this duty, which has ever since continued to be discharged by the organist.

Though Fuller's Christian name is never mentioned in MunB, whether as clerk, master of the choristers, deputy organist, or organist, it is hardly possible to doubt that he was the Robert Fuller who was put in charge of Trinity College choir in December 1717 (q.v.), and the Robert Fuller whom *Venn* records as having taken the Mus.B. degree in 1724 (yet the same authority notes that this graduate's will was proved in the Vice-Chancellor's Court in 1728). According to West (1921), our Robert Fuller died in 1743 and was buried in All Saints' Church, Cambridge.

John Randall 1742–99 (d. Cambridge, 18 Mar. 1799, aged 84). Randall was a chorister of the Chapel Royal under Bernard Gates, and it fell to him, as revealed in the libretto printed for the occasion (Pc, Rés. V.S.830), to assist in the birth of the Handelian dramatic oratorio by singing the name-part in the Crown and Anchor performance of Handel's *Esther* on 23 February 1731/2. 'Mr Randall' succeeded Fuller as organist and master of the choristers of King's College from Christmas 1742. His last payment was for the quarter ending Christmas 1798. He took the degrees of Mus.B. and Mus.D. in 1744 and 1756 respectively, and became professor of music in 1755 (*Venn*).

From 1762 to 1768 Randall shared the duty of organist of Trinity College with Tireman; he was appointed to the full post in 1777, holding this, together with his office at King's, until his death (q.v.). He was also organist of St John's College, Pembroke Hall, and St Mary's Church. In 1776 he subscribed to Burney's *History of Music*.

GM, 1799, p. 262.

John Pratt 1799–1855 (d. Cambridge, 9 Mar. 1855, aged 84). MunB records no payment to an organist from Christmas 1798 to Lady Day 1799. 'Mr Pratt' first received his stipend for the quarter ending Midsummer 1799. From 1815 he was also organist of Peterhouse.

GM, 1855, p. 544; West 1921.

William Amps 1855–76 (b. Cambridge, 18 Dec. 1824; d. Cambridge, 20 May 1910). While organist of King's, Amps matriculated at Peterhouse and took the degrees of BA and MA in 1858 and 1862 respectively. He resigned his appointment at King's in 1876, and his subsequent career is obscure, even to *BMB*, which was published during his lifetime. When *BMB* says that he was organist of St Peter's Church, Cambridge, this may be a misunderstanding for Peterhouse.

Records of Peterhouse, Cambridge.

Arthur Henry Mann 1876–1929 (b. Norwich, 16 May 1850; d. Cambridge, 19 Nov. 1929). Mann was a chorister of Norwich Cathedral, and afterwards an articled pupil of *Zechariah Buck. He was organist of St Peter's Church, Wolverhampton (1870), Tettenhall Parish Church (1871), and Beverley Minster (1875) before his appointment to King's College, where he served for the rest of his life. He took the FRCO diploma in 1871, followed by the Oxford degrees of B.Mus. (1874) and D.Mus. (1882). He received the honorary degree of MA from Cambridge in 1910, and was elected a fellow of King's College on 25 November 1921. A memoir, *Arthur Henry Mann*, was privately printed for the College in 1930.

The present fame of King's College choir rests in the first instance on Mann's unique contribution, and it was he who gradually accomplished the change from lay clerks to academical clerks or choral scholars.

He was no inconsiderable Handel scholar. His notes and books on Handel remain at King's, and he contributed the important section on Handel (in which he identified many fragments of works) to the *Catalogue of the Music in the Fitzwilliam Museum, Cambridge* (1893). His bound volumes of MS notes on

Norwich music and musicians are now in the Norfolk Record, Norwich (MSS 434–9).

Grove[2], *MT*, 71 (1930), 30; *MMR*, 60 (1930), 3; *DNB*, 1922–30; G. B. Smith 1955.

Bernhard (known as 'Boris') Ord, CBE, 1929–57 (b. Bristol, 9 July 1897; d. Cambridge, 30 Dec. 1961). From Clifton College, Ord won an organ scholarship to the Royal College of Music in 1914, which he resumed after World War I, and then went up to Corpus Christi College, Cambridge as organ scholar in 1920, winning the John Stewart of Rannoch scholarship in sacred music and taking the degree of Mus.B. in 1922. In 1923 he was elected fellow of King's College, proceeding to the degrees of BA (1925) and MA (1928). He had taken the FRCO diploma in 1916.

From 1927 to 1929 he was on the staff of the Cologne Opera House, but he returned to Cambridge as Mann's successor and was once again elected a fellow. He became a University lecturer in music in 1936, but most of his energy was devoted to the choir of King's College; building on Mann's work, he brought it to its celebrated reputation, then for the first time widely spread by radio. In 1957 his health failed and he relinquished the post of organist. But for one year, 1957–8, he held a specially designated post of 'director of music'. He retained his fellowship to the end of his life, living in College almost up to the time of his death.

In 1955 he received the honorary degree of D.Mus. from Durham University, and he was appointed CBE in 1958 upon his eventual retirement. In June 1960, on his last public appearance, he was conspicuously recognized by the honorary Cambridge degree of Mus.D.

Grove[3], *WWW*, 1961–70.

During Ord's absence on war-service, **Harold (Edwin) Darke**, D.Mus. (Oxon:) (1888–1976), acted as organist of King's College, 1941–5. He was a fellow of King's College, 1945–9, and in 1966 he was appointed CBE.

§Sir David (Valentine) Willcocks, CBE, MC, 1957–73 (b. Newquay, Cornwall, 30 Dec. 1919). Having been a chorister of Westminster Abbey, Willcocks then went to Clifton College, the Royal College of Music, the Royal School of Church Music (College of St Nicolas), and King's College, Cambridge, where he was organ student and held the John Stewart of Rannoch scholarship in sacred music. He completed his degree course after war-service, and was a fellow of King's College from 1947 to 1951. He took the FRCO and ADCM diplomas in 1938 and 1947 respectively, and the Cambridge degrees of BA, and Mus.B. (1946), and MA (1948).

He became organist of Salisbury Cathedral in 1947, and moved to Worcester Cathedral in 1950. Throughout his time at Worcester he was conductor of the City of Birmingham Choir (1950–7).

In 1957 he returned to Cambridge as fellow and organist of King's College, retaining these positions until the end of 1973. He was also a University lecturer in music, 1957–74, and was appointed CBE in 1971. From 1957 to 1974 he was conductor of the Bradford Festival Choral Society, and he has been conductor of the (London) Bach Choir since 1960. He became director of the Royal College of Music in April 1974, received a knighthood in 1977, and retired at the end of 1984.

The following honorary degrees have been conferred upon him: MA (Bradford, 1973), D.Mus. (Exeter, 1976; Leicester, 1977; Bristol, 1981). D.Litt. (Sussex, 1982). He became an honorary fellow of King's in 1979.

§Philip (Stevens) Ledger, CBE, 1974–82 (b. Bexhill-on-Sea, 12 Dec. 1937). Ledger went up to King's College, Cambridge from Bexhill Grammar School, and in 1959 won the John Stewart of Rannoch scholarship in sacred music. In the same year he took the FRCO diploma (Limpus and Read prizes), subsequently receiving the silver medal of the Worshipful Company of Musicians. Having read music, he took the Cambridge degrees of BA (1960), Mus.B. (1961), and MA (1964).

He was organist of Chelmsford Cathedral from 1962 to 1965, and then director of music at the University of East Anglia. He took up his appointment as fellow and organist of King's College in January 1974. He left Cambridge to become principal of the Royal Scottish Academy of Music and Drama (Glasgow) in 1982. In 1985 he was appointed CBE, and he received the honorary degree of LL D from the University of Strathclyde in 1987.

§Stephen (John) Cleobury, organist and director of music from 1982 (b. 31 Dec. 1948). After being a chorister of Worcester Cathedral, Cleobury went on to King's School, Worcester with a music scholarship and then became organ student of St John's College, Cambridge (1967–71), winning the John Stewart of Rannoch scholarship in sacred music. He read music and took the Cambridge degrees of BA (1970), Mus.B. (1971), and MA. On taking the FRCO diploma in 1968 he won the Limpus and Read prizes. From 1971 to 1974 he held the W. T. Best scholarship awarded by the Worshipful Company of Musicians.

Before taking up his post at King's College he held the following appointments: 1971–4, organist of St Matthew's Church, Northampton and director of music at Northampton Grammar School; 1974–8, sub-organist of Westminster Abbey; 1979–82, master of music, Westminster Cathedral.

CAMBRIDGE

The College of St John the Evangelist

Under its earliest statutes of Bishop Fisher (1530) and Henry VIII (1545), the College had no specific body of chaplains, clerks, and choristers for the service of its chapel. Instead, the two deans were required to designate a precentor and 'rectores chori', and to compel members of the College to practise in the choir (Mayor 1859).

But, possibly under the influence of the Laudian revival, there are indications of a choir before the Civil War. However, as at Peterhouse, Cambridge and St John the Baptist's College, Oxford, this development might have had no continuance had not Peter Gunning, master of the College, 1661–70, made the choir a special care. Both during his lifetime and under his will (he died as Bishop of Ely in 1684), he made provision first for six choristers and then for 'more voices for the Quire'. Furthermore, in 1681 John Ambrose, senior fellow, bequeathed part of the tithes of Addingham, Cumberland 'to be and remain for and towards the maintenance of a Quire in the chapel of the College'. Thus, a recognized endowment for the choral service of the College was created (Torry 1888: 50–1; 59).

We therefore begin our list at the time of Gunning's tenure as master, although before that there are traces of **(?James) Dunkin** as organist, 1637–9, and of one **Gibbons**, 1642–3 (information from College archivist).

——Loosemore 1661–? According to the *Victoria County History of Cambridgeshire* (ii. 337), the College rentals for 1661 show 'Mr Loosemore' as having been paid for 'learning the choristers' and for acting as organist; the college archivist notes that he was paid for teaching the organist in 1661–2, and for his pains in playing the organ on several occasions in 1666–7; also that he was paid for teaching the choir, 1661–82. Is he perhaps the George Loosemore who was organist of Trinity College, 1660–82 (q.v.), or maybe some relation of his?

Somehow into relation with these records has to be brought the following inscription in Peterborough Cathedral, as recorded by Willis (1742: ii. 481): 'Johannes Brimble, Col. D. Johannis Cant. Alumnus & Organista, Musis & Musicae devotissimus, ad coelestem evectus Academiam 25 Julii, Anno Domini 1670 Ætatis 39.' It is impossible to suggest how he might fit into the sequence of organists.

James Hawkins (I) 1681–? Hawkins was paid for teaching the choir in 1681 and 1682 (College archivist). This can hardly be other than the James Hawkins (I), organist of Ely Cathedral, 1682–1729, who, when he took his Cambridge degree of Mus.B. in 1719, did so as a member of St John's College (*Venn*). The connection with St John's has further testimony in the dedication of the anthem 'Behold, O God, our defender' (Lcm, MS 1719) 'to the very Revd Mr Tomkinson and the rest of the great, good, and just non-jurors of St John's College in Cambridge by Ja: Hawkins, organist of Ely'. Moreover, *Thomas Tudway, who knew Hawkins personally, described him in 1720 as 'sometime organist of St John's College, now . . . of the Cathedral Church, Ely' (Lbl, Harl. MS 7342, f. 296).

Thomas Williams 1682–1718→. The date 1682 is supplied by the College archivist. Writing in 1718, when he himself was organist of King's College, Cambridge, Tudway (Lbl, Harl. MS 7341, f. 235) speaks of 'Tho: Williams, one of the choirs of King's and Trinity, and organist of St John's College, Cambridge.'

Bernard Turner 1729–? Date supplied by the College archivist.

William Tireman 1777 (Feb. to April). Dates are supplied by Garrett (1891).

See under Trinity College, Cambridge.

Jonathan Sharpe 1777–94. These dates are supplied by Garrett (1891), who notes that Sharpe's tenure ended in September 1794. In 1793 the list of subscribers to *J. S. Smith's *Anthems* included 'Mr J. Sharp, organist of St John's College, Cambridge'.

What arrangements were made until the appointment of the next known organist one cannot say. From 1799 until 1856 the post was held jointly with Trinity College, and the choristers also were shared from 1819 (q.v.).

John Clarke (afterwards Clarke-Whitfeld) 1799–1820.

See under Hereford Cathedral.

William Beale 1820–1.

See under Trinity College, Cambridge.

Samuel Matthews 1821–32.

See under Trinity College, Cambridge.

Thomas Attwood Walmisley 1833–56.

See under Trinity College, Cambridge.

Alfred Bennett 1856 (June–Dec.). These dates are taken from Garrett (1891), who states that Bennett was a pupil of *S. S. Wesley. According to West (1921), he was later organist of St John's Church, Calcutta. From the time of his appointment, both the organist and the choir of St John's became once more independent of Trinity College. He was the son of *A. W. Bennett.

George Mursell Garrett 1856–97 (b. Cheesehill, near Winchester, 8 June 1834; d. Cambridge, 8 Apr. 1897). Garrett's father was a lay clerk of Winchester Cathedral, and he himself was a chorister of New College, Oxford under *Stephen Elvey. He was an articled pupil of *S. S. Wesley, 1847–54, and during that time he was organist in turn of two Winchester churches, St Thomas's (1848) and Holy Trinity (1852). He was organist of Madras Cathedral from 1854 to 1856. He took up his post at St John's College, as he himself recorded, on the last day of 1856. Almost immediately he took the Cambridge degree of Mus.B. (1857), proceeding Mus.D. in 1867. He became University organist in 1873. In November 1878 he received the Cambridge degree of MA, *propter merita*.

Grove[2]; *Venn*.

Edward Thomas Sweeting 1897–1901.

See under Winchester College.

Cyril Bradley Rootham 1901–38 (b. Bristol, 5 Oct. 1875; d. Cambridge, 18 Mar. 1938). Rootham's father, Daniel (1837–1922), was a lay clerk of Bristol Cathedral and a well-known Bristol musician who had been a chorister of both Trinity and St John's Colleges, Cambridge and a pupil of *T. A. Walmisley. Daniel's father was a bass singer in the choir of those two colleges, 1815–52.

C. B. Rootham was educated at Bristol Grammar School, Clifton College, and St John's College, Cambridge, of which he was a sizar. He read for the classical tripos, and took the Cambridge degrees of BA (1897), Mus.B. (1900), MA (1901), and Mus.D. (1910). On leaving Cambridge after taking his first degree he studied further at the Royal College of Music, and during this period he succeeded *H. W. Davies as organist of Christ Church, Hampstead, London, 1898–1901. In February 1901 he became organist of St Asaph Cathedral, but the Dean and Chapter released him after only a few months to become organist of his old college.

He became a fellow of St John's in 1914 and was a University lecturer in music, 1913–18 and 1926–38. Among several notable dramatic performances conducted by Rootham at Cambridge, the revival of Mozart's *The Magic Flute* in 1911 was specially important.

Grove[3]; *WWW*, 1929–40; *MT*, 79 (1938), 307; *Venn*.

§Robert ('Robin') (Kemsley) Orr, CBE, 1938–51 (b. Brechin, Angus, 2 June 1909). Orr was educated at Loretto School, Edinburgh, the Royal College of Music (1926–9), and Pembroke College, Cambridge, where he was organ scholar, 1929–32. He studied later with Casella and Nadia Boulanger. He took the Cambridge degrees of BA and Mus.B. (1932), MA (1938), and Mus.D. (1951).

From 1933 to 1936 he was director of music at Sidcot School, Somerset, and then (1936–8) assistant lecturer in music at the University of Leeds. He became organist of St John's College in October 1938 and was made a fellow of the College in 1948. From 1947 to 1956 he was a University lecturer in music and he was also on the staff of the Royal College of Music, 1950–6. Meanwhile, in 1951 he gave up his post as College organist. He left his other Cambridge posts in 1956 on becoming professor of music in the University of Glasgow, but he returned to Cambridge as professor of music and fellow of St John's College from 1965 until his retirement in 1976.

He was appointed CBE in 1972, and holds the honorary degrees of D.Mus. (Glasgow) and LL D (Dundee).

During Orr's absence on active service in World War II, **Herbert (Norman) Howells,** D.Mus. (Oxon.) (subsequently CH, CBE), acted as organist. He was made an honorary Mus.D. (Cantab.) in 1961 and an honorary fellow of St John's College in 1962.

§George (Howell) Guest, CBE, organist from 1951 (b. Bangor, 9 Feb. 1924). Guest was a chorister first of Bangor Cathedral (1933–5) and then of Chester Cathedral (1935–9). In his last year at King's School, Chester he was organist of

Connahs Quay Parish Church, Flintshire (1941–2). From 1944 to 1947, partly concurrently with war-service, he was organist of Christleton Parish Church, Cheshire and sub-organist of Chester Cathedral.

He went up to St John's College, Cambridge as organ student, 1947–51, and was awarded the John Stewart of Rannoch scholarhip in sacred music. He took the Cambridge degrees of Mus.B. (1951) and MA (1954), and holds the FRCO diploma (1942). Following his appointment as organist of St John's College, he also became a University lecturer in music (1953) and fellow of St John's (1956). He received the Lambeth degree of Mus.D. in 1977, and was appointed CBE in 1987. (See Addenda, p. 434.)

CAMBRIDGE

The College of the Holy and Undivided Trinity (Trinity College)

From 1682 up to and including the appointment of C. V. Stanford (see below), our source of information is the series of Conclusion Books of the Seniority (in effect, the governing body) of the College, from which the minutes referred to below under their various dates are derived. Evidence for the earlier appointments of 1594, 1628, and 1660 is specified in each instance.

Trinity College was founded by Henry VIII by letters patent of December 1546. A preliminary document 'Distributio Collegii', contains provision for an organist. Statutes given by Edward VI appear to say nothing about any musical establishment for the chapel, but those of Elizabeth I, dated 1560, generously provide for twenty-one people, including an organist/teacher of the choristers ('unus qui Organa pulset, Choristas docet').

A choir of lay clerks and boys (at one time in association with St John's College) was maintained until towards the end of H. S. Middleton's time (see below). At present, the College now being for both sexes, the Elizabethan provision for the chapel choir is represented by twenty choral exhibitions held by men and women undergraduates.

Information about the very earliest organist/teachers of the choristers seems irrecoverable.

John Hilton 1594–?1608. There is no mention of Hilton in any surviving College record, and hence he is not referred to by Ball and Venn (1916). But it is not reasonable to doubt that he was organist of the College. He had been a poor clerk (singingman of lower status than a junior vicar choral) of Lincoln Cathedral, and while there he had apparently assisted in the teaching of the choristers (q.v.). He also helped to produce two comedies acted by the choristers and other scholars (Lincoln CA3, f. 117, 21 January 1592/3). He evidently had a lease of a house in the Close of Lincoln, and because of the good service 'Johannis Hylton: nuper pauperis clerici et organiste dicte ecclesie cathedralis nuper in organistam Collegii Sancte Trinitatis Cantabrige assumpti' ('of John Hylton, formerly poor clerk and organist of the said cathedral church, recently chosen as organist of Trinity College, Cambridge', as a minute of 26 January 1593/4 puts it), he was allowed to dispose of this (ibid., f. 118v). If one translates the second *nuper* as 'recently', this is as clear an indication as could be wished of his appointment to Trinity College. (He had not, however, actually held office as organist of Lincoln Cathedral, a matter discussed on p. 157.)

The Triumphes of Oriana (1601) describes Hilton as a bachelor of music. No record of his taking such a degree survives, but he is not likely to have proclaimed it so publicly without justification. E. H. Fellowes (*Grove*[5]) pointed out that John Hilton, 'Mus: Bacc:', was living in the parish of St Sepulchre, Cambridge in 1604, and that an inventory of his possessions compiled in March 1607/8 in connection with the accounts of his administrators is now lodged with Cambridge University documents. This strengthens the case for his connection with a college of the University.

As between Hilton and *Richard Farrant, the attribution of the little anthem 'Lord, for thy tender mercies' sake' has been much debated. For a discussion, see *Church Music Society 76th Annual Report* (1981–2).

In their authoritative publication, Ball and Venn begin the list of College organists with Robert Ramsey (see below).

Robert Ramsey 1628–42. Ramsey took the Cambridge Mus.B. degree in 1616, and became a member of Trinity College in 1617. No further organist can be named until after the Restoration.

George Loosemore 1660–82. Cobb notes a payment to Loosemore as organist in the senior bursar's accounts for the quarter ending Christmas 1660, and *Thomas Tudway (Lbl, Harl. MS 7339) speaks of 'Mr George Loosemore, organist of Trinity College, Cambridge, at the Restoration'. Ball and Venn (1916) state that he was admitted a member of the College in 1666, having taken the degree of Mus.D. in 1665 and been a member of Jesus College since 1640. Shortly after his death the Seniority of the College ordered 'that five pounds be paid to Mrs Loosemore for the Through-Base Organ book made and pricked by our late organist deceased, as also that five pounds more be paid to her for the good service of the said Mr George Loosemore her husband' (Conclusion Book, 20 December 1682).

It is generally assumed that he was the son of *Henry Loosemore, organist of King's College, Cambridge (q.v.) but I am inclined to think that they were brothers.

Robert Wildbore 1682–8. The Conclusion Book minuted the appointment of 'Mr Wilbore' in 'Mr Loosemore's place lately deceased' on 11 September 1682.

Charles Quarles 1688–1717 (d. Cambridge, 1717). Quarles's appointment as organist, 'in the room of Mr Robt. Wildbore lately deceased', was entered in the

Conclusion Book on 26 December 1688. He became a member of the College in 1688 (Ball and Venn 1916), and took the degree of Mus.B. in 1698 (*Venn*). On 17 August 1705 it was resolved to pay him £10 'for repairing and fitting the organ in the chapel'. In August 1709 an arrangement was instituted whereby John Bowman was to 'perform upon the organ in the chapel for six months in the year alternately with Mr Charles Quarles, the College organist, and for his salary he shall have sixpence every quarter upon every name in the College butteries'. Later, from Michaelmas 1714, Bowman was allowed 1*s.* quarterly 'for his encouragement to improve himself in his skill'.

On 22 July 1717 the College resolved that £20 be given 'to the widow of Charles Quarles, late organist deceased'.

John Bowman 1717–30 (d. Cambridge, 1730). As already noted (see above), Bowman had acted as substitute organist from 1709. It was agreed on 4 July 1717 'that John Bowman be made College organist in the room of Charles Quarles deceased'. It seems, however, that he did not have charge of the choir, for it was ordered on 20 December 1717 'that [*]Robert Fuller [of King's College] do teach the whole choir to sing'.

James Kent 1731–7. On Bowman's death it was at first decided (17 December 1730) to appoint one Eblyn by name. However, Cobb (1913) notes that no payment was ever made to this man, and a Conclusion of 25 June 1731 'that Mr Kent have the place of College organist void by the death of Mr Bowman' confirms that the vacancy was still unfilled at that date. It was agreed that Kent should: teach the choristers; instruct the singingmen; secure suitable choristers and singingmen; take care of the music books; receive a salary of £50, plus the profits of one chorister's place and a further £10; be paid extra for music-copying; and prepare and deliver immediately a catalogue of the choir books.

See under Winchester Cathedral.

Edward Salisbury 1738–41. On 14 February 1737/8 it was agreed 'that Mr Jones be chosen into the place of College organist void by the cession of Mr Kent'. However, as with Eblyn in 1730 (see above), nothing seems to have come of this, and by a further Conclusion of 20 November 1738 it was agreed 'that Mr Edward Salisbury of York be chosen organist (the place being now declared vacant) upon the same terms and conditions that Mr Kent had the place'.

See under York Minster.

William Tireman 1741–62 (d. Cambridge, 16 Mar. 1777). Tireman's appointment to succeed Salisbury, 'deceased', was minuted on 27 July 1741. West (1921) states that he had been organist of Doncaster Parish Church from 1739. According to Williams (1893), he took the Cambridge degree of Mus.B. in 1757, but *Venn* does not record this. After some twenty years at Trinity his service was evidently not giving satisfaction, and on 9 October 1762 the following Conclusion was minuted:

> Whereas Mr Tireman our organist has several times received order from the Master in relation to playing the organ and accompanying the voices in the choir and has repeatedly

neglected them, the Master has summoned the Seniors on this occasion, who are come to this determination; that he shall be dismissed their service if he does not observe the orders given him for the future.

William Tireman and John Randall (joint organists) **1762–8**. A Conclusion of 13 November 1762 reads as follows:

Ordered . . . that Dr [*John] Randall, professor of music and organist of King's College for supplying our Chapel every surplice-morning and evening with four of the best singing boys out of the sixteen under his constant care; that is, with two first and second trebles; and for instructing them and the singingmen too to perform the chants, services, and anthems in the best manner and for accompanying them on the organ at every evening service shall be paid per ann. £30. That Mr Tireman for playing the organ at every morning service shall be paid per ann. £30 and have his chambers rent free as before.

This seems an unfavourable arrangement from Randall's point of view.

William Tireman (sole organist once more) **1768–77**. The joint arrangement with Randall came to an end by a Conclusion of 11 June 1768: 'Whereas it is found by experience that the appointment of two organists, as by Conclusion of 13 November 1762, has not answered the purposes intended; it is therefore agreed that from Midsummer day next Mr Tireman shall be the only organist upon the same terms as before the said Conclusion was made.'

John Randall 1777–99. Randall's appointment at an annual salary of £60 was minuted on 1 April 1777. He was required, among the various conditions of his post, to give 'as much variety of good chants, services, and anthems as may be', and to 'instruct the singingmen, if needful, about the manner of their singing'.

See under King's College, Cambridge.

John Clarke (afterwards Clarke-Whitfeld) 1799–1820. Though attested by plentiful external references, Clarke's appointment is not mentioned in the College Conclusion Books. In his autobiographical notes (Gu, R.d.85) Clarke mentions it between his departure from Dublin (1798) and the recognition of his Dublin doctorate at Cambridge, which took place in December 1799.

He became organist of St John's College at the same time as he was appointed to Trinity, thus beginning a series of joint appointments which lasted until 1856. A further joint arrangement was made in 1819 whereby not only the organist but also the choristers were shared by Trinity and St John's. On 12 June 1819 the master and seniors of St John's resolved that Clarke should 'instruct in music a sufficient number of singing boys for the service of the chapels belonging to the two Colleges, and that he be paid . . . £60 a year, viz: £40 by Trinity and £20 by St John's' (*Victoria County History of Cambridgeshire*, ii. 337). One must assume that this stipend refers solely to his duties as master of the choristers, and not as organist also, else he would have been paid for two posts what Randall in 1777 was paid for one.

See under Hereford Cathedral.

William Beale 1820–1 (b. Landrake, Cornwall, 1 Jan. 1784; d. London, 3 May 1854). Beale was a chorister of Westminster Abbey under *Samuel Arnold and *Robert Cooke. On 30 January 1816 he became a gentleman of the Chapel Royal (CB2). His appointment to Trinity (and St John's) was minuted on 1 November 1820. He resigned before the end of 1821 and returned to London, where he was successively organist of Wandsworth Parish Church and St John's, Clapham Rise.

Grove[1]; *BMB*.

Samuel Matthews 1821–32 (d. Cambridge, 9 Dec. 1832, aged 36). Like his predecessor, Matthews had been a chorister of Westminster Abbey. After a time as lay clerk of Winchester Cathedral he was appointed organist of Trinity College (and St John's) by Conclusion dated 29 December 1821. He took the degree of Mus.B. on 30 June 1828.

Bennett and Marshall 1829; *GM*, 1832, p. 581; *Venn*.

Thomas Attwood Walmisley 1833–56 (b. London (Westminster), 21 Jan. 1814; d. Hastings, 17 Jan. 1856). Walmisley was the grandson of William Walmisley, clerk of the papers to the House of Lords, son of Thomas Forbes Walmisley, organist of St Martin-in-the-Fields, London, 1814–54, and godson of *Thomas Attwood, whose pupil he became.

In 1830 he was appointed organist of Croydon Parish Church. On the advice and encouragement of Thomas Miller, a fellow of Trinity College, Walmisley broadened his education to include literature and mathematics. Rejecting an opportunity to compose for the London operatic stage, he made his career in Cambridge, being elected organist of Trinity College (and St John's) in 1833 (Trinity College Conclusion Book, 1 February). In that same year he took the Cambridge Mus.B. degree. Although organist of Trinity, on matriculation in 1834 Walmisley became a member of Corpus Christi College, migrating later in the year to Jesus College. He took the mathematical tripos (18th Junior Optime) and proceeded BA in 1838. Meanwhile (and this illustrates the unimportant status of the chair at that time), he had succeeded Clarke-Whitfeld as professor of music in 1836. On 2 May 1838 he became a member of Trinity College, taking the further degrees of MA and Mus.D. in 1841 and 1848.

Bumpus (1972: ii. 475) states that, in addition to his work at Trinity and St John's, Walmisley also deputized for *John Pratt at King's College and the University church of St Mary's. Bumpus tabulates Walmisley's Sunday duties during term-time thus:

St John's College	7.15 a.m.
Trinity College	8 a.m.
King's College	9.30 a.m.
St Mary's	10.30 a.m.
University Sermon (St Mary's)	2 p.m.
King's College	3.15 p.m.
St John's College	5 p.m.
Trinity College	6.15 p.m.

When the organ of Trinity College was rebuilt in 1836 by John Gray, two unusual features were introduced at Walmisley's suggestion. In the first place, the manual compass of the Great Organ was extended downward to approximate to that of a pianoforte, although there was a pedal-board of two octaves. Cobb (1913) remarks that

the art of pedal playing as now understood was at that time possessed by an extremely small number of organists, of whom Walmisley could hardly be reckoned one. The addition therefore of the extra octave on the manual enabled him to produce effects which were beyond the reach of the average player of that time. The subsequent rapid development of pedal playing, however, soon robbed our organist and his organ of their former advantage.

In the second place, there was a Choir to Pedal double-octave coupler, enabling a melody to be played by the feet, the accompaniment on the manuals.

Walmisley is commemorated by a memorial brass in the antechapel of Trinity College.

GM, 1856 p. 332; T. F. Walmisley, preface to *Cathedral Music by T. A. Walmisley* (1857); *Grove*[1]; *DNB*; *Venn*.

John Larkin Hopkins 1856–73 (b. London (Westminster), 25 Nov. 1820; d. Ventnor, Isle of Wight, 25 Apr. 1873). J. L. Hopkins was a chorister of Westminster Abbey under *James Turle. From 1841 to 1856 he was organist of Rochester Cathedral (q.v.). His appointment as organist of Trinity College was minuted on 31 March 1856, and marks the end of the joint arrangements with St John's. He took the Cambridge degree of Mus.B. in 1842 and proceeded Mus.D. in 1867 (*Venn*).

Sir Charles (Villiers) Stanford 1874–93 (b. Dublin, 30 Sept. 1852 d. London, 29 Mar. 1924). As a boy, Stanford, the son of a Dublin lawyer, was early influenced by *R. P. Stewart. He went up to Queen's College, Cambridge in 1870 with both an organ and a classical scholarship, but migrated to Trinity in February 1873. When J. L. Hopkins's health failed in that year, he gave assistance as organist along with G. F. Cobb, a fellow of the College. On 21 February 1874 the following Conclusion was minuted:

That Charles Villiers Stanford (undergraduate of the College) be appointed organist, at a salary of one hundred pounds per annum for the next two years in addition to rooms and commons when in residence. The organist to be allowed to be absent, during the two years mentioned, for one term in each and the vacations, for the purpose of studying music in Germany, the College undertaking to find a substitute during his absence.

Stanford availed himself of this opportunity during the last six months of 1874, 1875, and 1876, when he studied in Leipzig and Berlin; Alan Gray and Cobb supplied his place at the organ.

On 16 March 1877 Stanford was appointed permanent organist from 25 March. He took the degrees of BA and MA in 1874 and 1877 respectively, and in 1887 he succeeded Macfarren as professor of music. He had already been appointed teacher of composition at the Royal College of Music on its foundation in 1883, and it was in this capacity that his most influential work was done. He resigned as organist of Trinity College in 1892, retaining the chair of music, along with his work at the Royal College of Music, until his death. He was conductor of the (London) Bach Choir, 1885–1902, and of the Leeds Triennial Musical Festival, 1901–10.

He was granted the full Cambridge degree of Mus.D. by grace of senate. In view of the conflicting dates cited for this, a letter from the Registrary of the University, dated 11 September 1969, may be cited: 'He was admitted to the degree on 8 November 1888 and completed it by "creation" on 18 June 1889. The correct date of the degree is therefore 1889.' He received the honorary degrees of D.Mus. from Oxford in 1883 (at the Encaenia), DCL from Durham in 1893, and LL D from Leeds in 1904. In 1921 he was to have received the honorary degree of Mus.D. from Trinity College, Dublin, but was forbidden on medical advice to go to receive it. He received a knighthood in 1902, and is buried in Westminster Abbey in a grave adjacent to that of *Henry Purcell. There is a portrait of him in the hall of Trinity College by Orpen, and another at the Royal College of Music by Herkomer. The antechapel of Trinity College contains a tablet to his memory recalling that he composed 'novum canticum in laudem Dei'.

Stanford 1914; *Grove*[3]; *WWW*, 1916–28; *DNB*, 1922–30; Greene 1935.

Alan Gray 1893–1930 (b. York, 23 Dec. 1855; d. Cambridge, 27 Sept. 1935). Gray went to St Peter's School, York and studied music under *E. G. Monk. He went up to Trinity College in 1873 and took the degree of LL B in 1877. He was admitted a solicitor in 1881, but turned to music as his profession, becoming director of music at Wellington College in 1883. In that year he proceeded to the LL M degree, and he subsequently took the Cambridge degrees of Mus.B. (1886) and Mus.D. (1889).

Gray had deputized for Stanford when an undergraduate (see above), and on Stanford's resignation he left Wellington to become organist of the College. On his retirement he was elected an honorary fellow, an indication of a changed attitude towards musicians, such a compliment not having been extended to Stanford, though a more distinguished man. There is a memorial to Gray in the antechapel of the College.

Ball and Venn 1916; *Grove*[3] *MT*, 76 (1935), 1038; *WWW*, 1929–40.

Hubert (Stanley) Middleton 1931–57 (b. Windsor, 11 May 1890; d. Cambridge, 13 Aug. 1959). Middleton was educated at the Imperial Service College, Windsor, where he studied the organ under *Walter Parratt. After a time at the Royal Academy of Music he went up to Cambridge as a scholar of Peterhouse, reading classics and music and taking the degrees of BA (1916), MA, and Mus.B. (1920). He became organist of Truro Cathedral in 1920, and moved to Ely Cathedral in 1926, resuming his connection with Cambridge as a fellow of Peterhouse, and also teaching at the Royal Academy of Music.

He left Ely on appointment as organist of Trinity College in 1931, combining this post with a University lectureship in music. In 1946 he became a fellow of Trinity, the first organist of the College to do so. In 1937 he had taken the Oxford degree of D.Mus., and in 1943 he took the Mus.D. degree of his own university (not by incorporation from Oxford). Middleton played an important part in framing the syllabus for the music tripos instituted at Cambridge in 1945, and the wording of the tablet to his memory in the antechapel of Trinity College points to the nature of his influence: 'musicae tam intra quam extra Academiam fautor, doctrine ac studio parem suae inter ceteras artes honorem vindicavit' ('one who furthered the art of music both within and without the University, and by his teaching and zeal sought to establish it in an equal place of honour among the other arts').

MT, 100 (1959), 545; *WWW*, 1951–60.

Following Middleton's resignation, new arrangements were made for a time with regard to the music in Trinity College Chapel. Instead of a professional organist, a succession of organ scholars played for the services, and Raymond Leppard, then a fellow of the College, held the post of director of music in the College, 1958–68.

§**Richard (Kenneth) Marlow, organist from 1968** (b. Banstead, Surrey, 26 July 1939). Marlow was a chorister of Southwark Cathedral. On leaving St Olave's Grammar School, London he went up to Selwyn College, Cambridge as organ scholar, 1958–62, and in 1960 he won the John Stewart of Rannoch scholarship in sacred music. He took the following Cambridge degrees: BA (1961), Mus.B. (1962), MA (1965), and Ph.D. (1966). He also holds the FRCO diploma (Harding prize, 1958). From 1963 to 1965 he was a research fellow of Selwyn College. In 1965 he became lecturer in music at the University of Southampton, and from 1967 he was also master of the music of St Mary's Church, Southampton. He left these posts on his appointment as University lecturer in music and as fellow, organist, director of music, and lecturer at Trinity College. He is the editor of the keyboard works of Giles Farnaby (*MB*, xxiv).

ETON

The King's College of Our Lady of Eton beside Windsor (Eton College)

Our source of information about the earlier organists of Eton College is the series of Audit Books containing the annual accounts; these were made up to Michaelmas or mid-September until the eighteenth century, after which they ran to 30 November each year. These books provide the basis of the account of the early organists by M. R. James, himself provost of Eton College, 1918–36. Having consulted the Audit Books for myself as far as 1758, I have to say (with much diffidence in view of James's eminence as scholar and antiquary) that for the second half of the sixteenth century my own reckoning of the years differs occasionally from his by one year. However, from the appointment of Heather (1788) up to and including that of Johnson (1914), I have felt able to rely completely on James's dates.

Not infrequently, the clerk entered the names of two men against a single stipend. I have generally assumed this to mean that one man took over from the other during the course of the accounting year. But where, as with Walters and Lamb (see below), the same two names continue to share the stipend for a consecutive series of years, I have taken the alternative view that they simultaneously held a 'half place' each.

Eton College was founded by Henry VI in 1440 as 'The Royal College of Blessed Mary of Eton beside Windsor'. Besides the provost, fellows, and scholars, there were to be ten chaplains, ten clerks, and sixteen choristers for the fulfilment of the daily offices in chapel. Of the ten clerks, statute 10 of the 'Liber Originalis' ordained that six were to be able to sing, and four were also required to be expert in harmonized music (*cantus organicus*), for which they enjoyed a higher status and remuneration. One of the four was to be instructor of the choristers, and at least one of them was to be able to play the organ ('jubilare in organis'). Evidently some possible difficulty in finding one so qualified was envisaged, for it was expressly provided that, if another were not conveniently to be had, this clerk alone might be allowed to be married. Nevertheless, no extra stipend above that of his fellow clerks (4 marks) was allotted to the organ-player, though the instructor of the choristers was to receive £6. For these constitutional matters, see Heywood and Wright (1850).

There was a very close and long-standing relationship between the musical establishment of Eton College and that of nearby St George's Chapel, Windsor. Lay clerks frequently held appointments in both, and eventually the choristers were educated together. After about 1868, however, a separate school was established for the Eton choristers, and even though the revised statutes in force from November 1871 omitted any mention of the choir and organist, this endured until 1968, when it was abolished. At that point Eton College lost touch with the choral foundation of history, and its chapel choir has since been made up of masters and boys of the College, as in any other public school. Here, therefore, we chronicle no successor to K. F. Malcolmson.

——Janson ←1540→. In the accounting year ending 1540, 'Dominus' Janson (who was a chaplain, not a clerk), was paid 10*s*. 'pro pulsacione organorum' for two terms. He did not teach the choristers: in 1537–8 and 1539–40 Walter Detty, one of the clerks, was remunerated 'pro informatione choristarum'.

William Butler ←1542–61. After a two-year gap, the next account, 1542–3, shows Butler, a clerk, as having been paid 6*s*. 8*d*. 'in pulsandis organis', and 13*s*. 4*d*. as 'informator choristarum in cantu'. He continues in these capacities as far as Michaelmas 1561. Then, in a six-month account to Lady Day 1562, his name is found jointly with that of 'Dominus' Neale, a chaplain, which suggests that Neale took over temporarily, for those six months.

William Moyser 1562–74. Moyser, a clerk, was paid as both organist and *informator* for the six months from Lady Day to Michaelmas 1562, and continuously so up to September 1573. He was paid explicitly as organist for the first six months of 1573–4, and, together with William Young, as *informator* for the whole year—as if Young took over from him in that capacity for the second half of the year. After the first six months of 1573–4, only an *informator choristarum*, and no organist, is named until the year 1614–15. One might speculate that (whether under Puritan influence or not) the organ was not used in chapel during those years. The following are subsequently mentioned as teachers of the choristers: William Young, 1574–5; Harris, 1576–7; Randall Tinker, 1577–8; Fryer, 1579–86; Wagg, 1586–7; Walker, 1588–97, Robert Palmer, 1597–1628. Tinker was also a lay clerk of St George's Chapel, Windsor in 1596 (Windsor CA2), and became a gentleman of the Chapel Royal at some unknown date, dying of plague in 1606 (Rimbault 1872: 6).

Leonard Woodson 1614–47. The accounts for the year 1613–14 contain much detail about a new organ built by Dallam, and it is not surprising that in 1614–15 payment to an organist is once more found. Woodson, a clerk, was paid £5 with certain allowances, and he continued to be paid up to Michaelmas 1647. He had been a lay clerk of St George's Chapel, Windsor from January 1598/9, and in April 1605 he became deputy master of the choristers there. On 2 May 1614 he was called before the St George's Chapter and 'warned to keep the whole number of choristers and to see them brought up as they ought to be, in music, manners, and writing' (Windsor CA2). It is not clear how long he continued to be deputy master of the Windsor choristers after becoming organist of Eton College. But he was never teacher of the choristers at Eton; Palmer continued in that capacity up to 1628, and was followed by George Pretty, 1628–55.

In a manuscript in the Bodleian Library (Tenbury MS 791) there is a note that Woodson, 'organist of Eton College and one of the quire of Windsor', was born at Winchester.

Charles Pearce 1647–*c.*1660. Pearce is shown continuously as organist in the accounts from 1647–8 up to and including 1652–3. There was a Charles Pearce, or Pierce, who was a chorister of St George's Chapel, Windsor in 1636 and 1637 (Windsor CA2).

With the accounting year 1653–4 we enter a period of obscurity. For the years ending September 1656 to September 1662 there is no mention of an *informator*; there is, however, payment of £5 to an unnamed organist (quite likely, Pearce) in each year up to September 1657. Thereafter, up to September 1660, no stipend for an organist is included, perhaps not surprising at such a period. However, soon after the Restoration we find in the accounts for the year ending Michaelmas 1661: 'Mro Peirse et Mro Rogers organista et cler: £21. 11*s*. 2*d*.' (a sum which has the appearance of dealing with some arrears). Apparently, then, Pearce survived to resume his duties, but only for something less than a year, during which Rogers succeeded him.

Benjamin Rogers 1661–4. The 'Magister Rogers' mentioned in the accounts for Michaelmas 1661 (see above), who had been a clerk of the College since 1653, cannot be other than Benjamin Rogers. He is next shown, as both clerk and organist at a stipend of £8. 6*s*. 8*d*., in the accounts for 1661–2. From 1662 he combined his duties at Eton with a post as lay clerk of St George's Chapel, Windsor (Windsor CA3). There are further references to him at Eton, but not explicitly as organist. Thus, in 1662–3 he was reimbursed for 'being sent to London to try the organ', and shared the stipend of teacher of the choristers (an office now named for the first time since 1654–5) with 'Mr Tudaway' (perhaps the father of *Thomas Tudway; see King's College). He was sole *informator choristarum* in 1663–4, and shared the stipend with one Slaughter in 1664–5. This is the last time he is mentioned at Eton, which accords with his having taken up appointment at Magdalen College, Oxford in January 1664/5.

The accounts for 1661–2 until 1708–9 provide a continuous record of teachers of the choristers, but with the exception of a charge in 1669–70 for 'glazing of the organist's chamber', there is no mention of an organist. Yet someone must have played the organ. We know that Rogers, having been organist, taught the choristers until some date in the accounting year 1664–5. It therefore seems reasonable to think that he may have continued as organist until then, and that the clerk of accounts was not very exact in describing his post.

See under Magdalen College, Oxford.

——**Slaughter *c.*1663–*c.*1669**. The accounts for 1664–5 record the stipend of *informator choristarum* and of a clerk as shared between Rogers and Slaughter (who is sometimes named as Slater). Having assumed that Rogers remained as organist until then, one must now assume that Slaughter followed him not only as clerk and *informator* but as organist also, an assumption maintained for his successors, Sleech, Walters, and (in his earliest years) Lamb.

——**Sleech *c.*1669–1681**. Sleech took over from Slaughter as *informator* and, therefore, one assumes, as organist during the accounting year 1669–70.

John Walters 1681–1705. 'Mr Walter(s)', or Waters, is paid as Sleech's successor as *informator* from Michaelmas 1681. It was he who sent *John Weldon, one of the Eton choristers, to study with *Henry Purcell in 1693 and 1694 (see p. 11). The accounts for 1694–5 note a gratuity to 'Mr Walter for his continued care of the choristers for several years'. When Benjamin Lamb succeeded him as *informator choristarum* from Michaelmas 1705, the two of them shared the stipend of a clerk until Michaelmas 1708. Perhaps this represented a sort of pension to Walters.

There is every likelihood that he was the John Waters, one of the children of the Chapel Royal, whose voice had changed before February 1676–7 (Ashbee 1986–9: i. 169). The Eton musician clearly had an interest in the Chapel Royal repertory, for he was the scribe of an interesting score of anthems by *John Blow, now Ckc, Rowe MS 22.

Benjamin Lamb 1705–33. Lamb succeeded Walters as *informator* and (as we suggest) organist in 1705. When Walter's name finally disappears from the accounts in 1708–9, Lamb is designated 'organist' in the list of clerks, and his stipend as *informator choristarum* is separately entered under the heading of 'Officers'. At various times Lamb was paid for a good deal of music-copying, and some of his transcripts have survived. He was among the subscribers to Croft's *Musica Sacra* (1724). He received his final stipends for the financial year ending in 1733.

Lamb served as Golding's deputy as master of the choristers at St George's Chapel, Windsor during the later years of Golding's time as organist there, and when John Pigott became organist of St George's, Lamb continued to serve in this capacity, enabling Pigott to retain his post as organist of the Temple Church, London (Fellowes 1940: 56–7; see also St George's Chapel, Windsor).

John Pigott 1733–56. Pigott's name is recorded for the first time in the accounts for the financial year 1733–4.

See under St George's Chapel, Windsor.

Edward Webb 1756–88. Webb's name is entered for the first time in the accounts for the financial year 1756–7.

See under St George's Chapel, Windsor.

Stephen Heather 1788–1831 (b. 1748; d. Windsor, 14 Nov. 1831). Heather was also a lay clerk of St George's Chapel, Windsor. It may have been he who was described as being 'past duty' when *William Sexton acted as organist of Eton College (see p. 348).

M. R. James 1919; West 1921.

John Mitchell 1831–67 (b. Eton, 1809; d. Windsor, 6 Jan. 1892). Mitchell became a chorister of St George's Chapel, Windsor in 1815, and was afterwards a lay clerk there, completing seventy-five years with the Chapel choir in May 1890. In 1830 he was for a short time acting organist of St George's (q.v.). He sang at the Coronations of George IV, William IV, and Queen Victoria, and at Queen Victoria's Jubilee Service in 1887. New arrangements were made for the music of Eton College in 1868, and Mitchell retired with a pension (M. R. James 1919).

BMB.

Leighton George Hayne 1868–71 (b. Exeter, 28 Feb. 1836; d. Bradfield, Essex, 3 Mar. 1883). Hayne was educated at Eton College, and subsequently took the Oxford degrees of B.Mus. (1856) and D.Mus. (1860). He was organist of Queen's College, Oxford, 1857–61, exchanging this post for that of chaplain, 1861–6, on taking holy orders. From 1863 until his death he held the office of coryphaeus of the University (Foster 1887–92). He became vicar of Helston in 1866, but returned to Eton as organist the following year with the title of succentor, an office designated under the original statutes as to be held by one of the chaplains. On leaving Eton he became rector of Mistley-with-Bradfield, Essex.

Hayne made a particular study of the history and construction of the organ, and during his time a five-manual organ was built in the music room of Eton College.

BMB; Mellor 1929.

Charles Donald Maclean (formerly Macleane) 1872–5 (b. Cambridge, 27 Mar. 1843; d. London, 26 June 1916). Maclean was educated at Shrewsbury School and Exeter College, Oxford, where he was classical scholar and organist. He took the Oxford degrees of B.Mus. (1862), BA and D.Mus. (1865), and MA (1879). He also studied for a time under Hiller at Cologne. He joined the Indian Civil Service in 1864, and became organist and succentor of Eton (in effect, director of music) in 1872. After resigning from Eton he returned to India for some twenty-two years as a magistrate in the Civil Service. In 1880 he published some Latin and Greek verse translations. After his retirement he served as secretary of the Internationale Musikgesellschaft from 1908 until its disruption by World War I, having been the English editor of its publications since 1899. He died as a convert to Roman Catholicism. Maclean's son Alick and grandson Quentin became well known in the field of light music, the first as musical director of the Spa at Scarborough, the other as organist of a London cinema near Marble Arch.

Records of Exeter College, Oxford; Eton School lists; *MT*, 57 (1916), 378; *Grove*[3].

Sir Joseph Barnby 1875–92 (b. York, 12 Aug. 1838; d. London, 28 Jan. 1896). Barnby was a chorister of York Minster and then a student of the Royal Academy of Music. His first important posts were as organist of St Andrew's, Wells Street, London (1863) and of St Anne's, Soho (1871–86). From 1861 he was music adviser to Novello and Co., and in 1872 he became the first conductor of the Royal Albert Hall Choral Society (now the Royal Choral Society). On Maclean's retirement in 1875 his post at Eton was described as that of 'precentor' (Governing Body minutes), and it was under that title that Barnby and all his successors were appointed. He left Eton to become principal of the Guildhall School of Music in 1892, when he also received his knighthood.

DNB; *Grove*[2].

Charles Harford Lloyd 1892–1914.

See under Christ Church Cathedral, Oxford.

(Arthur) Basil (Noel) Johnson 1914–25 (b. Oxford, 1861; d. Wells, 10 Dec. 1950). Johnson was the son of G. H. S. Johnson, later Dean of Wells. He was educated at Malvern College and Magdalen College, Oxford, where he was an academical clerk. He took the Oxford degree of BA in 1883. He then studied for a time at the Royal College of Music, and held organist's posts at St James's, Norlands and St Gabriel's, Pimlico, London. In 1886 he went to Rugby School as organist and director of music, and he remained there until his appointment as precentor of Eton in 1914. Though including the ancient office of organist of the College, the post at Eton had by this time assumed the character of a directorship of music. Johnson's work at Rugby and Eton, spanning forty years in all, caused *The Times* (12 December 1950) to say that he ranked as 'one of the great pioneers of music in public schools'.

Johnson received the Lambeth degree of D.Mus. in 1928, and he was also an honorary FRCO.

MT, 92 (1951), 40.

Henry (George) Ley 1926–45.
See under Christ Church Cathedral, Oxford.

Sydney Watson, OBE, 1946–55.
See under Christ Church Cathedral, Oxford.

§**Kenneth Forbes Malcolmson 1956–71** (b. London, 29 Apr. 1911). Malcolmson was educated at Eton College, the Royal College of Music, and Exeter College, Oxford, of which he was organ scholar. He took the Oxford degrees of BA (1934), B.Mus. (1935), and MA (1938), and holds the FRCO diploma (1936). In 1936–7 he was temporary organist of St Albans Cathedral, and he was appointed organist of Halifax Parish Church in 1937. From 1938 to 1955 he was organist of Newcastle Cathedral. He took up his duties as precentor and director of music of Eton College in January 1956, remaining there until his retirement.

OXFORD

The College of St Mary Magdalen (Magdalen College)

There are three main sources of information about organists of Magdalen College. The first is the 'Libri Computi', a series of volumes each containing annual accounts (with some gaps) up to Michaelmas. These accounts were not generally compiled until the following February, and evidently rest on the basis of cash-books, some of which are still extant. The volumes consulted are those for 1543–59, 1560–80, 1586–1605, 1606–20, 1656–66, 1665, and 1684–96. For dates earlier than 1543 I rely on J. R. Bloxam's notes, now Magdalen College MS D.4.22. References in the text to 'the accounts for 1548' (for example) are to be understood as covering a period of twelve months from Michaelmas 1547. After the time of Thomas Hecht, these accounts do not mention the organist/instructor of the choristers by name.

The second main source of information is the Vice-President's Register (MS 730), which contains occasional references to the College organists. Lastly, from the time of William Hayes to that of J. V. Roberts (see below), I have relied on information from the College records gathered in the publications of Bloxam (1853–7) and Macray (1894–1915).

Magdalen College was founded by William of Waynflete in 1448, under letters patent of Henry VI. The chapel was to be served by four chaplains, eight clerks, and sixteen choristers. One of the chaplains or clerks, if qualified, was to instruct the choristers 'in plano cantu et alio cantu'; but, if necessary, the president of the College was to appoint someone additional (see *Statutes of the Colleges of Oxford*). This officer, who, by the time we reach our period, had come also to be organist, is mainly referred to in older documents as 'informator choristarum' or 'instructor choristarum'.

(?Thomas) Appleby 1539–41. In the course of the accounting year ending Michaelmas 1539 Appleby took over from one Jacquett, who had held office from 1536. He continued until Michaelmas 1541. These dates strongly suggest that he was the Thomas Appleby who was twice organist of Lincoln Cathedral (q.v.).

John Sheppard (1st tenure) **1541–2**. 'Magister Shepard' is found as instructor of the choristers (and therefore organist) in the accounts for 1542.

——**Preston 1542–3→**. The accounts for 1543 contain the name of Preston, but no account survives for the following year.

John Sheppard (2nd tenure) **←1544–*c*.1547**. On the assumption that the 'Magister Sheparde' who was paid for the year ending Michaelmas 1545 was the same man who had appeared in the 1542 accounts, the interruption in his service is unexplained. It raises the question of whether he was given leave of absence, with Preston filling a temporary appointment. Sheppard continues in the accounts up to 1548, when the stipend is allotted partly to him and partly to Games (see below), indicating the end of his time as organist.

He continued in some way to be connected with the College, however; and on 15 December 1554 (accounts for 1555) he was paid 20*s*. 'pro quibusdam canticis'. That is the last we hear of him at Magdalen. The idea that he was at any time a fellow of the College rests on a confusion dispelled by Macray (1894–1915: ii. 12).

Allowing for variant form of the surname, Sheppard was included in a list of gentlemen of the Chapel Royal in 1552 (Lbl, Stowe MS 571, f. 36), and was present in that capacity at the funeral of Edward VI and the Coronations of Mary I and Elizabeth I (PRO, E101/427/6; LC2, 4/3, f. 50). Also, on 21 April 1554 a John Shepheard, having been a student of music for twenty years, supplicated for the Oxford degree of D.Mus. (Bloxam 1853–7: ii. 187; Wood 1815–20: i. 142); Wood observes: 'whether he was admitted . . . appears not in our registers'. One should not make too much of that remark, as any such omission was probably nothing but the result of the anomalous status of music degrees at that time and for long after, and should certainly not be taken to imply that he failed to meet requirements in some way.

The documents of Magdalen College do not mention Sheppard's Christian name; it is supplied on the likely assumption that the College organist was the same man as the Oxford D.Mus. and the Chapel Royal musician.

——**Games 1548–50**. Games apparently took over from Sheppard during the accounting year ending 1548 (see above). His last stipend is recorded in the accounts for 1550, which also note an *ex gratia* payment to him on account of his imprisonment.

——**Veale 1550–1→**. Veale is named in the accounts for 1551; those for 1552 do not name anyone as *informator*/organist. He had been a chaplain of the College from 1548–9—hence the title 'dominus' by which he is designated in the accounts.

Thomas Clam 1552–3→. Clam's name appears in the accounts for 1553; other sources reveal his Christian name as being Thomas. The accounts for 1554 disclose no name.

Richard Ball ←1554–89 (d. Oxford, 1589). Ball is named in the accounts from 1555 to 1586, though no name is entered for some of the intervening years and from 1587 to 1590. Bloxam (1853–7: ii. 191) notes his death and burial in the College chapel in 1589, and one takes it that he remained in office until then. The various titles used to describe him are as follows: 'Musices Magister'; 'Moder[ator] scholae musicae'; 'Mag[ister] chor[istarum]'; 'Inf[ormator] chor[istarum]'; 'Mus[icae] prael[ector]'; 'Archimusic[alia]'.

William Parrat ←1590–4. Parrat's name is found in the accounts for 1591, 1593, and 1594. No name is given in 1592. I feel some reserve about identifying him, as Bloxam (1853–7) does, as the William Perrot, MA of Magdalen College, 1586, not because of the slight variation in the form of the name, but on account of the full graduate status.

Richard Nicholson 1594–1639 (d. 1639). Nicholson is the first *informator*/organist of the College whose appointment is officially recorded. The Vice-President's Register for 23 January, in what appears to be the year 1595/6, notes the admission of 'Joannes [*sic*] Nicolson . . . in locum Gulielmi Parret defuncti'. The Christian name is plainly a mistake. His first year's stipend is shown in the account for 1595. If the date of his formal admission was indeed January 1595/6, he must have begun work a fair time earlier. Wood (1815–20: i. 269) records that 'Richard Nicholson, organist of Magd. Coll.', took the Oxford degree of B.Mus. in February 1595/6, and adds that he died in 1639. His name appears for the last time in the accounts for 1638. When William Heather instituted the weekly University music practice in 1626, Nicholson (on Heather's nomination) was appointed to be the master of the music (Oxford University Convocation Register, 16 November 1626). This post soon came to be known as that of professor of music, held by no fewer than six organists or former organists of Magdalen College: Nicholson, Phillips, William Hayes, Philip Hayes, Stainer, and Parratt.

Arthur Phillips 1639–? (d. West Harting, Sussex, 27 Mar. 1695). The accounts for 1639 name Phillips alone as *informator*; but if Nicholson did not die until that year, perhaps the clerk did not trouble to show that the stipend was divided between two men. Wood (MS Notes) identifies him as a clerk of New College, aged 17 in 1622, and names his father as 'Will. Ph.' of Winchester, 'gent.'. (For the possibility that he was briefly organist of Bristol Cathedral from 1638, q.v.) Phillips succeeded Nicholson as 'professor of the musical praxis' on 18 November 1639 (Wood 1796: ii/2, 893), and took the Oxford degree of B.Mus. on 9 July 1640. In recording this, Wood (1815–20: i. 514) adds: 'Afterwards, upon the change of the times, and a perfect foresight of the ruin of the church, he changed his religion for that of Rome, and became organist to Henrietta Maria, queen of England. From whose service being dismissed, he returned into England, and was entertained by a Roman Catholic gentleman called Caryll of Sussex.' This account receives some degree of confirmation in John Caldwell's discovery that Phillips died in West Harting, Sussex in 1695 (*NG*). It seems likely that he left Oxford in about 1656, when his successor as professor (John Wilson) was appointed. Yet the College accounts are puzzling: those for 1657 and 1658 do not mention any *informator*, but Phillips's name is again found for 1659 and 1660. It was originally entered also for 1661, but then crossed out. If he did leave Oxford in 1656, and proceed as Wood says, then this leaves us with what seems extraordinary laxity on the part of the College accounts clerk.

Theodore Colby 1660–?1664. Colby is named in the accounts for 1661, when his name is substituted for that of Phillips, and the stipend is raised from £10 to £15. Wood (1815–20: ii. 305) describes him as a German, and clearly identifies him with the Theodore Colby who became organist of Exeter Cathedral in 1665.

There are no surviving accounts at Magdalen for 1663, and those for 1664 do not mention the master of the choristers by name. Bloxam (1853–7: ii. 192) records Acres and Edmund Slater as having been organists briefly in 1664 and 1665, though it is not clear how they might have fitted in, unless they were mere deputies. Wood (1815–20) leaves no doubt that Colby was the immediate predecessor of Rogers.

See under Exeter Cathedral.

Benjamin Rogers 1665–86 (d. Oxford, 1698, aged 84). Wood (1815–20: ii. 305) says that Rogers was born at Windsor, son of Peter Rogers of St George's Chapel, and that he was a chorister and then singingman there before going to Dublin. (Wood, by the way, was well acquainted with Rogers personally.) From 1638 to 1641 he was at Christ Church Cathedral, Dublin (q.v.). Then, according to Wood (1815–20), he returned to St George's Chapel as a lay clerk until disturbed by the Civil War, during which, 'by the favour of the men then in power, [he] got some annual allowance in consideration of his lost place'. He is next found as clerk, organist, and *informator choristarum* of Eton College from 1653 to 1664 (q.v.). In 1658 he was created Mus.B. of Cambridge by the favour of Oliver Cromwell (who, if anybody, was one of 'the men then in power') (Lbl, Harl. MS 7053, f. 152; Wood 1815–20). In his later years at Eton he was also a lay clerk of St George's Chapel, Windsor (Windsor CA3, 21 October 1662), and was granted the pay of 'a clerk and a half' because he could play the organ and the cornett. It was arranged that he should deputize there for *William Child, who was to pay him £1 a month for undertaking this duty.

In accordance with articles of agreement dated 22 July 1664 (as entered in the Vice-President's Register), Rogers ('of Eton in the county of Bucks., gent.') became *informator choristarum* of Magdalen College in January 1664/5, with the explicit duty of playing the organ (Bloxam 1853–7: ii. 196). He was allowed £60 a year and lodgings in College. Not only was this an unusually large sum, but it is curious that a married man should have been allowed residence in the College. The amount of money caused some demur, and the matter was referred to the Bishop of Winchester as visitor. He remarked that it 'was little enough for a man of that quality, and at a time when organists were scarce' (ibid. 197).

In July 1669 Rogers took the Oxford degree of D.Mus. (Wood 1815–20). His career at Magdalen came to a disastrous end, however, when he was dismissed in January 1685/6. This was in part on account of his daughter, whom he had already been told to remove from his lodgings and who was with child by the College porter, and also because of his noisy talk in the organ-loft and complaints from the choir that he would not play services 'as they were willing and able to sing, but out of a thwarting humour would play nothing but Canterbury tune'. It was also alleged that he had given it out that his lodging was haunted. He was considerately given a pension of £30 a year for life, two-thirds of which continued to be paid to his widow, who was buried at the College's expense (Bloxam 1853–7: ii, 198–9).

Rogers's memory is kept alive by his hymn, sung every May Day morning from the College tower.

Francis Pigott 1686–8. At the close of the meeting on 12 January 1685/6 at which it was decided to dismiss Rogers, 'Mr Pygott, the organist of St John's [College]', was brought to the president by one of the fellows. He offered his services in place of Rogers for £40 a year, with reversion of a further £20 on Rogers's death. Pigott was admitted on 18 January, and articles of agreement dated 21 January were signed on 29 January (Bloxam 1853–7: ii. 203). 'Mr Pigott, organista', is last mentioned in the Magdalen accounts for 1688, when he received £20, i.e., a half-year's stipend, suggesting that he left at about 25 March 1688. Such a date leaves one in no doubt that he was the Francis Pigott who became organist of the Temple Church, London in that year.

See under the Chapel Royal.

Daniel Purcell 1688–95 (d. London, Dec. 1717). After Pigott's departure, someone called Ramit was paid £5 as temporary organist for the remainder of the 1688 account, and 'Mr Purcell' is named in the account for 1689. The account for 1696 shows him as sharing the stipend with 'Mr Heicht', thus indicating the end of his tenure.

It is Hawkins (1853: ii. 759) who tells us that this Purcell is Daniel, brother of *Henry Purcell. As a boy he had been in the Chapel Royal choir with Francis Pigott (Ashbee 1986–9: i. 183, 186, 206). On leaving Oxford he settled in London, and from at least 1698 until his death he was organist of St Dunstan-in-the-East. From some date earlier than 1715 until his death he was also 'voluntary organist without election' of St Andrew's, Holborn (Dawe 1983).

Thomas Hecht 1695–1734 (d. Oxford, 5 Apr. 1734, aged about 70). Bloxam (1853–7: ii. 208) gives the precise date of 27 May 1695 for Hecht's admission at Magdalen, but it has proved impossible to verify this. Such a date conflicts with the division of stipend (between Hecht and Daniel Purcell) recorded in the accounts for 1696 (see above); yet that is clear enough to be relied upon. Hecht matriculated on 17 December 1714 (perhaps with some intention of acquiring a music degree), when he was described as 'Organista e co. Lincoln: gen: fil:' (Foster 1887–92). This means that he was the son of *Andreas Hecht, organist of Lincoln Cathedral, and had declined to accept the post vacated by his father's death (q.v.).

Under the date 6 October 1725, Hearne (1914) records some scandal to the effect that Hecht had left his rooms in College to have 'better convenience of conversing with and enjoying the company of a beautiful, comely, but impudent' girl, Betty Stonehill. Referring again to this girl, Hearne recorded on 8 March 1727/8 that 'though an elderly man, [Hecht] is much addicted to the flesh'. Nevertheless, no complaint about Hecht appears in the College records throughout his thirty-nine-year tenure.

It is Hearne (1914) who notes the date of Hecht's death. In his will dated 31 March 1734 he bequeathed £120 to the College to pay for the addition of four stops to the organ. He made his cousin *Edward Thompson, 'now organist of the Cathedral Church of Salisbury', his executor (Bloxam 1853–7: ii. 208–10). He signed his name as 'Tho. Hecht', though the varied forms of 'Hetcht' and 'Heicht' were in common use. For a few months after Hecht's death, someone named Phillips (perhaps the Matthew Phillips to whom he bequeathed 'one of my best spinets') acted as organist of the College. (For a speculative identification of Phillips, see under St David's Cathedral.)

William Hayes 1734–77 (b. Gloucester, Jan. 1708; d. Oxford, 27 July 1777). Hayes was baptized on 26 January 1707/8 in St John the Baptist's Church, Gloucester. He became a chorister of Gloucester Cathedral and was afterwards articled to *William Hine. His first post was as organist of St Mary's, Shrewsbury, presumably following the installation of an organ there in 1729 (Owen and Blakeway 1825: ii. 322). In 1731 he became organist of Worcester Cathedral (q.v.). According to the memoir by Philip Hayes prefaced to William Hayes's *Cathedral Music* (1795), William was appointed to Magdalen College on the recommendation of Jenner, Lady Margaret professor of divinity. There seems to be no formal record of appointment, but his successor at Worcester took over in 1734. He was admitted to the privileges of the University on 13 June 1735, and took the degree of B.Mus. on 8 July (Foster 1887–92). He became professor of music on 14 January 1741/2 (Philip Hayes, preface) and proceeded D.Mus. on 14 April 1749, following the official opening of the Radcliffe Camera (Foster 1887–92).

He was well known outside Oxford. He conducted the Festivals of the Sons of the Clergy in London and the 1763 Gloucester Music Meeting, as well as numerous performances of Handel's oratorios both in Oxford and the provinces. He was the owner of what is now known as the 'Goldschmidt' manuscript of *Messiah*. He subscribed to the first edition of Boyce's *Cathedral Music* (1760–77) and to Arnold's (1790); also to Burney's *History of Music* (1776).

Hayes was ill for some three years before his death, and was buried at St Peter-in-the-East, Oxford. The College granted his widow the sum of £21 (Macray 1894–1915: v. 28). In his will (Bloxam 1853–7: ii. 215) he bequeathed his pictures and musical library to his son Philip. There is a portrait of him in the Music School collection at Oxford (Poole 1912–25: i. 161).

Philip Hayes 1777–97.

See under New College, Oxford.

Walter Vicary 1797–1845 (d. Oxford, 5 Jan. 1845, aged 77 years). Bennett and Marshall (1829), drawing undoubtedly on personal knowledge, state that Vicary

> received his musical education under Dr [*James] Nares, organist of the Chapel Royal. In 1784 he came to Oxford as assistant to [*Thomas] Norris . . . He was appointed lay chaplain of New College in 1796 and organist of Magdalen College the following year. In 1805 he was admitted to the degree of B.Mus., and in the same year (Dr [*William] Crotch quitting Oxford to reside in London) he was appointed conductor of the Oxford Concerts.

Bloxam (1853–7: ii. 225) amplifies this a little, and also conflicts with it slightly, by saying that after leaving the Chapel Royal Vicary was in some way connected with Winchester Cathedral until he became assistant to Philip Hayes at Magdalen, and by saying that from 1830 he was also organist of the University church of St Mary's.

There is no official record of Vicary taking a degree, but he did matriculate on 2 November 1805, when he was described as the son of Walter Vicary of London (Foster 1887–92), and his anthem 'The heavens declare the glory of God' is stated by Bloxam (1853–7) to have been his degree exercise; his tombstone in Holywell churchyard, Oxford describes him as 'Mus. Bac.'. In view of the slackness with which music degrees were recorded at the time, one need not doubt this.

Benjamin Blyth 1845–c.1859 (d. Whitchurch, near Oxford, 20 July 1883, aged 58). The son of Benjamin Blyth, D.Mus., Blyth was chorister (1835–41) and then clerk (1842–5) of Magdalen College. He was formally admitted *informator choristarum* and organist on 26 January 1845. He took the Oxford degree of BA in 1845, proceeding MA in 1849. There is no explanation of his apparently early retirement.

Bloxam 1853–7: *BMB*.

Sir John Stainer 1860–72. Stainer was admitted organist of the College on 13 May 1860 (Macray 1894–1915: vii. 99).

See under St Paul's Cathedral, London.

Sir Walter Parratt, KCVO, 1872–82. Macray (1894–1915: vii. 101) notes only the year, not the precise date, of Parratt's appointment. The Vice-President's Register observes (in Latin) that he left for St George's Chapel, Windsor 'at the persuasion of Prince Leopold, also for the offer of a larger residence'.

See under St George's Chapel, Windsor.

John Varley Roberts 1882–1918 (b. Stanningley, near Leeds, 25 Sept. 1841; d. Oxford, 9 Feb. 1920). Roberts became organist of St John's Church, Farsley, near Leeds when he was only 12. He was subsequently organist of St

Barthlomew's, Armley, Leeds, 1862–8, before receiving his first important appointment as organist of Halifax Parish Church, 1868–82. While at Halifax he took the Oxford degrees of B.Mus. (1871) and D.Mus. (1876) and the FRCO diploma (also in 1876). He was elected organist of Magdalen College on 21 October 1882 from among twenty-one candidates (Macray 1894–1915: vii. 5). From 1885 to 1893 he was also organist of St Giles', Oxford.

In 1905 he was presented with a silver salver subscribed for by many members of Magdalen College; the Vice-President's Register described him in Latin phrases which may be rendered as: 'esteemed by his choristers on account of his kindliness, by the Fellows on account of his conscientiousness, and equally valued by all on account of his skill in the teaching and practice of music'. In 1916 the University conferred on him the honorary degree of MA.

The Magdalen choir achieved a celebrated reputation during Roberts's time as organist:

> Roberts's organ playing was poor, devoid of technique and second-rate in taste; in solemn marches a favourite effect of his was a queer deep rumble produced by swatting up and down the keys with his left fore-arm on a sixteen-foot Bourdon [cf. Zechariah Buck, p. 206] . . . But the choir was generally considered the finest in England, indeed famous throughout the world. Roberts dedicated the best part of his life to attain for Magdalen this high distinction. (Deneke 1951: 46–7.)

In some senses, Magdalen (under Roberts) and King's College, Cambridge (under *A. H. Mann) were contemporary counterparts to each other. In 1898 Roberts published *A Practical Method of Training Choristers*.

With his thick-set frame, bluff manner, and Yorkshire speech, Roberts was an Oxford character about whom many stories have been current (see, for example, Fellowes 1946: 63–4). There is a commemorative plaque to him beneath the organ-loft of Magdalen College, and a portrait of him in the practice room (Poole 1912–25: ii. 241).

BMB; *Grove*[2]; *MT*, 61 (1920), 193; *WWW*, 1916–28.

Haldane Campbell Stewart 1919–38 (b. London, 28 Feb. 1868; d. 16 June 1942). The son of a barrister, Stewart was a chorister of Magdalen College and then an exhibitioner there (1887–91). He read classics and took the degrees of BA (1893), B.Mus. (1915), MA, and D.Mus. (1919). Before his appointment to Magdalen College he was assistant master at Lancing (1891–6) and Wellington College (1896–8), and then director of music at Tonbridge School (1898–1919). During the later part of his time at Magdalen he was choragus of the University. Stewart returned to Magdalen to act as organist when Sir William McKie joined the RAF during World War II.

Register of Magdalen College; *MT*, 83 (1942), 224; *WWW*, 1941–50.

Sir William (Neil) McKie, MVO, 1938–41.

See under Westminster Abbey.

Philip John Taylor 1941–57 (b. 3 Feb. 1892; d. Fordingbridge, Hants., 12 July 1988). After attending King's School, Peterborough, Taylor became sub-organist of Peterborough Cathedral. He went up to St John's College, Oxford in 1914, returning after war-service to be organ exhibitioner there, 1919–22. He was then director of music at Sherborne (1922) and Cheltenham College (1932–41).

Register of Magdalen College.

§**Bernard (William George) Rose, OBE, 1957–81** (b. Little Hallingbury, Herts., 9 May 1916). Rose was a chorister of Salisbury Cathedral. After further education privately, he went to the Royal College of Music as an exhibitioner (1933–5) and to St Catharine's College, Cambridge as organ scholar (1935–9), where he also held the John Stewart of Rannoch scholarship in sacred music. He took the Cambridge degrees of Mus.B. (1938), BA (1939), and MA (1944).

In 1939 he was appointed organist of Queen's College, Oxford, becoming supernumerary fellow in 1949 and official fellow in 1954. He left Queen's to become organist, *informator choristarum*, and fellow of Magdalen College. Meanwhile he had taken the FRCO diploma (1954) and proceeded to the Oxford degree of D.Mus. (1955). He became a University lecturer in music in 1955, and from 1958 to 1963 he was also choragus of the University. He was appointed OBE in 1980.

Rose is the editor of two volumes of the music of *Thomas Tomkins (III) (*EECM*, v, ix), and of Handel's *Susanna* (Halle, 1967).

§**John (Martin) Harper, organist and informator choristarum from 1981** (b. Wednesbury, W. Midlands, 11 July 1947). Having been a chorister of King's College, Cambridge, Harper went to Clifton College with a music scholarship and an open exhibition in 1961 and then became organ scholar of Selwyn College, Cambridge, 1966–70. There he read music, taking the degrees of BA (1970) and MA (1972). Having taken the CHM diploma in 1969, he took that of FRCO in 1972. He then pursued further studies at the University of Birmingham, taking the degree of Ph.D. there in 1975. During this time he took up the post of organist and director of music at St Chad's (RC) Cathedral, Birmingham, which he held from 1972 to 1978. In 1978 he received a papal award for services to church music. After part-time appointments at the University of Birmingham, he was a full-time lecturer in music there from 1976 until taking up his duties at Magdalen College, where he is tutor in music and a fellow. He is the editor of the consort music of *Orlando Gibbons (*MB*, xlviii), and author of *A Historical Guide to Latin Liturgy for Musicians and Students* (1990) and *A History of Music in the English Church* (1990). (See Addenda, p. 434.)

OXFORD

St Mary College of Winchester in Oxford (New College)

The bursar's 'Long Books' ('Libri Bursariorum') constitute the primary source for information on the organists of the New College. They form a series of annual volumes of accounts for years running from Michaelmas to Michaelmas, divided into four terms or quarters. For the most part they are marked on the outside with the year ending at Michaelmas, but one or two (e.g., 1638, 1640) seem unclear, and in no instance does any volume open with a dated heading. They begin with the accounting year 1602–3 (i.e., a volume marked '1603'), and run with some gaps to the year ending 1860. Up to 1674, information about the organist and teacher of the choristers is found under the heading 'Solutio facta informatoribus', and thereafter under 'Custos capellae'.

At the time of my investigations (1969), the extensive College archives were being put into order, and the bursar's rolls, another potential source of information, were not available for consultation. They may perhaps shed further light on the period before 1660. It should be noted also that Mr R. Ll. Rickard, a former assistant in the Bursary and lay clerk of the College, made some annotations in the New College library copy of West (1st edition), without, however, giving any references. To judge from the dates quoted, these must have been derived not only from the Long Books, but also from the bursar's rolls. Those notes which I have not personally verified are cited below as '*Rickard*'.

New College was founded by William of Wykeham in 1379, under letters patent of Richard II. The statutes of 1400 provide for a college of 100 members, including the chapel establishment of ten priests, three clerks, and sixteen choristers. The educational aspect of the College was part of what was fundamentally a chantry foundation for the repose of William's soul, and by a notable provision (statute 68) he enjoined that, should the College income fall short, the twenty-nine chapel foundationers were to be retained.

It is not surprising that no organist was envisaged at the date in question, but it seems strange that there was no specific post of teacher of the choristers (cf. the twin foundation of Winchester College). No doubt it was taken for granted that the adult members of the College would undertake whatever was required, whether in grammar or music. However, by 1394 payments are found to one of the priests as *informator choristarum*, and presently the *informator* became additional to the 100 foundationers, acting also as organist (Buxton and Williams 1979: 267–8). Early in the seventeenth century the Long Books mention a teacher of the choristers (sometimes distinctively a teacher of the choristers in music, apart from their grammar master) who was also organist. Only in one instance (see Pinck below) was the holder of this post not additional to the foundation.

The earliest names within our period, all as noted by *Rickard*, are **Simon Vincent** (1592), **Alexander Heythwaite** (1594–6), and **Richard Bates** (1596).

William Wigthorpe 1598–1606→. When the series of Long Books opens in 1602–3, 'Mr Wigthorpe' is variously described as 'organista', 'informator choristarum et organista', and 'informator choristarum in musica'. Two indications strongly suggest that his appointment dates from some four years earlier. In the first place, 'William Wigthorpe of Hants., pleb.', aged 19, matriculated as a member of New College on 19 May 1598; and in the second place a new organ was built for the College during 1597–8. Wigthorpe took the degree of B.Mus. on 4 July 1605 (Foster 1887–92), and is named in the Long Books up to Michaelmas 1606, after which they break off until 1611–12, when he has disappeared.

William Meredith ←1611–37. The Long Books contain an entry for 'Dominus/ Magister' Meredith for the full year 1611–12, and continue to do so up to the end of the first term in the book marked 1637, that is, to Christmas 1636. But I suspect that this book may have been for the year ending Michaelmas 1638, and, if so, his last payment may have been to Christmas 1637. This would accord with the date on his tombstone, which must be read, of course, as OS. He is buried in the College cloisters, under a slab inscribed 'Hic jacet Gvliel Merideth huius Collegii nuper organista Vir pius facultate sua peritissimus 10 Jan 1637.' This is reproduced, not quite exactly, in Wood (1786–90: ii. 217), who also quotes a rhyming pun about him:

Here lies one blown out of breath
Who liv'd a merry life and died a merry death.

For the three terms following Meredith's death (whether in 1637 or 1638), there is a payment to a Mr Hosier, 'ex gratis domini custodis et seniorum', who in the following year (ending Michaelmas 1638, maybe 1639) received £1 for three terms as *informator* in music.

——**Pinck ?1638–40**. In the term ending Michaelmas 1638 (maybe 1639) Pinck, one of the priests or chaplains of the College, was paid as organist (Long Books). *Rickard*, however, gives 1637 as the date of his assumption of duties, which does not allow for what looks like the temporary employment of Hosier (see above). Pinck continues to Michaelmas 1640 (maybe 1641), after which there is a gap in the books until 1643–4, at which point he has reverted to being a chaplain only.

Simon Coleman ?1640–8. 'Mr Coleman' is recorded as organist and *informator* when the Long Books resume in 1643–4, but *Rickard* gives the year of his appointment as 1640. As a result of the parliamentary visitation of the College, begun in 1648, Coleman was displaced. Matthews (1948) specifically refers to a Simon Coleman in connection with New College.

The Long Book for the year ending Michaelmas 1649 mentions neither an organist nor a teacher of the choristers. 'Dominus' Miles is named as *informator in musica* from Christmas 1649 to Midsummer 1657; he is succeeded by 'Dominus' Grouch until Michaelmas 1660; and he is followed by 'Dominus' Flexney until Michaelmas 1661. As the organ had been dismantled as a result of the visitation, these men were obviously not also organists of the College.

——**Pickhaver 1662–4**. 'Dominus' Pickhaver is entered in the Long Books only as *informator* in music; he was paid as such from Easter 1662 (at a much improved salary of £20 as against the former £6. 13*s.* 4*d.*) up to Easter 1664. However, he is included in the list of organists here because of Wood's statement (MS Notes) that William King (see below) 'succeeded Piccover in the organistship of New Coll: in Oxon about 1664 when the said Piccover was promoted to the organist's place at Winchester Coll:'. Wood had personal knowledge of New College at this time, and his remarks help to identify this college organist with the Pickhaver who, according to our information, became organist of Winchester College at some date after 1665 (q.v.).

William King 1664–80 (d. Oxford, 17 Nov. 1680). The Long Books show 'Dominus' King as having been paid as teacher of the choristers and organist for the first time from Easter to Michaelmas 1664, with a stipend of £50 a year. Possibly his appointment coincided with the building of a new organ. Bloxam (1853–7: ii. 66) gives 10 December 1664 as the date of his admission as organist, but Buxton and Williams (1979) cite 31 December 1663. Anthony Wood, who knew him, says that he was 'son of George King, a musician and organist of Wykeham's College near Winchester' (Wood 1786–90: ii. 218; MS Notes, f. 80). Bloxam identifies him, strangely as it might seem, as a clerk of Magdalen College, 1648–52, and then chaplain, 1652–4, who took the degree of BA in 1649 and became a probationer-fellow of All Souls College in 1654. Foster (1887–92), however, has no knowledge of any Oxford graduate of this name at the time, but he agrees with Bloxam in identifying the clerk of Magdalen with the fellow of All Souls, though he does not mention any New College connection.

Bloxam (1853–7), apparently on the authority of *Stephen Elvey, states that, on King's appointment to New College, it was agreed 'that he should play the organ upon Surplice Days and Litany Days only, unless he should be by some of the House desired at any other time'. This would certainly make it easier for him to hold some concurrent post. On King's death the Long Books record a precisely calculated sum of £7. 5*s.* 10*d.* as due to him for the first seven weeks of the accounting year 1680–1. He is buried in the College cloisters, where there is the following inscription—making no mention of any degree: 'Hoc sub lapide obdormiscit quicquid mortale reliquum est Gulielmi King istius Collegii nuperrime Organistea Cujus in musica singularis eminentia ipsum Angelorum consortii participem fecit Die Mensis Nov. 17 Aetatis 57 Anno Domini 1680.' ('Under this stone there sleeps whatever remains mortal of William King, very recently organist of this College, whose singular eminence in music made him a partaker of the consort of angels. Aged 57, 17 November 1680.')

Richard Goodson (I) 1682–92. After King's death the bursar's Long Book speaks only of 'the organist' from Christmas 1680 to Michaelmas 1681, and no books survive for the years ending 1682 and 1683. From the year 1683–4 'Mr Goodson' received the full year's stipend, and continued to do so until Lady Day 1692. This is the Richard Goodson who became professor of music in 1682 and organist of Christ Church Cathedral from January 1692. As he was admitted to the privileges of the University in 1682, he was probably already organist of New College by then.

See under Christ Church Cathedral, Oxford.

——**Read 1694**. No immediate successor to Goodson seems to have been appointed. The bursar's Long Book does not record any stipend to an organist or teacher of the choristers from Lady Day to Michaelmas 1692. In the year ending Michaelmas 1693 there is a payment, for two terms only, to 'Mr Perry' for teaching the choristers; in the year ending Michaelmas 1694 no payment is mentioned up to Christmas 1693 and only one to 'the organist' for the quarter ending Lady Day 1694. Then, in the summer quarter of 1694, we find:

To Mr Read the organist	£7. 10*s*.
Towards Mr Read's funeral	£2. 12*s*.

This agrees with Wood's (1891–1900) entry under the year 1694: 'Apr 15, Low Sunday, in the afternoon ——Read of New Coll., organist, a young hot-head, ript up his own belly upon some discontent; died 18 day. W[ednesday].'

It is worth noting that during the apparent vacancy following Goodson's departure the Long Books record, under 24 June 1693, a payment of £5 'to Mr Alberici by order of Mr Warden'. Someone with a similar name was one of the musicians of the Roman Catholic chapel of James II and may have been seeking musical employment at New College.

John Weldon 1694–1701. 'Mr Weldon organist' received his stipend for the full year ending Michaelmas 1695, and was paid for the last time to Christmas 1701. His identification as John Weldon rests on information in Hawkins (1853: ii. 784).

See under the Chapel Royal.

Simon Child 1702–31. 'Mr Child' received his first stipend for the quarter ending Lady Day 1702. As Mrs Child received the pay for the quarter ending Michaelmas 1731, Child presumably died in office. His Christian name is found in a note made by *Philip Hayes (Lbl, Add. MS 33235, f. 2): 'This is one of the books I purchased of Mr Simon Child's widow at Oxford. NB, He was organist of New Coll: in that University and was succeeded by Mr Richard Church.' Another album of Child's is now Lbl, Add. MS 31460, while a third, endorsed 'Simon Child ejus liber', formerly belonging to Archdeacon Heathcote and then to J. S. Bumpus, was advertised by Kenneth Mummery in his catalogue of 1961 (NS 19).

The New College organist is in all probability the Simon Child who was a chorister of Christ Church Cathedral in the accounting year 1689–90 (Christ Church Disbursement Books). The list of subscribers to Croft's *Musica Sacra* (1724) describes him as organist of St John's as well as of New College.

Richard Church 1731–76. 'Mr Church' is found in the Long Books from Christmas 1731, but Hearne (1921) gives the date of his appointment to New College as 3 April 1732. His last payment was to Lady Day 1776; evidently, as at Christ Church, where he was also organist from 1741, he gave up his post shortly before his death.

See under Christ Church Cathedral, Oxford.

Philip Hayes 1776–97 (d. London, 19 Mar. 1797, aged 57). Philip Hayes was the son (according to Bloxam 1853–7, the second son) of *William Hayes. He was presumably born in Oxford, but the date of birth, though given in some works of reference as April 1738, is not precisely known. Rees's *Cyclopaedia* (i.e., Charles Burney) says that he was educated by his father, but *DNB* asserts that he was a chorister of the Chapel Royal under Bernard Gates. It is possible (see the family reminiscences below) that he was acting organist of Christ Church Cathedral shortly before the appointment of Thomas Norris in 1776, though the Christ Church Disbursement Books give no hint of this. On 30 November 1767 (CB2, p. 42) he was admitted a gentleman of the Chapel Royal, a post which he retained for life. As 'Mr Philip Hayes, Bachelor of Music, and Gentleman of the Chapel Royal', he subscribed to volumes 2 and 3 of the first edition of Boyce's *Cathedral Music* (1768–73). In 1776 he subscribed to Burney's *History of Music*. 'Mr Hayes' (later 'Dr') is found as organist in the Long Books of New College from the quarter ending Midsummer 1776 to Lady Day 1797. In 1777 he succeeded his father as organist of Magdalen College (q.v.). He also followed him as professor of music in the University (Wood 1796: ii/2, 894). To these two posts he added that of organist of St John's College in 1790. He was also 'during many years' (Parke 1830: i. 340) conductor of the Festival of the Sons of the Clergy. He took the Oxford degrees of B.Mus. (1763) and, following his succession to the chair, D.Mus. (1777). For some years during Hayes's tenure at New College the chapel and organ were out of use. The chapel was reopened on Trinity Sunday 1794, but, as Hayes himself noted, 'the organ was privately opened on the Monday before, with only the choir organ (all that was finish'd), after several years' cessation on account of the elegant alterations in the Chapel, organ, and gallery' (J. S. Bumpus 1972: 296).

Hayes was professor at the time of Haydn's visit to Oxford to receive the honorary degree of D.Mus. He inherited his father's music library, and was the owner of certain antiquarian albums of music (notably Cfm, Music MS 117 and Ob, Tenbury MS 791); he himself transcribed a good deal of earlier English music (e.g., Lbl, Add. MS 17839). A number of the portraits now belonging to the faculty of music (formerly the Music School collection) at Oxford were given by Hayes, including one of his father (Poole 1912–25: i. 161). He also caused the interior of the Music School (in the Schools quadrangle of the Bodleian) to be redesigned and furnished, and gave some pictures to Magdalen College, including one of Richard Fox, founder of Corpus Christi College.

Philip's great-nephew communicated to Bloxam the following reminiscences recorded by Hayes's nephews:

> Dr Philip Hayes was organist of New College (his favourite College), also of St John's College, and S. M. Magdalen College; was elected Organist of Christ Church and ousted by a man named Norris. Often went to London and purchased pictures, and presented them to the College. Very fond of works of *vertu*: a lazy dog, fond of good living, in fact a gourman: fine temper, good looking handsome man. Could have married well in his younger days, when his person was slender: during the latter part of his life very stout, weighing 20 stone.

He died suddenly on a visit to London, and is buried in the crypt (St Gregory's vault) of St Paul's Cathedral.

There are portraits of Philip Hayes in the faculty of music, Oxford, 'aetat 20, 1758' (Poole 1912–25: i. 163); in St John's College, Oxford (ibid. iii. 182), with a copy of the same at Magdalen College (ibid. ii. 231; the original is reproduced in Mee 1911, facing p. 72); and formerly at St Michael's College, Tenbury. The whereabouts of a further portrait, closely similar to this last, is unknown; it was reproduced in the programme book of the series of concerts given in Oxford to celebrate the Haydn centenary in 1932.

GM, 1797, p. 354; Bloxam 1853–7: ii.

Isaac Pring 1797–9 (d. Oxford, 18 Sept. 1799, aged 22). 'Mr Pring' received his stipend from the quarter ending Midsummer 1797 until Michaelmas 1798; he did not die until September 1799. According to some anonymous notes (Lcm, MS 1161, f. 184) compiled *c.*1830, Pring had been Hayes's assistant from 1794. Williams (1893) states that he took the Oxford degree of B.Mus. in 1799, but Foster (1887–92) notes only the matriculation of Isaac Pring as a member of New College on 1 March 1799. He was one of three brothers (another being *Joseph Pring, organist of Bangor Cathedral) brought up in the choir of St Paul's Cathedral under Robert Hudson. According to Lcm, MS 1161, he died of consumption.

In Warden Sewell's copy of Wood (1786–90) in the College Library, there is the following note: 'Isaac Pring, organist (d. 1799 aged twentytwo) buried in the south cloister', but no inscription can now be found.

William Woodcock 1799–1825 (b. Canterbury, *c.*1753; d. Oxford, 25 Apr. 1825. Mee (1911: 136) notes that Woodcock's appointment as organist of New College was reported in *Jackson's Oxford Journal* on 5 October 1799. The following account of him is given by Bennett and Marshall (1829):

> born at Canterbury, and received his musical education from Mr [Samuel] Porter, organist of that Cathedral. In 1778 he came to Oxford as assistant to [Thomas] Norris . . . and in 1784 was appointed lay clerk of Christ Church, New College, Magdalen, and St John's Colleges . . . and in 1806 was admitted to the degree of Bachelor in Music. He died in 1825, aged 72.

His degree, like some others in music, is not officially recorded. From 1791 (Mee 1911: 136) he was a singer and player at the Holywell Music Room. It appears that on his appointment as organist of New College he gave up his membership not only of the choir of that College but of St John's also.

Alfred William Bennett 1825–30 (b. Chichester, 1805; d. 12 Sept. 1830). Bennett was the elder son of *Thomas Bennett and the brother of *H. R. Bennett, who succeeded each other as organists of Chichester Cathedral. Following the death of Woodcock, the Long Books refer simply to 'the organist' for the two quarters ending Michaelmas 1825, mentioning 'Mr Bennett' by name only from the accounting year 1825–6. Bennett took the Oxford degree of B.Mus. in November 1825. According to Stephens (1882), he was also organist of the University church. He was among those involved in the fall of a runaway stage-coach near Worcester in September 1830, and died as a result of the injuries he sustained. The date of his death is usually given as 11 September, but Stephens (1882) deliberately corrects this to 12 September. He is buried in New College cloisters. His father and brother edited his *Cathedral Music*.

Stephen Elvey 1831–60 (b. Canterbury, 27 June 1805; d. Oxford, 6 Oct. 1860). Stephen was the elder brother of *G. J. Elvey, and had been a chorister at Canterbury Cathedral and a pupil there of *T. E. Jones. The Long Books do not disclose exactly when he became organist of New College; most reference books give 1830 as the date, but his brother's widow says he succeeded Bennett in 1831 (Elvey 1894: 180). At the age of 17 he was accidentally shot by a friend (whose sister he afterwards married), and had to have his right leg amputated. Nevertheless, 'with a wooden substitute he was enabled to manage the swell, having still the left at liberty for the pedal notes. Notwithstanding this disadvantage, few performers could give greater effect to Handel's choruses than the organist of New College' (ibid. 180).

As well as being organist of New College, Elvey was organist of the University church of St Mary (1845) and of St John's College (1846). He was choragus of the University, 1848–60 (not from 1840 or 1856, as variously stated).

GM (1869), i. 557; *Grove*[1]; *DNB*.

George Benjamin Arnold 1860–5. The Long Books end at Michaelmas 1860; but an 'Income and Expenditure Account' for 1860–1 shows Arnold as having been paid as organist from Christmas 1860—in effect from January 1861. One Pearson by name deputized for Arnold for the quarter ending December 1860.

See under Winchester Cathedral.

James Taylor 1865–1900 (b. Gloucester, 1833; d. 1 Aug. 1900). As a youth, Taylor became organist of St Mary-le-Crypt, Gloucester in 1850 (West 1921). 'He was a pupil of Sterndale Bennett and his pianism was remarkable: clear-cut, clean, of the restrained type, that showed to advantage in Mendelssohn's G minor Concerto. He was the leading piano-teacher of the Oxford of his day; exceptionally shy . . . and content with adequate achievement for the New College choir.' (Deneke 1951: 46.) After his appointment to New College he took the Oxford degree of B.Mus. (1873), and in 1894 the honorary degree of D.Mus. was conferred on him at the Encaenia. A tablet to his memory on the wall of the College cloister speaks of the gratitude of the warden and fellows, referring to his dedication both to his art and to the College.

Taylor's son Leonard was the artist of *The Rehearsal*, now in the Tate Gallery; another son, Colin, became principal of the Cape Town Conservatory of Music.

Sir Hugh Percy Allen, GCVO, 1901–18 (b. Reading, 23 Dec. 1869; d. Oxford, 20 Feb. 1946). Allen attended Kenrick School, Reading and, as a boy, studied the organ under *F. J. Read, then organist of Christ Church, Reading. When he was 11 years old he became organist of St Saviour's, Coley, near Reading, and then of Tilehurst (1884) and Eversley (1886). After a brief spell as assistant music master of Wellington College in 1887, he became assistant to Read at Chichester

Cathedral, 1887–92, during which time he worked for his Oxford music degree. In 1892 he went up to Cambridge as organ scholar of Christ's College, proceeding to the Oxford degree of B.Mus. in 1893 and taking the Cambridge degree of BA in 1895. In 1897 he was appointed organist of St Asaph Cathedral, moving after a few months to Ely Cathedral (1898). He took the Oxford degree of D.Mus. in 1898, followed by the Cambridge degree of MA in 1899.

He was appointed organist of New College in 1901, competing with *E. C. Bairstow, *H. W. Hunt, and others for the post. In 1908 he was made a fellow of New College (the first Oxford or Cambridge college organist to be made a fellow of his College, though *Stainer and *Parratt had already been made honorary fellows of Magdalen), but he preferred to resign the emoluments rather than be shackled by the obligation to do research. In the same year he became choragus of the University and was appointed director of music at University College, Reading.

In the summer of 1918 Allen was elected professor of music at Oxford, and in 1919 he also became director of the Royal College of Music. At the end of 1918, therefore, he resigned his appointment at Reading and his post as organist of New College, but he retained his Oxford chair and fellowship to the end of his life. Meanwhile he had became prominent as a choral conductor with the (London) Bach Choir (1907–20) and at the Leeds Festivals (1913, 1922, 1925, 1928).

In 1937 he resigned from the Royal College of Music. In his last years at Oxford he worked successfully to establish a faculty of music, thus securing for music, at last, its full University recognition.

He received numerous honours: Mus.D. (Cambridge, 1925), Litt.D. (Sheffield, 1926), D.Litt. (Reading, 1938), and Dr. Phil. (Berlin, 1936, so far as can be ascertained). He received a knighthood in 1920, followed by appointments as CVO in 1926, KCVO in 1928, and GCVO in 1935. His son, Sir Richard Allen, KCMG, became British ambassador to Burma.

Allen was a man of unusually powerful personality which cloaked great kindness. The memorial inscription to him in the cloisters of New College well expresses this by describing him as a 'devoted musician & wise counsellor who used his talent & the singular force of his personality in strenuously promoting the love and practice of his art'.

There is a fine drawing of him by Sargent (1926), and a portrait of him by L. Campbell Taylor is in the Royal College of Music.

Grove[3]; *MT*, 87 (1946), 65; Bailey 1948; *DNB*, 1941–50; *WWW*, 1941–50.

Sir William Henry Harris, KCVO, 1919–29.

See under St George's Chapel, Windsor.

Sir John Dykes Bower, CVO, 1929–32.

See under St Paul's Cathedral, London.

Sydney Watson, OBE, 1933–8.

See under Christ Church Cathedral, Oxford.

Herbert Kennedy Andrews 1938–56 (b. Comber, Co. Down, Ireland, 10 Aug. 1904; d. Oxford, 11 Oct. 1965). Andrews was educated at Bedford School and the Royal College of Music, and took the Dublin degrees of Mus.B. (1934) and Mus.D. (1935) as well as the FRCO diploma (1935). From 1934 to 1938 he was organist of Beverley Minster. Following his appointment to New College he took the Oxford degree of D.Mus. in 1942, and having read modern history in the meantime, he subsequently took the degrees of BA (1943) and MA (1944). In 1944 he was elected a fellow of New College. He also became a University lecturer in music, a post which he retained after his resignation as organist and fellow of New College, and was elected a research fellow of Balliol College. His death occurred while he was playing for the dedication of the organ in Trinity College, Oxford.

Besides a number of substantial articles on technical subjects for *Grove*[5], Andrews wrote *An Introduction to the Technique of Palestrina* (1958) and *The Technique of Byrd's Vocal Polyphony* (1966).

Grove[5]; *MT*, 106 (1965), 971; personal knowledge.

§'Albert) Meredith Davies, CBE, 1956–9 (b. Birkenhead, 30 July 1922). Davies entered the junior department of the Royal College of Music as an exhibitioner at the age of 8. He went up to Oxford as organ scholar of Keble College in 1941. There he read philosophy, politics, and economics, and took the degrees of BA (1946), B.Mus. (1946), and MA (1947). He holds the FRCO diploma, together with the silver medal of the Worshipful Company of Musicians.

After his first appointment as organist of St Albans Cathedral, 1947–9, he succeeded *P. C. Hull at Hereford Cathedral in 1950. While at Hereford he went to Rome to study conducting. In 1956 he moved to Oxford as organist and supernumerary fellow of New College. While holding this post he became associate conductor of the City of Birmingham Symphony Orchestra, 1957–9, and conductor of the City of Birmingham Choir in 1957, a post which he retained until 1964. He left New College in 1959 to devote himself to conducting. He was for some time prominently associated with Benjamin Britten's music, conducting, among other things, the first performance of *War Requiem*. He conducted at Covent Garden and Sadler's Wells, and was music director of the English Opera Group, 1962–4. From 1964 to 1971 he was conductor of the Vancouver Symphony Orchestra, while continuing free-lance work in the United Kingdom and abroad. He was chief conductor of the BBC Training Orchestra, 1969–72. In 1972 he became conductor of the Royal Choral Society. He took up the post of principal of Trinity College of Music in 1979, was appointed CBE in 1982, and retired in 1988.

§Sir David (James) Lumsden 1959–76 (b. Newcastle upon Tyne, 19 Mar. 1928). Before going up to Cambridge as organ scholar of Selwyn College (1948–51) Lumsden was a pupil of *Conrad Eden and *David Willcocks. In 1951 he was awarded the Barclay Squire prize for musical research. From 1951 to 1953 he was assistant organist of St John's College, Cambridge. He took the Cambridge degrees of BA (1950), Mus.B. (1951), MA (1954), and Ph.D. (1957).

From 1954 to 1956 he was organist and choirmaster of St Mary's, Nottingham and Nottingham University organist. He was then organist and *rector chori* of Southwell Minster, 1956–9, and part-time director of music at the University of Keele (1958–9). On moving to Oxford as fellow, organist, and tutor of New College in 1959 he was also appointed a University lecturer in music. He was on the staff of the Royal Academy of Music, 1959–61, and from 1968 to 1970 he was choragus of the University. He was appointed sub-warden of New College in 1970.

He left Oxford in 1976 on becoming principal of the Royal Scottish Academy of Music and Drama. In 1982 he became principal of the Royal Academy of Music, and received a knighthood in 1985.

§**Edward Higginbottom, organist from 1976** (b. Kendal, 16 Nov. 1946). From Leamington College for Boys, Higginbottom went up to Corpus Christi College, Cambridge as organ scholar, 1966–70, winning the John Stewart of Rannoch scholarship in sacred music, reading music, and taking the degrees of MA, Mus.B, and Ph.D. He won the Harding and Read prizes with the FRCO diploma (1966). He was a research fellow of his college from 1973 until his appointment to New College, where he is also tutor in music and a fellow.

WINCHESTER

St Mary College of Winchester (Winchester College)

Until *c.*1610, the College accounts (gleaned by Chitty 1912–13) represent the only source of (scanty) archival material available for our purpose. There are then the 'Long Rolls', lists of members of the College, compiled annually following the election week held between 7 July and 1 October. After an isolated roll for 1653, these run, with some breaks, from 1670 onwards. In published form they are available in Holgate (1899 and 1904). A little supplementary material is found in Kirby (1892), *passim*, and in Chitty's appendix ('College Register of Appointments') to volume 2 of Holgate (1904).

Winchester College was founded by William of Wykeham in 1382. Under its statutes of 1400, provision for the service of its chapel included the generous number of sixteen choristers (though these had not been envisaged in the charter of foundation). Besides performing their musical duties, they originally acted as servants to the scholars. It is not surprising that an organist is not mentioned at such a date, but it seems strange that at first there was no master of the choristers. The explanation may be that, in the earliest days of the College, the choristers were educated with the scholars. For these constitutional details, see Kirby (1892).

In course of time the College began to employ a master of the choristers and an organist, whose duties eventually merged with those of the twentieth-century director of music. (For most recent developments, see below under Cowan.) The earliest surviving trace of a master of the choristers is in the accounts for 1540–1, when a payment of £5 was recorded to 'domino Roberto Barber informatori choristarum' for three terms. But, as to an organist, the earliest ascertained name is that of Robert Moose (see below).

Robert Moose 1543–4. Payment to Moose, 'organista', was made at 10*s*. a quarter for two quarters in the accounting year 1543–4, a year in which 'Dominus' Goodwin (maybe Robert Goodwin, fellow of the College) became teacher of the choristers. This is doubtless the Robert Mos who had been paid as master of the choristers in 1542–3. The accounts for 1544–5 and 1545–6 have nothing to say about the organist or the master of the choristers. Payment to an unnamed organist is noted for 1546–7.

——**Hawkins ←1547–8→.** 'Dominus Hawkyns' is named as organist for the accounting year 1547–8. Subsequent accounts yield the following information: 1548–9, 1549–50, 1550–1, unnamed organist; 1551–2, no extant account; 1552–3 to 1556–7, no payment to an organist; 1557–8 to Christmas 1570, unnamed organist.

In 1571 Horne, Bishop of Winchester and visitor of the College, issued his injunction to give up using the organ; the organist's stipend was to be applied to what he considered more godly uses (Frere 1910: iii. 330).

Thomas Weelkes 1598–1600→. After Christmas 1570 no further payment to an organist is found for well over twenty-five years. Then, for the last three quarters of the year 1598–9 (i.e., from Christmas 1598), payment of 40*s*. is recorded to an unnamed organist. Payment at that same rate, 13*s*. 4*d*. quarterly, is found throughout 1599–1600. There is no extant account for 1600–1, but in 1601–2 the stipend dropped to 10*s*. a quarter, which may indicate a change of appointment.

Two clues enable us to name Thomas Weelkes as the recipient of the quarterly rate from Christmas 1598 until at least Michaelmas 1600. The first lies in his madrigal publication of 1600, in which he refers to 'the College at Winchester where I live' and describes himself as 'of the College of Winchester, organist'. The second is the payment in the College accounts for the year 1598–9 'pro vitro pro cubiculo mri. Weekes' ('for glass for master Weelkes's room'). There are grounds for thinking that he was established in Chichester by the end of 1602.

See under Chichester Cathedral.

William Emes 1606–9. The accounts for 1601–2 and 1602–3 do not mention the name of the organist; in 1603–4 no payment was made to an organist; but in 1604–5 the stipend became £4 per annum and in 1605–6 the officer was termed 'organist and instructor of the choristers'. For the three years 1606–7, 1607–8, and 1608–9 the name of William Emes is found as such. Hitherto he had been one of the three clerks of the chapel. He was buried in the College cloisters in 1637, and this led Chitty (1912–13) to suppose that he continued as organist until that time. However, as Betty Matthews has pointed out (the *Organ*, 51 (1971–2), 150–1), a William Emes became organist of Wimborne Minster in 1610, and it looks very much as if this was the same man. Miss Matthews herself states that he 'returned to Winchester in about 1622'. The question then arises of whether he was also the William Eames who was organist of Chichester Cathedral, 1624–35 (q.v.), perhaps returning yet again to Winchester, where he died in 1637.

At this point a speculative consideration must be taken into account. Among some names scratched or carved on the stonework forming the back of the organ-loft is found the inscription: 'MIO: OKER ORG:', and it has been neatly pointed out (Rannie 1970: 12–13) that this is capable of expansion as 'Magister Iohn Oker organista'. If indeed *John Okeover (or Oker) was at any time organist of Winchester College, it must have been in the years prior to 1616, when we know that he became a musician at Ingatestone Hall, Essex (see under Wells Cathedral).

George King ?1616–65 (d. Winchester, 10 May 1665, aged 70). After 1609, the available College documents are silent about the organist until the Long Roll for 1653 names 'Dominus' King in this capacity. There is no further roll until 1670, but King is identified by his memorial inscription in the College cloisters as George King, 'organista'. This inscription supplies the date of his death and his age.

It is not known exactly when King became organist. Rannie (1970: 13) suggests that the name George together with the date 1616 cut on the back of the organ-loft may refer to him and to the date of his appointment, pointing out also that he was named as organist in connection with the metropolitical visitation of 1635.

——**Pickhaver ←1670–6**. Pickhaver's name occurs in the next available Long Roll, 1670, and continues thus until 1677, when no organist is named. This seems to be the Pickhaver who was *informator in musica* and probably organist of New College, Oxford, 1662–4 (q.v.).

——**Jeferies 1678–80**. The Long Roll for 1677 names no organist, but 'Mr Jeferies' is named in the rolls for 1678, 1679, and 1680. It has been suggested that he may have been the Stephen Jefferies who was organist of Gloucester Cathedral, 1681–1712 (q.v.).

John Reading 1681–92. The name 'Mr Redding' occurs in the Long Rolls 1681–91. He may therefore perhaps be presumed to be the John Reading who left Winchester Cathedral in 1681. Hayes (1780) specifically identifies John Reading as the composer of the College Graces.

See under Winchester Cathedral.

Jeremiah Clarke 1692–5. The Long Rolls compiled in 1692, 1693, 1694, and 1695 specify 'Mr Clarke' as organist. Hayes (1780) identifies him outright as

Jeremiah Clarke, giving the 'College Accompt Books and School Rolls' as his general source of reference. Whether he saw some documents which included the Christian name Jeremiah, whether he simply knew the name to be thus as a result of information handed down through William Hayes, or whether he leapt to a conclusion is unknown. The surname alone might be thought too common for one to feel reasonably sure of this identification were it not for the note written by none other than William Croft (Lbl, Add. MS 30934), which states that Jeremiah Clarke wrote 'Come, come along for a song and a dance' when he was organist of Winchester College; this clinches the matter.

See under St Paul's Cathedral, London.

John Bishop 1695–1737 (d. Winchester, 19 Dec. 1737, aged 72). Hawkins (1853: ii. 767) states that Bishop 'was a scholar of Daniel Rosingrave, organist of Salisbury Cathedral'. A certain Mr Bishop became a lay clerk of King's College, Cambridge at Michaelmas 1687, and assumed the post of master or teacher of the choristers there in the spring of 1688 (King's College Mundum Books, 36). There appears to be no substance in West's statement (1921: 113, 125) that John Bishop (or any other Bishop) was ever organist of King's College; but it has been taken for granted, as indeed Hawkins (1853) states, that the King's College lay clerk was the same man as the Winchester musician.

The College Long Rolls record the name of 'Mr Bishop' as organist beginning with the year 1696 and continuing until his death in 1737; his memorial inscription (see below) discloses the Christian name. Like Reading before him, Bishop wrote music for the College Graces, printed by Hayes. In 1724 he subscribed to Croft's *Musica Sacra*.

In 1697 Bishop was appointed a lay clerk of Winchester Cathedral, and in 1729 he succeeded Richardson as organist of the Cathedral (q.v.), combining these posts with his work at the College. Hayes has this to say of Bishop's appointment at the Cathedral:

> His opponent for this last preferment was the late worthy Mr James Kent . . . who being at that time a younger man was esteemed a better player. Notwithstanding which, the age and amiable disposition of the former [Bishop], and, I might add too, some misfortune in his family, inclined the Dean and Chapter to decide the contest wholly in his favour.

The memorial to Bishop in the cloisters of Winchester College speaks of his honesty and uprightness of life, his gentle manners, and his faithful service throughout forty years.

Under the date 22 December 1737, Winchester PR records that 'Mr John Bishop, organist, was buried at the College.'

James Kent 1738–74. Kent is named in the Long Rolls 1738–74.

See under Winchester Cathedral.

Peter Fussell 1774–1802. Fussell is named in the Long Rolls 1775–1801.

See under Winchester Cathedral.

George William Chard 1802–49. Chard was admitted and sworn as College organist, 'loco Petri Fussel', on 2 August 1802, when he signed the following statement (Holgate 1904: appendix):

> The customary duties of the organist are, to teach the choristers chanting and singing; to assist the clerks in learning new choir music; to provide that the organ shall be played on all occasions of choir service throughout the year, without exception, of the vacations, if choir service is ordered in such vacations; to attend personally on all Saturday evenings and Sunday evenings of choir service; to assist at the performance of solemn Grace in the Hall; and to employ no deputy but such as shall be sanctioned by the Warden for the time being.
>
> These duties I undertake to fulfil, and hereby witness my engagement.

See under Winchester Cathedral.

Benjamin Long 1849–50 (d. Winchester, 20 Nov. 1850). Long, who was Chard's assistant at Winchester Cathedral, took over the College work on Chard's death. He himself died the following year, and was buried in the College cloisters. He took the Oxford degree of B.Mus. in June 1845, when he was 43 (Foster 1887–92).

Samuel Sebastian Wesley 1850–65. Wesley combined the duties of College and Cathedral organist from Long's death in 1850 until he left for Gloucester Cathedral. According to Sweeting (1924–5), he was 'generally present at Evensong [in the College] on Sunday. This overlapped with cathedral Evensong so the sermon in College was placed first to enable the organist and some of the choir to come over to College for the musical part of the service.'

See under Gloucester Cathedral.

William Hutt 1865–1901 (b. 25 Aug. 1843; d. Littlehampton, 18 Mar. 1904). Hutt was a chorister of Westminster Abbey and a pupil of *James Turle. He held several early posts as organist of churches in or near London: St Michael's, Queenhithe; Berkeley Chapel, Mayfair; Mitcham Parish Church. In July 1863 he was elected a lay clerk of Winchester Cathedral (Winchester CA10), and he succeeded Wesley as organist of the College in 1865. He seems to have been the first organist to have been regarded also as music master of the College. He retired in 1901.

BMB; West 1921.

Edward Thomas Sweeting 1901–24 (b. Alsager, Cheshire, 16 Sept. 1863; d. St Albans, 8 July 1930). Sweeting was a scholar of the National Training School for Music, the precursor of the Royal College of Music. He was organist of St Mary's, West Kensington from 1874, and in 1882 he became music master of Rossall School, Lancashire, where he taught the future Sir Thomas Beecham. In 1897 he became organist of St John's College, Cambridge, from where he moved to Winchester as organist of the College in 1901. Ranking as a don of the College, he enjoyed a more assured status than Hutt. He retired in 1924.

Sweeting took the Oxford degrees of B.Mus. (1889) and D.Mus. (1894), and held the FRCO diploma.

West 1921; *MT*, 71 (1930), 751.

Sir George Dyson, KCVO, 1924–37 (b. Halifax, Yorks, 28 May 1883; d. Winchester, 28 Sept. 1964). Dyson won scholarships to the Royal College of Music (1900–4), and was then awarded the Mendelssohn scholarship for composition which enabled him to travel in Italy and Germany. He held a succession of posts in public schools, at Osborne (1908), Marlborough (1911), Rugby (1914), Wellington (1921), and finally at Winchester (1924). He left Winchester to become director of the Royal College of Music (in succession to *H. P. Allen) in 1938, and retired in 1952.

Dyson took the Oxford degrees of B.Mus. (1909) and D.Mus. (1917); in 1940 he was made MA by decree. He received a knighthood in 1941 and was appointed KCVO in 1953. He was an honorary fellow of the Imperial College of Science and held the honorary LL D degree of the University of Aberdeen.

Among his writings are *The New Music* (1924), *The Progress of Music* (1932), and an autobiographical essay in *Fiddling While Rome Burns* (1954). He is widely reputed to have been the author of the anonymous *Manual of Grenade Fighting*, an official War Office publication of World War I. The Royal College of Music possesses a portrait of him by Anthony Devas, and also a sculptured head by Elizabeth Marks. His son Freeman became a distinguished scientist and fellow of the Royal Society.

Grove[5]; *MT*, 105 (1964), 838; *WWW*, 1961–70.

Sydney Watson, OBE, 1938–45.

See under Christ Church Cathedral, Oxford.

§Henry (Macleod) Havergal, OBE, 1946–53 (b. Hampton, Evesham, Worcs., 21 Feb. 1902; d. Edinburgh, 13 June 1989). After being a chorister of Salisbury Cathedral under *C. F. South, Havergal went to St Edward's School, Oxford and St John's College, Oxford, where he was exhibitioner (1920) and then organ exhibitioner (1923), taking the Oxford degrees of BA (1924) and MA (1929). Before his appointment to Winchester College he held posts as director of music at Fettes College, Edinburgh (1924–33), Haileybury (1933–6), and Harrow (1937–45). While at Fettes College he studied under Tovey and took the Edinburgh degree of B.Mus. He left Winchester in 1953 to become the first full-time principal of the Royal Scottish Academy of Music (now the Royal Scottish Academy of Music and Drama). He retired in 1969.

He received the honorary degrees of D.Mus. (Edinburgh, 1958) and LL D (Glasgow, 1969), and was appointed OBE in 1965.

Havergal is a member of a family which, though not otherwise represented in this book, has been connected with cathedral music for several generations. He was the great-grandson of W. H. Havergal (1793–1870), some of whose hymn-tunes are still well known, who published a useful collection called *Old Church Psalmody*; his grandfather, H. E. Havergal (1820–75), was a chaplain (corresponding to a minor canon) of Christ Church, Oxford and compiled the earliest catalogue of the manuscript music in the library there; and his great uncle F. T. Havergal, was a vicar choral of Hereford Cathedral and author of two works cited in our bibliography. Other members of the family have been choristers of Salisbury and Hereford Cathedrals and of St George's Chapel, Windsor.

Personal knowledge.

§**Christopher Home Cowan 1953–70** (b. Dalkeith, Scotland, 13 Nov. 1908). Cowan was educated at Winchester College (1922–7), Trinity College, Oxford (organ scholar, 1927–30), and the Royal College of Music (1930–2). He took the Oxford degrees of BA (1930), B.Mus. (1932), and MA (1934). Before his appointment as master of music at Winchester he held a series of posts in public schools, first as assistant music master at Winchester and Tonbridge, then as director of music at Dover College (1935–8), Sedbergh (1938–50), and Uppingham (1950–3). He retired from Winchester in 1970.

After Cowan's departure, new dispositions were made at Winchester College whereby the position of organist was no longer merged with that of master of music. The latter post was assumed by Angus James Watson, MA, Mus.B. (Cantab.).

§**Raymond George Humphrey 1970–9** (b. Redhill, Surrey, 24 Nov. 1916). Humphrey was educated at Reigate Grammar School, 1928–35, and took the FRCO and CHM diplomas (1937 and 1950) followed by the London degree of B.Mus. (1958). He was organist of St Matthew's, Redhill, 1930–46, and of St Michael's, Brighton, 1946–53. From 1948 to 1953 he was also assistant music master at Ardingly College. He was appointed assistant music master at Winchester College in 1953.

§**Christopher (John) Tolley, organist from 1979** (b. Birmingham, 8 June 1951). From King's School, Worcester, Tolley went up to New College, Oxford as organ scholar, 1969–72 and 1973–9, reading music and taking the degrees of BA (1972), MA (1976), and D.Phil. (1980). He took the FRCO diploma in 1970. Before leaving Oxford he was organist of the University church of St Mary, 1973–9, and of the Sheldonian Theatre, 1976–9.

APPENDIX I

ARMAGH

The Cathedral Church of St Patrick

Armagh Cathedral, see of the Primate of All Ireland, is a foundation of great antiquity which is unfortunate in having no extant records pre-dating the disestablishment of the Church of Ireland which are relevant here. Like all medieval secular cathedrals, it had its College of Vicars Choral, which Charles I refounded and enlarged in 1634, apparently including the organist in the foundation. His charter was cited as recently as when Frederick Carter was appointed in 1951 (see modern Chapter minutes), but enquiries have not enabled me to discover its whereabouts.

For appointments before 1916, therefore, we have to rely on derivative sources of information. In his pamphlet of 1881 Crawford tells us that he obtained his information from William Reeves, then Dean of Armagh. It seems obvious, however, that Reeves must have relied on the list of organists printed by Cotton (1848–9: iii. 69)—apart from the first officer named, where Cotton had clearly made a mistake. With that exception, Cotton represents our earliest source of information up to the time of Robert Turle (see below), with Crawford (1881) providing occasional supplementary details.

Richard Galway ←1634→. According to Crawford (via Reeves), the patent of Charles I (23 May 1634) constituting the College of Vicars Choral named Galway as 'primus et modernus organista dicti coenobi'. Cotton (1848–9), on the other hand, says John Hawkshaw was organist at the time of the Caroline charter. If the quotation given by Crawford is authoritative, as it seems to be, then Cotton must have made a slip. It is possible, no doubt, that Galway was already serving as organist under existing arrangements.

John Hawkshaw c.1661–95. There is no information about this man. One may conjecture that he was connected with John Hawkshaw of Dublin, for whom see Christ Church and St Patrick's Cathedrals.

Robert Hodge 1695–?1711. Hodge was appointed on 27 June 1695, by which time Hawkshaw had died. He may have been connected with Robert Hodge of Dublin, for whom see St Patrick's Cathedral.

William Toole 1711–22. Toole was appointed on 11 December 1711 and resigned in 1722. He was apparently organist of Cork Cathedral, 1703–11 (Caulfield n.d.).

Samuel Bettridge 1722–52. Bettridge was appointed on 26 May 1722. West (1921) says that he was organist of St Werburgh's and St John's, Dublin, 1715–20.

John Woffington 1752–?1759. Woffington was appointed on 14 May 1752, by which time Bettridge had died. West (1921) says that he was organist of St Werburgh's, Dublin.

Robert Barnes 1759–1774. Barnes held office from February 1759 until he resigned in 1774 on his appointment as a vicar choral.

Langrish Doyle 1776–80. A period of two years is now unaccounted for. Cotton (1848–9) gives the date of Doyle's appointment as 1774, the year of Barnes's resignation, but Crawford's (1881) date of 1776 is more reliable, for we know that Doyle left Dublin for Armagh in that year. He returned to Dublin in 1780.

See under Christ Church Cathedral, Dublin.

Richard Langdon 1782–94. Once more a period of some two years is unaccounted for. The assumption that this is the Richard Langdon who had been organist of Exeter Cathedral seems reasonably supported, bearing in mind that the Exeter man's wife was called Susanna and that John Stafford Smith's copy of his own *Anthems* (1793), now in the Royal College of Music, contains a torn fragment of a letter, dated Armagh, 23 November 1794, and signed 'Susanna Langdon'. It concludes: 'Mr Langdon is so ill, but if his health will permit intends to return here early in Spring.' Presumably his health did not improve, and this led to his retirement to Exeter.

See under Exeter Cathedral.

John Clarke (afterwards Clarke-Whitfeld) 1794–7. The dates cited by both Cotton (1848–9) and Crawford (1881) coincide with Clarke-Whitfeld's own general reference (*Cathedral Music*, ii) to a three-year tenure at Armagh. While there, he was granted the degree of Mus.D. from Trinity College, Dublin by diploma by private grace on 10 October 1795. Late in 1797 he moved to Christ Church Cathedral, Dublin as master of the choristers in succession to Langrish Doyle (Christ Church CA8), an appointment which was linked to a similar post at St Patrick's Cathedral (St Patrick's CA7, January and March 1798). On 4 June 1798 Christ Church gave him leave to go to England on private business; his letter of resignation was received on 26 December. He himself said that he left Ireland 'owing to the Irish Rebellion' (Gu, MS R.d.85).

See under Hereford Cathedral.

John Jones 1797–1816 (d. 21 Mar. 1830). Crawford (1881) notes that Jones relinquished appointment by resignation, and supplies the date of his death. He also designates him as Mus.D. (presumably of Trinity College, Dublin, though Burtchaell and Sadlier 1935 have no record of this). West (1921) says that Jones was born in 1767 and became a vicar choral of Armagh in 1796. According to Clarke-Whitfeld (*Cathedral Music*, ii), he had been a pupil of *Samuel Arnold.

Frederick William Horncastle 1816–22 (b. London, ?1790; d. 1850). Horncastle was a chorister of the Chapel Royal, London, and then organist of Stamford Hill Chapel and Berkeley Chapel, London. He was dismissed from his post at Armagh, but became a gentleman of the Chapel Royal in 1826 (CB2).

BMB; West 1921.

Robert Turle 1823–72 (b. Taunton, 19 Mar. 1804; d. Salisbury, 26 Mar. 1877). Robert was the younger brother of *James Turle. Before his appointment to Armagh he was organist of St Lawrence Jewry, London, 1821–2 (Dawe 1983); writing to the Vestry on 24 December 1822, he said that he had, 'through the interest and good opinion of a much respected and highly valued friend, my late master [*]Mr Greatorex, been honoured by the appointment of organist and master of the boys to the Cathedral Church of Armagh' (Vestry minutes, 31 December 1822, Lgh, MS 2590/5), and notified his resignation 'at Christmas next'—the following day! According to Sir Frederick Bridge (1918: 70): 'When the Irish Church was disestablished I believe he commuted his emoluments [from Armagh Cathedral] and retired with a considerable sum as compensation for the loss of his office. It is said that the old man drank the health of Mr Gladstone—to whom he owed this bit of good fortune—every night in a glass of port.'

There is a memorial to him in the north nave aisle of the Cathedral.

BMB, *sub* 'Turle' (James).

Thomas Osborne Marks 1872–1916 (b. Armagh, 6 Feb. 1845; d. Armagh, 12 Sept. 1916). Marks was a chorister of the Cathedral, and became deputy to Robert Turle when he was only 15 years old. Although he seems to have held office for forty-four years, his memorial in the north nave aisle speaks of him as organist for forty-two years. In 1870 he took the Oxford degree of B.Mus., and in 1874 the Dublin degree of Mus.D. He was the early teacher of Charles Wood, afterwards professor of music in the University of Cambridge.

BMB; *MT*, 57 (1916), 458.

George Henry Phillips Hewson 1916–20. Hewson was appointed by minute of the Cathedral Board dated 23 November 1916; his resignation was recorded on 5 March 1920.

See under St Patrick's Cathedral, Dublin.

Edred Martin Chaundy 1920–35 (b. Oxford, 1871). Chaundy was a pupil at Oxford of *C. H. Lloyd. He took the degrees of BA (1892), MA (1898), B.Mus. (1890), and D.Mus. (1908) as a non-collegiate student. Before his appointment to Armagh he was organist of Christ Church, Streatham Hill, London (1892), Enniskillen Parish Church (1895), Pershore Abbey (1898), Holy Trinity, Stroud (1899), St George's, Kidderminster (1901), St Mark's, Strandtown (1905), St George's, Belfast (1913), and Bangor Abbey (Ireland) (1919).

His retirement was discussed by the Cathedral Board in March 1935, and he gave up office at the end of that year.

West 1921.

§**Reginald (Harry) West 1936–51** (b. Hereford, 2 June 1904). West's appointment was minuted by the Cathedral Board on 17 June 1935. He had been a chorister of Hereford Cathedral and was educated at Hereford Cathedral School. He then served his articles to *P. C. Hull and was assistant organist of Hereford Cathedral, 1924–35. He resigned his appointment at Armagh in February 1951, and joined the staff of King's School, Worcester in that year. He retired in 1964.

§**Frederick (George) Carter 1951–66** (b. Enfield, Middlesex, 5 Mar. 1913). Carter received his general education at the George Spicer School, Enfield, and studied music under Harold Darke. He took the diplomas of FRCO (1948) and CHM (1949). From 1941 to 1948 he was organist of St Paul's Church, St Albans, and then, from 1948 to 1951, assistant organist of St Albans Cathedral. He left Armagh in August 1966 to become organist of St John's Church, Shaughnessy, Vancouver and music master of St George's School Vancouver.

§**(Eric) Christopher Phelps 1966–8** (b. Cheltenham, Glos., 21 May 1943). After attending King's School, Gloucester, Phelps went to the Royal College of Music, 1961–5, and in 1965 he took the diplomas of CHM and FRCO (with Turpin prize). He began his duties at Armagh in September 1966 and relinquished them at the end of May 1968 to study conducting at the Akademie für Musik, Vienna, where he received the *Kapellmeister Diplom* in 1971. Since then he has been a senior lecturer in the music department of the Colchester Institute.

§**Martin John White, organist and master of the choristers from 1968** (b. Southall, Middlesex, 26 Dec. 1941). White was educated at the Mercers' School, Holborn, 1953–8, and the Royal Academy of Music, 1961–5. He took the FRCO diploma in 1965 and that of CHM (with Brook prize) in 1967. In 1960 he became organist of Ruislip Priory Church, Middlesex, and from 1963 to 1968 he was organist of Harrow Parish Church. He took the degree of Mus.B. from Trinity College, Dublin in 1982.

APPENDIX II

DUBLIN

The Cathedral Church of the Holy and Undivided Trinity (Christ Church)

Main sources in this section (1967) (documents since deposited with the Representative Church Body (Church of Ireland), Braemar Park, Dublin):

Chapter Acts	
CA1	1574–1634 (transcript dated 1677).
CA2	1634–70 (unnumbered volume).
CA3	1686–1705. Not available to the present author; but see Crawford (1881) and Grindle (1989: 27–32).
CA4/5	1705–40.
CA6	1740–69.
CA7	1770–93.
CA8	1793–1809.
CA10	1818–25.
CA11	1825–34.
CA12	1834–55.
Proctor's Accounts	
Ac22 (etc.)	Bound volumes, beginning with No. 22 and continuing to No. 33, Sept. 1664–Sept. 1699.

In 1539 Henry VIII changed the constitution of Christ Church Cathedral from a priory of regular canons into a secular cathedral under a dean. The 'Regulae et Constitutiones' issued in that year (transcript by W. Monk Mason, National Library of Ireland, MS 98, f. 44), though containing some individual provisions, broadly foreshadow the statutes which Henry was shortly to prescribe for the cathedrals founded or refounded by him in England. There were to be eight vicars choral and four choristers, together with three 'clerici chorales' of whom the first was required to be learned in music, 'not only in organ playing, but in plainsong and discant . . . for instruction of the boys' ('tam in pulsatione organorum quam in canto plano et . . . in sufficienti discantu . . . pro instructione puerorum'), and to be master of the boys under the precentor.

Here we see the earliest example of the pattern followed in all the later Henrician foundations whereby an organist was provided by combining his duty with that of master of the choristers. The actual charter of the new foundation was issued in the form of letters patent on 10 May 1541, from which point we hear no more of the 'clerici chorales' from among whom the master of the choristers/organist was to be drawn. Instead, as we shall see, this officer was to be one of the vicars choral, who no longer had to be in holy orders. In later years, when it became necessary to supplement the choir of vicars, additional men were appointed under the name of stipendiaries, and it was found convenient to make separate appointments of organist and master of the choristers.

The musical establishment of Christ Church was closely intertwined with that of St Patrick's Cathedral, Dublin, and numerous examples will be recorded of those who were vicars choral/organists/masters of the choristers of both simultaneously.

Robert Heywood 1546→. Heywood's indenture of appointment was dated 16 March 1545/6. Report 24, Appendix 8 (1892) of the deputy keeper of the Public Records in Ireland furnishes the following calendared version of this document, the original of which perished in the Civil War of 1922:

> Thomas Lokwood, Dean, and the Chapter of the Holy Trinity, &c., in consideration of his instructing the chorister-children, grant to Robert Heywood of Dublin, singing-man, for life, a yearly stipend of £6 13*s*. 4*d*. [this was the sum provided in the 'Regulae' of 1539], twelve pecks of wheat, and eight pecks of malt . . . a livery coat, a cart load of wood at Christmas, and the chamber by the east of the churchyard; and the vicars-choral grant him four pecks of malt . . . his daily finding, table and board, sitting and taking the same with them. Grantee, who is empowered to distrain grantor's lands . . . for his stipend undertakes to play the organ, to keep Our Lady's mass and anthem daily, Jesus' mass every Friday, according to the custom of St Patrick's, and matins when the organs play on the eight principal feasts, and the feasts of 'major duplex' (grantors finding a blower); to procure at the expense of the church suitable songs . . . to instruct the choristers in pricksong and descant to four minims, and to play Our Lady's mass, all instruments being found for them during the time of their child's voice . . . to remain in the service of the church during his life, and not to absent himself without licence.

These provisions, though post-dating the dissolution of the monasteries, continue to reflect the medieval liturgy in the years preceding the 1549 Prayer Book.

Nothing further is heard of Heywood or any other organist for a spell of forty years.

Walter Kennedy 1586–95. Kennedy is named as organist in 1586 by Finlayson (1852), who had direct access to the Cathedral archives in the mid-nineteenth century. Cotton (1848–9) records Kennedy's admission as vicar choral in 1586. I could trace no reference to him under that date in CA1, though he is listed as such on 24 October 1592 (CA1, p. 75), and his resignation as vicar is noted on 19 October 1595 (p. 87). Curiously, on 17 May 1596 he was told to attend church on pain of losing his pension (CA1, 90).

John Farmer 1596–9. The minute in CA1 (p. 89), dated 16 February 1595/6, stating that 'John Fermor shall have as master of the choristers and organist for this year 15 pounds current money of England' probably marks his appointment. On 10 August 1596 (CA1, p. 92) 'John Farmor' was admitted vicar choral. Less than a year later it was ordered (18 July 1597) that if he did not return by 1 August 1597, 'then all excuses set apart his place to be void in the church for departing the land without licence' (CA1, p. 94). Fellowes (1921: 241) says that this order was obeyed and that Farmer remained in Dublin until the spring of

1599, when he left for London, after which he was permitted a deputy to perform his Cathedral duties. He adds that it was at the end of this year that Farmer's place as vicar choral was declared vacant and his successor was appointed. Fellowes is not likely to have invented this, but so far I have not traced these statements to their sources.

It was L. M'C. L. Dix who, in *Grove*[2], first suggested that this John Farmer was the composer of the set of four-part madrigals published in London in 1599 who was also a contributor to *The Triumphes of Oriana*. It has been stated that he was also organist of St Patrick's Cathedral, Dublin, but I am unable to confirm this (see p. 417).

Richard Myles 1599→. Myles was admitted vicar choral on 23 November 1599, and on 30 January next following he was allowed £3 'for training and instructing in singing and making fit for the choir such boys as the Dean and Chapter and Myles shall from time to time provide for the choristers' (CA1, p. 107). I include him somewhat tentatively as Farmer's successor, bearing in mind that he is not mentioned by either Finlayson (1852) or Crawford (1881).

Thomas Bateson 1609–30. Bateson was elected vicar choral on 24 March 1608/9, and almost immediately, on 5 April 1609, he was given a month's leave 'to pass into England about his necessary business'. On that same day an agreement was sealed whereby he was to be appointed organist and master of the choristers, with a yearly stipend of £8. 13*s*. 4*d*. above that of a vicar, and a house in the precincts, ('because the remuneration of a vicar-choral is not sufficient': CA1, p. 139). Some years later, on 22 October 1616, it was agreed that, when required, Bateson should 'make or cause to be made a sufficient instrument or organ' for the Cathedral at a cost of £35 (CA1, p. 153). He was admonished for using abusive language to one of the prebendaries on 16 May 1620 (CA1, p. 159). He died in office.

See under Chester Cathedral.

Randolph Jewett (1st tenure) **←1631–8**. On 27 August 1630 an unnamed organist was admonished 'not to walk in the body of the church in time of divine service' (CA1, p. 183). Jewett was named for the first time in a minute of 10 May 1631, when he was allowed £15 per annum 'conditionally, he being very diligent in his place of organist which he now holdeth' (CA1, p. 187). The stipend was increased to £20 from Michaelmas 1634, 'provided that he shall always be ready when he is required to sing among the vicars in the choir' (CA1, p. 266). He was admitted a vicar choral himself on 2 October 1638; he was already in deacon's orders (CA2, pp. 83, 89). But by then he seems to have ceased to be organist in fact, if not in name, for on that same day 'Benjamin Rogers organist' said that he had supplied the place of organist for a quarter without stipend (CA2, p. 82). Nevertheless, Jewett continued in charge of the choristers, at least for a time, for on 10 December 1639 he petitioned for an allowance for teaching them up to Midsummer 1639, whereupon he was allowed 20 nobles (£6. 13*s*. 4*d*.) until Christmas 1639 (CA2, p. 102).

It can only be assumed that he continued as vicar choral until he went to Chester Cathedral in 1643 (q.v.). For his presumed second tenure as organist of Christ Church, see below (after Rogers).

Benjamin Rogers 1639–41. Rogers seems to have been acting organist from mid-1638 (see above), and in that capacity he was allowed £20 per annum, the amount of Jewett's full salary (CA2, p. 82). On 9 September 1639, 'upon the humble petition of Benjamin Rogers to be established organist in this church absolutely', it was ordered that he should be admitted with that stipend (CA2, p. 99). According to Wood (1815–20: ii. 305), Rogers returned to England in 1641. The Cathedral was apparently in some financial difficulty, for on 9 November 1642, among various retrenchments ordered 'in respect of the church means', the organist's stipend was reduced to £10 a year (CA2, p. 130).

See under Magdalen College, Oxford.

Randolph Jewett (conjectured 2nd tenure) **?1646→**. Jewett reappears at Christ Church in 1646, by which time he is also to be found again at St Patrick's Cathedral, Dublin. On 24 July 1646 the Chapter received a letter from the Lord Lieutenant of Ireland (Ormonde), who stated that Jewett 'had suffered for his good affection towards his Majesty's service' (no doubt a reference to some event while he was in England), and, 'knowing how ably he is qualified in his profession and for the choir', asked for (and obtained) a place for him as vicar choral (CA2, p. 163). His inclusion here in the capacity of organist once more is speculative, yet one cannot but think it likely. He must have left Ireland for London before 1649.

See also under St Patrick's Cathedral, Dublin.

John Hawkshaw 1661–89. After the resumption of cathedral services following the Restoration, Hawkshaw was admitted vicar choral on 26 February 1660/1. This seems in fact to have been a readmission, for he was described as 'one of the ancient vicars of this church' (Cotton 1848–9). He was referred to as organist on 20 November 1662, when he was allowed arrears of salary (CA2). On 19 February 1663/4 (CA2) the following minute was passed: 'Ordered that if Mr Hawkshaw, being vicar as well as organist, do not attend with the choir daily in his vicar's stall unless or until the service of the church doth require him to go to the organ, the monitor for the time being shall take notice of and return his absence and tardy coming accordingly.' Ac24 shows that he was paid as organist up to Lady Day 1689.

See also under St Patrick's Cathedral, Dublin.

(Thomas) Finell 1689–92. Finell (whom one assumes to be the Thomas Finell named below in 1694) is included here somewhat tentatively, for he may have been only acting organist at this period. Thomas Godfrey (see p. 419) was paid as organist from Lady Day to Michaelmas 1689. 'Mr Finell organist' is named in the accounts for the year 1689–90. Between Michaelmas 1690 and the following

February there is simply the entry 'organist', with 'Mr Finell' reappearing until Michaelmas 1692. What happened was that on 2 January 1690/1 Thomas Morgan was appointed organist; but though it was resolved on 26 March 1691 to remit £5 sterling 'into England to Tho. Morgan for his relief and encouragement to use his best endeavour to attain the perfection of an organist' (CA3), he did not take up office and no more is heard of him.

Peter Isaac 1692–4. On 12 November 1691 the Dean and Chapter of Christ Church resolved to invite Isaac to come over from Salisbury. The accounts for the period February 1690/1 to September 1692 include the sum of £10 for 'Mr Isaac to bear his charges out of England', and he was admitted organist and vicar choral on 31 March 1692 'on account of his extraordinary skill in music' with a gratuity of 50*s*. (Ac25; CA3).

See under St Patrick's Cathedral, Dublin.

Thomas Finell 1694–8. Finell, already mentioned tentatively as officiating between 1689 and 1692 (see above), was admitted as organist on probation on 10 October 1694 (CA3). He had been a vicar choral of St Patrick's Cathedral from 1677 (St Patrick's CA2), and continued as such at least until January 1691/2 (ibid. 4). Ac28–32 confirm that he was organist at Christ Church, 1694–8. He was still in evidence in 1700, when on 3 September he was accused of assaulting his successor (CA3).

As the name is not a very common one, it is worth noting that a Thomas Finell was briefly one of the lay vicars of Westminster Abbey on the re-establishment of the choir there in 1660–1 (Westminster Abbey Muniment 33695).

Daniel Roseingrave 1698–1727. Roseingrave came to Dublin from Salisbury, and was admitted organist and stipendiary of Christ Church on 11 November 1698 (CA3) and organist and vicar choral of St Patrick's Cathedral four days later (q.v.). On 9 November 1699 a Chapter minute declared that he 'ought not to do any other duty . . . as a stipendiary . . . but only attend to the organist's place', presumably implying that his post of stipendiary was nothing but a sinecure to augment his emoluments as organist. Soon after, on 15 December, it was ordered that he was to be paid £3 'as a gratuity for writing three services and two Creeds for the use of the Church' (CA3). In this context, 'writing' may or may not mean copying as distinct from composing, and the works in question may very well be those for which St Patrick's also paid him in the same month (q.v.).

See under St Patrick's Cathedral, Dublin.

Ralph Roseingrave 1727–47. On 30 October 1727 Ralph Roseingrave was admitted as organist, at a salary of £50 a year, to run from the previous Michaelmas (CA4/5).

See under St Patrick's Cathedral, Dublin.

George Walsh 1747–65. Walsh was admitted organist, with an annual stipend of £50, on 24 December 1747 (CA6). In 1760 he became organist and vicar choral of St Patrick's Cathedral (q.v.), and he held both posts until his death. His colleague as master of the choristers at Christ Church was William Lamb (appointed on 13 August 1746 in succession to John Worrall), who had sung at the first performance of Handel's *Messiah* in 1742. Lamb was followed by Samuel Murphy (see below) in 1758.

Richard Woodward 1765–77 (d. Dublin, 22 Nov. 1777, aged 33). Richard Woodward 'the younger' was admitted organist on 7 March 1765, on Walsh's death (CA6). Earlier, on 11 June 1759, he had been given a present of £5 for having served an apprenticeship and behaved well as a chorister. In 1768 he became Mus.B. of Trinity College, Dublin, proceeding to Mus.D. in 1771 (Burtchaell and Sadleir 1935; but these authors confuse him with Richard Woodward, Bishop of Cloyne).

Richard Woodward's father (also Richard) succeeded Murphy as master of the choristers 5 December 1768, and on 8 September 1776 Richard (the younger) took over the post from his father (CA6). A memorial brass erected in the Cathedral by his father declares him to have been also vicar choral and master of the choristers of St Patrick's Cathedral.

Samuel Murphy 1777–80. Murphy had been master of the choristers from 1758 to 1768, a post which he resumed on his appointment as organist on 29 November 1777 (CA7). He was already organist and master of the choristers of St Patrick's Cathedral (q.v.). He took the degrees of Mus.B. and Mus.D. together in 1768 (Burtchaell and Sadleir 1935).

Langrish Doyle 1780–1814. Doyle had been a chorister of St Patrick's Cathedral, 1763–8 (St Patrick's CA5, 6) and of Christ Church, *c.*1766. Described as 'Dr Doyle', he became a substitute stipendiary of Christ Church on 12 November 1722 and a full stipendiary on 6 November 1775 (CA7).

The Christ Church Acts record his departure for Armagh (q.v.) on 8 September 1776, but his name recurs on 14 November 1780, when CA7 notes the resolution of both Christ Church and St Patrick's Cathedrals that 'Mr Langrish Doyle' should be appointed master of the boys and that he should be recommended to Trinity College as Samuel Murphy's successor as organist. On the same day he was also appointed organist and stipendiary of Christ Church. On 15 May 1781 he obtained a half place as vicar choral of St Patrick's, advancing to a full place on 5 February 1784 (St Patrick's CA6), In May 1791 he resigned his position as a stipendiary of Christ Church, receiving £40 a year more as organist in compensation (CA7).

On 18 December 1797 it was resolved (CA8) that from Christmas Day Dr Clarke (*John Clarke[-Whitfeld]) should succeed Doyle as master of the boys; and on 17 March 1798 (St Patrick's CA7) the St Patrick's authorities recorded their joint concern with Christ Church 'in appointing Dr John Clarke master of the choristers at the same salary as Dr Doyle had'. Doyle continued as organist of Christ Church, but on 25 November 1805 (CA8) he expressed a desire, 'from his age and long service', to have a deputy, and the Chapter, on his recommendation, appointed his nephew William Warren (see below). According to Finlayson (1852), Doyle ceased to be organist in 1814. There is no official record of his doctorate, but on the admission of his son, Garret Wesley Doyle, to Trinity College, Dublin in 1789, he was described as 'Musicae Doctor' (Burtchaell and Sadleir 1935).

William Warren 1814–41. There is very little information about Warren in CA8–12, and we have to rely on Finlayson (1852) for the date on which he succeeded Doyle. On 19 November 1841 (CA12) a confusing minute records that John Robinson, 'deputy organist to the late Dr Warren', was 'on his [Warren's] retirement with his full salary for life further appointed to be joint organist to him the said Dr Warren'. This makes sense if it is considered in the light of Finlayson's (1852) statement that Robinson became joint organist with Warren in 1834. Before that date, then, Robinson had deputized for Warren; in 1834 Warren effectively, though not technically, retired on full pay; and Robinson acted for him thereafter. Finlayson also says that John Robinson's eldest brother Francis (see p. 423) was Warren's assistant from 1816 to 1833, so John could not have been deputy for very long before Warren's retirement. His doctorate is not officially recorded.

John Robinson 1834–41 (jointly with William Warren) **1841–4** (sole organist) (b. Dublin, 1810; d. Dublin, 1844). John Robinson had already succeeded his brother as organist of St Patrick's Cathedral (q.v.) when he also became a stipendiary of Christ Church on 10 January 1832 (CA11). The minute of 19 November 1841 recording his appointment as joint organist (see above) not only explains that he was effectively organist after Warren's notional retirement, but goes on to say that he wished to arrange his work at Christ Church so that he would be organist there on Sundays and attend as stipendiary on weekdays. It was therefore arranged that Matthias Crowley should play the organ on weekday mornings.

On 19 December 1843 Robinson wrote to the Dean and Chapter to say that he was too ill to perform his duties, whereupon the Chapter, noting that he had suffered chronic disease for many months, asked for a medical certificate from the surgeon general. He had died by May 1844.

Sir Robert (Prescott) Stewart 1844–94 (b. Dublin, 16 Dec. 1825; d. Dublin, 24 Mar. 1894). The son of the librarian to the Honourable Society of King's Inns, Dublin, Stewart was educated as a chorister of Christ Church Cathedral. While still a boy he had deputized successfully for John Robinson at a moment's notice. He was appointed Robinson's successor on 15 May 1844 (CA12), and he also followed him as organist of Trinity College Chapel. On 9 April 1851 he accumulated the degrees of Mus.B. and Mus.D. from the University of Dublin. From 1852 to 1861 he was 'afternoon organist' of St Patrick's Cathedral (q.v.), and he continued unofficially to play for services there until his death, which is why the memorial window in St Patrick's speaks of him as having been 'for 43 years Organist of this Cathedral'. In 1861 he obtained the post of half vicar choral of St Patrick's (see introductory section to St Patrick's).

He was appointed professor of music in the University of Dublin (the first effective such appointment) in 1862, exerting his influence to raise the standard of the degrees in music and to require evidence of good general education as a prerequisite for them. In that respect, Dublin was ahead of both Oxford and Cambridge for some time. He was knighted by the Lord Lieutenant of Ireland on 28 February 1872, and after his death memorials to him were placed in St Patrick's Cathedral (a window) and Christ Church Cathedral (a brass). There is also a statue of him on Leinster Lawn, Dublin; he is probably unique among cathedral organists in being commemorated in such a way.

Stewart was a notable performer on the organ, especially when one considers the state of British organ technique when he was a boy. One of his pupils, W. G. Torrance, recalled his playing thus (Vignoles 1898: 41):

> Sir Robert's 'staccato pedal' was a remarkable feature in his organ playing. At times his feet seemed to glide over the notes with a lightness and softness which can only be described as a touch of velvet; and in rapid passages the pedals were *manipulated* with all the delicacy and dexterity of practised fingers. Another striking excellence, and one which all true musicians could appreciate, was his clever adaptation of orchestral effects in accompanying great classical works.

The well-known Dublin musician Joseph Robinson said (ibid. 57):

> On his [Stewart's] return from Paris in 1857, his style of organ playing seemed quite changed. The brilliant French school had attracted Dr Stewart very much, and so clever was he that he was able to adopt anything novel which had captivated his fancy. On the first Sunday after his return I could almost imagine that it was Wely of the 'Madeleine' that was at the instrument, so complete was the change from Stewart's former style of playing.

Vignoles 1898.

John Horan 1894–1904 (sole organist) **1904–6** (jointly with J. F. Fitzgerald) (b. Drogheda, 26 Feb. 1831; d. Dublin, 31 Jan. 1907). Horan was a chorister of Christ Church from 1841. Between then and his return as assistant organist in 1873 he had served, among other appointments, as solo bass of Limerick Cathedral and organist of Tuam (1857) and Derry Cathedrals (1862). He succeeded his former master, Stewart, in 1894. Latterly, from 1904, he was joint organist with J. F. Fitzgerald (see below). His years in office and the date of his death are found on the memorial to him in Christ Church. Other information about him is derived from West (1921).

James Ferrier Fitzgerald 1904–6 (jointly with J. Horan) **1907–13** (sole organist) (b. Dublin, 1873). Fitzgerald was educated at Uppingham School, Trinity College, Cambridge (1891), and the Royal College of Music. He took the Cambridge degree of BA in 1904. He became assistant organist of Christ Church Cathedral in 1901, joint organist with Horan in 1904, and sole organist in 1907. West (1921) says that he resigned in 1913 on taking holy orders in the Church of Ireland, but according to the records of Trinity College, Cambridge, he was a warrant-officer in World War I; possibly, then, his ordination was postponed until later. The date of his death is not known.

Thornsby 1912; West 1921; records of Trinity College, Cambridge.

Charles Herbert Kitson 1913–20 (b. Leyburn, Yorks., 13 Nov. 1874; d. London, 13 May 1944). After attending school in Ripon, Kitson became organ scholar of Selwyn College, Cambridge in 1893, and took the Cambridge degrees of BA (1896) and MA (1904). Between those dates he also took the Oxford degrees of B.Mus. (1897) and D.Mus. (1902).

He originally intended to take holy orders. But after teaching at Haileybury (1897–8) and St Edmund's School, Canterbury (1898–1901), he became organist of St John the Baptist, Leicester (1902, according to West 1921; 1906 according to *Venn*), from where he moved to Christ Church Cathedral, Dublin in 1913. In 1915 he also became professor of music at University College, Dublin (National University of Ireland). He resigned both these appointments in 1920 and settled in London, where he joined the staff of the Royal College of Music. In 1920 he was appointed to the (non-resident) chair of music at Trinity College (University of Dublin) in succession to *P. C. Buck. He retired from this in 1935. He was an honorary FRCO and wrote several widely used textbooks.

Kitson was in Dublin at the time of the Irish rising of 1916, and his eyewitness account of certain events is now Lcm, MS 4756.

Thornsby 1912; West 1921; *MT* 85 (1944), 191, 206; *WWW*, 1941–50; *Venn*.

Thomas Henry Weaving 1920–50 (b. Birmingham, 1881; d. Dublin, 26 Jan. 1966). Weaving was trained at the Royal Irish Academy of Music, and while there he was organist of Straffan Church (1897). He was appointed to Rutland Square Church in 1899, to Christ Church, Dun Laoghaire in 1910, and to Dublin Castle Chapel in 1917.

West 1921; *MT*, 107 (1966); 337; information from Mr A. McKiernan.

Leslie Henry Bret Reed 1950–5 (b. 7 June 1890; d. Jersey, 9 Nov. 1960). Reed went up to Selwyn College, Cambridge in 1911, becoming organ scholar in 1912 and taking the Cambridge degrees of BA and Mus.B. in 1914. He subsequently took the Dublin degree of Mus.D. in 1921, and also held the FRCO diploma. From 1915 to 1950 he was director of music at St John's School, Leatherhead, Surrey.

Records of Selwyn College, Cambridge and St John's School, Leatherhead; information from Mr A. McKiernan.

§Arnold (Thomas) McKiernan 1955–79 (b. Dublin, 30 June 1918). After leaving Dublin High School, McKiernan proceeded to Trinity College, Dublin (1936–40), and took the degrees of BA (1940), MA (1943), and Mus.B. (1950). He also holds the FRCO diploma (1954). He originally intended to pursue a career in the Royal Navy, and he served as a lieutenant in the RNVR from 1941 to 1946. In 1948 he became organist of St Canice's Cathedral, Kilkenny, from where he moved to Christ Church Cathedral, Dublin. In 1955 he joined the staff of the Royal Irish Academy of Music.

§Peter Sweeney, organist and master of the choristers from 1980 (b. Dublin, 7 Apr. 1950). Sweeney was educated at St Patrick's Cathedral Grammar School,

Dublin and then at Trinity College, Dublin (1968–72), where he took the degree of Mus.B. Later, from 1975 to 1977, he studied at the Conservatoire de musique, Geneva, winning, among other prizes, the *premier prix de virtuosité*. Meanwhile he was organist of St Mary's Church, Donnybrook, 1970–8, and from then until his Cathedral appointment, of St Francis Xavier Church, Dublin.

DUBLIN

The Collegiate and Cathedral Church of St Patrick

Main sources in this section (1967):

Chapter Acts

CA0 Unnumbered volume, 1643–9.
CA1 1660–70 (first page numbered 255).
CA2 1670–7; fair copy of original now in Trinity College, Dublin (MS F.i.17).
CA3 1678–90.
CA3b Unnumbered volume, 1678–1713, partly overlapping with CA3; original on parchment, with fair copy on paper.
CA4 1690–1719; held in Archbishop Marsh's Library, Dublin.
CA5 1720–63.
CA6 1764–92.
CA7 1793–1819.
CA8 1819–36.
CA9 1836–60.

Registers of Baptisms, Marriages, Burials

PR Printed as *Registers of the Collegiate and Cathedral Church of Dublin, 1677–1800*, Dublin Parish Register Society, 1907.

The existence of two cathedrals in one city is unique in Anglican ecclesiastical polity. Late in the twelfth century John Comyn, Archbishop of Dublin, built himself a palace outside the city walls where he was free to exercise civil jurisdiction, and hard by his new palace he founded and built a collegiate church in 1192. Early in the thirteenth century his successor raised it to cathedral status, with a secular chapter modelled on that of Salisbury and with a College of Vicars Choral, membership of which was open to laymen after the Restoration and included nearly all the organists named below. Perhaps it was intended that this cathedral, St Patrick's, would supersede Christ Church Cathedral, with its more independent monastic chapter. But this did not happen, and until the disestablishment of the Church of Ireland in 1871, the Archbishops of Dublin had their thrones in two cathedrals. However, there was an interruption in the history of St Patrick's, for it was swept away in 1547 by Henry VIII, who had remodelled Christ Church and evidently regarded one cathedral as sufficient for the diocese. It was refounded in 1555 under Philip and Mary.

After disestablishment, Christ Church became the sole cathedral of the Dublin diocese, and St Patrick's was formed into the 'national cathedral' of the Church of Ireland, each diocese of which nominates one of the canons. Though it no longer contains an episcopal throne, it is officially styled both a collegiate and a cathedral church.

From the late seventeenth century onwards, the emoluments of the choirs of St Patrick's and Christ Church Cathedrals were large enough, and the resulting stipends generous enough, to justify dividing the posts into two, thus explaining the many references below to a 'half place' as vicar choral.

West (1921) names **James White**, a vicar choral, as organist from 1540 until the surrender in 1547. Crawford (1881) names **William Browne** as the organist appointed at the Marian refoundation of 1555, while both he and Finlayson (1852) mention **Anthony Willis (or Wilkes)** as organist in 1606. West (1921) also included **John Farmer** as organist of St Patrick's from 1595 to 1599 (see under Christ Church Cathedral). The earliest extant Chapter records begin only at 1643.

Randolph Jewett (1st tenure) **1631–43** (2nd tenure) **1644→** (b. Chester, 1603; d. Winchester, 3 July 1675). Jewett's apparently complex career spanned, and was affected by, troubled times: the Civil War, the Commonwealth and Protectorate, and the Fire of London; and it must be traced in both Dublin cathedrals and in those of Chester, St Paul's (London), and Winchester. He is singular among the early figures in this book in possessing a pedigree attested by a recognized genealogist (Lbl, Harl. MS 2163, f. 76, reproduced by J. C. Bridge 1913). Springing from 'Heyton' (Heaton) in 'Bradforde-dale', Yorkshire, the family settled in Chester, where William Jewett became mayor in 1578. Not only was he a lay clerk of the Cathedral (J. C. Bridge 1913), but he was also 'one of the Queen's Majesty's Chapel' (sworn 18 June 1568 as 'Wm. Iuett of West Chester' (Rimbault 1872: 2, 55)). His son Randle, 'a singer in King's Chapel' (not noted by Rimbault) who died at Chester in 1619, was the father of our present subject, who, according to J. C. Bridge (1913), was a chorister of Chester Cathedral, 1612–15.

Randolph Jewett began his adult career in about 1631 as organist of Christ Church Cathedral, Dublin, acquiring deacon's orders *c.*1638; he apparently ceased to be organist there at about the same time, though he continued for some indeterminate period to have charge of the choristers (q.v.). Meanwhile, though there are no extant documents for the period, he appears to have developed an association with St Patrick's Cathedral. Crawford (1881) says that he became organist there also in 1631, and it is on this testimony, though unsupported, that he is included here at this point. Cotton (1848–9: ii) states that his name occurred as a vicar choral there in 1639, that the archbishop deprived him of this post, but restored him to it in 1641.

The next we know of him is that he was paid as organist of Chester Cathedral from Lady Day 1643 (q.v.). How long he remained there cannot be determined, for the Chester documents break off at Midsummer 1643. However, extant records at St Patrick's, Dublin begin in 1643 (CAo), and his name appears in the roll-call of vicars choral in January 1644/5, so it is reasonable to conclude that he returned from Chester during 1644. He continues to be named thus up to and including January 1649/50, and on 18 March, just before this volume of Acts breaks off, we find an entry recording that 'upon a petition of Randall Jewett organist it is ordered that he shall receive £4 sterling . . . as soon as the same can be raised' (f. 46). One might assume, then, that he had been organist since his return as vicar choral in 1644. Meanwhile, in July 1646, powerful influence had been exerted on his behalf to obtain his renewed appointment at Christ Church Cathedral as vicar choral—and, very likely, as organist also (q.v.).

Yet this did not secure his loyal attachment to Dublin. A post-Restoration minute (see below under Hawkshaw) shows that Jewett was absent from St Patrick's during the Marquis of Ormonde's tenure as Lord Lieutenant of Ireland—i.e., November 1643–July 1647, and February 1649–December 1650. (By that time Parliament had prohibited the Prayer Book liturgy and imposed the 'Directory of Public Worship'; but even if that was effective in far-off Dublin, an organist might still have been used to accompany metrical psalm-singing.)

When St Patrick's Cathedral began to function again in 1660, after the Restoration of Charles II, it clearly regarded Jewett as still being its organist and one of its vicars, thinking of him merely as being absent (see minute of March 1660/1 below under Hawkshaw). But—how surreptitiously we cannot tell— some time before 1649 (the year in which cathedral bodies were disbanded by the Long Parliament) he must have secured a minor canonry of St Paul's Cathedral, London on the strength of his diaconate. There is no record of this; but it must have been thus that he qualified for the £4 compensation allotted him in respect of that cathedral by the Trustees for the Maintenance of Ministers in April 1655 (and a further £2 in 1657) (Matthews 1948). It is clear that he felt no further loyalty to St Patrick's, for when St Paul's remustered after the Restoration, he was immediately (11 July 1660) made almoner and master of the choristers (St Paul's Cathedral, Pridden Collection, i), and on 16 May 1661, since he was one of only three surviving minor canons, he was made junior cardinal notwithstanding that he was only in deacon's orders (Lgh, MS 25664/1). He may have remained in London during the Interregnum, for in 1651 he was included in the list printed in John Playford's *Musical Banquet* of teachers of the organ or virginals available there.

In 1666, soon after the Fire of London, treating St Paul's with more courtesy than St Patrick's, he asked leave to go to Winchester as organist 'until it shall please God to make St Paul's Cathedral in a condition for him to discharge his duty'. Leave was granted, preserving his rights as almoner and cardinal (Lgh, MS 25738/2, 22 November 1666). This was a good arrangement, for he continued to draw his emoluments at least until 1674 (Lgh, MS 25650/2). Later, in May 1669, there was a dispute about his entitlement to the rent of the Almonry, and he was ordered to come back to teach the boys. When he refused, the Chapter inconsistently argued that as there were now no boys, the rent was at its own disposal. The affair was settled by his being allowed a quarter of the revenue of the Almonry (Lgh, MS 25738/2).

Meanwhile he had been duly and promptly appointed to Winchester Cathedral (q.v.), where, as 'generosus' not 'clericus', he put his holy orders behind him. He was buried in the Cathedral there.

John Hawkshaw 1660–86. On 24 October 1660 (CA1) Hawkshaw, who had been a vicar choral before the Interregnum, was (re)admitted as the first of the nine vicars and was 'nominated organist during the absence of Mr Randall Jewet'. On 15 March 1660/1 (CA1) it was ordered that 'in lieu of Mr Hogshaw's two years service in the Lord of Ormond's time he the said Mr Hawkshaw shall receive from the Proctor of this Church the half year's salary (as organist) ending at Michaelmas last. And that for the time to come he shall in the absence of Mr Jewet receive the salary allowed while he shall officiate as organist.'

Hawkshaw became steward of the College of Vicars Choral in 1661. For a long time (there are references on 6 September 1664, 24 January 1664/5, and 11 May 1669) he kept pursuing arrears of salary which he claimed were due to him from 1659. He is named as vicar in every January roll-call, with the exception of 1684/5, up to and including 1687/8 (CA2, 3), after which his name vanishes. But by then he had ceased to be organist. Against his name as vicar choral in January 1685/6 is written 'offic: organisti seq: in manus Thomas Godfrey', and below the list there is an order that John Hawkshaw, 'propter manifestum contemptum', is to be sequestered from his post of organist and replaced by Godfrey.

Hawkshaw was never master of the choristers (or master of the song, or tutor of the boys, as it was known as St Patrick's). At the time of the Restoration that post was held by Richard Hosier, and when he died it was given to Nicholas Saunderson, both vicars choral (CA2, 17 March 1676/7).

Hawkshaw was also vicar choral and organist of Christ Church Cathedral, 1661–89 (q.v.). Crawford (1881) conjectured that there may have been two John Hawkshaws as organist of St Patrick's between 1660 and 1685—one up to 1678, the other from that date. On whatever evidence this may rest, I noticed nothing to substantiate it.

Thomas Godfrey 1686–8→. Godfrey's formal election as organist took place on 1 May 1686 (CA3). In December 1688 he was admonished to attend. Crawford (1881) states that he was succeeded as organist of St Patrick's in 1668/9 by Thomas Finell (see p. 410), who in turn was followed by William Isaac, 1691–2, and that Thomas Finell was once more organist of St Patrick's, 1692–4. The first two of these statements canot be confirmed, and the third is clearly wrong, as Peter Isaac was the next named organist of St Patrick's.

Peter Isaac 1692–4 (bur. Chester, 26 Aug. 1694). It is possible that this is the Peter Isaack, a Chapel Royal chorister under *John Blow, whose voice had broken by December 1670 (Ashbee 1986–9: i. 107). He was first connected with St Patrick's on his appointment to a half place as vicar choral on 18 June 1672 (CA2), leading to a full place on 8 April 1673 (CA2). He was not present at the roll-call of January 1687/8, and on 24 April the archbishop reported that Isaac 'had accepted of a place in England and was settled there' (CA3), a reference to his move to Salisbury, where he was Cathedral organist, 1687–92 (q.v.). But he was back in Ireland by 4 April 1692, where he was admitted organist and vicar choral of St Patrick's (CA4). At about the same time he also became organist of Christ Church Cathedral (q.v.), holding both posts until his death. The burial of 'Mr Peter Isaack, organist of Dublin', is entered in the registers of Chester Cathedral.

Robert Hodge 1694–8 (b. Exeter; bur. Dublin, 26 May 1709). This can hardly be other than the Robert Hodge, organist of Wells Cathedral, 1688–90, who then became a lay clerk of Durham Cathedral in April 1691 and set out from there for 'Hibernia' in April 1692 (Durham University Library, Mickleton MS 32). (For his career up to that time, see under Wells Cathedral.)

He became a vicar choral of St Patrick's on 19 April 1693 (CA4), and was admitted organist on 19 October 1694 (CA3b, original). We know from subsequent references that he became 'master of the song' either then or later, but no official record of appointment seems to exist. He was also connected in some way with Christ Church Cathedral as early as the accounting year 1692–3 (Christ Church Ac26), and Cotton (1848–9: ii) says that he became a vicar choral there on 4 June 1695. On 15 November 1698 he resigned as organist of St Patrick's (CA4), having been appointed master of the choristers of Christ Church (Ac32), but he continued as vicar choral of St Patrick's and evidently continued to teach the boys. He clashed with Daniel Roseingrave, who succeeded him as organist, and CA4 (5 December 1699) records how they 'lately gave each other very scurrilous language in Christ Church, Dublin, and afterwards went to the tavern and there fought'. Although Roseingrave was judged chiefly to blame and was required to beg Hodge's pardon publicly, Hodge himself was not held blameless.

These two men, both with English experience, and both connected with Christ Church as well as with St Patrick's, seem to have exerted their influence to improve the music of the two cathedrals. On 17 March 1697/8 Hodge, having brought some anthems and services from England, was not only paid for transcribing them but given a gratuity for his pains in obtaining them. CA3b notes that these included Blow's 'I was glad', performed at the opening of the choir of St Paul's Cathedral as recently as 2 December 1697. Hodge was also paid for providing some anthems (perhaps these same ones) for Christ Church (Ac32). On 7 February 1705/6 he brought two choirboys from England for St Patrick's (CA4).

Evidently he was regarded as having something worth while to offer on special occasions, for the Christ Church accounts (26 and 27, 1692–3 and 1693–4) note payments to him 'for the first day of Lord Justice coming to church' and for three 'State Days'—5 November, Thanksgiving Day, and Christmas Day, when no doubt the Lord Lieutenant attended, since Christ Church was at that time the Chapel Royal of Ireland.

The burial of 'Mr Robert Hodge, vicar of St Patrick and master of the song', is recorded in PR.

Daniel Roseingrave 1698–1719 (d. Dublin, May 1727). It is possible that Roseingrave was of Irish origin: the surname is not unknown in the seventeenth-century leases granted by Christ Church Cathedral, Dublin (see MS Calendar in the Public Record Office, Dublin). Hawkins (1853: ii. 771) says that he was 'educated in the Chapel Royal, London, and a fellow-disciple of Purcell'. Nevertheless, his name is not to be found in any Chapel Royal record (Ashbee 1986–9 or Rimbault 1872, *passim*). However, he is certainly the 'old Roseingrave' who recounted the story of how Renatus Harris's supporters cut the bellows of 'Father' Smith's organ on the night before the celebrated trial of the two organs in the Temple Church, London in 1684 (Burney 1776–89: iii. 438). That incident took place when Roseingrave was organist of Winchester Cathedral; but he may have had at least some contact with the Blow–Purcell group other than as a Chapel Royal boy. Certainly, his first appointments as organist were in England: Gloucester Cathedral, 1679–81; Winchester Cathedral, 1681–92; and Salisbury Cathedral, 1692–8 (q.v.).

He was admitted organist and vicar choral of St Patrick's Cathedral on 15 November 1698 (CA4), combining these posts with similar ones at Christ Church Cathedral (q.v.). His quarrel with his colleague Hodge is recounted above. On 14 December 1699 it was resolved to pay him for transcribing the following repertory for use at St Patrick's: Aldrich's Service in G; Byrd's 'Full' Service (presumably the 'Short' Service); Farrant's 'High' Service (i.e., in G minor); and Wise's Communion Services in E minor and F major.

The following extract from CA4, 14 December 1709, reveals the enlightened attitude of the Cathedral (but with a view to the future) towards Roseingrave's most noted son:

> Ordered that whereas Thomas Roseingrave son of Daniel Roseingrave the present organist . . . being minded to travel beyond the seas to improve himself in the art of music and that hereafter he may be useful and honourable to the said Cathedral, ten guineas be by the Proctor of the said Œconomy given him as a gift from the said Œconomy towards bearing his charges.

On 12 February 1718/19 Daniel wrote to ask permission to resign as organist of St Patrick's for reasons of health, and asked that his son Ralph (whom he had 'bred to understand playing on the organs') might succeed him (CA4). He retained his posts at Christ Church Cathedral until his death. He is buried in St Bride's Church, Dublin.

He had three sons: Daniel (b. 1685), who became organist of Trinity College, Dublin in 1705; Thomas (b. 1690), organist of St George's, Hanover Square, London for some years from 1725, composer, and admirer of Domenico Scarlatti; and Ralph (b. 1695), his father's successor at both Dublin Cathedrals.

Ralph Roseingrave 1719–47 (bur. Dublin, 7 Dec. 1747). When his father's request was agreed that Ralph might succeed him as organist, he was appointed vicar choral in April 1719 (CA4). Though nothing was expressly said about the post of organist, it was surely implicit in that appointment. Ralph also succeeded his father as organist of Christ Church Cathedral in 1727 (q.v.). He himself is buried in St Patrick's churchyard. Father and son between them covered the period when Jonathan Swift was Dean of St Patrick's, 1713–45.

Richard Broadway 1747–60 (d. Dublin, 1760). Broadway was appointed organist of St Patrick's on 12 December 1747 and admitted vicar choral a month later (CA5).

George Walsh 1760–5. George Walsh was appointed organist on 18 November 1760 on the death of his predecessor, and was admitted vicar choral four days later (CA5). During his tenure the stipend of organist, which had gone down to the low figure of £5 per annum in Broadway's time, was restored to £30, with the proviso that the organist was to copy out music books for the organ (CA5, p. 241).

See also under Christ Church Cathedral, Dublin.

Henry Walsh 1765–9. Henry Walsh's appointment was minuted on 18 March 1765. There seems to be no record of his having been made a vicar choral. His name appears for the last time in the roll-call for January 1769 (CA6).

Samuel Murphy 1769–80 (d. Dublin, 9 Nov. 1780). Murphy is listed as a chorister of the Cathedral at the roll-call in January 1743/4 (CA5). There seem to be no such lists for 1741/2 and 1742/3, but it has been stated that he was one of the choristers who took part in the first performance of Handel's *Messiah* in 1742, and this is not unlikely. There was Samuel Murphy (whose voice was reported changed in April 1744) who was a chorister of Christ Church Cathedral (Christ Church CA6), and this is probably the same boy. He was a vicar choral of St Patrick's by January 1762 (CA5), and on 13 June 1766 he is mentioned as being already master of the choristers. The following minute is dated 14 January 1768: 'Mr Samuel Murphy, master of the choristers, having composed a piece of music and requested permission from the Dean and Chapter that the boys may be permitted to assist in the performance, ordered that on account of his extraordinary care of the boys and diligence in instructing them that they be permitted for this time accordingly.' More than twenty-five years earlier, at the time of Handel's visit to Dublin, there had been rumblings at both cathedrals about singers taking part in outside performances without permission (see, for example, Christ Church CA6, 22 December 1741).

'Samuel Murphy, Dr of Music' and vicar choral, is first listed as organist in January 1770. Thus Finlayson (1852) (followed by Crawford 1881) cannot be right in saying that a Michael Sandys was organist of St Patrick's, 1769–73, and that Murphy was appointed after him. Murphy had become master of the choristers of Christ Church Cathedral by 1758, and was also made organist in 1777 (q.v.). He received his doctorate from Trinity College, Dublin on 9 September 1768 (Burtchaell and Sadleir 1935). For the date of his death I rely on Crawford (1881).

Philip Cogan 1780–1810 (b. Cork, *c.*1747; d. Dublin, 3 Feb. 1833, aged 85). Cogan (or Coogan) was a stipendiary of Christ Church Cathedral from 14 June 1771 until he was dismissed on 12 June 1772 (Christ Church CA7). Earlier he had been in the choir of Cork Cathedral. West (1921) states that he was organist of St John's Church, Dublin in 1778. His death is noted in *Freeman's Journal*, 9 February 1833 (reference from Nicholas Temperley).

At the St Patrick's roll-call of 1781 'Phil: Coogan' is named as organist and *Langrish Doyle as master of the choristers (see under Christ Church Cathedral). He seems not to have been a vicar choral. The list for 1793 describes both men as doctors of music. It is interesting to note that by January 1798, when Doyle, though still a vicar, had given way to *Clarke(-Whitfeld) as master of the choristers (see Armagh Cathedral), the number of musicians enjoying the style of doctor of music at St Patrick's was unsurpassed anywhere or at any time: Cogan, organist; Clarke, master of the choristers; S. Carter, L. Doyle, J. Parkinson, and Sir John Stevenson, vicars choral. They are all described thus in CA7, but (other than Clarke) not known to Burtchaell and Sadleir (1935).

Michael Kelly says of Cogan, who was his pianoforte teacher: 'His execution on that instrument was astonishing and his compositions, although not generally known in this country [England], possess great merit', and that he was 'highly esteemed by all his connections' (Kelly 1826; i. 11). Later, speaking of an occasion when Catalani sang in Dublin, Kelly says: 'At the pianoforte sat my old, revered, and first teacher, Dr Cogan.' (Ibid. ii. 259.)

John Mathews 1810–27→. When Mathews was appointed organist on 11 April 1810 the minute stated that Cogan had resigned (CA7). It is possible that Mathews was the son of an elder John Mathews, who obtained a half place as vicar choral on 5 February 1777 and who was the transcriber of a particularly interesting score of Handel's *Messiah* now in Marsh's Library, Dublin. At the roll-call of January 1819 the younger man appears as sole organist; yet in March of that year 'Messrs Mathews and Warren' were entered as organists (CA8). On 25 January 1827 'John Mathews, organist', was appointed half vicar choral in place of William Warren. That is his last mention. Exactly how one should interpret these entries is uncertain. Perhaps they are the origin of Finlayson's statement (1852; also Crawford 1881) that William Warren (for whom see Christ Church Cathedral) was organist in 1827–8.

Francis Robinson ←1829–30 (b. Dublin, 1799; d. Dublin, 1872). Francis Robinson, having ceased to be a chorister of the Cathedral on 31 March 1815 (CA7), was named as master of the boys in the roll-call of January 1819. There is no minute of his appointment as organist, but he is named as such in January 1829. On 18 March 1830 he became a half vicar choral, but he relinquished the post of organist at the same time (CA8), while retaining that of master of the choristers until 1844. Cotton (1848–9) notes that he became a full vicar in 1843 and that from 1833 he was also a vicar choral of Christ Church Cathedral. His name is included in the memorial to several members of his family there. He became an honorary Mus.D. of Trinity College, Dublin in 1852.

John Robinson 1830–44. The younger brother of his predecessor, John was appointed organist on 18 March 1830 (CA8).

See under Christ Church Cathedral, Dublin.

Richard Cherry 1844–5. John Robinson died about the beginning of May 1844. On 28 May the Chapter Acts refer to 'Mr Sherry' as 'the present organist'. On the same day Francis Robinson (see above) was given a retirement allowance as 'master of the song', and Sherry (Cherry) succeeded him in that capacity. The same minute mentions William Murphy (see below) as assistant organist. At the January roll-call of 1845 the organist's name is given as 'Richard Cherrie'. Vignoles (1898: 122–3) quotes a letter of Sir Robert Stewart stating that Cherry emigrated from Ireland.

William Henry White 1845–52. Though I have found no trace of White in the Chapter Acts, there can be no doubting Finlayson, who was writing in 1852, when he names him as organist in succession to Cherry from 1845. He had been organist of Dublin Castle Chapel, 1833–45. Sir Robert Stewart recalled that 'poor White drank himself into his grave' (Vignoles 1898: 122–3).

Sir Robert (Prescott) Stewart and William Murphy (joint organists) **1852–61.** On 28 May 1852 (CA9) Stewart was appointed to be 'afternoon organist' and William Murphy to be 'morning organist' and master of the choristers. According to West (1921), it was to obtain a place as vicar choral that Stewart relinquished this appointment in 1861, though he was only given a half place. Nevertheless, he continued unofficially to play the organ at St Patrick's (Vignoles 1898: 196).

For Stewart, see under Christ Church Cathedral, Dublin.

William Murphy (sole organist) **1861–78.** Having been assistant organist (in Cherry's time) and then joint organist with Stewart, Murphy now received the complete appointment (West 1921). He took the Dublin degree of Mus.B. in 1847, and was in office at the time of disestablishment. Writing in 1879, Sir Robert Stewart said: 'We recently got William Murphy a bene dicessit in the shape of a gold watch, and we sent him away rejoicing. He also obtained a pension of £60 per annum.' (Vignoles 1898: 122–3.)

Charles George Marchant 1879–1920 (b. Dublin, 23 Sept. 1857; d. Dublin, 16 Jan. 1920). Marchant, who was of Huguenot descent, was a chorister of St Patrick's, afterwards becoming organist of Holy Trinity, Rathmines (1874), Christ Church, Bray (1876), and, only a week before his appointment to the Cathedral, St Matthias, Dublin. He was also organist of Trinity College, Dublin, from which he received the honorary degree of Mus.D. in 1911. There is a memorial brass to him on the wall of the north aisle of the Cathedral.

West 1921: *MT*, 61 (1920), 119.

§**George Henry Phillips Hewson 1920–60** (b. Dublin, 1881; d. Dublin, Nov. 1972). Hewson became a chorister in St Patrick's Cathedral in 1889 and was later sub-organist there. He was educated at Trinity College, Dublin, taking the degrees of Mus.B. (1903), BA (1905), Mus.D. (1914), and MA (1928). In 1907 he became organist of Dublin Castle Chapel, and he was appointed to Armagh Cathedral in 1916. He returned to Dublin as organist of St Patrick's in 1920. In 1927 he assumed the post of organist and choirmaster of Trinity College in addition to his other duties. In 1935 he became professor of music in the University of Dublin (Trinity College) in succession to *C. H. Kitson. He resigned as organist of St Patrick's and Trinity College in 1960, but he retained the chair of music until 1962. In that year, to mark his long association with the College, he was elected an honorary fellow. Hewson was also an honorary FRCO.

§**William (Sydney) Greig 1960–76** (b. Dublin, 25 Nov. 1910; d. Dublin, 6 Mar. 1983). After attending St Patrick's Cathedral Grammar School, Greig studied at the Royal Irish Academy of Music with an organ scholarship, 1928–31, and in 1934 took the Dublin degree of Mus.B. From 1929 to 1960 he was organist of Abbey Presbyterian Church, Dublin. He was also assistant organist of Christ Church Cathedral, 1934–43, and of St Patrick's, 1943–60.

§**John (Anthony) Dexter, organist and master of the choristers from 1977** (b. Guildford, Surrey, 25 Aug. 1954). As a boy, Dexter was in Guildford Cathedral choir and attended the Royal Grammar School there, proceeding to Oxford as organ scholar of Jesus College, 1972–5, and reading music. He then spent a year at the Royal College of Music and a further year at Goldsmith's College, London, during which time (1975–7) he was organ scholar of St Paul's Cathedral. He took the FRCO diploma with CHM in 1975, and the Oxford degrees of BA and MA in 1975 and 1982 respectively.

BIBLIOGRAPHY

Except where otherwise stated, the place of publication is London. In addition to works cited in the text, a few additional titles are included for further reading.

ARKWRIGHT, G. E. P., 1893, *The Old English Edition*, x.

—— 1898, *The Old English Edition*, xxi.

—— 1913–14, 'Elizabethan Choirboy Plays and Their Music', *PMA*, 40, p. 117.

ASHBEE, ANDREW, 1986–9, *Records of English Court Music*, 3 vols. (Snodland, Kent).

ASHMOLE, ELIAS, 1927 (new edn.): *The Diary and Will of Elias Ashmole*, ed. R. T. Gunther (privately printed, Oxford).

ATKINS, IVOR, 1918, *The Organists and Masters of the Choristers of Worcester Cathedral* (Worcestershire Historical Society).

—— 1946, 'The Authorship of the XVIth century description of St David's printed in Browne Willis's "Survey" (1717)', *National Library of Wales Journal*, 4, p. 1.

BAILEY, CYRIL, 1948, *Hugh Percy Allen* (Oxford).

BAILLIE, HUGH, 1962, 'Some Biographical Notes on English Church Musicians, chiefly working in London (1485–1560)', *Royal Musical Association Research Chronicle*, 2.

BALL, W. W. ROUSE, and VENN, J. A., 1916, *Admissions to Trinity College, Cambridge*, 5 vols.

BATES, FRANK, 1930, *Reminiscences and Autobiography of a Musician in Retirement* (Norwich).

BAX, P. B. I., 1904, *The Cathedral Church of St Asaph*.

BENNETT, ALFRED, and MARSHALL, WILLIAM (eds.), 1829 (2nd edn.), *Cathedral Chants* (contains biographical notes on some contemporary composers).

BENNETT, F. G., et al. (eds.), 1904, *Statutes and Constitutions of the Cathedral Church of Chichester* (Chichester).

BENNETT, WILLIAM, 1933, 'Music in the Provinces, 1700–1750', *MMR*, 63, p. 155.

BENTHAM, JAMES, 1812 (2nd edn.), *The History and Antiquities of the . . . Cathedral Church of Ely*.

BIGLAND, RALPH, 1792, *Historical, Monumental, and Genealogical Collections . . . of Gloucester*.

BLOMEFIELD, FRANCIS, 1805–62, *History of Norfolk*, 11 vols.

BLOXHAM, JOHN ROUSE, 1853–7, *A Register of . . . Magdalen College . . . Oxford*, i, ii (Oxford).

BREWER, A. H., 1931, *Memories of Choirs and Cloisters*.

BRIDGE, JOSEPH C., 1913, 'The Organists of Chester Cathedral', *Journal of the Architectural, Archaeological, and Historic Society for the County and the City of Chester and North Wales*, NS 19/2.

BRIDGE, J. F., 1918, *A Westminster Pilgrim*.

BROWN, A., 1948, 'Notes on John Redford', *Modern Languages Review*, Oct.

—— 1949, 'Three Notes on Sebastian Westcott', *Modern Languages Review*, Apr.

BROWN, DAVID, 1959, 'Thomas Morley and the Catholics', *MMR*, 89, p. 53.

—— 1969, *Thomas Weelkes: a Biographical and Critical Study*.

BUMPUS, JOHN S., 1891, *Organists of St Paul's Cathedral*.

BUMPUS, JOHN S., 1972 (repr.; orig. edn., 1908), *A History of English Cathedral Music, 1549–1889*, 2 vols.

BUMPUS, THOMAS FRANCIS, 1903, *Cathedrals of England and Wales*, 3 vols.

BURNE, R. V. H., 1958, *Chester Cathedral from its founding by Henry VIII to the accession of Queen Victoria*.

BURNEY, CHARLES, 1776–89, *A General History of Music*, 4 vols.

—— 1785, 'Sketch of the Life of Handel', in *The Commemoration of Handel*.

BURTCHAELL, G. D., and SADLEIR, T. U., 1935, *Alumni Dublinienses, 1593–1860* (Dublin).

BUXTON, J., and WILLIAMS, P. (eds.), 1979, *New College, Oxford, 1379–1979* (Oxford, New College).

(CAMBRIDGE, TRINITY COLLEGE) 1773, *Statuta Collegii sanctae et individuae Trinitatis in Academia Cantabrigiensi* (Cambridge).

(CANTERBURY) 1925, *The Statutes of the Cathedral and Metropolitical Church of Christ, Canterbury* (Canterbury).

CAULFIELD, RICHARD, n.d., *Annals of St Fin Barre's Cathedral, Cork*.

CHAMBERS, JOHN, 1820, *Biographical Illustrations of Worcestershire* (Worcester).

CHANTER, J. F., 1933, 'The Custos and College of the Vicars Choral of the . . . Cathedral Church of Exeter', *Transactions of the Exeter Diocesan Architectural and Archaeological Society* (Series 3) 5.

CHARLTON, PETER, 1984, *John Stainer and the Musical Life of Victorian Britain*.

CHESTER, J. L., 1876, *The Marriage, Baptismal, and Burial Registers of the Collegiate Church . . . of St Peter, Westminster* (Harleian Society, 10).

C(HITTY), H(ERBERT), 1912–13, 'The Organist and the Queristers' Master', the *Wykehamist*, 11, 523.

CLARK, ANDREW (ed.), 1887, *Registers of the University of Oxford*, ii (Oxford Historical Society).

COBB, G. F., 1913, *A Brief History of the Organ . . . of Trinity College, Cambridge*, ed. Alan Gray (Cambridge).

COLLES, H. C., 1942, *Walford Davies*.

(COOKE, HENRY), 1837, *Some Account of Doctor Cooke*.

CORRIE, G. E., 1864, 'Reasons for the Completion of Dr Tudway's Degree in Musick', *Antiquarian Communications*, 2, pp. 345–9 (Cambridge Antiquarian Society).

COTTON, HENRY, 1848–9, *Fasti Ecclesiae Hibernicae*, ii, iii, and supplement (Dublin).

COX, H. B., and COX, C. L. E., 1907, *Leaves from the Journal of Sir George Smart*.

CRAWFORD, G. A., 1881, 'Succession of Organists', in *Cathedral Anthems published for the Cathedrals of . . . Dublin* (Dublin).

DAWE, DONOVAN, 1968, 'New Light on William Boyce', *MT*, 109, p. 802.

—— 1983, *Organists of the City of London 1666–1850* (privately printed).

DENEKE, MARGARET, 1951, *Ernest Walker*.

DEUTSCH, O. E., 1955, *Handel: A Documentary Biography*.

DICKINSON (formerly DICKINSON RASTALL), W., 1787, *History of the Antiquities of Southwell*.

DICKSON, W. E., 1894, *Fifty Years of Church Music* (Ely).

DRAKE, FRANCIS, 1736, *Eboracum*.

DRENNAN, BASIL ST G., 1970, *The Keble College Centenary Register 1870–1970* (Oxford, Keble College).

DUGDALE, WILLIAM, 1658, *History of St Paul's Cathedral.*

—— 1917, *Visitation of Yorkshire*, ed. J. W. Clay.

EATON, T. D., 1872, *Musical Criticism.*

ELVEY, MARY (Lady Elvey), 1894, *Life and Reminiscences of George J. Elvey.*

(ELY) 1867, *Statuta Ecclesiae Cathedralis Eliensis recognita per . . . Carolum Secundum* (Cambridge).

FALKNER, J. M. (ed.), 1929, *The Statutes of the Cathedral Church of Durham*, with an introduction by A. Hamilton Thompson (Surtees Society, 143).

FELLOWES, E. H., 1921, *The English Madrigal Composers.*

—— 1940, *Organists and Masters of the Choristers of St George's Chapel in Windsor Castle* (Windsor).

—— 1946, *Memoirs of an Amateur Musician.*

—— 1948 (2nd edn.), *William Byrd* (Oxford).

—— 1951, *Orlando Gibbons and his Family.*

FINLAYSON, JOHN, 1852, *A Collection of Anthems as sung in the Cathedral of the Holy Trinity . . . Dublin* (Dublin).

FLOOD, W. H. G., 1925, *Early Tudor Composers.*

FORD, W. K., 1957–8, 'The Life and Works of John Okeover', *PRMA*, 84, p. 71.

FOSTER, JOSEPH, 1887–92, *Alumni Oxonienses, 1500–1714; 1715–1886*, 8 vols.

FOWLER, J. H. (ed.), 1900, *Durham Account Rolls* (Surtees Society, 103).

—— 1902, *The Rites of Durham* (Surtees Society, 107).

FREEMAN, ANDREW, 1977, *Father Smith, Edited . . . with new material by John Rowntree* (Oxford).

FRERE, W. H., 1910, *Visitation Articles and Injunctions*, 3 vols. (Alcuin Club).

FROST, W. A., 1925, *Early Recollections of St Paul's Cathedral.*

FULLER, THOMAS, 1662, *The Worthies of England.*

GARDINER, WILLIAM, 1838–53, *Music and Friends*, 3 vols.

GARRETT, G. M., 1891, 'The Choral Services in Chapel', the *Eagle* (journal of St John's College, Cambridge), 16, pp. 224–9.

GOODMAN, A. W., and HUTTON, W. H. (eds.), 1924, *The Statutes Governing the Cathedral Church of Winchester Given by King Charles I* (1638) (Oxford).

GREENE, HARRY PLUNKET, 1935, *Charles Villiers Stanford.*

GRETTON, F. E., 1889, *Memories Hark Back.*

GRINDLE, W. H., 1989, *Irish Cathedral Music* (Belfast).

HAVERGAL, F. T., 1869, *Fasti Herefordenses and other Antiquarian Memorials of Hereford* (Edinburgh).

—— 1881, *Monumental Inscriptions in the Cathedral Church of Hereford* (London, Walsall, and Hereford).

HAWKINS, JOHN, 1853, *A General History of the Science and Practice of Music.* A New Edition with the Author's posthumous notes. 2 vols.

HAYES, PHILIP, (ed.), 1780, *Harmonica Wiccamica.*

HEARNE, THOMAS, 1914, *Remarks and Collections*, ix (Oxford Historical Society).

—— 1921, *Remarks and Collections*, xi (Oxford Historical Society).

(HEREFORD) 1882, *The Statutes of Hereford Cathedral, Promulgated 1637* (privately printed).

HEYWOOD, J., and WRIGHT, T., 1850, *The Ancient Laws . . . for King's College, Cambridge and . . . Eton College.*

HIBBERT (afterwards HIBBERT-WARE), S., 1834, *History of the Foundations in Manchester*, 3 vols. (London and Manchester).

HOLGATE, C. W., 1899, *Winchester Long Rolls, 1653–1721* (Winchester).
—— 1904, *Winchester Long Rolls, 1723–1812* (Winchester).
HOPPE, HARRY R., 1954, 'John Bull in the Archduke Albert's Service', *ML*, 35, pp. 114–15.
HORTON, PETER, forthcoming, *S. S. Wesley*.
HUDSON, F., and LARGE, W. R., 1970, 'William Child: A New Investigation of Sources', *MR*, 31, p. 265.
HUDSON, H. A., 1917, 'The Organs and Organists of the Cathedral and Parish Church of Manchester', *Transactions of the Lancashire and Cheshire Antiquarian Society*, 34.
HUNT, J. E., 1939, *Cranmer's First Litany, 1544, and Merbecke's Book of Common Prayer Noted, 1550*.
HUNTER, JOSEPH, 1819, *The History and Topography of the Parish of Sheffield* (new edition by Alfred Gatty, n.d.).
JACKSON, N. G., 1964, *Newark Magnus: The Story of a Gift* (Nottingham).
JAMES, M. R., 1919, 'Organs and Organists in the College Accounts', *Etoniana*, 24 (22 Oct.), 369–76.
JAMES, W. A., 1927, *Schools of the Collegiate Church of Southwell* (Lincoln).
JEBB, JOHN, 1847–57, *The Choral Responses . . . collected from authentic sources*, 2 vols.
KELLY, MICHAEL, 1826, *Reminiscences*, 2 vols., ed. T. E. Hook.
KING, A. HYATT, 1950, 'The Importance of Sir George Smart', *MR*, 91, p. 461.
—— 1963, *Some British Collectors of Music* (Cambridge).
KIRBY, T. F., 1892, *Annals of Winchester College* (London and Winchester).
KITCHIN, G. W., and MADGE, F. T., 1889, *Documents relating to the foundation of the Chapter of Winchester, 1541–1547* (Hampshire Record Society, London and Winchester).
KITTON, FREDERIC, G., 1899, *Zechariah Buck . . . A Centenary Memoir*.
KNOWLES, J. W., *Records of the Musicians . . . in York Minster* (York Minster Library, MS Add. 157/1–5).
LAFONTAINE, H. C. de, 1909, *The King's Musick* (more correctly, 'Cart de Lafontaine, H.', though generally known in later life as, and entered under, 'Lafontaine').
LANGFORD, J. A., 1868, *A Century of Birmingham Life* (Birmingham and London).
LANDON, H. C. ROBBINS, 1959, *The Collected Correspondence and London Notebooks of Joseph Haydn*.
LONSDALE, ROGER, 1965, *Charles Burney: A Literary Biography* (Oxford).
(LICHFIELD) 1863, *Statuta et consuetudines Ecclesiae Cathedralis Lichfieldiae* (privately printed).
LYSONS, DANIEL, 1812, *History of the . . . meeting of the Three Choirs* (Gloucester).
MACKERNESS, E. D., 1956–8, 'William Jackson at Exeter Cathedral, 1777–1803', *Devon & Cornwall Notes and Queries*, 27, p. 7.
MACLEAN, C. D., 1908–9, 'Sir George Smart, Musician-Diarist', *Sammelbände der Internationalen Musik-Gesellschaft*, 10, p. 287.
MACRAY, W. D., 1894–1915, *Register of . . . Magdalen College, Oxford* (NS).
MACRORY, EDMUND, n.d. (2nd edn.), *A few notes on the Temple Organ*.
MADDISON, A. R., 1889, 'Lincoln Cathedral Choir, 1640–1700', *Associated Architectural Societies Reports*, 20.
MANN, A. H., MS Notes on Norwich Music and Musicians (Norwich Record Office, MSS 434–9).

MATTHEWS, A. G., 1948, *Walker Revised: being a revision of John Walker's 'Sufferings of the Clergy during the Grand Rebellion', 1642–1660* (Oxford).

MAYOR, J. E. B. (ed.), 1859, *Early Statutes of the College of St John the Evangelist in the University of Cambridge* (Cambridge).

MEE, JOHN H., 1911, *The Oldest Music Room in Europe.*

MELLOR, ALBERT, 1929, *A Record of the Music and Musicians of Eton College* (Eton).

MELLOWS, W. T., 1940, 'The Last Days of Peterborough Monastery', *Northamptonshire Record Society*, 12.

—— 1941, 'The Foundation of Peterborough Cathedral', *Northamptonshire Record Society*, 13.

MICKLETON, Mickleton MS 32 (Durham Cathedral Library).

MILLER, EDWARD, 1804, *History of Doncaster.*

MOODY, C. H., 1926, *The Organs of Ripon Cathedral.*

NEWMAN, FRANK, 1932, *Two centuries of Mancroft Music* (privately printed).

NICHOLS, JOHN, 1788–1821, *Progresses of Queen Elizabeth*, 3 vols.

NOAKE, JOHN, 1866, *The Monastery and Cathedral of Worcester.*

(NORWICH) n.d., *The Statutes of the Cathedral Church of Norwich* (privately printed, Bungay, Suffolk).

ORMEROD, G., 1882 (2nd edn.), *History of the County Palatine and City of Chester.*

OWEN, H., and BLAKEWAY, J. B., 1825, *A History of Shrewsbury.*

(OXFORD) 1851, *A Catalogue of all Graduates . . . in the University of Oxford between 1659 and 1850* (Oxford).

—— 1853, *Statutes of the Colleges of Oxford* (Oxford and London).

PARKE, W. T., 1830, *Musical Memoirs*, 2 vols.

PARKER, MATTHEW, 1928, *Registrum Matthei Parker*, transcribed by E. M. Thompson, edited by W. H. Frere (Canterbury and York Society).

PAYNE, H. T., *Collectanea Menevensia* (MS SD/Ch/B27–8, National Library of Wales).

PEARCE, C. W., 1909, *Old London City Churches.*

PEARCE, E. H., 1928 (2nd edn.), *The Sons of the Clergy.*

PECKHAM, W. D., 1937, 'The Vicars Choral of Chichester Cathedral', *Sussex Archaeological Collections*, 78, p. 126.

PERKINS, C. C., and DWIGHT, J. S., 1893, *History of the Handel and Haydn Society of Boston, Massachusetts*, i (Boston).

PHILLIPS, HENRY, 1864, *Musical and Personal Recollections during half a century*, 2 vols.

PINE, EDWARD, 1953, *The Westminster Abbey Singers.*

PONSONBY, FREDERICK (LORD SYSONSBY), 1951, *Recollections of Three Reigns.*

POOLE, RACHAEL (MRS REGINALD LANE POOLE), 1912–25, *Catalogue of Portraits in the possession of the University . . . of Oxford*, 3 vols. (Oxford).

PRESCOTT, J. E., 1879, *Statutes of the Cathedral Church of Carlisle.*

PRESTIGE, G. L., 1955, *St Paul's in its glory.*

RAINE, JAMES (ed.), 1900 (2nd edn.), *The Statutes . . . of the Cathedral Church of York* (Leeds).

RANNIE, ALAN, 1970, *The Story of Music at Winchester College, 1394–1969* (Winchester).

RENNERT, JONATHAN, 1975, *William Crotch* (Lavenham).

REYNOLDS, H. E., 1881, *Wells Cathedral: Its Foundation, Constitutional History and Statutes* (Leeds).

RIMBAULT, E. F. (ed.), 1872, *The Old Cheque Book . . . of the Chapel Royal from 1561 to 1744* (Camden Society).

ROBERTSON, DORA H., 1938, *Sarum Close.*

RUSSELL, RAYMOND, 1959, *The Harpsichord and Clavichord.*

SALISBURY, E. G., 1880, *Border County Worthies*, 2nd series (London and Oswestry).

SANDFORD, FRANCIS, 1687, *The History of the Coronation of James II and Queen Mary.*

SAUNDERS, W. H., 1932, 'Gloriana in 1578', *Report of the Friends of Norwich Cathedral.*

SCHOLES, PERCY A., 1953, *Sir John Hawkins.*

SHAW, WATKINS, 1954, *The Three Choirs Festival* (London and Worcester).

—— 1963–4, 'Blow, Purcell, and the Exeter Choristers', *Mus. Op.*, 87, p. 485.

—— 1963–4, 'Musical Life in Durham Cathedral', *Mus. Op.*, 87, p. 35.

—— 1965, 'Thomas Morley of Norwich', *MT*, 106, p. 669.

—— 1967, 'William Byrd of Lincoln', *ML*, 48, p. 52.

SHEPPARD, EDGAR, 1894, *Memorials of St James's Palace*, 2 vols.

SIMPSON, W. SPARROW, 1873, *Statutes . . . of St Paul's Cathedral.*

SMITH, ALAN, 1964, 'Parish Church Musicians in England in the reign of Elizabeth I', *Royal Musical Association Research Chronicle*, 4.

SMITH, G. B., 1955, 'Memories of King's', *ECM*, 25, p. 73.

SONNECK, O., 1914, *Report on the Star-spangled Banner* (Washington).

SPARK, WILLIAM, 1892, *Musical Reminiscences: past and present.*

SPINK, GERALD W., 1970, 'Walter Scott's Musical Acquaintances', *ML*, 51, p. 61.

STANFORD, C. V., 1914, *Pages from an Unwritten Diary.*

STEPHENS, C. E., 1882 (enlarged issue), *Bemrose's Choir Chant Book.*

STEPHENS, W. R. W., and MADGE, F. T., 1897, *Documents relating to the history of the Cathedral Church of Winchester in the seventeenth century* (Hampshire Record Society, London and Winchester).

STEVENS, DENIS, 1957, *Thomas Tomkins.*

STOW, JOHN, 1580, *Chronicles.*

STRYPE, JOHN, 1821, *Life and Acts of Archbishop Parker*, 3 vols. (Oxford).

—— 1720, *Continuation of Stow's 'Survey of London'*, 2 vols.

SWEETING, E. T., 1924–5, 'The Organs of Winchester Cathedral and College', the *Organ*, 4, p. 211.

TANNER, L. E., 1969, *Recollections of a Westminster Antiquary.*

THOMAS, D. R., 1908–13, *Esgobaeth Llanelwy: The History of the Diocese of St Asaph* (Oswestry).

THOMPSON, A. HAMILTON, Introduction to *The Statutes of the Cathedral Church of Durham*: see Falkner, J. M.

THOMPSON, H. L., 1900, *Christ Church.*

(THORNSBY, F. W.), 1912, *Dictionary of Organs and Organists* (Bournemouth).

TORRE, JAMES, *The Antiquities of York Minster* (York Minster Library, MS L1(7)).

TORRY, A. F., 1888, *Founders and Benefactors of St John's College* (Cambridge).

TOVEY, D. F., and PARRATT, G., 1941, *Walter Parratt: Master of Music.*

TURNBULL, E., 1955, 'Thomas Tudway and the Harleian Collection', *Journal of the American Musicological Society*, 8.

VAUGHAN, J., 1919, *Winchester Cathedral: its monuments and memorials.*

VENABLES, E. M., 1947, *Sweet Tones Remembered: Magdalen Choir in the Days of Varley Roberts* (Oxford).

VIGNOLES, OLINTHUS, J., 1898, *Memoir of Sir Robert Stewart* (London and Dublin).

WAGNER, A. R., 1967, *Heralds of England.*

WATKINS MS (Ely Cathedral).

WEST, JOHN E., 1921 (new and enlarged edn.), *Cathedral Organists Past and Present.*

WESTRUP, J. A., 1968 (rev. edn.), *Purcell.*

WILLIAMS, C. F. ABDY, 1893, *A Short Historical Account of the Degrees in Music at Oxford and Cambridge.*

WILLIS, BROWNE, 1719, *A Survey of the Cathedral-Church of Llandaff.*

—— 1720, *A Survey of the Cathedral-Church of St Asaph.*

—— 1721, *A Survey of the Cathedral-Church of Bangor.*

—— 1727, *A Survey of the Cathedrals of York, Durham, Carlisle, Chester, Man, Lichfield, Hereford, Worcester, Gloucester and Bristol*, 2 vols.

—— 1742, *A Survey of the Cathedrals of York, Durham, Carlisle, Chester, Man, Lichfield, Hereford, Worcester, Gloucester, Bristol, Lincoln, Ely, Oxford, Peterborough, Canterbury, Rochester, London, Winchester, Chichester, Norwich, Salisbury, Wells, Exeter, St David's, Llandaff, Bangor, and St Asaph*, 3 vols.

WILSON, JOHN (ed.), 1959, *Roger North on Music.*

WOOD, ANTHONY, 1786–90, *The History and Antiquities of the Colleges and Halls in the University of Oxford*, ed. J. Gutch, 2 vols. (Oxford).

—— 1796, *The History and Antiquities of the University of Oxford . . . now first published in English . . . by John Gutch* (Oxford).

—— 1815–20, *Fasti Oxonienses . . . a new edition with additions and a Continuation by Philip Bliss*, 2 parts (contained in *Athenae Oxonienses*, ed. Bliss, 1813–20) (Oxford); numbers refer to columns, not pages.

—— 1891–1900, *Life and Times of Anthony Wood*, ed. A. Clark, 5 vols. (Oxford Historical Society).

—— MS Notes (Bodleian Library, MS Wood D.19(4)).

WOODRUFF, C. E., and DANKS, W., 1912, *Memorials of Canterbury Cathedral.*

(WORCESTER) 1879, *Statutes of Worcester Cathedral* (privately printed).

YARDLEY, EDWARD, 1927, *Menevia Sacra*, ed. Francis Green (Cambrian Archaeological Association, supplemental volume).

YOUNG, JOHN, 1928, *The Diary of John Young*, ed. F. R. Goodman.

ZIMMERMAN, FRANKLIN B., 1967, *Henry Purcell, 1659–1695: His Life and Times.*

—— 1962, 'Purcell and the Dean of Westminster—Some New Evidence', *ML*, 43, p. 7.

ADDENDA

(*October 1989 to 1 January 1991*)

(p.19). Richard Popplewell was appointed MVO, Birthday Honours list, 1990.

(p.42). Malcolm Archer resigned as organist of Bristol Cathedral at the end of 1989 and was succeeded in September 1990 by Christopher (John) Brayne, MA (Cambridge), FRCO(CHM) (b. Wolverhampton, 30 June 1954), formerly assistant organist of Wells Cathedral.

(p.43). Mark (Laurence James) Blatchly, BA (Oxford), FRCO (b. Shepton Mallet, Somerset, 21 February 1960), formerly assistant organist of Gloucester Cathedral, became organist of Bury St Edmunds Cathedral in September 1990.

(p.96). William Smith had been cantor of the pre-dissolution cathedral priory.

(p.106). Arthur Wills was appointed OBE, Birthday Honours list, 1990.

(p.129). John Sanders was awarded the Lambeth degree of D.Mus., 1990.

(p.144). Roy Massey: award of Lambeth degree of D.Mus. announced December 1990.

(p.182). Christopher Dearnley was appointed CVO, New Year Honours list, 1990. His successor, John (Gavin) Scott, MA, Mus.B. (Cambridge), FRCO, was born at Wakefield, 18 June 1956.

(p.272). E. H. Warrell was appointed MBE, New Year Honours list, 1991.

(p.353). Christopher Robinson is to leave St George's Chapel, Windsor in the summer of 1991 to become organist of St John's College, Cambridge.

(p.365). George Guest is to retire at the end of the summer term 1991, and will be succeeded by Christopher Robinson.

(p.386). John Harper became professor of music, University College of North Wales, Bangor in January 1991.

INDEX OF NAMES

Main extries are given in **bold**.

Acres, —— 381
Alberici, —— 390
Alcock, John 148
Alcock, Walter Galpin 18, 268
Allen, Hugh Percy 104, 246, **393**
Allen, John (Chester) 63
Allen, John (Lincoln) 157
Allinson, Thomas 161
Amner, John 99
Amott, John 125
Amps, William 359
Andrews, (Herbert) Kennedy 395
Angel, Alfred 116
Appleby/Appilby, Thomas **155**, 379
Archer, Malcolm David 42
Armes, Philip 79, 94
Armstrong, Thomas Henry Wait 117, **216**
Arne, Thomas Augustine 67
Arnold, George Benjamin **302**, 393
Arnold, Samuel 13, 14, 20, **335**
Ashfield, Robert James **240**, 279
Atkins, Ivor Algernon 312
Atkins, Robert Augustus 246
Atkinson, Frederick Cook 206
Attwood, Thomas 16, 20, **177**
Awman, Robert 284
Avison, Charles 192
Ayleward, Richard 202
Aylward, Theodore 347
Aylward, Theodore Edward 80, **167**
Ayrton, Edmund 19, **277**
Ayrton, Nicholas Thomas Dall 230
Ayrton, William 229
Ayrton, William Francis Morell 230

Badham, John 136
Bailey, Edward (Chester) 68
Bailey, Edward (St Asaph) 245
Bailey, John 68
Bairstow, Edward Cuthbert **323**, 394
Baker, Edmund 67
Baker, Henry 200
Baker, Reginald Tustin 270
Ball, Cyril James 194
Ball, Richard 380
Banks, Ralph 238
Barber, John 209
Barber, Robert 397
Barber, Thomas 79
Barcroft(e), George 99
Barcroft(e), Thomas 99
Barnby, Joseph 377
Barnes, Robert 404
Barnes/Barneys), Thomas 61
Barrett, John 253
Bartlett, John 260
Barton, Christopher Michael John 195
Barton, Matthew 356
Base, Richard 72
Bassett, Peter 34
Batchelor, Chappell 278
Bate, Donald William 195
Bates, Francis/'Frank' 206
Bates, George 230
Bates, Richard 387
Bateson, Thomas **62**, 409
Bath, George 295
Bath, William 294
Batten, Adrian 173, 294
Beale, George Galloway 168
Beale, William 363, **369**
Beard, Kenneth Bernard 279
Beckwith, *see also* Beckwyth
Beckwith, John Charles 205
Beckwith, John 'Christmas' 204
Beckwyth, —— 258
Bedsmore, Thomas 152
Beeston, John 274
Belcher, John Theodore 247
Belcher, William Edward 246
Bellamy, Richard 182
Benbow, John/Robert 209
Bennett, Alfred 363
Bennett, Alfred William 392
Bennett, George John 163
Bennett, Harold Aubie 239
Bennett, Henry Roberts 79
Bennett, Robert 269
Bennett, Thomas 79
Benson, Thomas 318
Berlioz, Hector 16
Bertalot, John 29
Best, Hubert 28
Bettridge, Samuel 404
Betts, Edward 186
Bevin, Elway 36
Bielby, Jonathan Leonard 282
Birch, John Anthony 82
Birchley, *see* Byrcheley
Bird, Francis 151
Bishop, John 299, **399**
Bishop, William 252
Black, George 69
Blackwell, Isaac 174
Blagrove, Thomas (Oxford) 210
Blagrove, Thomas (Westminster) 331
Blair, Hugh 311
Blatchly, Mark Laurence James 434

Blith(e)man, John 3, 209
Blow, John 1, 2, **9**, 19, 20, 182, 331, 333
Blundell, Ropier 233
Blundeville, John (Ely) 100
Blundeville, John (Lincoln) 159
Blundeville, John (York) 318
Blyfer, Thomas 77
Blyth, Benjamin 384
Bolton, Thomas 21
Bond, Capel 83
Bond, John Henry 230
Boorman, Peter 256
Booth, John Stocks 240
Booth, Richard 185
Bottomley, Joseph 30, 269
Boulter, *see* Butler
Bower, *see* Dykes Bower
Bower, Richard 19
Bowers, Robert 236
Bowman, John 367
Boyce, William 11, 12, 20
Boyle, Malcolm Courtenay 70, 351
Boys, William 157
Braddock, Edward 331
Brameley, Richard 355
Bramma, Harry Wakefield 272
Braye, Oliver 210
Brayne, Christopher John
Brearley, Hermann 29
Brewer, (Alfred) Herbert 83, 128
Brian, *see* Bryne
Bridge, (John) Frederick 189, **337**
Bridge, Joseph Cox 69
Briggs, David John 281
Brimble, John 362
Brimley/Brymley, John 88
Brind, Richard 176
Broadway, Richard 421
Brod(e)horne (alias Goring), Thomas 72
Broderip, John 289
Broderip, William 289
Brooksbank, Hugh 168
Brown, *see also* Browne
Brown, William 151
Browne, —— 316
Browne, John 287
Browne, Richard (Wells) 286
Browne, Richard (Worcester) 307
Browne, William (Dublin) 417
Browne, William (Durham) 89, 90
Bruce-Payne, David Malcolm 28
Bryan, *see* Bryne
Bryne/Brian/Bryan, Albertus **173**, 331
Buck, Percy Carter 41, **290**
Buck, Zechariah 205
Bucknall, Cedric 278
Bull, John 1, 4, **132**
Bull, Thomas 44
Bullbrick, —— 13
Bullis, Thomas 101
Bullock, Ernest 117, **338**
Bunnett, Edward 206
Burry, Hugh Ambrose 225
Burstall, Frederick Hampton 164
Burton (Claud) Peter Primrose 241
Burton, Richard 355
Bussell, Humphrey 36
Butcher, (Albert) Vernon 168
Butler/Boulter, Thomas 157
Butler, William 373
Byas/Byers, Cuthbert 315
Byrch(e)ley, John 61
Byrd, William 2, 3, **155**
Byrne, Nicholas 221

Calah, John 222
Camidge, John (I) 321
Camidge, John (II) 321
Camidge, John (III) 322
Camidge, Matthew 321
Camidge, Thomas Simpson 321
Campbell, Sidney Scholfield 52, 105, 272, **352**
Campion/Campyon, William 72
Cantrell, Derrick Edward 60, **191**
Capell, Thomas 78
Carden, John Humphrey 31
Carr, George 166
Carter, Frederick George 406
Carter, William 184
Chamberlayne, Robert 258
Chambers, Peter 108
Chappell, Edward 275
Chappell, George 275
Chard, George William **301**, 400
Chaundy, Edred Martin 405
Cheese, Griffith James 188
Cherrington, Richard 307
Cherry/Sherry, Richard 423
Child, Simon 390
Child, William 8, **344**
Chipp, Edmund Thomas 104
Chomley, Richard 46
Church, John 333
Church, Richard **211**, 390
Churchman, Thomas 233
Clack, Richard 138
Clam, Thomas 380
Clark(e), *see also* Clerk(e)
Clarke, Charles Erlin Jackson 93, **310**
Clarke, Jeremiah (St Paul's, London) 10, **175**, 182, 398
Clarke, Jeremiah (Worcester) 27, **309**
Clarke, John, *see* Clarke-Whitfeld
Clarke, Laurence 36
Clarke-Whitfeld, John **240**, 363, 368, 404
Claypole, Arthur Griffin 85
Claxton, Robert 99
Cleobury, Stephen John 361

Clerk(e)/Clark(e), John 285
Coates, Henry 30
Cobbold, William 200
Cock(e), Arthur **5**, 45, 108
Cocker, Norman 190
Codner, D. John D. 255
Cogan/Coogan, Philip 422
Colberke, William 274
Colborne, Langdon 81, 142
Colden, John 305
Col(e)by, Theodore **111**, 381
Coleman, (Richard) Henry Pinwill 29, **224**
Coleman, Simon 388
Combes, George 39
Coningsby, Eric Arthur 169
Coningsby, Gilbert 77
Conway, Marmaduke Percival 81, **105**
Coogan, *see* Cogan
Cook, Edgar Tom 271
Cook, (Alfred) Melville 143
Cooke, Benjamin 334
Cooke, Henry 19
Cooke, Robert 336
Cool, Henry 355
Cooper, *see also* Cowper
Cooper, David Anthony 29
Cooper, George 17
Cooper, James 203
Cooper/Cowper, John 73
Corfe, Arthur Thomas 267
Corfe, Charles William 214
Corfe, John 266
Corfe, John Davis 40
Corfe, Joseph 266
Cotterell, Robert 305
Cottrell, Thomas 148
Cotton, Humphrey 203
Coulder, *see* Golder
Cowan, Christopher Hume 402
Cowper, *see also* Cooper
Cowper, John 162
Coyle, Miles 139
Craw(e), James 155
Creser, William 18
Croft, William 1, **10**, 19, 20, 333
Cross, William 214
Crossland, Anthony 291
Crotch, William 213
Crow, Edwin John 230
Crowe, Frederick Joseph William 81
Culley, Arnold Duncan 94
Cutts, John 160

Dakers, Lionel Frederick **117**, 231
Dalton, Robert (I) 53
Dalton, Robert (II) 53
Dare, Charles James 139
Darke, Harold Edwin 360
Darlington, Stephen Mark **217**, 242
Davies, David Gwerfyl 31
Davies, Hugh Hooper 247
Davies, (Albert) Meredith 143, 241, **395**
Davies, Samuel 66
Davies, (Henry) Walford 339, 350, **351**
Davis, Hugh 136
Davis/Davys, Richard 307
Davis, Thomas Henry 291
Davis, William 319
Davison, John Armitage 225
Davys, *see* Davis
Day, John (St Asaph) 243
Day, John (St David's) 253
Day, Thomas 19, 330
Deane, Thomas (Bristol) 37
Deane, Thomas (Coventry) 83
Dearnley, Christopher John **182**, 269
Demonterat, *see* Monnterratt
Detty, Walter 373
Dexter, Harold 272
Dexter, John Anthony 425
Dickinson, Robert Duke 247
Dobinson, Abraham 55
Dodshon, —— 90
Dodgson, Francis 275
Done, Michael 63
Done, William 311
Dove, Robert 155
Doyle, Langrish 404, **412**
Duerden, Thomas Lucas 29
Dunkin, James 362
Dunnill, William Frederick 27
Dupuis, Thomas Sanders 13, 20
Dussek, Ronald Walter 130
Dykes Bower, John 95, **181**, 280, 394
Dyson, George 401

Eames, *see also* Emes
Eames, William 75
East/Este, Michael 146
Ebdon, Thomas 93
Eblyn, —— 367
Eden, Conrad William **95**, 291
Edge, Edward 186
Edmonds, Thomas 150
Edwards, Richard 19
Elbonn, John 102
Elliott, Graham John **60**, 247
Elliott, Richard 120
Elliott, Thomas 248
Ellis, Robert 255
Ellis, William 193
Elmore, Arthur 27
Elvey, George Job 349
Elvey, Stephen 393
Emes, *see also* Eames
Emes, William 75, 397
Este, *see* East.
Eusden, Laurence 357

Eusden, Matthew 357
Evans, William 289
Eveseed, Henry 2

Farmer/Fermer/Fermor, John **408**, 417
Farrande, Henry 316
Farrant, John (I) **34**, 98, 134, 259, 285
Farrant, John (II) 260
Farrant, Richard 343
Farrell, Timothy Robert Warwick 19
Fellowes, Edmund Horace 40, 351
Ferguson, Barry William Cammack 240
Fermer/Fermor, *see* Farmer
Ferrabosco, John 100
Ferrer, —— 22
Fidge, John 74
Fido(w), John 134, 135, 285, 306
Finell, Thomas 410, 411
Fisher/Fyssher, Richard 304
Fisher, Roger Anthony 71
Fitzgerald, James Ferrier 414
Fletcher, Eric Howard 169
Flexney, —— 388
Flood, David Andrew **52**, 163
Floud. John 76
Ford, Henry Edmund **57**, 238
Foster, John 91
Foster, Thomas 274
Fox, Robert 326
Fox, William 99
Francis, Charles Cooper 224
Francis, George Thomas 279
Froggatt, James Anthony 226
Frye, Frederick Robert 59
Fryer, —— 374
Fuller, Matthew 293
Fuller, Richard 260
Fuller, Robert 358, 367
Fussell, Peter **300**, 399
Fyssher, *see* Fisher

Gabb, (William) Harry **19**, 168
Gaccon, John Augustus 194
Gale, Thomas 108
Gaffe, George 240
Galway, Richard 403
Games, —— 379
Garland, Thomas 204
Garrett, George Mursell 363
Garton, Frederick S. 255
Gates, Bernard 13, 19, 333
Gedge, David Patrick 32
George, David 250
George, John 289
Gerard, *see* Jarred
Gerrard, Alexander 244
Gerrard, John 245
Gibbons, —— 362
Gibbons, Christopher 8, **296**, 332
Gibbons, Edward 37, 109, 355
Gibbons, Orlando 3, **6**, 330
Gibbs, *see also* Gibbes
Gibbs, John (Hereford) 135
Gibbs, John SSt Paul's; Westminster) 182, 328
Gibbs, Richard 202
Gibbs/Gibbes, Thomas (Canterbury) 46
Gibbs, Thomas (Norwich) 202
Gibson, Joseph 38
Giles/Gyles, Nathaniel 19, 305, **343**
Giles/Gyles, Thomas 182
Gladstone, Francis Edward 80, **167**, 206
Gleson, Walter 33
Godfrey, Thomas 410, 419
Golder/Coulder, Robert 342
Golding/Goldwin, John 346
Goldwin, *see* Golding
Godwin, Matthew 44, **107**
Gomester, Richard 355
Goodman, Peter 129
Goodson, Richard (I) **211**, 389
Goodson, Richard (II) 211
Goodwin, Andrew John 26
Goodwin, Robert 397
Goring, *see* Brod(e)horne
Goss, John 20, **178**
Goss-Custard, Walter Henry 164
Gostling, John 49
Gostling, William 49
Gould, Peter David 86
Gower, Christopher Stainton **224**, 226
Grace, Harvey 81
Grant, Willis 27
Gray, Alan 371
Gray, George Charles 145
Greatorex, Thomas **56**, 336
Green, Gabriel 288
Green, Matthew 344, 345
Green, William 326
Greene, Maurice 11, 20, **176**
Greening, Richard George 153
Greggs, William **92**, 318
Greig, William Sydney 424
Grier, Francis John Roy 217
Grew(e), Thomas 197
Grouch, —— 388
Guest, Douglas Albert 269, 312, **340**
Guest, George Howell 364
Guise, Richard 335
Gunn, Barnabas 27, **123**
Gunter, Thomas 34
Gunton, Frederick 69, **278**
Gyles, *see* Giles

Hake, John 342
Hale, Paul Robert 280
Hall, Henry (I) 111, **137**, 288
Hall, Henry (II) 138
Hall, Richard 78

Hallam, Edward Percy 42
Hallford, Thomas 168
Hamond, Thomas 355
Hancock, Charles 144
Handel, George Frideric 20, 301
Hanforth, Thomas William 270
Hardy, Joseph Naylor 281
Harker, (Arthur) Clifford 41
Harper, John Martin 386
Harris, —— 374
Harris, Joseph John 29, **189**
Harris, William Henry 216, **352**, 394
Harrison, Mrs A. L. 59
Harrison, Stephen 161
Harwood, Basil 104, **215**
Hasted, John 162
Havergal, Henry Macleod 401
Hawes, William 19, 182
Hawkins/Hawkyns, —— 397
Hawkins, Horace Arthur 82
Hawkins, James (I) **101**, 362
Hawkins, James (II) 222
Hawkins, John 228
Hawkshaw, John (Armagh) 403
Hawkshaw, John (Dublin) 410, 418
Hawkswell, —— 317
Hawkyns, *see* Hawkins
Hayden, Henry 245
Hayden, William 246
Haydn, Franz Joseph 14, 391
Hayes, Henry 209
Hayes, Philip 384, **391**
Hayes, William 308, **383**
Haylett, Thomas 69
Hayne, Leighton George 376
Hayter, Aaron Upjohn 140
Hayward, *see* Heywood
Heardson, John 159
Heath, John 234
Heath, Paul 37
Heath, Thomas 107, 327
Heathcote, Edward 277
Heather, Stephen 376
Heath-Gracie, George Handel 86
Hecht/Heicht/Height, Andreas 160
Hecht, Thomas 161, **382**
Helmore, Thomas 16, 20
Henman, Richard 112
Henshaw, William 94
Henstridge, Daniel 47, 121, **235**
Hesford, (Michael) Bryan 32
Hesletine, James 92
Hewson, George Henry Phillips 405, **424**
Heythwaite, Alexander 387
Heywood, Robert 408
Hicks, John 113, 114
Higginbottom, Edward 396
Higgins, Edward 39
Hill, David 303
Hill, Thomas 57
Hillarye, Jacob 73
Hillye, Thomas 233
Hilton/Hylton, John 157, **365**
Hinde, Henry 147
Hine, William 123
Hoddinott, John 308
Hodge, Robert (Armagh) 403
Hodge, Robert (Wells; Dublin) 288, 420
Hodges, John 132
Holder, William 160
Holland, James 185
Holmes, George 161
Holmes, John 261, **294**
Holmes, Thomas 295
Hone, Timothy Graham 194
Hooper, Charles 30
Hooper, Edmund 3, 4, 6, **328**
Hopkins, Charles 307
Hopkins, Douglas Edward **51**, 224
Hopkins, John 238
Hopkins, John Larkin 238, **370**
Hopwood, William 109
Horan, John 414
Horn, Karl Friedrich 348
Horncastle, Frederick William 405
Horsey, Alan Graham 31
Hosier, —— 388
Hosier, Philip 119
Hosier, Richard 419
Howard, Michael Stockwin 105
Howe, John 55
Howe, Joseph 237
Howe, Richard 237
Howe, Timothy 55
Howells, Herbert Norman 364
Hoyle, Walter 83
Hudson, Robert 182
Hughes, John Thomas 70
Hughes, Thomas 244
Hull, Percy Clarke 143
Humfrey, Pelham 19
Humphrey, Raymond George 402
Hunnis, William 19
Hunt, Donald 312
Hunt, Hubert Walter **41**, 394
Hunt, John 142
Huntley, George Frederick 193
Hurford, Peter John 241
Husbands, Charles 211
Husbands, William 211
Hush, George 76
Hutcheson/Hutchinson, Richard 90
Hutchinson, John (Southwell, fl.1540) 274
Hutchinson, John (Southwell, fl.1628) 275
Hutchinson, John (York) 316
Hutt, William 400
Huxley, Marcus Richard 28
Hylton, *see* Hilton

Hylton-Stewart, *see* Stewart.
Hywel, John 26

Ingham, Richard 57
Inglott, Edmund 197
Inglott, William 135, **199**, 201
Ions, William Jamson 192
Irons, Herbert Stephen 278
Isaac, Elias 308
Isaac(ke), Peter 264, 411, **419**
Isaac, William 419
Iuett, *see* Jewett

Jackson, —— 100
Jackson, Francis Alan 323
Jackson, John 100, 287
Jackson, Nicholas Fane St George 256
Jackson, William 114
James, Robert 53
Jameson, John 160
Janes, Robert 103
Janson, —— 373
Jarred/Gerard, Richard 23
Jeferies, —— 398
Jefferies/Jeffries, Stephen (I) **122**, 263, 398
Jefferies/Jeffries, Stephen (II) 38
Jeffries, John Edward 193
Jekyll, Charles Sherwood 17, 20
Jewett, Randall 63, 182, 298, 409, 410, **417**
Jewett/Iuett, William 417
Johns, Charles St. Ervan 195
Johnson, Basil 377
Johnson, Hugh 21
Jones, John (Armagh) 404
Jones, John (St Paul's, London) 177
Jones, John (St Asaph) 245
Jones, Thomas 63
Jones, Thomas Evance 49
Jordan, John William 60
Joyce, Robert Henry 169
Juxon, George 45

Kay, *see also* Key(s)
Kay, William 65
Keeton, Haydn 223
Kelway, Thomas 77
Kemp, Joseph 40
Kempton, Thomas 102
Kenge, William 310
Kennedy, Walter 408
Kent, James **299**, 367, 399
Key(s), William 185, 244
King, Charles 176, 182
King, George 398
King, William 389
Kingston(e), Thomas **157**, 316
Kir(k)by, Thomas 313
Kitson, Charles Herbert 415
Knight, Gerald Hocken 51
Knight, Thomas (Peterborough) 223
Knyght, Thomas (Salisbury) 258
Knyvett, Charles 14, 20
Knyvett. William 14, 20
Kyng, *see also* King

Lamb, Benjamin 346, **375**
Lamb, George 148
Lamb, William (Lichfield, I) 66, 147
Lamb, William (Lichfield, II) 147
Lamb, William (Dublin) 412
Lamkyn, Robert 327
Lambert, Thomas 73
Lancelot, James Bennett 95
Langdon, Richard 39, 103, **114**, 222, 404
Lant, Bartholomew 209
Lant(e), John 295
Larkin, Edmund 223
Lavington, Charles Williams 290
Ledbury (alias Ludby) 132
Ledger, Philip Stevens 60, **361**
Lee, William 276
Leeve, Henry 328
Lee Williams, *see* Williams
Leigh, John 184
Lemare, Edwin Henry 269
Lepine, David Foster 84
Leppard, Raymond 372
Lewes, Thomas 75
Lewis, Thomas 76
Ley, Henry George **215**, 378
Lichfield/Leichfield, Robert 118
Lide, *see* Lyde
Liddle, Robert William 279
Linsey, Richard 34
Little, Ian Donald 84
Lloyd, Charles Harford 18, 127, **214**, 377
Lloyd, Llewellyn 246
Lloyd, Richard Hey 95, **144**
Lloyd, Thomas 23
Long, Benjamin 400
Longhurst, William Henry 49
Loosemore, —— 362
Loosemore, George 366
Loosemore, Henry 356
Lott, John Browning 152
Lowe, Edward 8, **210**
Lowe, Thomas 121
Luard Selby, *see* Selby
Ludby, *see* Ledbury
Lugg(e), John 108
Lugg(e), Robert 109
Lumsden, David John 279, **395**
Luttman, William Lewis 240
Lyde, William 284

Mace, Henry 158
McKie, William Neil **339**, 385
McKiernan, Arnold Thomas 415

Maclean, Charles Donald 377
Macpherson, Charles 180
Madokes, Thomas 134
Madox, Matthew 252
Major, Leonard 209
Malcolmson, Kenneth Forbes 193, **378**
Manestie, Edward 275
Mann, Arthur Henry 359
Marbeck, *see* Merbecke
Marchant, Charles George 424
Marchant, Stanley Robert 180
Marker, John 284
Marks, Thomas Osborne 405
Marlow, Richard Kenneth 372
Marriott, Arthur (or W.) 279
Marrock, Richard 250
Marshall, George 356
Marshall, (Joseph) Philip 163, **231**
Marshall, William 214
Marson, George 45
Marson, John 209
Martin, George Clement 180
Martin, Jonathan 11
Mason, Thomas 132, 133
Massey, Roy Cyril 28, **144**
Masterman, *see* Maysterman
Matthew, John 209
Matthews, Graham Hedley 271
Matthews, John 423
Matthews, Samuel 363, **369**
Maycock, Thomas 209
Maycock, William 209
Mayne, John 108
Maysterman, Robert 88
Menzies, Maxwell Graham 226
Merbecke, John 341
Mercer, E. G. 58
Meredith, William 388
Merifield, John 308
Mersham, George 45
Middlebrook, William 161
Middleton, Hubert Stanley 105, 280, **371**
Middleton, (James) Roland 59, 71, **247**
Miles, *see also* Myles
Miles, —— 388
Millington, Barry Thomas Seager 130
Mineard, Samuel 39
Miro, Richard 36
Missin, Russell Arthur 194
Mitchell, John 348, **376**
Mitternacht, Joachim Jeremiah 263
Monk, Edwin George 322
Monk, Mark James 280
Monnterratt/Montr(i)ot/Demonterat, John 66
Moody, Charles Harry 50, **231**
Moore, —— 36
Moore, George 108
Moore, Philip John 130, **323**
Moore, Reginald 117
Moose/Mos, Robert 397
Mordant, Henry (I) 251
Mordant, Henry (II) 252
More, Thomas 109
Morgan, Thomas 411
Morgan, Tom Westlake 26, 50
Morley, James 38
Morley, Thomas 172, **198**
Morres, *see* Morris
Morris, Herbert Charles 255
Morris/Morres, Lewis 248
Mos, *see* Moose
Moyser, William 373
Mozart, Wolfgang Amadeus 177
Mudd, Henry 172
Mudd, John 219, 274
Mudd, Thomas **110**, 159, 220, 317
Mundy, John 343
Murgatroyd, Charles **161**, 319
Murphy, Samuel 412, **422**
Murphy, William 424
Mutlow, William 124
Myles, Richard 409

Nailer, Matthew 285
Nares, James 12, 19, 20, **320**
Naylor, John 322
Neale, —— 373
Neary, Martin Gerard James 303, **340**
Nethsingha, Lucian 117
Newbold, Richard 64
Newboult, Thomas 225
Nicholas, Michael Bernard 207
Nicholls, John 92
Nicholson, Richard 380
Nicholson, Sydney Hugo 50, 58, 190, **338**
Noble, Thomas Tertius **104**, 323
Norris, Thomas (Lincoln 161
Norris, Thomas (Oxford) 212
Norwood, John 316

Olive, Edmund 24
Okeover/Oker, John 119, 286, 398
Ord, Bernhard/'Boris' 360
Orme, Edward 68
Ormond, (Francis) Guillaume 280
Orr, Robert/'Robin' 364
Osmond, Cuthbert Edward 241
Ottey, Thomas 243
Otty, Thomas 65
Oxley, (Thomas Frederick) Harrison 42

Paddon, James 115
Paine, *see also* Payne
Paine, Christopher 73
Painter, Giles 36
Palmer, Clement Charlton 50
Palmer, Henry 91
Palmer, John 34

Pardo, Marmaduke 250
Pardo, William 250
Parfitt, Peter 289
Parrat, William 380
Parratt, Walter **350**, 384
Parry, Robert **266**, 289
Parsons, John 329
Parsons, Robert 3
Pas(s)more, Peter 111
Pat(t)rick(e), Nathaniel 305
Paul, Leslie Douglas 26
Payne/Paine, William 72
Peach, Charles 237
Pearce/Peirse, Charles 374
Pearce, Edmund 182
Pearson, James 53
Pearson/Peirson, Samuel 77
Peasgood, Osborne H. 339
Peerson, Martin 173, 182
Peirse, *see also* Pearce
Peirson, *see also* Pearson
Pepusch, Johann Christoph 334
Perkins, Abednego 243
Perkins, Dodd 289
Perkins, William 290
Perrin, Harry Crane **50**, 83
Perrin, Ronald Edward 231
Perronet, Edward 24
Perry, William 139
Phelps, (Eric) Christopher 406
Phillips, *see also* Philpott
Phillips, —— 383
Phillips, Arthur 37, **380**
Philpott/Phillips, Matthew 252
Pick, Charles 56
Pickhaver/Pickover 388, 398
Pigott, Francis 9, 382
Pigott, John **346**, 376
Pink, —— 388
Pinnock, Stephen Drew 192
Piper, Edward 72
Pitt, Thomas 309
Pleasants, Thomas 203
Plomer, Francis 46
Plumley, James 232
Polley, Richard 355
Ponsonby, Noel Edward 105, 216
Popely, William (I) 276
Popely, William (II) 276
Popplewell, Richard John 19
Porter, Ambrose Propert 153
Porter, Samuel 48, 177
Porter, Walter 330
Porter, William 47
Portman, Richard 330
Pouncey, Denys Duncan Rivers 291
Pratt, John 359
Prendergast, William 302
Preston, —— 342, 379
Preston, Simon John **217**, 340
Preston, Thomas (Ripon, I) 228
Preston, Thomas (Ripon, II) 229
Preston, Thomas (York) 317
Pretty, George 374
Priest, —— 22
Priest, Nathaniel 22, **38**, 346
Pring, Isaac 392
Pring, James Sharpe 25
Pring, Joseph 24
Prinn, *see also* Prynne
Prinn, Anthony 36
Propert, William Peregrine 253
Prynne, Nicholas 284
Purcell, Daniel 382
Purcell, Henry (the elder) 331
Purcell, Henry 9, **332**
Purvage, James 34
Pyne, James Kendrick 80, **189**
Pysing, William 46

Quarles, Charles (Trinity, Cambridge) 366
Quarles, Charles (York) 319

Railton, *see* Raylton
Ramsey, Robert 366
Randall, Greenwood 108
Randall, John **358**, 368
Randall, William 1, 4
Rathbone, —— 66
Rathbone, John 22
Rathbone, William 23
Raylton/Railton, William, 47
Rawsthorne, (Christopher) Noel 165
Raynor, Lloyd 162
Read, —— 390
Read, Frederick John 81
Reading, John (Chichester) **76**, 160
Reading, John (Winchester) 160, **298**, 398
Reading, John (St John's, Hackney) 77, 161, 175
Redford, John 171, 182
Reed, Leslie Henry Bret 415
Rees-Williams, Jonathan 153
Rese, —— 165
Rhodes, Harold William **83**, 303
Rhodes, Keith Vernon 30
Rhys, Philip ap 172
Richardson, Arthur 253
Richardson, Alfred Madeley 271
Richardson, John Elliott 267
Richardson, Vaughan **299**, 307
Ringrose, William Weaver 278
Riseley, George 40
Roberts, John, *see* Benbow.
Roberts, John Varley 384
Roberts, Nicholas 252
Roberts, Robert 25
Roberts, Thomas 21

Robinson, Christopher John 312, **352**
Robinson, Francis 413, 423
Robinson, John (Dublin) **413**, 423
Robinson, John (Rochester) 234
Robinson, John (Westminster) 333
Robinson, Robert 100
Rodgers, James 102, 222
Rogers, Benjamin 345, 374, **381**, 410
Rogers, Roland 25, 26
Rooke, Edward 39
Rookes, Nicholas 355
Rootham, Cyril Bradley 246, 364
Roper, (Edgar) Stanley 18
Rose, Barry Michael 130, 242
Rose, Bernard William George 386
Roseingrave, Daniel 121, 264, 299, 411, **420**
Roseingrave, Ralph 411, **421**
Roseingrave, Thomas 421
Ross, Colin Archibald Campbell 193
Ross, Wallace Michael 86
Rtther, Valentine 46
Rothwell, William 234
Rowle, Peter 233
Runnett, (Henry) Brian 207

Sale, John 182
Sale, John Bernard 16
Salisbury, Edward **319**, 367
Sanders, John 113
Sanders, John Derek 71, **129**
Sandley, Peter 202
Sandys, Michael 422
Saunders, Percy George 282
Saunderson, Nicholas 419
Savage, William 12, 182
Saywell/Sewell, Richard 61
Schwarbrick, *see* Swarbrick
Scott, John Gavin 182, 434
Seal, Richard Godfrey 269
Seivewright, (Robert) Andrew 58
Selby, Bertram Luard 239, **267**
Selbye, William 44
Senny, John 33
Sewell, *see* Saywell
Sexton, William 348
Shann, Charles John Harold 42
Sharp, Carter 222
Sharpe, Jonathan 363
Shaw, —— 228
Shaw, Alexander 91
Sheppard/Shepherd, John 379
Sherry, *see* Cherry
Shrubsole, William 23
Silver, John 296, **297**, 357
Silvester, John 113
Sinclair, George Robertson **143**, 280
Skeats, Highmore (I) **49**, 103
Skeats, Highmore (II) 103, 348
Skelton, George 162
Slater, Edmund 381
Slater, Gordon Archbold **145**, 163
Slaughter, —— 375
Sleech, —— 375
Smart, George Thomas 14, **15**, 20, 349
Smart, Henry 29
Smedmore, John 263
Smith, —— 22
Smith, Bernard 47, 244
Smith, Edward 90
Smith, Elias 119
Smith, George Townsend 142
Smith, John Stafford **15**, 19
Smith, Martin 15, **124**
Smith, Michael John 170
Smith, Thomas 258
Smith, William (Durham) 89
Smith, William (Durham minor canon) 90, 91
Smith, William (Ely) 96
Smith, William (Manchester) 185
Smyth(e), *see* Smith
Soar, Joseph 256
Sorrell, William 228
South, Charles Frederick 268
Southwick(e), Thomas 53
Sowerbutts, John Albert 129
Spain, John 236
Speechly, John 223
Spence, Charles 245
Spenceley, Christopher 316
Spofforth, Samuel **152**, 223
Spofforth, Thomas 277
Stainer, John **179**, 384
Standish, David 220
Standish, Francis 221
Standish, Ralph 158
Standish, Roger 221
Standish, William 221
Stanford, Charles Villiers 370
Stanley, Thomas 158
Statham, Heathcote Dicken 207
Stephens, John 265
Stephenson, Alan 84
Stephenson, Edwin 27
Stevenson, John 433
Stevenson, Peter Anthony Stanley 226
Stevenson, Robert 62
Stewart, Charles Henry Hilton/Hylton 80
Stewart, (Arthur) Charles (Lestoc) Hylton 43, 70, **239**, 352
Stewart, Gordon Brodie 192
Stewart, Haldane Campbell 385
Stewart, Robert Prescott **413**, 424
Stimpson, James 57
Stocks, Harold Carpenter Lamb 247
Ston(n)ard, William 210
Stores, Thomas 45
Storey, Richard 219
Stringer, John 65

Stringer, Peter 64, 184
Strugnall, William 186
Sudlow, William 188
Sumsion, Herbert Whitton 128
Surplice, Reginald Alwyn 41, **303**
Swarbrick/Schwarbrick, Henry 138
Sweeney, Peter 415
Sweeting, Edward Thomas 363, **400**

Tallis, Thomas **2**, 44
Tanner, Robert 92
Tanner, Thomas 285
Targett, James 79
Taverner, John 208
Taylor, Philip John 385
Taylor, James 393
Taylor, John (Salisbury) 259
Taylor, John (Westminster) 327
Tetlow, Edward 185
Thaxton/Thexton, George 342
Thetford, George 274
Thexton, *see* Thaxton
Thompson, Edward 138, **265**
Thomson, *see* Tomson
Thorne, Edward Henry 79
Thorne, Henry 315
Thorne, John 314
Thurlow, Alan John 83
Thynne, Robert 211
Tiller, Richard 219
Tinker, Randall 374
Tireman, William 363, **367**, 368
Tolley, Christopher Joen 402
Tomkins, Giles (I) **261**, 356
Tomkins, Giles (II) 306
Tomkins, John 7, 172, **356**
Tomkins, Richard 252
Tomkins, Thomas (I) 249
Tomkins, Thomas (II) 249
Tomkins, Thomas (III) 2, 6, 7, **306**
Tomkis, John 305
Tong, Thomas 318
Tooker, *see* Tucker
Toole, William 403
Tracey, Ian Graham 165
Travers, John 11
Tremaine, Thomas 794
Trepte, Paul **43**, 106
Trye, James 330
Tucker, Edmund/Edward 260, 285
Tudway, Thomas 357
Tunnard, Thomas Newburgh 28
Tunstall, Thomas 46
Tupper, Harry William 279
Turle, James 336
Turle, Robert 405
Turner, —— 184
Turner, Bernard 362
Turner, Charles Kenneth 169
Turner, John 76
Turner, William 160, 333
Tusser, Thomas 198
Tye, Christopher 2, **96**
Tyesdale, John 219
Tysoe, Albert Charles 241

Vann, (William) Stanley **59**, 224
Veale, —— 379
Vicary, Walter 384
Vincent, Robert William 191
Vincent, Simon 387

Wadeley, Frederick William **50**, 58
Wagg, —— 374
Wainwright, John 186
Wainwright, Richard 164, **187**
Wainwright, Robert 164, **187**
Wake, William 108, 109
Walkeley, Anthony 264
Walker, —— 374
Wallbank, Newell Smith 282
Walley, Humphrey 33
Walmisley, Thomas Attwood 363, **369**
Walond, William 79
Walrond, Theodore Hunter Hastings 58
Walsh, Colin Stephen **163**, 242
Walsh, George 411, 421
Walsh, Henry 422
Walker, —— 374
Walter(s)/Waters, John 10, **375**
Wanlass/Wanless(e), Henry 227
Wanlass/Wanless(e), John 158
Wanlass/Wanless(e), Thomas 318
Warrell, Ernest Herbert 272
Warren, William **413**, 423
Warrock, Thomas 7, 133
Warwick, Thomas 7
Wasbrough, John 40
Wasbrough, Rice 39
Wass, Robert 12
Waters, *see* Walters
Watson, —— 342
Watson, Sydney **217**, 378, 394, 401
Watts, Malcolm Gryffydd 257
Weare, James 285
Weaver, Geoffrey John 31
Weaving, Thomas Henry 415
Webb, Bartholomew 76
Webb, Edward 347, **376**
Webb, Robert 120
Webb, Thomas 289
Weber, Carl Maria von 16
Weddle, Robert George 84
Weeley, Thomas 161
Weelkes, Thomas **73**, 397
Wencelow, —— 344
Weldon, John **10**, 20, 390

Wesley, Samuel Sebastian 116, **125**, 141, 301, 349, 400
West, Reginald Harry 406
Westcott(e), Sebastian 171, 182
Whall, Benjamin 182
White, Edmund 66
White, James 417
White, John 112
White, Martin John 406
White, Peter Gilbert 145
White/Whyte/Witt, Robert 62, **97**, 327
White, William Henry 424
Whyte, *see* White
Wicks, (Edward) Allan **52**, 191
Wigthorpe, William 387
Wilcock, Alfred William **85**, 117
Wildbore, Robert 366
Wilkes, *see also* Willis
Wilkes, John Bernard 167
Willcocks, David Valentine 269, 312, **360**
Williams, Charles Lee 81, **127**, 360
Williams, George Ebenezer 336
Williams, Henry 252
Williams, John 234
Williams, Thomas 362
Willis/ Wilkes, Anthony 417
Wills, Arthur William 106
Wilson, —— 228
Wilson, Archibald Wayet 105, **190**, 246
Wilson, John 243
Winslade, Richard 293
Winter, John Charles 281
Wise, Michael 182, **262**
Wise, Samuel (Lincoln) 161
Wise, Samuel (Southwell) 276
Witt, *see* White
Woffington, John 404
Wood, Daniel Joseph 80, **116**
Wood, David 102
Woodcock, Clement 72
Woodcock, William 392
Wood(e)s, Michael 72
Woodson, Leonard 344, **374**
Woodward, Richard 412
Woot(t)on, Nicholas 47
Worrall, Benjamin 67
Worrall, John 412
Wren, Charles 121, **235**
Wren, Robert 47
Wrench, —— 166
Wrench, Berkeley 119
Wright, (Anthony) Paul 85
Wright, George 222
Wright, Peter Michael 273

Young, John Matthew Wilson 162
Young, William 374